# STUART DYNASTIC POLICY AND RELIGIOUS POLITICS 1621–1625

# STUART DYNASTIC POLICY AND RELIGIOUS POLITICS 1621–1625

edited by
MICHAEL C. QUESTIER

CAMDEN FIFTH SERIES
Volume 34

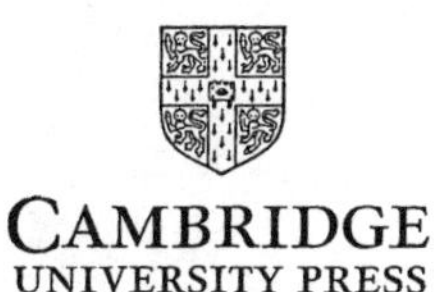

CAMBRIDGE
UNIVERSITY PRESS

FOR THE ROYAL HISTORICAL SOCIETY
University College London, Gower Street, London WC1 6BT
2009

Published by the Press Syndicate of the University of Cambridge
The Edinburgh Building, Cambridge CB2 8RU, United Kingdom
32 Avenue of the Americas, New York, NY 10013-2473, USA
477 Williamstown Road, Port Melbourne, VIC 3207, Australia
Ruiz de Alarcón 13, 28014 Madrid, Spain
Dock House, The Waterfront, Cape Town 8001, South Africa



First published 2009

*A catalogue record for this book is available from the British Library*

ISBN 9780 521 19403 7 hardback

SUBSCRIPTIONS. The serial publications of the Royal Historical Society, *Royal Historical Society Transactions* (ISSN 0080–4401) and Camden Fifth Series (ISSN 0960–1163) volumes, may be purchased together on annual subscription. The 2009 subscription price, which includes print and electronic access (but not VAT), is £109 (US $183 in the USA, Canada, and Mexico) and includes Camden Fifth Series, volumes 34 and 35 (published in July and December) and Transactions Sixth Series, volume 19 (published in December). Japanese prices are available from Kinokuniya Company Ltd, P.O. Box 55, Chitose, Tokyo 156, Japan. EU subscribers (outside the UK) who are not registered for VAT should add VAT at their country's rate. VAT registered subscribers should provide their VAT registration number. Prices include delivery by air.

Subscription orders, which must be accompanied by payment, may be sent to a bookseller, subscription agent or direct to the publisher: Cambridge University Press, The Edinburgh Building, Shaftesbury Road, Cambridge CB2 8RU, UK; or in the USA, Canada, and Mexico: Cambridge University Press, Journals Fulfillment Department, 100 Brook Hill Drive, West Nyack, New York, 10994–2133, USA.

SINGLE VOLUMES AND BACK VOLUMES. A list of Royal Historical Society volumes available from Cambridge University Press may be obtained from the Humanities Marketing Department at the address above.

*Printed and bound in the United Kingdom at the University Press, Cambridge*

# CONTENTS

# ACKNOWLEDGEMENTS

The newsletters which I have reproduced in this volume are retained in the archives of the archdiocese of Westminster. I am very grateful to Westminster Cathedral's new archivist, the Reverend Nicholas Schofield, and also to the former archivist, the Reverend Ian Dickie. They have both been extremely helpful in allowing me access to the collections in their charge. I am quite certain that, had it not been for the cathedral archivists' readiness to provide regular assistance and advice, this project would have been quite impossible to contemplate.

I was fortunate enough to be able to finish the editing process with a period of sabbatical leave from Queen Mary, University of London, supported by the Arts and Humanities Research Council. The text was finally completed while I was a visiting fellow at All Souls College, Oxford, in Michaelmas Term 2007. I am also grateful to the Scouloudi Foundation for financial assistance with the costs of publication.

Many people assisted me by reading through and commenting on the text, and by providing references: in particular, Geoff Baker, Caroline Bowden, Thomas Cogswell, Alexander Courtney, David Cressy, Pauline Croft, Robert Cross, Kenneth Fincham, Andrew Foster, Gabriel Glickman, Simon Healy, Michelle Howell, Peter Lake, Lynne Magnusson, Noel Malcolm, Thomas McCoog, Jeanne Shami, Paul Stevens, Christopher Thompson, Sara Wolfson, and Rivkah Zim.

# NOTE ON THE TEXT

The manuscripts published here are printed in full with routine openings and terminations, and with endorsements and annotations, usually, though not invariably, in the hand of the recipients of the letters. (In the letters received by Thomas Rant, however, many of the marginal annotations which he made on them are purely routine, and have not, therefore, been reproduced in the text of this volume.) The original spellings have been retained, except that modern usage is employed for *u* and *v*, and for *i* and *j*.[1] Punctuation and capitalization have also been modernized. Most abbreviations have been expanded through the use of italics and square brackets. Interlineations are indicated by the use of brackets <thus>. Deletions (where the deleted word is still legible) are indicated ~~thus~~. Other deletions and obliterations are noted in square brackets. Cross-references to other letters printed here are made by citing the number of the letter in italic type: for example, *Letter 23*. Underlining of words and passages of text in these letters has been preserved.

The letters are printed in chronological sequence. In the absence of other evidence, I have assumed that letters which were written on the Continent were dated according to the New Style and those written in England were dated Old Style. (With Old Style dates, I take the year to begin on 1 January and not 25 March.)

[1]In these newsletters, 'than' is frequently written as 'then', and 'whether' as 'whither'. I have changed the spelling in these cases so as to aid the sense.

# ABBREVIATIONS

| | |
|---|---|
| AAW | Archives of the Archdiocese of Westminster |
| ABSJ | Archivum Britannicum Societatis Jesu |
| Adams, FP | S. Adams, 'Foreign policy and the Parliaments of 1621 and 1624', in K. Sharpe (ed.), *Faction and Parliament* (London, 1978), pp. 139–171 |
| Adams, PC | S. Adams, 'The Protestant cause: religious alliance with the west European Calvinist communities as a political issue in England, 1585–1630' (unpublished DPhil thesis, University of Oxford, 1973) |
| Albion, *CI* | G. Albion, *Charles I and the Court of Rome* (London, 1935) |
| Alexander, *CLT* | M. van Cleave Alexander, *Charles I's Lord Treasurer* (Chapel Hill, NC, 1975) |
| Allison, QJ | A.F. Allison, 'A question of jurisdiction: Richard Smith, bishop of Chalcedon and the Catholic laity, 1625–1631', *RH*, 16 (1982), pp. 111–145 |
| Allison, RS | A.F. Allison, 'Richard Smith, Richelieu and the French marriage: the political context of Smith's appointment as bishop for England in 1624', *RH*, 7 (1964), pp. 148–211 |
| Allison, RSGB | A.F. Allison, 'Richard Smith's Gallican backers and Jesuit opponents', I (*RH*, 18 (1987), pp. 329–401), II (*RH*, 19 (1989), pp. 234–285) |
| Anstr. | G. Anstruther, *The Seminary Priests*, 4 vols (Ware and Great Wakering, 1968–1977) |
| *APC* | J.R. Dasent *et al.* (eds), *Acts of the Privy Council of England (1542–1628)*, 32 vols (London, 1890–1907) |
| ARCR | A.F. Allison and D.M. Rogers, *The Contemporary Printed Literature of the English Counter-Reformation between 1558 and 1640*, 2 vols (Aldershot, 1989–1994) |
| ARSJ | Archivum Romanum Societatis Jesu |
| ARSJ, Anglia MS 1 | Letters of the Jesuit general to members of the English province of the Society of Jesus (summaries at ABSJ, XLVII/3 (vol. I: 1605–1623) and XLVII/4 (vol. II: 1624–1632)) |
| *BIHR* | *Bulletin of the Institute of Historical Research* |
| Birch, *CTCI* | T. Birch, *The Court and Times of Charles I*, 2 vols (London, 1948) |
| Birch, *CTJI* | T. Birch (ed.), *The Court and Times of James the First*, 2 vols (London, 1848) |

| | |
|---|---|
| BL | British Library |
| *Cabala* | *Cabala, Mysteries of State, in Letters of the Great Ministers of K. James and K. Charles* (London, 1653) |
| *CCE* | H. Lonchay, J. Cuvelier, and J. Lefèvre (eds), *Correspondance de la Cour d'Espagne sur les Affaires des Pays-Bas au XVII$^{e}$ siècle*, vol. II (*Précis de la correspondance de Philippe IV avec l'Infante Isabelle (1621–1623)*) (Brussels, 1927) |
| *CGB* | B. de Meester (ed.), *Correspondance du Nonce Giovanni-Francesco Guidi di Bagno (1621–1627)*, 2 vols (Brussels, 1938) |
| Cogswell, *BR* | T. Cogswell, *The Blessed Revolution* (Cambridge, 1989) |
| Cokayne, *CP* | G.E. Cokayne, *The Complete Peerage*, 13 vols (London, 1910–1959) |
| CRS | Catholic Record Society |
| CRS, 10–11 | E.H. Burton and T.L. Williams (eds), *The Douay College Diaries*, CRS, 10–11 (London, 1911) |
| CRS, 37 | W. Kelly (ed.), *Liber Ruber Venerabilis Collegii Anglorum de Urbe: Annales Collegii Pars Prima: Nomina Alumnorum I. A.D. 1579–1630*, CRS, 37 (London, 1940) |
| CRS, 54–55 | A. Kenny (ed.), *The Responsa Scholarum of the English College, Rome*, 2 vols, CRS, 54–55 (London, 1962–1963) |
| CRS, 68 | A.J. Loomie (ed.), *Spain and the Jacobean Catholics*, vol. II: 1613–1624, CRS, 68 (London, 1978) |
| CRS, 74–75 | T.M. McCoog (ed.), *English and Welsh Jesuits, 1555–1650*, 2 vols, CRS, 74–75 (London, 1994–1995) |
| *CSPD* | R. Lemon and M.A.E. Green (eds), *Calendar of State Papers, Domestic Series*, 12 vols [for 1547–1625] (London, 1856–1872) |
| *CSPV* | H.F. Brown and A.B. Hinds (eds), *Calendar of State Papers, Venetian Series*, 11 vols [for 1581–1625] (London, 1894–1912) |
| Dirmeier, *MW* | U. Dirmeier (ed.), *Mary Ward und ihre Gründung: die Quellentexte bis 1645*, 4 vols (Münster, Westphalia, 2007) |
| Dodd, *CH* | C. Dodd [*vere* Hugh Tootell], *The Church History of England*, 3 vols (Brussels [imprint false, printed at Wolverhampton], 1737–1742) |
| *DSSD* | E. Bourcier (ed.), *The Diary of Sir Simonds D'Ewes (1622–1624)* (Paris, 1974) |
| ED | 'The diary of Sir Walter Earle', BL, Additional MS 18,597 (transcript supplied by Simon Healy of the History of Parliament Trust) |
| Foley | H. Foley, *Records of the English Province of the Society of Jesus*, 7 vols (London, 1875–1883) |
| Gardiner, *NSMT* | S.R. Gardiner (ed.), *Narrative of the Spanish Marriage Treaty*, Camden Society 101 (London, 1869) |
| Hacket, *SR* | John Hacket, *Scrinia Reserata* (London, 1693) |

*HJ* — *Historical Journal*
HMC — Historical Manuscripts Commission
*HMCMK* — H. Paton (ed.), *Supplementary Report on the Manuscripts of the Earl of Mar & Kellie* (HMC, London, 1930)
*HR* — *HR Historical Research*
*LJ* — *Lords' Journals*
McClure, *LJC* — N.E. McClure (ed.), *The Letters of John Chamberlain*, 2 vols (Philadelphia, 1939), vol. II
*NAGB* — M. Questier (ed.), *Newsletters from the Archpresbyterate of George Birkhead*, Camden Society, 5th series, 12 (Cambridge, 1998)
*NCC* — M. Questier (ed.), *Newsletters from the Caroline Court*, Camden Society, 5th series, 26 (Cambridge, 2005)
nd — no date (of publication)
np — no place (of publication)
*ODNB* — *Oxford Dictionary of National Biography*
OP — Order of Preachers
OSB — Order of St Benedict
PRO — Public Record Office (recently rebranded as the 'National Archives')
*Proceedings 1625* — M. Jansson and W.B. Bidwell (eds), *Proceedings in Parliament, 1625* (New Haven, CT, 1987)
Pursell, ESP — B.C. Pursell, 'The end of the Spanish match', *HJ*, 45 (2002), pp. 699–726
Pursell, *WK* — B. Pursell, *The Winter King: Frederick V of the Palatinate and the coming of the Thirty Years War* (Aldershot, 2003)
Questier, *C&C* — M. Questier, *Catholicism and Community in Early Modern England* (Cambridge, 2006)
Ransome, PPNF — D.R. Ransome, 'The Parliamentary Papers of Nicholas Ferrar 1624', in *Camden Miscellany XXXIII*, Camden Society, 5th series, 7 (Cambridge, 1996)
Redworth, *PI* — G. Redworth, *The Prince and the Infanta* (London, 2003)
*RH* — *Recusant History*
Ruigh, *1624* — R.E. Ruigh, *The Parliament of 1624* (Cambridge, MA, 1971)
Russell, *PEP* — C. Russell, *Parliaments and English Politics, 1621–1629* (Oxford, 1979)
*Salvetti* — H.B. Tomkins (ed.), *The Manuscripts of Henry Duncan Skrine, Esq.: Salvetti Correspondence*, HMC, 11th report, appendix, part I (London, 1887)
Schreiber, *FC* — R.E. Schreiber, *The First Carlisle* (Philadelphia, 1984)
SJ — Society of Jesus
*SRP*, I — J.F. Larkin and P.L. Hughes (eds), *Stuart Royal Proclamations: royal proclamations of King James I, 1603–1625* (Oxford, 1973)

| | |
|---|---|
| *SRP*, II | J.F. Larkin (ed.), *Stuart Royal Proclamations: royal proclamations of King Charles I, 1625–1646* (Oxford, 1983) |
| TD | M.A. Tierney, *Dodd's Church History of England*, 5 vols (London, 1839–1843) |
| Thompson, *HA* | C. Thompson, *The Holles Account of Proceedings in the House of Commons in 1624* (Orsett, Essex, 1985) |
| Thompson, *RD* | C. Thompson, *Sir Nathaniel Rich's Diary of Proceedings in the House of Commons in 1624* (Orsett, Essex, 1985) |
| Tillières, *ME* | M.C. Hippeau (ed.), *Mémoires Inédits du Comte Leveneur de Tillières* (Paris, 1863) |
| Whiteway, *Diary* | William Whiteway, *William Whiteway of Dorchester: his diary, 1618 to 1635*, Dorset Record Society, 12 (Dorchester, 1991) |
| Zaller, *1621* | R. Zaller, *The Parliament of 1621* (London, 1971) |

# INTRODUCTION

The newsletters which are reproduced in this volume are retained in the Westminster Diocesan Archives (in the A Series, volumes XVI–XIX; the B series, volumes 25–27, 47, and 48; and the OB series, volume I/i).[1] They were penned by English Catholic clergymen and laymen during the first half of the 1620s. At this time, these writers, and indeed many others, expected that sweeping political changes would occur in the wake of the twists and turns of the Stuart court's dynastic marriage negotiations abroad. The present series of letters begins at the point when, in late 1621, with the parliament on the verge of dissolution, the English secular clergy dispatched an agent to Rome in order to persuade the papal curia that this was the right moment to appoint a bishop to exercise direct and local episcopal authority over English Catholics. The secular clergy's efforts to secure episcopal power for one of their number generated a stream of correspondence between them over the next few years. Their letters dealt both with their frenetic lobbying in Rome in order to secure their suit and also with the course of events in England and on the Continent as the Stuart court tried to construct a dynastic alliance which would supply a bride for Prince Charles.[2]

I have no intention in this introduction of using this material to construct a full narrative of the negotiations during 1621–1625 for the failed Anglo-Spanish treaty or for the successful Anglo-French treaty. This can be done much more effectively by exploiting the ministerial and diplomatic correspondence retained in official, and particularly foreign, archives.[3] The point of this volume is to demonstrate, as far as possible, how the English Catholic community's understanding of

[1]AAW, B 25–26, and B 47 have no regular foliation. There are two sets of numbering for the documents in B 26. The first set ceases with B 26, no. 50. In the second set, B 26, no. 50 is also numbered B 26, no. 53. However, rather than regarding B 26, according to the first set of document numbers, as unnumbered after B 26, no. 50 (as does Allison, RS), I have used the second set of numbers in B 26 for documents after no. 50/53.

[2]In the footnotes to the text of these newsletters I have tried to identify individuals where there is any uncertainty about their identity (for example, if they are mentioned via an alias), though this is done only on the first occasion that they are thus mentioned in each letter. I have not, however, for reasons of length, supplied detailed biographical information about such individuals unless it is directly relevant to the newsletter in which they are cited.

[3]See e.g. Adams, PC; Cogswell, *BR*.

these diplomatic manoeuvres can be integrated into our account of mainstream politics during this period. I wish to show how Catholics attempted to negotiate with the Stuart regime and with the papal court in order to achieve some of their own aims for the reform of the English Catholic community and to attain a (perhaps quite broad) measure of tolerance for the Stuarts' Catholic subjects. I also want to indicate how Catholic interventions of this kind became part and parcel of contemporary politics.

Many of these letters do not contain a great deal of information or material which cannot be garnered from other sources.[4] They are important, however, because they reveal a crucial (Catholic) component of 'public-sphere' politics, in other words the range (and means and modes of expression) of opinions and discourses which were deployed in reaction to the Stuart court's highly controversial attempts to secure the future of the dynasty through a marriage for Prince Charles. In the often fraught conditions of the late Jacobean polity, Catholics, like certain Protestants, availed themselves of the opportunity to agitate and lobby for public and official approval and confirmation of their particular glosses on and attitudes to the questions raised by royal foreign policy.[5]

Historians have occasionally noted that King James, while theologically a Calvinist, showed himself 'sympathetic to Catholics';[6] and, indeed, both before and after his accession in England, many English Catholics argued that they were loyal supporters of the Stuart cause and dynasty. But the relationship between the king and his Catholic subjects was far from stable. At various points earlier in his reign James had shown complete ruthlessness in dealing with Catholic dissent, even while he argued publicly that he would tolerate those who were of a 'moderate' disposition, Catholics as well as puritans. After he came to England, James had, to many Catholics' way of thinking, soon reneged on promises which he had made to them while he was still in Scotland. During the years 1610–1614, his regime showed itself determined to punish Catholic disobedience. As was made clear by the marriage which he secured for his daughter, Princess Elizabeth, with the Calvinist Frederick V, elector palatine, James was

[4]Several of these letters were printed, in part or whole, in Mark Tierney's edition of Charles Dodd's *Church History* (TD, IV, V). Antony Allison also used them in his essays published in *RH* on English Catholicism in the early 1620s.

[5]For recent analysis of the issue of the public sphere in the context of English history, see P. Lake and S. Pincus, 'Rethinking the public sphere in early modern England', *Journal of British Studies*, 45 (2006), pp. 270–292; P. Lake and M. Questier, 'Puritans, papists, and the "public sphere" in early modern England: the Edmund Campion affair in context', *Journal of Modern History*, 72 (2000), pp. 587–592.

[6]G. Bernard, 'The Church of England *c.* 1529–*c.* 1642', *History*, 75 (1990), p. 194.

still prepared at this point to pose as a leading light of the pan-European 'Protestant cause' (the long political tradition of alliance between European Protestants, which operated on the principle that a shared religious position on certain central doctrinal issues underwrote a more general common interest among them).

Catholics were pessimistic about their own prospects in the wake of the palatine marriage. Toleration seemed as far away as ever. Nevertheless, the failure of the 1614 parliament allowed the Spanish ambassador, the count of Gondomar, to play upon James's fears and suspicions of 'popularity' and of the unquiet parliamentary spirits which had, it seemed, wrecked the session. Their attitudes were, the Spaniard claimed, very different from the loyalism of James's Catholic subjects.[7] During the 1614 débâcle, critics of royal government pointed to the maladministration of the fiscal measures which were supposed to discipline Catholic separatists. Gondomar argued, however, that if concessions were made to Catholics they might show their gratitude by seeking to ensure that some of the crown's revenue requirements were satisfied.[8] It was impossible, of course, that Catholics' generosity could even begin to relieve the king's financial wants. But Gondomar was deploying a version of the arguments which were being advanced not only by English Catholics themselves but also by officials within the central administration whose duties included the regulation and fiscal exploitation of the legal penalties for Catholic separatism.[9] There was, here, an identifiable link and likeness to Gondomar's other claim, namely that James could seek to augment his sovereign authority through the financial and political implications of an Anglo-Spanish dynastic union. In both cases, the crown's fiscal and other political difficulties could be resolved, or so it was argued, without the king being held to ransom, as it were, by his own subjects. In March 1615, the king's ambassador in Madrid, Sir John Digby, received a treaty proposal for such a union. Digby subsequently became an ardent supporter of the project.[10]

The mid-Jacobean regime suffered from a series of horrendous public-relations disasters, the most notable of which was the Overbury scandal. The resulting censures of the regime were compatible with, if not directly informed by, standard contemporary anti-popish

[7] Redworth, *PI*, p. 15.

[8] *Ibid.*

[9] M. Questier, 'Sir Henry Spiller, recusancy and the efficiency of the Jacobean exchequer', *HR*, 66 (1993), pp. 257–258, 261–262.

[10] Redworth, *PI*, pp. 15–16, 148 n. 14. Digby advised the king in early 1618 that, since the Spaniards had made their demands concerning religion explicit and were 'likewise resolved to satisfye' him 'in temporall regards and poynt of portion', he (Digby) was 'of opinion that the calling of a parliament wilbe in no kynde usefull': PRO, SP 94/23, fo. 5v.

discourse.[11] Then, after 1618, the onset of the troubles in Europe, generally referred to as the 'Thirty Years War', confronted the Stuart court with a number of near-insoluble quandaries and problems.

Bohemia had challenged the authority of the emperor Matthias, arguing that promises made as the result of disputes settled in 1609 and 1611 had been broken; and it sought aid from the Dutch and from the German Protestant princes.[12] James's difficulties were made considerably worse by the decision of his son-in-law, the elector palatine, to accept the Bohemian crown from those who had rebelled against imperial authority and had then deposed Archduke Ferdinand of Austria.[13] In October 1619, Henry Erskine observed in Paris that there was 'great gladness', especially among the Huguenots, at the elector's acceptance of the Bohemian crown, and 'no less gladness that our kings Majestie' would 'draw his shourd in his auld dais in the king of Bohemia his defence'.[14] European Protestants looked to James to play the champion of the European Protestant cause, a role which he no longer wanted. These events and the Jacobean regime's reaction to them transformed the political status of Catholics within the Stuart realms, not least because they allowed Catholics of various kinds to engage in a series of public debates about royal policy.

Of course, according to many historians, by the early 1620s English Catholicism had become politically inert. Protestant fears of popery therefore had little to do with actual Catholics in England. Such people, it is usually assumed, were excluded from public life and distracted by factional disagreements among themselves. Catholics could hope for no more than that perhaps, one day, they might be granted a modicum of tolerance and partial relief from the penal statutes, certainly not a full legal toleration in the sense of a parliamentary repeal of those statutes.[15] When Protestants identified a popish conspiracy to subvert true religion and monarchical authority, they were, it is said, really referring to two things. The first of these was the trials and tribulations of the Protestant cause in Europe and the willingness of the Stuart court to discard much of the Elizabethan tradition of enmity towards Spain. The second was the dislocation caused within the English Church as, or so it seemed to some contemporaries, a strain of doctrinal thought (sometimes referred to as 'Arminianism') started to challenge the supposedly dominant

[11] A. Bellany, *The Politics of Court Scandal in Early Modern England* (Cambridge, 2002).

[12] G. Parker, *The Dutch Revolt* (London, 1988), p. 262; Pursell, *WK*, ch. 2.

[13] J.V. Polisensky, *The Thirty Years War* (London, 1974), pp. 103–113; Pursell, *WK*, pp. 45, 49–50; Adams, PC, pp. 280–282.

[14] *HMCMK*, p. 93.

[15] I am grateful to Pauline Croft for discussion of this point.

species of Calvinist belief and practice which had been inherited from the Elizabethan era.[16]

Yet the glaring fractures in English and British politics that were created by royal foreign policy in some respects actually revitalized the Catholic issue because, inevitably, that issue both affected and was informed by the conduct of royal negotiations with the court in Madrid. As Simon Adams has made clear, by the early 1620s there were serious arguments both for and against a Spanish alliance. For those who believed that the Spanish branch of the Habsburgs did not aim at global dominance, it seemed reasonable to treat the current European political crisis as a set of territorial disputes and not as part of a massive ideological confrontation between the forces of light and darkness.[17] (This, of course, was a difficult argument to sustain once Spanish troops were used in the invasion of the Palatinate.) Those who feared the burgeoning power of Spain could point instead to the need to maintain Protestant coherence and unity, and in particular the safety and security of the United Provinces, something which was now an immediate and pressing issue because the Truce of Antwerp was set to lapse in April 1621.[18]

James did not veto all military action to secure the return of the elector palatine's territory. But he absolutely would not countenance being dragged into the conflict between Spain and the United Provinces, in part because it would redound to the benefit of the French state. In any case, for James to wage a land war against the Habsburgs was financially impossible. Inevitably, there was an alignment between the financial retrenchers within the Stuart regime and those who had ideological reasons for supporting a Spanish marriage, including some who were or could be classed as papists. (Their critiques of the regime's war effort, once hostilities commenced, turned out to be largely correct.[19])

Here, naturally, was fertile ground for those who wanted to claim, and had always claimed, that English Catholics were part of a wider popish conspiracy. Each proposal, in the course of the negotiations with the Spaniards, to grant a measure of toleration to James's Catholic

[16]See N. Tyacke, *Anti-Calvinists* (Oxford, 1987). For the type of Arminianism in the Low Countries which served as a reference point for the English variety, see J. Israel, *The Dutch Republic* (Oxford, 1995), pp. 480–482, 486–525.

[17]For a discussion of the meaning of 'Spanish party' or 'Spanish faction' in mid- and late Jacobean politics, see C.H. Carter, 'Gondomar: ambassador to James I', *HJ*, 7 (1964), pp. 193–194; CRS, 68, pp. xiv–xix.

[18]For the failure of the archdukes' regime to secure an extension of the truce, see P. Arblaster, *Antwerp & the World: Richard Verstegan and the international culture of Catholic reformation* (Louvain, 2004), pp. 138–139.

[19]Adams, FP, pp. 148–151.

subjects could be represented as part of an attempt to fragment the political coherence of the realm and to make it ungovernable. The Spanish court tried to insist on a full legal toleration for James's Catholic subjects as a condition of any Anglo-Spanish marriage treaty, and was backed up by Rome's refusal of a papal dispensation for the marriage until evidence of such a toleration was forthcoming.

It is worth asking, therefore, how far English Catholics were part of these political equations. To what extent were they a coherent component of a pan-European 'Catholic cause', diametrically opposed to the Protestant one? How did they perceive the increasingly frenetic manoeuvres of James and his closest, though often mutually hostile, counsellors as they tried to solve the contradictions into which the king's apparent half-heartedness about European religious divisions had plunged them all? Was the Spanish match the summit of Catholics' hopes? Was its failure the end of their aspirations and dreams? Was the marriage treaty with the House of Bourbon, seemingly so much less concerned with matters of religion, for them no more than a damp squib in this regard? Did it signal the end of Catholics' political ambitions? It would not be difficult to fashion an argument that this was yet another occasion when the devious and unscrupulous French let down their English co-religionists as, arguably, they had done during the Anjou marriage negotiations in 1579–1581.[20]

In fact, as the crown searched – sometimes desperately – for support, a number of different Catholic parties and factions were able to pose as the bulwarks of the monarchy, the regime, and the state, of order, security, and authority. They stood against a (supposed) puritan and popular threat, which was expressed through carping criticism of James's prerogative, particularly as it was used to make foreign-policy decisions.

It is impossible, unfortunately, to estimate what fraction or proportion of 'public opinion' Catholics represented (even assuming that we could arrive at a working definition of Catholicism which would satisfy most historians of the period). But we can glean from surviving clutches of Catholics' correspondence, and especially their newsletters, the extent to which they were capable of intervening in contemporary politics, and of spinning and glossing specific events, just as their enemies tried to spin and gloss such events against them.[21]

[20] See J. Bossy, 'English Catholics and the French marriage, 1577–81', *RH*, 5 (1959–1960), pp. 2–16.

[21] See Cogswell, *BR*, pp. 20f. for the mechanisms of contemporary news culture. For the translation and transmission of English newsletters to the curia, via the secular clergy's agent in Rome, see *NAGB*, introduction; *Letter 34*.

Catholic accounts of the intentions of James's regime were a valuable source of information for foreign diplomats in London; and the Stuart court could and did use Catholics, including the writers of some of these newsletters, to push forward its dynastic negotiations abroad. The flow of news generated by Catholics thus became a means by which they could insert themselves and their agenda into the political process and, into the bargain, ingratiate themselves with the regime in London. Some Catholics, for example, searched for and recorded every sign that the Jacobean regime really meant to allow Catholics the freedoms for which they regularly petitioned. In Rome, John Bennett reported, in a letter of May 1622 to William Bishop (the leading secular priest and future bishop of Chalcedon), that he had 'putt certayne clauses' of Bishop's most recent letter and enclosures into Latin and had given them to Cardinal Ottavio Bandini. Bandini 'was very glad of the newes and the next day, being congregacion day for the Holy Office, read [. . .] publickly' the information conveyed to him by Bennett, 'and he tould me after that it gave much content, specially that clause wherin it was sayd that his Majesty had taken order for the quiete of Catholiques'.[22] This was the sort of news which would make the Roman curia favourably inclined towards the Stuart court and more likely to grant a dispensation for the proposed Anglo-Spanish dynastic union.

The problem was that news was not always favourable. A certain amount of spinning might have to be done in order to make it palatable to its eventual recipients. 'Nowe', said Bennett, in the same letter, 'the same newes makers saye that our king hath sent souldioures to the Palatinate and his banner is there display[e]d against the emp[e]ror but this we assure ourselves by other lettres to be false, yet this doth serve there turne to putt doubtes and lettes for the present'.[23] A week later, Bennett informed his brother Edward that he had received two of his letters (which brought better tidings) and 'your newes I putt in Latyne' and showed it to 'these greate men' in Rome 'whoe were very glad therwith'.[24] Catholic news reports could, therefore, from time to time, acquire the capacity to influence the regime's foreign-policy agenda. Equally, the regime calculated that Catholics might well be relied upon to tell inquisitive foreign ambassadors and their masters abroad what the regime wanted them to hear, since it would be in the Catholics' interests to see that James's present foreign-policy objectives were realized.

[22] AAW, B 25, no. 55.

[23] *Ibid.*

[24] AAW, B 25, no. 57; see also AAW, A XVI, no. 156, p. 605 (cited in *Letter 8*).

## Dynastic Matches and Religious Politics

In recent years, a self-consciously 'revisionist' account of the early 1620s has claimed that conflict between crown and parliament during this period did not cause the kind of political instability which Whiggish narratives once described and celebrated. And yet, even while we might want to accept substantial parts of the revisionists' analysis, what is clear is that, as Peter Lake points out, in spite of the theoretical extent of the royal prerogative over the Church and foreign policy, 'James I was [. . .] unable even to arrange the marriage of his son' to a Spanish infanta 'without rousing a storm of protest from his subjects'. The expression of traditional anti-popish tropes and opinions (in response to royal policy-making) came to represent 'a real limitation on the crown's autonomy'.[25]

In the years after the Overbury scandal, there was, as Simon Adams has described in some detail, a revival of the 'puritan' political faction at court (grouped around the earl of Pembroke, Sir Ralph Winwood, and the earl of Southampton), just as the Howard family's star appeared to go into steep decline.[26] That faction's victory, however, was a pyrrhic one. There arose 'two mutually antagonistic factions on the council, one committed to rapprochement with Spain and the other to political puritanism, whose struggles for supremacy were to form the underlying framework of politics for the remainder of the reign'. The 'puritan core wished to institute major changes of policy, summon a parliament, and reform the finances', but those who had been temporarily allied with them were satisfied with the earl of Somerset's disgrace after his implication in Sir Thomas Overbury's murder. In addition, the earl of Arundel had gravitated back to the other Howards by 1619, following the fall of the earl of Suffolk.[27]

As Adams also observes, 'the decision to seek a Spanish marriage [. . .] saw the emergence of a new element in the Spanish faction, together with the Howards and the Catholic sympathisers, a party which in part represented' a throwback to the realpolitik of the earl of Salisbury up to 1612. Lord Chancellor Bacon was in the forefront here, supported by Lord Digby (ennobled in November

[25] P. Lake, 'Anti-popery: the structure of a prejudice', in R. Cust and A. Hughes (eds), *Conflict in Early Stuart England* (London, 1989), p. 87. For the different sets of negotiations for dynastic alliances entered into by the Stuart regime during the period up to 1621, see A. Thrush, 'The French marriage and the origins of the 1614 Parliament', in S. Clucas and A. Davies (eds), *The Crisis of 1614 and the Addled Parliament* (Aldershot, 2003), pp. 25–35; *idem*, 'The personal rule of James I, 1611–1620', in T. Cogswell, R. Cust, and P. Lake (eds), *Politics, Religion and Popularity in Early Stuart Britain* (Cambridge, 2002), pp. 84–102.

[26] Adams, PC, ch. 7.

[27] *Ibid.*, pp. 247–249.

1618). Their motivation can be ascribed to their hostile attitudes towards the French and the Dutch, and a belief that a Spanish match would be commercially advantageous. At least as far as Bacon was concerned, it would also underpin some of James's more absolutist claims about the nature of monarchical authority.[28] Many of those who supported the Spanish marriage alliance in fact had no investment in Catholicism as such. As Adams remarks, 'the legends of bribery and secret Catholicism connected with the "Spanish faction" have tended to obscure much of the significance of support for an alliance with Spain'.[29] Some of the match's exponents regarded the Catholic issue as a positive obstacle. Even those who did subsequently turn out to have an ideological investment in it, such as the secretary of state, Sir George Calvert (who converted to the Church of Rome in 1625 and was evidently sympathetic to Catholicism long before that), were quite happy to mislead and hinder resident Spanish diplomats when they agitated for concessions to be made to English Catholics. For Adams, 'the attitude taken to the Roman Church by such important members of the Spanish party' as Calvert, and also by Sir Richard Weston and Sir Francis Cottington, in the early 1620s was 'far from clear'. Arguably, such people were primarily influenced by a belief that the Habsburgs represented 'social order and monarchical legitimacy and stability in a world threatened by Dutch and presbyterian republicanism'.[30]

It was natural that the opposition to the proposed Anglo-Spanish treaty would seek to appeal to a wider public when it found itself forced onto the defensive in court and council.[31] One means of gathering support was through parliament. Inevitably, a parliamentary solution to the crown's foreign-policy and financial difficulties would have Hispanophobe characteristics. Divines such as George Abbot assumed that parliament would always function as a bulwark against popery:[32] parliament had traditionally served as a forum for voicing demands that rigour should be used against English papists. It was obvious to all that a visible harshness towards Catholics, so visible that not even the most myopic foreign ambassador could miss it, would serve as a means to hinder a Catholic dynastic marriage for the Stuart heir. James's belief in the free exercise of his prerogative inevitably led him to raise parliamentary hackles in both 1621 and 1624 when he showed

[28] *Ibid.*, pp. 250–251.

[29] Adams, FP, p. 140.

[30] *Ibid.*, pp. 140–141.

[31] For an excellent account of how the criticism of the regime's foreign policy was voiced in the pulpits, see J. Shami, *John Donne and Conformity in Crisis in the Late Jacobean Pulpit* (Cambridge, 2003), ch. 2.

[32] Lake, 'Anti-popery', p. 91.

himself unwilling to allow the rigorous enforcement of the law against Catholics.

As we shall see, both Spanish and French negotiators used the issue of toleration to test and determine how enthusiastic the Stuart regime was about the proposed treaties, and whether those, including Catholics, who might be regarded as having most interest in the success of the negotiations – and the defence of whatever polity emerged from them – would be given access and influence. Would, for instance, known Catholics be allowed onto the privy council? This would serve as a sure indication of how committed the Stuarts would be to the non-domestic clauses of whatever alliance was concluded, for example the military guarantees made to their new ally, who was, supposedly, making an equal commitment to them (which, in the early 1620s, meant assistance with the resolution of the question of the Palatinate).

Sir Basil Brooke, a prominent Catholic, drew up a position paper on this subject, apparently for the eyes of a Spanish diplomat. He claimed that 'the Spanishe party and the Catholike party [in England] are one and the same thing', so that the advancement of 'Spanish designes dependant on the amity with England will consist principally in advancing the Catholicke party'. It was vital, then, that the oaths of supremacy and allegiance should, for them, be set aside. Brooke added that 'it is not desired (for the present) that offices of importance should be conferred upon Catholikes, but only [that] the disabilities and incapacities of Catholickes to serve in offices be taken away, leaving the disposicion of offices wholly in his Majesties pleasure'. Brooke envisaged the entry of Catholics to parliament as a means of overthrowing the penal legislation. He thought Protestants' 'tender consciences', opposed to the royal supremacy, might be enlisted for this project.[33] William Bishop speculated in early 1623 about which English Catholic noblemen might be admitted to the privy council.[34]

To many observers, both Protestant and Catholic, it seemed certain that, if the negotiations were to proceed successfully, the ideological composition of the regime itself would be fundamentally altered, as would the character of the English Church. Another Catholic advice paper, written when it seemed that the marriage negotiations were about to succeed, anticipated not just that the marriage would be a means to protect Catholics but also that moderate Protestants would support the marriage proposals. The less moderate ones,

[33]BL, Additional MS 21203, fo. 12r; cf. Redworth, *PI*, pp. 41–42. Brooke's commercial interests predisposed him to be hostile to the Dutch, who had complained in early July 1619 about a patent, held by him from the crown, 'for the makeing of steele [. . .] and prohibiting the importacion of forraine steele': *APC, 1619–1621*, pp. 2–3, 77–78.

[34]AAW, B 25, no. 82 (cited in *Letter 7*).

identified as 'puritans', would be astounded and downcast when the marriage worked inevitably to undermine the cause of pan-European Protestantism. The moderates – the ones who appeared to be favourable to, and sometimes even praised, Catholic modes of worship – would, of necessity, be approached by the crown in order to push through the Anglo-Spanish treaty.[35]

This statement of English Catholic opinion argued that 'the nature and disposition of these two nations, English and Spanish, doe tend and incline unto mutual friendship, as it were by a natural propension'; furthermore 'they have seldome or never had enmities for anie cause till the difference of religion did separate them'. Anglo-Spanish amity would spawn a universal peace, or at least peace in northern Europe, for 'it is evident that England only being quiet from warres, France, Germanie and Flanders have much prevailed in restraining rebels and establishing sure peace, which certainely, whiles England was in armes, for more than 40 yeares last past could never be performed'.

One imagines that this is not how some of those old enough to remember the 1580s and 1590s would have seen it. This document claimed, however, that it was only malice, self-interest, and the love of conflict which had led German and Dutch heretics and 'English puritans' to do 'all they can [. . .] to breake of[f] that treatie' and to persuade the prince to marry a Protestant and to risk conflagration in Europe. For

> we have lately seene how fatal and almost deadly to the Christian world hath beene the mariage of the Ladie Elisabeth [. . .] with the prince palatine, and how greate tumults the [. . .] prince palatine and his consorts (all relying upon the authoritie and power of the king of England, by reason of the foresaide mariage) have raysed in Bohemia, Germanie, Hungarie and other neighbour countries.

Within James's own realm, if the Spanish marriage were to fail, the 'puritans' would 'persequute and rage against us English Catholiques much worse than ever before'. A papal endorsement of the match would assuredly prevent this. But the success of the match would greatly increase the Catholic faith in Britain. This was because 'all English men who are not Catholiques are either indeed true heretiques, to witt the puritans, or doe professe them selves to be Protestants, for feare of the severe lawes, being in hart Catholiques'. Or, through 'licentiousnesse', they are of no religion at all. The number of the puritans 'is verie small' while the 'number [. . .] of the second

[35]BL, Harleian MS 1583, fos 291r–294r; AAW, B 25, no. 39. This document, which seems to have been drawn up by, or on behalf of, the English Catholic secular clergy, argued that the papacy should grant a dispensation for the proposed Anglo-Spanish marriage; it was sent to Rome for curial perusal there, and appears to have been written in late 1622.

sort' is 'verie great', even if the entirely uncommitted were more numerous still. The marriage would impel those Protestants inclined to moderation 'presently to the Catholique Church, and ecclesiasticall discipline', while many of those inclined to puritanism through ignorance would rapidly be disabused. Indeed, 'by the connivencie' of 'a fewe months and some small suspension of penall lawes' in 1622, 'a great number be alreadie united to the Catholique Church in so much that manie, of whom before there was verie litle or no hope, nowe have reconciled themselves to the Catholique Church, for which the puritans [...] alreadie dayly doe complaine'. The process of national conversion would be assisted, furthermore, by the good and transformative effects which the prince of Wales's bride would have on him. Even if he did not convert to Catholicism, the children of the marriage would undoubtedly be 'trained and accustomed to Catholique pietie'. Then, across Europe, the Protestant dominoes would start to fall: 'other neighbour countries which have taken their false doctrine from our infection [...] when Catholique religion shall be restored unto us [...] will feele the holesome fruict thereof, with great benefit of soules'.

Inevitably, too, the prevailing definitions of appropriate religious demeanour and inclination, as well as of what constituted true loyalty to the Stuart dynasty, would start to change. This would certainly happen when the king moved to silence the puritan slurs on his government, reined in the rapacious officials who enforced the law against Catholics, and took 'into his privie councell more moderate men', ones who were 'better affected to Catholique religion'. James had already punished some puritan preachers and 'by quips and jeasts [...] he hath made them contemptible'. Also 'he sendeth abroade preachers who speake modestly of Catholique matters, and such as sometime doe affirme the reall presence of our Saviours bodie in the Blessed Sacrament'. These men taught 'the worship of the holy crosse to be approved by all antiquitie' and they commended 'to the people other points and mysteries of Catholique faith'. Such preachers were the ones whom the king advanced to 'ecclesiasticall dignities'. Recently,

> one of the chiefest of their bishops, famous among them for his learning [Lancelot Andrewes, one assumes] did celebrate their service somewhat like the exteriour forme of a Masse, and imitated the consecration and elevation and other ceremonies of the Masse before all the people, looking and admiring thereat, so that many thought the Masse it self to be brought againe in practise.

If anyone doubted that all this was by the king's command, it was necessary only to observe the termination of the 1621 parliament (an inevitable step 'when he could not remove' the puritans 'from their purpose') to know that the king positively endorsed these developments.[36]

Of course, this was special pleading. Andrewes is unlikely to have thought that he was celebrating the Roman Mass, while those who objected to the Anglo-Spanish dynastic negotiations were not exclusively puritans. Yet signs of change had been evident during the spring and summer of 1622, when distinctly (on some accounts) moderate Protestant divines, rather than seasoned godly polemicists, were chosen to engage in debate with the noted Jesuit evangelist John Percy (better known by his alias of Fisher) in order to persuade the countess of Buckingham to pledge her allegiance to the Church of England.[37] In addition, Catholics knew what they were doing when they warned against the quasi-republican dangers represented by the Bohemian party in England.[38] The secular clergy advised that 'our northerne sectaries, Germans, Flemmings, French and English puritans doe all endevour by their united forces that the succession of the crowne of England should be derived unto the palatine and his children'. They thought that this could not but encourage James and Charles both to seek alliance with Spain and to allow the Catholics to 'encrease in power and number, upon whose strength the safegarde of themselves and their succession doth relie', and to ensure 'that the strength and power of the puritans [. . .] may be diminished'.[39]

The certainty that some measure of toleration for Catholics would be stipulated by the Spaniards and by the papacy as an essential prerequisite for a Catholic dynastic union for Prince Charles was central to the debates within the Catholic community about reform and particularly those about the alleged need for more ecclesiastical hierarchy within the community in order to regulate both clergy and laity. The agitation for a grant of toleration to James's Catholic subjects was therefore integral to the campaign at Rome to secure an award of episcopal authority to an English priest who would reside and exercise his authority in James's English realm. Indeed, from the time of the appellant controversy at the turn of the century, a number of Catholic clergymen had argued that the papacy should put the English Catholics' house in order by reinstating a hierarchy there.[40] They declared that this would not only increase the true faith but

[36]BL, Harleian MS 1583, fos 291r–294r.

[37]See *Letter 14*; and below, p. 30.

[38]For the popularity of Frederick and Elizabeth in English politics, something which 'provided the Spanish faction with one of their more useful propaganda weapons: the claim that the palatines and their English allies were aiming at the succession and even the overthrow of James', see Adams, PC, p. 291.

[39]BL, Harleian MS 1583, fo. 295r; cf. *Letter 22*.

[40]See *NAGB*, introduction and *passim*.

also restrain hot and unbridled Catholic spirits of the kind who most offended and provoked the regime and state.

The opponents of a reinstated episcopal jurisdiction – mostly members of the religious orders and their lay sympathizers and patrons – claimed that the time was not right for such a development in a still manifestly heretical country where such jurisdiction could not be properly exercised and where its inevitable failings would weaken the faithful. The appointment of such a prelate, they said, would enrage the authorities against the Catholics and would bring down on the faithful a more grievous persecution than that which they were already suffering.

One typical position paper on the topic, written in the mid-1630s either by a Jesuit or by someone who sympathized with the Society of Jesus, argued that, even if a newly appointed English Catholic bishop should 'imploy himself onely upon ministring the sacrament of confirmation and making chrisme and holy orders and the lyke, we hould it [...] to be very unfitte and unsaufe'. For even the bishop's exercise of this spiritual function would be 'commonly very publique, and bothe the bishoppe must have diverse servants and officers about him, and many are assembled to receve that sacrament'. Wherever the bishop resided it would be impossible to maintain adequate security. Of course, many argued that the king was himself tolerant and irenic, 'very mercifull and full of goodnesse'. However, 'many inferiour magistrates and bishoppes and judges are full of their zeale against us'. Furthermore, while Catholics might enjoy a de facto toleration (by means of compounding for their forfeitures), 'yet wee have noe certeynty at all that the same kinde of moderation shall [...] last'. For 'the lawes are still in force against us for performing any act of our owne religion'. Trouble could flare up at any time 'as upon some difference with a pursevant or the offending of any Protestant officer'; and 'the offence which is taken nowe maye be punished even to our undoing a dozen or twenty yeares hence'. Even if the king were inclined to interfere in the judicial process, he would often have to refrain 'bicause he cannot doe it [...] without publique notice; the which he is carefull to avoyde and so the Catholique is forced to sufferre, though it be even against the kings owne will'.[41]

There were suspicions, too, about exactly how far the new bishop would restrict his activities to the realm of the spiritual. The writer of the same memorandum feared 'howe easy it wilbe for a bishoppe, whoe commeth in limitted and restrayned at the first, to enlarge perhappes his commission, or else to erre in the execution therof, through some passion or other'. Even if the bishop were not at fault,

[41] ARSJ, Anglia MS 36/i, fo. 11r–v.

his grandiloquent exposition of his own ecclesiastical authority would induce 'the great jealousye of the Protestant bishoppes', who would 'persecute both the sayd bishoppe himself and all such others as they shall discover to have relation to him'.[42]

Here the Jesuits publicly paraded their concern for the health and safety of all English Catholics. More privately, and far from inaccurately, some Jesuits said that their enemies wanted to get their hands on this kind of authority in order to exercise an unnatural and damaging dominion over English Catholicism, and primarily over their own enemies in the religious orders and among those orders' lay patrons. It was not, however, a great leap from this observation to a more general (and, to some, definitely offensive) thesis that those who entered the religious orders had a superior spiritual vocation themselves and were less inclined to interfere in politics to the detriment of the wider Catholic community.

By contrast, the leading secular clergy proponents of a restored hierarchy argued that, notwithstanding all the outward appearances of royal and parliamentary hostility to any such thing, an English Catholic bishop (a prelate who would not have 'that compleat authority which other bishopps have and may exercise over all that are in their diocesse' – in other words, a spiritual man, and one without temporal political power and pretensions) would not be offensive to the English state in the way that, as so many assumed, the meddlesome Jesuits were. One of the secular clergy's position papers on the topic, written during Charles's reign, argued that, 'considering [. . .] his Majesty hath no small number of subjects in his realmes of Great Brittane who professe the Catholick Roman religion', it was necessary for the good of the whole commonwealth for them to have spiritual direction and sacramental ministration. The writer stressed how

> the state useth to distinguish betweene priest and priest, and betweene Catholick and Catholick, houlding some more disinteressed than others, and of a truer zeale towards their king and country. There seemeth to be noe question but that the king and state, upon due consideracion, will judg[e] it much safer and more conducing to their ends that the said Catholicks and priests should bee subject to a spirituall superiour of their owne profession, residing ordinarily within the realme, than permitted to live confusedly without any setled governement or subordination amongst themselves.[43]

[42] *Ibid.*, fo. 11v.

[43] AAW, B 27, no. 105 ('Reasons to induce the court of Rome to beleeve that a Catholick bishop in England will not bee offensive to the king and state'). The writer of this paper argued that 'the king and state doe very well know that episcopall governement is the naturall and ordinary governement of the Catholick Church in all places, and that it belongeth to the integrity of Catholick religion to include discipline noe lesse than doctrine and governement togeather with beliefe'. It had always been a maxim of the English state's

The rhetoric of the Catholic community's proponents of augmented hierarchal authority shared some of the resonances of the style of ecclesiology in the Church of England which historians now seem to call 'avant-garde' conformity. It is worth noting that, throughout this period, a certain section of the English Catholic community tended to recall James's words at the Hampton Court conference (and particularly the phrase 'no bishop, no king').[44] Certain Catholics' accounts of the Jesuits' attempts to prevent Rome's appointment of a Catholic bishop to govern in England were undoubtedly intended to resonate within the context of rumours that puritans still aspired to destroy the religion established by law in the English Church, and particularly that there was a dark lay conspiracy to appropriate the wealth of the Church through the agitation of malign clerical cat's-paws. Even the secular clergy's complaints about the prominence and influence of Catholic laymen (meaning the patrons of the religious orders) mimicked the style and arguments of conformists within the Church of England who sometimes glanced unfavourably at the power of the laity over the Church.

In October 1624, as the seculars were still waiting for Rome to nominate a successor to the recently deceased William Bishop, George Fisher wrote a long exhortatory letter to his friend Thomas More in Rome, in which he warned of the evil effects of the regulars' lay patrons' interference in the election of a new bishop.[45] It had become known that Rome was consulting quite widely on who should replace Bishop; among those contacted were leading lay Catholics, some of whom tended to side with the regulars. Some seculars complained bitterly about the 'motions and conceipts of particular persons, and those lay people too'. They even feared that Bishop's successor might be a member of one of the religious orders, or one of their clerical sympathizers, thus prostituting the newly established episcopal authority to the control of lay patrons of the religious, particularly of the Jesuits.[46]

There was here, however, an opportunity to construct an image of Catholic loyalism which was not phrased in the distasteful and embarrassing terms of the recent debate over the oath of allegiance (a

proceedings against Catholics that they were not punished 'for any point belonging meerely to religion'. So, 'upon this sole consideracion, it might happily be presumed that the king and state will take noe offence to see the Catholicks of England governed according to the ordinary principles of their owne religion, and to live under the same forme of discipline, which is usually observed by all other their Catholick brethren through out the whole world': *ibid.*

[44] See, e.g., Questier, *C&C*, p. 439.

[45] AAW, B 47, no. 156.

[46] AAW, B 26, no. 50 (cited in *Letter 45*).

debate in which the Jesuits had been all too prominent) but, instead, of the arguments about how far an episcopal Catholic system of Church government in England would coincide with and underpin the purposes of the Jacobean state. In the 1620s, and even more in the 1630s, some Catholics argued that a Catholic bishop, tolerated by the state, would commend obedience to monarchical authority and would compel it from Catholics in England as a matter of conscience. He would preserve Catholics in 'peace and good order among themselves' and also 'in perfect obedience to the king and in a generall good temper of mind towards the state'.[47] Bishop Richard Smith's supporters asserted that 'the wisest and most moderate of the Protestant clergy are so farr from being offended or thinking it straunge to see Catholickes governed by a bishop of their owne, as they rather much wonder that the matter hath bin formerly so long neglected'.[48]

Of course, this is not the same as saying, and should not be taken to signify, that those of a conformist cast of mind in the Church of England all positively sympathized with Catholics on religious or political grounds. William Laud was, from time to time, genuinely hostile towards the Church of Rome.[49] Yet this does not mean that we should ignore the convergence, at various points, of the ideological agendas of these lobbies within the two Churches.[50] Contemporaries could easily perceive the common ground in the ecclesiological arguments and rhetoric which were deployed, on the one hand, by avant-garde conformists and, on the other, by certain sorts of Catholics.

As for King James, his attitude towards the papacy was arguably rather inconsistent, though undoubtedly he did not think it was. At times he had claimed to regard the pope as Antichrist: he had done so very publicly during the course of the controversy over the oath of allegiance. But at other times he had declared himself ready to accept the pope as the patriarch of Western Christendom.[51] In February 1621, Gondomar wrote that, in a conversation with James about how far the

[47] AAW, B 27, no. 105; *NCC*, *passim*. It was claimed that King James, perceiving the benefits of having a Catholic hierarchical authority within his English realm, gave 'tacite way to the restoring of this episcopall governement': AAW, B 27, no. 105.

[48] *Ibid.*

[49] See, e.g., Russell, *PEP*, p. 164.

[50] See M. Questier, 'Arminianism, Catholicism and Puritanism in England during the 1630s', *HJ*, 49 (2006), pp. 53–78.

[51] As Adams points out, even James's *Premonition* of 1609, defending the 1606 oath, was not entirely straightforward in its identification of the pope as Antichrist. Richard Montagu was able to claim, at the York House conference in 1626, that James's description of the papacy in that publication did not actually mean what godly Protestants generally took it to mean: Adams, FP, p. 148.

king could move towards détente with Catholicism and the papacy, James had said that he would recognize

> the pope [. . .] as his universal head and of all Christianity in the spiritual and ecclesiastical, and that there might be appeals to the pope from all of the bishops in his dominions provided that the pope did not mingle in the temporal jurisdiction of his states, especially in the removal and deposition of kings at his pleasure.

He had, he said, called the pope Antichrist in his published tracts on the oath of allegiance only because of the pope's temporal ambitions, and, 'were he not so acting, he would hold the pope as the universal head'.[52] A formal letter from James to Gregory XV, written on 30 September 1622, addressed the pope warmly, stressed the compatibility of their faiths, and urged him to join with James in an attempt to put an end to 'these calamitous discords and bloodsheds which for these late years by-past have so miserably rent the Christian world'.[53]

Even after the Spanish match had failed, James still publicly described the new pope, the recently elected Urban VIII, as a 'marvailous good prelate, wise, myld and judicious'.[54] John Jackson, perhaps the most outspoken monarchist among the secular clergy newsletter writers, added a postscript to a dispatch written by his friend Thomas More that 'owr k[ing] saieth that this pope is more than a scholler, v[i]z a statesman also, for if he were onely a scholler he shold doe well enowgh'.[55] In some senses, then, the Catholic activists in the religious politics of the early 1620s were simply following a royal lead.

## The Anglo-Spanish Negotiations and the 1621 Parliament

Negotiations for a Catholic European dynastic match for Prince Charles had continued, on and off, from the middle years of James's

[52] CRS, 68, p. 146.

[53] G.P.V. Akrigg (ed.), *Letters of King James VI & I* (London, 1984), p. 384; W.B. Patterson, *King James VI and I and the Reunion of Christendom* (Cambridge, 1997), pp. 313–314. The letter also supplied diplomatic credentials for the Roman Catholic priest George Gage.

[54] *Letter 46*. Of course, in early 1624, the Stuart court (in the course of negotiations with the Bourbon family for an Anglo-French marriage treaty) had every reason to persuade the French that it was not riddled with anti-popery.

[55] AAW, B 26, no. 10.

reign.[56] Once Gondomar had indicated, in early March 1617, that the Spanish court had sought its own theologians' approval for a treaty, Digby was dispatched to Spain in order to contract a dynastic marriage alliance.[57] Then, as we have noted, there occurred the revolt against Ferdinand and against Habsburg rule in Bohemia, situated next to the elector palatine's territory of the Upper Palatinate, which meant that James's son-in-law had a considerable interest in intervening in this dispute, and James himself was virtually under an obligation to reaffirm his support for Europe's Protestants.[58] In turn, if the Bohemian question were to be resolved, the Spaniards would have more freedom to renew the pressure on the Dutch, following the end of the Truce of Antwerp.[59] This might make the Dutch more ready to negotiate with James when it came to questions of competition in trade matters.[60] Yet, as Adams argues, James's dilatory response to the crisis, in the form of Viscount Doncaster's embassy to Frederick in May 1619, meant that James, in effect, 'abdicated the leadership' of the European Protestant cause.[61] The political dominance of *dévot* opinion in France at this point meant that no aid would come to the Bohemian cause from the French court, even though some Huguenot leaders offered their assistance to James if he would command a Protestant alliance against the Habsburgs.[62]

During the summer of 1619, however, negotiations were conducted in order to secure some sort of armistice. Initially, the Bohemian rebels had proved remarkably successful against imperial troops, though the defeat near Budweis in early June of the roving military entrepreneur and warlord Count Ernst von Mansfelt temporarily handed the

[56] T. Cogswell, 'England and the Spanish match', in Cust and Hughes, *Conflict in Early Stuart England*, p. 111, citing S.R. Gardiner, *The History of England, 1603–1642*, 10 vols (London, 1883–1884), II, pp. 216–258, 314–369, III, 37–106; Thrush, 'Personal rule'.

[57] Thrush 'Personal rule', p. 94; TD, V, pp. 115–116; Albion, *CI*, pp. 16f.; McClure, *LJC*, p. 64; Bodleian Library, Tanner MS 74, fos 92r–93r. According to John Chamberlain, Digby departed 'having alredy apparelled all his followers *alla Spagnuola*'. He carried 'with him a troupe of notorious Catholiques, which is not so well disgested [*sic*] of divers that heretofore hoped and promised themselves better of him': McClure, *LJC*, p. 82.

[58] Pursell, *WK*, pp. 48–53. When Christoph von Dohna, Frederick V's agent, came on embassy in late 1618, arriving in early 1619, James agreed to the renewal of his treaty with the German Protestant Union. This, as Adams points out, made some believe, wrongly, that 'he would in time come to the assistance of the Bohemians': Pursell, *WK*, p. 54; Adams, PC, p. 278; A. Courtney, 'Court politics and the kingship of James VI & I, c. 1615–c. 1621' (unpublished PhD thesis, University of Cambridge, 2008), p. 176.

[59] Parker, *The Dutch Revolt*, pp. 263–264; Pursell, *WK*, p. 134.

[60] Schreiber, *FC*, p. 24. Maurice of Nassau had been anticipating a possible Anglo-Dutch alliance, following the end of the Truce of Antwerp in 1621, by trying to put an end to extant colonial disputes: Adams, PC, p. 288.

[61] *Ibid.*, p. 279.

[62] *Ibid.*, p. 289.

advantage to the imperialists.[63] Frederick then, in late September 1619, accepted the Bohemian crown, contrary to James's publicly expressed wishes and the advice of some of his own supporters. On 16/26 August, the estates of Bohemia had voted for Frederick to be their king, and he was crowned in Prague on 25 October/4 November.[64] Meanwhile, Ferdinand was himself elected to the imperial throne on 18/28 August, ironically with the vote of Frederick's representative at the election in Frankfurt. (The emperor Matthias had died in March 1619.) This was one reason for Ferdinand's deposition by the Bohemians in the same month: they did not know of his election but were anticipating it.[65] The Spaniards now had a reason for supporting Ferdinand because, by a treaty in 1617, he had agreed that, if Spanish support for his imperial candidacy were forthcoming, he would, with other concessions, cede Alsace to his Spanish cousins. In turn, this would facilitate their forthcoming renewal of hostilities against the Dutch.[66]

Despite the intervention of Bethlen Gábor, who marched on Vienna in October 1619, the Bohemian cause faltered. The army which they had dispatched against the imperial capital was, with the Hungarians and their other allies, compelled to fall back.[67] James's son-in-law was expelled from Bohemia and, gradually and painfully, from his own domain of the Palatinate. Imperial forces conquered Bohemia, while troops from Flanders, at the direction of Ambrogio Spinola, marquis of Los Balbases, took the Lower Palatinate on the Rhine. Troops provided by the Catholic League (set up in 1609 to confront the Union of German Protestants) and raised through the agency of Maximilian I, duke of Bavaria, subsequently acquired the Upper Palatinate. The battle of the White Mountain was fought outside Prague on 29 October/8 November 1620. The actual military confrontation was short, but the rebels were forced from their positions back into the city. Frederick and Elizabeth fled their capital almost immediately, and Prague fell soon thereafter.[68]

[63]Schreiber, *FC*, pp. 26–31; Pursell, *WK*, pp. 49, 56, 58–59, 81.

[64]Pursell, *WK*, p. 85.

[65]Schreiber, *FC*, pp. 5, 6; Pursell, *WK*, pp. 54, 58–59, ch. 3, *passim*.

[66]Schreiber, *FC*, p. 25; *CCE*, p. 126; M.S. Sánchez, 'A house divided: Spain, Austria, and the Bohemian and Hungarian successions', *Sixteenth Century Journal*, 25 (1994), pp. 887–903; Pursell, *WK*, p. 47.

[67]G. Parker, *Europe in Crisis 1598–1648* (Brighton, 1980), pp. 164–166; Pursell, *WK*, pp. 81, 107, 108.

[68]Cogswell, *BR*, pp. 18–19; Parker, *Europe in Crisis*, pp. 167–169; Polisensky, *The Thirty Years War*, p. 129; B. Pursell, 'War or peace? Jacobean politics and the parliament of 1621', in C. Kyle (ed.), *Parliaments, Politics and Elections, 1604–1648*, Camden Society, 5th series, 17 (Cambridge, 2001), p. 149; Pursell, *WK*, pp. 33, 104, 115, 141; PRO, SP 77/14, fo. 239r. An embassy led by Sir Richard Weston and Sir Edward Conway in July 1620 had tried,

Increasingly, the Anglo-Spanish match became a necessity for James, who could not now hope to influence the situation in central Europe in any other way, particularly as he came under pressure from the elector's supporters to intervene militarily in his favour.[69] The Spaniards were, it appeared, potentially amenable to the restitution of the elector palatine's territories – Roger Lockyer argues that the Spaniards 'recognised that Frederick must either be restored or compensated' – but they could not, on their own, hand back the Lower Palatinate since they did not have exclusive possession of it.[70] At the same time, the apparent incoherence of James's policy allowed others, particularly the Franco-Bohemian faction, to make a bid for influence which they would not otherwise have; and it seemed to give the Spanish ambassador, Gondomar, extraordinary sway over the king. Ironically, therefore, the eruption of godly pro-palatine sentiment augmented the power of those whom contemporaries identified as part of a Spanish faction in English politics.[71]

In order to make the Habsburgs negotiate with him, James had to have popular (and ultimately parliamentary) backing for a war. But, in making a pitch in this way to belligerent godly Protestant public opinion, he risked convincing people that he really intended to fight, which was not the case.[72] Predictably, therefore, James faced serious problems when the 1621 parliament assembled, in the wake of the crown's recent inadequate attempt to raise revenue via the device of a loan, the news of Frederick's defeat at the battle of the White Mountain, and, also, Louis XIII's military campaign against the Huguenots (itself a response to the war in Germany which would prevent foreign interference as the French court moved to crush Huguenot resistance).[73]

unsuccessfully, to avert the invasion of the Lower Palatinate: PRO, SP 77/14, fos 163r–164r; Pursell, *WK*, p. 110. Some bastions held out against Spinola in the Lower Palatinate until September 1622: Schreiber, *FC*, p. 49. For the imperial–Spanish treaty in February 1620 concerning the joint conquest of Frederick's territories, see Zaller, *1621*, p. 11. For the Spanish strategic incentives, objectives, and strategy in invading the Lower Palatinate, see Pursell, *WK*, pp. 105–106, 115; Zaller, *1621*, p. 16; Redworth, *PI*, pp. 21, 22; and, for the geography of the Palatinate, see Pursell, *WK*, p. 23; Redworth, *PI*, p. 11.

[69] For the Bohemian faction in English politics, see Adams, PC, pp. 285–288.

[70] R. Lockyer, *Buckingham: the life and political career of George Villiers, first duke of Buckingham 1592–1628* (London, 1981), pp. 125–126; Adams, PC, p. 303; Cogswell, *BR*, pp. 18–19. For the strategic considerations raised for the Spaniards by their successful invasion of the Rhineland Palatinate, see J.H. Elliott, *The Count-Duke of Olivares* (London, 1986), p. 205; Pursell, *WK*, p. 106.

[71] Adams, PC, p. 304.

[72] Russell, *PEP*, p. 87; Lockyer, *Buckingham*, p. 107; Adams, PC, p. 304; Courtney, 'Court politics', p. 99.

[73] Zaller, *1621*, pp. 30–31; Pursell, *WK*, pp. 138–139; Adams, PC, pp. 305–307, 312.

The 1621 parliament has been the subject of quite intense modern historiographical controversy. Some scholars have wanted to argue that the Commons had no intention of seizing the initiative in foreign policy from the crown, and were even prepared to follow the crown's lead,[74] whereas the traditional narratives have always stressed that, during the session, a serious ideological and constitutional conflict arose between crown and parliament. There was certainly sufficient expression of Hispanophobe sentiment there, and also of other traditional styles of anti-popish invective, notably during the Edward Floyd case. Some of this invective demanded the rigorous enforcement of the law against Catholic nonconformity: new recusancy legislation was introduced, which passed both Houses in May 1621. The belief in some quarters that the proper prosecution of Catholic nonconformity was being corrupted, deflected, and undermined expressed itself in attacks on the veteran and allegedly crypto-Catholic exchequer official Sir Henry Spiller. At the same time, there was agitation over monopolies and other varieties of corruption.[75] Buckingham, who had conspicuously become alienated from the leading members of the Bohemian party and was threatened by the corruption investigations directed against monopolies, 'faced the opening of the session as an ally of Gondomar'.[76]

For much Protestant public opinion, both in and outside parliament, James's response in the period up to the end of the first sitting of 1621 was hardly encouraging.[77] Those of a Hispanophobe temperament would not have been reassured by the sight of circulating Catholic pamphlets, notably those written by Richard Verstegan in reply to Thomas Scott.[78] The regime certainly attracted adverse criticism as it moved against those (the earl of Southampton, Sir Edwin Sandys,

[74] Russell, *PEP*, p. 87.

[75] Zaller, *1621*, pp. 41, 42, 43, 53–59, and *passim*. For the Floyd case, see Russell, *PEP*, p. 117; Zaller, *1621*, p. 104. For the draft recusancy legislation, see Zaller, *1621*, p. 132; *CSPV, 1621–1623*, pp. 54–55; McClure, *LJC*, p. 379. For Spiller, see Questier, 'Sir Henry Spiller', p. 256. Spiller, together with Sir Lewis Lewkenor, had taken command of a force of three hundred men in December 1620 in order to guard Gondomar's residence, following the revelation of an alleged plot to murder him and his entourage: *CSPV, 1619–1621*, pp. 501–502. Spiller's expertise was crucial in the drawing up of the pardons for recusants in the summer of 1623: PRO, SP 14/151/27.

[76] Adams, PC, p. 306.

[77] Zaller, *1621*, pp. 43–44; McClure, *LJC*, p. 345.

[78] See A.F. Allison, 'A group of political tracts, 1621–1623, by Richard Verstegan', *RH*, 18 (1986), pp. 128–142; P. Lake, 'Constitutional consensus and puritan opposition in the 1620s: Thomas Scott and the Spanish match', *HJ*, 25 (1982), pp. 805–825. Russell argues that the Commons's anti-Spanish emotionalism was formal and traditional rather than strongly ideological: Russell, *PEP*, pp. 119–120. But, for the enthusiastic puritan reception of Scott (as well as other anti-popish writers and preachers), see, e.g., *DSSD*, pp. 125–126, and *passim*.

and John Selden) who had opposed it during the first sitting.[79] From within the regime, people such as Thomas Murray and George Hakewill continued to agitate surreptitiously against the marriage proposals.[80]

Digby had gone on embassy to Vienna in May 1621 to try to broker a cease-fire with the emperor. The infanta-archduchess Isabella, established by her father, Philip II, as autonomous ruler with her husband the archduke, Albert (d. July 1621), of the Spanish Low Countries, had already assented to this proposal after Digby had visited Brussels in March to ask for a suspension of arms. This had resulted in a withdrawal of some of the Spanish troops in the Lower Palatinate and a three-month cessation of military activities. But Digby's embassy in Vienna failed, not least because of Frederick's utter intransigence and the provocation offered both by Mansfelt's troops in the Upper Palatinate sallying across the Bohemian border and by Gábor's military operations near Vienna. Digby, though hardly an enthusiast for Frederick's cause, was forced to conclude that a military defence of the Palatinate was required, even though the German Union of Protestants had recently dissolved itself. Digby himself contributed to the successful, though temporary, protection of Frankenthal by Mansfelt's troops.[81] He returned to London in October 1621 and called for the reinforcement of the soldiers, led by Sir Horace Vere, who had been recruited for the Palatinate in early and mid-1620.[82] Digby's account of the Habsburgs' intentions

[79]For the proceedings against Southampton, Sandys, and Selden (which involved Sir Henry Spiller and another crypto-papist, Sir John Weston), and also against the earl of Oxford, see Zaller, *1621*, p. 139; Russell, *PEP*, pp. 122–123, 133; PRO, SP 14/121/136; Adams, PC, p. 315; McClure, *LJC*, pp. 384–385. Emily Rose has made a convincing case that the action taken against Southampton, Sandys, and Selden was motivated by the question of tax revenues generated by the Virginia Company rather than by opposition to the regime's foreign policy, although it seems likely that the two sets of concerns were, in practice, connected: E. Rose, 'Betting on the New World' (forthcoming). I am very grateful to Dr Rose for allowing me to read her work in draft.

[80]PRO, SP 14/122/46, 88; Bodleian Library, Rawlinson MS D 853, no. 13 (George Hakewill, 'The Wedding Ring: or, a treatise touching the unlawfulness [. . .] of Protestants marriages with papists, devided into three parts [. . .]'); McClure, *LJC*, pp. 393, 394; *CSPV, 1621–1623*, p. 107.

[81]Adams, PC, pp. 319–320; Pursell, *WK*, pp. 134–135, 136, 140–144, 149–150; *Letter 1*. For the constitutional implications of Archduke Albert's death, see *CGB*, I, pp. xvii, 29, 101.

[82]Adams, PC, pp. 300–302; Redworth, *PI*, p. 25; PRO, SP 77/14, fo. 300r; *CSPV, 1619–1621*, pp. 262, 291–292, and *passim*; Pursell, *WK*, p. 109. For the attempts to raise funds for the elector palatine, see Adams, PC, pp. 296–299. English Catholics contributed financial aid to the imperial cause (though some were more enthusiastic than others) as a counterweight to the funds which were being raised by the Bohemian party: see McClure, *LJC*, p. 326; PRO, SP 15/42/22; *CSPV, 1619–1621*, p. 479; Zaller, *1621*, p. 19; Whiteway, *Diary*, p. 31.

also meant that James was forced to recall parliament.[83] However, as Adams comments, there had been a minor 'purge of the Bohemian party' earlier in the year, and the replacements of the dismissed ministers 'were to form the core of the Spanish faction of the 1620s'.[84]

Parliament reassembled in November 1621.[85] James relied on Digby, Calvert, John Williams, and Sir Lionel Cranfield to put the line to the parliament that the forces currently defending the Palatinate should be kept in being, and that nothing should be done to forestall the proposed dynastic treaty with Spain.[86] However, there was a distinct mismatch between the moderate rhetoric of councillors such as Cranfield and Digby – who announced that the Habsburgs seemed merely uncooperative, making it advisable to prepare for military action – and the bloodcurdling calls to arms of speakers such as Sir Robert Phelips, who demanded war against Spain.[87] In the provinces, there were overt displays of anti-popish zeal.[88] The Commons was saturated with demands for effectual punishment of Catholic nonconformity – of a piece with the calls for military endeavour abroad – notably as a result of Sir George Goring's famous intervention in the lower House on 29 November. All of this culminated in the petition of 1 December, read in the Commons on 3 December, the king's vitriolic response, the declaration of 8 December, the royal replies of 11 and 17 December, and, finally, the protestation of 18 December, leading to

[83] Adams, PC, p. 320. Via a seizure of imperial correspondence, it was established that – as was already expected – Ferdinand intended to allocate the Palatinate and the electoral title that went with it to Maximilian I of Bavaria (the title was formally conveyed to him in February 1623) as the price of Maximilian's services. Thus, as Adams says, 'any hope for a negotiated settlement now rested on a successful defence of the Palatinate, and financial support from England was vital if Frederick's army was to survive the winter' (Adams, FP, p. 162). See also Pursell, *WK*, p. 150; M. Lee (ed.), *Dudley Carleton to John Chamberlain 1603–1624* (New Brunswick, NJ, 1972), p. 307; Lockyer, *Buckingham*, pp. 110, 126; *CSPV, 1619–1621*, p. 115; Pursell, ESP, p. 708; *HMCMK*, pp. 149, 150; *CGB*, I, pp. 51, 90, 274, 281, 295, 300; Redworth, *PI*, p. 71; *Letter 1*.

[84] Adams, PC, p. 322.

[85] See Zaller, *1621*, p. 144. There has recently been a debate about whether James, advised by Buckingham, called the parliament specifically with the intention of sabotaging it. But the consensus seems to be that he proposed to dissolve it only if it proved uncooperative, and did so when, as Alexander Courtney comments, 'the Commons went further' than Sir George Goring suggested in his motion that the House should petition the crown over foreign policy. See B. Pursell, 'James I, Gondomar and the dissolution of the parliament of 1621', *History*, 85 (2000), pp. 428–445; cf. Redworth, *PI*, pp. 28–30; Courtney, 'Court politics', pp. 121–122.

[86] Adams, PC, pp. 323–324; Zaller, *1621*, p. 145; *CGB*, I, pp. 116–117.

[87] Zaller, *1621*, p. 146; Adams, PC, pp. 324–326.

[88] See, e.g., PRO, SP 14/123/115, 116.

the dissolution.[89] The regime again reacted harshly against its critics once the members had dispersed.[90]

This, then, was the immediate political context for the dispatch of the new Roman Catholic secular clergy agent, John Bennett, to Rome. His agency initiated the writing of the series of newsletters reproduced in this volume. He was charged with securing a replacement for the recently deceased archpriest William Harrison, and with ensuring that the man appointed should have episcopal authority.[91] But Bennett had another purpose as well. His pass to travel, dated 12 September 1621, was obtained from the secretary of state, Sir George Calvert. It specifically said that 'this bearer John Bennett, gentleman, is upon spetiall occasion concerning his Majesties service to make his repaire into forraigne partes'.[92] Francisco de Jesús noted the terms of Bennett's licence and observed that, although 'publicly, it was given out that' Bennett 'had come in the name of the English clergy to assist in soliciting the dispensation', this was itself a 'pretext', for Bennett was in fact acting as a personal envoy from James. Once at Rome, Bennett claimed that 'the king was well inclined towards the Mass, which was news which had much influence upon all who heard it'.[93]

By October 1621, Gondomar was corresponding with Bennett from London, and William Bishop was communicating with Diego de Lafuente in Rome. Lafuente had been sent back to Spain by Gondomar to expedite the marriage. He had then, on the Spanish

[89] Zaller, *1621*, pp. 150–151, 152–153, 165, 172; Adams, PC, pp. 326–328; PRO, SP 14/124/27; Redworth, *PI*, p. 34; Russell, *PEP*, pp. 132–133, 134–135; J.P. Kenyon, *The Stuart Constitution* (Cambridge, 1966), pp. 29, 43–48; TD, V, p. 119; Adams, FP, pp. 163, 164; Cogswell, *BR*, p. 58; Akrigg, *Letters of King James VI & I*, pp. 377–380; BL, Harleian MS 1580, fos 166r–168v, 170r–172r. Cf. C. Russell, 'The foreign policy debates in the House of Commons in 1621', *HJ*, 20 (1977), pp. 289–309; R. Cust, 'Prince Charles and the second session of the 1621 parliament', *English Historical Review*, 122 (2007), pp. 432–437. For the timing of the proclamation of the dissolution, see Courtney, 'Court politics', pp. 121–124. See also J.F. Merritt (ed.), *The Political World of Thomas Wentworth, Earl of Strafford, 1621–1641* (Cambridge, 1996), for T. Cogswell's essay ('Phaeton's chariot: the parliament-men and the continental crisis in 1621') and C. Russell's essay ('Sir Thomas Wentworth and anti-Spanish sentiment, 1621–1624').

[90] Cogswell, *BR*, p. 163.

[91] TD, V, p. 83. It was initially suggested that the best candidate was Gondomar's chaplain, Diego de Lafuente, who was involved in the shuttle diplomacy at this time to secure the necessary dispensation from Rome for the proposed Anglo-Spanish dynastic marriage: see *CSPV, 1619–1621*, p. 458; Gardiner, *NSMT*, pp. 161–162; *Letter 1*; see also *CSPV, 1621–1623*, p. 403.

[92] AAW, A XVI, no. 63, pp. 221–222; BL, Additional MS 37028, fo. 41v.

[93] Gardiner, *NSMT*, pp. 168–169; *CGB*, I, pp. 57–58, 87. Sir Henry Wotton remarked, however, that, after Gregory XV had set up the congregation of cardinals for considering the issue of the dispensation for the marriage, 'no Englishman of any fashion (if he be one of their Catholics) can come thither, but they baptize him straight an ambassador': L.P. Smith (ed.), *The Life and Letters of Sir Henry Wotton*, 2 vols (Oxford, 1907), II, p. 222.

court's orders, travelled to Rome in order to obtain the dispensation.[94] Before Gondomar left London for Spain in mid-1622, with a promise from Prince Charles that, when Gondomar judged fit, he would travel to Madrid to secure the marriage treaty, Gondomar was approached by the patrons of the secular clergy, especially Lady Elizabeth Dormer, to whom the Bennett brothers were chaplains.[95]

Bennett then proceeded to engage with those who opposed the establishment of an English Catholic hierarchy, notably George Gage, as he and they presented their credentials and arguments to the relevant curial committees in Rome.[96] With the backing of cardinals such as Bandini, Bennett managed to persuade the curia to change its mind about the appointment of a bishop for the English nation.[97] In June 1622, it was decided, in principle, that an episcopal appointment should be made for England and Scotland.[98]

## The Toleration of 1622 and the Papal Dispensation

For Catholics, any sign that they were likely to obtain toleration was evidence that the king had decided to drive hard for a 'Spanish' solution to his difficulties. Even before the beginning of the second sitting of the 1621 parliament, it looked as if the regime might be moving in this direction. As William Bishop noted on 14 December 1621, 'before the beginning of the parlement the lay Catholikes in prison were sett' at liberty 'on their own bands', and the times were 'very calme'.[99] As early as February of that year, Gondomar had thought that, although the situation in Ireland was bad, there was a kind of toleration – at least an unofficial one – in England: 'each day [. . .] countless persons are being converted and [are] declaring themselves Catholics during the lull in persecution', and the same was true in Scotland. Furthermore, James had done 'many [. . .] generous acts on behalf of the Catholics without permitting any harassment or

[94] TD, V, p. 120; AAW, A XVI, no. 91, pp. 397–398; CRS, 68, p. 144. For the setting up of the papal commission to study the dispensation issue, see *CSPV, 1621–1623*, p. 158.

[95] *Letter 4*; Questier, *C&C*, pp. 392, 399–400; Redworth, *PI*, p. 45. Another patron to whom the seculars sued for assistance was the archdeacon of Cambrai, François de Carondelet. He came to England for a time in the service of the ambassador Carlos Coloma. In mid-August 1623, Carondelet sought to be appointed almoner to the infanta, if she should come to England: PRO, SP 14/151/4. He defended Matthew Kellison when Kellison was attacked for his book *The Right and Iurisdiction of the Prelate, and the Prince*: AAW, A XVII, no. 6, p. 21 (cited in *Letter 27*).

[96] Questier, *C&C*, pp. 394, 397–398; Gardiner, *NSMT*, p. 164.

[97] Questier, *C&C*, pp. 397–400.

[98] TD, V, p. 87; and see below, p. 31.

[99] *Letter 1*.

annoyance to any one'.[100] The Flanders nuncio had commented in August that it seemed certain there would be a successful conclusion of the Anglo-Spanish treaty, and 'on constate déjâ, en Angleterre, un commencement de tacite liberté de conscience; la Messe se dit plus librement que de coutume et l'inquisition contre les Catholiques a presque pris fin'.[101] Late in the year, Richard Broughton, a leading secular priest, published his *English Protestants Plea*, provocatively dedicated to parliament;[102] in it, he declared that the parliament was riddled with anti-monarchical puritanism.[103]

The animosity between James and the parliament seemed to augur well for Catholics, though informers against them were still active in January 1622.[104] Royal favour was being shown to leading members of the community such as Lord Vaux: with the earl of Argyll, Vaux was allowed to raise troops for Spanish service in Flanders.[105] The Vaux family became the target of local Protestant hostility in Northamptonshire, not least because Lord Vaux appeared to be

[100]CRS, 68, pp. 144–145.

[101]See *Letters 1, 6*; *CGB*, I, pp. 46, 52, cf. p. 57.

[102]Edward Bennett remarked on its appearance in the third week of December: *Letter 2*.

[103]Richard Broughton, *English Protestants Plea, and Petition, for English Preists and Papists* (Saint-Omer, 1621), p. 4.

[104]*Letter 3*.

[105]*Letters 3, 5, 13*; *APC, 1621–1623*, p. 191. In early February 1622, the Venetian diplomat Girolamo Lando observed that, in order to facilitate the levies of troops for the earl of Argyll, 'orders were issued to the ports of the realm to allow English recusants' as well as others 'to pass without the customary examination and oath'. Lando also said that rumours were being spread that the levies were to be deployed against the Turks: *CSPV, 1621–1623*, p. 233. For Argyll's recent attempts to recruit a regiment of Scottish soldiers for Habsburg service, see PRO, SP 94/23, fo. 241v. He had returned in April 1620 from a visit to Spain and, William Trumbull recorded, 'he magnifieth and extolleth to the skyes the courteous entertainment and liberallityes of Spaine' and also the 'sollid counsells and resolutions taken there to pursue the warres in Germany': PRO, SP 77/14, fo. 78r. By the end of December 1621, Argyll's regiment was 'augmented to 20 companyes of Englishe and Scottishe, each company of 200 or 150 at the leaste, for the leavying [...] whereof into these countryes there is requyred the terme of 4 or 6 monethes': *ibid.*, fo. 577r; cf. PRO, SP 77/15, fo. 32r. In March 1622, Argyll called Trumbull to his house in Brussels and relayed to him news of a conspiracy, reported by Richard Verstegan (who was standing by), in which two assassins (one Burgundian and one Italian) were to be sent from the United Provinces to England 'to laye violent handes' upon the king and prince of Wales, and to kill Gondomar. For the 'particulars' of this conspiracy, Verstegan 'alleaged one Dr [Thomas] Wright as his author, an Englishe preiste' in Antwerp: *ibid.*, fo. 52r–v. In the autumn of 1623, the nuncio del Bagno reported that Argyll had shown him two letters from William Alexander, James's master of requests for Scotland, in which it was claimed that, 'depuis les négociations du mariage Anglo-Espagnol', the king 'désire accommoder Protestantisme et Catholicisme', an assertion which was taken seriously in Rome: *CGB*, I, pp. 349, 359, 369. For Argyll's conversion to Catholicism (which he announced in 1618), see *ODNB*, *sub* 'Campbell, Archibald' (article by John Callow); Thomas Scott, *Vox Populi. Or newes from Spayne* (np, 1620), sig. C2r.

recruiting a Catholic army.[106] On 25 January/4 February 1622, Henry Clifford understood that 'a brother of my Lord Vaux was committed to the common gaole in Northampton by two precise justices of peace who presented him the othe of allegeance which he refused to sweare, but he is freed out of prison and, as I am advertised, the justices [are] putt out of commission'.[107]

Actually, the record of these Catholic-cause warriors was rather patchy. Joseph Mead recorded on 27 April 1622 that some of the men enlisted in Lord Vaux's companies had pulled out, 'utterly refusing to serve against the Hollanders, complaining they were cozened, being taken up to serve in the Low Countries, which they conceived to be all under the Hollanders'.[108] Nevertheless, it appeared that the king had allowed Catholic soldiers to set sail (though hardly with his blessing, according to Lando) to help the Habsburgs to crush the cause of European Protestantism.[109]

It was at this point also that Archbishop Marc'Antonio de Dominis, who had arrived in England in late 1616 in a blaze of anti-popish publicity, departed for Rome, evidently with the intention

[106]Many of those enlisting in Vaux's and Argyll's regiments were prominent Catholics: for example, Sir Edward Parham. He was the dedicatee of Richard Verstegan's tract of 1623 entitled *A Toung-Combat, lately happening, between two English Soldiers; in the Tilt-boat of Gravesend. The one go-ing to serve the King of Spayn, the other to serve the States of Holland* (Mechlin, 1623), pp. 3–6; see also Allison, 'A group of political tracts', pp. 139–140. Among the others were Sir William Tresham, Roger Tirwhit, John Timperley, Thomas Bedingfield, Henry Gage, Sir Edward Easton, and Sir Richard Huddlestone. Vaux obtained his licence to embark on 8 April 1622, and warrants for his captains came on 10 April. There were supposed to be 8,000 men in all, divided between Vaux and Argyll: G. Anstruther, *Vaux of Harrowden* (London, 1953), pp. 431–433; PRO, SP 77/15, fos 92v, 137r, 161r; PRO, SP 77/16, fo. 113r. For those officers who were nominated by Gondomar, see A. Loomie, 'Gondomar's selection of English officers in 1622', *English Historical Review*, 88 (1973), pp. 574–581 (I am grateful to Alexander Courtney for this reference). For the attempt to convert to Catholicism those recruits who were not Catholic, see *CGB*, I, p. 199.

[107]AAW, A XVI, no. 96, p. 410. The Vaux family was one of the victims of John Gee's humour in his *New Shreds of the Old Snare* (London, 1624), pp. 3–6.

[108]Birch, *CTJI*, II, pp. 306–307; see also *CSPV, 1621–1623*, p. 386. William Trumbull, in early June 1622, reckoned that Argyll's outfit numbered only 1,200 men: PRO, SP 77/15, fo. 177r. In mid-August, having admitted that it had started with 1,400 or 1,500, Trumbull claimed that desertions were rife and that it was now reduced to fewer than 600. From Vaux's regiment, likewise, there were 'at leaste 600 runne away': *ibid.*, fos 237v, 242v, 246v, 282v; PRO, SP 77/16, fo. 13v; see also *Letter 76*.

[109]*APC, 1621–1623*, p. 191; *CSPV, 1621–1623*, p. 307. One of Vaux's first objectives was the besieged town of Bergen-op-Zoom, which the imperial commander Spinola was trying, unsuccessfully, to reduce: Anstruther, *Vaux of Harrowden*, pp. 432–433; Israel, *The Dutch Republic*, p. 483; *CCE*, pp. 91, 93, 96; see also PRO, SP 77/15, fos 200r, 231r, 282r, cf. fo. 238r. Sir Dudley Carleton commented bitterly, at the end of August 1622, on the presence of both Vaux's and Argyll's levies 'in the ennemyes camp before Berghen': BL, Harleian MS 1580, fo. 245v.

of influencing Rome's opinions about the grant of the dispensation.[110] The Spaniards had allegedly had a hand in his new-found enthusiasm for the papacy. In mid-February 1622, John Chamberlain understood that de Dominis had permission to go to Rome, and now 'pretends auncient acquaintance and familiaritie with this pope, and that the kinges of Spaine and Fraunce have undertaken for his securitie'. Gondomar was 'saide to be the cheife architect in this busines' and the wily Spaniard had 'inchaunted' the archbishop 'into this fooles paradise'.[111] The new pontiff, Gregory XV, was supposedly more moderate than his predecessor. De Dominis had said, when he was summoned to appear at Lambeth before George Abbot and others on 30 March, that 'now there is a goode pope whose eares are open to heare and redresse what is amisse'. The archbishop's return seemed to indicate that good relations between the Court of St James and the Holy See were going to be firmly established, even though, after the accession of Maffeo Barberini as Urban VIII in August 1623, de Dominis was treated with much less sympathy in Rome.[112]

Most contemporary accounts, both Catholic and Protestant, of de Dominis's motives were extremely disdainful. John Hacket summarized them when he described him as both exceptionally greedy and also theologically confused.[113] But de Dominis claimed that there was a significant body of Protestant opinion in England which favoured reunion with Rome. He had had discussions with, among others, Richard Montagu about the points which their Churches held in common.[114] There was evidently a connection between the kind of reports which the secular clergy were sending to Rome about the rise of 'moderate' opinions within the Church of England and de Dominis's own account of the possibility of healing confessional divisions there

[110]PRO, SP 14/128/97, 103; *CSPV, 1621–1623*, pp. 263, 493, 494; *CGB*, I, p. 148; R. Ferrini and E. de Mas (eds), *Lettere a William Cavendish (1615–1628)* (Rome, 1987), pp. 146, 218, and *passim*.

[111]McClure, *LJC*, pp. 423–424; N. Malcolm, *De Dominis* (London, 1984), ch. 12; Ferrini and de Mas, *Lettere a William Cavendish*, p. 175. The nuncio in Flanders understood, in January 1622, that Philip IV had recently dispatched a substantial financial gift to de Dominis: *CGB*, I, p. 148. For the earl of Kellie's scepticism about Rome's intentions towards the archbishop, see *HMCMK*, p. 144.

[112]McClure, *LJC*, p. 431; *DSSD*, p. 64; Richard Neile, *M. Ant. De Dominis Arch-bishop of Spalato, his Shiftings in Religion* (2nd edition, London, 1624), pp. 79f.; Ferrini and de Mas, *Lettere a William Cavendish*, pp. 282–283.

[113]Hacket, *SR*, part I, sig. O2r–4r.

[114]A. Milton, *Catholic and Reformed: the Roman and Protestant Churches in English Protestant thought, 1600–1640* (Cambridge, 2002), pp. 347, 352, 353, 359–360; Ferrini and de Mas, *Lettere a William Cavendish*, p. 176.

('wind-mills of union to concord Rome and England, England and Rome', as Hacket put it).[115]

By the middle of 1622, when the Jesuit John Percy was invited to debate theological matters at court in the presence of, and actually with, the king (though Percy's efforts attracted the derision of several Catholic secular clergymen),[116] it was also known that some kind of official toleration was imminent.[117] John Colleton, who already enjoyed a form of unofficial liberty, had secured a formal warrant on 31 March to allow him to reside with Gondomar.[118] A lobbying campaign for the liberation (without, in the case of the priests, the obligation of exile) of Catholics in prison had been running since late 1621. Anthony Champney passed the news to John Bennett in a letter of 30 May/9 June 1622 that 'the warrant for the deliverie of the lay prisoners was under the broad seale some dayes before' Champney's informant had

[115]Hacket, *SR*, part I, sig. O3v.

[116]See *Letters 5, 14, 54.*

[117]The three days of debate (24–26 May) were occasioned by the rumours concerning the countess of Buckingham's decision to convert to Rome. See John Percy, *True Relations of Sundry Conferences had betweene Certaine Protestant Doctours and a Iesuite called M. Fisher* (np, 1626). The audience on the first day included Buckingham, his mother the countess, Buckingham's wife (Katherine Manners), and, it seems, the king. It was significant that it was William Laud, Francis White, and John Williams who were chosen to argue with the Jesuit, and not, for example, one of the equally theologically qualified clients of Archbishop Abbot, such as Daniel Featley. See T.H. Wadkins, 'The Percy–"Fisher" controversies and the ecclesiastical politics of Jacobean anti-Catholicism, 1622–1625', *Church History*, 57 (1988), pp. 153–169; Francis White, *A Replie to Iesuit Fishers Answere to Certain Questions propounded by his most gratious Ma[jes]tie* (London, 1624); Hacket, *SR*, part I, pp. 171–173. Williams was a confidant of the countess and a client of Buckingham, through whose influence he had aimed at and acquired high office: Ruigh, *1624*, pp. 137–138; *CSPV, 1621–1623*, p. 88. For Francis White's Arminian tendencies, see Tyacke, *Anti-Calvinists*, pp. 174–180, 222–223, although White was well regarded by, for example, the puritan Simonds D'Ewes: *DSSD*, *passim*.

On 25 May, James was the principal disputant against Percy. According to the count of Tillières, James took Francis White's place after White had failed to convince the countess: PRO, PRO 31/3/56, fo. 47v. This day's conference did not find its way into print: ARCR, II, no. 603; T.H. Wadkins, 'King James I meets John Percy, S.J. (25 May, 1622.): an unpublished manuscript from the religious controversies surrounding the countess of Buckingham's conversion', *RH*, 19 (1988), pp. 146–154. On 26 May, the main Protestant disputant was William Laud and the topic for discussion was the compatibility of the Roman and English Churches: Patterson, *King James VI and I*, pp. 342–344; William Laud, *An Answere to Mr Fishers Relation of a Third Conference betwene a Certaine B. (as He Stiles Him) and Himselfe* (London, 1624). For James's subsequent admonition to Percy not to put anything in print, see *Cabala*, p. 75; ARSJ, Anglia MS 1, fo. 166r. Buckingham himself had shown interest in the arguments which Jesuit debaters, such as Percy, were using at this time in order to make converts: see Bodleian Library, Rawlinson MS D 853, fo. 172r (Richard Corbet to the marquis of Buckingham [date uncertain]). In mid-October 1622, Williams sent Buckingham 'a copie of the conference' which Williams had 'procured' from Percy 'without his privity, onely to make his Majestie and your lordship merrie': *Cabala*, p. 75.

[118]PRO, SP 14/128/100; cf. *APC, 1621–1623*, p. 184.

left London 'and, as he sayd, was presently to be put in execution'.[119] On 8 June 1622, Joseph Mead remarked that 'all the Jesuits and priests, which were in prison at London and elsewhere, were this week set at liberty'. It was said that 'their number was 400', although 'they were under bail to be forthcoming when they should be called for'.[120] In Madrid, five weeks later, Sir Walter Aston recorded that, while the elector palatine's and Mansfelt's recent activities had caused no little irritation in the Spanish court, it had nevertheless 'been extreamly well taken heere by this king' that James had 'been pleased to conferr' his 'grace' on 'divers Romish Catholicks that weare prisoners in England'. They were now known to be 'at liberty upon the instance of the conde of Gondomar'.[121]

The negotiations by the secular clergy's agent for a grant of episcopal authority proceeded in Rome exactly in tandem with the haggling over the dispensation and the prospect in England of a royal grant of toleration to Catholics. Almost inevitably, the conflict between the secular clergy and their opponents within the religious orders soon included accusations by each side that the other's lobbying at Rome threatened to impede both the dispensation and toleration and must logically mean that ill-intentioned Catholics were actually trying to hinder the progress of the marriage and the treaty. On 8/18 May, Bennett wrote that 'our [Catholic] opposites' were still spending their time 'in spreading tales' in order to disrupt both the episcopal suit and the dispensation necessary for the success of the match.[122]

A week later, Bennett announced (rather too optimistically as it turned out) that the dispensation 'is indeed agreed upon, and here will be no difficulty made, if there be no let elsewhere'.[123] At the end of July 1622, Bennett recorded that 'about the midst of June, I had a decree [. . .] for a bishop' and, 'if I would have been importunate, I could have got more, as I verily think'. At last the nomination of the man who would be invested with episcopal authority was 'in deliberation'.[124] The different factions within the community were now directly in competition with each other in order to show that they, rather than their opponents, had pursued the path which most closely tallied with

[119] *Letter 5*.

[120] Birch, *CTJI*, II, p. 313.

[121] PRO, SP 94/25, fo. 147r; Pursell, *WK*, pp. 172–180.

[122] TD, V, p. ccxxxv.

[123] *Ibid.*, p. ccxxxvii. For the letter of 13 June 1622, from the secular clergy via John Bennett to the curial committee of cardinals considering the dispensation, urging how beneficial the grant of the proposed dispensation would be to English Catholics, see BL, Additional MS 37028, fo. 41r.

[124] TD, V, p. ccxlv.

the king's wishes and would guarantee royal tolerance for the Catholic community.[125]

As Thomas Cogswell puts it, so determined was James to secure the Anglo-Spanish treaty that acceptance of it became 'the litmus test of loyalty, a test which many, notwithstanding their own best efforts, failed'. Among those who passed the test with flying colours were Catholics. Some kind of toleration was the logical political reward for them. James reversed a whole generation's expectations and assumptions by ordering the lord keeper, John Williams, to suspend, by formal letters, the branches of the statutes which defined and punished Catholic recusancy and also, in certain cases, the section of the 1606 act which had promulgated the Jacobean oath of allegiance.[126]

James's letter to Williams, authorizing the order to the judges, explained the grounds of this grant. James regarded it as fit that, in the light of the marriage, his Catholic subjects 'should be treated and used with all clemencie and mildnes'. James said that

> because wee will give example to other princes to extend the like grace and favour to such of theire subjectes as are of the religion which wee ourselfe professe, wee have resolved to mitigate the severitie of those lawes which doe inflict on them anie penalties in respect of theire religion.

He hoped that these Catholics would be encouraged to show themselves loyal 'towardes us and our milde and mercifull governement'. James intended 'to grant pardons and dispensacions to such of our subjectes and Romishe Catholiques as, within the space or terme of five yeares next ensueinge the date hereof, shall desire the same, according to the tenor and forme of a pardon and dispensacion heereunder written'.[127] Catholics such as Arthur Pitts argued that James's wise, principled, and irenic statesmanship 'should move his Holinesse to hasten the consecration of the bishop with authority to drawe all us that be abrode to retourn to their country'.[128] Indeed, Catholics would do all that they could to play up the king's action as genuinely irenic rather than purely a matter of practical politics. On 30 September/10 October, John Bennett wrote from Rome to his brother Edward that 'my lord keeper his letter I putt in Latin, and gave it to these greate men, which they were well pleased with. Our

[125] *Letter* 7.

[126] Cogswell, 'England and the Spanish match', p. 118; *Letter* 7. For the king's efforts to extend the toleration to Scotland and Ireland, see PRO, SP 14/150/113.

[127] AAW, OB I/i, no. 79, fo. 150r–v; Dodd, *CH*, II, p. 439. Williams's toleration letter was publicized by the British embassy at Brussels, as the nuncio there reported on 10/20 August 1622: *CGB*, I, pp. 238–239.

[128] AAW, A XVI, no. 145, p. 563.

adversaryes would fayne have made the matter doubtefull, for they would not that this court should conceave well of his Majesty.'[129]

Many Protestants were, unsurprisingly, very suspicious of James's actions and motivation. Williams felt compelled, on 17 September 1622, to assure John Murray, first Viscount Annan (who had informed Williams the day before of the 'offence taken by many people' in England and Scotland at Williams's letter) that the tolerance offered was only temporary. Catholics would be rearrested if they tried to take political advantage of the king's clemency. Toleration of papists did not mean toleration of popery. It was hardly a toleration at all: 'a toleration lookes forward to the tyme to come', but 'this favor' looks 'backward to the offences past'. Thus, 'if any papist now set at liberty shall offend the laws again, the justices may, nay must, recommitt him and leave favour and mercy to the king, to whom they properly belong'. If people were to read the writs to the judges they would find that the 'papists are not otherwise out of prison than with their shackles about their heels' and 'sufficient sureties and good recognizaunces to present themselves again at the next assizes'. If the 'lay papists do wax insolent with this mercy, insulting upon the Protestants, and translating this favour from the person to the cause', Williams was sure that the king would return them to their 'former state and condition, and renew his writ no more'. Lastly, Williams believed that his own letter to the judges had been misconstrued. It 'recited four kinds of recusants only' who were

> capable of his Majesties clemency, not so much to include these as to exclude many other crimes [. . .] as using the function of a Romish priest, seducing the king's liege people from the religion established, scandalizing and aspersing our king, Church, state, or present government, all which offences (being outward practises, and no secret motions of the conscience) are adjudged by the laws of England to be meerly civil and political

and therefore excluded from the scope of those writs. The king was and always would be a true Protestant.[130] Significantly, the letter from Williams to Annan, which was intended for circulation, was obtained by Catholics and appeared in print.[131]

[129] AAW, A XVI, no. 156, p. 605. (For the Latin version of Williams's letter retained in AAW, see AAW, A XVI, no. 128, pp. 511–514.)

[130] Hacket, *SR*, part I, pp. 92–93; TD, V, pp. ccxcvi–ccxcix; PRO, SP 14/133/20; BL, Additional MS 22591, fos 222r–223r; cf. *CSPD, Addenda 1580–1625*, p. 646.

[131] ARCR, II, no. 920; *A Letter Writt[en to] the L. Viscunt Anan, Decl[aring the] Nature and Reason of the late [Clemency] extended to the Lay-Recus[ants in] England* (np [printed secretly in England], 1622); BL, Additional MS 34727, fo. 43r (for which reference I am very grateful to Alexander Courtney). See also Shami, *John Donne*, p. 106.

Directions on preaching were also issued in August 1622.[132] The king's letter to Archbishop Abbot that ordered the enforcement of the directions was dated 4 August, only two days after Williams's toleration directive was sent out. Inevitably, the toleration inflected public understanding of the directions.[133] On 15 September, John Donne preached a sermon at Paul's Cross which explained and justified the directions and also the king's command that there should be an end to many of the punitive restrictions in force against Catholics.[134] Catholics could soon observe the prohibition of anti-Catholic preaching starting to bite.[135] On 12 October 1622, Thomas Locke reported to Sir Dudley Carleton that the Catholics in Ireland were also hoping for a toleration.[136]

The correspondence of the secular clergy, and in particular a long account by one John Hazell, an agent and go-between for those interested in acquiring the proffered immunity, set out in detail how tortuous a process this was.[137] William Bishop, however, had, on 22 August/1 September 1622, dashed off a missive to Bennett in Rome with a copy of the lord keeper's letter. Optimistically, he commented 'now doth our king begin to do some thing for the Catholikes'. Inevitably, thought Bishop, 'the next point wilbe a releasement of the penalties of the lawes against recusants' – in other words, an overturning of recusants' convictions; and Bennett immediately translated it to show to the relevant cardinals.[138]

Of course, the regime had no desire to implement a full legal toleration, although Buckingham insisted to Gondomar, in the context of an appeal for the Habsburg troops in the Palatinate to be called off, that 'priests and recusants' were 'all at liberty', and 'all the Roman Catholics [were] well satisfied and, which will seem a wonder unto

[132]The directions were issued in response to Hispanophobe sermons preached at Paul's Cross in the wake of the collapse of the defence of the Palatinate: Adams, PC, p. 331; Shami, *John Donne*, ch. 4; *Letter 11*; K.C. Fincham, *Prelate as Pastor* (Oxford, 1990), p. 245. As Fincham notes, 'sermons were to be based squarely on the Articles of Religion and the Homilies, and preachers were to avoid contentious topics, especially the power and exercise of temporal authority, and the technicalities of predestinarian theology': *ibid.* See also Cogswell, *BR*, pp. 32–33; *idem*, 'England and the Spanish match', pp. 118–119.

[133]Shami, *John Donne*, p. 106.

[134]Chamberlain sarcastically observed that Donne's sermon was supposed to reassure his audience of the king's 'constancie in the true reformed religion, which the people (as shold seeme) began to suspect'. For the court's strategy in appointing Donne to preach on this occasion, see Shami, *John Donne*, pp. 12, 102–138 (esp. pp. 107–108, 111f.); Adams, PC, pp. 331–332.

[135]*Letter 22*. Cf. Cogswell, 'England and the Spanish match', p. 119.

[136]PRO, SP 14/133/49. See also G. Redworth, 'Beyond faith and fatherland: "The appeal of the Catholics of Ireland", c.1623', *Archivum Hibernicum*, 52 (1998), pp. 3–23.

[137]*Letter 6*.

[138]AAW, A XVI, no. 136, p. 541; TD, V, p. cclii; *Letter 7*.

you, our prisons are emptied of priests and recusants and filled with jealous ministers for preaching against the match'.[139]

Bishop Williams had been extremely unwilling to grant immunity to recusants in as full a form as was eventually, under pressure, conceded to them. As we have seen, he had a great deal of difficulty justifying it to Protestant sceptics such as Viscount Annan. As a result, stories and rumours circulated among Catholics which claimed that 'persecution' had not ceased. This allowed the Jesuits to argue that an episcopal appointment, as proposed by the secular clergy's leadership, would be unwise at this time. Such opinions were vigorously refuted by some secular clergy, who declared that instances of persecution were becoming the exception rather than the rule (though there was no objective test to measure at what precise point signs of tolerance constituted a real and irrevocable toleration, nor whether accounts of sporadic localized anti-popery showed that persecution persisted).[140] This situation was exploited by the secular clergy leadership. They used it to persuade the Stuart regime not to hinder their attempts to secure the grant of episcopal jurisdiction to one of their number (because such hindrance could be interpreted at Rome as persecutory) and also to refute and discredit the Jesuits' assertions and the regime's own worries – voiced at Rome through the agency of the Spanish ambassador in England, Carlos Coloma – that the secular priests' ambitions were a direct threat to royal authority over the English Church.[141]

[139]Redworth, *PI*, p. 42; *Cabala*, p. 233. Buckingham's letter to Gondomar is undated but the reference to Protestant preachers evidently locates it after the issuing of the directions on preaching, although (as noted above) the release of Catholic clergy from London prisons had begun earlier in the year.

[140]See, e.g., *Letter 15*.

[141]See *Letter 8*. John Hacket noted that Catholic agitators had 'put a paper into my lord of Buckingham's hands' to 'assist them for the erection of titulary popish praelates in this kingdom': Hacket, *SR*, part I, p. 94. Hacket claimed that the agitators 'did not hope to obtain' their request. But even the approach 'would make the council table odious' and 'contribute much to embitter the subjects and to raise divisions'. According to Hacket, Buckingham consulted Williams. Williams (echoing almost exactly the arguments put forward by some members of the religious orders against the institution of English Catholic bishops) 'damned the project' because it would 'set all the kingdom on fire and make his Majesty unable to continue those favours and connivencies to peaceable recusants'. It would also deprive the crown of the exclusive right to invest bishops; and 'it is a far greater mischief in a state (I mean in regard of the temporal, but not of the spiritual good thereof) than an absolute toleration', because, as a result of the institution of a Catholic episcopate, 'this invisible consistory shall be confusedly diffused over all the kingdom'. Inevitably, many of the king's subjects would, 'to the intolerable exhausting of the wealth of the realm, pay double tithes, double offerings and double fees'. (Ireland and its widespread poverty, he said, were a demonstration of precisely this.) Williams also argued that, 'if the princes match should go on, this new erected consistory will put the ensuing parliament into such a jealousie

A number of people, however, were willing to heed the admonitions which came from the Society and its patrons: Sir George Calvert and Sir Francis Cottington were clearly sympathetic to their warnings.[142] As part of this campaign against the secular clergy's programme, someone had also denounced Matthew Kellison's *The Right and Iurisdiction of the Prelate, and the Prince*. This book, first published in 1617, was a reply to the regime's apologist Thomas Preston's *Theologicall Disputation* of 1613. Kellison's tract vigorously endorsed the doctrine of the indirect power of the papacy to depose temporal rulers.[143] In November 1622, the secular priest Joseph Haynes had to approach Lord Keeper Williams in order to put the seculars' case on these matters to him directly.[144]

Full toleration (in other words, suspension of the penal law in its entirety) was, of course, not implemented. What the regime was prepared to concede was something akin to what the more moderate members of the English Catholic community had been demanding in 1603 – in other words, a relaxation of the law by direct grant from the crown. Nevertheless, the constraints on the crown's freedom of manoeuvre had allowed an admittedly rather divided and fractious Catholic coalition to extract a visible form of toleration from the king. No wonder, then, that certain preachers, notably Richard Sheldon, were so bold as to express their horror at such developments. Sheldon, a royal chaplain (and former seminary priest), had publicly renounced Rome in 1612. He had also published justifications of the 1606 oath of allegiance and had thus become a living symbol of what many Protestants would have regarded as an appropriate fusion of godly Protestant conversion and support both for the royal supremacy and for James's own reading of his sovereignty against the claims of the papalists. On 1 September 1622, however, Sheldon preached

and suspition, that it is to be feared that they will shew themselves very untractable upon all propositions'. James ordered Williams to inform Coloma of the proposed hierarchy. This resulted in the diplomat's warning delivered at Rome against the project to appoint a bishop: *ibid.*; see also *Letter 24*. Sir George Calvert, at the king's direction, had instructed Lord Digby in Madrid, via a letter of 16 August 1622, to try to prevent the dispatch into James's dominions of 'titularie English bishops': BL, Additional MS 48166, fo. 155r.

[142] See *Letters 20, 25*.

[143] See *Letters 25, 27*; Matthew Kellison, *The Right and Iurisdiction of the Prelate, and the Prince. Or, a treatise of ecclesiasticall, and regall authoritie* (Douai, 1617). A second edition (of 1621) incorporated material which replied to Preston's attack on the first edition, Thomas Preston, *A New-Yeares Gift for English Catholikes* (London, 1620); see ARCR, II, nos 470, 471, 657. Kellison had originally written the book in 1614, and its printing had been delayed by the refusal of the bishop of Saint-Omer's approbation: P. Milward, *Religious Controversies of the Jacobean Age* (London, 1978), pp. 105–106; ARCR, II, no. 470. See also J.P. Sommerville, 'From Suarez to Filmer: a reappraisal', *HJ*, 25 (1982), pp. 525–540; Allison, RS, pp. 154–155, 176–177.

[144] TD, V, p. ccliv; Questier, *C&C*, p. 400; *Letter 24*.

an inflammatory sermon at Paul's Cross, in which he lambasted those who compromised with Rome. Sheldon's sermon brought him immediate disgrace, though he had tried to cover himself – and to justify his assault on Rome and the papacy – by citing James's own defence of the oath of allegiance in his *Premonition* of 1609.[145]

## The Prince's Journey to Spain

George Gage had left Rome on 18/28 July 1622 carrying the text of the dispensation issued by the Roman curia. It had been made more stringent than James expected, so Gage was subsequently dispatched back to Rome via Madrid.[146] In late August, Lord Digby, who had arrived at the court in Madrid in early June, expressed concern at what was going on: 'I have here lett them knowe that I conceave this hath not beene the right way, for that, by the articles, the dispensation is to bee procured merely by the industry of the king of Spayne'. James, by contrast, should not become embroiled in argument with the papacy: 'whatsoever the pope should have pretended, he should have made the king of Spaine the meanes of it'.[147]

In November, Gage came through Paris. He informed his secular clergy critics there, in no uncertain terms, that his manner of dealing was the one which would produce results. James was determined to force the marriage through and would do Catholics 'all the favour that can be reasonably demanded of him'. But, if the project failed, 'he must needes deale by way of parlement', in other words, sue to the 'puritans'. The Catholics would suffer grievously in consequence. So, if the Catholics had any common sense, they 'must labour that the match be not hindered', by which Gage clearly made an oblique reference to the seculars' project to obtain episcopal authority for one of their number.[148]

In Madrid, Digby argued that there was a potential and radical disjuncture between the aims of the Spaniards, on the one hand, and the pope and English Catholics, on the other. The Spanish court's

[145] M. Maclure, *The Paul's Cross Sermons 1534–1642* (Toronto, 1958), p. 244; Shami, *John Donne*, pp. 108–109; Richard Sheldon, *A Sermon Preached at Paules Crosse* (London, 1625).

[146] *Letters 7, 12*; TD, V, p. 124; McClure, *LJC*, pp. 452, 458, 460–461; Gardiner, *NSMT*, pp. 176–184; *CSPV, 1621–1623*, pp. 412, 485, 490; *HMCMK*, p. 139; PRO, SP 94/25, fos 166v, 199v.

[147] PRO, SP 94/25, fos 199v–200r; *CSPV, 1621–1623*, p. 350. At this stage, Digby could not ascertain what the terms of the dispensation were, since Gage, 'at his going from Rome, either omitted to write unto me or else his letters have miscarried': PRO, SP 94/35, fo. 200v; see also BL, Harleian MS 1580, fo. 122v.

[148] *Letter 22*.

purpose was to 'mainetaine [...] peace' and to secure advantages for 'both theise estates'. The clauses of the treaty governing religion were purely to secure Spanish honour in a mixed dynastic union. But, 'for the pope, it is without question that as a temporall prince he desireth not so strict a conjunction betwixt' the 'two crownes' but 'approveth of the match only for the good and advantage which he thinks may therby bee procured to the Catholique cause'. This, Digby believed, was the aim of English Catholics as well. He advised the Spanish negotiators to bring pressure on the pope, if need be, to make the terms of the dispensation more accommodating (though, in the event, during the following year the Spanish court persuaded the papacy to make the wording of the dispensation more severe).[149] Digby was livid when, by mid-September, he learned of 'theise unexpected and indeede impossible demands of the pope'. He claimed that the Spaniards were highly offended that Gage had gone straight to England without returning first to Madrid. On 3/13 October, the count-duke of Olivares made Digby believe that Philip IV would 'induce the pope to content himself with those conditions which shall bee esteemed fitting and reasonable'.[150] The earl of Kellie thought that Philip IV was as irate as James at the way in which the dispensation had been presented in London.[151]

At this point, however, it appeared – at least outwardly – that the marriage still had some chance of succeeding. Even the recent taking of Heidelberg in September 1622 by imperial forces (where a number of English troops, led by Sir Gerard Herbert, had been cut down)[152] had stalled the Anglo-Spanish negotiations only briefly.[153] Digby was told in October that the Spanish court had positively disapproved of the siege but could not prevent it, despite all the negotiations during the summer at Brussels, in which Sir Richard Weston had tried to secure an armistice. Digby credited his Spanish hosts with 'integrity and uprightnes' when letters were, though with little prospect of any success, sent off from Madrid to the archduchess Isabella for dispatch to the Habsburg commanders in the Palatinate, telling them to halt the advance of their troops there. (The count of Tilly replied that he would not obey any such order without a direct command from the emperor; and Isabella herself thought it impossible that the Spanish

[149] PRO, SP 94/25, fos 201r–202r; and see below, p. 49.

[150] PRO, SP 94/25, fos 214r, 216r, 223r–v, 242r; see also *Letter 13*.

[151] *HMCMK*, pp. 139–140.

[152] Cogswell, *BR*, p. 20; Pursell, *WK*, p. 184; *CSPV, 1621–1623*, pp. 467, 469–470; Patterson, *King James VI and I*, pp. 312–313; PRO, SP 94/25, fo. 244r; *CGB*, I, p. 79; *Letter 13*.

[153] *Letters 15, 17, 18, 22*. For the subsequent loss of Mannheim and Frankenthal, see *Letter 15*.

king should want to commit himself 'contre la Ligue Catholique et les Catholiques d'Allemagne, du côté des Protestants'.)[154]

Draft articles for the marriage were, despite heated arguments between Lord Digby (now the earl of Bristol) and the junta appointed to oversee the negotiations, drawn up in November/December 1622 and sent from Madrid to London.[155] Gage appeared briefly in Madrid on his way to Rome and, much to Bristol's satisfaction, posed as an out-and-out loyalist. He 'behaved himself very discreetlie here [...] and hath freelie told' the Spaniards 'that all good and discreete Catholikes' in England 'do so much relie uppon the goodnesse and sinceritie of the king['s] and princes promises that they desire no further securitie than their words' alone.[156]

In England, by early 1623, the leading opponents of the marriage, notably Archbishop Abbot, were being publicly and embarrassingly thwarted at every turn. Even Abbot's attempt to dismiss Catholic musicians from Prince Charles's service had failed.[157] Routine searches of the London prisons, designed to disrupt the activities of the Catholic clergy who remained incarcerated there, were thwarted by royal command.[158]

For some time, in fact, there had been an alternative (though unworkable) set of proposals to resolve the question of the Palatinate. According to this scheme, the elector's son and heir would be brought up at the imperial court and would contract a marriage with the emperor's younger daughter, while Charles himself would marry the emperor's elder daughter, Maria Anna. (For Olivares, says Glyn

[154]PRO, SP 94/25, fos 264v–265r, 266r, 360r; PRO, PRO 31/3/56, fos 148v–149r; Adams, PC, p. 330; Pursell, *WK*, p. 184; Alexander, *CLT*, pp. 24–28; *CCE*, pp. 105–106, 111, 112.

[155]Redworth, *PI*, p. 177; Gardiner, *NSMT*, p. 332; PRO, SP 94/25, fos 312r–315v.

[156]PRO, SP 94/25, fo. 325r. See also Hacket, *SR*, part I, p. 130.

[157]William Harewell reported in February 1623 that 'the prince of Wales his musitions <did hether to> sing a solemne Masse at the Sp[anish] embassadours on Christmas day, for the which, being complained of by the bishop of Canturburie and some other sticklers like himselfe, they were dismissed the princes service'; but Charles, said Harewell, when informed of the ambassador's reaction, 'entertained them againe, restoring them to their former place': AAW, A XVII, no. 6, p. 22. The Venetian ambassador, Alvise Valaresso, said four musicians had been sacked (while Jean Beaulieu and Sir George Calvert put the number at two, and Calvert said that one was English and the other was an Italian). They had then been reinstated. Although the 'prince seemed very determined upon their exclusion [...] the king interposed his authority': *CSPV, 1621–1623*, pp. 555, 558; BL, Additional MS 72255, fo. 7v; CRS, 68, p. 185. The musicians had assisted 'with there voyces and musicke' at the Midnight Mass for Christmas: CRS, 68, p. 185; PRO, PRO 31/3/57, fo. 164r–v. Coloma requested, though unsuccessfully, that they should offer their services again at Easter: PRO, SP 14/139/111; PRO, SP 14/140/20; see also *NCC*, p. 68.

[158]*Letters 27, 29*; *CSPV, 1621–1623*, pp. 573, 578.

Redworth, this would have served to resolve the difficulties posed at the Spanish court by the draft Anglo-Spanish treaty.)[159]

It was now that Charles and Buckingham undertook their journey to Madrid. The hardly impartial French ambassador, the count of Tillières, thought that the whole country heard the news 'avec admiration, crainte et désespoir [...] non seulement le simple peuple, mais les plus grands, non seulement les puritains et les Protestans mais aussy les Catholiques'. It does seem to have caused consternation among some of the Spanish diplomatic service and the Hispanophile members of the English privy council, and indeed it was hardly welcome to the earl of Bristol.[160] Hispanophobe European sentiment condemned the journey as utter folly.[161] Sir Edward Conway commented, in a letter of 29 March which followed Buckingham to Spain, that 'a thousand conjurers could not have raised soe many severall spiritts as that journey of yours did; all the affeccions and passions of mankinde' were 'commenting upon it', though many critical voices were silenced 'when you had safely passed France' and even more 'upon the knowledg[e] of your good reception at the court of Spaine'.[162]

Many historians have concluded that the journey to Spain was idiotic. But some contemporaries, including English Catholics, saw it differently. William Harewell interpreted what has since become the stuff of ridiculous romance as 'one of the greatest pointes of pollicie that the king hath yet shewed for the securing of himselfe and his sonne'.[163] As Thomas Cogswell points out, Charles Emmanuel of Savoy saw the venture as a daring political manoeuvre to cut

[159] AAW, A XVII, no. 6, p. 22 (cited in *Letter 25*); *CGB*, I, pp. 274, 280, 282; Redworth, *PI*, pp. 69–72; Pursell, *WK*, p. 169; Lockyer, *Buckingham*, p. 130; PRO, PRO 31/3/56, fo. 135v; PRO, PRO 31/3/57, fo. 161r; PRO, SP 94/25, fos 277v–278r.

[160] PRO, PRO 31/3/57, fos 173r, 221v; Adams, PC, p. 334; Redworth, *PI*, ch. 8. Hacket argued that it would have been virtually impossible for any privy councillor, apart from Buckingham, to advise this course, because it was such a high-risk strategy. Secrecy, therefore, was a way of protecting those who would have been reluctant to endorse it publicly: Hacket, *SR*, part I, p. 114.

[161] See, e.g., *CSPV, 1621–1623*, pp. 575, 576.

[162] BL, Harleian MS 1580, fo. 332r. For the range of reactions in France to Charles's appearance there, see Sir Edward Herbert's report to James on 4/14 March 1623, and the letter of the same date written by James Hay, earl of Carlisle: PRO, SP 78/71, fos 66r–v, 69r–70r. Herbert argued that it was only the 'Jesuited' party which wanted to detain Charles in France (in order to force him to convert or, if he refused, until he had renounced the Stuart claim to the French crown): *ibid.*, fo. 66r; for Tillières's account of Herbert's report, which claimed that 'la faction des Jésuistes' also wanted to force Charles to wed Henrietta Maria, see PRO, PRO 31/3/57, fo. 190r–v. Herbert also noted that the proposals for a marriage between Henrietta Maria and the infante of Spain, Don Carlos, were being renewed at this point: PRO, SP 78/71, fo. 67r.

[163] *Letter 27*; see also *Letter 28*; cf. Schreiber, *FC*, pp. 48–49.

through the verbiage and tedium of endless delays in negotiation and to establish once and for all whether the Spaniards were serious about resolving the Palatinate issue at the same time as the celebration of the marriage.[164] Buckingham was, as Simon Adams notes, already 'suspicious of Bristol and wished to force the issue one way or another'. This explains the extension of his patronage at this time in 'a puritan direction' towards those who were regarded as opponents of the match, including Conway, Sir Horace Vere, the earl of Oxford, and Sir Robert Naunton, either to restrict opposition to the proposed treaty or to prepare 'a party in the event of a breach with Spain'.[165]

The rationale which, according to Sir Balthazar Gerbier, Buckingham himself advanced for the journey was 'to putt the Spaniards to it once for all to know what satisfaction they were like to have in the businesse of the Palatinatt [. . .] and to discover whether the ambassadors had entertayned the king with reallities or no'. Charles was in no danger in Madrid 'because of the queene of Bohemia and her numerous issu resyding in Holland'.[166] Among modern commentators, Robert Cross avers that the journey to Madrid was not 'a farce' but 'a serious attempt to bring some closure to the negotiations'.[167]

Some of the Spaniards also thought the Stuarts' strategy was annoyingly astute.[168] The French court evidently felt compelled by it to come to an accord with the Huguenots, since it appeared that an Anglo-Spanish alliance was very close.[169] Hispanophiles on the Continent celebrated the prospective union in advance.[170] There was a degree of courtier sentiment in England which professed to believe, even if only to flatter Buckingham, that the journey was a stroke of genius. Sir Humphrey May rejoiced on 23 April 1623 that the course taken by Charles and Buckingham had 'much disappointed the censorious wisedome' of carping armchair critics in England 'who were prepared to be wise accordinge to the event, and if anything but well had happened would have said that they did forsee it'. Rather presciently, May observed that 'so unhappy ar all greate men in all greate actions' for they 'ar never justified in their enterprises by the prudent motives and reasons by which they were induced to undertake them but by their successes'. Nevertheless, May was convinced that

[164] Cogswell, *BR*, pp. 60–61.

[165] Adams, PC, pp. 333–334. For Buckingham's enmity towards Bristol, noted by Tillières in a dispatch of 24 April 1622, see PRO, PRO 31/3/56, fo. 30r–v.

[166] BL, Additional MS 4181, fos 17v–18r; Adams, PC, p. 334; Redworth, *PI*, p. 65.

[167] R. Cross, 'Pretense and perception in the Spanish match, or history in a fake beard', *Journal of Interdisciplinary History*, 37 (2007), p. 572.

[168] Gardiner, *NSMT*, p. 202.

[169] Adams, PC, pp. 332–333; though cf. PRO, SP 78/71, fo. 87r–v.

[170] Arblaster, *Antwerp & the World*, p. 145.

'this match wilbe a happy meanes to compose the miserable fractures of Christendome and restore peace againe unto it and that it will conduce somwhat to allay the cruell hatred and detestations and prosequutions that ar on all sides amongst Christians', even though May emphasized that he was a firm adherent of the Church of England.[171]

The Spanish court was seriously divided on the issue of whether to proceed with the negotiations once Charles had arrived in Spain. While, for Gondomar, it served as a ticket to dizzying heights of influence, only a minority of the council of state was really in favour. Olivares certainly was not.[172] The anticipated dowry, though a crucial element of James's calculations and, in effect, a massive European subsidy, was surely never likely to be handed over without major concessions by the Stuart court. It is difficult to see how any amount of diplomatic double-speak would ever have got round the fact that Charles was probably not going to show himself in the religious colours which the Spaniards would ultimately have required in order to proceed with the treaty. The furious negotiating over the papal dispensation suggests that they did not actually expect him to convert to Catholicism, although there was a body of opinion in Europe which affected to believe that he would.[173] Indeed, the earl of Bristol, as he reported on 3/13 December 1622, had had it made clear to him how generous the Spaniards thought that they were already being towards the Stuart family. Gondomar had urged Bristol to tell Prince

[171]BL, Harleian MS 1581, fos 358r–359r.

[172]Pursell, ESP, p. 713; Cross, 'Pretense', pp. 569–570. For an assessment of Gondomar as 'one of the best-informed and most well-connected men' in the Spanish court, see Cross, 'Pretense', p. 570.

[173]For Ranier Zen's note, on 5/15 April 1623, that the Jesuit general Muzio Vitelleschi was spreading rumours that King James was near death and that Charles 'will readily become a Catholic, and so that kingdom will return to the obedience of the Catholic Church', see *CSPV, 1621–1623*, p. 632. For the conversion issue, see Redworth, *PI*, pp. 89–95; Cross, 'Pretense', p. 567. Redworth argues that the short-lived conferences in Madrid about religion were the product of misunderstanding, and he describes Charles as 'a contented, even smug, Anglican'. The connections between smugness and Anglicanism are, of course, well established. But it is at least arguable that such encounters were part of an elaborate diplomatic duel, and provided a language whereby the two sides could test out, via religion, each other's intentions concerning the match. Through Charles's and Buckingham's attendances at the conferences arranged to discuss religion, and their appearances at ceremonial religious occasions, both sides were able to make, in effect, quite belligerent public statements about their intentions without exposing the arcana imperii of international treaty negotiations to public scrutiny. (For Buckingham's aggressiveness at this point towards the Spaniards, see Gardiner, *NSMT*, pp. 210–211, 225–226.) Rumours in France, retailed for example by Louis XIII to Sir Edward Herbert in April 1623, that Charles was on the verge of converting to Catholicism in Spain and had 'given monney to the Jesuits', were clearly no more than a gloss on the irenic front adopted, from time to time, by the English royal party in Madrid: PRO, SP 78/71, fo. 121r.

Charles 'what difficultye' Philip IV 'had overcome in satisfying his people for the matching of a daughter of Spayne with a prince of a differing religion', and with such a large dowry ('a thinge unheard of in Christendome'). For all the advantages that the Stuarts would reap through the marriage, 'there was nothing required [...] but the ease and quyett of your owne subjects that the infanta might not live to see a persecution for the religion she professed'.[174]

Olivares's line, and an entirely reasonable one, was that English and Spanish interests should, under normal circumstances, not be in conflict. The marriage therefore only made sense if it brought them closer together, and it appeared to him that this would probably not happen via the proposed dynastic union. The problem was that James wanted things from it which the Spaniards would not deliver: 'if a necessary consequence of the conclusion of the marriage should be to introduce a contrariety of interests in this friendship where there has hitherto been a community, the opening of the negotiation has been pernicious and its conclusion will soon be worse'. What Olivares meant was that, if James engaged in war against the empire, the result would be either that the Spanish Habsburgs would have to fight the Viennese branch of the House of Austria, or that Spain would be compelled to remain neutral (thus risking disgrace for not supporting the European Catholic cause), or, of course, that Spain would simply turn against the English altogether.[175]

Many contemporary commentators could hardly be blamed, therefore, for their scepticism even while Charles was in Spain and while a fleet was being fitted out to go to bring him and the infanta home; and they were proved right in the end. Philip III had, before his death, it turned out, instructed his son not to contemplate concluding the marriage.[176]

On the other hand, this should not conceal the fact that other observers, even those who were not enthusiastic Catholics, thought for a time that the marriage really would take place. (Although Olivares insisted that the king of Spain would not go to war with the emperor, Glyn Redworth points out that the Spaniards had a genuine incentive to rein in the rampant forces of the duke of Bavaria, as well as to prevent a strengthening of Anglo-Dutch amity.[177]) Brennan Pursell argues, extremely convincingly to my mind, that it is wrong to assume

[174] PRO, SP 94/25, fo. 310r.

[175] Gardiner, *NSMT*, pp. 224, 194–195; Thompson, *HA*, p. 8; Lockyer, *Buckingham*, p. 134; see also PRO, SP 94/25, fos 275v–276r; PRO, SP 94/29, fo. 157r–v.

[176] Redworth, *PI*, pp. 66, 67, 68; Gardiner, *NSMT*, pp. 192, 321–322; PRO, SP 94/25, fo. 269r.

[177] Redworth, *PI*, pp. 56–57; PRO, SP 78/71, fos 31r, 32r; PRO, SP 78/72, fo. 15r; PRO, SP 94/25, fo. 239v; *CGB*, I, p. 90. Bristol claimed on 8/18 October 1622 that, at a recent

that 'the Spanish monarchy had never been serious about the match' (the view set out by Gardiner in his account of the Spanish marriage negotiations), even though there were profound disagreements among the Spanish monarchy's advisers. Pursell suggests that the Spaniards did not set out simply to dupe the Stuart court but had a very different idea from Prince Charles about the way in which the linked issues of the Palatinate and the proposed marriage should be handled. If anyone was to blame for the negotiations' failure it was Charles himself. This, rather than the Spaniards' allegedly 'pathologically mendacious' nature or the, again alleged, political insight of the duke of Buckingham in worming out Spanish lies, was what caused the negotiations to break down.[178] Although Philip IV had indeed been instructed by his father to prevent the marriage under anything except the most propitious circumstances, Pursell claims that, by late 1622, the young king 'seemed to be warming to the idea' and certainly had enough motivation to prevent the elector palatine and his wife succeeding Prince Charles should he die childless.[179]

Moreover, Robert Cross has recently argued that, while Paul V may have had ideological objections to the marriage, Gregory XV evidently did not. Cross rejects the idea that 'talk of anything less than Charles's conversion' was 'simply Gondomar's wishful thinking'. He suggests instead that, 'at the time, virtually everyone in the Spanish government and Church seemed to think that the match would require merely a deal involving toleration of English Catholics (be it *de facto* or *de jure*) and that the prince's conversion would not be a necessary condition'.[180]

The point is that there was no reason for contemporaries necessarily to conclude, as the negotiations progressed, that they were mere window-dressing. In the politically contingent circumstances of 1622–1623 this was, at least in the context of English and British domestic

audience, Philip IV had said that James's demands concerning the Palatinate would be met, if necessary, by the deployment of Spanish military force against imperial troops: PRO, SP 94/25, fos 243v, 257v; Lockyer, *Buckingham*, p. 131. (On 9 October 1622, the earl of Kellie had noted Cottington's report that 'the king of Spaine hes saide plainlye that, if the emperoure and Baviere will not surrander the pallatinate [...] Spinola shall goe as from him to assiste the recovery of it againe': *HMCMK*, p. 140.) For Pursell's reconstruction of the scenario in which, following a submission to the emperor by the elector palatine, it was possible that, if the duke of Bavaria did not accept the emperor's subsequent restoration of the elector (something which a majority of Philip's council of state desired to see), then Habsburg troops might force the duke of Bavaria to comply, see Pursell, ESP, pp. 717–718; see also *CGB*, I, p. 346 (for the nuncio del Bagno's report in August 1623 of Spinola's hostility to the duke of Bavaria).

[178] Pursell, ESP, pp. 699–701, 725–726.

[179] *Ibid.*, pp. 703–704.

[180] Cross, 'Pretense', pp. 566, 567.

politics, probably just as important as whether the treaty was actually agreed and implemented in the end. As early as March 1623, Secretary Conway could be found making arrangements for the reception and lodging of the prince and the infanta (though, later in the year, Venice's ambassador, Alvise Valaresso, noted that 'the Spaniards hate' Conway 'extremely').[181] In April, Conway believed that the dispensation would soon arrive and 'then hee that supposeth a delay is either desperately envious or a vile almanack maker that out of a false colleccion of the conjunction of the planetts feares us with a fowle day when it prooves faire'.[182] Furthermore, during April and May 1623, absolutely contrary to the elector palatine's wishes, a treaty was hammered out between James and Isabella, a treaty which was also signed by the emperor. It established a period of peace and a cease-fire in which an attempt would be made to work out a final settlement.[183]

The fleet which was now being commissioned to go to Spain to bring the royal party home was to be officered by Catholics: for example, the earl of Rutland (Buckingham's father-in-law) as admiral, and Lord Windsor and Lord Morley as, respectively, vice- and rear-admirals.[184] Tillières described how the fleet was ordered to sail from London rather than from Plymouth 'pour faire croire au peuple que les dicts vaisseaux' were going to bring back the infanta and the prince of Wales.[185] Chamberlain commented on 19 April that there was a whole gaggle of courtiers rushing for Spain. Among them were Lord Kensington and Sir George Goring who

[181] PRO, SP 14/139/63; *CSPV, 1623–1625*, p. 106.

[182] PRO, SP 14/142/34, fo. 70v.

[183] Pursell, ESP, pp. 709–710; Patterson, *King James VI and I*, p. 334; see below, p. 50.

[184] *CSPD, 1619–1623*, p. 558; McClure, *LJC*, pp. 491, 499; *CSPV, 1623–1625*, p. 8; PRO, SP 94/26, fos 159r, 160r–v; *DSSD*, pp. 131, 138. The news about the fleet was conveyed to Simonds D'Ewes by 'one of Lord Windsors gentlemen': *DSSD*, p. 131. D'Ewes's diary remarks disdainfully on the 'popish' command of the fleet. In mid-June 1623, news had reached him that 'ther had been latelye a mutinie at the ships which weere going for Spaine and lay yett upon the Downes' about the type of divine service to be celebrated on board. It was 'saied my Lorde Morley would have hindred' the recital of the prayer book and 'would have brought inn his damnable Masse instead of it'; and 'the marriners weere soe farr provoked as his lordshipp was verye near throwing over boorde': *ibid.*, p. 141; see also Whiteway, *Diary*, p. 52; Birch, *CTJI*, II, p. 407. D'Ewes also noted how the court jester, Archibald Armstrong, mocked the popish lords for the expenditure which they had personally incurred over setting forward the fleet 'in hope of great rewards': *DSSD*, p. 156. See also *CSPV, 1623–1625*, p. 33 (for the claim that Rutland, Windsor, and Morley, departing from the court to their ships, had 'a numerous company composed almost exclusively of Catholics'). The earl of Rutland denied that there had been any 'interruptions and scandalls [. . .] given to inferiour officers and marrinours when theie were att common praier and singing of psalmes': PRO, SP 14/147/84 (fo. 103r), 84. i, 85. For the orders issued to Rutland, see BL, Harleian MS 1584, fos 4r–8v.

[185] PRO, PRO 31/3/57, fo. 219r.

were religiously quite sound; but others had opportunistically turned Catholic.[186] The liturgical arrangements made for the prince in Madrid were deliberately designed to appear as Catholic in character as possible.[187]

Soon Chamberlain was informing Carleton that the infanta would have 'prerogative and privileges [. . .] more than ever quene of England had'. Coloma 'had ben at St James and Denmarke House to fit and apoint her lodgings with many alterations'. There would be 'a new chappell built in either place, for which order is taken with the surveyor Innigo Jones to have them don out of hand, and yet with great state and costlines'. The Savoy chapel 'likewise shalbe converted to the use of her household'. Diego de Lafuente, Gondomar's chaplain, would be in charge, or any other 'that shalbe as yt were bishop or superintendent over her priests and chaplains'.[188] At the end of May, Chamberlain saw that all the preparations for the infanta's arrival

[186] McClure, *LJC*, p. 491.

[187] Two chaplains, Leonard Mawe and Matthew Wren, had been sent to attend the royal party. They had been instructed to behave in a manner 'agreeable to the puritie of the primitive Churche and yett as neare the Romane forme as can lawfullie be done'. They were to use a room 'decently adorned chappellwise with an altar [. . .] palls, lynnen coverings, demy carpet, 4 surplices, candlesticks, tapers, chalices, pattens, a fine towell for the prince, other towells for the household [. . .] wafers for the communion', and so on. In particular there were to be no 'polemicall preachings'. Lord Keeper Williams arranged for the English liturgy to be translated into Spanish. The translation was made by the convert Fernando de Tejeda, formerly the protégé of Daniel Featley (his tract, *Scrutamini Scripturas* (London, 1624) was dedicated to Williams): CRS, 68, pp. 185, 186; PRO, SP 94/26, fo. 80r; Hacket, *SR*, part I, pp. 126–127; Birch, *CTJI*, II, p. 375. (Williams went through the same rigmarole for the French when the marriage between Prince Charles and Henrietta Maria was being negotiated; he employed a minister of the French church in Norwich to produce a translation of the prayer book to 'clear the Church of England [. . .] from the gross slanders of fugitives': Hacket, *SR*, part I, p. 209.) Simonds D'Ewes remarked that the chaplains selected for Charles's service 'weere choosen as men altogether free from the suspition of being puritans': *DSSD*, p. 128. Disparate rumours about the prince's chaplains (both that they were 'not suffred to come to him' and that 'they had accesse twise a day') filtered back from Spain, and Simonds D'Ewes commented that 'what to beleeve was uncertaine': *DSSD*, pp. 136–137; cf. Albion, *CI*, pp. 36–37. (Leonard Mawe suffered an injury during the course of his journey and never reached Madrid: Redworth, *PI*, pp. 93–94.) For Mawe and Wren, see also Tyacke, *Anti-Calvinists*, pp. 46, 48–49.

[188] McClure, *LJC*, p. 494; cf. BL, Harleian MS 1581, fo. 260r; see also *CSPD, 1619–1623*, p. 560; PRO, SP 14/143/13, 31; PRO, SP 14/144/42. In mid-May, Calvert was dealing with the layout of the chapels at St James's and Denmark House (formerly Somerset House, which had been Anne of Denmark's residence until 1619): PRO, SP 14/144/42. The infanta would live primarily at Denmark House, but her private chapel would be near St James's palace: Redworth, *PI*, pp. 100–101, 127 (citing M.D. Whinney and O. Miller, *English Art 1625–1714* (Oxford, 1957), p. 27). The proposed chapel would be fifty-five feet long and would have 'width in proportion'. The Flanders agent van Male commented that if 'these three buildings are built according to the drawings of the king's architect then we shall have nothing to complain of': CRS, 68, p. 186. By contrast, in June 1623, the count of Tillières

were going on apace. Coloma himself had laid the first stone of the chapel being constructed for her at St James's.[189] A newsletter of 30 May to Joseph Mead in Cambridge made a connection between this and the cross which was being restored in the chapel royal, and also the king's direction to the bishop of Winchester that the chapel at Greenwich should be 'new repaired and gilded'.[190]

The public impact of these things was amplified greatly by the dispatch of a formal papal letter, of 10/20 April 1623, to the prince in Spain. The letter was formally presented to Charles on 8/18 May by the nuncio in Madrid. It was much copied, translated, and circulated. In it, Gregory XV enthusiastically addressed Charles, dwelling on his decision to marry a Habsburg:

> whereas you are come to Spayne to the Catholique kinge to desire a marriage with the House of Austria, this your desire wee much commend; and also, upon this present occasion offered, testifie that you appertayne to the speciall care of our papall dignitie. For, since you are resolved to joyne to you in marriage a Catholique mayden, wee may easilie conjecture that those seedes of piety which so happelie florished in the myndes of the Roman kinges may also [. . .] spring up in your hart. Neyther would hee seeke after such a match who hated the Catholique religion and delighted in the oppression of the sea of Rome.[191]

An equally gushing response from the prince to the pontiff followed. It was also much copied and circulated, though the pope died before it reached him.[192] Chamberlain was still fuming, even at the end of August 1623, that

> here goes a letter up and downe in the princes name in aunswer to that [which] the pope sent him three or fowre moneths since, which, yf yt be true, is somwhat

alleged that the chapel which was under construction at St James's palace was 'une maison pour le diable': PRO, PRO 31/3/57, fo. 224v.

[189]McClure, *LJC*, p. 500; *CSPV, 1623–1625*, p. 40. In France it was being said, at the end of May, that Philip IV would 'demand some cautionary touns in England for the securinge of the covenants to be performed' by James (including the recall of James's subjects who were serving with the Dutch and the toleration of those 'who shall come to the infantas chappell'): PRO, SP 78/71, fo. 161r.

[190]Birch, *CTJI*, II, p. 400; cf. *Letter 1.*

[191]BL, Additional MS 72286, fos 176v–177r; PRO, SP 14/142/59, fo. 118r; TD, V, pp. 130–132; ARCR, I, nos 1575–1593; Hacket, *SR*, part I, pp. 128–129; *Cabala*, pp. 212–214; *The Popes Letter to the Prince: in Latine, Spanish, and English* (London, 1623). Simonds D'Ewes recorded in his diary for 20 June that he 'had sight of a letter in Lattine which was sent from the pope to the prince which afterwards came into print': *DSSD*, p. 142.

[192]TD, V, pp. 132–134; ARCR, I, nos 1594–1600; Hacket, *SR*, part I, pp. 128–129; PRO, SP 14/147/10, 11; PRO, SP 94/27, fo. 85r–v; *Cabala*, pp. 214–215. For the diplomatic consequences of Gregory XV's death, see Redworth, *PI*, p. 128; Lockyer, *Buckingham*, p. 161; PRO, SP 78/71, fos 208r, 220r, 231v.

straunge, for (besides other passages) yt geves him the title of Holines and most holy father divers times and kisses his Holines feet.[193]

John Hacket admitted that the prince's reply allowed 'some of our hot-heads in England' to make 'it a quarrel and a calumny', although Hacket, and indeed the Stuart regime, could claim with some justice that Charles, within the polite formula of goodwill which his reply adopted, maintained a position of complete ecclesiological independence.[194]

There was undoubtedly an air of triumphalism among Catholics and those who were associated with the 'Spanish' faction. Sir William Monson's son, John, was alleged by the earl of Nottingham to have said in May 1623, in front of a group of twenty or thirty people, that, 'whatsoever the kinges Majestie did shew himselfe, yet he was of theare religion'. Nottingham remarked, if rather inaccurately, that William 'Watson the priest was executed at Winchester for the very same wordes', and he added that John Monson's 'delight' was 'in seeking whome he may perswade'.[195] Juan Hurtado de Mendoza, marquis of Inojosa, who had been recalled from Navarre in March and had been appointed extraordinary ambassador to the Stuart court in London, landed at Dover. He was welcomed with considerable pomp and ceremony, and arrived at Canterbury in June 1623. It was claimed that 'a greate many papists [. . .] declared themselves at Canterbery at the embassadors being there'. One of them 'dranke a health to the confusion of all Protestants'.[196] Chamberlain noted on 28 June that Inojosa went to lodge at Ely House, where Catholics had established a London church for themselves. The Catholics began 'to be very confident and talke lowde of such a toleration as that they expect to have the tenth church of the land'.[197] Such was their exuberance that, in mid-July, Secretary Calvert tried to ensure that the Spanish ambassador would 'labour to prevent all cause of his Majesties displeasure' and to persuade the Catholics to 'behave themselves with that modesty, meeknesse and humility' which they owed to a 'gratious souveraigne'.[198] Conway observed on 17 July that Catholics were making the marriage articles 'as common as the balletts sung in

[193] McClure, *LJC*, p. 513.

[194] Hacket, *SR*, part I, p. 128.

[195] PRO, SP 14/145/22, fo. 39r; McClure, *LJC*, p. 500; *CSPD, Addenda 1580–1625*, p. 654; *APC, 1623–1625*, pp. 6–7.

[196] PRO, SP 14/146/87, 88; PRO, SP 14/147/35, fo. 41r; PRO, SP 94/26, fo. 106r. The count of Tillières thought, however, that, when Inojosa arrived in London, 'les honneurs que l'on luy a faicts n'ont aucunement esgalé ceux que l'on rendist' to the former French ambassador extraordinary, the marquis of Cadenet: PRO, PRO 31/3/57, fos 226v–227r.

[197] McClure, *LJC*, p. 504.

[198] PRO, SP 14/148/124, fo. 153r.

the streets, and [. . .] with such inventions and addicions as deforme them past knowledge'.[199]

It was at this point that leading Jesuit polemicists such as John Percy were becoming more visible as they disputed semi-publicly with leading Protestant ideologues such as Daniel Featley.[200] Even in late summer, Valaresso was commenting that one of the 'chief results' of the match was 'the open declaration by many who before were only secret Catholics'. It was believed that, 'since the prince left, about a hundred families have declared themselves, noted down by his Majesty himself'.[201]

The progress of the negotiations at Madrid did not, however, warrant some English Catholics' enthusiasm. George Gage secured the final text of the dispensation at Rome and it was sent off to the nuncio in Madrid, Innocenzo Massimi;[202] but its effect was now vitiated by a change in Spanish policy, the news of which reached Rome just after the dispensation had been dispatched.[203] Whether this was always the Spaniards' intention – namely, to lead the English a merry dance – or whether the new policy was actually the product of the hostility generated, mainly by Buckingham, in Madrid, is a matter for interpretation.[204] Further conditions, drawn up by Cardinal Luigi Ludovisi at Spanish request, were added to those of the extant dispensation and, as Charles Dodd put it, 'by a skilful management of the difficulties that would thus arise, the negotiation might still be protracted'.[205] A theological 'junta' had been set up soon after Charles arrived in Madrid, superseding the earlier and much smaller body which had met in the past to consider the question of the marriage. Buckingham showed considerable irritation when Olivares told him how the junta must necessarily guide the king's conscience; Buckingham informed Olivares 'that it was all a plot to mock and betray them'. Olivares then told Buckingham that it would have been better to leave the diplomacy to Bristol, who had been ready to trust the Spanish court to deal with the papacy about the terms of the dispensation.[206]

[199] PRO, SP 94/27, fo. 113r.

[200] McClure, *LJC*, p. 507. See also Henry Rogers, *An Answer to M^r. Fisher the Iesuite his Five Propositions concerning Luther. By M^r. Rogers, that worthy Oxford divine* (np, 1623).

[201] *CSPV, 1623–1625*, p. 103.

[202] *Letter 28*; Redworth, *PI*, p. 103; *CSPV, 1621–1623*, p. 569; PRO, SP 94/26, fo. 106v.

[203] Redworth, *PI*, p. 103.

[204] For a discussion of this issue, and of the diplomatic reasons why Rome was likely to accede to Madrid's wishes concerning the text of the dispensation, see *ibid.*, pp. 101–104.

[205] TD, V, pp. 135–136; *CSPV, 1621–1623*, pp. 623–626; *CSPV, 1623–1625*, p. 20; Redworth, *PI*, pp. 102–104; Lockyer, *Buckingham*, p. 144; Pursell, ESP, p. 710.

[206] *CSPV, 1623–1625*, pp. 32, 36, 37; Lockyer, *Buckingham*, p. 148; Redworth, *PI*, p. 108; Pursell, ESP, pp. 710, 711–713. For Lord Rochford's warning to Buckingham in Spain about

The new conditions did not immediately halt proceedings, but the effects of the procrastination threatened havoc in English domestic and foreign policy.[207] In early June 1623, Sir Edward Herbert warned that, if James should concede by treaty what the Spanish court desired 'before the match betwixt his Highnes and the infanta bee consummated', the Spaniards would 'protracte the tyme with so many and artificiall delayes' that 'all the affaires betwixt your [. . .] Majestie' and Philip IV would 'remaine more than ever in suspense'; and therefore James should insist on the return of Charles with the infanta before 'the least speech of any other busines with the Spaniarde', and particularly of a 'league offensive', which would commit James 'against all your [. . .] Majesties neighbors and antient allyes at once'.[208] In the same month, the Venetian ambassador in Spain commented that, through delay, the Spaniards would 'discover various things and chiefly the strength of the Catholics, who need not longer conceal themselves out of fear'.[209] In other words, while Olivares might well be counselling that the match was not feasible, it was nevertheless crystal clear to some observers what the Spaniards might do if they chose to press the issue, and how they might damage, for example, the relationship between the king and parliament – a relationship which Protestants such as Thomas Scott were proclaiming was essential to preserve the monarchical authority with which they believed James was invested.[210]

The armistice of May 1623 stipulated a cease-fire for fifteen months, during which time, at the direction of the regime in Brussels, negotiations would be conducted at Cologne. Frederick and the prince of Orange were unwilling participants, and the former, who was utterly desperate to see the Spanish match fail, finally agreed only after his adherent Christian of Brunswick was defeated at Stadtlohn in August.[211]

the danger represented by Bristol, who, said Rochford, 'hath a greater [. . .] partie in court than you imagine, in so much that [. . .] were the kinge a newter, he would prevail', see BL, Harleian MS 1581, no. 115, fo. 379v.

[207] For the complexity of the negotiations at Madrid between May and July, see Redworth, *PI*, chs 10–12.

[208] PRO, SP 78/71, fo. 175r.

[209] *CSPV, 1623–1625*, p. 37.

[210] Lake, 'Constitutional consensus', p. 814. An open letter to the king, put about in Archbishop Abbot's name in August 1623, declared that 'this toleration [. . .] which you endeavour to set up by proclamation cannot be decided without a parliament'. The letter asked 'Does your Majesty mean to show your subjects that you intend to arrogate to yourself the entire authority to reverse the laws of the realm at your pleasure?': *CSPV, 1623–1625*, p. 91; PRO, SP 14/150/54–57, 81, 105; *CGB*, I, p. 348; BL, Harleian MS 1583, fo. 89r–v.

[211] *CSPV, 1623–1625*, pp. 43, 44, 56–57, 96, 98, 105, 107; *CGB*, I, p. 356; PRO, PRO 31/3/57, fos 247r, 253v; Pursell, *WK*, pp. 201–203; Adams, PC, p. 335.

In spite of the accumulating mistrust, two treaties – one with a public set of articles and the other with a private set – were now drawn up in Spain and were dispatched to London for ratification by James. The public treaty contained the provisions for, among other things, the infanta's clerical entourage and chapel. The private treaty had the more sensitive provisions concerning the extent of the toleration which the crown would grant to Catholics.[212] On 17 July 1623, Sir Edward Conway wrote to Buckingham about the 'great [. . .] distress' caused to James by the 'articles brought' from Spain, by Peter Killigrew, 'upon three poynts'. The first concerned 'the perpetuitie of time for the abrogation of all lawes concerning the Romaine Catholiques in noe time to bee renewed against them, nor any other to bee raised in their place upon any occasion'. Secondly, a guarantee was required from James that the articles 'in favour of Romaine Catholiques' would be 'confirmed by parliament within three yeares [. . .] and sooner if the constitution of affaires would permit it'. The third dealt with the oath to be taken by the privy council. The first, 'a perpetuall imunity', would bring the Catholics 'to a daungerous encrease'; the second was simply impossible to procure; and, as for the third, if the council would not concur, the king's authority might 'receave prejudice' by his councillors' refusal to co-operate. The marriage had, in effect, been negotiated by Prince Charles in Spain. In consultation with specific councillors on the previous Sunday, at which he had voiced his concerns about these issues, James had been advised that the prince's 'wordes and articles must bee made good', that the 'oath by the councell must bee taken', and, in addition, that 'the prince must marry and bringe his lady away with him this yeare'.[213]

Some members of the privy council, notably Lord Zouch, had to be forced to take the oath by which they swore that they would allow the proposed toleration to work, or that at least they would not impede it.[214]

[212] TD, V, pp. 137–138; Gardiner, *NSMT*, pp. 327–344; *CSPV, 1623–1625*, pp. 82–85.

[213] BL, Harleian MS 1580, fo. 307r–v; PRO, PRO 31/3/57, fos 231r, 235r–236v; Redworth, *PI*, pp. 124–125; TD, V, pp. 138–139.

[214] PRO, SP 14/149/12, 31; McClure, *LJC*, pp. 509–510; *Letter 30*. The dissent on the council over the oath was informed by knowledge of Buckingham's change of opinion about the proposed treaty: Adams, PC, p. 335. Zouch made his opinions known by doggedly sticking to the absolute letter of the law concerning the release of Catholic prisoners, and by trying to prevent the carriage of Catholic books and letters through Dover: PRO, SP 14/153/59; PRO, SP 14/152/42. He had, up to this point, in his capacity as lord warden of the Cinque ports, been zealously administering the oath of allegiance to those passing through the ports, especially those who were known to have been involved in Catholic military activity on the Continent. Zouch bitterly criticized Lord Keeper Williams for agreeing to bail such people (and in particular one who was a soldier serving in one of the companies under the command of Lord Vaux) after they had been arrested: PRO, SP 14/148/31, 31.i–iv; PRO, SP 14/149/19. In July 1623, Zouch informed Conway that he had arrested the Jesuit Thomas

Sir George Calvert, on 18 July, arranged for the attorney-general to draw up a dispensation for the oath of allegiance.[215] On Sunday 20 July, at Whitehall, James 'tooke his oath to observe all the articles agreed upon, which were read by Secretarie Calvert in Latin and lasted almost an howre'. Additional articles concerning the toleration of Catholics were sworn by the king later in the day 'in some private roome apart where', as Calvert had noted a few days before, only the ambassadors were to attend, accompanied by 'some few' of James's 'councell such as his Majesty shall thinke fitt'. Chamberlain had heard only extracts of the articles, but 'one among the rest' was that 'the infanta is to be allowed 24 priests, which are to have as yt were a bishop over them and not to be any way subject to our lawes'. She was also 'to have the education of her children till they be ten yeares old, with many other points concerning her joynter, and favorable toleration toward the Romish Catholikes'. Even at Whitehall, Catholic pride and effrontery had been displayed for all to see. For, complained Chamberlain, 'the ceremonies beeing ended and the antheme sung', when the bishop of London 'began the prayer for the king, the ambassadors confessor or Jesuite (that stood by him within the traverse) clapt on his hat and so continued all the while though the king and ambassador were bare'.[216]

The Spanish diplomats, however, continued to agitate for more speedy and thorough implementation of thc toleration clauses than the regime and even genuine supporters of the marriage such as Calvert were prepared to concede.[217] All was clearly not well. Conway's letter

Everard who had come from Calais, disguised as a soldier, with a pass from Sir Edward Parham (sergeant-major of Vaux's regiment): PRO, SP 14/148/57, 57.i–ii.

[215]PRO, SP 14/149/6, 7.

[216]McClure, *LJC*, p. 510; BL, Harleian MS 1580, fo. 187r; BL, Harleian MS 1581, fo. 292r; PRO, PRO 31/3/57, fo. 239r–v; *DSSD*, pp. 147–148; *HMCMK*, p. 175; TD, V, p. 139; Cogswell, *BR*, p. 46; Redworth, *PI*, p. 126; Akrigg, *Letters of King James VI & I*, p. 417; Pursell, ESP, p. 714; BL, Harleian MS 1583, fos 268r–271r; BL, Additional MS 72255, fo. 45v; see also PRO, SP 14/149/30; Birch, *CTJI*, II, p. 416. According to Jean Beaulieu, 'in the afternoone all the lords of the councell', except the earl of Pembroke and Lord Brooke 'who were both sicke at that tyme', 'tooke oath [. . .] to conforme themselves' to the king's 'will therein': BL, Additional MS 72255, fo. 63r. A compromise on the toleration issue was rather hastily arranged with the Spanish ambassadors (on the same day, it appears, as the treaty was signed). On 23 July, Conway reported to Buckingham that the Spanish ambassadors had been leaned on to send word to Spain that 'favour to the Romaine Catholiques was already put in execution'. They 'fayntly accorded', but 'withall prayed to have some actes done which might bee publique and authenticall', to which James seemed to accede: BL, Harleian MS 1580, fo. 311v.

[217]BL, Additional MS 35832, fos 114r, 116r; PRO, SP 14/149/79; and see below, pp. 57–63. Tillières reported on 13 July that James, speaking to the judges about to go on circuit, had insisted that, as for Catholics, 'ce n'est pas que je les ayme ny la religion qu'ilz professent, au contraire [. . .] j'abhorre plus et l'un et l'autre'; and James instructed the judges to proceed harshly against Catholics 's'ils font quelque scandale': PRO, PRO 31/3/57, fo. 232r–v.

to Buckingham of 23 July carried a postscript: 'the acts of favour are gone this day' for 'the kings signature, which knowne, will create cold swett and feare untill the returne of his Highnes and your Grace'.[218] On 27 July, the marquis of Inojosa penned a letter to Calvert asking, yet again, that he should 'procure the resolution that is to be taken with the Catholiques'.[219] On 29 and 30 July, according to Tillières's secretary, leading Catholics met with the Spanish ambassadors 'pour donner leur advis de la forme en laquelle ilz requerroient du roy de la Grande Bretagne la publication des articles dont il a juré l'observation', and some of these Catholics insisted that it must be by way of a general pardon and proclamation. George Gage, who was present, gave his opinion (which he said was also that of the king) that 'cela estoit impossible'. James 'ne leur accorderoit jamais telle chose qui offenseroit son peuple' and instead 'il falloit trouver quelque autre expédient'. It was concluded 'il faudroit se contenter de la volonté du roy'. Gage proposed, on behalf of Secretary Calvert, that the king 'donneroit un pardon aus dicts Catholicques' under the great seal, and that those who wanted it would have to purchase it.[220]

Almost simultaneously, however, the two sides in Madrid had manoeuvred themselves into irreconcilable positions, although there was a show of consensus in early July as Charles appeared to accept the Spanish court's terms.[221] Charles prepared to leave Spain, though there was further haggling as the news of Pope Gregory XV's death arrived and, therefore, of the need for a new dispensation. Charles actually put his signature to the treaty, even in the face of the absolute refusal of the Spanish court to allow the infanta to leave for England before the following spring.[222]

It had never made sense to the Spaniards simply to restore Frederick to the Palatinate. As we have seen, Olivares's preferred dynastic solution to the Bohemian and Palatinate question was to make the Stuarts deal directly with the Habsburg court in Vienna. In July, even as the Spanish marriage negotiations started to break down completely, the proposal that Charles should marry the emperor's

[218] BL, Harleian MS 1580, fo. 312v.

[219] PRO, SP 94/27, fo. 127r. Calvert had, according to Carondelet, said that James had ordered 'warrants to bee made as are requisite for the execution of that which is granted in favour of the Roman Catholiques for the time to come, reserving that which concernes the remission of the penalties by-past'. Inojosa was incensed because he had understood that all penalties had been remitted: *ibid.*

[220] PRO, PRO 31/3/57, fo. 242r–v.

[221] Pursell, ESP, p. 714; Lockyer, *Buckingham*, p. 158; Redworth, *PI*, pp. 122–123.

[222] Redworth, *PI*, pp. 119–133; Pursell, ESP, p. 715. A letter of 10 August from James had ordered the prince and the duke to return: Akrigg, *Letters of King James VI & I*, p. 424. For Pursell's discussion of whether the infanta Maria herself ever desired or intended to go through with the proposed marriage to Prince Charles, see Pursell, ESP, pp. 719–720.

elder daughter, the archduchess Maria Anna, was renewed.[223] Charles's merely diplomatic assent on 27 June/7 July to all Madrid's conditions (not long before he left the city) also had the effect of preventing this alternative, Viennese dynastic solution favoured by Olivares.[224] Just before Charles departed, the Spaniards put forward again the equally pointless proposal for Frederick's eldest son to be educated in Vienna and marry a daughter of the emperor.[225]

On his journey home, Charles sent orders back to the earl of Bristol in Madrid. Bristol was not to hand over Charles's proxy for going ahead with the marriage, on the technical grounds that assurances were still required that the infanta would not, after the betrothal, be incarcerated in a house of religion. Back in England, further orders were issued that the proxy should not be delivered until the Spaniards rendered satisfaction over the Palatinate; in other words, never.[226]

## The Appointment of William Bishop as Bishop of Chalcedon

Before the Anglo-Spanish negotiations began to break down irretrievably, William Bishop had been consecrated in Paris on 25 May/4 June as bishop of Chalcedon. He set off on 18/28 July for his home country, which had also, in some sense, become his new diocese.[227]

[223] Redworth, *PI*, pp. 122–123.

[224] *ibid.* For Charles's departure, see *ibid.*, pp. 128–129, 132–136. There is, perhaps, a disparity between Glyn Redworth's evidence of the sophistication of the Stuart court's international diplomacy and his claim both that the journey to Madrid was merely 'foolhardy' and that it was not primarily concerned with the resolution of the Palatinate question: *ibid.*, p. 74; cf. Pursell, ESP, *passim*. For Robert Cross, 'despite the importance of emphasizing the match as a distinctive event, Redworth goes too far in portraying the concurrent conflict in central Europe as largely irrelevant to the negotiations between London and Madrid. In fact, most of the key participants at the time saw them as inextricably intertwined': Cross, 'Pretense', pp. 569, 578–579.

[225] Pursell, *WK*, pp. 204–205.

[226] Ruigh, *1624*, p. 17; Lockyer, *Buckingham*, pp. 164, 169, 171; Redworth, *PI*, pp. 135–136.

[227] Anstr., I, p. 37; TD, IV, pp. cclxx–cclxxv. Sir Edward Herbert, reporting Bishop's consecration, also commented on the advancement of William Gifford (who, since 1621, had been archbishop of Rheims only at the French king's pleasure) 'absolutely into the charge' of his archdiocese. There was speculation that King James would be persuaded that Gifford's promotion was intended to 'give encouragement to, or draw dependance from, the Englishe Roman Catholiques'. Herbert also commented that some at the French court genuinely feared that this would simply encourage James to take the Huguenots 'into his more particular protection'. But it was Herbert's own opinion that, should Gifford prove capable of winning 'the English Catholiques rather to the Sorbonne than [to] Jesuiticall doctrine', the English state could 'make use of this faction to discover their designes on eyther side'. At that time, the French court had no 'intention or hope to gayne the English Catholiques to their partye': PRO, SP 78/71, fo. 183r–v.

Bishop's progress in England can be followed through the newsletters and other documents that he and his officials dispatched to the secular clergy's agent in Rome. Despite his advanced age, Bishop showed considerable vigour in trying to recruit support among Catholics. He set up fledgling hierarchical structures (notably an episcopal chapter) through which his authority might be exercised. He gave rhetorical assurances to the regime that his authority was primarily 'spiritual' and therefore was not a challenge to the royal supremacy. He attempted some measure of reconciliation with the regulars. The Jesuits, however, were unwilling to trust him, perhaps because they knew that proof of Bishop's capacity to heal divisions among the Catholic clergy would itself increase his power.[228]

Bishop's position was, in fact, far from secure. There was doubt within the Catholic community about the wisdom of some of his actions. It was clear that he did not have authority from Rome to do all that he now did, in particular his establishment of an episcopal chapter. He had not, in fact, had ordinary jurisdiction conferred upon him; rather, he had been granted delegated power, to be held and exercised under the authority of the papal nuncio in Paris.[229] But Bishop soldiered on. He attempted to secure the dismissal of the pro-Jesuit Cardinal Giovanni Garzia Millini from his office as one of the cardinal protectors of the English nation; and he tried to ensure a new appointment to that post, first of Cardinal Bandini, and then of Cardinal Francesco Barberini, the new pope's nephew.[230] He petitioned for the appointment of more bishops.[231] He also sought to exploit the 'Fitton' rebellion at the English College in Rome,[232] which became a test case for his new authority. On 15/25 October 1623, a number of students at the college had been expelled by the Jesuit rector, Thomas Fitzherbert. One of these students, Francis Haynes, was a cousin or nephew of one of the inner circle of seculars in London, Joseph Haynes.[233] Another, Anthony Shelley, was a cousin of the Elizabethan martyr Edward Shelley.[234] Peter Biddulph (better known by his alias of Fitton) eventually rose to prominence as secretary of the English episcopal chapter. Ralph Fowler, another of those caught up in the fracas in Rome, was a cousin of both Biddulph and Thomas White (alias Blacklo), the future political theorist and agent in Rome

[228] *Letter 35*; Questier, *C&C*, pp. 406–408.

[229] TD, IV, pp. cclxxxiv–cclxxxvi.

[230] *Letter 31*.

[231] *Letter 32*.

[232] *Letter 33*.

[233] AAW, B 26, no. 21; *Letter 33*.

[234] Anstr., II, p. 291. Shelley had already been involved, while at Saint-Omer, in a dispute with the Jesuit superiors there: *ibid.*

for the secular clergy;[235] it was no secret that Biddulph was from a Jesuit-oriented gentry household. Another of the rebels, John Faulkner, was a nephew of the Jesuit of the same name.[236] As Dodd relates it, the simmering discontent against the Jesuit administration of the premier English Catholic seminary on the Continent broke out when John Bennett arrived in Rome. The appearance of the secular clergy's agent in the city provided an opportunity for discontented scholars to press their grievances.[237] So the seminary issue became part of the contemporary debate over the governance of English Catholicism at exactly the same time as the other and related questions of authority, hierarchy, and conformity were being fought out at home.[238]

The English critics of the Society of Jesus had been stoking their petitions for years with complaints about how the entire Counter-Reformation in England was distorted and undermined by the insidious manner in which the Jesuits extracted the best students from the seminaries and placed them in their own novitiates. This left the dunces to be ordained as secular clergy and to become a laughing-stock in England, derided by the Catholic gentry, who chose instead to rely on members of the religious orders to satisfy their spiritual needs.[239] Furthermore, the control exerted by the Jesuits and their agents over so many seminaries and schools gave the impression that English Catholicism was so badly fractured and disunited (whereas, the seculars claimed, only a small faction was disrupting the efforts of the rest) that it was impossible to take major decisions affecting and reforming the whole body. A series of visitations led first to the expulsions of the rebel students and then to an arbitration which saw the evicted scholars transferred to Douai.[240] Many secular clergymen

[235] AAW, B 26, no. 54; AAW, B 47, no. 49.

[236] Anstr., II, pp. 99, 100; *NCC*, pp. 66, 102. A cousin of the rebel Faulkner, Thomas Dingley, also joined in the agitation in the college. Dingley was regarded by Thomas Fitzherbert as mad, since Dingley believed, from time to time, that he was the pope and 'hath made us all cardinalls', and he was sent back to England via Douai: PRO, SP 77/17, fo. 210v; see also AAW, B 25, no. 102, for Rant's 'catalogue of our Inglish schollers made madd in the Inglishe colledge in the space of five yeare[s]'.

[237] Among the papers in the possession of the rector of the Jesuit college at Liège in 1637 was 'a malitious manuscript (wanting one sheete) agaynst the superiors and government of the seminarie' at Rome, 'written about 1623 by P. Fitton, J. Faulconer, F. Harris, Ant. Shelley and Ant. Hoskins': ABSJ, Stonyhurst Anglia MS VI, no. 98.

[238] TD, V, pp. 98–100.

[239] Lists compiled by Thomas Rant alleged that, of the forty-seven students who left the college between 1616 and 1623, thirty-three went to the Jesuit novitiate and, as Dodd put it, 'fourteen only, of the most incompetent, were added to the body of the clergy': TD, V, p. 99. Cf. L.J. Hicks, 'The English College, Rome and vocations to the Society of Jesus: March, 1579–July, 1595', *Archivum Historicum Societatis Iesu*, 3 (1934), pp. 1–36; *NAGB*, p. 4.

[240] *Letters 35, 38.*

would only have had their suspicions of Jesuit perfidy confirmed if they had seen a letter written in June 1624 by Thomas Fitzherbert to another Jesuit, John Knatchbull, in Brussels. Fitzherbert was clearly pleased by the 'great evacuation we have made of late of the subjects of this colledge'. He urged Knatchbull to ensure that students to fill the ejected rebels' places were sent from the Jesuit college at Saint-Omer. He also said how relieved he was that the Congregatio de Propaganda Fide had withdrawn its threat to have replacements sent from the seculars' own college at Douai.[241]

## The Illusion of Toleration, the Failure of the Spanish Match, and the Turn towards France

The desperate attempt to resolve the toleration issue during the summer months of 1623, in order to facilitate the increasingly impossible treaty, had finally exposed how far apart the Spanish and English negotiators really were. On 1 August, Conway reported to Buckingham that James had recently 'made a select comittee' to deal with the mechanics of the toleration. The committee

> fell upon all the poenaltyes and forfeitures and did desire by Mr Secretary Calvert's lettre his Majesties declaracion how farre his Majestie would extend his grace, wheather onely to thinges to come or further to thinges past; and if onely to the tyme and thinges to come they prayed order for actes and warrantes accordingly.

James had to decide whether the toleration would take effect only from the present time or would be retrospective. He desired that, for the 'time to come', the crown would 'confirme and assure the immunityes of the Romaine Catholiques from all those poenaltyes and molestations' cited in the marriage articles. But, as for 'the tyme past' and the 'forfeitures and poenalties setled as part of his Majesties revenue long before the treaty, and fynes sett upon them for contempt', and 'for want of appearance in the high commission court', James 'conceaved himself not bound by the articles [...] but did declare that hee did reserve himself in those points untill some occasion of extraordinary greate joy for the good proceedings in this busines'. Yet the Spaniards evidently found this to be unacceptable. According to Conway, the marquis of Inojosa had immediately demanded 'the present execution of all'.[242] The count of Tillières narrated how the

[241] PRO, SP 77/17, fo. 209r–v; Anstr., I, p. 200.
[242] PRO, SP 94/27, fo. 140r.

day before, on 31 July, Coloma and Inojosa had gone to court, and had obtained promises that 'chasque evesque et autres officiers' would be instructed not to trouble Catholics 'directement ou indirectement pour leur religion'.[243] Conway lamented that the

> pretence of this hasty execution hath raised the Romaine Catholiques to a greate confidence; and caused examination of the advantage and disadvantage of and in the forme and matter of the treaty; here being a visible actuall greate alteration in the auncient face of this goverment, and nothing heard of the temporall conditions or certaynty of the marriage or returne of the prince.

Conway emphasized that, at James's direction, he had ordered Calvert 'with all [...] dexterity possible to solicite and gaine of the ambassadors by their lettres to satisfy the king and councell of Spaine of the full satisfaction they have receaved and reall possession the Romaine Catholiques are in of the grace intended them', all in order, of course, to hasten the prince's return. This, it seemed, the ambassadors had more or less promised to do.[244]

Secretary Calvert confirmed on 2 August that the crown's official position was still that Catholics should enjoy 'a pardon for all penalties whatsoever, incurred by vertue of any statute made against priestes and recusantes untill this present, which pardon, to so many as would sue it out, should discharge them of all rentes, debtes and sommes of money due from them as recusantes'. This would put an end to all 'seazures' and 'duties' due from them to the king and also of all 'treasons, fellonies [and] premunir[i]es whereof they may stand guilty' under the law 'for being priestes, harbouring priestes, reconciliation to the Church of Rome', and for 'refusing the oathes of supremacy and allegiance', as well as other offences, so that judges and royal officials would not proceed against them concerning such matters. However, the Spanish diplomats had demanded that, instead of 'pardon[s] and privie seale[s]', there should be a

> proclamation for all, whereby his Majesty shall declare the grace he intendes to the Romane Catholiques in respect of the present conjuncture of his affayres, and that his expresse pleasure is not to have them molested or troubled with any exactions or demaundes of any penalties already incurred, nor by any proceeding against them heerafter

for any reason. For they said that if Catholics sued for pardons they would risk declaring themselves; moreover, it would also be

[243] PRO, PRO 31/3/57, fo. 243r.
[244] PRO, SP 94/27, fo. 140v.

very expensive. Calvert had done his best to persuade them that a proclamation was not possible.[245]

During the afternoon of 4 August 1623 a series of arguments took place between the English and Spanish negotiators about the legal security which Catholics would have if James were to proceed by way of 'pardon and dispensacion' rather than via the Spaniards' preferred method of a royal proclamation. Conway wrote to Calvert on the following day that

> wee shewed them the authoritie and inviolable dignitie of a greate seale which his Majestie would make good against himself and his successors and the weaknes of a proclamacion, which was but a suspencion of the lawe, might be made voyde by an other proclamacion and did not bynd a successor.

Furthermore, 'the judges, justices of peace and other inferior officers were the men that did [...] molest the recusants, and to them the pardon and dispensacion were to be directed, whereas the proclamacion was only to the vulgar sort of people that had no interest in the busines', or rather had no capacity to understand such things and were susceptible only to 'feare and rumor'. It was agreed that the Spanish ambassadors should have the services of a Catholic lawyer, assisted by George Gage, in order to 'looke into the validitie of the pardon and dispensacion', and the ambassadors then 'lett fall their pretence to a proclamacion', though they made a number of other requests. Conway believed here that they had managed to compromise, particularly over the issue of what would happen in the case of recusants who had compounded for their sequestrated property and had seen those compositions granted to third parties. Inojosa promised to certify the agreement on these issues to the court in Spain.[246]

[245] PRO, SP 14/150/10, fo. 12r–v; PRO, SP 94/27, fo. 152r; BL, Additional MS 72255, fo. 71r. Cf. Calvert's queries of 24 July 1623 concerning how to execute the king's promise about recusants, i.e. exactly how the extant fines should be remitted, and whether other penalties, inflicted, for example, by high commission, should be discarded: PRO, SP 14/149/38.

[246] PRO, SP 94/27, fos 150r–151r; PRO, SP 14/150/29 (calendared in *CSPD, 1623–1625* under 6 August); PRO, SP 14/150/82; Akrigg, *Letters of King James VI & I*, p. 421. For Conway's much more detailed account of the meeting, which he sent to Buckingham (itself a fuller narrative than the one in the Domestic State Papers series), see BL, Harleian MS 1580, fos 318r–322v; PRO, SP 94/27, fos 152r–155v (in which Conway related that the ambassadors protested 'theire care of the peace of the state' and cited the 'orations they had made to the Romaine Catholiques to receave this grace thankfully as a meere grace of the king': PRO, SP 94/27, fo. 153v). On 6 August, Conway reported that Gage had been with him to arrange another meeting, between the ambassadors, Carlisle, and Conway himself, in order 'to accord upon some limitations of the matters to bee comprehended in the pardon and dispensation'. In return, Inojosa would write 'effectuall lettres [...] for the assurance of the full accomplishment of all on his Majesties part and hastening of the match': BL, Harleian MS 1580, fo. 324r.

On 7 August, James Hay, earl of Carlisle, together with Conway, made a declaration that James intended to 'pass a free pardon to all his Roman Catholic subjects, whether priests or laymen, for offences of conscience only; and to include in the marriage treaty a suspension of all penal laws against them'. The same conditions were to apply in Ireland and Scotland as well, as the Spanish ambassadors had specifically required three days before.[247] On 8 August, a statement (counterparts of which were signed by Inojosa, Coloma, and Carlisle) was issued at Salisbury as part of an attempt to placate the Spaniards. It promised that a 'legall authenticall pardon' would pass under the great seal,

> wherein shalbee freely pardoned all those penaltyes, forfeitures and seisures, indictments, conviccions and incombrances whatsoever whereunto the Romaine Catholiques are lyable, and have bin proceeded against, or might bee, aswell preists as others for matter of conscience merely, and for which the rest of his Majesties subjects are not lyable,

though James insisted that grants of sequestrated recusants' property to crown nominees were not reversible. James promised a 'present suspention [...] under his Majesties seale of all those poenall lawes, chardges and forfeitures whereunto the Romaine Catholiques, subjects of his Majestie, have hitherto bin subject'. He guaranteed 'in the same graunt [...] a dispensacion and immunity' to all Catholics, both clergy and laity, from the laws which interfered with the 'exercise of theire [...] religion in their private howses without noise and publique scandall'. Similar, though rather more vague, promises regarding Catholics in Ireland and Scotland were incorporated in the document.[248]

All was not, in fact, settled by this agreement. The Spaniards remained very suspicious about the exact form in which the dispensation for Catholics would be cast.[249] Inojosa was far from happy about what seemed to him like deliberate prevarication concerning

[247] PRO, SP 14/150/47; PRO, SP 94/27, fo. 150v, see also *ibid.*, fo. 179r.

[248] BL, Harleian MS 1583, fos 287r–289r; BL, Harleian MS 1580, fo. 179r–v. For Conway's account of the meeting at Salisbury, see BL, Harleian MS 1580, fo. 326v.

[249] On 13 August, we find Conway fuming that the Spaniards had said that, 'instead of a lawier' (as James had promised them on 31 July to secure the pardons promised to Catholics), they wanted 'to have for [a] councellor the Lord Arundell of Wardour'. The day before, they had badgered Calvert to approach Arundell because, they said, it was 'the dead time of the vacation' and 'all the lawiers' were 'out of towne'. But Arundell's nomination was blocked. Calvert was instructed to inform the ambassadors that it would not 'sort with that privatenes and silence' which the king 'directs and expects this busines should be carryed in, to imploy a baron and peere of the realme': PRO, SP 94/27, fos 171r–v, 214r–v, 215r; PRO, PRO 31/3/57, fo. 243r; *CSPD, 1623–1625*, pp. 53, 54; PRO, SP 14/151/5; McClure, *LJC*, p. 513; Questier, *C&C*, pp. 389–390.

the toleration.[250] By 18 August, the ambassadors were threatening to inform their masters in Spain that the regime in London was not taking the issue seriously and could not be trusted.[251] They had noticed that the terms of the agreement meant that Catholics were 'exempted' only 'from such lawes and penalties to which the rest of his Majesties subjects are not lyable': this would not shield them from the acts of supremacy and uniformity. Calvert had to beg Conway to resolve this rather glaring deficiency, and James was not best pleased with this aspersion on his integrity. On 19 August, the attorney-general was ordered to rectify perceived defects in the format of James's proposed grant of toleration.[252] Calvert was dispatched to tell Inojosa that James's royal word could be relied upon. Inojosa attributed his spleen to his own 'naturall plainnesse', and said that he would, if necessary, behave in the same way with his own master. Calvert, who was far from unsympathetic towards the Spaniards, still took the opportunity to make a complaint about Philip IV's and the archduchess Isabella's delivery of their congratulations to the duke of Bavaria after his acquisition of the palatine electoral title. Inojosa and Coloma claimed that either it was not true or that it was merely a compliment and that Philip still intended to offer his protection to the elector palatine once a settlement was reached.[253]

After yet another dressing down of Inojosa from James, delivered in writing by Conway on 29 August, a further compromise was struck, in part through the intervention of George Gage. The period until which the toleration would commence was now lengthened from three months, as the Spaniards had understood it would be, to six months.[254] There was something close to desperation, though, in the

[250] Calvert reported on 14 August that the Spanish diplomats were irritated because he had refused to let them see the 'Englishe copie of those articles which were delivered unto them in Spanishe at Salisbury', i.e. the grant of toleration on the basis of which 'pardons and dispensacion' would be given to Catholics: PRO, SP 14/150/105, fo. 168r. A week earlier, Conway had informed the attorney-general that James still wanted to keep recusants 'in awe', and that the relevant warrants authorizing toleration should reflect the king's intention: PRO, SP 14/150/45; *CSPD, 1623–1625*, p. 47. On 16 August, Conway was trying to delay the extension of the same favour to Scottish Catholics: PRO, SP 14/150/113. (There had been a stormy confrontation between two Scottish Catholic clergymen and Inojosa and Coloma in early August over the Spaniards' refusal to intervene on behalf of Scottish Catholics: PRO, PRO 31/3/57, fo. 243v. A Scottish priest saw Inojosa subsequently, on 4 September, 'and spoke strongly to him about the ostentation and worldly aims of Spain in benefiting the religion in London alone, without caring about the provinces and still less for Scotland, just as if they were bastards of the Church': *CSPV, 1623–1625*, p. 111.)

[251] PRO, SP 94/27, fos 215v–216r.

[252] PRO, SP 14/151/5, 6; PRO, SP 94/27, fos 215r, 216r–v, 216v–217r, 218r.

[253] PRO, SP 14/151/27, fos 36v–37r; PRO, SP 94/27, fo. 218r–v.

[254] PRO, SP 94/27, fo. 224r–v; BL, Harleian MS 1583, fos 315r–316r; PRO, SP 14/151/61; cf. Schreiber, *FC*, pp. 52–53. For the format of the proposed dispensation whereby Catholics

crown's efforts to avoid conceding more than was politically necessary. On 30 August, Williams informed the still-absent Buckingham of the roundabout procedural course held with English Catholics, of which mode of proceeding 'there are 20 of the privye counsaile [who] knowe nothinge as yet'. Williams, who wanted a general grant of toleration to be delayed until after the infanta's arrival, explained that it was the perception which mattered rather than whether Catholics actually obtained royal favour. By deciding to grant favour gradually, and by extending tolerance only to individual Catholics, Williams argued that the crown could avoid a hostile public reaction (perhaps even a 'tumult in three kingdoms'). It would also be very difficult to forbid the judiciary 'to execute the lawe of the land', though this was precisely what Williams had done in 1622.[255]

As for the bishop of Chalcedon, Williams understood that he was 'come to London privatelye'. The lord keeper was 'much troubled thereabouts, not knowing what to advise' the king. If the duke were 'shipped (with the infanta) the onely councel were', suggested Williams, 'to let the judges proceed with' the bishop 'presently, hang him out of the waye', and for 'the king to blame' the archbishop of Canterbury 'or my self for it'. But, before the royal party returned, Williams said that he dared not 'assent or connive at such a course'. Williams told the duke, however, that

> it is a most insolent part and an offence (as I take it) against our common law (and not the statutes onely which are dispensed withall) for an English man to take such a consecration without the kings consent, and especially to use any episcopal jurisdiction in this kingdom without the royall assent, and bishops have beene, in this state, put to theyr fine and ransom for doinge so three hundred yeares agoe.[256]

On the same day as Williams dispatched this letter to Buckingham, Chamberlain noted that 'our papists are verie busie and earnest (by the Spanish ambassadors meanes) to have a publike toleration, but yt seemes the king will not allow yt', and indeed 'suspects that our papists (for their owne ends) are the greatest hinderance of the speedie

were to be permitted freedom from vexation concerning Roman Catholic worship in their own houses and exemption from any requirement to attend church or take communion or take the two oaths (of supremacy and allegiance), see PRO, SP 14/151/76, 77. Conway admitted, in his account of the negotiations in the first week of August, that Gage had helped, 'by good interpretation' and 'by bearing witnes to the truth of the allegations concerning formalityes and condition of our state and lawe', to fend off the Spanish ambassadors' demands for a more extensive toleration: BL, Harleian MS 1580, fo. 321r.

[255] Hacket, *SR*, part I, p. 157.

[256] *Cabala*, p. 81. See Ruigh, *1624*, p. 140; BL, Additional MS 34727, fos 47r–48r; Hacket, *SR*, part I, p. 94.

dispatching the match, and sayes he will make them repent yt, yf he find they continue to crosse him'.[257]

On 4 September, Conway assured Inojosa that the toleration measures agreed with the Spaniards had passed the great seal, though the marriage would have to go through before Catholics could draw any benefit from them. Two days later, Conway reminded Williams that, although James had indeed signed the toleration warrant for releasing imprisoned priests, it was not to be put into effect until certain news arrived from Spain about the betrothal or marriage of Charles and the infanta (and, of course, by this point, it was known that Charles was returning from Spain unwed). This had, unsurprisingly, infuriated the Spanish ambassadors.[258] Nevertheless, a commission was drawn for Williams on 8 September to grant 'pardons and dispensations [. . .] to Catholics, for five years [. . .] on account of the intended marriage between the prince of Wales and the Lady Mary of Spain'.[259]

The Spanish diplomats were being made increasingly aware of their unpopularity in London. Whereas, in general, apprentices had merely shouted ruderies at Gondomar, their coaches were now being stoned when they appeared in public. (In the first week of September, one of their men got into a fight with, and killed, a baker in the Strand.[260]) Inojosa and Coloma knew well enough that diplomatic failure on their part might lead to their own political demise. They were furious that the Spanish council of state was being so tardy, and they badgered James to allow real evidence of the toleration to be seen.[261] In mid-September, Williams was quite candid about the fact that he was deceiving the Spaniards by making them think that the delays were the result of administrative hiccoughs and that the king was himself urging his officials to expedite matters.[262]

[257]McClure, *LJC*, p. 513.

[258]PRO, SP 14/152/4, 19, 20; BL, Harleian MS 1580, fo. 85r–v; PRO, PRO 31/3/57, fos 246r, 247r.

[259]PRO, SP 94/28, fo. 10r; *CSPD, Addenda 1580–1625*, p. 657; *CSPD, 1623–1625*, p. 76; *CSPV, 1623–1625*, pp. 137–138.

[260]PRO, SP 14/152/4, 18; Cogswell, 'England and the Spanish match', p. 125; cf. Birch, *CTJI*, II, p. 392.

[261]PRO, SP 14/152/36.

[262]PRO, SP 14/152/46, 46.i, cited in *Letter 30*; see also PRO, PRO 31/3/57, fo. 249r. Though Conway commanded Williams on 7 October 1623 (two days after Charles's return from Spain) to execute the order releasing Catholic clergy from the prisons, a few days later Conway told the lord keeper that James had now directed the requisite letters to bishops and justices to be held back: *CSPD, 1623–1625*, p. 89; PRO, SP 14/153/39; PRO, SP 94/28, fo. 133r; PRO, PRO 31/3/57, fo. 259r; though cf. *CSPV, 1623–1625*, p. 131; Hacket, *SR*, part I, p. 166. In fact, subsequently (on 8 November 1623), the exchequer was ordered to suspend recusants' payments of fines due at Michaelmas: PRO, SP 14/154/15. On 6 December, Chamberlain recorded that 'our papists of Cheshire and Lancashire, beeing called upon

Thomas Cogswell has evoked the euphoria which greeted Charles's return from Spain. General celebration spontaneously broke out when, clearly unmarried, he appeared back in the country on 5 October, although his return was being anticipated at least three weeks beforehand. The public rejoicing, the sheer apparent unanimity of opinion that the nation had been saved at the last minute from the jaws of the Habsburgs and of popery, was a sign that 'many saw the passing of the Anglo-Spanish alliance as the advent of an Anglo-Spanish war'.[263]

The new mood was demonstrated by the popular reaction to the 'fatal vespers', the collapse of a building in the gatehouse of the French embassy in Blackfriars in which Catholics had gathered to hear a Jesuit sermon. Official tracts on the incident deployed a rhetoric of moderation;[264] other publications about the event were much less sympathetic.[265] It certainly allowed anti-popish elements in the London crowd an opportunity to vent their frustrations at the rudderless drift in official policy towards Spain and English Catholics. A hostile mob attempted to stone the survivors and even tried 'to set an injured lady afire when she was travelling in her coach as they attempted to fix a broken wheel'.[266] Inojosa complained that, upon this 'tragic event', the 'heretics have begun to build a case to attack the Catholic religion'.[267] François de Carondelet lamented that Bishop George Montaigne had refused burial to the Catholic dead in London churchyards and directed that 'as excommunicates they [should] be

for certain payments and debts to the king for recusancie, had recourse to the Spanish ambassador as their mediator, upon whose motion the king gave order those payments shold be respited till our Lady-day when his pleasure shold be further knowne, but I heare those gentlemen are sent for by pursevants to aunswer their dooings': McClure, *LJC*, p. 530.

[263]Cogswell, 'England and the Spanish match', pp. 107–111, 126; *idem*, *BR*, introduction, ch. 1; PRO, PRO 31/3/57, fo. 248r.

[264]See W.C., *The Fatall Vesper* (London, 1623); Thomas Goad, *The Dolefull Even-Song* (London, 1623); T.H.B.M. Harmsen (ed.), *John Gee's Foot out of the Snare (1624)* (Nijmegen, 1992).

[265]For less moderate Protestant accounts, see, e.g., Thomas Scott, *Boanerges. Or the humble supplication of the ministers of Scotland* (Edinburgh [false imprint; *vere* London], 1624), which strongly implied (p. 26) that 'it was a judgement of God [...] to kill a hundred people with the fall of a loft', and warned the parliament of 1624 that 'at Rome there hath been solemne procession, and from Rome letters of discovery, that in England God hath beene so angrie with the hereticks [...] that churches and lofts have overwhelmed many of them in their ominous falls'. For D'Ewes's remark in his diary that 'S[t] Giles Church by Blomesburye fell downe, but a little before, a great parte which had slaine manye, if they had been ther when it fell, which would have been if it had fallen in a sermon time', see *DSSD*, p. 168.

[266]CRS, 68, p. 160.

[267]*Ibid.*, p. 157.

buried on the refuse pile and that the clothes they wore were to be stripped off'.[268]

Catholics retaliated with allegations that puritans had been responsible for the tragedy.[269] A Jesuit pamphlet claimed that all those who had perished there might be presumed to have died in a state of grace, listening to a Jesuit sermon.[270] The Spanish diplomats used the incident to push on, however vainly, with their suit for official toleration. They argued that the English Catholics, 'being denied safer places for their exercises', were 'constrained to adventure themselves in such dangerous ones'.[271]

With Buckingham's volte-face over the match, support for war was now virtually incompatible with opposition to the duke.[272] His authority at court was almost complete. The downfall of the ministers who had supported the marriage would, eventually, leave him to advise on, if not in effect to make, their successors.[273] For Charles and Buckingham, however, it was also going to be a war where tight control would be kept over strategic objectives. They wanted a limited campaign, in alliance with the Catholic French. They did not intend to invoke a Protestant–Catholic Armageddon.[274]

[268] *Ibid.*, p. 160. Most of the dead were interred in the courtyard of the French embassy, with some thirty being taken for burial to the Spanish embassy at Ely House: Harmsen, *John Gee's Foot out of the Snare*, p. 82, n. 70.

[269] Joseph Mead was told that John Price, a Catholic doctor who practised in Chancery Lane, had alleged that 'the puritans of Blackfriars' had caused the accident 'by unpinning' of the 'great main beam' underneath the room: Birch, *CTJI*, II, p. 427. Daniel Featley likewise recorded the Catholic claim that 'the Protestants at Blacke-fryers, by knocking certaine pins out of the timber, caused that late and lamentable fall of the floar wherin about 200 papists were assembled, and neere a 100 slaine': Daniel Featley, *The Romish Fisher Caught and Held in his Owne Net* (London, 1624), sig. Ar. The rector of St Anne's, Blackfriars, William Gouge (who was a prominent supporter of the elector palatine and his wife), was asked to investigate the allegation that the supports of the room had been deliberately weakened: Harmsen, *John Gee's Foot out of the Snare*, pp. 53–54; Adams, PC, pp. 316–317. Thomas Knyvett wrote that, although 'it was a most fearefull judgment of God', 'for all this the papists gives [*sic*] out that it was a plott of the puritanes': B. Schofield (ed.), *The Knyvett Letters (1620–1644)* (London, 1949), p. 62.

[270] John Floyd, *A Word of Comfort* (Saint-Omer, 1623); *Relacion de un caso en que murieron muchos Catolicos oyendo la palabra de Dios* (Valladolid, [1623]); ARCR, I, nos 382–383; McClure, *LJC*, p. 520.

[271] *CSPV, 1623–1625*, p. 150.

[272] Russell, *PEP*, pp. 147–149.

[273] Cogswell, *BR*, pp. 64–65. For Buckingham's break with Lord Keeper Williams, see *Cabala*, pp. 86–90; K. Sharpe, 'The earl of Arundel, his circle and the opposition to the duke of Buckingham, 1618–1628', in K. Sharpe (ed.), *Faction and Parliament* (London, 1978), p. 221.

[274] Cogswell, *BR*, pp. 69f.

Recent developments, such as the ceding of the Bergstrasse in the Lower Palatinate ('the prime flower of our sonne in lawe's revenue', as James described it) to the archbishop of Mainz, had made it clear that Spain was not thinking in terms of restitution at all. In December, even the ever-optimistic Bristol had to admit that the Spaniards were preparing for a breach of amity. At the end of the month it was known that the infanta had given up trying to learn English.[275] During November and December 1623 there were proposals from Bavaria entertained in London that the eldest son of the elector palatine should marry the niece of Duke Maximilian. James appeared ready to consider this suggestion, since it would still allow him to avoid entanglement in a military confrontation with the Habsburgs. However, the diplomatic difficulties in the way of a Palatine–Bavarian match proved predictably insurmountable.[276]

Yet, to the bafflement of many, although the treaties with Spain were clearly suspended, James's Hispanophile policy was not actually abandoned.[277] Francophiles such as Sir Edward Herbert had, of course, immediately begun to lobby for an Anglo-French dynastic union. He advised the king in late October 1623 that the Spaniards had been insincere all along and that he should consider the response in France of the 'bons François' and of the Huguenots who rejoiced at the return of Prince Charles from Spain. The Huguenots devoutly wished that 'the same greatnes which the king of Spaine doth so affect over all the worlde [. . .] your [. . .] Majestie would imbrace' instead, 'in beeinge defender of our faithe'.[278] In the first week of November, the count of Tillières anticipated that the English would now turn to France, though he was hardly enthusiastic about the prospect of such an alliance. A week before Christmas, he thought that approaches made to him by Carlisle and Buckingham were 'un artifice de ce roy pour donner subject à l'Espagne de renouer avec luy'.[279] But, as late as 30 December, Conway recorded the king's fury at the 'forged bruite of the princes treating for marriage in France'.[280] Even in January 1624, most observers agreed that the privy council was divided over how to proceed. The court seemed to be reverting to something like

[275] Ruigh, *1624*, p. 26; Pursell, *WK*, pp. 167, 207; PRO, C 115/107/8485; PRO, SP 94/29, fos 10r–v, 27r–v, 106r–108r, 130r–131r, 148v, 189r. For Bristol's continuing diplomatic efforts to broker a deal over the Palatinate and to salvage the marriage treaty, see Patterson, *King James VI and I*, pp. 332–334; PRO, PRO 31/3/57, fo. 272v.

[276] Pursell, *WK*, pp. 208–210, 218–221; PRO, PRO 31/3/57, fo. 265r; *Letter 41*.

[277] PRO, SP 94/29, fos 209r–212v.

[278] BL, Harleian MS 1581, fos 21r–22r.

[279] PRO, PRO 31/3/57, fos 262v, 283v.

[280] PRO, SP 94/29, fo. 190v.

business as usual, namely a complex balancing act of simultaneous negotiation between foreign powers in a seemingly endless search to extract better conditions and political advantage by playing the one off against the other. James had still not given up hope that a deal might be worked out with the Spaniards.[281] The decision to summon a parliament, which (according to Ruigh) was being considered in the second week of November 1623, was regarded, it seems, as a lever to bring the Spaniards to some kind of accommodation, rather than as a forum to break the treaties.[282]

Certainly, there is evidence that English Catholics had not despaired of the Anglo-Spanish alliance. In early October, shortly before Charles disembarked, Tillières remarked that some Catholics were in cloud-cuckoo-land, thinking that Charles was 'grandement amoureux de l'infante' and would persuade James to secure 'sincèrement les points nécessaire à donner fin au mariage'.[283] In early December, Chamberlain conceded that Tillières, who, after the embarrassment of the 'fatall vespers' in the French embassy complex, had transferred to other premises, now 'admitts no more of our Romish Catholikes to his Masse or mattens'. He would 'have no more to do with them for, do them what favor or goode offices he can, yet still he sayes he finds them all Spanish'.[284]

One of James's reactions to the impending return of the prince had been to consider seriously one of the other Habsburg proposals which had been put forward in order to resolve the Palatinate question. During early October, James had made a formal approach to the elector to consider again Madrid's suggestion of a marriage between his son Frederick Henry and the emperor's younger daughter.[285] There was, of course, no possibility that Frederick would assent to it in the form that the Habsburgs demanded, in other words without restoration of the Palatinate to himself.[286] On 20 November, James tried, yet again, and equally unsuccessfully, to persuade the elector to agree to his son being set up in the Palatinate, and that the boy should marry into the Habsburg family on the condition that the crucial

[281]Russell, *PEP*, p. 148; Cogswell, *BR*, pp. 118–119.

[282]Ruigh, *1624*, p. 27.

[283]PRO, PRO 31/3/57, fo. 253r.

[284]McClure, *LJC*, p. 529.

[285]See Pursell, ESP, p. 722; *CGB*, I, pp. 372, 378. For Olivares's proposal of this scheme to the Spanish council of state in August 1623 (something which Charles accepted in principle, as Pursell says, on 10/20 August), see Pursell, ESP, p. 716.

[286]Schreiber, *FC*, p. 53; Cogswell, *BR*, p. 109; Pursell, ESP, p. 722; Adams, PC, p. 336; PRO, SP 94/28, fo. 188r.

period of his education was reassigned to the English court, though under the tutelage of the infanta.[287]

The Spanish diplomats were still regularly closeted with Buckingham, the king, and the prince, although, on 28 November, Valaresso was saying that Coloma had 'remarked that in the long run a war would be better for the Catholics than the marriage'.[288] In the third week of December, William Bishop reported that 'there be some that thinke' the Anglo-Spanish treaty 'wilbe peeced up againe one way or other, bicause it is holden in reason of estate so convenient both for the one king and thother'. The Spaniards were still making arrangements for the wedding to go ahead by proxy, and, indeed, the new dispensation, issued by Urban VIII, was brought to Madrid in late November. However, as we remarked above, on 26 November/6 December the earl of Bristol received instructions to link the marriage inseparably with a deal over the Palatinate. His immediate notification of this to the Spanish council of state was taken as a breach of the treaty.[289]

In mid-January 1624, quite extraordinarily, the Spaniards raised the stakes by offering that the infanta would land on English soil in March and that the Spanish-dominated part of the Palatinate would be handed back in August. At the same time, they promised 'to make urgent representations for the surrender of the rest to the palatine' under conditions laid down by the English diplomats in Spain. Furthermore, they consented to the marriage of the elector's son with the emperor's daughter, and to the supervision of Frederick's son at the English court. According to Valaresso, who reported this on 2 February, 'the king seems determined, the ambassadors revitalised and the Hispanophiles relieved'. Conway alone stood out against this. In the end it was Charles's utter refusal, as Buckingham suffered one of his many nervous collapses, to go along with this proposal that stymied the threat to the emergent war party.[290]

To the consternation of the war party, James seemed never to lose hope that he could reach a settlement based on negotiation rather than bloodshed. Only a slim majority on the privy council foreign affairs

[287] Ruigh, *1624*, p. 28; *CSPV, 1623–1625*, pp. 156, 158–159; PRO, PRO 31/3/57, fo. 270v. Charles soon declared himself opposed to this project: *CSPV, 1623–1625*, p. 164; PRO, PRO 31/3/57, fo. 274v; cf. *Letter 36*.

[288] *CSPV, 1623–1625*, pp. 156–158, 165. Back in May 1623, Tillières had claimed that Coloma 'ne favorise pas le mariage', partly out of spite towards Gondomar and partly because he thought Spain's interests would not be served by it: PRO, PRO 31/3/57, fo. 205v.

[289] *Letter 35*; Pursell, ESP, p. 723; BL, Additional MS 72286, fo. 119r.

[290] *CSPV, 1623–1625*, pp. 207–208; BL, Additional MS 72255, fo. 111r; *CCE*, pp. 147–148, 151; McClure, *LJC*, pp. 539–540; Cogswell, *BR*, pp. 128–130, 133; Ruigh, *1624*, pp. 39–40.

committee endorsed the decision that parliament should be called.[291] In late January, councillors were divided even over the question of how the treaties with Spain should be broken. While some simply wanted a 'public declaration' from Charles, others wanted 'detailed information about the whole affair'. They believed that Buckingham would thereby be ruined.[292]

From late December, however, Catholic newsletter writers avidly followed the progress of a new set of dynastic marriage negotiations, namely with the French court. William Bishop observed on 18 December that Buckingham and Carlisle had already conferred with the French ambassador 'about matching our prince in France as many do presume'.[293] Lord Kensington was sent to France in February to pursue the matter, though he had no formal commission to do so because the Anglo-Spanish treaties had not yet been broken. He appears to have made, initially, a number of negotiating errors: for example, he suggested that the marriage should be concluded separately from a military alliance between the two realms.[294]

It was hard, at least for the Catholics, to believe that Buckingham would manage to dazzle parliament in the way that he had obviously captivated the prince. Thomas More, the former secular clergy agent, now back in London, noticed on 9 February 1624 that 'great bandying ther is against the duke, and much opposition is like to be against him in the parlament' even though he had apparently 'won the puritan faction in great part' by his quarrel with the Spaniards. Moreover, on the privy council, only Carlisle and Conway seemed to be taking his side; the others, especially the earls of Pembroke and Arundel, were against him.[295] John Lockwood had heard that Buckingham was in disgrace because he had sent a message to the Spanish ambassador and had represented it as the word of the king. This had forced Buckingham to grovel before James. In Cambrai it was being rumoured that Buckingham was in the Tower.[296] On 5/15 February 1624, Anthony Champney affected to believe that James was listening to Spanish promises about the Palatinate, and that the earl of Bristol had been told to stay in Spain.[297]

[291] Ruigh, *1624*, p. 34.
[292] *CSPV, 1623–1625*, p. 211.
[293] *Letter 35*.
[294] Ruigh, *1624*, pp. 38–39; PRO, SP 78/72, fo. 20r; *Letter 43*; R.E. Shimp, 'A Catholic marriage for an Anglican prince', *Historical Magazine of the Protestant Episcopal Church*, 50 (1981), pp. 5, 6–7. For the difficulties encountered by Kensington, see also Adams, FP, pp. 157–158.
[295] AAW, B 26, no. 10; *Letter 37*.
[296] AAW, B 26, no. 11.
[297] *Letter 37*.

When the Catholics did realize how far things had changed, it was undoubtedly, for many of them, a shattering blow. But the dislocations and incoherences within the court gave them a breathing space in which to revise their attitudes to the crown's dynastic policy, as well as to renegotiate their contacts with the foreign embassies in London. The French ambassador, Tillières, who had allowed the Jesuits the use of French embassy property, now offered entertainment to the leading secular clergy.[298] William Bishop opined that 'we must alwaies joyne with them whom our king most respecteth; which some now imagine to be rather the Frenc[h]e than the Spanish'. Bishop instructed the new clergy agent in Rome, Thomas Rant, to tell Urban VIII that Tillières was 'a very honest and zealous Catholike, and favoreth recusants and priest[s] so farr forth as he may, and is very ready to assist us all'.[299]

The secular clergy's opponents were, however, not going to be outdone easily, and started to realign themselves as well. To Bishop's disdain, Sir Tobias Mathew, 'who was knighted for his good service in Spain, declares himself openly to be for the duke of Buckingh[am] and saith he hath reason to do as he doth, that is, to be against the Spanish match, and that our prince was not well used there', and that Olivares was 'a darke and dull felow'.[300]

One of the conditions for this new match was obviously going to be some form of French military assistance for the recovery of the Palatinate. At the same time, the French court had to avoid concluding an alliance which could be construed as, in any sense, confessionally Protestant.[301] Thus it was with reasonable optimism that the leadership of the secular clergy could lobby at Rome and ask the papacy to persuade Louis XIII, Marie de Médicis, and her increasingly independent client Cardinal Richelieu to stand as firmly for the Catholics in England as ever the Spaniards had done. (In fact, very shortly before his own death, Bishop himself wrote to Louis, on 10 April 1624, begging him to secure the repeal of the penal laws as a condition of the marriage treaty.[302]) It was devoutly to be hoped that the pope would not show weakness over the dispensation which would now be demanded by the French. Tillières, who was a *dévot* Catholic (even the Spaniards admitted that he did not quite fit their picture of

[298] For some years, Tillières had employed the secular priest John Varder as a chaplain: Anstr., II, pp. 326–327; *Letters 35, 47*.

[299] *Letter 40*.

[300] *Letter 38*. Subsequently, the marquis of Effiat recorded that Mathew's knighthood had been procured by Buckingham, and confirmed that Mathew had thrown off his affection for Spain: PRO, PRO 31/3/60, fo. 329v.

[301] Tillières, *ME*, pp. xvi–xvii.

[302] Allison, RS, p. 165; Shimp, 'A Catholic marriage', p. 8.

the archetypal unprincipled Frenchman), had been informed of the conditions which the Spaniards had demanded.[303]

Tillières had of course been in contact with Francophile English courtiers, particularly with the staunchly Protestant earl of Carlisle.[304] His stock began to rocket once the Spanish match failed. Roy Schreiber claims that Tillières could not reconcile his *dévot* Catholicism with his country's national interest sufficiently to take advantage of the English break with Spain; and certainly he was extremely vocal about the difficulties of an alliance with a regime which was riding a wave of Protestant enthusiasm.[305] Thomas Cogswell argues, however, that his equivocal attitude to the proposed Anglo-French match was at least partly a response to his own political instructions; and his doubts were informed by political realism as well as by religious principle. He was in a good position to watch Londoners' displays of anti-popery. Of course, such displays were grist to the mill of a French diplomat who had no desire to see the Anglo-Spanish negotiations succeed, and who argued consistently that the proposed treaty would undermine the British state. But, equally, there was no reason to think that English Protestants would necessarily be any less anti-popish about a French princess.[306] Tillières had told François de Carondelet that, although he had been directed from Paris to negotiate an Anglo-French dynastic treaty in order to forestall the Spanish one, he was personally opposed to the idea, since he feared the consequences of an English alliance with the Huguenots 'if the king of France and his brother died without sons'.[307]

The French therefore avoided putting their cards on the table until they were sure that the Anglo-Spanish treaty was finally broken.[308] In January 1624, Sir Edward Herbert had summarized the position in France thus: 'the bigot partie tell the kinge that he ought to take this time to settle his affaires at home by reducinge' the Huguenots 'to an entier subjection', while the 'bons François [. . .] wish him not to loose this opportunitie to enter into league with' James 'for remittinge the affaires of Christendome into the state in which they were' in the reign of Henry IV. However, 'the graver sort of counsailors' believed that

[303]CRS, 68, p. 157; AAW, A XVII, no. 110, p. 355 (cited in *Letter 42*).

[304]Among Tillières's friends at court was also the Catholic Robert Maxwell, 1st earl of Nithsdale: PRO, PRO 31/3/58, fos 71v, 73r.

[305]Schreiber, *FC*, p. 56; PRO, PRO 31/3/58, fos 73r–74v.

[306]Cogswell, *BR*, p. 125. For Tillières's scepticism about the Spanish match, see, e.g., PRO, PRO 31/3/56, fo. 26v: PRO, PRO 31/3/57, fos 223r–224r.

[307]CRS, 68, p. 161.

[308]Cogswell, *BR*, p. 125.

Louis should remain 'undeclared' until James's breach with Spain was overt.[309]

## The 1624 Parliament

The new parliament assembled on 19 February. It had been postponed first by the hard frost and deep snow and then by the sudden death of the second duke of Lennox on 16 February. Thomas More remarked that he 'was a noble man of such worthie disposition that he carryed with him generallie the hartes of all and particulerly the Catholickes because of his good affection and furtherance of the match with Spayne', an odd judgment considering his presence among the 'Bohemian' faction and his reputation for opposing the Spanish match.[310] Those who did take their places in the session were definitely not so charitably inclined, particularly when stories flooded in from around the country that papists were preparing to challenge the rule of law and perhaps even to raise rebellion.[311]

As Cogswell notes, the opening of the parliament witnessed the extraordinary spectacle of former opponents (Sir Dudley Digges, Sir Edwin Sandys, Sir Robert Phelips, and Sir Edward Coke) rallying to Charles's and Buckingham's standard.[312] James's speech on 19 February denounced the false dealing of the Spaniards. He professed also that he had never intended anything more than a temporary reduction of the force of the laws against the practice of Catholicism, although, as Conrad Russell and Simon Adams point out, exactly how far he was prepared to go in following the Commons's anti-Spanish line was not clear.[313] Lord Keeper Williams, who was in some sense the architect of the limited toleration previously granted to Catholics, applauded James's speech but remained under attack throughout the session.[314]

[309] PRO, SP 78/72, fo. 9r.

[310] *Letter 39*. Lennox had, however, with Pembroke, Belfast, and Hamilton, abstained when Buckingham urged the junta for foreign affairs in January 1624 to endorse the breach of the treaties with Spain before parliament met: Adams, FP, p. 156; see also *CCE*, p. 165.

[311] Cogswell, *BR*, p. 139; *Letter 39*.

[312] Cogswell, *BR*, p. 149.

[313] PRO, SP 14/159/55; *CSPV, 1623–1625*, pp. 228–229; Russell, *PEP*, pp. 155–156; Adams, FP, pp. 164–165; Ruigh, *1624*, p. 155; ED, fos 1r–4r; *Letter 39*. For Conway's attempts to ensure that Inojosa and Coloma did not take 'ombrage ou offense par faux rapports' of James's speech, see PRO, SP 94/30, fo. 121r.

[314] See *Letter 39*; *LJ*, III, p. 269; Lockyer, *Buckingham*, p. 193. For Sir George Calvert's admonitory message from James, delivered on 1 March, concerning petitions against Williams 'allreddy in the hows', see Thompson, *HA*, pp. 13–14; see also Russell, *PEP*, pp. 160, 166. Buckingham was now openly hostile to Williams: Lockyer, *Buckingham*, p. 175.

Cogswell emphasizes, however, how extraordinary were the concessions which James made in this address, in the sense that he 'gave parliament *carte blanche* to discuss the domestic religious situation as well as the diplomatic one abroad'.[315] The speaker of the Commons, Sir Thomas Crew, made the not-unexpected request, in his response of 21 February, for legislation against monopolies and other evils, and for the execution of penal statutes against the Catholics.[316] James's toleration of all this was, says Cogswell, apparently an official sign of 'approval of a campaign against the recusants'.[317] There were calls that papists should have their military hardware taken from them;[318] and, at the opening of convocation on 21 February, Joseph Hall delivered a strongly anti-popish sermon.[319]

One Commons member, Sir Thomas Gerard, MP for Liverpool, was ejected because of suspicions about his religion.[320] Some members directed their barbs against the bishop of Chalcedon. Valaresso reported in mid-March that this was not surprising because William Bishop had 'passed all bounds and perhaps exceeded his commissions in consecrating priests, dispensing titles, dressing in the episcopal vestments and finally erecting a public tribunal', though it is not clear that he did any of these things except, perhaps, use episcopal apparel.[321] The parliament also heard complaints against Matthew Kellison, the president of the English College at Douai. Kellison was known to be in England on financial business.[322]

This, then, was the context for the ensuing denunciations of Spanish treachery and hostility, denunciations which came from the heart of the regime. Buckingham addressed the House of Lords on 24 February, and was extremely scathing about the earl of Bristol's dealings in Spain. The duke and Prince Charles placed themselves at the head of a prospective war party.[323] Following a series of committee reports

Williams complained on 2 February 1624 about the 'report of the Venecian embassador that [...] your Grace intended to sacrifice me this parliament to appease the dislike of immunityes exercised towards the Catholiques': BL, Harleian MS 7000, fo. 140r.

315 Cogswell, *BR*, p. 167.

316 PRO, SP 14/159/66; Ruigh, *1624*, pp. 158–159; *CSPV, 1623–1625*, pp. 235–236. Crew had come back from Ireland, whither he had been sent for his opposition in the previous parliament: Russell, *PEP*, p. 156; Cogswell, *BR*, p. 168.

317 Cogswell, *BR*, p. 168.

318 Ruigh, *1624*, pp. 169–170.

319 Cogswell, *BR*, p. 169.

320 *Letter 40*; Ruigh, *1624*, pp. 89, 259–260.

321 *Letter 39*; *CSPV, 1623–1625*, p. 249.

322 AAW, B 26, no. 27 (cited in *Letter 39*).

323 T. Cogswell, 'The people's love: the duke of Buckingham and popularity', in Cogswell, Cust, and Lake, *Politics, Religion and Popularity*, pp. 216–219; *CSPD, 1623–1625*, pp. 169, 171, 172; Ruigh, *1624*, pp. 162f.; *Letter 39*.

and conferences, rehearsing the perfidy of the Spaniards, on 5 March, Archbishop Abbot, in the name of both Houses, urged the king to break the treaties.[324]

A succession of speakers then called for war against the Spaniards in retaliation for their trickery and their recent deliberate encouragement of the growth of popery in England. In particular, a joint report from Lords and Commons stated that 'whereas heretofore' the Catholics 'have bene devided amongst themselves in the partie of the Jesuitts, depending uppon Spayne, and the secular preists', who did not, now 'they are generally [. . .] strongly united together, depending no lesse on Spayne for temporall respects than uppon Rome for spirituall' ones.[325]

But it was far from clear that the regime was necessarily going to follow the Commons's lead on religion. Catholics said that Lord Keeper Williams had censured the speaker of the House, Crew, for his godly zeal against papistry on the grounds that it would make a nonsense of the crown's future foreign-policy plans.[326] James replied to the deputation from Lords and Commons on 5 March, with its address urging the rupture of the treaties with Spain, in part by justifying his courses towards Catholics.[327] He told his hearers that he knew best how to handle such matters, though he guaranteed that revenue voted for the recovery of the Palatinate should be administered by the Commons's commissioners.[328] James still wanted a negotiated settlement and he warned of the perils of war.[329] There ensued a suspicion-driven round of bargaining about how much war revenue should be generated through taxation, on whom the burden would principally fall, and how the money would be used.[330] For Russell, this showed that the Commons was not fully committed to war; for Cogswell, it meant that the members would not commit themselves to

[324] ED, fos 41r–51v; PRO, SP 14/160/29; *CSPV, 1623–1625*, p. 248; Russell, *PEP*, p. 176; *LJ*, III, pp. 246–247. A copy of Abbot's speech was sent to Thomas Rant in Rome: AAW, A XVII, no. 107, pp. 347–350.

[325] Ruigh, *1624*, pp. 178–180, 181–182; PRO, SP 14/160/27, fo. 42r; ED, fos 41r–42r. Christopher Brooke claimed on 2 March that 'oure papists were not as the papists in France, Italy etc., for oure papists ar all Spanish papists': Thompson, *HA*, p. 14.

[326] *Letter 39*; PRO, SP 14/169/67.

[327] James's reply (reported in the Commons on 8 March) was 'the first occasion in the parliament when James had publicly to declare himself and to reveal how little he was prepared to concede': Adams, FP, p. 167. According to Holles's diary, James would 'have no warr, but upon necessity, as wemen ar called necessary evils': Thompson, *HA*, p. 25; ED, fos 57v–60v.

[328] Lockyer, *Buckingham*, p. 185; *Letter 40*.

[329] *Letter 40*.

[330] Adams, FP, pp. 167–170.

voting a large revenue grant before they knew that there was definitely going to be a war.[331]

Most contemporaries, however, were certain that there would be a disjuncture between James's likely courses and some of his godlier subjects' expectations. James's meaning in his 5 March address had to be carefully re-explained by Charles.[332] Another deputation, led by Abbot, confronted the king on 14 March and demanded a breach of the treaties. Again James was noncommittal. He wanted five subsidies and ten fifteenths and then an annual grant of one subsidy and two fifteenths. Of James's speech of 14 March, Edward Nicholas remarked that it 'was thought to contradict all that had been said by the prince or Buckingham; the papists begin to brag'. Abbot was so disconcerted 'that he was sick, and absented himself for a day from the House'.[333] The Spanish ambassadors, who had not shown 'their heads out of doores for a fortnight together', went out and 'passed as it were in triumph through Cheapeside'.[334] James's demand had to be frantically renegotiated, largely through Buckingham's efforts, to an overall grant of six subsidies and twelve fifteenths.[335] Following the long subsidy/war debate on 19 and 20 March,[336] James tried to repair the damage further with a somewhat convoluted reply to a delegation from Lords and Commons on 23 March concerning the Houses' joint declaration of the same day.[337] The preamble attached to the eventual subsidy bill did contain a statement that the alliance and treaties with Spain were indeed broken, as Buckingham himself insisted to both Houses on 24 March.[338]

The parliament broke up briefly for Easter (between 26 March and 1 April). At this point, Charles ordered Lord Kensington to open formal negotiations for a dynastic match with France. Instructions were then drawn up for Kensington and Carlisle to deal with the French both for a treaty of arms (though the French ultimately balked at this) and for

[331] For Russell's account of the debates on the topic of supply and foreign policy, see Russell, *PEP*, pp. 177f.; cf. Cogswell, *BR*, p. 186. For Buckingham's controversial use of the subsidy revenue, granted in this session, to support Mansfelt, see Adams, FP, pp. 158–159, 170–171.

[332] Cogswell, *BR*, p. 193; ED, fos 76r–77r.

[333] PRO, SP 14/160/77, 81; Cogswell, *BR*, pp. 195, 196; Ruigh, *1624*, pp. 210–211, 218; Adams, PC, p. 342; Thompson, *HA*, p. 36; *Letter 41*.

[334] PRO, SP 14/160/89, fo. 147r. See also McClure, *LJC*, pp. 548–549.

[335] Cogswell, *BR*, pp. 195, 197–198; Adams, PC, p. 342; Lockyer, *Buckingham*, p. 186; *CSPV, 1623–1625*, pp. 254–255; PRO, SP 14/160/79, 80, 81, 89; ED, fos 78v–80r, 83r–86r; *LJ*, III, pp. 265–266; *Letter 41*.

[336] Cogswell, *BR*, pp. 200f.; Adams, PC, p. 343; Ruigh, *1624*, pp. 216f.; Adams, FP, pp. 168–169; ED, fos 92v–100r.

[337] PRO, SP 14/161/19, 24; Ruigh, *1624*, pp. 229–233; ED, fo. 104v.

[338] Adams, PC, p. 345; Ruigh, *1624*, pp. 233–234, 248, 253.

a marriage, while negotiations were also conducted with the Dutch.[339] Kensington tried to persuade the French court that the whole business was not simply a device to exert pressure on the Spaniards to make concessions. Bristol, however, came through Paris on his way back from Spain; he told the French that that was exactly what it was. In this, he was backed up, from London, by Tillières.[340] James had met the Spanish diplomats on 29 March and had refused to declare the treaties completely at an end.[341]

When parliament reassembled on 1 April, it heard warnings from Buckingham about the danger of a Spanish invasion. There were demands for redress of commonwealth grievances, one of which was the problem of Catholicism;[342] and there was extensive debate on 2 April about the danger from popery. A parliamentary petition followed on 3 April, drawn up in the Commons for immediate removal to the Lords. As well as citing (ironically rather briefly) the military danger from Spain, it warned at great length of the indigenous papist threat, and in particular that the Catholics were flocking together in London, especially to the ambassadors' houses. It demanded the expulsion of the Romish clergy from the realm, the disarming of 'all popish recusants, legally convicted or justly suspected', the removal of popish officials and office-holders, and the general enforcement of the laws against Catholics without delay.[343] Its language was too violent and, after prompting by Charles in the Lords, another version (with significant changes) was hammered out there by 6 April, just as the impeachment process against Lord Treasurer Cranfield was gathering pace. This version merely called for execution of the statutes against Catholic clergy and recusants. The Commons was not unanimous in endorsing it – they insisted, for example, on the need for a proclamation against Catholic clergy – but by 10 April a deal had been done. The absolute demand for a proclamation was withdrawn in return for a promise that a day would be fixed for the ejection of Catholic clerics. In part, this was because it had been

339 Ruigh, *1624*, p. 234; *CSPV, 1623–1625*, pp. 323–324; Lockyer, *Buckingham*, p. 207; *Letters 42, 43*; PRO, SP 78/72, fos 214r–220r; BL, Harleian MS 1584, fos 10r–15r. Dutch ambassadors had arrived in England in February 1624 and had been 'antagonized by the lack of interest shown towards them': Adams, FP, p. 170.

340 Schreiber, *FC*, p. 59.

341 Ruigh, *1624*, p. 235.

342 Cogswell, *BR*, pp. 230, 231–232; Lockyer, *Buckingham*, p. 189; ED, fos 109r–v, 121r.

343 ED, fos 113r–114r; PRO, SP 14/162/9; Ruigh, *1624*, pp. 238f.; *LJ*, III, pp. 287, 289–290; TD, V, pp. cccxli–cccxliii; *Letter 44*. On 1 March, Sir Francis Seymour had warned of the 'concourse of recusants to ambassadors houses': ED, fo. 36v. In the context of Catholic rallies at some of the London embassies, the anger of MPs such as Seymour is quite comprehensible. See also, e.g., BL, Harleian MS 1583, fo. 293v.

decided to deal with papist office-holders separately.[344] On 6 April, James had personally sent an explanation to Sir Walter Aston in Madrid (and through him to Philip IV) that he had consented to the breaking of the treaties on the advice of parliament, 'having not found anie example that anie king hath refused the councell of the whole kingdome composed of faithfull and lovinge subjects'.[345]

The breach of the treaties with Spain accelerated the proposals to deal with Catholics. The parliament's petition against recusants was presented to James by a deputation from both Houses on 23 April.[346] James then acceded to the request for a proclamation and he promised to deal with the scandal of public displays of Catholicism.[347] Wild overestimates were in circulation about the number of priests within the realm, especially in London, a situation on which John Gee's *The Foot out of the Snare* capitalized. Gee had been one of those who survived the 'fatal vespers' at Blackfriars on 26 October 1623. His 'conversion' to godly Protestantism was managed by Archbishop Abbot and his chaplains Thomas Goad and Daniel Featley. It is clear that Gee's revelations about the extent of the Catholic clerical network in London were supposed to confirm and amplify the complaints in parliament about the de facto toleration of the Catholic clergy – for example, Thomas Wentworth (MP for Oxford)'s exclamation on 25 February, 'is it not wonderfull that traytors should walke up and downe with impunit[i]e?'[348]

The proclamation was finally issued on 6 May.[349] An attempt was now made to purge the kingdom of popish officials. Lists were compiled of those who were suspected of popery but nevertheless exercised authority in their localities: prominent among them were the earls of Rutland and Castlehaven, Viscount Colchester, and Lords Windsor, Eure, Petre, Morley, Teynham, Wotton, and Scrope.[350]

[344] Ruigh, *1624*, p. 245; *CSPV, 1623–1625*, p. 275; ED, fos 116r, 118r, 129v; *LJ*, III, pp. 291–292, 297–298; TD, V, pp. cccxli–cccxliv; AAW, A XIII, no. 75, p. 191.

[345] PRO, SP 94/30, fos 167r, 171v.

[346] Ruigh, *1624*, p. 250; Lockyer, *Buckingham*, p. 191; *LJ*, III, pp. 317–318; PRO, SP 14/163/32, 33; TD, V, pp. cccxliii–cccxliv; *Letter 44*.

[347] TD, V, pp. cccxlv–cccxlvi. On 30 April, Jean Beaulieu said that he had heard that 'the Spanish ambassadors, to breede a jealousie in the myndes both of the parlament and of the people of the kings intent therein, have taken upon them to assure their clients the papistes' that the king 'will never be brought to put anie such thing in execution against them, but that it behoveth him at this point to putt on such a shewe for the necessitie of his affaires': BL, Additional MS 72255, fo. 142r.

[348] *CSPV, 1623–1625*, p. 303; Harmsen, *John Gee's Foot out of the Snare*; Thompson, *RD*, p. 13. Cf. McClure, *LJC*, p. 556, for Chamberlain's claim on 30 April that '1,400 friers, Jesuites and priests are certainly knowne and discovered in the land'.

[349] See *Letters 44, 45, 47, 48*.

[350] *Letter 44*; TD, V, pp. 152–153; *LJ*, III, pp. 394–396.

At this time, news was leaking out that there had been an attempt to overthrow Buckingham. At an audience with James over two months before, on 26 February, Inojosa and Coloma had bitterly reviled the duke.[351] They sent messages to James via Carondelet, Coloma's chaplain, that Buckingham was working behind James's back to organize the Anglo-French treaty. On 1 April, Carondelet handed over a general diatribe which claimed that Buckingham was usurping the king's power and function, and that there was a proposal to force James into retirement, even a form of house arrest.[352] A follow-up visit from Diego de Lafuente took place on Saturday 3 April to reinforce the prejudices against Buckingham that, the Spaniards trusted, had now taken root in James's mind.[353] The Spaniards hoped for assistance from those at court whom they thought might be sympathetic to them. This turned out rather unsuccessfully in the case of Lord Keeper Williams because, as soon as Carondelet approached him, Williams revealed everything to Buckingham.[354] Lafuente met James again on 20 April and launched another withering attack on Buckingham, alleging that the two-faced duke was supplanting James by posturing as a Protestant saviour. He claimed that the Protestant cause looked not to Charles for leadership but to the elector palatine, and in fact desired him as James's heir. He also said that Buckingham was scheming to divert the succession to his own family via a marriage between the elector's elder son and his own daughter. (This was a rumour which Tillières had reported in January.)[355]

The conspiracy culminated with an audience on 24 April. On that day, Inojosa and Coloma insisted that Buckingham and Charles would depose James if he declined to accept the breach of the treaties with Spain.[356] Charles's intervention in Buckingham's favour proved crucial, in that it prevented privy council members from joining in the

[351] Ruigh, *1624*, p. 265. According to Sir Balthazar Gerbier, the conspiracy was undertaken when the archduchess Isabella's agent, van Male, obtained from 'one of the men at the post office att London' an unciphered copy of a letter from Buckingham to James's daughter, explaining that the Spanish match was broken and that a military assault on the Spaniards was imminent: BL, Additional MS 4181, fos 20r–22r. For a copy of the representations made against Buckingham by Inojosa and Coloma, dated 9 March, see BL, Harleian MS 1583, fos 329r–330v.

[352] Ruigh, *1624*, pp. 271–272; PRO, SP 94/30, fo. 230r.

[353] Ruigh, *1624*, pp. 272–273; *CSPV, 1623–1625*, p. 273; McClure, *LJC*, p. 553.

[354] Ruigh, *1624*, pp. 273–276; see also Hacket, *SR*, part I, pp. 198–199; *Cabala*, pp. 90–93.

[355] Albion, *CI*, p. 52; Lockyer, *Buckingham*, p. 194; Ruigh, *1624*, pp. 279–281; PRO, SP 14/164/8; PRO, PRO, 31/3/58, fo. 14r.

[356] Ruigh, *1624*, pp. 282f.; Cogswell, *BR*, p. 251; Lockyer, *Buckingham*, p. 195; BL, Harleian MS 1580, fo. 443r. It was suspected that the disgraced lord treasurer, Cranfield, was involved in the conspiracy: PRO, SP 14/163/50; PRO, SP 14/164/12; Lockyer, *Buckingham*, p. 193. For Lafuente's reinforcement of the charges against Buckingham, see PRO, SP 14/164/8, 12; for Inojosa's backtracking in early May, see PRO, SP 14/164/44. Sir Francis Nethersole

attack. The council collectively swore on 2 May that Buckingham was innocent of the ambassadors' accusations.[357] The Spaniards, despite a last-ditch attempt to get the recently returned Bristol to approach James in their cause, had failed.[358] The courtier Sir Lewis Lewkenor, who in mid-1618 had gone to the Spanish embassy and reconciled himself sacramentally to the Church of Rome, was sent to the Tower for, on his own initiative, writing to Sir Richard Bingley 'to furnish [...] a shippe for the Spanish ambassador to goe over', in what appeared to be an attempt to get Inojosa out of the country and off the hook for the plot against Buckingham.[359] Inojosa had already reported to Madrid that James intended to declare war, and had given his opinion as to where the English and Dutch would attack first.[360]

It was obvious that James was nothing like as hostile to the Spanish diplomats as Charles and Buckingham were. The Jesuit Thomas Fitzherbert remarked in Rome in June 1624 that the Spaniards' accusations might prove true and that this would 'happely worke other effects than yet have been designed by the parlament'. Fitzherbert speculated that 'perhaps the king may take occasion hereby to breake of[f] the parlament re infecta, and yet fynd meanes to recover the money graunted him, which may be [...] the cheefe marke he aymed at from the beginning'.[361] Inojosa, and subsequently Coloma, of necessity prepared for their departure, although Diego de Mendoza, Gondomar's nephew, was soon on his way to replace them.[362]

The Spanish faction at court was, however, being comprehensively ejected from office. Williams had already lost favour with Buckingham, who could not brook the lord keeper's continued espousal of the match or forgive his attempt during 1623 to resolve the spat between Bristol and Buckingham in Spain. Williams was temporarily retained because Charles intervened on his behalf, but he never fully regained favour, and fell, finally, in October 1625.[363] Bristol was already disgraced for his rivalry with Buckingham. His case was referred to the foreign-policy junta in early June 1624. A show trial was considered but

claimed that the Spanish ambassadors blamed Carondelet for the vigour of the allegations against Buckingham: PRO, SP 14/164/46, fo. 81r.

[357] Ruigh, *1624*, pp. 286–294, 359; Lockyer, *Buckingham*, pp. 195–196.

[358] Ruigh, *1624*, p. 359.

[359] PRO, SP 14/164/92, fo. 151r; CRS, 68, pp. 104–106; see also PRO, SP 16/164/86, fo. 141v.

[360] *CCE*, pp. 152, 160.

[361] PRO, SP 77/17, fo. 209r.

[362] *CSPV, 1623–1625*, p. 301; PRO, SP 14/167/28; *Letter 44*. Inojosa was ordered, before he left, to set up 'un service d'espionage, afin de rester au courant des projets du monarque anglais': *CCE*, pp. 168, 174. At Brussels, Inojosa received instructions to return to Spain 'to declare the necessity and commodity of a warr': BL, Harleian MS 1581, fo. 312r.

[363] Ruigh, *1624*, pp. 140–144; Adams, PC, p. 384; Hacket, *SR*, part I, p. 150.

postponed (until 1626) because of the risk of embarrassment to the prince and the duke, and evidently because Bristol made it known that he would not go down without a fight.[364] Lord Treasurer Cranfield was impeached after he launched a challenge to Buckingham's monopoly at court via his brother-in-law Arthur Brett, a groom of the bedchamber.[365] His had been a largely financial commitment to the Spanish match, but his support for it was one of the things which publicly damned him, although the allegations brought against him of financial mismanagement and peculation indicated how widely he had made enemies. Cranfield's trial in the Lords began on 7 May. Sentence was given a week later. He was dispatched to the Tower.[366] Subsequently, Calvert was levered out of his secretaryship; he had refused to take the oath of allegiance.[367] Sir Francis Cottington became an enemy of Buckingham by continuing to side with the king and to argue for the maintenance of good relations with the Spaniards.[368]

The freelance military commander Count Ernst von Mansfelt had come to London and was lodged at St James's, near to the prince's own chambers.[369] His special skills were to be employed to regain the elector palatine's territories. As Simon Adams argues, Buckingham had no clear ideological standpoint in the matter of European religious division; or, rather, he had no incentive to follow an ideological commitment to the European Protestant cause. He bound himself to the French alliance in order to underwrite and justify the reaction against Spain, even though it was far from obvious that this reorientation would secure the Stuart court's other foreign-policy objectives. Adams comments that, 'since neither success in parliament nor the break with Spain was assured', Buckingham could not afford a setback to the alliance with France. But his 'grand alliance' against Habsburg power, via the Anglo-French dynastic treaty, surrendered a great deal of the initiative to the French; the alliance 'would be dominated by French political considerations, one of the most important of which was the weakening of international Calvinism', something which threatened to alienate godly Protestant opinion in Britain. In order to retain political momentum and to engage the Stuart court in a war which would prevent any revival of the former Hispanophile policy, Buckingham sanctioned the employment

[364] Ruigh, *1624*, pp. 362f.

[365] Cogswell, *BR*, p. 233; Alexander, *CLT*, pp. 58–64; *CSPV, 1623–1625*, p. 343; *HMCMK*, p. 198; AAW, A XVII, no. 133, p. 421.

[366] For Cranfield's impeachment, see M. Prestwich, *Cranfield* (Oxford, 1966), pp. 448f.; Alexander, *CLT*, pp. 60–62.

[367] *Letter 81*.

[368] Ruigh, *1624*, p. 288.

[369] *Letter 44*; Adams, PC, p. 348; Pursell, *WK*, p. 222.

of Mansfelt, who in April 1624 set out his proposal for an Anglo-French military expedition, from French territory, to retake the Palatinate. James was prevailed upon to hope that Mansfelt's 'expedition might become the basis for the Anglo-French military alliance'. Mansfelt travelled to France in May 1624 with an advance of £20,000, out of the subsidy, in order to guarantee English commitment to the scheme.[370]

The British thinking behind the proposed dynastic alliance with France was relatively simple. The French could challenge the Habsburgs militarily but they were, of course, a Catholic nation. An alliance with them would not appear to commit the British state to a Protestant crusade. Meanwhile, Habsburg victories were threatening to leave the Bourbon realm encircled. The French would look for the resolution of the Valtelline question in their favour. In return, they were prepared to commit themselves to the restoration of the Rhineland Palatinate, though that was not, of course, one of their own military objectives.[371] Moreover, the Gallican temper of much of the French Church was sufficiently anti-papal to offer a platform for friendship and understanding with the English Church and state, even if at a respectable distance.[372] In April 1624, Charles had, as Chamberlain narrated, given 'great satisfaction' in parliament with his assurance that 'yf he did treat of mariage with any of contrary religion, yt shold be with that caution that there shold be no manner of connivance but for herself and her servants straungers'.[373]

In all probability, the internal contradictions of the Anglo-French alliance were not immediately evident to Catholics, even though negotiations with the Dutch States-General were opened at this point.

[370]Adams, FP, pp. 154, 156, 157–158; *idem*, PC, pp. 345, 346, 347, 349; *Letter 44*; Shimp, 'A Catholic marriage', p. 11; BL, Egerton MS 2596, fo. 3r. As Adams explains, Mansfelt's scheme for a military expedition to the Palatinate was attractive because it was comparatively cheap and his proposals 'for joint action with France and vague promises of French interest would provide the functional basis for the alliance with France': Adams, PC, p. 348.

[371]Shimp, 'A Catholic marriage', pp. 4–5. The problem for the English negotiators who joined the issue of the stand-off between the French and the Spaniards in the Valtelline to that of the Palatinate was succinctly summed up by the Venetian ambassador in Paris, Zuane Pesaro. He noted in March 1624 that the English thought 'the French want to lead others into war while keeping at peace themselves' and therefore the English wanted 'to unite the Palatinate and the Valtelline into one common cause, owing to the fear that, if the French receive satisfaction, they will be left to fight alone': *CSPV, 1623–1625*, p. 245.

[372]Cogswell, *BR*, p. 122; D. Lunn, 'The Anglo-Gallicanism of Dom Thomas Preston, 1567–1647', in D. Baker (ed.), *Schism, Heresy and Religious Protest*, Studies in Church History, 9 (Cambridge, 1972), p. 239. See also PRO, SP 78/74, fo. 242r–v ('The exemptions of the Church of France from the jurisdiccion of the pope [. . .]'); *Letter 81*.

[373]McClure, *LJC*, p. 553; Albion, *CI*, pp. 52, 54; Thompson, *RD*, p. 62.

All that they could immediately hope for was that parliament would be dissolved.[374]

In fact, it gradually became clear that religion would be an issue in the treaty and that English Catholics' influence would be far from negligible. As all commentators on the French match – both Catholic and Protestant –were well aware, the still-unresolved predicament of the Huguenots in France was a crucial part of the equation. The position of the English Catholics was, in some ways, analogous to theirs. The French negotiators' contacts with and support for the English Catholic minority could hardly be kept separate from the assistance which might be rendered to the Huguenots by the Stuart regime. Sir Edward Herbert had predicted in April 1624 that the French court, in the forthcoming negotiations, would 'hope to drawe a dependance from the Englishe papists for whome (that they may not seeme lesse Catholique than the Spaniard) they intend to require the same priviledges' as had been recently promised to the Spanish negotiators. Indeed, the 'Jesuits and their adherents' in France argued that this was a 'profitable' project for Louis XIII since, 'by this means, hee will ever have a partie in England to counterballance' the Huguenots. The bait which the French court held out to James was that French patronage 'would divide and distracte' the English Catholics 'from their dependance on Spaine and consequently raise a faction by which they might more easily bee governed'.[375]

At the same time, the regime headed by Richelieu had to deal with the fury of the Habsburgs' friends in France, who believed that a war against the House of Austria was quite simply incompatible with the duty of the French king to suppress heresy within his own kingdom. Richelieu was, it appears, never ideologically committed to either side of the argument between the *dévots* and those who called themselves *bons Français*.[376] In the end, he decided to crush the Huguenot challenge to the French state before turning to confront the threat of Habsburg supremacy in Europe. In the process, it was essential for the French crown not to be seen to be committing itself to what could be viewed as

[374] *Letters 44, 47*; Adams, PC, pp. 349, 364; Pursell, *WK*, p. 236. The conclusion of the agreement with the Dutch, a defensive alliance only, was delayed for quite some time, in fact until September of the following year.

[375] PRO, SP 78/72, fos 127v–128r; Adams, PC, p. 362. See also PRO, SP 78/72, fos 279v–280r; *Letter 75*. Tillières was able to report in early June that the 'principalles et plus zellés Catholiques' who had been to visit him now offered their thanks to the French king and his ministers 'touchant la loy que les puritains voulaient, que l'on passait contre eulx ce dernier parlement'; and also that they recognized 'les artiffices des Espagnols': PRO, PRO 31/3/59, fo. 125r.

[376] Shimp, 'A Catholic marriage', p. 7; R. Briggs, *Early Modern France 1560–1715* (Oxford, 1977), pp. 95–96.

a Protestant alliance with a Calvinist king. Hence the long-drawn-out arguments over compliance with the terms of the papal dispensation and the visible implementation of concessions to James's Catholic subjects which had been written into the treaty.

As Adams points out, Richelieu was initially presented with a real difficulty when it appeared that the enthusiasts in the 1624 parliament had secured 'a full-scale war' against the Habsburgs 'on a religious basis'. However, 'Buckingham's commitment to a French alliance and marriage surrendered the initiative and allowed Richelieu to hamstring the English leadership'.[377] The cardinal would soon come to dominate the negotiations.[378] The English priest Richard Smith, who was about to succeed William Bishop as bishop of Chalcedon, served as one of Richelieu's chaplains; and he used his influence with the cardinal to intervene on the English Catholics' behalf.[379]

In the initial stages of the negotiations, however, there was little to encourage the English Catholic community. The strategy of the French court was, at first, to allow the diplomatic bargaining with the Stuarts not to be pegged to the issue of toleration for James's Catholic subjects.[380] (English Catholics were, of course, desperate that the two should not be separated.[381])

On 1/11 May, Kensington informed Conway that he had used a recent meeting with Louis XIII to feel 'once againe their pulse in

[377] Adams, PC, pp. 426–427. Herbert predicted that the French would try to take advantage of the forthcoming Anglo-Spanish war to 'settle their owne affairs at home to the assured detriment' of the Huguenots, and he advised that James should 'bringe them [...] to some reall and infallible proofes' that they would assist him 'in the recovery of the Palatinate', for otherwise they would take advantage of their existing double marriage alliance with Spain in order to 'keepe themselves in [...] peace and neutrality': PRO, SP 78/72, fo. 128r.

[378] *CSPV, 1623–1625*, pp. 313–314; PRO, SP 14/167/28.

[379] Questier, *C&C*, pp. 378–379, 418, 420, 421, 423, 425, 444, 453, 465, 466, 471, 493; *Letter 48*.

[380] Albion, *CI*, pp. 52–53. The instructions issued to Carlisle and Kensington on 17 May 1624 insisted that 'the constitution of our estate cannot beare any generall change or alteration in our ecclesiasticall or temporall lawes touching religion', even though, temporarily, such an offer had been made (for special considerations – namely the restoration of the Palatinate) to the Spaniards. Instead, James's ambassadors were told to promise Louis XIII that, 'in contemplation of' the marriage, James would 'bee the rather inclined' to treat his Roman Catholic subjects 'with all favor, soe long as they shall behave themselves moderately' and keep 'their consciences to themselves'. The quid pro quo was, by implication, that James would not intervene on behalf of the Huguenots: PRO, SP 78/72, fos 215v–217r; cf. BL, Harleian MS 1584, fos 11v–13r.

[381] Back in early February, William Bishop had informed Thomas Rant that 'we do request the Frenc[h]e ambassador that he will procure his king to write unto our kings Majestie to protect us, because that of the Spanish is [...] more hatefull to the puritans'. Rant should, said Bishop, 'obtaine, if you can, his Holines['s] letters to the king of France that he may write to our king to favour his Catholike subjects as our king hath written to him in favour of his Calvinists': AAW, A XVII, no. 96, pp. 314, 315; TD, V, pp. cclxxvi–cclxxvii.

matters of religion' and found the attitude of the French court to be broadly favourable. Kensington dealt 'plainely with the marquis de La Vieuville' concerning the course that James might 'be driven to hould against Jesuites and priests, of banishing them the kingdome, and of quickening the lawes against the other Catholiques', partly in order to reduce them to obedience, and partly in order to keep 'good intelligence with his parlement, without which he could not possibly goe through with such a weighty worke as he is now to undertake'. Charles Coskaer, marquis de La Vieuville, 'approoved of the course for the ends sake', though he hoped 'notwithstanding that his Majestie would not tye his owne hands from some moderate favour heerafter'. The Frenchman trusted that even a limited toleration might 'flowe from the mediation' of the French state following the treaty 'for the saving of their honour, who otherwise wilbe hardly reputed Catholiques' at all.[382]

Towards the end of June, some observers, such as Sir Francis Nethersole and Dudley Carleton, thought that the French would not even insist on a papal dispensation for the proposed marriage.[383] Tillières, who was a friend of Pierre Brûlart, vicomte de Puisieux (displaced, with Nicolas Brûlart de Sillery, in January 1624), was recalled. Gordon Albion comments that it was 'a wonder he had stayed so long'. Tillières was succeeded by the more flexible Antoine Coiffier de Ruzé, marquis of Effiat. The change of ambassadors was taken by some, quite wrongly in fact, as an indication that the French court would inevitably make concessions on religion in order to secure the match.[384]

Parliament was now adjourned until 2 November.[385] James hardly concealed his irritation with the members before they dispersed, although superficially his speech to them on 29 May made a few conciliatory noises. Sir Francis Nethersole's account of the speech put the best possible gloss on it. He stressed that James had refused only four bills, though this included the legislation against recusants; he

[382] BL, Harleian MS 1581, fo. 28r.

[383] PRO, SP 14/168/40, 48; Cogswell, *BR*, pp. 122–123; *HMCMK*, pp. 212, 218, 224. For the question of whether such a dispensation was in fact required for a valid marriage, see Redworth, *PI*, p. 53; Albion, *CI*, pp. 74–75; *CSPV, 1623–1625*, p. 362. As Antony Allison points out, 'theological opinion in France was solidly against the view that the dispensation was strictly necessary. Many theologians maintained that there was no obligation *in foro interno* and that France had fulfilled her obligation *in foro externo* by the act of asking for the dispensation'. Cardinal de la Rochefoucauld and Pierre de Bérulle were of this opinion: Allison, RS, pp. 192–193.

[384] Albion, *CI*, p. 53; Tillières, *ME*, p. 57. Schreiber notes that Tillières 'volunteered his own recall': Schreiber, *FC*, pp. 56, 65. For the instructions issued to Effiat, see PRO, PRO 31/3/59, fos 143r–147v.

[385] PRO, SP 14/165/61.

also noted that the king had commended the controversial dealings of Bishop Samuel Harsnett in the diocese of Norwich.[386] Most of the Commons's charges against Harsnett dealt with central conformist issues (preaching, catechizing, images, and so on), but it was also said that 'his lordship connived at recusants'.[387] Catholic commentators, like others, were not slow to remark on these tensions.[388]

Valaresso observed that, three days after parliament adjourned, Cranfield was released from the Tower. The Venetian commented that 'this is the way in England: hardly has the ink dried of a sentence fulminated by parliament than the king annuls it'. The earl of Arundel, Bristol's friend, appeared to be rising 'hourly in the king's favour'; James was still seeing the shortly-to-depart Spanish diplomats and was expressing doubts about the proposed treaty with the Dutch; the 'council of war' was 'nothing but a name'; and Buckingham appeared physically very ill and was believed to be on the verge of falling from grace.[389] All would depend on the deal shortly to be struck with the French.

## English Catholics, the Anglo-French Marriage, and War in Europe

While these events were in train, the English Catholic community was plunged into crisis yet again. William Bishop had expired at Bishopshall in Essex on 13 April 1624.[390] His death reopened the debate about the authority and function of a Catholic bishop in England, a debate which could not but be informed by the twists and turns of the negotiations for the Anglo-French dynastic treaty. Bishop's demise led to a furious struggle at Rome over who should succeed him. The leading secular clergy now enjoyed the backing of the French crown, although they anticipated considerable opposition, both in England and at Rome, to their own nominations for the

[386] *Ibid.*; PRO, SP 14/167/10; Ruigh, *1624*, pp. 255–256; McClure, *LJC*, pp. 561–562; *CSPV, 1623–1625*, p. 342. For Harsnett, see Fincham, *Prelate as Pastor*, pp. 245–246.

[387] *LJ*, III, p. 388.

[388] AAW, B 26, no. 77 (Thomas More to Thomas Rant, 18/28 June 1624).

[389] *CSPV, 1623–1625*, pp. 343–344; Cogswell, *BR*, p. 251; *HMCMK*, pp. 201, 203, 205. On 5 June, Chamberlain observed that 'the papists geve out malicious reports that' Buckingham 'shold be crased in his braine', although there was 'no such matter, but that the suspicion grew by reason of his often letting bloud': McClure, *LJC*, p. 563.

[390] Anstr., I, p. 38; AAW, B 26, no. 40A; AAW, A XXVIII, no. 58, p. 224.

appointment.[391] Richard Smith alleged that the Jesuits persuaded Inojosa to oppose the secular clergy's suit there.[392] At the end of July 1624, Edward Bennett wrote to Rome concerning the rumours that Thomas Fitzherbert was obstructing their suit for an episcopal appointment.[393] Smith alleged that the Jesuits in Rome, by which he principally meant Fitzherbert, were still repeating the old slanders that he (Smith) held heterodox opinions about the nature of the papal deposing power.[394] In early August, John Jackson claimed that there was a co-ordinated campaign in England both to secure gentry opposition to the appointment of another bishop and to prove that William Bishop himself had been a cause of division within his flock.[395] On 8/18 August, Smith complained that Sir Tobias Mathew had accused him of helping to secure Tillières's recall to France, thus making way for Tillières's supposedly more pliable successor, the marquis of Effiat, and thereby facilitating the French match without doing anything to help English Catholics.[396] The secular priest John Cecil added his voice to those who were critical of Smith.[397] Some enemies of the seculars also argued that the appointment of another bishop would impose a heavy financial burden on the Catholic gentry, who would be called on to support him, something which they could ill afford.[398]

As Antony Allison has shown, somebody put up an alternative slate of candidates to that proposed by the members of the deceased William Bishop's episcopal chapter. The alternative list named Cuthbert Johnson, William Smith, Oliver Almond, and John Roberts. Only Almond was a member of the episcopal chapter; Johnson was said by Richard Smith to be the Jesuits' nominee.[399]

Allison's definitive account of Richard Smith's election demonstrates how that election fitted into the strategy of the French undertakers of the Anglo-French treaty. Smith was not the preferred candidate of the English secular clergy. The French, however, intervened to force his election as part of their diplomacy to secure the marriage between Prince Charles and Henrietta Maria. In fact,

[391] See, e.g., *Letter 59*; cf. Allison, RS, pp. 155–157. There is comparatively little archival material for the English Jesuits in the 1620s and so it is hard to gauge their response to the seculars' campaign for another episcopal appointment.

[392] *Letter 45*.

[393] AAW, B 26, no. 94 (cited in *Letter 59*).

[394] *Letter 59*; *NAGB*, p. 8.

[395] *Letter 50*. See also AAW, B 27, nos 30, 42 (cited in *Letter 58*).

[396] AAW, B 26, no. 105 (cited in *Letter 53*). In October 1624, Mathew complained to Cardinal Barberini about the watering down of protection for English Catholics in the wording of the treaty's articles: Albion, *CI*, p. 56; *Letter 53*.

[397] AAW, B 27, no. 28.

[398] Questier, *C&C*, p. 419; AAW, B 27, no. 9.

[399] Allison, RS, pp. 158–159; *Letter 53*.

the French secretary of state, Henri-Auguste de Loménie, seigneur de Villeauxclercs, had written, when it became known that Bishop was dying, to ask Tillières to 'let me know whom you judge suitable to be appointed successor [...] so that we can dispose matters at Rome'. The right candidate would be able to influence the course of the treaty negotiations and to prevent Hispanophile Catholics from obstructing the marriage. Tillières, who had already urged on 14 April, the day after Bishop's death, that the new bishop must be a Francophile, replied on 4 May that the candidate who was most likely to be amenable to the French court's agenda was Smith himself.[400]

In a list of reasons drawn up by Thomas Rant for Smith's preferment over the heads of the others who had also been recommended, it was argued (in ascending order, as it were) that he was less aged, more vigorous, better known in England, better acquainted with the court of Rome, *and* that the king of France demanded him.[401] Rather than entrusting the case of Smith's alleged heterodoxy to the Inquisition's permanent commissary, Urban VIII appointed the French Cardinal de La Valette to oversee the Inquisition's investigation of the accusations which were being levelled against him.[402] This virtually guaranteed that Smith would be appointed. Some of the secular clergy were perturbed that Smith's preferment should have been so openly at the direction of the French court; it laid him and them open to charges of bias and faction. William Harewell lamented 'that his Hol[iness] should designe the persons of the bishops at the instance of princes (as it is presumed he hath)'. From this it would be deduced that

> the bishop and clergie shall be accounted as interessed in that princes faction by whose endeavours the saied bishop is made, and so the bodie inforced to loose all creditt and authoritie with the princes of the contrarie faction and disinhabled by their letters or advocats to effect any thing in the behalfe of their seminaries, or other their members, residing within their provinces or dominions.[403]

Far more serious, however, for the secular clergy party, which saw in this grant of episcopal authority another opportunity to invoke the cause of reform among English Catholics and to clear up what they called the 'chaos Anglicanum', was the fact that, when Rome finally made up its mind to appoint him, the authority granted to Richard Smith was limited in the same way that William Bishop's had been.

400 Allison, RS, p. 165; PRO, PRO 31/3/58, fos 81v, 100v; Shimp, 'A Catholic marriage', pp. 8–9.

401 AAW, A XVIII, no. 57, p. 345; Allison, RS, p. 181.

402 Allison, RS, p. 185; Shimp, 'A Catholic marriage', pp. 14–15; *Letter 59*.

403 AAW, B 47, no. 89 (cited in Allison, RS, p. 182).

Smith was consecrated on 2/12 January 1625 by the Paris nuncio, Bernardino Spada, with Richelieu and Claude de Rueil, bishop of Bayonne, present to assist him. Smith's faculties had been granted to him ten days before. He was nominated as Bishop's successor to rule over the clergy and laity of England and Scotland. His powers were set out in a papal breve of 25 January/4 February 1625; it reached him in early March. But the breve stated that his authority was, like Bishop's, held during the pope's pleasure and that he was, in effect, subordinate to the papal nuncio in Paris.[404]

As we noted above, Tillières was recalled to France (temporarily, as it turned out) and the marquis of Effiat was sent in his place.[405] Effiat left Calais on 28 June/8 July 1624 and was in London by 3/13 July.[406] The secular clergy and their friends were concerned that Effiat was a cynic and that the French court would pursue the treaty without considering the interests of English Catholics. By contrast, Effiat and others, notably the Venetian diplomat Valaresso, believed that reports of persecution were being exaggerated by Hispanophile English Catholics, and by the Spaniards themselves, in order to thwart the negotiations for the marriage.[407] In fact, soon after his arrival, Effiat consulted Coloma about the English Catholics and then saw various Catholic representatives, mainly, it seems, from the religious orders. They gave him to understand that 'leur misères estoient telles qu'ils n'espéroient d'avoir jamais soulagement à leurs maux que par l'ayde de Dieu' and of Louis XIII. They had the temerity to insist that, while the Anglo-Spanish negotiations were in train, 'ils n'avoient respiré que douceur et liberté' but now that 'on avoit pourparlé du mariage' with the sister of the French king the cruelty with which they were treated was insupportable. Effiat decided that, since he had been officially instructed 'de les détacher d'avec Espagne', he should tell them that Louis XIII 'porte le tiltre de très Chrestien, et n'a plus grande gloire que de procurer à ceux qui ont ce saint nom, secours et soulagement en leurs afflictions'. How dare they suggest that he was the source of their misery, especially when they had thrown themselves

[404] Allison, RS, pp. 188–190; *Letter 64*; AAW, A XIX, no. 5, pp. 13–16.

[405] *Letter 47*; Schreiber, *FC*, p. 65. Tillières returned to serve (if rather briefly) as chamberlain of Henrietta Maria's household, and his wife also entered her service: Albion, *CI*, p. 50; PRO, PRO 31/3/60, fo. 223r.

[406] PRO, SP 14/169/2; *CSPV, 1623–1625*, p. 382; PRO, PRO 31/3/59, fos 157r–158r.

[407] AAW, B 26, no. 85; AAW, B 27, no. 15. See also Tillières, *ME*, pp. 79–87; *CSPV, 1623–1625*, pp. 394, 399, 411, 443–444, 451 (for Effiat's and Valaresso's views). An exchequer drive against recusants followed the collapse of the Spanish marriage negotiations, although, as Terence Smith demonstrates, 'hardly any money was ever received' from the 'new seizures' of Catholic separatists' property: T.S. Smith, 'The persecution of Staffordshire Roman Catholic recusants: 1625–1660', *Journal of Ecclesiastical History*, 30 (1979), pp. 330–331.

'inconsidérérement entre les bras du roy d'Espagne'? The Spaniards had deceived King James with a mere illusion of an alliance purely for their own purposes. No one could doubt 'les malicieux artifices' which the Spanish king had used towards James, and it was not surprising that he had now retaliated against 'les principaulx instruments' which they had used to mislead him, namely the Catholics. Effiat told these Catholics that it was 'nécessaire pour vostre salut' that the prince should marry the French king's sister, and 'si Dieu bénit ce dessein [. . .] vous mettans en la protection du roy mon maistre', then their concerns would be taken into consideration.[408] These Catholics assured Effiat that 'en leurs assemblées secrettes, ils avoient résolu de s'attacher entièrement' to the French, despite 'les impressions mauvoises qu'on leur avoit données' that Effiat himself favoured the Huguenots. Effiat promised them that France would protect them 'd'une manière differente à celle d'Espaigne qui donne des promesses sans effect', and that Louis 'donniez des effects sans promesses'.[409] Effiat informed Buckingham of what had been said at this meeting, and then went for an audience with James at Windsor.[410]

In the round of negotiations which had begun in June 1624, the English had put forward a treaty based on the rather limited model of the proposals advanced in 1613 for Prince Charles and Henrietta Maria's sister Christine.[411] The French negotiators countered with proposals based on those which had been agreed in principle with the Spaniards. The English objected to some of the terms and especially to the suggested guarantee of toleration, by royal grant, for English Catholics. The French then made a concession: their compromise was that James's pledge would be kept secret, though it would be in writing. This initiative, offered via the agency of Lord Kensington, procured La Vieuville's downfall in early August 1624. Richelieu and Villeauxclercs moved to supplant him on the grounds that he had gone beyond his brief by assuring the English that French support for English Catholics was no more than gesture politics.[412] Carlisle, however, remarked that 'perhaps his greatest crime is to have aspired

[408]PRO, PRO 31/3/59, fos 159r–160r; Albion, *CI*, p. 58.

[409]PRO, PRO 31/3/59, fo. 160v. On 18/28 July, Effiat repeated his opinion that the English Catholics were beginning to detach themselves from their former reliance on Spain: Bodleian Library, Carte MS 82, no. 410b.

[410]PRO, PRO 31/3/59, fos 160v–161r, 161r–163r; *CSPD, 1623–1625*, pp. 295–296. On 9 July, however, the Venetian ambassador narrated a visit he had received from Effiat, and said that Effiat still believed 'that the Catholics here are undoubtedly Spanish' and 'some of them had presumed to maintain Spanish interests in his presence': *CSPV, 1623–1625*, pp. 394–395.

[411]Albion, *CI*, p. 55.

[412]Schreiber, *FC*, pp. 69–70; Albion, *CI*, p. 57. As Anthony Champney described it, La Vieuville fell from power because he had, 'contrarie to his kings will, assured the king of

to that glory which the queen mother and the cardinal desired to appropriate'.[413]

Some interpreted the religious issue in the negotiations as no more than a matter of French honour. Nethersole commented, soon after La Vieuville's disgrace was known, that,

> although they did in France insist upon the same conditions for matter of religion which were yielded unto in the treaty with Spayne, yet, to shew that this was onely for honors sake, they were contented to have all the articles concerning religion put apart in a treaty by themselves, unto which there should be no confirmation by oathe required, and not onely so but to have them couched in such generall wordes as that they might be observed without any great prejudice: for example, that the lawes against Catholiques should not be executed tandis qu'ils se comportent en bons sujets.[414]

But others, and notably the secular clergy and their friends, were happy to gloss La Vieuville's fall by reference to his alleged lack of enthusiasm for the Catholic cause. On 10/20 August 1624, Richard Smith observed that the negotiations were 'in my cardinals hands, who laboureth al he can to get good conditions for us and hopeth to obtaine [them]. The king hath put downe' La Vieuville 'cheefly for having so litle care of the Catholiks of England when he delt for the mach'.[415] Three days earlier, Carlisle himself had conceded that 'this change turned the streame of affaires heer into the cardinals hands, who now sweighs every thing as he pleases'. This had caused Carlisle and Kensington to wonder how to carry forward the negotiations, and even 'whether we should first addresse our selves to the king or to' Richelieu, in order to 'communicate with them the articles as they came reformed from England'. The cardinal assured the English negotiators that the change of personnel in the Bourbon regime would not lead to change of 'affections' towards the English.[416]

With Richelieu in charge, however, the English would have to take seriously the French strictures against the continuation of anti-Catholic measures and practices. La Vieuville's pledges to the English

Ingland that the king of France did not stand much' in the defence of the Catholic religion, 'which treacherie, being discovered', he was disgraced: AAW, B 26, no. 104; see also D.L.M. Avenel (ed.), *Lettres, Instructions Diplomatiques et Papiers d'état du Cardinal de Richelieu*, 8 vols (Paris, 1853–1877), II, pp. 20–26.

[413]Schreiber, *FC*, pp. 64–65; Albion, *CI*, pp. 56–57; C. Burckhardt, *Richelieu and his Age*, 3 vols (London, 1967), I, pp. 155–157; Shimp, 'A Catholic marriage', p. 11; PRO, SP 78/73, fos 1r–2r, 6r, 7r, 11r–v, 94r–95v. (For other accusations against La Vieuville, see, e.g., PRO, SP 78/73, fo. 193r.) For Louis XIII's concessions on other issues, notably the education of the children of the marriage, see *ibid.*, fo. 262v.

[414]PRO, SP 14/171/60, fo. 91r.

[415]AAW, B 26, no. 106.

[416]PRO, SP 78/73, fos 5r–7r.

over the issue of toleration were withdrawn. Louis himself told Carlisle and Kensington that the pope's dispensation would not be issued unless the pontiff were convinced that the Stuart court would guarantee some mode of toleration for James's Catholic subjects.[417]

The ambassador Effiat, who had been sent as a representative of an essentially politique French lobby, found that his position had become more complicated. He had made clear to Buckingham, almost immediately after his arrival, that there would have to be concessions over the question of religion before any treaty could be signed.[418] On 11 August, Effiat reported the long discussions which he had had with James about the required papal dispensation and the ways in which the penal laws against Catholics would have to be modified. He believed that he had extracted worthwhile guarantees that the laws against Catholics would be suspended.[419] La Vieuville's dismissal, however, threw all into doubt. Effiat told Buckingham about it on 8 August. The duke was astonished, though Effiat tried, initially with some success, to persuade him that nothing had changed.[420] But the French appeared to become so obdurate over the toleration issue that the negotiations threatened to stall altogether.[421] Kensington's and Carlisle's letter of 7/17 August 1624 (concerning the new French stipulations about toleration) provoked James into a decision to break the match, and Conway issued an order to this effect to the English ambassadors in Paris. James's angry letter was recalled and substantially rewritten only when Buckingham intercepted the messenger. Effiat then engaged James at Derby in a tense conversation over how the negotiations could be fruitfully restarted.[422]

There was a meeting on 20/30 August between Marie de Médicis and Kensington, who had proved more amenable than Carlisle to a compromise with the French. After a series of witty initial remarks and ripostes over Prince Charles's recent journey to Spain, and whether he was badly treated there, Kensington 'smilingly added [...] yow heer, madame, use him farre worse [...] in that yow presse [...] upon' him 'the same, nay more unreasonable, conditions'. For what the Spaniards

[417]Schreiber, *FC*, pp. 70 (citing PRO, SP 78/73, fo. 8r), 71; *CSPV, 1623–1625*, pp. 361–362, 429; PRO, SP 78/73, fos 5r–6r, see also *ibid.*, fos 57v–58r. The English ambassadors made haste to seek an audience with the queen mother. They argued that pressing this issue would make Henrietta Maria less well received in England: PRO, SP 78/73, fos 8v–9v.

[418]Tillières, *ME*, pp. 79–87; PRO, PRO 31/3/59, fos 163r–165r.

[419]PRO, PRO 31/3/59, fos 174r–177v, 180v.

[420]*Ibid.*, fos 182v–183r, 183v.

[421]Albion, *CI*, pp. 59–60; AAW, B 26, no. 97; see also *Letter 50*; *CSPV, 1623–1625*, p. 431.

[422]Schreiber, *FC*, pp. 72–75; Lockyer, *Buckingham*, p. 203; PRO, SP 78/73, fo. 5r; PRO, PRO 31/3/59, fos 197v–199r.

'traced out for the breaking of the match, yow follow pretending to conclude it'. This was, claimed Kensington, unacceptable

> in this conjuncture of tyme especially when the jealousies that such great changes in state are apt to begett are cunningly fomented by the Spanish embassador in England who vaunts it forth that there is not soe great a change in La Vieuvilles particular person as there is in the generall affections which did but follow before the streame of his greatnes and credit, thus casting in the kings mynde the seed of doubts.

Olivares was alleged to have boasted to the English ambassador in Madrid that, 'if the pope ever graunted a dispensation for the match with France, the king of Spaine wold march with an army to Rome and sack it'. The queen mother tartly replied 'nous l'en empecherons bien'. Kensington went on to insist that the seventh and last articles of the proposed treaty, as they then stood, were impossible for the Stuart court to accept, and that they must be altered, or at the very least that she must 'procure the allowance of this protestation by the king our master, when he should swear them, that he intended no further to oblige himself by that oath than might well stand with the surety, peace, tranquillity and conveniency of his state'. The queen mother thought this was reasonable and she promised to speak to the king and cardinal.[423]

Thus the English insistence that a concession of toleration, in the form which the French had demanded, was simply impossible was balanced by Buckingham's capacity to persuade James that the French proposal of an *écrit particulier* (outside the main treaty document) would suffice, and would be compatible with his guarantees made to the 1624 parliament. This served to keep the negotiations going. At the end of August, the French made a limited funding commitment to Mansfelt.[424] The new version of James's pledge (extremely vague and capable of a variety of interpretations), in the form of the *écrit particulier*, to show favour to his Roman Catholic subjects was phrased in such sort that James would merely promise rather than swear favour and liberty to Catholics.[425] The formula adopted was, ironically, virtually the same as the compromise originally advanced by La Vieuville.

[423] Schreiber, *FC*, pp. 76–77; BL, Harleian MS 1581, fos 31v–32v; PRO, PRO 31/3/59, fo. 174v.

[424] Shimp, 'A Catholic marriage', p. 12; Schreiber, *FC*, p. 77; Albion, *CI*, p. 60; Adams, PC, p. 352; *CSPV, 1623–1625*, p. 434.

[425] Schreiber, *FC*, pp. 77–78; Albion, *CI*, pp. 60–64; Shimp, 'A Catholic marriage', p. 11; Lockyer, *Buckingham*, p. 205; PRO, PRO 31/3/60, fo. 227v; BL, Egerton MS 2596, fo. 67r. For Kensington's and Carlisle's account, of 18/28 August 1624, of this attempt to find a compromise over the guarantee that James would give for the liberties of his Catholic subjects, sufficient to persuade the pope to issue a dispensation for the marriage, see PRO, SP 78/73, fos 63r–69r. There was considerable debate also over the difficulties presented by

James approved the new version of the marriage treaty (now in the form of twenty-six articles) by 1 September 1624. It was sent off to the French court, though the arguments about how far James was to be obliged to abrogate the penal law rumbled on.[426] Two days before, in Paris, Kensington had written to James that, in his opinion, Richelieu was playing a double game, posing as a protector of Catholics but in fact undermining *dévot* hardliners in France.[427] Nevertheless, on the same day, Conway wrote to Coventry with a list of recusants and priests for whom Effiat had petitioned the crown for favour.[428]

One practical effect of these delays was to give the English Catholics in London and in other European capitals a window of opportunity to snatch, if not victory, then at least some acceptable compromise from the jaws of defeat. The Catholics saw the possibility of inserting themselves back into the body politic from which the euphoric Protestant enthusiasts of 1624 had thought to eject them. But this would happen not only through a struggle with their Protestant critics but also by engaging with the French (who did not necessarily share English Catholics' views about how their Catholicism and French political interests should coincide) and with each other. Once it was clear that the French match was going to take place, the various Catholic interest groups moved swiftly into an end game where they tried to demonstrate that their religious concerns and ambitions were not just acceptable to the Stuart state but were a corollary of their support for the regime, even when, on the face of it, the purpose of the match was to confront the Habsburgs.

The irony here, of course, was that the Anglo-French treaty negotiations had initially made swift progress because those on the

the loyalty oath that the queen's servants and James's Catholic subjects would take: *ibid.*, fos 67r–v, 262v; see also *ibid.*, fos 105r–108r, 315r; PRO, PRO 31/3/60, fo. 236r.

[426]Schreiber, *FC*, p. 78; Albion, *CI*, pp. 60–61; PRO, PRO 31/3/60, fos 216r–218v, 227r, 230r. For the problems caused by the English court's demand, accompanying the return to Paris of the *écrit* ('framed' by James 'into the fashion of a letter'), that the French should 'give an explanation in writing that the oath of alleageance is not contradictory to the Roman religion' or 'to the conscience of Romane Catholiques' (to which, Carlisle and Kensington advised on 18/28 September, the French would not agree), see PRO, SP 78/73, fo. 183r–v. For Conway's reply to this objection, see *ibid.*, fos 199r, 200r; see also *ibid.*, fos 229r–v, 262v–263r.

[427]*Ibid.*, fo. 103r; see also *ibid.*, fo. 105r; Lockyer, *Buckingham*, pp. 204–205. On 4/14 September, Kensington told Conway how Richelieu had given assurances that he was 'bon François'. The cardinal had even claimed that, in the context of the difficulties raised in the negotiations over what oath of loyalty (contained in the *écrit particulier*) would be stipulated for Catholics, and particularly for servants of Henrietta Maria, the 1606 oath of allegiance was 'in no way contrary to the Roman faith'. He 'affirmed' this 'to be the generall tenent of the Sorbonne', though it was still impossible to incorporate any such oath in the treaty articles themselves: PRO, SP 78/73, fo. 132r.

[428]PRO, SP 14/172/1.i.

French council of state – principally Sillery and Puisieux – who were favourable to the Habsburgs had been levered out back in January 1624.[429] Their replacements were new men who wanted French differences with the Habsburgs settled with less diplomacy and more force: for example, over the question of the Valtelline.[430] Such people included La Vieuville and Villeauxclercs and, of course, Richelieu, though La Vieuville was, as we have seen, soon displaced and disgraced.[431]

There were, in fact, two agreements between the English and the French. One was the marriage treaty itself. The other was an accompanying military compact in which the French designs on the Valtelline would be combined with the military entrepreneur Mansfelt's assault on the Palatinate, even though, as Brennan Pursell points out, the actual Anglo-French marriage treaty 'did not include a provision for the restitution of the Palatinate'.[432] The problem was, as Simon Adams has shown in some detail, that the Stuart court's strategy, which revolved around an alliance between itself, the French, and the Dutch, was essentially a pipe dream in Buckingham's head. The French were still extremely reluctant at this point to engage in full-scale hostilities against Spain and the empire.[433] As Carlisle and Kensington (recently created earl of Holland) were compelled to report in early October 1624, the French negotiators of the treaty still argued that English concessions over the terms to be accorded to James's Catholic subjects and over the regulation of the entourage of Charles's bride were absolutely essential to prevent European condemnation of Louis XIII for an apparent betrayal of the Catholic cause. The French would not even concede a 'league offensive' 'till the marriage shall be consummate'. As Richelieu had recently said, 'donnez nous des prestres [. . .] et nous vous donnerons des colonels'. Now they claimed that 'to capitulate with us in writing would but cast rubs in

[429] See PRO, SP 78/72, fos 16r, 19r–v; Tillières, *ME*, pp. 57–58. For Puisieux's entertainment in early 1624 of Spanish proposals for a Franco-Spanish alliance directed against the forces of European Protestantism, designed to obviate the Anglo-Spanish dynastic treaty but dependent on restoring the Valtelline to French control, see PRO, SP 78/72, fo. 36r; *CSPV, 1623–1625*, pp. 214–215. The French ambassador in Rome, Noël Brûlart, had negotiated (contrary to the 1621 Treaty of Madrid) for the Spaniards' demolition of their forts in the Valtelline while retaining the right to 'have [. . .] passage free' through the region: PRO, SP 78/72, fo. 74r. For Brûlart's self-justification in this respect, see *ibid.*, fo. 96r–v. For the Valtelline issue, see *Letter 76*.

[430] The French and the Dutch signed the Treaty of Compiègne in the summer of 1624: Pursell, *WK*, p. 230.

[431] Schreiber, *FC*, pp. 59–60.

[432] *Ibid.*, pp. 61, 78; Pursell, *WK*, p. 230; see also *CSPV, 1623–1625*, pp. 350–351, 613; Albion, *CI*, p. 63; Shimp, 'A Catholic marriage', p. 9.

[433] Adams, PC, p. 351.

the way of the dispensation, and make it alltogether impossible, sith it must needs highly offend the pope to heare they should enter into an offensive league with heretiques against Catholiques'. It 'was like so farre to scandalize the Catholique princes of Germany', and Louis would 'loose all credit with them, whom yett he hoped to winne to the better party'.[434]

This was why Mansfelt was so important. He was the focal point for an Anglo-French military consensus, and he would shoulder most of the organizational difficulties and the risk of his proposed expedition to the Palatinate. He simply needed to be financed. The money would not be forthcoming until the partners to the alliance, notably the Dutch, put up funds as well. Using him did not necessarily mean – and this was crucial for James as much as for Louis – an outbreak of general hostilities with Spain.[435]

But the employment of Mansfelt was, as Adams says, Buckingham's 'most disastrous error in foreign affairs'.[436] Although the English and French negotiators discussed Mansfelt's proposals during the summer, the fall of La Vieuville temporarily threw the whole project into doubt. Carlisle had had serious qualms about continuing the discussions, but Buckingham had boxed himself in. If the negotiations with the French came to grief, then it was possible that James might decide to approach the Spaniards again.[437]

The raising of troops and the appointment of officers for a new English expeditionary force to the Netherlands had begun earlier in the year, in fact as the 1624 parliament was ending.[438] Clearly, English Catholics wanted the French match to proceed; but even the Francophiles among them did not want to see the treaty lead to a Protestant resurgence in mainland Europe. What Mansfelt did or did not accomplish was therefore extremely significant.[439] The Catholics in London had watched Mansfelt very carefully when he was in the

[434]PRO, SP 78/73, fo. 230r.

[435]Cogswell, *BR*, pp. 243–245, 250f.; Adams, PC, p. 351.

[436]Adams, FP, p. 158; and see below, pp. 104–105, 114–115. While Buckingham wanted Mansfelt's expedition to constitute the 'basis for a revival of the Grand Alliance' which the duke had tried to create in 1623, in fact he had to make so many concessions to Richelieu to secure the treaty that the whole policy ended in a débâcle in 1625: Adams, FP, p. 158.

[437]*Ibid.*

[438]McClure, *LJC*, p. 562. For the recruitment and delivery of troops to the Dutch, allowing them to release their own veteran soldiers from garrison service, see *CSPV, 1623–1625*, pp. 403, 422, and *passim.*

[439]Thomas Cogswell argues that Mansfelt has probably been underestimated as a commander: Cogswell, *BR*, p. 239. For his performance, for example, at Frankenthal in late 1621, at Wiesloch against Tilly in April 1622, and at the battle of Fleurus in late August 1622, see *Letter 1*; Adams, PC, p. 329; *CSPV, 1621–1623*, pp. 318, 414, 420; Pursell, *WK*, p. 172; PRO, SP 77/15, fo. 282v; BL, Harleian MS 1581, fo. 160v; Lee, *Dudley Carleton to John*

capital in April 1624; they continued to do so when he returned in September. They recorded the names of those whom he was seeing, where he was allowed to stay, whether he was receiving the trappings of honour, and how much cash was being allotted to him.[440]

As this sweeping reorientation of royal diplomacy was in train, a flood of anti-popish literature poured from the presses. Such works had no doubts about what should be done with the popish caterpillars of the commonwealth, even though James had shown himself so unenthusiastic about the recent parliament's calls for more effective measures against Catholics.[441]

What did the state do to fulfil popular expectations in this respect? Even if the regime did not, to a man, entirely share the sentiments of the tractate literature against the Catholic menace, Catholics claimed that they were again subject to the terror of house-to-house searches and of commissions dispatched here, there, and everywhere to assess what convicted recusants possessed, with follow-up commissions to enforce sequestration, and a whole series of middlemen taking their cut at each stage.[442]

Furthermore, a priest, one William Davies, had been arrested on 17 June and, in spite of his bad health and advanced years, had been sent to Newgate by the recorder of London.[443] In itself, the arrest of a Catholic clergyman was nothing new. However, in the circumstances of the Anglo-French treaty negotiations, it became something of a test case. Some Catholic commentators insisted that, despite the evidence of an imminent return to the bad old days, the king was still unlikely to concede the full onslaught against Catholics which the recent parliament had demanded.[444] As we have already seen, a proclamation against the Catholic clergy had been issued on 6 May. It commanded them into exile (by 14 June), and Davies was arrested for not complying with it.[445] But would it really be enforced? As John

*Chamberlain*, p. 293; *CCE*, pp. 98–99; BL, Additional MS 72254, fos 143r, 145r; cf. Adams, FP, p. 158.

[440] See, e.g., *Letters 44, 55, 60*; see also Cogswell, *BR*, p. 241.

[441] Cogswell, *BR*, pp. 281–307. A proclamation was issued in mid-August 1624 against seditious books and pamphlets. James had intervened to direct it equally against popish and puritan tracts. On 21 July 1624, Sir Edward Conway informed the attorney-general that the draft proclamation, on the king's order, had to be 'altered and, in all places where mencion is made of popish scandalous bookes, theis wordes are precisely to bee added: "as alsoe all sedicious bookes and scandalous to our person and state such as have ben lately vented by some puritanicall spiritts"': PRO, SP 14/170/35, fo. 53r; *SRP*, I, no. 256; S. Lambert, 'Richard Montagu, Arminianism and censorship', *Past and Present*, 124 (1989), p. 53.

[442] AAW, B 26, no. 72 (cited in *Letter 49*).

[443] Anstr., I, p. 99; *Letter 47*.

[444] *Letter 45*.

[445] CRS, 68, p. 171.

Colleton speculated, 'som hope that before the expiration of the dayes apointed there wilbe published a kind of mitigation or revocation' and 'others thinke that nothing wilbe don'.[446] It was not just Catholics who believed that the proclamation of 6 May had been issued purely to secure the parliamentary subsidies. The king had more or less admitted it himself.[447]

Despite John Gee's recent warnings about the swarms of Catholic clergy in the metropolis,[448] there was no mass round-up of clergy. When the aged cleric Davies was dragged off to Tyburn for execution, in front of a huge, expectant crowd, he was reprieved at the last moment. Sir Francis Nethersole lamented on 3 July that this had done more damage than if he had not been proceeded against in the first place.[449]

The only other priest who was arrested and detained at this time was Thomas Cole. Cole ran into the self-obsessed self-publicist John Gee in a London street, was arrested, and, like Davies, was sent to Newgate by the lord mayor after he refused the oath of supremacy. But, despite the protests of the recorder of London, Cole was allowed to go to live with one of the ambassadors.[450] At the beginning of August it was reported that two gentlewomen from the leading Yorkshire recusant family of Tankard had been condemned for helping a priest to escape. Execution of sentence was stayed by order of the judge.[451]

The issue of 'persecution' was, therefore, largely a matter of perception, just as it had always been. The earl of Carlisle had explained to Louis, at an audience early in the morning on 22 July/1 August, that the French had to be realistic about prevailing political conditions in England. Carlisle denied that there was a 'great persecution', such as Louis professed to believe that there was, of English Catholics. Carlisle himself had heard of no such thing. In any case, 'howsoever it were likely enough that there was some quickening and reviving of the lawes', Louis should not concern himself with it. James 'did but therby putt himself into a fitt posture of satisfying his desires, that so the thancks of any future ease' in the condition of James's Catholic subjects might not be attributed to Spain 'but rather

[446] *Letter 46*. On 12 June, Tillières described how he had presented to James two petitions, drawn up by English Catholics and by himself, against the enforcement of the proclamation: PRO, PRO, 31/3/59, fos 136v–137r.

[447] *Letters 45, 48*; *SRP*, I, p. 592, citing PRO, SP 14/163/30 and PRO, SP 14/164/72.

[448] Harmsen, *John Gee's Foot out of the Snare.*

[449] *Letter 49*; PRO, SP 14/169/14.

[450] Anstr., II, p. 68; *Letters 50, 54*. In a Paul's Cross sermon of 31 October 1624 (the published version of which was dedicated to Sir Robert Naunton), Gee mentioned his encounter with Cole, and alleged that Cole had attacked him: John Gee, *Hold Fast* (London, 1624), p. 51 (cited in *Letter 50*).

[451] *Letter 50*; CRS, 68, p. 172.

to this match'. Carlisle asserted that 'to take away the lawes was not' within James's power, at least 'without his parlement'. If he were to 'exercise his grace against the penalty and execution therof [. . .] this must follow the match and not precede' it, and 'so follow that it might appeare to flow out of the clemency and sweetnes of his owne royall heart, and not anothers stipulation'. Louis should remember how much he had resented one of James's recent intercessions, via Carlisle, on behalf of the Huguenots.[452]

A letter arrived on 6 August for Lord Keeper Williams from Conway, who was staying at the earl of Rutland's house at Belvoir. Conway condemned the 'complaintes' which had been 'made to his Majesty of great persecutions lately upon the Roman Catholikes'.[453] (Indeed, as Conway noted, on that very day, in an audience with the king, Effiat denounced the 'furious persecucion of the Romaine Catholicks in England', and explained the 'traverse it would give to the negociacion at Rome'.[454]) Conway and the king could hardly believe it to be true, considering that James remembered 'well the directions he gave conserning the stay of all executions'. The judges also knew 'how far' it was 'from his Majestys [. . .] nature to suffer anny persecution' of 'his subjects espessially in case of religion'. But Conway instructed Williams to find out exactly what the judges had done on circuit.[455]

On the same day, Conway wrote in a similar vein to Sir Richard Weston, the chancellor of the exchequer, asking to know how the king's directions concerning Catholics had been fulfilled.[456] On 7 August, at James's direction, he instructed Carlisle and Holland in Paris to assure the French king that there was no persecution. For the sake of James's honour and the upholding of the law, and for the 'satisfaccion of his parlament', however, some measures were necessary to 'keepe in order the overswellinge humors of some Romaine Catholicks'. In fact, it was all for their own good. Conway insisted to the English ambassadors in Paris that they should remind Louis of the 'art which is imployed to breed misunderstandinge in this soe necessarie and soe usefull treatie for the good of all Christendome for the conservacion of theis crownes'. Those who made these claims that James was a persecutor did not intend 'the good and peace of the Romaine Catholick religion'. Instead, they sought, by 'practize and sedicions', to 'fish for the ends of a Catholick monarchie': in other words, the interests of Spain.[457]

[452] PRO, SP 78/72, fo. 366r; *Letter 49*.
[453] PRO, SP 14/171/22, fo. 28r.
[454] PRO, SP 78/73, fo. 15r; *Letter 53*.
[455] PRO, SP 14/171/22, fo. 28r.
[456] PRO, SP 14/171/21.
[457] PRO, SP 78/73, fo. 15r–v.

The following day, Williams replied to Conway that, since the judges were out of London, he could not yet ascertain what was going on. But the recusants were 'a veryie cunninge and ever whyninge generacion, complayninge rather out of custome than anie true and reall cause'. For 'not one Romaine Catholick' had 'suffred this last circuite in anie countrey of England or Wales'. The judges had had precise instructions 'before their goinge this last circuite'. It was possible that some might have been 'more tart and pressing in their charges and speeches upon the bench than others according to the speciall natures and disposicions of men. But their speeches' had 'drawen noe blood nor anie one severe accion'. The 'messingers of the hiegh comission in both the provinces of Canterburie and Yorke' were 'soe restrayned and brydled up with instruccions for the ease of the Romaine Catholicks as they never have ben before this sommer sithence their first institucion'. The king 'hath ben in the opinion of most men but too too carefull for' the 'ease and immunitie' of the Catholics. At the very most, some of the judges might have 'commaunded the justices to informe themselves exactly of all the recusants in their severall divisions and to present unto them the names of such recusants at the beginning of the next tearme'. Williams opined that it was possible (in fact it was a racing certainty) that 'some justices' might have been

> forward enough in this service, and that the recusants are thereupon startled, and afrayd to bee all forthwith indicted and convicted. But the judges have noe intent at all to proceede in anye rigorous course against them more than to present their names unto his most excellent Majestie and to receave his royall pleasure and direccion what they are to doe therein.[458]

On 9 August the attorney-general, Sir Thomas Coventry, attested that he had not 'violated one syllable' of the king's 'gracious direction'. He thought that the judges on circuit had not done so either, 'and sure I am that att the first assises they can but indite and proclaime for recusancy and they which were indicted and proclaimed this assise are not convicted until the next assises'. The court of exchequer, for its part, had done no more than award

> those ordinary commissions which went of course every yeare until the late connivence for the goods and two parts of the lands of the recusants which commissions will not be returned until the next terme, and then his Majesty may receive an accounte of that which is or will bee donne therupon, and may declare his pleasure for the ease of any to whome hee shall thinke good to extende his grace and favor.

[458] PRO, SP 14/171/27, fo. 35r–v.

'In all this', Coventry could not imagine 'what it is which is accounted a greate persecution'.[459] On that same day, Conway drafted a letter from James to Louis declaring that, 'in contemplation of the marriage', he would 'give all convenient favor' to Roman Catholics as long as they behaved like good subjects.[460] In fact, some priests were undoubtedly now receiving what amounted to royal favour: one week later, John Clare SJ obtained a warrant for his protection, releasing him from the need to obey the May proclamation (which had ordered the Catholic clergy to go into exile) and licensing him to go to Bath to take the waters.[461]

Weston certified on 12 August that he had received no special orders about recusancy revenue but simply took his cue from the king's direction to the judges. He had inquired of the exchequer officials as to 'the ordinary course with recusants for their arrieres due to his Majestie before the late connivence', and 'they brought me an usuall forme of a warrant which I signed'. Its purpose was to 'direct commissions into every county according to the ordinary manner, but how they are proceeded in I know not, but they cannot be said to take effect before they be retourned into the exchequer'. Then, as Coventry had insisted, 'his Majestie may use what clemency' he pleased, 'according to his owne goodnes, or the reason and condition of the times'. Weston, however, had no intention of simply making a 'stay of the generall' course of the law concerning Catholic separatism.[462] On 13 August, Prince Charles wrote to Carlisle that, if the French persisted 'in this new way [. . .] in making an article for our Roman Catholique subjects', then he should 'breake [. . .] the treatie of marriage, keeping the frendshipe in as faire tearmes' as he could.[463]

These attempts at compromise did not deflect French fears that, unless the terms agreed were, at least publicly, as favourable towards James's Catholic subjects as those recently granted, in principle, to the Spanish court, Louis would suffer from the 'calumnies of Spaine' and of 'Jesuitically-affected persons'.[464] Some English Catholics were

[459] PRO, SP 14/171/28, fo. 37r–v.

[460] PRO, SP 14/171/29, fo. 39r; see also PRO, SP 78/73, fo. 16r.

[461] *CSPD, 1623–1625*, p. 328. Smith believed, in mid-August 1624, that priests walked the streets in London 'as freely as before', and that Effiat had done very well for Catholics: AAW, B 26, no. 105.

[462] PRO, SP 14/171/42, fo. 60r–v. Ten days later, on 22 August, Williams was still asking Buckingham 'howe to demeane my selfe to the French embassador in matters concerning recusants' (especially since the judges remained on circuit). The day before, Effiat had 'sent unto me to knowe if I hadd received any order from his Majestye to staye this (as he tearmed it) perseqution', though Williams had denied that there was any 'such matter in this estate': BL, Harleian MS 7000, fo. 159r.

[463] PRO, SP 78/73, fo. 40r.

[464] PRO, SP 78/72, fo. 373r.

well aware how they might exploit this. In the third week of August, as the negotiations over the treaty articles were proceeding in Paris, John Jackson introduced himself to the new French ambassador. He assured him that, in some respects, the secular clergy had been ill-served by the Spaniards and that they could be trusted to work for the conclusion of the Anglo-French treaty.[465] All through September 1624, Effiat proceeded to intervene, on behalf of Catholics, with the duke of Buckingham and the king himself.[466]

This did not mean that the Catholic networks of news gatherers in the counties had desisted from their complaints that there was widespread popular hostility to them. Nor did such complaints come only from those Catholics who tended to look to Spain rather than to France. But the Francophile Catholics who believed that, in some sense, there was still a persecution of themselves and of their co-religionists needed to work hard in order to prevent the French from glossing over it and over them. They certainly tried to force the French negotiators to take more notice of English Catholics' alleged or actual plight than the French would have liked and than their instructions allowed for. The leading secular clergy in England vigorously protested, from time to time, that the French were not doing enough for them.[467] Valaresso suggested to Effiat in September, as they contemplated the Catholics' irritating insistence that there was a terrible persecution in progress, that 'the best plan to get at the real truth was to ask for particulars, making them name some one who had suffered persecution, the time and the place'. Effiat 'entirely agreed'.[468]

What this represented, however, was a sophisticated public debate about politics and religion, as various parties, including Catholics, tried to define what a 'persecution' was and to prove that it either did or did not exist. They did this not merely by comparison, for instance, with the Tudor past but in the context of what contemporaries of different ecclesiological stripes assumed or feared should or might be an entirely new status quo created by an Anglo-French dynastic union.

All the prevarication and arguments in the summer and autumn of 1624 over the exact terms of the treaty did not stop some English Catholics from anticipating the good effects which the treaty would

[465] *Letter 51*; PRO, SP 78/73, fos 63r–68r; PRO, PRO 31/3/59, fo. 210v; Questier, *C&C*, pp. 415–417.

[466] AAW, B 26, no. 139 (cited in *Letter 55*); CRS, 68, pp. 167, 168.

[467] See, e.g., *Letter 56*. On 23 August, two days after John Jackson's visit, Effiat, however, was complaining of the secular clergy's tendency to put their interests before those of the French state: PRO, PRO 31/3/60, fo. 213r [*bis*].

[468] *CSPV, 1623–1625*, p. 444.

finally bring. As early as 13/23 July 1624, Richard Smith could rejoice that, in 'the mach with France', James had 'agreed to all the articles which the French proposed'; and 'the summe for Catholiks' was 'that they shal not be persecuted for practise of their religion in privat'. But 'more the duke wold not agree unto lest he shold offend the puritans of whome he hath made him self head'. Yet, 'if the Catholiks carie them selves moderatly, more in time wilbe graunted'.[469]

Indeed, it seemed, as the marriage negotiations began to move towards a conclusion, that Catholics had a good deal to be optimistic about. On 4/14 August, Matthew Kellison wrote that he had heard from Anthony Champney in Paris that the French match was concluded and that Louis XIII's envoy, Pierre de Bérulle, was being sent to Rome to seek the dispensation.[470] On 28 August/7 September 1624, Thomas More had reported from Rome that Bérulle, on his journey, had written from Turin that he 'will favour us all he maye and attendeth onlie to the procuring of the dispensation'. The secular clergy could confidently rely on the French ambassador in Rome, Philippe de Béthune, count of Sully. He had been their patron during the appellant controversy over twenty years before. More and Rant had been to call on him 'and ther he discoursed with us above an howre and an half'.[471] On the same day, John Colleton in London informed Rant and More that he had (on 1 September) formally written to the pope in favour of the proposed Anglo-French marriage. He had laid 'downe the generall desire of the whole bodie of Catholicks that his Holiness would be pleased to graunt the foresaid dispensation', and the sooner the better.[472] Champney, in Paris, wrote to assure Rant and

[469] AAW, B 26, no. 90.

[470] AAW, B 26, no. 100. Bérulle, the superior of the French Oratory, arrived in Rome in late September: Schreiber, *FC*, pp. 81–82. The use of Bérulle to persuade the pope that the dispensation should be granted was a shrewd French calculation that he would be seen as disinterested and principled, in a way that Philippe de Béthune, count of Sully (the French ambassador in Rome, and brother of the Huguenot duke of Sully) was not: *ibid.*, p. 81; PRO, SP 78/72, fo. 388r–v. Carlisle mentioned to Conway, in a letter of 29 July/8 August 1624, that he intended to persuade Bérulle that the Spaniards, 'pretending to procure a dispensation, suggested extravagant conditions to the pope [...] purposely to crosse the match'; and therefore Carlisle proposed to 'give him withall a brief discourse of the true state of things in England, actuall and possible, that it may serve as a healp to remove such obstacles as may be offred': PRO, SP 78/72, fo. 388v. For Bérulle, see P.A. Klevgard, 'Society and politics in Counter-Reformation France: a study of Bérulle, Vincent de Paul, Olier and Bossuet' (unpublished PhD thesis, Northwestern University, 1971), ch. 2.

[471] *Letters 52, 59*. For the negotiations for the dispensation, conducted in Rome by Bérulle and Béthune, see Albion, *CI*, pp. 68–72.

[472] AAW, B 26, no. 118; Albion, *CI*, pp. 58–59; PRO, PRO 31/3/59, fo. 208v. The offer by the secular clergy to write to Rome had been made by John Jackson to Effiat on 21 August: *Letter 51*. For Colleton's subsequent letter of 22 September 1624, directed to Urban VIII, which urged that, if the dispensation were not granted, this would unleash a new

More that they 'must both help [...] to procure the dispensation'. This should be done 'in the name of our whole clergie', even without specific directions from their clerical colleagues to do so.[473]

As long as Smith remained secure in Richelieu's favour and the secular clergy seemed able to deliver support for the match without provoking the Jacobean regime into direct and overt retaliation, the French would find it worthwhile to deliver the quid pro quo of assisting their suit for a successor to William Bishop, as well as urging the Stuart court to honour its tolerationist promises.[474] At one stage, Richelieu and the nuncio in Paris even considered sending Smith to Rome in order to lobby for the dispensation.[475] On 2/12 September 1624, Smith rejoiced that the match was concluded and signed by both parties, with good conditions for Catholics 'and in some points better than thos of Spayne'.[476]

A special papal curial committee was assembled in late October 1624 to discuss the two topics of whether Henrietta's religion was adequately ring-fenced and whether and how English Catholics would benefit from the marriage.[477] Initially, the papacy accepted the terms hammered out by English and French negotiators. But the real difficulties over the way in which the treaty would work in practice – something which, as we saw, had already threatened to halt the negotiations in August– now surfaced again. During October, heated arguments took place in Paris over the exact terms and mechanisms by which the English crown's guarantees to James's Catholic subjects would be made, and about how far French promises to assist the English military proposals to recover the Palatinate should be set out in a formal diplomatic document.[478] Subsequently, on 21 November/1 December 1624, Rome decided to impose further conditions which would have to be agreed by both regimes – principally that the English promise of toleration for Catholics should be public, not private. James objected strongly. In Paris, Carlisle and Villeauxclercs had a shouting match about it.[479]

wave of persecution by the 'puritans', see AAW, A XVIII, no. 62, pp. 357–358. For Matthew Kellison's letter of 16/26 August 1624 to the pope, requesting the dispensation, see AAW, A XVIII, no. 49, pp. 325–326 (cited in *Letter 51*).

[473] AAW, B 26, no. 103.

[474] *Letter 54*.

[475] *Ibid.*

[476] *Letter 53*; PRO, SP 78/73, fo. 299r. For the other conditions of the treaty, e.g. the dowry, see PRO, SP 78/73, fo. 261r; Tillières, *ME*, p. xiv.

[477] Allison, RS, pp. 190–191; *CSPV, 1623–1625*, pp. 619, 620; Albion, *CI*, p. 65.

[478] PRO, SP 78/73, fos 229r–232v.

[479] Albion, *CI*, pp. 67–74; Allison, RS, pp. 190–191; AAW, B 47, no. 159 (cited in *Letter 75*); AAW, B 47, no. 78 (cited in *Letter 78*).

## The Conclusion of the Anglo-French Treaty

The Stuarts' military exploits during the early stages of the Thirty Years War were a critical index for Catholics to work out what their own political position would be like once the French match was concluded. Catholics could point to the withering uncertainties inside the Jacobean regime as to what kind of war English forces were supposed to be fighting. As Russell comments, the end of the 1624 parliament allowed James to regain some of the initiative he had lost while it was in session. One of the effects of this reassertion of royal authority was that 'the supposed war on which Buckingham had expended so much effort slowly degenerated into one mercenary expedition to the Palatinate'. As we have already seen, the employment of Mansfelt was arguably Buckingham's crucial strategic error at this point. Moreover, Mansfelt's campaign, 'when it might have contributed effectively to war against Spain by relieving the key siege of Breda', as the French suggested, 'was forbidden to do so by James', who would not sanction the use of military force against troops deployed by the Spaniards.[480]

The prolonged and ghastly siege of Breda had started in August 1624. The archduchess Isabella could, by 17/27 October, boast that Breda was completely isolated, and that the prince of Orange was failing to dislodge the forces surrounding it.[481] Starvation and the plague had already set in. As Spinola increased his stranglehold on the town, the battle of wills between him and the defenders, and the question of whether Mansfelt could intervene, even if hardly related to the Palatinate issue, became a way of assessing how far the entire British war strategy was going to work.[482] For all James's professions that he would not allow the military forces at his disposal to be used

[480] Russell, *PEP*, p. 202; Ruigh, *1624*, p. 386; Lockyer, *Buckingham*, pp. 222–224. For James's guarantee, finally issued by Conway on 29 December 1624, that Mansfelt would not engage in hostilities in the dominions of Philip IV or of the archduchess Isabella, see PRO, SP 78/73, fo. 366r; *CGB*, II, pp. 590–591. The Spanish council of state initially disapproved of the apparently rash decision of the Habsburg administration in Flanders to besiege Breda: *CCE*, pp. 180, 187; see also Elliott, *The Count-Duke of Olivares*, p. 236. The Brussels administration had itself been uncertain in July and August that the proposed siege was feasible, but Spinola insisted upon it: *CGB*, I, pp. 505, 507, 510.

[481] *CCE*, p. 185; see also *ibid.*, p. 188.

[482] For the arrangements at the French court, recorded by Carlisle on 21/31 August 1624, for regular payments to be made to Mansfelt, see PRO, SP 78/73, fo. 71r–v. On 23 September/3 October, the English ambassadors in Paris reported that the French 'desire an answerable proceeding in England' to the support which Mansfelt was receiving in France: *ibid.*, fo. 193v; for James's guarantees of financial aid to him, and for recruitment of men to be shipped to France, consequent on Louis's declaration of his 'conjunction in the accion', see *ibid.*, fo. 225r.

directly against Spanish troops, the archduchess was not so sure. She wrote to Philip on 16/26 November that James was raising a large number of soldiers under Mansfelt's command and, even though he had disclaimed any intention of levying war against Spanish military power, she thought that James 'veut secourir Bréda soit directement, soit en faisant une diversion'. The Dutch were recruiting around Breda. The siege was becoming a crucial trial of strength. The levying of additional troops, insisted the archduchess, was inevitable: 'il n'y a pas moyen de faire face autrement à tant d'ennemis'.[483] A month later, she feared that Mansfelt's force would establish 'sa jonction avec une troupe française', and she believed it would head straight for Breda, even though James had declared that his sole purpose was to set up the elector once more.[484]

The Catholics around London had, as we saw earlier, followed Mansfelt's movements almost obsessively as he came and went raising money and men. Every apparent hiccough in the recruitment process, every mishap with his shipping arrangements, and every incident of public disorder as his low-quality recruits for his expeditionary force (unpaid until they reached Dover) were assembled and taken to their rendezvous point allowed Catholic observers to pour scorn on the apparent schizophrenia in the crown's foreign policy, which was concluding a 'Catholic' dynastic marriage for the prince of Wales but could not even make its mind up about whether it wanted to be fully involved in a 'Protestant' military conflict.[485] James's understanding of the general thrust of the proposed campaign appears to have been quite different from that of many of his subjects, although it was clear that the French were also reluctant to commit themselves to war against the Habsburgs.[486]

It was in the middle of this somewhat half-hearted military exercise, as Mansfelt raised his army and hobnobbed with the great and the good in the capital, that arrangements were made for representatives of the French crown to cross the Channel and finalize the treaty. Several weeks before the French secretary of state, Villeauxclercs, arrived for this purpose, it appeared that Effiat had already secured something like a toleration. Zuane Pesaro, Valaresso's replacement as Venetian ambassador in London, reported on 1 October that the Catholics had been badgering Effiat to demand 'a *supersedeat* [*sic*] under the public seal for non-execution, as being entirely contrary to the laws and to the decisions and promises made to the parliament'.

483 *CCE*, p. 191.

484 *Ibid.*, p. 192.

485 *Letters 67*, *68*, *70*; Lockyer, *Buckingham*, p. 210.

486 Albion, *CI*, p. 63; Lockyer, *Buckingham*, pp. 206–207, 222–223.

Effiat was proud, instead, to have 'obtained an order to withdraw all commands for executions against the Catholics for the chancellor of the exchequer who has charge thereof, thus obtaining actual relief for them without upsetting anything'. Effiat himself had described it on 26 September as 'un supersedeas qui est une cessation générale', one which even Catholics had not expected. It was 'une chose signée de la main du roy et scellé de son grand sceau, en somme un acte très publicque et qui fut résolu en plain conseil, le dit roy l'ayant assemblé exprès pour cela'. James had told him that he would 'non seulement cesser la persécution mais que l'on rendroit tout ce que l'on pouvait avoir exigé des Catholiques en vertu de commissions qui avoient esté expediés mesme avant qu'il m'eust donné sa parole'. Effiat lost no time in telling his Catholic contacts what he had done; and he wrote to Béthune 'cette bon nouvelle' in response to two letters from Béthune 'par lesquelles il me prie de l'advertir soigneusement de ce qui se faict en faveur des Catholiques touchant leur persécution'.[487]

On 9 October, a perplexed if not disgusted John Chamberlain mentioned that 'our papists begin to hold up their heads again, for wheras writts were gon out to inquire' of

> their lands and arrierages for not payeng according to the statut, letters are gon downe to suppresse that course and, yf any have payed, to restore yt: yt beeing (as is saide) the first article of this new alliance that no Romish Catholikes be troubled or molested for their conscience in body or goods.[488]

'There will be, as we gather, a calme', remarked Thomas Roper on 14 October. In fact, Roper had heard that 'the preistes and prisoners in Newgate are this daye to be released, and that there is order come to my lord keeper how to directe the judges for their carriadge about recusantes'. Furthermore, 'all the informers are of a sudden repressed'.[489] In mid-October, a priest, exiled but now returned from abroad, was (to the astonishment of Lord Zouch) ordered to be released on a writ from the king's bench prison. Zouch could not believe that James intended this to happen; Conway assured him that he did.[490]

487 *CSPV, 1623–1625*, p. 456; PRO, PRO 31/3/60, fo. 255r–v.

488 McClure, *LJC*, pp. 581–582. On 24 September, the Venetian ambassadors could note that, of the Anglo-French treaty's twenty-six articles, eleven were 'in favour of the Catholic religion, either for the service of Madame or the advantage of the Catholics'; also, Effiat claimed to have done even more for them than his instructions allowed 'and much more than the Spaniards', especially in the arrangements for the education of the children of the marriage, in provision of chaplains for Charles's bride, and 'even in the sureties for the liberties of the Catholics': *CSPV, 1623–1625*, p. 451. For the articles as they were eventually signed on 10/20 November, see Albion, *CI*, p. 63.

489 AAW, B 27, no. 15.

490 PRO, SP 14/173/59.

Conway told Lord Keeper Williams on 22 November 1624 that, now that the marriage articles were signed in France and that Villeauxclercs was expected at any time to arrive to ratify them, James intended, the moment the Frenchman disembarked, 'in contemplacion of that joyfull allyance [. . .] to give libertie to all the priests, saving those that by libertie' might 'bee exposed to dainger, which are those who have taken the oath of allegeance'. Williams was to see to the necessary paperwork, but it must 'appeare' that 'this libertie and favour' had been granted 'for things past, which they might forfeit if hereafter they' failed to 'governe themselves modestly and without scandall'.[491]

On 22 November also, Colleton wrote to More and Rant in Rome with the news that the order had gone out the previous day for bonfires and bells to celebrate the conclusion of the match. In a letter to More, his cousin Thomas Roper recorded that the ordnance at the Tower was discharged, 'and a ballette for joy mayde which here I send you'.[492] On 25 November, Colleton was also able to declare that Effiat had recently told the seculars that 'his Majestie had graunted the cessation of all penall statutes and other troubles for religion untill the 15 daye of Februarie next', in other words 'before the daie that the parliament' was expected to meet.[493]

When Villeauxclercs arrived on 6 December, he staged a public-relations coup by insisting on the release of several Catholics who had recently been put under restraint at Dover.[494] Prominent secular priests, including Colleton, Edward Bennett, Joseph Haynes, and William Shelley, visited the new ambassador, who carried directions to make contact with the leaders of the English Catholic community.[495] He

[491] PRO, SP 14/175/30, fo. 40r.

[492] AAW, B 27, nos 57, 58; *CSPV, 1623–1625*, pp. 503–504.

[493] AAW, B 27, no. 59.

[494] See *Letters 62, 64*. As R.E. Shimp points out, Villeauxclercs was briefed also to 'cajole James into open war with Spain', though James still refused: Shimp, 'A Catholic marriage', p. 13; for the purposes of Villeauxclercs's embassy, set out in a document of 17/27 November 1624, see PRO, PRO 31/3/60, fos 284r–295r. John Hacket argued that Villeauxclercs was 'a fervent zealot in his own religion' and listened too readily to the grievances of 'our nimble-headed recusants': Hacket, *SR*, part I, p. 212. For Hacket's account of the case made by Lord Keeper Williams to Villeauxclercs in justification of the legal status quo concerning recusancy and the technical proscription of the Catholic clergy, see *ibid.*, pp. 213–222. Hacket claimed that Villeauxclercs pushed the toleration issue so hard that James was 'observed to begin to be cooler in the treaty for the marriage than he had been': *ibid.*, p. 213.

[495] Albion, *CI*, p. 64. Hacket scornfully claimed that the English Catholics resorted 'daily to Mass in the embassadors house', and that they 'found access unto him and sighed out their grievances before him that their priests, who adventured to come to them for their souls health, were executed for traytors; and themselves were set such fines for their conscience that they were utterly impoverished', and begged him to alleviate their suffering: Hacket, *SR*, part I, p. 212.

made a commitment that he would do what he could for them and that they should not thereafter be troubled for religion.

On 12 December, Roper remarked, Villeauxclercs and Effiat 'after dinner were some three houres in private with the kinge in Trinity Colledge at Cambridge, none being presant but the duke and the prince'. Roper had heard that 'certayne articles were presented by them to the king, which his Majestie seigned, and that night they dispatched an expresse post into France with them, and thence they were to be sent to Rome'. The hope was that 'uppon the seight of them, his Holinesse' would 'graunte a dispensation'. Roper sent to More 'his Majesties graunte unto the ambassador in the behalfe of recusantes'. Catholics trusted that the ambassador would 'see these thinges performed by his Majesties officers before his departure'. If, commented Roper, 'these thinges be performed, his Majesties subjectes that are recusants will then say viva viva la France'.[496] Roper further noted that Villeauxclercs took a far harder line than Effiat over the performance of the royal guarantees of toleration to Catholics.[497] The earl of Kellie understood, on 15 December, that 'their is derektione gevin' to the lord treasurer and the chancellor of the exchequer 'that noe more processes' should 'goe out against recusants', and 'sutche be recalled that are out, and their bands takin bakke that wes gevin'; and 'this makes men believe that the same courss goes on now with the Frenche that was concludit with the Spainyard'.[498]

On 24 December 1624, following his meeting with the French ambassadors in Cambridge, James instructed Conway (who, Pesaro said subsequently, was blamed by the French for the impediments cast in the way of an effective toleration) that the law officers of the crown should be told to 'forbeare and cause to be forborne all manner of persecution' of Roman Catholics 'for the exercise of their religion', even though, on the same day, a commission went out to Abbot, Williams, and others to exile such clergy as had been 'convicted or attainted of or for any high treason or other offences whatsoever, and

[496] AAW, B 27, no. 79. See also AAW, B 47, no. 53; Hacket, *SR*, part I, p. 210; PRO, SP 78/73, fo. 362r–v; Lockyer, *Buckingham*, p. 209. In Paris, on 22 December 1624/1 January 1625, Anthony Champney was still complaining that 'the French conceive and utter their conceipt playnly that the Catholikes in Ingland are Spaniards': AAW, B 47, no. 45.

[497] *Letter 65*; see also *CSPV, 1623–1625*, p. 504. Both James and Charles signed the private agreement which granted relief to Catholics: Albion, *CI*, p. 63. For the French ambassadors' account of their meeting at Cambridge, see PRO, PRO 31/3/60, fo. 305r *et seq*. They recorded that they had been assured that 'les Catholiques de ce pays ne seront jamais inquietés pour raison de serment de fidelité': *ibid.*, fo. 305v.

[498] *HMCMK*, p. 216; cf. McClure, *LJC*, p. 589.

also all other' Catholic clergymen whom it 'shalbe thought convenient or fitt to be soe dealt withall'.[499]

Villeauxclercs's insistence really does seem to have been the prime motivation for the toleration order which went through in late December. No more money was to be received for recusancy fines; discharges were to be issued for recusancy debts due at the exchequer; all money paid since the previous Trinity term was to be returned; no further proceedings against recusants were to be allowed; and all cash to be refunded was to be delivered to two Catholic middlemen.[500] The proceedings of the high commission were halted. Instructions went out that the fines levied on recusants under the act of uniformity should cease, and James ordered Williams to make out the necessary writs for releasing imprisoned Catholic clergy.[501]

Thus, as the new year came in, some Catholics thought that they could discern the outlines of a new and tolerant order. In fact, the debate continued throughout early 1625 among Catholic observers as to whether they had obtained toleration or not. It was not entirely clear whether they had, in any sense, won real rather than theoretical concessions from the crown. If they had, was this invalidated by sporadic instances of recusants being imprisoned or harassed again? Was the crown really trying to put a stop to such incidents? Was the supposed toleration merely a sham?[502]

Bérulle had left Rome in January 1625. On 4 February, Conway observed that Bérulle had 'arrived at last with the dispensation', but the document was being retained in the hands of the papal nuncio in Paris.[503] The nuncio, Bernardino Spada, had sent sceptical reports to Rome about the French intentions in the treaty. As a result, the official and final version of the dispensation (granted by Urban VIII on 21 November/1 December 1624), which had been sent to Spada

[499] PRO, SP 14/177/10, fo. 13r; PRO, SP 14/177/11, fo. 14r; *CSPV, 1623–1625*, p. 539; PRO, C 231/4, fo. 173v. For the promises made to Villeauxclercs and Effiat that Conway had been ordered to dispatch warrants to free imprisoned Catholics and to restore property to them which had been sequestrated 'depuis ledit traicté', see PRO, PRO 31/3/60, fo. 307v.

[500] PRO, SP 14/177/37, 39.i; *Letter 60*; Albion, *CI*, p. 64. Subsequently, on 1 February 1625, Conway directed James, Baron Ley, and Sir Richard Weston to implement the promised discharges of recusants' property; at the same time, Ley and Weston ordered the exchequer to 'give dischardge for all rentes and revenues for which any money hath bin receaved, bonds taken, lands or goods seized, or onely inquisicions taken'; and all money taken by virtue of commissions issued since the previous Trinity term should be redelivered, 'the bonds given up and the lands and goods dischardged as cleerely from the power [...] of these seizures, and from any burthen or incumbrance to rise by them, as possibly and legally may be done': *CSPD, 1623–1625*, p. 465; BL, Additional MS 35832, fo. 149r.

[501] PRO, SP 14/177/22, 23, 24, 25, 28, 29, 31, 36, 39, 45; Albion, *CI*, p. 64.

[502] See, e.g., *Letters 72, 73, 74*; AAW, B 47, no. 187.

[503] PRO, SP 78/74, fo. 51r.

(whereas Bérulle had carried an unofficial one), was a great deal tougher. It effectively altered the treaty as it had been signed between the two crowns.[504] On 14/24 February, Carlisle and Holland relayed to Conway how Villeauxclercs had presented them 'with a copie of the articles [. . .] which he said he was ashamed to reade unto us, but [. . .] they were the conditions as the pope had limited the dispensation unto, and they were bound to present them unto us'. Louis himself apologized to them; but he said it was 'not in his power to alter it'. The English ambassadors were convinced that they were seeing a repeat of the final absurdity of the Anglo-Spanish negotiations. They believed that 'all these new condicions have beene forged here' in France, and advised James to 'reject these presumptuous and unreasonable demandes with a sharpe stoute negative, not admitting of any the least of them, for that would be to enter into a new treaty to the losse of tyme' and 'hazard to the whole busines, and to give them courage and appetite to presse for more'.[505]

There was a genuine possibility that the treaty might founder at this late stage. However, as Simon Adams says, Richelieu 'reasoned that Buckingham was so committed to the French alliance that he could not refuse'.[506] In the third week of February, Effiat lodged a protest about the slowness of the Jacobean regime to deliver on its promises of toleration, even though, on 1 March, he bitterly complained to his master that the English Catholics displayed 'une grande ingratitude' towards their royal benefactor and had forgotten that Louis had stopped 'le cours de la plus cruelle persécution'.[507] On 24 February/6 March, Carlisle and Holland had reported from Paris that Villeauxclercs, a 'false ingratefull fellowe', was semi-publicly averring that, although Louis XIII had given his royal word in the matter of the treaty, he would do better to break the compact 'for that therby he might make himself cheif of the Catholique league, and being so, he need not feare the kinge of Great Brittayne and the king of Spayne both'.[508] It was clear to the English that, while Richelieu gloried 'to have been a principal actor' in the conclusion of the match, a cabal was gathering which wanted both to remove the cardinal and the queen mother and radically to change French foreign policy.[509]

[504] *CSPV, 1623–1625*, pp. 576, 588, 597, 615; Albion, *CI*, pp. 72–73; Allison, RS, pp. 190–191; Shimp, 'A Catholic marriage', p. 15; *HMCMK*, p. 222; PRO, PRO 31/3/61, fo. 63v; *Letter 75*.

[505] PRO, SP 78/74, fos 60r–61r; see also Philip Yorke, *Miscellaneous State Papers from 1501 to 1726*, 2 vols (London, 1778), I, pp. 551–555.

[506] Adams, PC, p. 362. Effiat had advised Louis on 1 March that 'la fortune dudit duc estoit perdu s'il venoit à se rompre': PRO, PRO 31/3/61, fo. 64v.

[507] PRO, SP 78/74, fos 68r–v, 74r, 80r; *Letter 72*; PRO, PRO 31/3/61, fo. 72r.

[508] PRO, SP 78/74, fo. 78r.

[509] *Ibid.*; see also AAW, B 47, no. 78.

On 11 March, Conway tried to assure Effiat that the toleration order was on the verge of going through and that, if James 'escrivoit sa [*sic*] lettres aux juges, sheriffes et autres officiers, ce seroit la mesme chose qu'une proclamation'. The king would keep the promises made in favour of the Catholics. Effiat should not try to prescribe the means by which the king's beneficence should be distributed, as this would be counter-productive.[510] The next day, Conway wrote to the attorney-general with a list of Catholics whom the French ambassador had demanded should have freedom. The regime was happy in principle to grant favour but, added Conway, 'not in the public way they desire'.[511] On 14 March, Henry de Vic described the attorney-general's irate questioning of the Catholics' representatives about those who had been identified as prisoners exclusively because of their religion. The attorney-general launched an inquiry among the keepers of the London prisons in order to ascertain whether the Catholics' assertions were true.[512] A day later, a still angry attorney-general wrote back to Conway that he had looked into the cases which the French ambassador had specified and found that few of the people named were imprisoned for religion alone. He knew 'no cause why those that abuse his Majesties clemency by terming it persecution should, by such an importunity to my lord ambassador, procure greater favour than they have' already.[513] On 17 March, Williams complained to Buckingham that Effiat was 'fired with some complaints of our recusants, who (I verily beleeve) worke upon him purposelye, findinge him to be of a combustible disposition'. The lord keeper cited the letter he had received from Archbishop Mathew 'which shewes howe reallye his Majestyes promise hath beene in that kinde performed'. Williams advised Buckingham to reiterate to Effiat that the judges' proceedings against Catholic separatists were no more than 'orations [. . .] opening all the penal lawes; and the inditements, being presented by the countrey, cannot be refused by the judges. But the judges are ordered to execute nothing actuallye against the recusants nor will they doe it during the negociation'. Williams claimed that, with each of the ambassador's secretary's visits, he ordered those thus indicted to be transferred to the king's bench, 'out of the power and reach of the justices of the peace'; and, 'beinge there, the kinge maye and doth release them at his pleasure'.[514]

[510]PRO, SP 78/74, fo. 106r.

[511]*CSPD, 1623–1625*, p. 496; *Letter 73*.

[512]PRO, SP 78/74, fo. 124r–v.

[513]PRO, SP 14/185/54, fo. 83v; see also PRO, SP 14/185/95.

[514]BL, Harleian MS 7000, fo. 174r–v. On 5 April, however, Conway ordered Abbot to discharge specific prisoners, as named by the French ambassador, or to produce evidence that they were held for temporal causes: *CSPD, 1625–1626*, p. 6.

The basically unsympathetic Pesaro noted, towards the end of March 1625, that 'some unhappy accidents are always happening in the persecution of the Catholics' and that 'those of the county of York have complained bitterly of the measures from which they have recently suffered'. Pesaro thought that the French diplomatic service was genuinely and generally doing its best and had even 'obtained royal letters under the seal with orders to the archbishop of York', Tobias Mathew, 'to stop the persecution'. Although there were rumours that 'free worship may not be authorised in any form', Effiat 'always works hard for the benefit of the Catholics, but they never cease making representations to the contrary at Rome to the despair of those who wish them well'.[515]

These delays and difficulties fomented more rumours, namely that the Spanish match would be revived. James himself had fuelled such rumours by dispatching envoys to Spain on 11 March to request a re-opening of the negotiations. They carried an invitation for Gondomar to return.[516] Predictably, Richard Smith suspected that the Jesuits had encouraged the incorporation of conditions in the dispensation which would prove politically unacceptable.[517]

There was an eleventh-hour diplomatic compromise whereby James, in fraught discussions with Effiat, refused to alter the treaty conditions as the papal dispensation required, in particular the demand that the *écrit particulier* should be 'confirmed by a public declaration'. But he agreed to write a private letter to the French king with a guarantee concerning how the existing articles would be interpreted. This was apparently enough. For various reasons – not least, the impending arrival of Cardinal Barberini to broker a Bourbon–Habsburg agreement in Italy – the French were now determined that the marriage should go ahead. In the end, it was the Roman curia and Spada who were forced, by English and French intransigence, to give in. The new papal conditions for granting the dispensation were withdrawn, and the document was handed over.[518]

Despite this last-minute compromise and the real uncertainty over how far the religious clauses of the treaty were likely to take effect, the anxiety caused to some of the regime's officials by this new course was clear for all to see. The attorney-general's correspondence shows how worried some ministers were by the prospect of implementing

[515] *CSPV, 1623–1625*, pp. 620–621.

[516] Allison, RS, p. 191; *CSPV, 1623–1625*, pp. 468, 472, 474, 484, 486, 493, 495, 499, 522, 610, 616; Shimp, 'A Catholic marriage', p. 15; Adams, PC, p. 345; see also *Letter 77*.

[517] Allison, RS, p. 191; *Letter 78*.

[518] Schreiber, *FC*, pp. 83–86; cf. Albion, *CI*, pp. 72–76; Allison, RS, pp. 191–193; Bodleian Library, Tanner MS 73, fo. 516r; AAW, B 47, no. 154.

the regime's promises. Already, on 15 March, Coventry had written to Conway asking whether they genuinely meant to suspend the act of uniformity's one-shilling fine and also not to levy the forfeitures of £20 each month on convicted recusants' estates. Coventry thought it inadvisable to suspend the one-shilling fine since it would 'cause so generall a divulging of his Majesties purpose in these matters'.[519]

In the midst of the bargaining over the dispensation, King James died, relatively unexpectedly, on 27 March 1625. On 1 May, Charles sent orders to the increasingly beleaguered lord keeper that, on the pretext supplied by the impending marriage, all the crown's officers should be directed to suspend proceedings against Catholics.[520] Pardons began to be dispatched to specific recusants and priests, including, for example, John Percy SJ.[521] Of course, this did not prevent those officials who were less than convinced by the crown's proceedings from enforcing what they, correctly, believed the letter of the law still to be. During the summer months, recusancy prosecutions did in fact continue, temporarily ensnaring even some Catholic notables such as the earl of Clanricarde.[522] Charles's Protestant subjects did not want to believe that he was simply going to give effect to whatever had been promised to the French on the issue of toleration. On 13 April, Joseph Mead had been optimistic that Charles would be a new broom, for he understood that the king had 'ordered under his hand that no recusant papist shall have any mourning' for King James, 'of what rank soever he be'.[523] On 6 May, Mead believed that Charles had expelled from his household an Irish earl who would not attend divine service with him.[524]

Of course, this somewhat unstable state of partial de facto toleration does not look all that different from the position and condition of Catholics throughout much, though by no means all, of the early Stuart period. What was different was that the context for it was

[519] PRO, SP 14/185/54, fo. 84r–v. By 25 March, Pesaro understood that, although the lord treasurer had 'ordered repayment to the Catholics by degrees', the Catholics 'were not satisfied'. They wanted 'a general order for the restitution of their goods also, which would amount to a declaration against the laws, such as the king cannot make', nor was Effiat 'inclined to go to this extreme': *CSPV, 1623–1625*, p. 625.

[520] PRO, SP 16/2/1.

[521] PRO, SP 16/2/22. Albion notes that, 'in fulfilment of his promises', Charles ordered Williams to 'stay the execution of the penal laws', whereupon '3,000 letters were sent out to the judges and bishops', although, informally, many Catholics who expected to benefit were told that they would have to wait until the end of the forthcoming parliamentary session: Albion, *CI*, p. 76.

[522] PRO, SP 16/4/63, 64, 68; J.S. Cockburn (ed.), *Calendar of Assize Records: Kent indictments: James I* (London, 1980), no. 993; Questier, *C&C*, pp. 425–426.

[523] Birch, *CTCI*, I, p. 10.

[524] *Ibid.*, p. 20.

entirely novel: a dynastic marriage to a princess whose government's representatives had made some very public statements about the necessity of actual tolerance of Catholics as a condition for the marriage.

On 12 May 1625, the recently arrived Richard Smith found it encouraging that 'I have bene here this forthnight and I heare not that the state taketh any notice of me'. Amazingly, Effiat 'offered me divers times to present me to his Majestie and the duke, if I wold', though Smith preferred to 'stay that til the coming of our queene'.[525]

## The Arrival of Henrietta Maria

The new queen's imminent appearance had already provoked a good deal of speculation within the English Catholic community about the likely composition of her entourage.[526] It had seemed at one point that her confessor would be a Jesuit.[527] In the end, however, there was no Jesuit chaplain provided for her, even though the Jesuits had, Smith claimed, been in communication with the countess of Buckingham in order to get close to the new queen.[528] (In fact, Bérulle became her confessor.[529]) With a bad grace, the seculars suspected, the Jesuit provincial Richard Blount approved the choice – for the queen's liturgical and spiritual service – of the bishop of Mende (Richelieu's nephew Daniel Du Plessis), Bérulle, and the Oratorians.[530]

Just before the finalization of the marriage, the defence of Breda became unsustainable. The siege had been a test of how far the British commitment to the anti-Habsburg cause would hold up. Champney wished the town would fall, for then 'Mansfeilts armie would goe into smoake and [. . .] the day would growe clere that our kings intentions might be seene'.[531] James had, as we have seen, forbidden Mansfelt to take part in the attempt to lift the siege, and although this order was rescinded by Charles after James's death by then it was far too late.[532]

[525] *Letter 80*.

[526] See, e.g., *Letter 62*.

[527] AAW, A XIX, no. 2, p. 3. Richard Ireland had mentioned in his letter to Rant of 25 November/5 December 1624 that her confessor would be a bishop, 'which must be a Jesuit as it is commonly reported even by some of the Societye': AAW, B 27, no. 69; see also *Letter 64*.

[528] *Letter 69*.

[529] AAW, A XIX, no. 32, p. 105.

[530] AAW, B 47, no. 123 (cited in *Letter 85*); see also *Letter 53*; *CSPD, 1625–1626*, p. 67; C. Hibbard, 'Henrietta Maria and the transition from princess to queen', *Court Historian*, 5 (2000), p. 23; Albion, *CI*, pp. 81, 108; Tillières, *ME*, pp. 63–64.

[531] AAW, B 47, no. 47.

[532] Adams, PC, p. 354; Lockyer, *Buckingham*, p. 243.

On 2/12 April 1625, Champney observed that Mansfelt had arrived at Flushing with his troops in an appalling state. He was unlikely to 'doe anie thing either for the releiving of Breda or the recoverie of the Palatinate'. This would 'make our king and prince' (Champney was unaware that James had died) 'think they have committed an errour in going so farr that way after the puritaynes conduct'.[533] On 24 April/4 May, William Trumbull set down how, in Brussels, 'this day hath ben taken up with extraordinary devotion, espetially by our Englishe Romishe Spanishe Catholicks, for the good successe of the Marquis Spinola' in the siege of the hapless town.[534] An attempt in early May to relieve Breda, led by Sir Horace Vere, the earl of Oxford, and William of Nassau failed completely.[535]

Soon it was clear that the Anglo-French alliance was worth little more, militarily, than the paper on which it was written. The French and their allies had, even if only temporarily as it turned out, already achieved their immediate military objectives in the Valtelline during late 1624 and 1625: in other words, before the English could call on them to honour their promises over the Palatinate. In consequence, the French drew back from their commitment to assist James's son-in-law.[536] Breda capitulated, and the archduchess Isabella entered in triumph.[537]

[533] AAW, B 47, no. 49; *Letter 76*. Mansfelt had departed in late January 1625, taking his men to Holland. Those who had the misfortune to be sent to Geertruidenberg were unable to disembark and were struck down by infection on the ships: Lockyer, *Buckingham*, p. 228.

[534] PRO, SP 77/17, fo. 92r.

[535] *CSPV, 1625–1626*, pp. 46–47, 61; *Letter 82*. For the account (dated 8/18 May) of the failed attempt, written by the Catholic Captain John Langworth, who was serving under Sir Edward Parham in the English regiment stationed in front of Breda, see PRO, SP 77/17, fo. 121r–v; see also *CSPD, 1625–1626*, p. 154.

[536] Allison, RS, p. 197; Schreiber, *FC*, p. 82; *CSPV, 1623–1625*, pp. 520, 536, 562, and *passim*; *HMCMK*, pp. 214, 219, 235; Ferrini and de Mas, *Lettere a William Cavendish*, pp. 294, 297; Shimp, 'A Catholic marriage', p. 13. Some English Catholics were horrified at the atrocities committed by French troops against Catholics in the Valtelline (in pursuit of the French court's alliance with the region's Protestants): *Letter 76*. In fact, the French military initiative in the region, after initial successes, subsequently ground to a halt for lack of naval support. Richelieu was forced to negotiate the Treaty of Monzón (March 1626) with the Spaniards, prior to turning to deal with the Huguenots: Richard Bonney, *The European Dynastic States, 1494–1660* (Oxford, 1991), pp. 207–208; Albion, *CI*, p. 5; T. Osborne, 'Abbot Scaglia, the duke of Buckingham and Anglo-Savoyard relations during the 1620s', *European History Quarterly*, 30 (2000), p. 19. Conrad Russell interprets the breakdown of the Anglo-French amity primarily from a domestic angle. He argues that the French had required tolerationist concessions from the regime in England which could not but irritate Hispanophobe sentiment. However, they had also demanded that Charles should sustain a war effort. This was something which he could not easily do once he had thus alienated those elements of the political nation which would be asked to provide the necessary revenue: Russell, *PEP*, pp. 209–210.

[537] *Letter 82*.

Meanwhile, the marriage compact had been sealed in Paris on 1/11 May 1625. The ceremony took place at Notre Dame and was based on the ritual provided for Marguerite de Valois and Henri de Navarre in 1571. The duke of Chevreuse acted as proxy for Charles.[538] Buckingham set off for France in order to greet Charles's bride and, at the same time, to try – though in the event unsuccessfully – to give life and a measure of permanence to the military alliance between the two realms.[539]

On 8/18 June, Champney heard that Charles was 'between London and Dover, expecting the arrivall of his queene'. The countess of Buckingham 'with divers ladies' had gone to meet Henrietta Maria.[540] The ladies in question included some notable Catholics, for instance Jane Savage (the wife of John Paulet, Lord St John) and her mother Elizabeth Darcy, the wife of Sir Thomas Savage.[541] Henrietta Maria landed at Dover on 12 June (as George Fisher remarked, she and Charles 'bedded togeather the second night') and the royal couple reached London on 16 June.[542]

What was immediately obvious was that the political manoeuvring and bickering which had marked the Catholics' struggle for favour and influence before the marriage would continue with a vengeance after Henrietta Maria arrived. The clergy were no shrinking violets in their determination to gain access to this new source of favour. For, noted Fisher on 17 June, 'the very day of ther arrivall here, our new master', Bishop Richard Smith, 'attended with 5 of us, visited' Bérulle, the duke of Chevreuse, and Villeauxclercs. They all 'promised to doe ther utmost endeavour and all good offices for Catholikes so that now we are laboring how to setle matters, and to free our selves from the burden of persecution wich hath hitherto pressed us'.[543] It must have been encouraging for the secular priests that, as Pesaro remarked,

538 Hibbard, 'Henrietta Maria', p. 17; Allison, RS, p. 193; PRO, SP 78/73, fo. 261r; PRO, PRO 31/3/61, fo. 69v.

539 *Letter 80*; Shimp, 'A Catholic marriage', pp. 16–17; Lockyer, *Buckingham*, pp. 236–238; Adams, PC, pp. 362–363; *Salvetti*, p. 17.

540 *Letter 83*.

541 *Letter 82*; L. Boothman and Sir Richard Hyde Parker (eds), *Savage Fortune* (Suffolk Records Society, Woodbridge, 2006), pp. xxxix–xl.

542 Allison, RS, p. 193; AAW, B 48, no. 34, fo. 97r; *Letter 84*; PRO, SP 16/3/69. For the ceremonial and ritual accompanying Henrietta's arrival, notably in Canterbury, see Hibbard, 'Henrietta Maria', p. 18, citing M. Toynbee, 'The wedding journey of King Charles I', *Archaeologia Cantiana*, 69 (1955), pp. 75–89; see also C. Hibbard, 'Henrietta Maria in the 1630s: perspectives on the role of consort queens in *ancien régime* courts', in I. Atherton and J. Sanders (eds), *The 1630s* (Manchester, 2006), pp. 94–95.

543 AAW, B 48, no. 34, fo. 97r (cited in *Letter 85*). See also *CSPV, 1625–1626*, p. 81.

the queen's train consisted of 'a bishop and twenty-four Bérullists or fathers of the Oratory, Jesuits being absolutely excluded'.[544]

For Catholics such as Thomas Roper, all seemed bright. He exulted on 23 June that, 'on Sonday last [. . .] about 12 a clocke', the queen came 'by water from Whitehall to Somersette House to the duke of Cheverous where she heard service performed with great reverence by Monsieur Berule. There wanted some cairefull attendantes at the doore of the chapell, beinge present there halfe Protestantes, yet I heare not of any great misbehavior amonge them'. On Tuesday, the king and queen dined at the banqueting house, and 'the two dukes did contend who should exceede the other, yet Chevrous was judged to surpasse our duke, since Chevrous hathe feasted the kinge and queene at Sommersette House and Buckingh[am] hathe don the like at Yorke House'. Chevreuse had been angered by the evidence of continued legal proceedings against Catholics, in particular the case of one of Roper's neighbours. This man had been 'committed to the Counter for a debte to the kinge contracted for [. . .] recusancy'. Chevreuse 'complayned to the kinge, and his Majestie was informed that there was none troubled for recusancy, but that it was for debte, and so Cheverous was told, who hathe furder enquired of the truthe, and founde it to be for recusancy and no other cause'. Both Chevreuse and Villeauxclercs were 'zealous' even though, it had to be conceded, they were ultimately pessimistic about royal guarantees of toleration to Catholics.[545]

Some Catholics affected to believe that only meagre provision had been made for the formal and ceremonial expressions of the queen's Catholicism, certainly nothing compared with what had been envisaged for the infanta in 1623.[546] Contemporaries were noting as early as June 1625 that Charles was distinctly unsympathetic towards

[544] *CSPV, 1625–1626*, p. 82.

[545] AAW, A XIX, no. 56, p. 166; see also AAW, B 47, no. 132; Avenel, *Lettres*, II, pp. 94–95 (Chevreuse's statement on behalf of English Catholics at his first audience with Charles I, asking him to honour the concessions which had been made to them). For proceedings against Catholics reported by the duke of Tuscany's agent, Amerigo Salvetti, on 24 June, see *Salvetti*, p. 24. Salvetti commented that 'those who had charge of the negotiations in France' had failed to provide adequately for this situation, and they 'apparently believed, or induced others to believe, that the English [Catholics] are a sort of Spanish Catholics, different from the French'. A week later, however, he recorded that, although some English Catholics were deeply critical of the French diplomats, the diplomats themselves had lodged protests with the court about the proceedings against Catholics: *ibid.*, pp. 24, 25.

[546] AAW, B 47, no. 190. See also Birch, *CTCI*, I, p. 33; *CSPV, 1625–1626*, p. 34. For the arrangements for Henrietta Maria's chapel, see Hibbard, 'Henrietta Maria', p. 17; PRO, PRO 31/3/60, fos 309r, 320r. She was entitled to a chapel in each royal abode, with as many as twenty-eight chaplains in all, and a bishop to serve as her almoner.

his wife's liturgical requests and requirements.[547] On the other hand, for many Protestants, any expression of Catholicism at court was too much. In the same month, complaints about the queen's chapel were voiced in parliament.[548] On 4 July, the earl of Pembroke, the lord steward, informed the upper House that 'the kinge hath certified him and others that such servaunts as she had when she was princes[s]' would be the only ones allowed 'to waite on her'. She would have no subjects of his to serve her 'without they goe to church'. He also said that Charles had 'given strict comaund to his porter at St James his house, where the q[ueen's] chapell is to bee erected, that no one subject whatsoever should bee suffered to come to the Masse'.[549]

While different Catholic factions had calculated how they might best insinuate themselves into the queen's entourage and favour, precautions had been taken to make sure that Henrietta Maria met only the right sort of English Catholics. For example, the regime sent for a cantankerous Benedictine called John Barnes, promising him both 'securitie' and 'preferment'. Barnes was renowned for his anti-Jesuit views; he also favoured Thomas Preston's opinions about the 1606 oath of allegiance; and he had been presented to Buckingham in Paris. It seemed that the regime would offer patronage to those who countenanced the Jacobean loyalty oath, and it was rumoured that such clerics would replace Henrietta Maria's Oratorian chaplains.[550] Initially, though, the queen's Oratorians seemed to be a great success.[551]

## The 1625 Parliament and the Aftermath of the Anglo-French Treaty

The 1625 parliament was deferred several times before it finally assembled on 18 June. The principal reason was the royal marriage, although the plague, raging in London, contributed to its delay.[552]

[547] Birch, *CTCI*, I, p. 33; Albion, *CI*, p. 80; cf. *Salvetti*, p. 25.

[548] TD, V, p. 160.

[549] F.H. Relf (ed.), *Notes of the Debates in the House of Lords* (London, 1929), p. 58. In a newsletter of 1 July, Joseph Mead was informed that this was in response to Henrietta Maria's officials dismissing all the English Protestants who attended upon her: Birch, *CTCI*, I, p. 39. For the ambiguities about what exactly the situation was with regard to the queen's chapel, see *CSPV, 1625–1626*, p. 118.

[550] *Letter 81*; D. Lunn, *The English Benedictines, 1540–1688* (London, 1980), pp. 108–110.

[551] *Letter 85*.

[552] Russell, *PEP*, pp. 204–205. Buckingham wrote to Lord Nithsdale that the postponing of the parliament was 'for manie waightie considerations' but mainly to allow for the arrival of Henrietta Maria, so that her 'graces and virtues [. . .] will not onlie stay the exorbitant or ungentle motions that might otherwise bee made in the house of parlement but will facilitate, in his Majesties proceeding, those passages of favors, grace and goodness which

According to Conrad Russell, the combination of the postponements and the completion of the French treaty created a fertile ground for suspicion that true (Protestant) religion was in danger. This was, as he points out, the period when 'theologically alert' members of the Commons, such as John Pym, began to be aware that there was a dangerous species of doctrinal novelty creeping in among English Protestants and creating serious dissent within the Church of England.[553] For Russell, however, the sudden and violent anti-popery scare of 1625, if it did not quite come out of nowhere, emerged from normal and traditional anti-popish feeling but at a time when there was no visible 'external' enemy to fight, and when the regime, though outwardly led by a godly Protestant sovereign who had broken with Spain, was forced to prevent the full implementation of that anti-popish impulse.[554]

Of course, we might wonder whether this was not the first time that this had happened in the 1620s. Within rather recent memory, in fact, the regime had committed itself to honouring tolerationist promises made to a foreign power, namely Spain. But when an opportunity for rapprochement with the parliament was provided by the plague and the resulting adjournment to Oxford in August, Charles failed to take advantage of the breathing space offered to him.[555] Simon Adams's account of Buckingham's packing of the council and royal household, from mid- to late summer 1624 onwards, helps to explain why the Protestant enthusiasm for the breach of the treaties with Spain turned so quickly to disillusion.[556]

Charles's speech at the opening of the session was, as John Chamberlain noted, short. The king told the members that the war was, financially, parliament's responsibility. The fleet was in readiness and it was for them to fund its expedition properly. He also said that they should 'not doubt nor suspect his religion seeing he was brought up at the feet of Gamaliel'.[557] Parliament's response was a stream of anti-popish invective. The speaker of the House of Commons,

his Majestie hath promised for the ese of the Romaine Catholickes'. This would make diplomacy with the French court easier. It would also allow 'the beginning of a straighter correspondence' with 'him you went to', i.e. Urban VIII, 'than could be hoped for these manie yeres past': BL, Harleian MS 7000, fo. 179r. The marquis of Effiat had urged (for example, in a dispatch to Villeauxclercs of 29 February) that parliament should not meet before Henrietta Maria's arrival, in part because 'les puritains', who were 'offencés des graces que nous faisons recevoir aux Catholiques', could afford to speak their minds now that the Spanish match was irretrievably broken: PRO, PRO 31/3/61, fo. 58r.

[553] Russell, *PEP*, pp. 204–207.

[554] *Ibid.*, pp. 208–209.

[555] Schreiber, *FC*, p. 89.

[556] Adams, PC, pp. 359–360.

[557] McClure, *LJC*, pp. 625–626; Lockyer, *Buckingham*, p. 242.

Sir Thomas Crew, was presented on 20 June. Despite the context of a loyal address and of the slew of petitions which were customary at the beginning of a session, he inveighed 'bitterly against recusantes'; and the 'lower House did propose unto his Majestie that the penall lawes might be putt in execution against them'. But Charles, via Lord Keeper Williams, told them that this was not 'the businesse for which they were cauled', though he would do 'what was fittinge'.[558]

The mismanagement of the war effort provoked intense and hostile criticism. Furthermore, the French crown had requested English naval assistance in late 1624: Louis wanted ships for service against the Genoese. Then the proposed target changed from Genoa to the Huguenots. Initially, faced with Soubise's pre-emptive rebellion against the military action planned against La Rochelle, Buckingham did not object, particularly since it did not appear, at first, that the majority of Huguenots desired conflict with the French crown, especially when it seemed that Louis might go to war with Spain, and could not do so if threatened by a Huguenot revolt. In the end, the French received the ships, though without their crews. But Buckingham had been manipulated and outwitted by Richelieu, who had talked up the prospect of peace with the Huguenots as a prelude to the transfer of control of the ships. The episode raised, during the summer of 1625, the possibility that English forces would wage war against the cause of European Protestantism.[559]

On 23 June, 'an act for explanation of a branch of 3 Jac. concerning the discovering and repressing of popish recusants was twice read together'. MPs demanded that loopholes in the law must be closed.[560] This was essentially the same as the bill which had been introduced and lost in both 1621 and 1624.[561] Chamberlain noted that, on 24 June, the members were 'with the king about yt'. They 'began to mutter about matters of religion that the king promised them when he was prince that he wold never contract any mariage with conditions derogatorie to that we professe'. Some were actually saying that 'all goes backward since this connivence in religion came in, both in our wealth, valor, honor and reputation, and that yt is visiblie seen that God blesses nothing we take in hand wheras, in Quene Elizabeths

[558]AAW, A XIX, no. 56, p. 166 (cited in *Letter 85*); Russell, *PEP*, pp. 219–220; Hacket, *SR*, part II, pp. 11–13; *Proceedings 1625*, pp. 34–35.

[559]Russell, *PEP*, pp. 211–212; Adams, PC, pp. 361, 363; Lockyer, *Buckingham*, pp. 229–231, 252–255; Shimp, 'A Catholic marriage', pp. 13–14; Avenel, *Lettres*, II, pp. 63–64. In September 1625, the Huguenots under Soubise were defeated at the Ile de Rhé: Adams, PC, p. 376; *Salvetti*, p. 33.

[560]*Proceedings 1625*, pp. 232–233, 504–505; C. Thompson, 'Court politics and parliamentary conflict in 1625', in Cust and Hughes, *Conflict in Early Stuart England*, p. 186; *LJ*, III, p. 446.

[561]*Proceedings 1625*, p. 226, n. 4; *LJ*, III, p. 248.

time, who stoode firme in Gods cause, all thinges did flourish'.[562] As early as 25 June, Thomas Roper recorded parliament's reluctance to make the full customary grant to Charles of the one shilling in the pound in tonnage and poundage duty which they 'formerly gave his father unlesse he will graunte them their desiers'. More generally, Roper thought that the 'common wealthe is sicke and muche distempered'.[563]

Between 25 and 28 June, a subcommittee drew up various articles to be presented to Charles. These mainly concerned the 'great increase' of papists in the realm. It was claimed that these papists aimed at 'the possessing themselves of the whole power of the state'. For the umpteenth time, the standard and not necessarily inaccurate anti-popish mantra of the period was trotted out – 'such is the restlessness of their spirit that, if they gain but a connivancy, they will press for a toleration, then strive for an equality and lastly aspire to such a superiority as may work the extermination both of us and our religion'. Commenting on the extent to which the various Catholic factions had intruded into recent diplomatic processes, the articles stated that the danger from papists was much increased by their 'dependency upon foreign princes'. Their aspirations would open 'a way of popularity to the ambition of any who shall adventure to make himselfe head of so great a party'. The fundamental cause to which these articles pointed was the weakness displayed by the crown as it negotiated for treaties with those same foreign powers. The crown's spinelessness was principally displayed in 'the late suspension of the execution of the laws against the Jesuits, seminary priests and popish recusants'. It was compounded, even when those laws were enforced, by the frauds practised by popish officers of the crown. This encouraged the recusants in their boldness. Foreign ambassadors had 'interposed' in the English Catholics' favour. Catholics had been audacious in their resort to London and in 'their frequent conventicles and conferences heare'. The Commons also cited the distribution of popish books, the harm caused by popish schoolteachers, the freedom of the popish clergy to come and go as they pleased, and the bad state of the Church of England ministry. Significantly, the agitation over religion now included proposals that the Church of England should be made more amenable to godly Protestants. Sir Nathaniel Rich, for example, suggested that ministerial subscription should be compelled only to those of the Thirty-Nine Articles which parliament had confirmed by statute. As Russell says, this subject had not been touched in 1621

[562] McClure, *LJC*, p. 626.

[563] AAW, B 47, no. 190 (cited in *Letter 85*); Thompson, 'Court politics', p. 176; Alexander, *CLT*, pp. 82–83.

and 1624. The 1625 parliament also saw the storm over the Arminian polemicist Richard Montagu.[564]

It was urged that public expressions of Catholicism should be strictly curbed. In particular, Charles was to be petitioned 'that no popish recusant be permitted to come within the court', except upon specific royal warrant. Significantly, in the light of the Catholic episcopacy campaign and the arrival of Bishop Smith, the Commons also demanded that Charles should be requested 'to take such order [. . .] that no bishop, stranger, nor any other by authority derived from the see of Rome, confer ecclesiastical orders or exercise any ecclesiastical function whatsoever towards or upon any of his Majesty's natural subjects within any of his Majesty's dominions'.[565]

Although statutes had already codified all the possible penalties that had ever been imagined for dealing with Catholic offenders against the law which governed religious conformity, the petition rehearsed most of them. All that was necessary, it was declared, was to enforce them. The question, as ever, was what implementation of the law would mean in practice. Enforcement to the absolute limits of the statutes against Catholics implied what was impossible even in the late 1580s under Elizabeth, namely a 'terror' of Jacobin proportions. In other words, despite the qualifying and respectful phrases used by the Commons, all such advice, coupled with claims about the increase in the number of recusants, was a critique of royal government. A select committee for drawing up a petition concerning religion was appointed on 28 June; it reported, with the text of the petition to the king, two days later.[566] The Commons's petition against recusants, which had been sent to the Lords on 1 July after a request for a joint conference, was read on 4 July. It was discussed and amended after yet another conference between the two Houses' representatives. Measures were considered for restricting the Catholic impact that Henrietta Maria would have.[567]

Also on 28 June, the Lords heard the reading of a petition brought in by Lionel Farrington. It concerned a recusant against whom Farrington was proceeding 'pro domino rege quam pro seipso'. But the

[564] *Proceedings 1625*, pp. 260–264; Russell, *PEP*, pp. 230, 231–233. On 28 June, a draft bill was introduced by Sir John Strode 'for the educating of the children of popish recusants': *Proceedings 1625*, p. 257.

[565] *Ibid.*, p. 263. On 4 July, at a conference between the Commons and the Lords, it was decided that the provision concerning foreigners executing episcopal jurisdiction should be 'extended to natural subjects': *ibid.*, p. 305. On the same day, Bishop George Carleton complained about Richard Smith: Questier, *C&C*, p. 424.

[566] *Proceedings 1625*, pp. 265–266, 274.

[567] *Ibid.*, pp. 155, n. 12, 78–79, 80, 84, 85, 86, 88, 89, 297, 298, 299, 300, 301, 305, 314, 316; *LJ*, III, pp. 451, 453, 456, 457, 458, 460, 465.

recusant, one William Andrewes, had, when arrested at Farrington's request, produced a 'protection [. . .] subscribed by [. . .] Lord Eure'. Eure was one of the popish office-holders who had been named and shamed in May 1624. The Lords took the opportunity to pronounce that 'none are to be privileged against any statute of recusancy'.[568]

Following the extremely ill-received royal request on 8 July for an additional grant of supply, and a simultaneous announcement of the adjournment of the parliament from plague-ridden London to Oxford, the members reconvened there after intermission (11 July to 1 August).[569] There, the regime experienced a barrage of criticism over how it had conducted its recent business.[570] One of the topics which kept recurring was the issue of Catholicism. On 4 August, Charles addressed both Houses in Christ Church. They were promised that the petition against recusants would be dealt with, though there were protests the following day about pardons obtained for recusants by the French ambassador.[571] In the extensive debates in the Commons on 5 August, about a range of controversial issues (including the war and financial supply), Sir Robert Phelips openly demanded an explanation of the purpose of the Anglo-French alliance, and of why Charles had married a Catholic.[572] Sir Simon Weston demanded that 'papists' estates' be subjected to a greater tax burden.[573] On 6 August, Sir Nathaniel Rich, seconded by Phelips, put forward five demands. They dealt with the apparent de facto toleration for Catholics, the absence of a coherent war strategy, evil counsellors, and royal finances. Others, such as Sir Henry Mildmay, referring to the plague, lamented that 'our coldness in religion [is] one of the principal causes of the grievous visitation now upon us'. He suggested that the king should, 'upon no instance, give any connivance to the papists'.[574] On 8 August, in the context of a long speech from Buckingham in defence of the regime's proceedings, both Houses were (as part of a strategy to instigate a grant of supply) advised by the lord keeper that the king and privy council

[568] *Ibid.*, pp. 446–447. Farrington had come to grief at the hands of the allegedly crypto-papist Sir Henry Spiller early in the 1621 parliament, when Farrington joined in the petitioning against alleged maladministration of the exchequer procedures for fining recusants and sequestrating their property: Questier, 'Sir Henry Spiller', p. 256.

[569] Russell, *PEP*, pp. 235–237; Adams, PC, pp. 366–367; Thompson, 'Court politics', pp. 176–179.

[570] Russell, *PEP*, pp. 238–252; Lockyer, *Buckingham*, pp. 260–267.

[571] Thompson, 'Court politics', pp. 180–181; Russell, *PEP*, p. 241; Alexander, *CLT*, p. 84; Lockyer, *Buckingham*, pp. 255, 260; *LJ*, III, pp. 470–471.

[572] Adams, PC, p. 368; Thompson, 'Court politics', p. 181; *Proceedings 1625*, pp. 395–396. For the debates about financial supply, see Alexander, *CLT*, pp. 84–88.

[573] *Proceedings 1625*, p. 391; Adams, PC, p. 368.

[574] Adams, PC, p. 369; Lockyer, *Buckingham*, p. 261; *Proceedings 1625*, pp. 412, 549.

were considering remedies to satisfy the petition against recusants.[575] The petition was read in full on 9 August 1625 and Charles's reply was delivered.[576] 10 August found John Delbridge still complaining in the Commons about 'pardons to Jesuits' and the afflictions of the Huguenots at La Rochelle.[577] Archbishop Abbot reported from the recent conference between delegates from both Houses (requested on 8 August) that the lower House was extremely concerned about these issues and could point to recent prerogative pardons extended to Catholics.[578]

In fact, following Charles's answer to the petition concerning religion, it was decided by the Lords that this matter should, in effect, be allowed to drop.[579] On 11 August, Sir Edward Coke, back from conference with the Lords, was still protesting about the terms obtained by the French for English Catholics, although the Lords had 'resolved to move the king never to pardon any Jesuit or other papist til they be attainted'.[580] As Schreiber and Russell stress, the regime was quite ready to breach the toleration clauses of the Anglo-French treaty if that was the price of both supply and popularity. This did not serve, however, to protect Buckingham from attack; and it was the attacks on Buckingham which played a major part in forcing Charles to dissolve the parliament. The session ended on 12 August.[581]

In the face of Protestant parliamentary hostility, the new king had tried very hard to head off charges of dalliance with popery. But would the crown now allow the resumption of proceedings against Catholics? Apparently, the answer was that it would. The law would be enforced as usual against Catholic nonconformists, in spite of (or perhaps in part because of) the occasional French protest and, of course, the overt *dévot* Catholicism of the queen.[582]

It was far from clear, however, that the royal administration of the law against nonconformity was now exactly as it had been. On 14 August 1625, Charles issued a proclamation which ordered those at

[575] Relf, *Notes of the Debates in the House of Lords*, pp. 61–62; Russell, *PEP*, p. 248; Lockyer, *Buckingham*, pp. 262–265; PRO, SP 16/5/28; *Proceedings 1625*, pp. 147, 148; Thompson, 'Court politics', p. 183; *Salvetti*, p. 27.

[576] *Proceedings 1625*, pp. 155f., 170, 177, 433; *LJ*, III, pp. 477–481.

[577] *Proceedings 1625*, pp. 448, 556, n. 181; *Salvetti*, p. 29.

[578] *Proceedings 1625*, pp. 146, 152, 169, 171–172, 375, 412, n. 10.

[579] *Ibid.*, p. 172.

[580] *Ibid.*, pp. 458, 461; *LJ*, III, p. 487.

[581] Schreiber, *FC*, p. 90; Russell, *PEP*, pp. 248–252; Adams, PC, p. 370.

[582] Allison, RS, p. 197; Hibbard, 'Henrietta Maria', pp. 19, 20, 23, 24; Birch, *CTCI*, I, p. 52; *CSPV, 1625–1626*, p. 129; Albion, *CI*, pp. 79–85; TD, V, pp. 161–162. A good deal of the opposition to Buckingham at court came from within the queen's entourage (before it was diminished through dismissals): Hibbard, 'Henrietta Maria', p. 23; Schreiber, *FC*, pp. 96–98.

the seminaries to return to England and commanded that the penal laws be enforced against the Catholic clergy.[583] On 8 September, Sir George Goring advised Carleton that the Catholics believed that the game was up and that 'they have offered underhand 3 hundreth thousand pounds sterling presently to be leavyed for regaining the peace they did injoy but were not contented then withall'.[584] In Michaelmas term, an order was delivered to the judges that, in their circuits, they should execute the penal laws against Catholic separatists. This was Charles's response to the parliament's petitioning. Charles could interpret those statutes according to a particular set of commonplaces in contemporary commonwealth theory. Here, it was argued, the Catholic nonconformists' fines and sequestrations would make amends (for the rent in the social and political fabric that Catholic nonconformity had caused) by being employed for national defence.[585] In some ways, this anticipates the composition schemes of the later 1620s which, to many Protestants, did appear to be a form of de facto toleration.

Even as these orders were being issued, stories flooded in from around the country that papists were plotting all manner of treasons. Their power and their lawlessness undermined, it seemed to some, the nation's capacity to defend itself as it anticipated a full-scale war against the Spaniards.[586] In October, instructions were issued that leading Catholics should be disarmed.[587]

In Northamptonshire, on 31 October, this attempt to seize papists' weapons had resulted in a brawl at the house of Lord Vaux, with 'blowes exchanged betwene the said lord and Mr Knightly, a justice of the peace who assisted the deputy lieutenants in that action'.[588] The

[583] *SRP*, II, no. 23; Albion, *CI*, p. 79; *Salvetti*, p. 31; BL, Harleian MS 1581, fo. 66r–v.

[584] PRO, SP 16/6/35, fo. 50v.

[585] AAW, A XIX, no. 89, pp. 273–274; *CSPD, 1625–1626*, p. 142 (Charles's commission of 3 November 1625 to the lord keeper and others 'to see the laws against popish recusants put in execution according to the petition of the parliament; with a declaration of the king's pleasure that all fines and forfeitures of recusants' goods be set apart for certain specified public services'); PRO, SP 16/9/51 (a similar commission of 11 November 1625, which specifically directed that 'all sums received for pecuniary forfeitures' of recusants should be 'applied towards the provision of gunpowder and repair of fortifications'); see also Hacket, *SR*, part II, p. 7.

[586] PRO, SP 16/6/41, 41.i, 46, 57, 68, 68.i, ii, iii, 104; PRO, SP 16/7/37, 69; PRO, SP 16/10/42, 42.i–iv; PRO, SP 16/11/42; PRO, SP 16/12/71; BL, Harleian MS 1580, fo. 201v; Birch, *CTCI*, I, p. 58.

[587] Questier, *C&C*, p. 429; *APC, 1625–1626*, pp. 188–189; Durham University Library, Mickleton and Spearman MS II/2, fos 355r, 363r–365r, 371r–372r. For the two separate orders to disarm papists at this time, on 2 October and 30 October, see Anstruther, *Vaux of Harrowden*, pp. 441, 449. See also B. Quintrell, 'The practice and problems of recusant disarming', *RH*, 17 (1985), pp. 208–222; Boothman and Parker, *Savage Fortune*, p. xxxix.

[588] BL, Harleian MS 1580, fo. 201r.

search was clearly motivated and informed, in part, by Vaux's recent military exploits on the Continent. As Godfrey Anstruther comments, there was a fear that 'soldiers equipped in Flanders might be bringing [. . .] weapons' back home and 'putting them by for future reference'.[589] On 3 November, the searchers wrote up their own account of what had happened, and sent it to the privy council. Conway sent a version of it to Buckingham:[590] in it, he described how the quarrel developed following the search for 'martiall munition'. Initially, the Vauxes 'respectfully consented to the search' and 'noe armes [were] found'. But Lord Vaux's brother, William, opined loudly that the searchers 'gave to the recusants the worst usage they could, except they should cutt theire throates, and with divers other oathes wished it were come to that day'. Richard Knightly, who was also a deputy lieutenant, replied that there 'were divers statutes against recusants which they were not troubled withall'. When Vaux's brother denied this 'with greate oathes', Knightly cited the 1581 recusancy statute as one of which they were free but 'further told him there was a late statute against swearing which putt a penalty of 12$^{d}$ upon every oath and told him he must exact that from him'. More expletives followed, and Knightly demanded satisfaction from Lord Vaux and his mother. They refused, and so Knightly commanded a 'counstable to distreyne soe much of Mr Vaux his goods as would satisfy three shillings and give that to the poore according to the statute'. Lord Vaux 'tooke Mr Knightley aside and told him that if hee found him in another place hee would call him to a reckoning for this. To which Mr Knightley replyed, you knowe where I dwell.' In the hall, however, Lord Vaux gave Knightly a push, and told him to 'bee gone', to which Knightly retorted that he would search some more if he felt like it, 'and when hee had done his office hee would more willingly bee gone than hee would have him'. At this point Lord Vaux 'gave him a good blowe on the face'. They grappled with each other and were dragged apart. But that only provided the opportunity for the noble lord to obtain a 'cudgell out of anothers hand' and strike 'Mr Knightleyes man' and, according to Conway's account, Vaux 'broke his head and knockt him downe'. This persuaded the search party to leave the house in haste.[591]

In the context of the recent uncertainty over the status and enforcement of the law against Catholic separatism, this was a high-profile incident. The king directed that the matter should be dealt with in the star chamber. As the parties left the 'councell chamber', Vaux

[589] Anstruther, *Vaux of Harrowden*, p. 441.

[590] PRO, SP 16/9/18; BL, Harleian MS 1580, fo. 342r–v; Anstruther, *Vaux of Harrowden*, pp. 441–445.

[591] BL, Harleian MS 1580, fo. 342r–v; Anstruther, *Vaux of Harrowden*, pp. 441–445.

implied that Sir William Spencer, who had testified against him there, had perjured himself, and Vaux was sent to the Fleet prison. Yet this was hardly evidence of a determined drive against Catholic dissent. 'In the disarming of the lords recusants, there was as much respect had', Carlisle assured Buckingham, 'of some who have relacion to your lordship as yow yourself would desire'.[592] Significantly, Conway informed Buckingham that Knightly, being soon after appointed sheriff, was 'perplext' and argued 'that all the world would thinke it was a punishment laid upon him for my Lord Vaux'.[593]

There was, nevertheless, evidently supposed to be some kind of equivalence in the public mind between the sequestration of arms and armour from recusants' households and the provision of military equipment for the war with Spain, even though recusants in general had very little in the way of military hardware and the war effort needed a great deal more, and was not receiving it. It was this kind of thinking which lay behind the suggestions of MPs such as Sir John Eliot in the 1624 parliament and Christopher Sherland at the very end of the 1625 parliament that forfeited recusant property might serve to pay for a fleet to fight against Spain.[594]

In January 1626, there was a proclamation against recusants in anticipation of the meeting of the 1626 parliament.[595] Mass indictments of Catholic nonconformists took place at this time. Late February saw public brawling between the French diplomats' servants and royal officials over the resort of Catholics to the French embassy at Durham House for Mass. In March, there were prison searches once again.[596]

In the meantime, Buckingham had tried to rescue himself from the disaster of the Anglo-French alliance. He did this by attempting, in the latter part of 1625, to construct a new alliance, one which replaced the French with the United Provinces and with Denmark; in the course of its construction, Mansfelt's troops were reassigned to Danish service, though this led to yet another defeat for him (at Dessau Bridge in April 1626). This new strategy was also what had spawned the failed expedition to Cadiz in late 1625.[597]

[592] BL, Harleian MS 1580, fo. 201r–v.

[593] *Ibid.*, fo. 343r; Anstruther, *Vaux of Harrowden*, p. 448. For the subsequent conduct of the case, removed from the star chamber to the House of Lords after Vaux took the oath of allegiance in the 1626 parliament, see Anstruther, *Vaux of Harrowden*, pp. 448–453.

[594] Russell, *PEP*, pp. 174, 251–252; ED, fo. 37r. Cf. the implementation, in the subsidy bill passed on 8 July, of the proposal that recusants should pay double subsidy: *Proceedings 1625*, pp. 276, 279, 391, n. 5.

[595] *SRP*, II, no. 36.

[596] PRO, SP 16/21/23, 63; PRO, SP 16/22/112 (see also BL, Harleian MS 161, no. 30, fo. 93r); PRO, SP 16/23/125.

[597] Adams, PC, pp. 371–376; Pursell, *WK*, p. 240; Lockyer, *Buckingham*, pp. 278–279.

The eventual war between England and France severely tested the English Catholics' political coherence. Charles managed, of course, to drift into war with France (in the form of the Ile de Rhé expedition, undertaken in the belief that assisting the Huguenots would bring down Richelieu) while he was still at war with Spain. And he did this at one of the few times in the period when the Bourbons and the Habsburgs were not at war with each other – in other words, before the Mantuan succession conflict meant that normal service was, as it were, resumed.[598]

The 'approbation' controversy, when Bishop Richard Smith challenged his Catholic critics and spectacularly lost, destroyed a good deal of the vision of the leading secular clergy and their patrons for the renascence of a unified hierarchical version of the Catholic Church in England.[599] On the other hand, the Caroline regime did not now readily identify, if it ever had, its ideological enemies as being primarily among the king's Catholic subjects.

## Conclusion

The period after 1625 lies beyond the scope of the texts reproduced in this volume. However, the newsletters written by the secular clergy in the late Jacobean and early Caroline period demonstrate how far Catholicism in England was politically wired into national and popular politics. The programme of these clerics was itself, on one reading, a resurrection of Catholic aspirations at the accession of James in 1603. At that time, it had briefly appeared that the condition of Catholics might change irreversibly. What had seemed possible in the years 1603–1604 (in the sense of a toleration for the Catholic community) actually happened, albeit briefly, during the early 1620s.

Here, also, we have a contribution to the 'post-revisionist' critique of certain recent accounts of parliamentary politics in the 1620s. As Thomas Cogswell has pointed out in a series of ground-breaking studies of the period, looking beyond the narrow confines of Westminster gives us not just a wider perspective but a view which is different in kind from one which is constructed by concentrating on parliament and the court. He argues that 'the pronounced polarization of the realm during the Spanish match [...] was not a passing aberration in early Stuart politics'. Certainly, the conduct of royal policy in the early 1620s would come to be regarded by contemporaries as a direct prequel to the 1630s – 'the stress on the blessings of peace, the

[598] Schreiber, *FC*, pp. 102–103; Bonney, *European Dynastic States*, pp. 208–210.
[599] Questier, *C&C*, ch. 13.

tight episcopal control over preachers, the campaign against puritans amid a de facto toleration of Catholics, and [. . .] the reliance on Spain'.[600]

As the above exposition of Catholic attitudes to central political themes in British politics at this time has attempted to show, behind the rhetoric of heretical depravity and depictions of ruthless puritans intent on maliciously vexing and mulcting innocent and helpless Romanists, there was a clear political awareness among Catholics of a radical discrepancy between the crown's approach to the conduct of foreign policy and the supposed religious and ideological underpinning of that policy. The Stuarts' Catholic subjects realized at least as well as, if not better than, others that the crown's response to the parliamentary demand for a war against the Habsburgs was not in tune with the agenda of the Commons as it emerged in, and was expressed all through, the 1620s.[601]

The late Jacobean and early Caroline period had seen the further opening up of an already deep and public political fracture over the relationship of Britain to Europe and also over the function of religion in interpreting this relationship. Through this gaping breach, a number of Catholics – even if often deeply at odds with each other – could easily drive a coach and four, finding now that many of the previous blocks and obstacles in their way were no longer there.

Here we have the basis of an explanation of the relationship between the crown and the Catholics which is compatible with the period's anti-Catholicism, and with anti-popery's opposites as well. As Anthony Milton has shown, the post-Reformation anti-Catholic canon was never particularly secure. Many of the images which anti-papists used to establish their demand for zero tolerance had very visible contemporary antitheses. These antitheses had existed for a long time; but it was only in the 1620s and 1630s that it seemed that they were being established somewhere near the centre of the political and ecclesiastical establishment – even at the heart of the royal court.[602]

Furthermore, as is clear from, for example, Simon Adams's account of the policy manoeuvres sponsored by Buckingham in this period, what the crown did served to create a series of ideological fractures which were in the end irremediable and were heavily informed by contemporary religious debate. It was this, rather than the simple fact that the Stuart war policy was strategically disastrous and

[600] Cogswell, 'England and the Spanish match', pp. 110–111.

[601] Adams, PC, p. 431.

[602] A. Milton, 'A qualified intolerance: the limits and ambiguities of early Stuart anti-Catholicism', in A. Marotti (ed.), *Catholicism and Anti-Catholicism in Early Modern English Texts* (London, 1999), pp. 85–115.

financially unsustainable, which caused the crown so many problems. Buckingham's contribution to the contracting of an alliance with Spain (manipulating though not ideologically sympathizing with members of the Spanish faction) and then to the breaking of the Anglo-Spanish treaties and the contracting of a French alliance (without, however, being prepared to hold the French to a credible Protestant-cause raft of policies) inevitably made the crown liable to attack, and not just from former supporters of the Spanish match such as Arundel and Bristol. This was made infinitely worse when Buckingham and Charles tried, unsuccessfully, to rely on parliament to underwrite their increasingly confused programme and then were forced to fall back on a much smaller nexus of political supporters. Among these supporters were known Catholics who clearly appreciated the political and ideological significance of the crown's strategies here, as, of course, did the so-called 'Arminians' who looked to the new regime, and specifically to Buckingham, for favour.

It is not exactly a revelation that the Caroline regime infuriated Protestants of a certain kind (increasingly referred to by some contemporaries and some modern historians as puritans); nor that the Caroline court admitted entry both to those who were overtly Catholic and to those who might be suspected of harbouring popish tendencies; nor that the Laudian experiment (however appropriate a term that is) seemed, to some people, popish by association, if nothing else. However, a review of the political priorities of certain strands of English Catholicism during the early 1620s can tell us a great deal about how these connections and equivalences began to be made.

# THE NEWSLETTERS

## 1. William Bishop to John Bennett, 4/14 December 1621

[*AAW, A XVI, no. 72, pp. 247–248*]

Very much respected and worthy s*ir*,

We long to heare of yo*ur* safe arrivall at Rome,[1] w*hi*ch I hope we shall do ere th[ese] come to your handes. I will first tell you what letters I have already addres[sed] towards you, then what I have now to say. I sent you the nuncios[2] letters to Card[inal] Lodovicy,[3] the popes nephew, by the meanes of the Spanish ambassadors[4] secretary. The packet was endorsed unto Padre Maestro[5] at the Spanish amb[assador's] house in Rome. Afterward I sent you one of mine, with another out of England to M[r] Franks,[6] by M[r] Wainmans[7] means. It was addressed unto Monsig*no*r Cursino, the agent in Rome, at Cursino House hard by S[t] Lewes Church. Item, the nuncio himself being at Toulouse with the king[8] did, upon the receit of that l[etter] w*hi*ch you sent him from o*ur* brethren in England, write a second letter unto Card[inal] Lodovicio in your favour, w*hi*ch he addressed unto the rector[9] of the Engli[sh] college in Rome to be deliv*er*ed unto you at yo*ur* arrivall

[1]John Bennett, the recently appointed agent of the English secular clergy, had arrived in Rome on 11/21 November 1621: TD, V, p. ccxxxii.

[2]Ottavio Corsini, archbishop of Tarsus and papal nuncio in France.

[3]Luigi Ludovisi, nephew of Pope Gregory XV.

[4]Francisco de la Cueva, duke of Alburquerque, Spanish ambassador in Rome.

[5]Diego de Lafuente OP, chaplain to Diego Sarmiento de Acuña, count of Gondomar. He had been dispatched to Rome to obtain a papal dispensation for the proposed marriage of Prince Charles to the infanta Maria. See *CSPV, 1621–1623*, p. 158; CRS, 68, pp. 144, 148–151; AAW, B 25, no. 17. On 18/28 July 1622, William Bishop had requested Gondomar that Lafuente should be appointed 'great almoner' to the infanta, in part because of 'the credit that he hath gotten already with our king', and that Lafuente might 'be made a byshope aswell': AAW, A XVI, no. 124, p. 501.

[6]Identity uncertain.

[7]Probably a reference to Thomas Wenman. A letter from William Bishop to John Bennett in October 1622 mentioned that Wenman was with Bennett in Rome: AAW, A XVI, no. 168, p. 633. Wenman, with William Seton and John Browne, signed a letter to Urban VIII in September 1624 in favour of the proposed Anglo-French dynastic marriage treaty: AAW, B 26, no. 146.

[8]Louis XIII.

[9]Thomas Fitzherbert SJ. See Anstr., I, p. 117. Fitzherbert was on bad terms with some of the English Catholic secular clergy. In December 1623, Thomas Rant claimed that

at Rome. The last weeke I writt to Mr Mailer[10] another about you and our affaires, thinking him to send [it] ere this come to Rome, but I p*er*ceive sence that they are yet at Florence and p*er*haps will not come to Rome of [*sic*] one moneth, for w*hi*ch I am sorie, for that he and his going by shipe would have assisted you to the uttermost of their powers. There is, within his, a letter of father prior[11] of the Benedictines to there agent, who went up with you, which I hope he will sent [*sic for* send] him. Thus much of that w*hi*ch is past. Now to the present. The Lord Digbie, at his returne from the emperour,[12] did bring downe into the Lower Palatinate Count Mansfild, with 14,000 souldiers, who at h[is] arrivall did raise the siege of Frankenvale; w*hi*ch was evill taken of the Spaniard[s]; and the Lord Digbie therefore much denied in Flanders as one that p*re*tended love to the Spaniards and yet underhand did maligne them.[13] But, having better judgment, that can hardly be gathered out of Mansfild['s] fact. For o*ur* king hath alwaies p*re*tended to defend the Palatinate, and to gett it for some one of his grandchildren, either by intreaty or by strong hand. Therefore his agents can be no more accused for seeking to defend that, than thothers be for endevoring to take it. Wherefore, it being at liberty to ech p*ar*ty alike either to gett it, or to kepe it, neither can be justly offended with [each] other for doeing their best both in their kinds. That he[a]ringe of the L[ord] Digbie was very gratefull to his king and state,[14] whereupon he hath ~~called~~ <caused> the parlement to [be] held at the 20 of their November, albeit he had before put it of[f] unto February, that he may uppon so good an occasion gett some more subsides to maintaine the said count in the Lower Palatinate.[15] Before the beginning of the parlement the lay Catholikes in prison were sett

Fitzherbert had told John Bennett that 'hee woulde gett him putt out of Rome', and 'Ben[nett] replyed, yow are a cokscombe': AAW, B 25, no. 102.

[10] Henry Mayler. See Anstr., I, pp. 223–224; *NCC*, p. 98.

[11] This is presumably a reference to Robert (Sigebert) Bagshaw OSB, the prior of St Edmund's in Paris, since Henry Mayler was still in Paris before setting out for Rome, where he arrived by mid-March 1622: D. Lunn, *The English Benedictines, 1540–1688* (London, 1980), p. 233; AAW, B 25, no. 54.

[12] Ferdinand II.

[13] For Count Ernst von Mansfelt's contribution to the raising of the siege of Frankenthal, see *CSPV, 1621–1623*, p. 159, and for John Digby, 1st Baron Digby's part in this enterprise, see *ibid.*, pp. 161–162; McClure, *LJC*, p. 401; Adams, PC, pp. 319–320; *CCE*, p. 47. Henry Clifford commented on 25 January/4 February 1622 that Digby had 'effected litle by his' recent failed 'ambassage to the emperour' and 'had brought downe the C[ount] Mansfyelde to annoy the contrary part what he coulde', which 'deprived himselfe of good giftes that were ordayned for him': AAW, A XVI, no. 96, p. 409.

[14] See *CSPV, 1621–1623*, p. 161.

[15] For the 1621 parliament's second sitting, see Russell, *PEP*, pp. 124–144; Adams, PC, p. 320; and for Digby's address delivered there concerning the Palatinate, see Russell, *PEP*, pp. 125–126; *CSPV, 1621–1623*, pp. 167, 174; McClure, *LJC*, p. 410.

at liberties [*sic*] on their own bands.[16] And Mr Colleton[17] hath leave to choose what house he will to remaine in, as I have heard other men say, but not from our agent or himself.[18] And other priests at libertie write that the times are very calme. Yet I for my p*ar*t do feare thend of the parlement, for the Houses be both against us and have passed terrible lawes, but I hope the king will not confirme them.[19] The false archbishope[20] hath greased the favorite[21] in the fist, and made his peace, though I hold him for ever disgraced;[22] and the disgraces given to thothers[23] at thend of the last session may happ to make them all more moderate. Thus much of England. Here ~~one~~ Mr [*name illegible*], one of our companie,[24] without our knowledge, went to Orleans and there proceeded doctor in both lawes, w*hi*ch we tooke verie ill at his handes because it is against the popes breve.[25] And [we] do not to this day salute <him> by the name of doctor, nor meane not to do untill the nuncio hath seen the breve (w*hi*ch we have to shew him) and have passed his judgment thereupon. This I thought good to advertise you of, that if [*MS torn:* any (?)] imputation should be laid upon our

[16] See *Letter 6*; PRO, SP 14/123/116; *CGB*, I, p. 46.

[17] John Colleton.

[18] By September 1622, Colleton had left London and had 'gone to the Bathes': AAW, A XVI, no. 135, p. 539.

[19] For the anti-Catholic draft legislation of the first sitting of the 1621 parliament, see *CSPV, 1621–1623*, pp. 54–55; CRS, 68, p. 150; McClure, *LJC*, p. 379.

[20] George Abbot, archbishop of Canterbury.

[21] George Villiers, 1st marquis of Buckingham, later 1st duke of Buckingham.

[22] In July 1621, Archbishop Abbot had accidently shot a gamekeeper, Peter Hawkins, on the Hampshire estate of Lord Zouch. For the commission which dealt with Abbot's case, and for James's decision to exonerate him, see McClure, *LJC*, pp. 394, 395, 399–400, 406; Hacket, *SR*, part I, pp. 67–68. A copy of the royal dispensation which cleared Abbot was sent to Rome: AAW, B 25, no. 43; *CSPD, 1619–1623*, p. 311. John Hacket pointed out that 'our hierarchy was much quarrel'd with and opposed by our own fugitives to the Church of Rome, who would fasten upon this scandal, and upon it pretend against our constant succession'. Hacket said that the lord keeper, John Williams, made the same point in his letter (to Buckingham) in which he refused consecration by Abbot: Hacket, *SR*, part I, pp. 65, 66; cf. *NCC*, p. 226; PRO, SP 14/123/107. For the damage to Abbot's reputation, see PRO, SP 14/122/97; PRO, SP 14/123/5; McClure, *LJC*, p. 406. (William Whiteway heard a rumour that Abbot had been 'remooved fom his place, and in his steed came' Bishop Lancelot Andrewes: Whiteway, *Diary*, p. 40.)

[23] Bishop refers to the proceedings against the regime's critics during the first sitting of the 1621 parliament, primarily those who were subsequently imprisoned: the earl of Southampton, the earl of Oxford, John Selden, and Sir Edwin Sandys. See Russell, *PEP*, pp. 122–123; McClure, *LJC*, pp. 384–385, 388; Hacket, *SR*, part I, pp. 68–69; *Cabala*, pp. 57–59, 61.

[24] i.e. one of the members of the English secular clergy's writers' institute, the Collège d'Arras in Paris, for which see *NAGB*, p. 8.

[25] For the papal breve governing the award of higher degrees to the English secular clergy, see *NAGB*, pp. 8, 259; L. Hicks (ed.), *Letters of Thomas Fitzherbert, 1608–1610*, CRS, 41 (London, 1948), pp. 52–53.

companie for his audacious fact you may excuse us as altogether cleare ~~for all~~ <from any> consenting or approving of it.

Father Leander[26] writ[t]e unto Doctor Cicill[27] a letter wherin he did, undiscreetly in my judgment, say that it were meet, ere bishops were granted us, that it should be p*ro*posed both to religious men and lay gentlemen to heare their advises therein; he not being ignorant, as I thinke, that all those gentlemen who affect the Jesuites would be against the having of them.[28] And, as for religious, if they will not be under them, what should they have to do with the choise of them more than we do meddle with the [*MS damaged:* [mak]ing (?)] of their superiors, ours being the ordinary rulers in Gods Church, theirs being extraordinary father vicars and viceprovinciall[s]? This letter was sent to F[ather] Fitzherbert and may happ to be p*ro*duced [*p. 248*] against us. I will cause him to be spoken withall that he may declare their opinion categorically by their agent there, w*hi*ch is that they mislike not bishops but rather thinke them convenient for England now, p*ro*vided that they may enjoy their accustomed priviledges and exemptions. This they have often said, wherefore some doubt may bee made of that letter.

I heard even now that o*u*r king of England should of late demand of some <of his> bishops and chaplaines whether they thought that the papists did committ idolatry in that worshipping of images w*hi*ch they used, and willed them to consult of it seriously and to returne him their answer, <who>, after deliberation among themselves, answered that they thought the papists did not committ idolatry therein. Which answer he liked and, shortly after, gave order that his chappell at Whitehall[29] should be of new decked up and all the images that had been there this hundreth yeare[s] should be decently painted and sett in the places accustomed. This chappell will agree well with their Lutheran Masse in a cope with candels and crucifix, of w*hi*ch you heard before, with elevation and adoration of the sacrament w*hi*ch was said by <D[octor]> Andre[w]s, bishop of Winchester, by the kings order as it is commonly thought.[30]

[26] John (Leander) Jones OSB, prior of St Gregory's, Douai.

[27] John Cecil.

[28] John Bennett had informed Matthew Kellison in late November 1621 that 'the Jesuits here are making catalogues of lay people's names, who forsooth would have no bishops; and this, as a great weapon, they purpose to use': TD, V, p. ccxxxii. In the same month, the Jesuit general, Muzio Vitelleschi, promised Richard Blount SJ that he would do his best to frustrate Bennett's agitation in Rome: ARSJ, Anglia MS 1, fo. 148r.

[29] The old chapel royal at the east end of Whitehall Palace. See B. Schofield (ed.), *The Knyvett Letters (1620–1644)* (London, 1949), p. 56, citing J.E. Sheppard, *The Old Royal Palace of Whitehall* (London, 1902), p. 65.

[30] See above, p. 12; AAW, B 25, no. 39; BL, Harleian MS 1583, fo. 294r. Thomas Knyvett had remarked, on 9 October 1621, that 'the kings chappell at Whithall is curiously painted

When Mr Mailer shall come to Rome you may by his meanes most conveniently sent [*sic for* send] yo*ur* letters to me, for the Spanish ambassador[31] is often abroad with the king, and p*er*haps will not so willinglie send unto us yo*ur* letters as the others agent will.

I will add here this my observation of o*ur* kings p*ro*ceeding of late w*hi*ch gave me hope that he meanes we[ll]. First he hath disgraced them that were hottest against us: Canterbury,[32] <another bishop puritan>,[33] Nanton,[34] Southampton,[35] etc.

Secondly he hath provided to the chief offices men better affected to o*ur* religion, the L[ord] Tresurer <Cranfild>,[36] the L[ord] Keeper Williams,[37] the great secretaries [*sic*].[38]

Thirdly he did countenance Winchester seeming to say Masse, and hath given order that his owne chappell be dressed up ~~after~~ with pictures after th*e* old maner, and hath bespoken a crucifix of gold to be sett in it.

and all the images newe made and a silver crusifix amaking to hange therin, against the Spanish ladys coming': Schofield, *The Knyvett Letters*, p. 56; see also PRO, SP 14/123/27; N. Tyacke, 'Lancelot Andrewes and the myth of Anglicanism', in P. Lake and M. Questier (eds.), *Conformity and Orthodoxy in the English Church, c.1560–1660* (Woodbridge, 2000), pp. 31–32.

[31] Diego Sarmiento de Acuña, count of Gondomar.

[32] George Abbot, archbishop of Canterbury.

[33] Thomas Morton, bishop of Coventry and Lichfield: see *ODNB*, *sub* 'Morton, Thomas' (article by Brian Quintrell).

[34] Sir Robert Naunton. The elector palatine's representatives at the English court had recently put forward proposals for an Anglo-French marriage in order to forestall the projected Anglo-Spanish treaty. Initially, it appears, James exploited this as a bargaining counter with the Spaniards. The marquis of Cadenet, brother to the duke of Luynes, Louis XIII's favourite, visited the English court in late December 1620: Schreiber, *FC*, pp. 35–36; *CSPV, 1619–1621*, pp. 534–535, 572; Tillières, *ME*, pp. 30–49. But, in late January 1621, Gondomar persuaded James against such a proposal. This led to Naunton's dismissal: *CSPV, 1619–1621*, pp. 548, 553; R.E. Schreiber, *The Political Career of Sir Robert Naunton 1589–1635* (London, 1981), pp. 68–84.

[35] Henry Wriothesley, 3rd earl of Southampton.

[36] For the recent appointment of Sir Lionel Cranfield as lord treasurer, see McClure, *LJC*, p. 403.

[37] John Williams, bishop of Lincoln (consecrated on 11 November 1621).

[38] Sir George Calvert, a crypto-Catholic, had been appointed secretary of state in February 1619, in succession to Sir Thomas Lake. In March 1621, Chamberlain had remarked that among the competitors for the other secretaryship, after the disgrace of Sir Robert Naunton (who technically retained his post at this time, although he was suspended from it), was 'Master Gage (Tobie Mathewes deare frend) though most say he is rather reserved for that place about the infanta when she comes': McClure, *LJC*, p. 339. In late July, Chamberlain could write that 'all this last weeke, Sir Richard Weston was secretarie (as far as common fame could make him) insomuch that yt was saide not to be in dooing, but don, but now the report cooles again': *ibid.*, p. 392. In mid-October there were rumours (again) that Sir John Suckling would be appointed to the post: *ibid.*, p. 399, cf. p. 339; Adams, PC, p. 322. (It was even claimed, in January 1622, that Tobias Mathew had been appointed to the secretaryship: *Letter 3*.)

Fourthly he hath sett at liberty all <lay Catholikes> that were in prison, and M$^{r}$ Colleton. Other priestes imprisoned hath also such liberty that they be absent a moneth, as I heare, and go out, whosoever will go, over the seas.

It is also com*m*only voiced that the Lord Digbie is very shortly to returne into Spaine to make an end of the match.[39] He hath 15 daies since sent thither an extraordinary post to prepare his way.

It is here greatly feared lest Cou[n]t Mansfild wil, by Lorrayne, passe into France to aid the Hugonots. Some say that he <is> already entred into Lorraine.

Thus with my very harty commendac[i]ons unto you both,[40] desiring you to remember my harty good affection unto Padre Maestro, I rest.

The 14 of December, 1621.

Yo*u*rs most assured,

W*illia*m Bishope

If you can find any better means of directing o*u*r letters to you, I pray you advertise us. M$^{r}$ D[octor] Smith[41] com*m*ends himself to you.

*Addressed*: Admodu*m* r*everen*do viro d*omi*no Johanni Bennetto, sacerdoti Anglo.
Romae.

*Endorsed*: 14 Decemb*er* 1621.

## 2. Edward Brown [Bennett] to John Bennett, 19 December 1621

[*AAW, A XVI, no. 75, pp. 253–256*]

Good syr,

Yo*u*rs of the 7 of November from Millayn I have receaved, being very glad that you soe well passed the difficulties of those mountayns w*hi*ch I allwayes conceaved to be soe daungerous. Boath my frendes[42] give

[39] See *CSPV, 1621–1623*, pp. 162, 166.

[40] i.e. to John Bennett and also to William Harewell, who had travelled to Rome with Bennett: TD, V, p. ccxxxii.

[41] Richard Smith.

[42] Presumably a reference to Lady Elizabeth Dormer (widow of the 1st Baron Dormer, and cousin, by marriage, of the duke of Feria, whose mother was Jane, the daughter of Sir William Dormer and Mary Sidney) and to her grandson Robert Dormer, 2nd Baron Dormer.

you many thankes for your frendly discourses of this familye[43] to the governour,[44] who as yeat hath not written to the ould lady,[45] but when he dothe she will give hym humble thankes for the many favours he showed yo*u*.[46] To the embassadour[47] he hathe written how that he will write to the king of Spayn and desyer his letters to o*ur* king abowte the younge lord[48] and so intreat hyme to followe the bussines.

My younge lady liketh well of the cowrse but is desirous that for this haulf yeere it should not be sett a foote, while that[49] there be more certaintye of the Spanish match. For, if that should breake of[f], this is not like to succeed. Withall my L[ord] of Mongymry,[50] havinge notice of such a cowrse to have been undertaken for the younge lordes travaile, it would move hime, it may be, to deale hardlier with the younge ladye, as supposing all this to be plotted to defeate him of what he most desirethe, and soe labour not only to have the younge lord into his p*ro*tection, but alsoe restrayne hyme, that she should not have the comforte of hime as she desireth.[51] Therefor yo*u* are intreated to give the duke thankes, withall to showe hyme that as yeat it is not thought convenient his excellency should move the kinge <of Spain> till he heer further from the embassadour who will, and can, best informe his excellency of the tyme most fittinge for such a p*ro*ject.[52]

Heere[53] we have been this 4 days, wher at o*ur* first cominge we fownd all thinges uncertayne, the parlement men having drawen such

[43]i.e. the Dormer family of Wing in Buckinghamshire, whom Edward Bennett served as a chaplain.

[44]Gomez Saurez de Figueroa, duke of Feria and governor of Milan.

[45]Lady Elizabeth Dormer.

[46]On 16/26 November, John Bennett had assured Matthew Kellison that he had made representations to Feria at Milan concerning the finances of the secular clergy's college at Douai: TD, V, p. ccxxxii. On 1/11 January 1622, Kellison wrote to Bennett to thank him for his 'carefull remembraunce of our affaires with the duke of Feria', who had 'promised my Ladie Dormer once before' to write to the king of Spain on behalf of the college at Douai in order to secure the payment of its Spanish royal pension. Kellison hoped that the duke would now write to the Spanish court to procure that the pension might be paid either at Milan or at Antwerp: AAW, A XVI, no. 92, p. 399. See also *Letter 4*.

[47]Diego Sarmiento de Acuña, count of Gondomar.

[48]Robert Dormer, 2nd Baron Dormer.

[49]i.e. 'until'.

[50]Philip Herbert, 1st earl of Montgomery.

[51]Sir William Dormer, the 1st Baron Dormer's heir, had died in October 1616. The first baron himself died soon afterwards and the earl of Montgomery was granted the wardship of Sir William Dormer's son: McClure, *LJC*, pp. 30, 39, 41; PRO, SP 14/89/55. For the marriage, in 1625, of the 2nd Baron Dormer and Montgomery's daughter, Anna Sophia Herbert, see *Letter 75*.

[52]For the formal request to Feria to deliver the young Lord Dormer from the perils in which he found himself (in other words, the danger of apostasy while he remained under the control of the earl of Montgomery), see AAW, A XVII, no. 77, pp. 239–240. I am grateful to Caroline Bowden for assistance with this point.

[53]i.e. in London.

positions against recusantes[54] that, if his Ma*jes*ty had given way unto them, it had not been morally possible for them to have given any releefe for the maintenaunce of any good people.[55] But he checkt them withe a shorte letter, wherof my nephew[56] saieth he hath sent you a coppye.[57] Since, they have replied.[58] But he soe catechised them with a letter of 3 sheetes of pap*er* that they all held down there heades. In the same he willed them not to medle with his p*re*rogatives and misteries of estate, nor yeat w*i*th the matching of his sonne, or direct hyme how to make his warres; that he would match w*i*th Spayn if the kinge of Spayn would keepe all conditions agreed upon; that they had too long a peace under hyme w*hi*ch made <them> soe desirous of alterations; that bellum was dulce inexp*er*tis w*i*th many other thinges.[59] The coppy bye the next post it may be I shall send yo*u*. Soe that heer be good hopes all will goe well.

The Jesswetes give owt that the dispensation is grawnted,[60] withall that M^r^ Gage[61] hath made a speech to Gregory[62] against the having of b*ishop*s w*hi*ch heer is litle regarded.[63]

[54] In addition to the unsuccessful recent draft recusancy legislation (see *Letter 1*), it was proposed in the subsidy bill that recusants (and those with recusant wives, children, or servants) should pay double the ordinary rate, 'and be counted as aliens', as Chamberlain remarked on 1 December, observing that this was all that the Commons could 'do to shew the apprehension and dislike of the incredible increase of that faction': McClure, *LJC*, p. 412; see also AAW, A XVI, no. 92, p. 401.

[55] i.e. Catholic clergy.

[56] Joseph Haynes.

[57] Matthew Kellison forwarded the copy, sent by Haynes, to John Bennett (AAW, A XVI, no. 71, pp. 243–245) of James's letter of 3 December 1621 to the speaker of the Commons (commanding 'fierie and popular spirittes' there to desist from debating 'matters farre beyond their reache and capacitye'), and also of the remonstrance which the Commons had drawn up on 3 December to be sent to James and had been forced to withdraw, AAW, A XVI, no. 92, p. 399 (printed in TD, V, pp. cclxxxviii–ccxc; J.P. Kenyon, *The Stuart Constitution* (London, 1966), pp. 43–47); Russell, *PEP*, p. 135; B. Pursell, 'War or peace? Jacobean politics and the parliament of 1621', in C. Kyle (ed.), *Parliaments, Politics and Elections, 1604–1648*, Camden Society, 5th series, 17 (Cambridge, 2001), pp. 174–175.

[58] For the petition taken to the king on 11 December, see Kenyon, *Stuart Constitution*, p. 29.

[59] See *ibid.*, p. 29; McClure, *LJC*, p. 414.

[60] For the papal commission (comprising the cardinals Millini, Bandini, Cobelluzio, and Sacrati) appointed to deal with the issue of the dispensation for the proposed marriage of Prince Charles and the infanta Maria, see *CSPV, 1621–1623*, p. 158; PRO, SP 77/14, fo. 500v. From Rome, on 1/11 September 1621, George Gage had notified Lord Digby that the Roman curia had 'no aversion from this busines' of the Spanish match. Bandini in particular was well affected towards King James and 'as affectionat to England as can be wished': PRO, SP 94/24, fo. 292r.

[61] George Gage, secular priest, son of Edward Gage of Bentley, East Sussex. See Anstr., II, pp. 120–121; P. Revill and F. Steer, 'George Gage I and George Gage II', *BIHR*, 31 (1958), pp. 141–158.

[62] Pope Gregory XV.

[63] For George Gage's audiences with the pope in July and August 1621 concerning the dispensation for the Spanish match, see CRS, 68, pp. 149–150. Gage had argued to Digby

[*p. 254*] Of yo*ur* last from Millayne I sent a coppye to yo*ur* frend[64] by Jenkyn who since 10 dayes <agoe> was withe me. She is very well, God be thancked. As we came from the cuntrey I writt unto her againe by M^r^ Bowes who is gon to keepe Chrismas with her.

M^r^ Collington[65] comendeth hime self to yo*u*. He would have written but that he hath nothing to saye, w*hi*ch p*er*chaunce yo*u* will think impossible for sup*er*iors who have dew care of the comon. But, to deale plainly w*i*th you, I think he hath nothing to write.

Withe the embassadour[66] I have been, who used me after his maner. He showed me yo*ur* letter from Millain, and hopeth shortly to heer from you.[67]

Ther is a book latly come fowrth called the P*ro*testants Plea,[68] directed to the parlament. The autor as [*sic*] is sayed (w*hi*ch I alsoe beleeve) to be hime who writ[t]e those letters for p*re*eminence of place.[69] Many marvaile it came owt at this tyme, but he saieth M^r^ Archpreest[70] left it hyme for a legacye to sett it fowrth.[71]

I pray reme*m*ber me to Pater Maister (who they say heer is bushop) and to M^r^ Franckes. John Meredith is like to fall to some truble as

that Spanish diplomatic assurances in Rome (that Spain was persuaded and satisfied that James would grant toleration to his Catholic subjects after the match was concluded) would secure the dispensation; but here Gage interpreted toleration as, essentially, no more than the liberty to worship in private according to conscience: PRO, SP 94/24, fos 291v–293v. Many secular priests believed, by contrast, that the success of the Spanish match ought to lead to a grant of episcopal authority to one of their number, and that this would be an essential component of a more comprehensive and far-reaching toleration: AAW, A XVI, no. 95, p. 407. For the long-standing enmity between George Gage and some of the secular clergy, see AAW, A XIV, no. 142, p. 445; TD, V, p. 90; *NCC*, pp. 80, 144–145.

[64] Lady Elizabeth Dormer.

[65] John Colleton.

[66] Diego Sarmiento de Acuña, count of Gondomar.

[67] Gondomar had written to John Bennett in early October 1621: AAW, A XVI, no. 64, p. 225.

[68] Richard Broughton, *English Protestants Plea, and Petition, for English Preists and Papists, to the Present Court of Parlament* (Saint-Omer, 1621). The book is an answer to the sermon preached at St Margaret's, Westminster by Archbishop James Ussher at the opening of the 1621 parliament on 18 February: ARCR, II, no. 80; P. Milward, *Religious Controversies of the Jacobean Age* (London, 1978), no. 682; James Ussher, *The Substance of that which was Delivered before the Commons House*... (London, 1621); McClure, *LJC*, p. 347; J. Shami, *John Donne and Conformity in Crisis in the Late Jacobean Pulpit* (Cambridge, 2003), pp. 61–62. Ussher's sermon condemned idolatry, remonstrated against toleration of Catholics for reasons of state, and demanded the enforcement of the recusancy statutes.

[69] For the authorship of *English Protestants Plea*, see ARCR, II, no. 80; *Letter 13*.

[70] William Harrison.

[71] See Broughton, *English Protestants Plea*, p. 3, where the author claims that William Harrison 'bequeathed as a legacie to mee unworthie this chardge: to write and publish to the world this [...] treatise'.

alsoe his brother about beating of a minister at Abergeyney who complayned of them to the parlament.[72] M^r^ Smith remembreth hym self unto yo*u*, as also to M^r^ Franckes.

The owld frend,[73] young frend[74] and M*istr*es Fr:[75] most lovinglye salute yo*u*. My Lady St Johns is maried to M^r^ W*illia*m Arundell by whom I have been very kindly intertayned.[76] Josephe[77] liketh hyme well.

Even as I write this, I heer the parlament is p*ro*rowged to the 8 of Februarye, his Ma*jes*tye being this night expected to the town. Sig*no*r Licentiato saluteth yo*u* and M^r^ Franckes kindlye. This

[72]In late 1621, the House of Commons received a deposition from Eleazar Jackson, 'a public preacher in Abergavenny', who claimed to enjoy 'the popularity and approbation of the inhabitants of that town'. He alleged that two of the town's numerous recusants had assaulted him at night in his own chamber and had inflicted serious injuries upon him. Because of the local magistrates' sympathy for the recusants, and because of further threats to his life, he was constrained to leave Abergavenny. They had 'sought to deterre and drive me from my place', he said, 'by scandalous aspersions, hereby labouringe to perswade the common sorte of people to entertaine a dislike of my doctrine'. Finally 'when they sawe their menacing would nott prevaile, two noted recusants (one of them suspected to be a seminarie priest) came upon mee in myne own chamber, intending to murther mee, which if they had effected they had a horse of one John Meridith redie sadled att a recusants doore neare unto my lodginge, where hee, the said John Meridith, stood at a windowe in an upper chamber to see the event, butt by Gods providence att that tyme I escaped from them'. After dark on 14 October 1621, another two convicted recusants forced their way into his room and demanded 'a quarrell by way of disputation, viz concerning Purgatorie and the blessed virgin Marie'; but soon they 'reprehended mee for handling matters of controversie in the pulpitt and further charged mee with the procuring of a warrant of the peace against one Roger Howell, one of the recusants which first attempted to murther mee'. Then they resorted to violence, 'beating and sore wounding mee in the head with a dagger and a candlesticke, besides a dangerous stabb in the forehead'; and they warned Jackson 'to leave the contrie forthwith'. His opponents said that 'if they had a king which would favoure theire religion they would putt us all to the fire and faggott, styling us obstinate and damnable heretiques': M.S. Giuseppi *et al.* (eds), *Calendar of the Manuscripts of the Most Honourable the Marquess of Salisbury*, 24 vols (HMC, 1888–1976), XXIV, pp. 242–243; see also PRO, SP 14/124/58; W. Notestein, F.H. Relf, and H. Simpson (eds), *Commons Debates 1621*, 7 vols (New Haven, CT, 1935), II, pp. 544–545, V, pp. 245–246.

[73]Lady Elizabeth Dormer.

[74]Robert Dormer, 2nd Baron Dormer.

[75]Identity uncertain.

[76]Matthew Kellison remarked in January 1622 on the recent marriage between the 2nd Viscount Montague's widowed daughter, Mary, Lady St John (whom Kellison referred to as Joseph Haynes's 'landladie', i.e. patron) and William Arundell, the second son of Sir Thomas Arundell, 1st Baron Arundell of Wardour. He regarded it as 'an unequal match [...] and prejudicious to her [...] reputation'. Lord Arundell, however, emerged as one of the most vociferous supporters of the secular clergy leadership and their proposals to reform the English Catholic community: AAW, A XVI, no. 92, p. 400; see also Questier, *C&C*, pp. 388–389 and *passim*; McClure, *LJC*, p. 396.

[77]Joseph Haynes.

is all that occurreth. Soe, with my best wishes to you boath, I cease.

Your very assured,

Ed[ward] Brown

December 19, 1621 our stile.

*[on p. 256]*

*Addressed*: Admodum reverendo domino, D[omino] Joanni Bennetto.

*No endorsement.*

## 3. Joseph Hervey [Haynes] to John Bennett, 20 January 1622

*[AAW, A XVI, no. 94, pp. 405–406]*

My good uncle,

Wee are much comforted to heare that you are safely come to your jornies eand. I have letters from you but they are not dated, at which your brother[78] is much troubled. That to your best freind[79] I sent immediately to her. She is well, as also the rest of our freinds, God be thanked. This weeke we received a letter from F[ather] M[aste]r[80] to the a*rch*p*riest*[81] and [his] assistents wher, acknowledging the receipt of our letter to him, he desireth to be excused in the busines we intreated him. I hope it is but a modest refusall. You can advise whether it be necessary for us to renew our request unto him or no.[82] He speaketh very comfortably of you in his letter. As yet we are not quite out of feare whether some of your letters which should have mett you there have miscaried in the way or no. All things here goe well; only informers are busy and, as I am for certaine told, some 40 writts are taken out of the crowne office against Catholiques. But it is very like they will be stopped. The puritans out of a hatred and feare they have of it doe ordinarily report that papistry is setting up againe. Here is a gentelman called Mr Tobias Mathew in greate request and is, as I am

78 Edward Bennett.

79 Lady Elizabeth Dormer.

80 Diego de Lafuente OP.

81 William Harrison, who had died on 11 May 1621.

82 William Bishop had written to Diego de Lafuente on 25 December 1621/4 January 1622: AAW, A XVI, no. 91, pp. 397–398.

tould, made secretary of state in S*ir* [Robert] Nantons place, w*hi*ch is thought a very strainge thing, being that he is com*m*only reputed both a preist and Jesuite.[83] The parlament you here is quite dissolved and the L[ord] Cooke[84] in the Tower, and some others of them. It is sayed that we shal shortly have another parlament. Ther is a report that an Inglish regement of souldiers[85] shal goe into the Low Countries on the archeduk[e]s side and the gentelman[86] who married my lady is amongest others named to be coronell and then your nephew[87] is to be capelliano major. Your brother and his company went forth of [the] towne the last weeke. He was here very sick, and in some dainger, w*hi*ch hath renewed their resolution to come here no more. I have at this p*re*sent no other newes. By the last the Carmelite[88] did write a letter for you and we are now talking of writing a com*m*on letter for the busines of bushops. My lady remembers her love to you and to M^r^ Franks to whome I also desire to be kindly remembred and so doth M^r^ Pecker when you have well dispatched your busines. I wish I were w*it*h you to accompany you home. Be carefull of your health, w*hi*ch I forgett not dayly to remember. W*it*h my service and best love, I leave you to the p*ro*tection of our Saviour, and will ever be your nephew, to be com*m*aunded,

Joseph Hervey

20 of Jan[uary].

[*on p. 406*]

*Addressed*: Admodum r*everend*o domino, D*omin*o Johanni Bennetto. Roma.

*No endorsement.*

[83] John Chamberlain noted Tobias Mathew's arrival from Paris, and also that he was politically tainted because of his association with the disgraced lord chancellor, Sir Francis Bacon: McClure, *LJC*, p. 419; PRO, SP 14/124/82, 84. Mathew had been secretly ordained, with George Gage, by Cardinal Bellarmine in May 1614:, Anstr., II, p. 120; *NCC*, p. 50.

[84] Sir Edward Coke.

[85] See *Letter 5*.

[86] Haynes appears to refer here to William Arundell (see *Letter 2*), but Edward Vaux, 4th Baron Vaux was the colonel of the English regiment which went to Flanders.

[87] i.e. Joseph Haynes himself.

[88] This may be a reference to the Carmelite friar Thomas Dawson (Simon Stock), a friend of the secular clergy: see *NCC*, p. 12. In June 1624, Carlos Coloma, the Spanish ambassador, took Dawson as his chaplain: TD, V, p. cclx.

## 4. Anthony Champney to John Bennett, 1/11 May 1622

[*AAW, A XVI, no. 108, pp. 449–452*]

Worship*full* and r*everen*d s*i*r,

In my last I signifyed Mr P*re*sident[89] his sicknesse w*hi*ch I doubt not maketh you longe to heare of his recoverie.[90] His fever hath quitt him and he only nowe expecteth to recover his strength. Here past yesterday S*i*r Rich[ard] Weston, embassatour for Ingland, to meete w*i*th other embassatoures of Spayn, France and the emperoures at Bruxelles to treat of accom*m*od*at*ing matters in these partes of Christendom.[91] The Lord Hayes[92] is in France; Lord Digbie in Spayne.[93] The governoure of Cambray[94] is gon for Ingland[95] whence the count of Gondomar departethe about the 10 of their May ~~March~~.[96]

[89] Matthew Kellison, president of the English College at Douai.

[90] See *Letter 5*.

[91] On 10/20 April, Champney had recorded that 'Sir Richard Weston and, as some say, the earle of Rutland ar expected here about the Palatinate'; the imperial ambassador, Count Georg Ludwig von Schwarzenberg, had also arrived in Brussels following an embassy to the court in London where he had 'commission to propose a match betwixt a daughter of the emperour and the [...] p[a]latin his sonn upon condition that he be brought up with the emperour whereupon will folowe the restoring of the Palatinat at least to the sonn': AAW, A XVI, no. 107, p. 447; see also *CSPV, 1621–1623*, pp. 294, 325; Birch, *CTJI*, II, p. 303; PRO, SP 77/15, fos 85v, 92r, 94v; *CGB*, I, pp. 151, 178, 193; BL, Additional MS 72254, fo. 101r; *The Oration or Substance of that which was Delivered before his Majestie of Great Brittaine, by the Emperours Embassador...* (London, 1622, *Revised Short-title Catalogue*, nos 21828.5, 21829); Pursell, *WK*, pp. 170–171. For Weston's embassy in May, and his return, empty-handed, in late September 1622, the purpose of which journey had been, in part, to prevent the elector palatine joining Mansfelt and encouraging him, as he did, to refuse a peace accord, see Adams, PC, p. 329; Alexander, *CLT*, pp. 24–28; R. Lockyer, *Buckingham: the life and political career of George Villiers, first duke of Buckingham 1592–1628* (London, 1981), p. 126; W.B. Patterson, *King James VI and I and the Reunion of Christendom* (Cambridge, 1997), pp. 311–312; Inner Temple Library, Petyt MSS 538, vol. 48, no. 3; PRO, SP 77/15, fos 221r, 296r–306r; *CCE*, p. 78; *CGB*, I, pp. 166, 169, 179, 180, 188, 193, 202, 233; BL, Harleian MS 1581, fo. 200r–v.

[92] Sir James Hay, 1st Viscount Doncaster and future 1st earl of Carlisle. See *CSPV, 1621–1623*, p. 276; Schreiber, *FC*, pp. 39–47.

[93] See *CSPV, 1621–1623*, pp. 323, 326, 329; *CCE*, p. 66.

[94] Carlos Coloma.

[95] See *CSPV, 1621–1623*, p. 320; *CCE*, pp. 66, 89.

[96] For Gondomar's departure from London, on 16 May, see Redworth, *PI*, p. 45. Champney mentioned to John Bennett, in a letter of 22 May/1 June 1622, that Lady Elizabeth Dormer had come 'to London expressly to take leave of the co[u]nt of Gondomare and to be acquaynted with his successour' and that 'shee would commend unto him ernestly the cause of <the> [secular] clergie'. Edward Bennett, her chaplain, had said that Gondomar 'telleth him that all things goe well and he hopeth they will goe better and that he liketh nothing the padri', i.e. the Jesuits: AAW, A XVI, no. 112, p. 463. Several commentators noted how Gondomar was socializing with the prominent Catholic peer and nephew of Lady Dormer, the 2nd Viscount Montague. Simonds D'Ewes was told that Gondomar had been

The governoure afore me*n*tioned, passing this way, did us the honoure to come to our colledge,[97] heard Mass in our church and accepted of a fewe verses, Greeke and Latin, and promised all good offices possible. M$^{r}$ P*re*sident, by me, p*re*sented him the names of divers of our bretheren w*i*th whome he might deale co*n*fidently: M$^{r}$ Colleton, y*our* brother,[98] M$^{r}$ Harvey,[99] M$^{r}$ Musket[100] and M$^{r}$ Bretain.[101] M$^{r}$ John Loe his brother[102] is gon [as] <his> chaplayne. He would not visit the colledge of S$^{t}$ Omers though he was invited. M$^{r}$ Colleton hath his absolute libertie and hath taken a howse nere Clerkenwell. M$^{r}$ Blackloe his brother[103] writeth to his brother[104] her[e] that they live in greate peace for the p*re*sent and in hope of better; that they expect a generall pardon from the king of all penalties of ~~confiscatione~~ co*n*victions w*hi*ch he saythe they long to see effected.[105] He addeth that the earle of Oxford[106] was sent to the Towre [*word deleted*] two dayes before the date of his letter w*hi*ch was the 2 of the p*re*sent

at Godalming with Montague, and they 'strove soe long to give each other the best inn, ther being but two good ones in the towne'. Gondomar 'tooke upp an alehowse and the viscount a clothiers howse and ther men jovialised in the two best inns'. Then Gondomar went down to Cowdray 'wher desiring to see Chichester church, hee was at first kept out and I thinke altogether by a poor sexton whoe shutt the doores against him'. Afterwards Gondomar, it was said, went to visit the Cotton family at Warblington in Hampshire, after which he departed for Portsmouth: *DSSD*, p. 79; *Letter 5*; PRO, SP 14/130/85; cf. Questier, *C&C*, pp. 392, 399–400. The Venetian ambassador, Alvise Valaresso, noted in early September 1622 that Gondomar had had differences with the Jesuits, while his successor, Coloma (who, the count of Tillières claimed in May 1623, referred to Gondomar as a liar and a charletan), was on much better terms with the Society: *CSPV, 1621–1623*, p. 403; PRO, PRO 31/3/57, fo. 205v. Subsequently, however, as it appears from a letter from Coloma to Cardinal Millini in 1624, Coloma changed his opinions somewhat: TD, V, pp. cclx–cclxii. On 10/20 August 1622, the Jesuit general, Muzio Vitelleschi, wrote to Richard Blount SJ that the English secular clergy were trying to alienate Gondomar from the Society: ARSJ, Anglia MS 1, fo. 161v.

[97] The Collège d'Arras.

[98] Edward Bennett.

[99] Joseph Haynes.

[100] George Fisher. Fisher had been ordered into exile by the privy council in February 1621 but had not left the country, and had subsequently taken part in a debate with George Abbot's chaplain, Daniel Featley: Anstr., II, p. 103.

[101] Matthew Britton.

[102] William Law. See TD, V, p. cclxi; *NAGB*, p. 97; Anstr., II, p. 204.

[103] Presumably a reference to Richard White, brother of Thomas White, alias Blacklo. See *NCC*, pp. 7, 128.

[104] i.e. Thomas White.

[105] Champney reported on 22 May/1 June 1622 that Catholics in England 'speake still of a pardon to come forth for all convictions, and that there is a commission granted to 8 of the counsell to determin upon the deliverie of all prisoners as well preistes as others', but nothing, apparently, had been done to effect this: AAW, A XVI, no. 112, pp. 463–464; cf. *Letter 6*.

[106] Henry de Vere, 18th earl of Oxford.

[month].[107] The palatin[108] is for certayn in the Palatinate where he and Mandsfeild will doe what mischeife they ca*n*.[109] I know not whether the expedition of his p*ro*ceedinges may not hinder the good course of things aswell in Ingland as els where. But all must be referred to Gods holy disposition. You heard of the king of France his happy successe agaynst his rebelles wherein if he goe forward, w*hi*ch we are to pray for, will bring them under his obedience.[110] Our bretheren in Ingland co*m*playne much of the Jesuites p*ro*ceedinges agaynst Mr Newma*n*[111] in Lisboa, whereof I suppose you are informed by Mr Newman him self.[112] For Mr Messenden[113] in <his> last wrote [*p. 450*] that he hadd a large paquet to send to Rome from him. They use the p*ro*tectoures[114] letters and authoritie to putt Mr Newma*n* out of his residence. I pray you have a*n* eye to his affayres and assist him all you ca*n* according to the informations you shall receave from him self. You see howe occasions fall out for our countries servise to hold you there longer than you expected. And certaynly thence you must <not> part till you have a successoure, howsoever your mayne busines goeth for this p*re*sent. The p*re*sident of the Benedictaynes,[115] haveinge beene lately at Parise, hath p*ro*mised them there to write to their p*ro*cter there at <Rome> to joyne w*i*th you in the matter of b*ishop*s, w*hi*ch, if they doe, will help salte*m* removendo p*ro*hibens. They can*n*ot yet jumpe together amongst them selves w*hi*ch doth them harme.[116] Even nowe was there heare a doctour of the Dominicanes to bidd farewell to Mr P*re*sident and to com*m*end him self unto the prayers of the howse, he being sent into Denmarke to preach. God graunt them good successe. He sayth that he is sent by the nu*n*cio[117] by his Holiness his

[107] See McClure, *LJC*, p. 433; PRO, SP 14/129/50; *DSSD*, p. 75; BL, Additional MS 48166, fo 142v; PRO, PRO 31/3/56, fo. 32r; G.P.V. Akrigg (ed.), *Letters of King James VI & I* (London, 1984), pp. 409–410.

[108] Frederick V, elector palatine.

[109] See *CSPV, 1621–1623*, pp. 267, 324, 326; *CCE*, p. 73; BL, Harleian MS 1581, fo. 160r.

[110] See *CSPV, 1621–1623*, pp. 294, 317.

[111] William Newman.

[112] For Thomas More's account, dated 8/18 March 1622, of the conflict in Lisbon over the semimary founded there through the beneficence of Pedro Coutinho, see AAW, A XVI, no. 102, pp. 427–429; see also TD, IV, pp. cclviii, cclx, cclxv; J. Kirk and W. Croft, *Historical Account of Lisbon College* (Barnet, 1902); *NCC*, p. 258.

[113] Edward Maddison. He had been sent to Madrid in November 1619 as agent for the English College at Douai. See Anstr., II, p. 207.

[114] Edouardo Farnese, cardinal protector of the English nation. See Questier, *C&C*, pp. 326, 327, 345; *NAGB, passim*.

[115] William (Rudesind) Barlow OSB.

[116] According to John Ducket, writing on 1/11 May 1622, the Benedictines at Paris were saying that 'there will be bishop[s] if the match hould, otherwise not': AAW, A XVI, no. 109, p. 453.

[117] Giovanni Francesco Guido del Bagno, archbishop of Patras.

order.[118] We have your acquittance of the 23 of March, as I reme*m*ber, for 35 crownes, receaved of o*ur* agent[119] there. I pray you keepe a*n* accompt of that [which] you receive, that our accompts may be entire w*i*th him. Noe more nowe but my love and best wishes to y*our* self and Mr Farrare,[120] telling you both that all y*our* freinds could willingly co*m*playne of y*our* seldom writing. God ever keepe you both.

Doway, this 11 of May 1622.

Yours ever,

Champney

If the match goe forward it would be convenient we hadd some honest frend nere the queene. For w*hi*ch purpose we have thought of Mr Clifford[121] of Antwerpe who, as you knowe, by y*our* and y*our* freinds meanes was p*re*ferred to the duches of Feria[122] and quitt himselfe well.[123] I wrote hereof to y*our* brother and <he> liketh verie well both of the thing and of the ma*n*. The duke of Feria wilbe both able and willing to sett <it> forward if you ca*n* co*n*venien[t]ly dispose the business that we be not p*re*vented therein; if the thing fall out you shall do well. Here is a speech that Mrs Ward[124] has put her self in the Inquisition.[125] We knowe not in what sense it may be true. The Lord Digbie is, by this, in Spayn w*i*th his wife and eldest sonn and daughter.[126]

[118] The nuncio reported to Propaganda Fide on 8/18 June 1622 that he had appointed the Dominicans Jacques de Brouwer and Nicolas Janssens 'pour faire une enquête au Danemark et en Norvège': *CGB*, I, pp. 212, 261–262, see also *ibid.*, p. 296.

[119] Giovanni Battista Scanarolio, the agent in Rome for the English College at Douai. See *CGB*, I, p. 54. For Scanarolio's letter to John Bennett of 19/29 June 1622, see AAW, A XVI, no. 115, p. 471. For letters to Scanarolio from English secular priests, see PRO, PRO 31/9/90, *passim.*

[120] William Harewell. Harewell had left Rome on 28 April/8 May 1622: CRS, 10, p. 191.

[121] Henry Clifford.

[122] Jane Dormer, duchess of Feria.

[123] On 23 April 1623, William Trumbull provided Henry Clifford with a letter of recommendation to Sir George Calvert, describing Clifford as 'a very sufficient and honest gentleman', who had attended on the duchess of Feria until her death, and subsequently resided in Flanders but wanted briefly to return to England 'to followe his particuler affaires': PRO, SP 77/16, fo. 145r–v.

[124] Mary Ward.

[125] For Mary Ward's arrival in Rome in 1622, and her interview with Gregory XV, see M. Chambers, ed. H.J. Coleridge, *The Life of Mary Ward (1585–1645)*, 2 vols (London, 1885), II, pp. 2–3; *CGB*, I, pp. 69, 136. For the discussion during 1622 of Ward's institute by the congregation of bishops and regulars, headed by Cardinal Bandini, see M.M. Littlehales, *Mary Ward* (London, 1998), pp. 110, 114; Chambers, *Life*, II, p. 59; Dirmeier, *MW*, I, pp. 661–662, 684–685, 698–699, and *passim.*

[126] McClure, *LJC*, p. 432.

[*on p. 452*]

*Addressed*: Perillustra et admodu*m* rev*erend*o d*omi*no, D[omino] Johanni Benetto, cleri Anglicani in curia Romana procuratori. Romae.

*Endorsed*: D. Champ[ney]. Maii xi$^{o}$.

## 5. Anthony Champney to John Bennett, 20/30 May 1622

[*AAW, A XVI, no. 113, pp. 465–466*]

R*everen*d and respected s*ir*,

M$^{r}$ P*re*sident[127] had y*our*s of the last of Aprill and 7 of May. We are sorie of yo*ur* solitude but <glad> of [your] co*n*stancie and corage. God, I hope, will <give> effect to all yo*ur* good endevores. M$^{r}$ P*re*sident doth still co*n*tinue ill. God graunt we may see him one [*i.e.* on] his feete agayne, for w*hi*ch I beseech you pray in those holy places.[128] Yesternight came one hither who was in London the Su*n*day before and brought a message from my Lord Vaux that he did rely upon M$^{r}$ P*re*sident for a chaplayn major of his regiment.[129] For he will not have anie of the Jesuites p*ro*viding.[130] He brought newes of the count of Gondemoors his being at Plimmouth in his way to Spain, likewise of the countess of Buckinghams being Catholike for w*hi*ch the king, he sayth, is angrie. But I pray God her religione be sincere.[131] He telleth also of a booke[132] writen in Latin in France of the co*n*veniencie of the match <which> ~~with~~ Canterburie[133] p*re*sented to the kinge, thinking to p*ro*cure his dislike thereof, but it fell owt quite co*n*trarie. For he liked it so well that he hath caused it to be printed in Inglishe. The

[127]Matthew Kellison.

[128]William Bishop reported Kellison's recovery on 18/28 July 1622: AAW, A XVI, no. 124, p. 501. John Bennett understood on 24 September/4 October 1622 that Kellison had 'fallen backe into his ague': AAW, A XVI, no. 151, p. 587. But cf. *Letters 13, 15*.

[129]Emerging out of the marriage negotiations with the Spaniards was a concession that Lord Vaux (with another Catholic peer, the earl of Argyll) could raise troops for service in Flanders: see Cogswell, *BR*, p. 20; McClure, *LJC*, p. 428; PRO, SP 94/30, fo. 64r; *CGB*, I, p. 312; see also above, pp. 27–28, 51–52.

[130]The Vaux family tended, however, to function as a patron of the Society of Jesus. See also *Letter 13*.

[131]The count of Tillières recorded that the countess of Buckingham had converted to Catholicism at Easter 1622: PRO, PRO 31/3/56, fo. 44v. See *Letter 14*.

[132]Michel Du Val, *Hispani-Anglica seu Malum Punicum Angl'Hispanicum* (Paris, 1622, translated and published in London in the same year). See Cogswell, *BR*, pp. 39, 41–42, 46, 48, 50.

[133]George Abbot.

warrant for the deliverie of the lay prisoners was under the broad seale some dayes before his departure from London and, as he sayd, was p*re*sently to be put in execution.[134] He sayd further that the Jesuites hadd made a*n* assembly in London about y*o*ur business to co*n*sult what they showld answer to the reasons for b*ishop*s, whereby I gather that your business is not so nere a*n* end. For I imagin they will p*ro*cure delay till these mens answers come to Rome. They have showed a great deale of violence agaynst M^r^ Newman in Lisboa whereof I doubt not that [you] have heard. You must in the behaulf of all the clergie, who is [*sic*] wronged in him, defend him agaynst their violence.[135]

[*p. 466*] M^r^ More[136] is upon his way hither, and then for Ingland to set forward that house of Lisboa.[137] M^r^ Farrare,[138] when he cometh, shalbe most hartely welcome. It is pitie such mynds or sowles showld not be in better bodies, sed ipse fecit nos ut [*word illegible*: no*n* (?)] ipsi nos. When you were here my leysure was small but, nowe M^r^ P*re*sident is sick, I ame quit[e] opprest. God will either give strength or help, to whose holy grace I committ you this 9 of June 1622.

Yours ever,

Champney

*Addressed*: Admodu*m* r*everen*do d*omi*no, D[omino] Johan*n*i Benetto cleri Anglicani procuratori in curia Romana. Roma.

*No endorsement.*

## 6. John Hazell[139] to Diego de Lafuente, [after 25 July] 1622

[*AAW, OB I/i, no. 64, fos 125r–126v*]

Very r*everen*d s*i*r,

Bycause I have intreated yo*u*r favo*u*r and [*MS damaged*] I will geve yo*u* a true accompt of what I have undertaken and p*er*formed.

[134] See *Letter 6.*
[135] See *Letter 4.*
[136] Thomas More.
[137] Anstr., I, p. 234.
[138] William Harewell.
[139] See H. Bowler (ed.), *London Sessions Records, 1605–1685*, CRS, 34 (London, 1934), pp. 105, 106, 386.

The embassadour of Poland,[140] having [*MS damaged*: obtained from our (?)] kinges Majestie the liberty of the lay Catholique prisoners, commended the procuring of [*MS damaged*] to Count Gondomar and Sir Arthure Aston.[141]

But bycause there wanted a solli[citor] [*MS damaged*] was neglected, whereuppon the Catholiques of the New Prison earnestly intreated me to [*MS damaged*] whereunto I gave consent apprehending it to be a busines of small labor and lesse charge.

Thereupon I went to the embasador of Spayne[142] in their name to intreat his assurance aswell bycau[se] the busines concerned the Catholique cause, as also because the embassador of Poland had left [?] it recommended to his lordshipp and he [accord]ingly promised his best helpes, and for a beginning sent one of his follow[ers] with me to Mr Secretary Calvert[143] to make me knowne unto him. And withall to lett him understand that I was the man appointed to sollicytt the busynes for the Catholiques.

Mr Secretary then promised he wold moove the king and bad[e] me attend at Hampton Court, which I did for the space of foure or fyve dayes, but could gett none other answere than that he had no tyme oportune to moove the king.

This was before Michaelmas. And those dilatory answeres I receaved dyvers other tymes, twice or thrice a week for a month or fyve weekes together. At last, upon a lettre from his Majesty concerning this busynes, he answered his graunt was to be understood by way of banishment.

[140]Jerzy Ossolinski, count of Teczyn. See *Oratie van ... Georgius Ossolinsky Grave Palatijn van Tenizijn ende Sendomyria ... ende Ambassadeur aende Koninckklijcke Majesteyt van Groot-Brittaignien ... den 11 Martij, 1621* (The Hague, 1621); *A True Copy of the Latine Oration of the Excellent Lord George Ossolinsky* (1621). For the ideological significance and objectives of the Polish court's soliciting of military aid from James – namely the possibility of a 'crusade against the Infidel', something which James welcomed and which could be construed, at this point, as part of 'the public critique of the Protestant cause' – see S. Pincus, 'From holy cause to economic interest and the invention of the state', in A. Houston and S. Pincus (eds), *A Nation Transformed: England after the Restoration* (Cambridge, 2001), pp. 281–282, for which reference I am grateful to Paul Stevens.

[141]See Sir W. Fraser *et al.* (eds), *Reports on the Manuscripts of the Earl of Eglinton* (HMC, London, 1885), p. 118. For Gondomar's involvement in the securing of this concession for imprisoned Catholics, see CRS, 68, p. 152; *CGB*, I, p. 46. Sir Arthur Aston co-operated with the Polish ambassador in raising Irish troops for Polish military purposes. A formal complaint against Aston was lodged by the Russian ambassador in June 1622: PRO, SP 14/120/38, 107; McClure, *LJC*, pp. 352, 353, 388; *APC, 1621–1623*, pp. 32, 246; C.W. Russell and J.P. Prendergast (eds), *Calendar of the State Papers Relating to Ireland, 1615–1625* (London, 1880), pp. 334–335; BL, Harleian MS 1581, fo. 164r–v; see also *CGB*, I, pp. 100–101. For Aston's royalism during the civil war, see P.R. Newman, *Royalist Officers in England and Wales, 1642–1660* (London, 1981), p. 10.

[142]Diego Sarmiento de Acuña, count of Gondomar.

[143]Sir George Calvert.

But this answere gave soe small contentment to my lord embassador that he took that graunt rather for a punishm*en*t than a grace, and for his p*ar*t wold not accept of it whereupon, at his Ma*jes*t[i]es next com*m*ing to towne, he renued the suit againe to his Ma*jes*ty and obtayned a promise of their lib*er*tyes upon bonds.

Afterwards, diligently solliciting p*er*formance of this p*ro*mise from tyme to tyme, my answere still was that they were devising a course to doe it in some sufficyent legall manner, for w*hi*ch it was necessarie to consult w*i*th my l[ord] chief justice,[144] the other justices and the attorney generall,[145] and theire opynions to be delivered to his Ma*jes*ty. Soe difficult a matter it was made that in those consultaci[ons] there were fyve months spent, though I did followe it most importunelye from daye to daye, attendi[ng] oftentymes whole dayes w*i*thout audyence or speeche.

At last, upon Easter Monday, M^r^ Secretary tolde me there was nowe a course resolv[ed] [up]on w*hi*ch [h]e had not com*m*ission to declare unto me, but badd me come to him the next daye, and th[en he to]ld mee I was to attend upon my l[ord] keep*er*[146] who wold acquaint me w*i*th the course, w*hi*ch was that all [*MS damaged*] of othe[r] prisons w*i*thin the kingdome should be by wrytts of habeas corpus remooved to the kin[g's bench], and thence deliv*er*ed by the justices of that benche upon their bonds as aforesaid by vertu[e of a w]rytt unde[r] the great seale, devised for this speciall purpose, w*hi*ch onely wrytt my l[ord] keep*er* told me wold cost them iii^li^ a peece besides the charge of the habeas corpus w*i*th other charges belonging thereunto and besides all other fees aswell of keep*er*s as officers.

This charge being considered to be verie great and such as a great p*ar*t could not undergoe, I enformed my l[ord] embassado*ur* thereof, and mooved him that the wrytt might be gotten gratis, which accordinglie he p*ro*cured for the poorer sorte. But this difference betwene poore and rich being likely to breed p*er*plexitie and confusion, we made further suit to p*ro*cure this favo*ur* for all, w*hi*ch also was obtained; onely my l[ord] keeper badd me paye the clarks for wryting.

The wrytt being made, it concerned onelie such as were in prison for refusing the othe w*hi*ch, though it were a principall matter, yet manie being prisoners for other matters, though lesse offensive, we had reason to doubt that these wold not be suffred to have the benefitt of the wrytt, where upon we were forced to make suite that the wrytt might be enlarged and renewed to comprehend all other cases concerning

[144] Sir James Ley.
[145] Sir Thomas Coventry.
[146] John Williams, bishop of Lincoln.

recusancye, w*hi*ch was at last graunted, but there were still excepted all other cases, as printing, selling of books, speeches against ministers and the like.

This newe wrytt being made, I p*ro*cured habeas corpus for them of the Newe Prison. But, bycause their remoove from that prison to the kings bench wold have bene both troblesome and chargeable, I p*ro*cured that they might be onlie brought to the kings bench barr where, being presented w*it*h their causes, 2 dayes they were turned back, some p*re*tence of impedyments being still found, whereupon I was still dryven to goe to the secondary of the crowne office and to other officers and to promise them recompence of their fees w*hi*ch were taken awaye, a gratuity for their favo*ur* and furtherance and soe the next tyme of their apparance they were discharged.

Afterwards I proceeded to p*ro*cure the lib*er*tyes and discharge of other prisoners, and soe in those two termes of Easter and Trynitye 1622, w*it*h much importunitie and labor, there were released 4 or 5 and thirtye, for div*er*[s] of w*hi*ch number I was dryven to p*ro*cure from my l[ord] keep*er* speciall warrants, ether bycause there was no cause [*fo. 125v*] of their com[mittal] specified in the Mitt[imus or by]cause some other cause of the aforesaid was added to the cause of their refusin[g the] oathe or recusancye.[147]

The busines in towne [*MS damaged*] it remayned that a course should be taken for such as were prisoners in the contrye [*MS damaged*] [re]moove by habeas corpus may easily appeare to be [a] matter of much trouble and more charge. Therefore I petitioned my l[ord] keep*er* to take [in] to his considerac*i*on the difficultyes of it, especially that many of the Catholique prisoners were not able to beare the charge of their jorney to London, and some through sicknes and age not able to to travell at all. For those that were able to travell it was first graunted by my lord keep*er* that they should be brought up at the kings charge. And soe, to husband the matter well for the kings purse, my lord keep*er* sent to my l[ord] chief justice to drawe a l*ett*re that might be sent w*it*h the wrytts, com*m*aunding that none should be brought up but such as were capable of the kings grace, whereupon my l[ord] chief justice, consulting w*it*h my l[ord] treasorer concerning this l*ett*re, he opposed this course as chargeable for his Ma*jes*ty, notw*it*hstanding

[147] For those Catholics released from prison in 1622–1623, see CRS, 68, pp. 152–154; PRO, C 181/3, fos 70v–71v (lists contained in the docquet books of the crown office in chancery). For the writs in late June and the first week of July 1622 directed to the judges of king's bench 'to take baile' of large numbers of Catholic prisoners for recusancy and for refusing the oath of allegiance, see PRO, C 231/4, fos 141r, 143r. Further writs of this kind (and pardons to Catholic clergy) were issued in late November 1622 and (to judges on circuit as well as in London) from mid-February 1623 onwards: *ibid.*, fos 146r, 146v, 153r, 157r, 157v, 158r, 174r.

it was concluded that the king should beare the charge of the poorer sort and th*a*t the richer should beare their owne.

But finding in this course dyvers difficultyes w*hi*ch may easily appeare to any mans understanding, aswell for the troble as the charge,[148] I p*ro*posed to my l[ord] keep*er* another w*hi*ch was that the wrytts might be dyrected to the judges of the assizes, to enlarge in their sev*er*all circuit[s] such Catholique prisoners as the wrytts concerned, w*hi*ch course my lord allowing for his part (especially bycause it saved the kings purse) promised to moove the kings Ma*jes*ty in it, w*hi*ch he accordingly did. And soe his Ma*jes*ty com*m*aunded that that course should be taken.[149]

But whereas at first the wrytt was retornable cr*astin*o a*nim*ar*um*, the retorne being soe short, I sollicited anewe for a longer retorne and soe it was graunted to be quindena pasche. I further p*ro*cured my l[ord] keep*er*s *lett*re unto the judges to declare more expresly and fully his Ma*jes*ti[e]s intencyon that no occasion might be left to interprett the wrytt otherwise than according to the meaninge of that letter.

Moreover, the graunt being made to the embassador of Poland, it was onely understood <onely> [*sic*] of such as were prisoners then, to wytt at the tyme of the grace obtayned, w*hi*ch was about the [f]irst of August 1621, soe that all such as were com*m*itted afterwards were decreed incapable [t]hereof. And therefore, that they also might receave the benefitt of it, we were dryven to make the execuc*i*on of the graunt w*hi*ch was about the first of July 1622.

Thus difficult, troblesome and tedyous a busynes it prooved, and indeed, if it be well considered, it wilbe found a matter of great consequence not onelie for the benefytt that many poore Catholique prisoners enjoyed thereby a legall course, being newly and for this sole purpose devised to bayle those that were condempned in praemunire, but for the countenance it gave to religion, and it did incredibly moderate the passion and malice of the especiall enemyes thereof aswell officers of all qualletty as others.

[148] John Hacket memorialized and celebrated the 'mazes wherein' Williams 'led the Spanish embassador, with whom he shifted so cunningly that they could obtain nothing for the toleration of popish recusants but delays and expectations from time to time': Hacket, *SR*, part II, p. 6.

[149] An order from the king to the lord keeper, dated 25 July 1622, admitted that the directions which had been issued concerning the release of imprisoned Catholic separatists on bail 'before the king's bench' were 'very chargeable' to the 'poorer sort of recusants'. Assize judges were empowered to free them 'on the sureties and conditions before ordered': *CSPD, 1619–1623*, p. 429; PRO, SP 14/132/57, fo. 92r; BL, Additional MS 48166, fo. 154r.

Besides this I sollicited and brought to p*er*fection an other matter of great consequence w*hi*ch was that after the wrytts of *ad melius inquirendum* were sent and deliv*er*ed to the sheriffs of all the countyes of Wales, I procured a sup*er*sedeas to stay all p*ro*ceedings and messingers at the kings charge to carry them downe. In recompence whereof I receaved bare thanks from one onely man.

Lastly I have now labored in the matter of the informers, no man els willing to shewe himself in it, much lesse to take any great paynes therein or to be at anye charge. I may well saye that nothing had bene done in the generall had I not undertaken it.

Besides I rann hazard of incurring the displeasure of the state, in following with soe much importunitye a busines soe lyttle grateful and pleasing to them. And de facto the bishopp of Durham,[150] w*i*th the judges of that circuit, made great complaints of me to his Ma*jes*tye for my earnestnes and forwardnes in the cause.

I may well add that, to prosecute this, I neglected my owne pryvate affayres as also dyvers good occasions of preferments, as in p*ar*ticuler in any course wherein my l[ord] embassador [*fo. 126r*] Gondomar could have furthered me, w*hi*ch he voluntarilie [*MS obscured*] to doe in any course I should undertake, aswell for the paynes he knewe I took in the [*MS damaged*] busynes as also for some speciall service I had done his l*ordshi*pp.

Seing therefore, r*everen*d good s*ir*, I have taken soe long and great paynes w*i*th so much hindrance and hazard to my self, seing I have disbursed so much moneyes, and ingaged my credytt for much more to gratefie officers and others whose labo*u*r and helpe I used in the busynes, I humbly intreat your charytable furtherance that in recompence of all my labo*u*rs I may not be too much p*re*judiced both in my credytt and state, and I shall ever remayne,

Y*ou*r poore frend and servant [to] be com*m*aunded,

John Hasell

S*ir*, th*a*t yo*w* may the better understand the benefytt I did the Catholiq*ue* prisoners and what charge I saved them, aswell in the fees of the sheriffs as in their remoove from their severall prisons to the kings bench, I thinck good to lett yo*u* knowe that it cost one David East, being a poore man, remooved but from S[t] Albans to the kings bench, and therat bayled, himself alone six pounds and upwards, and yet the fees of the wrytt was [*sic*] forgeven him.[151] According to which proportyon let it be judged what it wold have cost such as had

[150] Richard Neile.

[151] For the writ in early May 1622 to release David East from the king's bench prison, see PRO, C 231/4, fo. 134v, which also records others (Sir John Webb, William Matthews,

come from the remote parts, brought up by sheriffs and officers, their charges and all their fees reckoned.

[*on fo. 126v*]

*Addressed*: R*everendissi*mo in Christo patri D[omino] Didaco de Fuentes espiscopo Madriti.

*Endorsed*: Mary Q[ueen] Mother.
John Hasel his account about his soliciting for Catho[lics].
Com*m*on Cathol[ics].
Artis intoriatus sive tabelliorum libri duo spirum.

## 7. William Bishop to John Bennett, 15/25 August 1622

[*AAW, A XVI, no. 133, pp. 533–534*]

Very deare s*i*r and as much respected,

Being to send the inclosed I thought good to add these first to let you understand that Mr Gage dined with us yesterday, with whom we had much talke for he taried with us 2 howers before and three howers after dinner.[152] For other matters we found him indifferent, but he thought it not expedient that we should have any bishope before his imbassy were passed. He is very confident that he shall p*er*swade his Ma*jes*tie to condescend to all that he hath p*ro*mised in the favour of Catholiques and so to worke that the mariage shalbe presently concluded. He would not have the newes of a bishop to be bussed into the puritans eares before all were concluded, for feare lest they should thereupon cause a new cry against the mariage and so trouble the king. We replied that their malice was rather against Spaniards than o*u*r having of bishops, and that therefore it should be better to ha[ve] bishops before the match, that they might not be hated more for the match and <the> Spaniards sake than for their owne. And that if his Ma*jes*tie would, for ~~the~~ <o*u*r> having of bishops, breake with the king of Spaine, then it were better he should breake with him before the match were made than after, when it should ly in his hands to afflict also the infanta, maried, at his pleasure, when they were better to kepe out of his power, if for any so necessary

William Martin, Barnardine Peppey, Margaret Field, and Grace Cooper) freed by the same means a few days later.

[152] See Questier, *C&C*, p. 397.

a point of o*ur* religion he would be so much moved. Diverse other reasons passed to and fro, he sometimes, between, p*ro*testing that he had not done any evill offices that way. To say the truth he is like to find our king in very good disposition, for he hath promised the Spanish ambassadour[153] that he will take away all penall lawes against recusants, and de facto hath commanded the judges of assise not to meddle with any recusants in this summers circuit. All lay Catholikes be deliv*er*ed on their bondes out of prison.[154] And all priests in prison do walk and rid[e] too, abroad, as Mr Hewes[155] assured me, at their pleasure. But no assurance from his Ma*jes*t[i]e of any continuance.[156] That must be wrought by his Holines or the king of Spaine. For the co[u]ntenance of Catholik[es] and continuance of their ease it wilbe necessary that his Holines do add to his conditions that three or four Catholike lords may be sworne on the privy councell where all <such> matters are <soe> principally handled.[157] Item, that we may have in ev*er*y shire some two or three justices of peace, either Catholike or Catholikely affected, to defend the country Catholikes in ev*er*y shire.[158] To w*hi*ch end the old oath of <the kings> supremacy and new [oath] of false fidelity must be suppressed in all Catholikes

[153]Carlos Coloma.

[154]On 2 August 1622, Lord Keeper Williams had issued an official instruction to the judges: AAW, A XVI, no. 127, p. 509; AAW, OB I/i, no. 80; TD, V, pp. ccxcv–ccxcvi; PRO, SP 14/132/84. Williams cited reason of state for the king's command to him to pass two writs under the great seal to release imprisoned Catholics. The judges were to comply in the cases of those imprisoned for recusancy, for refusing the oath of supremacy, for having or dispersing popish books, for hearing Mass or 'any other parte of recusancy which doth concerne religion only and not of state, which shall appeare unto you to be totally civill and politicall': AAW, A XVI, no. 127, p. 509; see also above, pp. 30–37.

[155]This appears to be a reference to the writer ('E. Hew[es]') of AAW, A XVI, no. 165, pp. 625–626, whom Matthew Kellison seems to cite as the agent in England for the English College at Douai: AAW, B 26, no. 139; see also AAW, B 27, no. 3; cf. Anstr., I, p. 178, II, pp. 164–165.

[156]Simonds D'Ewes recorded on 4 August 1622 that one of the judges at the Winchester assizes had said that 'the king disliked a rumour of toleration, and was sorrye for his peoples feares, and that hee himselfe was farr from poperye': *DSSD*, p. 89.

[157]In an undated missive (AAW, B 25, no. 82) which was dispatched to Gondomar in Madrid (though written in English) after the count's return there, and which commented on the marriage articles of December 1622 (see Redworth, *PI*, p. 177; Gardiner, *NSMT*, p. 332), William Bishop advised that it should be arranged, 'if it may bee, that two noblemen at the least be made 2 of the kings privy councell, that they may there deale for Catholikes'. The 'fittest' men, according to Bishop, were 'the Lord William Howard, the Lord [Thomas] Arundell of Warder, the Lord Harbert [Henry Somerset], the Lord Ewers [William Eure] and Sir Thomas Savage', and also 'the Lord Clenrichard [Richard Burke]'; Bishop added that the first two were 'the wisest, the gravest and fittest men'. (This modifies Questier, *C&C*, p. 389.)

[158]William Bishop argued that such men might 'winne credit so that, when a parlement is called, they may be chosen knightes of the shire': AAW, B 25, no. 82.

cases. For these, and some such like, it were very expedient that either o*ur* bishope were established, to take order for these orders, or that some of us were deputed by his Holines to go in and treat about them, leave being gotten by his Holines or the Spaniards meanes of the king for our safe entry. M$^{r}$ Gage doth make us to feare, albeit you have many hopeful wordes given you, ~~yf~~ <lest> you shall not gett the bishop named before they are fully accorded, w*hi*ch is like to be about or before All Saints as he verily thinketh. If you be forced to stay so long, or otherwise [are] willing enough to have about for the Roman college [*sic*],[159] certify them in England so much and you shall not want either comission or instructions to compass it, as I verily hope. Other newes there is none worth the writing w*hi*ch you shall not heare of Mons*ieu*r d'Aire,[160] for some say that the Cardinal de Rets[161] is dead, a great losse to France but, may be, a plaice to Mons*ieu*r de Lusons cardinalate, w*hi*ch Mons*ieu*r d'Aire greatly desireth, to whom I pray you com*m*end me hartely. And so with my best wishes to yo*ur*self, I do rest.

Yo*ur*s alwaies assured,

W*illia*m Bishope

I do hold it most expedient that you daily make instance for o*ur* bishope, albeit I wish it should be holden as secret as may bee among o*ur* selves for, within a month or two after you have obtained it, his bulles will not be dispatched, and order in p*ar*ticular sett with all due circumstances for his consecration. I thinke it wilbe best cheape in Paris even for D[octor] Chelison[162] or any that come out of England. For here we never want the presence of three bishops, w*hi*ch wilbe hard to find in any p*ar*t of Flanders.

The 25 of August 1622.

[*on p. 534*]

*Addressed*: A monsieur, Monsieur Bennett, agent du cleargy d'Ingleterre ches Monsig*no*r l'evesq*ue* d'Aire auprès le Mont de la Trinité. A Rome.

*No endorsement.*

[159] The English College in Rome.

[160] Sébastien Bouthillier, bishop of Aire.

[161] Henri Gondi, cardinal de Retz, who had died on 2/12 August 1622.

[162] Matthew Kellison.

## 8. Eaton [Edward Bennett] to John Bennett, 31 August 1622

*[AAW, A XVI, no. 134, pp. 535–538; printed in TD, V, pp. ccxlviii–ccl]*[163]

Sir,

Wee receave greate content of your industrious negotiation in the matter of b*ishop*s, ~~but~~ and the happie success thereof.[164] Neverthelesse, our adversaries, who have not bene able to prevayle againste you there, have not omitted to stirre up coales here and, as is very p*ro*bablie thought, have stirred up the kinge and state to oppose in the businesse. The lord keeper[165] hath bene lately w*i*th the Spanish embassadour,[166] complaininge, as from the kinge, that the pope went about to sett up b*ishop*s in his kingdome againste his will, w*hi*ch in former ages was not wonte to bee done but by the princes nomination; and w*i*thall signified that he understood they should be created w*i*th titles of Canterburie, Lincolne etc., w*hi*ch must neede cause great exasperation in the state and would by noe meanes bee

[163] Only the postscript of this letter is in the hand of Edward Bennett.

[164] In reply to a previous letter sent by Edward Bennett on 4 August, John Bennett notified him on 30 September/10 October 1622 that, 'for our suite of bishops', the secular clergy leadership's opponents 'leave nothing untryed to hinder it; and, having bene foyled here (for we have a decree before his Hol[iness] for it), they fly to his Majesty of England for help, and here give out that his Majesty is offended with the motion; and all to delaye'. John Bennett advised that 'you must helpe there, that from thence we be not hindred. They oppose themselves to his Majestyes designes what they can, and yet will make him by art serve their turne. There is no meanes to assure his Majesty against there slightes but to bring in bishops whome his Hol[iness] will charge soe to governe his people that it be without offence to his Majesty. And, if bishops had governed hertofore, his Majesty had not bene troubled w*i*th such plotts as have bene discovered to the hazard of his Majesty and the ignominy of Catholicke relligion. I praye putt that in exequution which in my last I did soe earnestly desire and gett, if you can procure it, a testimoniall from the Spanish embassad[or] for the present want of bishops and send it to me'. John Bennett instructed his brother to 'forgett not alsoe to drawe reasons to satisfy his Majesty. 1. We seeke but one bishop. 2. Titular in partibus infidelium, not in England, soe as there wilbe no cause of emulation with them at home. 3. His jurisdiction will not be larger than that of the archpriest. 4. It wilbe limited and knowne. 5. It will serve to keep our opposites in order. 6. It will oblige the superior to accounte of his owne and his subjectes actions and consequently [p]reserve his Majesty and estate from all trouble that way': AAW, A XVI, no. 156, p. 605. He further instructed him to warn James that 'if he should be against ordinary jurisdiction, without which Catholick relligion cannot stande, they here presently will take heed therof and bring his Hol[iness] into jeleousy that his Majesty meaneth not well towardes Catholickes and that all is but a shewe; and soe make him doubtefful to proceede in the matter of dispensation; specially, his Majesty suffering soe many bishops in Ireland and that without inconvenience': *ibid*; see also Questier, *C&C*, pp. 399–400.

[165] John Williams, bishop of Lincoln.

[166] Carlos Coloma.

suffered.[167] The embassadour answered he had not bene informed concerninge the state of this bussinesse and therefore could, for the present, give him noe full answere. Only this, he sayd, hee had heard, that the clergie p*re*tended bishops but not w*i*th any such titles as he spoke of, but only w*i*th episcopall authori[ti]e to minister the sacrament of ~~extreame u[nction]~~ confirmation and performe other things pertaininge to such a function. Neverthelesse he promissed to informe himselfe better concerninge the whole matter and afterwards give the kinge and his lordship ~~better~~ a fuller answer. Upon this the embassadour hath writ[t]e to the Spanish embassadour[168] there w*i*th you to knowe in what termes ~~that~~ the matter stands.[169] Some

[167] Williams, said Hacket, was inspired by 'so great [. . .] disaffections to that corrupt and unsound Church' that he 'watched' the Catholic clergy 'more narrowly than any other counsellor'. He intervened when they petitioned Buckingham 'to assist them for the erection of titulary popish prelates in this kingdom'. Buckingham consulted Williams, and Williams advised that it 'would set all the kingdom on fire and make his Majesty unable to continue those favours and conveniences to peaceable recusants'; and that it would take away 'from his Majesty an hereditary branch of the crown', namely 'the investitures of bishops'; and furthermore it would be worse than an 'absolute toleration'. For whereas, in France, toleration 'doth so divide and distinguish towns and parishes that no place makes above one payment to their church-men [. . .] this invisible consistory shall be confusedly diffused over all the kingdom'. The result would be that 'many of the subjects shall, to the intolerable exhausting of the wealth of the realm, pay double tithes, double offerings and double fees'. This was one reason, in fact, why the Irish nation was so impoverished. Also, 'if the princes match should go on, this new erected consistory will put the ensuinge parliament into such a jealousie and suspition that it is to be feared that they will shew themselves very untractable upon all propositions'. Finally, it was against 'the fundamental law of the land' for 'the pope to place a bishop in this kingdom'. Hacket claims that James ordered Williams to put these arguments 'with his best skill to the Spanish embassador', and that Williams pretended to Coloma that he 'was startled at a heady notion that came from Savoy, as he thought', concerning Catholic bishops. Williams urged Coloma 'to send for the Savoyan [ambassador] and to wish him to throw aside his advice for titulary bishops lest it should hinder the king of Spain's desire in accommodating the Catholics with those courtesies which had been granted': Hacket, *SR*, part I, p. 94. James had heard, remarked Alvise Valaresso, of a petition to the curia to appoint four bishops, and that the pope would grant two, one of them being Diego de Lafuente. The king was infuriated at the proposal to give those who were appointed 'the title of the bishoprics of this realm': *CSPV, 1621–1623*, p. 403. William Bishop, however, argued that Williams had 'a good affection to our religion', and that the fault lay with Coloma: AAW, A XVI, no. 164, p. 623.

[168] Francisco de la Cueva, duke of Alburquerque, Spanish ambassador in Rome.

[169] Lord Keeper Williams had told Buckingham on 23 August 1622 that Coloma 'took the alarum very speedily of the titulary Romish bishop, and before my departure from his house at Islington [. . .] did write both to Rome and Spain to prevent it'. Williams said that the regime's information about the suit for bishops with the titles of established sees had in fact come from Tobias Mathew. Williams observed that Mathew would 'prove but an apocryphal and no canonical intelligencer, acquainting the state with this project for the Jesuites rather than for Jesus['s] sake': *Cabala*, p. 70; BL, Harleian MS 7000, fo. 98r; see also *Letter 23*. Mathew had revealed the project initially to his friend Sir Francis Bacon: TD, V, p. 90. In a letter to Buckingham of 29 September 1622, Mathew denounced 'those indiscreet

of ours, who live about this towne, have bene too negligent in not preoccup[y]inge the embassadour[170] w*it*h the substance of our designes, and stayinge his hand from intermedlinge, to the p*re*judice [*p. 536*] of our affayres in a businesse alreadie determined by the sea apostolike. But, neverthelesse, wee hope all will goe well. For althoughe he bee much addicted to the Jesuits, as he himselfe confesseth, yet he seemeth a noble and honeste minded man and hath promised to favour us in all juste pretensions, and w*it*hall to informe our kinge and his ministers what we pretende, to see if we canne gaine the state by fayre meanes w*hi*ch, if wee cannott, we shall [*word deleted*] have his helping hand to further our designe however, w*hi*ch is all wee doe desire. This wee have, from his owne mouth, this morninge, M^r^ Broughton, who is nowe very forward for b*ishop*s,[171] M^r^ Harvie,[172] M^r^ Barker[173] and my selfe haveinge bene w*it*h him to treate about this businesse. The newes of the Spanish embassadour interposinge himselfe in this affayre after such a maner troubled us all. But the greatest feare is paste and wee have not spared to speake playnely and signifie unto him expressly that the Jesuits are the only men that oppose us and therefore have desired him he give noe eare unto them in our matters, to our prejudice, w*hi*ch he hath promised he will not, w*it*hout our knowledge. And soe wee departed from him w*it*h greate contentement and satisfaction.[174] Afterwards, I went to the

English Catholicques which I declared to your lordship heertofore to have drawn a purpose from the pope to consecrate and send hither some English Catholicque bushops', for they had 'proceeded so farr as to name the men', namely Matthew Kellison, William Bishop, Richard Smith, John Bosvile, Cuthbert Trollop, and Edward Bennett. Mathew claimed that 'the Jesuits have had no part in this negotiation' but that, 'if the business proceed, some one or more of them will also gett to be made bushops heer': BL, Harleian MS 1581, fo. 82r.

[170] Carlos Coloma.

[171] On 22 August/1 September 1622, William Bishop reported from Paris that Richard Broughton 'hath even now written unto the nuncio of France and among <other> things doth tell him that matters amend apace in England and that now it wilbe no danger to have bishops if it so please his Holines. He estemeth Doctors Kellison, Bishope, Smith and Champeney to be very gratefull to the cleargy and that any of them wilbe acceptable': AAW, A XVI, no. 136, p. 541. In a letter of 23 October 1622, Broughton explained to John Bennett that 'I was never against bishops but onely I wished yt had beene stayed a little longer before begunne'. Broughton added that, 'since our first beeing with' Coloma, he (Broughton) had 'beene there agayne to putt hym in mynde to bee and continue our frend'. John Colleton, with Cuthbert Trollop and Roger Strickland, had also been to visit Coloma: AAW, A XVI, no. 167, p. 631.

[172] Joseph Haynes.

[173] Oliver Almond. Elsewhere his alias is given as Parker: Anstr., I, p. 7.

[174] William Bishop sent word on 26 September/6 October 1622 that Coloma had dropped his objections: AAW, A XVI, no. 153, p. 595. On 29 September, Edward Bennett commented to his brother that the king had shown Coloma 'a letter written by Secretary Calvert in the name of the king to show the kings dislik as before. Now we know that there is a Jesswet [a

Dutch embassadour,[175] acquaintinge him w*i*th what the l[ord] keeper had delivered to the embassadour, and desireinge him, in occasions, to signifie to the kinge and his ministers that wee pretend noe more but what the Spanishe embassadour hath alreadie signified to the lord [*p. 537*] keeper, that is, to have a b[ishop] ~~who may~~ or b*ishop*s, w*i*th some forraine title, who may exercise amongst us the function of episcopall authoritie, who hath promised all favour.[176] Wee are upon p*re*sent departure; and soe, in haste, I end.

London, this 31 of Auguste, 1622.

Yours,

Eaton

I use another hand because I am soe busye. It is two a clock, and am to goe 27 miles this night. All this morninge I was w*i*the these embassadours and, [I] hope, [they have] don us som good.

[*on p. 538*]

*Addressed*: Admodu*m* r[everendo] d[omino], D[omino] Joanni Bennetto cleri Anglicani apud sedem apostolicam agenti. Romam.

*Endorsed*: M^r^ Faringt[on].[177] Aug[ust] 31.
I had in mine that the lord keeper sayd we went about to make an archbishope of Canterburry and of Yorke and, when the ambassadour told him that they p*re*tended [*three words illegible*] onely to [*word illegible*] and to kepe order among priestes, he was appeased.

reference, presumably, to Mathew] who is well acquainted with the sayed secretary, whom we vehemently suspect in this bussines. It is certayn if [. . .] [Gondomar] had been heer, he had soe satisfied the king as that a bushop might have come in withowt any notice of the estate taken of hym'. The way was now clear for the pope to appoint a bishop, and 'it must not be in the estate['s] liking or disliking whether we have bushops or no. If it were soe, we should have no goverment at all heere': AAW, B 47, no. 30; *CSPV, 1621–1623*, p. 403.

[175]Jean-Baptiste van Male. For van Male, see C.H. Carter, *The Secret Diplomacy of the Habsburgs, 1598–1625* (London, 1964), ch. 11.

[176]Van Male promised Edward Bennett that he would speak to the lord keeper to 'shew him how litle cause they have to except against the priestes for seeking for bishops': AAW, A XVI, no. 147, p. 567.

[177]The name Farrington was one of the aliases used by Edward Bennett.

## 9. Caesar Clement[178] to [John Bennett], 31 August/ 10 September 1622

[*AAW, A XVI, no. 137, pp. 543–544*]

Verry wor*shipfu*ll syr,

W*i*th the occasion of directinge unto yow th*is* l*ett*re, I lett yow knowe t*ha*t I sent an answer to y*o*u th*e* 28 of Aug[ust] and t*ha*t here be many discourses uppon whose head th*e* mytre off th*e* graunted b[ishop] shall lyght, amonge whome su*m* would make to believe that yow labour onlie for y*ou*r brother,[179] and t*ha*t th*e* ende off this business is to seeke y*ou*r selves, and t*ha*t itt hathe not th*e* com*m*on consent. I do as a frende warne yow what is sayde, even by su*m* verry grave men off th*e* clergie. We hope itt is otherwyse, thowgh th*e* hydinge off th*e* parson[s] from us th*a*t ar interessated in itt, and th*e* pretendinge to have an anomalu*m* com*m*ended by th*is* nuncio,[180] maketh th*e* mattre not a little suspect. Iff yow go thus to worcke yow will marr all and make th*e* m*att*re of b*ishop*s odious agayne. Yow be discrete ynowgh to looke well abowtt yow t*ha*t yow be not founde partiall in th*e* carriage off so waightie a busines. Th*e* best were th*e* election wer as neare canonicall as o*u*r state will permitt, t*ha*t nott onlie th*e* assistents butt others allso off respect t*ha*t ar abrode wer harde theyr opinion in individuo, t*ha*t he myght be a parson pleasinge and off partes requisite. For iff yow make him amonge y*ou*r selves onlie, yow must allso looke t*ha*t he shall stande by himself when yow shall need concell and helpe off those who hetherto have assisted yow. Wee knowe who be uppon th*e* liste and who ar borne in hand t*ha*t ar not. To doo well, itt showlde go by the voyces off th*e* gravest and off most respect, w*hi*ch his Holl[iness] and protect*o*r can easilye have iff itt wer so propounded. Remembre th*e* sturres past, because they instituted an archpriest[181] in th*e* begin*n*inge w*i*thowtt hearinge th*e* clergie, w*hi*ch clergie yow must not thincke is

[178] Caesar Clement was, at this point, vicar-general of the Spanish army in Flanders, as well as dean of the church of St Gudule in Brussels: *CGB*, I, pp. 8, 120–121.

[179] Edward Bennett.

[180] For the unwillingness of the Flanders nuncio (Giovanni Francesco Guido del Bagno, archbishop of Patras) to become involved in the process of nomination for an English bishop, and his opinion that it was primarily the concern of the Paris nuncio (the 'ordinarie of England'), see AAW, A XVI, no. 144, pp. 561–562; TD, V, pp. 88, 89. The Flanders nuncio was, from time to time, tacitly sympathetic towards the vicar apostolic in Holland, Philip Rovenius, whom the English secular clergy regarded as a friend, principally because of his hostility to some of the religious orders; on the other hand, the nuncio was not (in general) a critic of the Jesuits and was also an enthusiastic supporter of Mary Ward: *CGB*, I, pp. 68–69, 107, 136, 162, 245, 251, cf. p. 514.

[181] George Blackwell.

in Inglande onlye, w*hi*ch opinion wer a grounde off division to th*e* wronge off many, w*hi*ch therfore I have laboured w*i*th M^r D*oct*or Kellison to take awaye all we cowlde to bringe in true correspondence between those at huome [*sic*] and abrode, t*ha*t so th*e* com*m*on cause myght have more poise, and speed th*e* better, w*hi*ch I wowlde had so ben observed in this off b*ishop*s. Off w*hi*ch no more, w*i*th my kyndest com*m*end*ations*.

From Brussels, the 10 off Sept[ember] 1622.

Y*ou*r unfayned frende,

C[aesar] Clement

*No address or endorsement.*

## 10. Oliver Almond to John Strong [Matthew Kellison], 31 August/10 September 1622

[*AAW, A XVI, no. 138, pp. 545–546*]

R[ight] worthie sir,

I am right glad of your recoverie, and the 3 lynes you wryt did co*m*fort me much, beinge a tooken of some amendme*n*t. I have thought good to lett you understand in respect my name is used in Rome (as appeareth by a l*ett*er written by Don Anselmo[182] unto M^r Presto*n*[183]) co*n*cerning some speaches had betweene the sayd M^r Presto*n* and myselfe[184] of the death of D[octor] Kinge, b[ishop] of Londo*n*.[185] I reme*m*ber I related [*word omitted:* them] unto the r[ight] r[everend] archpriest, D[octor] Harreson deceased. And the truth was, as I can nowe call to mynd, th*a*t M^r Presto*n* never co*n*fessed unto me but denyed th*a*t ever he reco*n*ciled or in th*a*t kynd dealt w*i*th the b[ishop] of Londo*n*.[186]

[182] Robert (Anselm) Beech OSB.

[183] Roland (Thomas) Preston OSB.

[184] In November 1613, Anthony Champney had suspected Almond of being in agreement with Preston's opinions concerning the 1606 oath of allegiance: *NAGB*, p. 117.

[185] For the circulation of the rumour of Preston's involvement in the alleged conversion of Bishop John King, see D. Lunn, *The English Benedictines, 1540–1688* (London, 1980), pp. 51–52; *Letter 13*. John Gee claimed that he had asked among the London Catholic clergy which priest had reconciled the bishop and 'they named to me F[ather] Preston': T.H.B.M. Harmsen (ed.), *John Gee's Foot out of the Snare (1624)* (Nijmegen, 1992), pp. 143, 91.

[186] In May 1621, John Chamberlain had commented that the reason for the story was that Bishop King had 'out of charitie (both before and in his sicknes) [...] relieved some priests that were in prison'; a correspondent of William Trumbull said that Preston was one of them: McClure, *LJC*, p. 376; Harmsen, *John Gee's Foot out of the Snare*, p. 91.

But he sayed that he thought that he myght be prayed for, yf at his death he required a priest and were contrite. But I doe not know that eyther he sayed Masse for him or caused others to doe it. I moved a doubt yf he were not reconciled nor absolved ab excommunicatione, havinge binn a notorius percussor clericorum, and as it were nominatis excommunicatis per bullam coenae, that we could not offerre sacrificium pro [?] anima eius but only praye privatly for his soule and remember him in our memento. This was the passage of those busines[ses] at that tyme, so fare as I remember. I have credibl[i]e h[e]ard, but I did not see it, that in March last, or end of Februarie, there was a booke uppon the presse, or prynted, intituled the Bishop of Londons Legacie, wherein was probablie proved that the b[ishop] recanted his errors and dyed a Catho[lic]; but it was suppressed and came not publickly to lyght although some have privatly seen it.[187]

For the sermon, preached on 25 November 1621 by Henry King, which refuted the rumour of the conversion, see *DSSD*, p. 58; Henry King, *A Sermon Preached at Pauls Crosse* (London, 1621).

[187]For George Fisher's *The Bishop of London his Legacy* (Saint-Omer, 1623), see ARCR, II, no. 557; A. Davidson, 'The conversion of Bishop King: a question of evidence', *RH*, 9 (1968), pp. 245–246; *Letter 13*. Antony Allison and David Rogers (ARCR, II, no. 557) attribute the tract to Fisher, although cf. *Letter 23*, which perhaps implies that Richard Broughton (who had cited the alleged conversion in his *English Protestants Plea*, p. 19) may have been the author or have had a hand in it. For Broughton's defence of the book, see AAW, A XVII, no. 3, pp. 9–10; *Letter 13*. Broughton wrote to Thomas Rant on 28 April 1624 that 'I thinke you have h[e]ard' that, during John Bennett's agency in Rome, 'the author of the booke to the last parlament' (i.e. Broughton himself) 'was complayned of in the consistory for writeinge [that] D[octor] Kinge, Protestant bishop of London, dyed a Catholick'. (Rant believed that the complaint came from Thomas Preston.) However, Broughton successfully 'justified himself', and now 'the Jesuits at S. Omers have published that b[ishop] his book of the authors of his chaunge in religion. Yt came publick hither about Christmas last but with a new preface; for, in the first which came forth in the beginning of March was 2 yeares and then was in the archb[ishop] of Canterburyes hands, it sayd the booke was delyvered to the publisher by the b[ishop] of London to bee published after his death; in the second, onely they say constantly that hee dyed a Catholicke, not affirming the other': AAW, B 26, no. 45. For the second edition of *The Bishop of London his Legacy*, see ARCR, II, no. 558; *Letter 20*.

The book was printed on the Saint-Omer Jesuit college press. However, some Jesuits may have been dismissive of it. According to John Gee, the Jesuit Lawrence Anderton believed that it was too obviously a forgery: 'he was sorrie that ever any such booke should be suffered to come forth: for it would doe them more hurt than any booke they ever wrote': Harmsen, *John Gee's Foot out of the Snare*, p. 144; cf. Thomas Scott, *Boanerges: or the humble supplication of the ministers of Scotland, to the High Court of Parliament in England* (Edinburgh [false imprint; *vere* London], 1624), p. 24. Nevertheless, the book appears to have been exploited by the secular clergy in order to argue at Rome that the Protestant episcopate in England was no longer as resolutely anti-Catholic as it had once been. William Bishop, in a letter to John Bennett, enclosing the volume, assumed that it could be used in this way: *Letter 23*.

The k[ing's] M*aje*stie sent the l[ord] keeper[188] of the great seale of England unto the Spanish embassador[189] (as I think, misenformed) th*a*t they [*sic for* the] priests sought to have manie b*ishop*s w*i*th Englishe titles, as it were to affront the b*ishop*s of England. The embassador hath wrytten to Rome to be enformed of this matter.[190] It is thought co*n*venient, yea necessarie, th*a*t we have on[e] b[ishop] (intituled of Hippo or Alexandria, it is no matter where), in place of the archp[riest][191] deceased, to be a sup*e*ri*ou*r and governe eccl*esiastic*es more s*ecundum* cannones eccl*esi*ae, and lett not o*u*r suyte in any case surcease in this kynd, but pursue the grant and gett the man no*min*ated. Thus mu[ch], yf you think good, you maye signifie to M^r^ Ben[nett] or send him this my l*ett*er. And so w*i*th all good wishes, especially the recoverie of your streng[t]h and health, I tak[e] my leave.

London, this 10*th* of Sept[ember] 1622.

Yours ever to use,

Ol[iver] A[lmond] or J. Bark[er]

[*In hand of Anthony Champney*] S*i*r, this letter coming so fitly and the author desiring it should be sent to you, we would not omitt to send it. Here w*i*th it is M^r^ Oliver Almond[s] letter, alias Jo[hn] Barker. We have not leasure to copie it; therefore reserve the leter.

[*on p. 546*]

*Addressed*: To his worthie good frend M^r^ John Stronge at Dowe.

*Endorsed*: [*on p. 545*] Oliver Almond, assistant, who amongst many of his worthy labours converted the Lord Stafford[192] and lived with him till his death.[193]
[*on p. 546*] M^r^ Barker. Septemb[er] 10^th^.

[188] John Williams, bishop of Lincoln.

[189] Carlos Coloma.

[190] See *Letter 8*.

[191] William Harrison.

[192] Edward Stafford, 4th Baron Stafford. See *NCC*, p. 193.

[193] Oliver Almond died before June 1625: Anstr., I, p. 7. Lord Stafford died in September 1625: Cokayne, *CP*, XII/i, p. 186. In mid-1621, Stafford's sister Dorothy, following her unfortunate marriage to a lawyer from Lincoln's Inn, was in Spain and seeking to 'gett entertaynment under the Lady Doña Maria [...] and so to rayse a fortune if happily the match shold succeed with England': PRO, SP 94/24, fo. 176r.

## 11. William Farrar [Harewell] to [John Bennett], 4/14 September 1622

[*AAW, A XVI, no. 139, pp. 547–548*]

Very reverend and respected sir,

It is now a moneth since M^r^ President[194] had any letter from you. In my last[195] I advertised you that the king had given a charge unto all ministers in England not to speake in their sermons any thinge against the pope or Catholickes. This was writt us from England. Since, we have receaved a copie of the directions given by the kings appointement in this behalfe unto the ministers,[196] which I send you hereinclosed, whereby you shall see whereuppon that report rose and how farre it is verified. All the lay Catholickes throughout the realme are now sett at libertie. There arrived heere 3 dayes agoe a scholler out of the North, who affirmes it for those partes;[197] by whome also I understood of a peece of busines <happened lately in that countrie> w*hi*ch I thought good to give you notice of, and therefore have caused him to sett it downe in writing, w*hi*ch I send you togeather w*i*th this. He reportes also that some moneths agoe the bishop of Durrham,[198] accom*m*odating the quire of the <cathedrall> church, tooke up a stone w*hi*ch bare the inscription of a bishop (whose name was Shirley[199]) buried under the same some 200 and odde yeeres agoe. The workemen digging under that stone light uppon the bishops bodie, w*hi*ch was found entire lapt up in lead, the intirenesse whereof one of the workemen trying w*i*th his finger found it firme and solid flesh. The bodie was buryed againe in the same place and the matter silenced as much as they could.

[194] Matthew Kellison.

[195] This letter does not appear to have survived.

[196] For King James's directions concerning preaching, see K. Fincham (ed.), *Visitation Articles and Injunctions of the Early Stuart Church*, 2 vols (Woodbridge, 1994, 1998), I, pp. 211–213; Cogswell, *BR*, pp. 32–35, 37; Shami, *John Donne*; McClure, *LJC*, p. 449. Simonds D'Ewes remarked with sarcasm that Richard Sheldon, in his provocative anti-popish sermon of 1 September 1622, concluded (as did 'allsoe all our ministers') that 'the late articles the king had sett foorth, especiallye that of preaching in the afternoone upon the points of the catechisme, would bee of [. . .] good use for the beating downe of poperye': *DSSD*, p. 95.

[197] For the virtual cessation in September 1622 of the proceedings of the high commission at York against Catholics, see Borthwick Institute of Historical Research, High Commission Act Book, 16, fos 300r–322v.

[198] Richard Neile.

[199] Walter Skirlaw, bishop of Durham (d. 24 March 1406). He was buried in a chantry tomb at the altar of St Blaise and St John of Beverley: *ODNB*, *sub* 'Skirlaw, Walter' (article by M.G. Snape).

Their is some variance and hart burning in England amongst some (you know whome <Mr [*name deleted*], Mr Rouse[200] et[c].>) about the settling of the affaire of b*ishops*.[201] Heere also some have averted D*octo*r Clement[202] from the same by wronge information. But this day Mr President hath writt to him at large to make all straight againe.[203] Mr President salutes you and desires you againe to remember his indulgences, agnus Deis, medals <pardon for S*i*r Charles [*name obscured*]> etc. Mr D*octo*r Champney also remembers himselfe unto you. The post is ready to goe and I have no more time, having all this day been troubled partely w*i*th Mr President[s] letter to D*octo*r Clement, partely w*i*th other encombrances. So, w*i*thout more ceremonie, I take my leave.

Y*ou*rs ever,

W[illiam] Far[rar]

Doway, 14 Sept[ember] 1622.

*No address.*

[*on p. 548*]

*Endorsed*: Mr Farrar. Septemb[er] 14th.
Matheus.

## 12. Eaton [Edward Bennett] to John Bennett, 14 September 1622

[*AAW, A XVI, no. 140, pp. 549–552; printed in part in TD, V, pp. 124–125*]

Syr,

I was glad to see y*ou*rs to o*u*r good frend Mr D[octor] Bushop, of the 15 of August, and that you are soe well in healthe. The last weeke I writt unto yo*u* from London. Now I am to awnswer this <of yo*urs*>

[200] Richard Broughton.

[201] See *Letter 8*.

[202] See *Letter 9*.

[203] On 14/24 September 1622, William Harewell advised John Bennett that Caesar Clement (who, Harewell noted in a letter four days later, was 'of great authoritie with the nuncio, and in that court, and one who must be respected, els our cause is like to fare the worse': AAW, A XVI, no. 147, p. 567; cf. *CGB*, I, p. 32) was 'no friend of the Theatins', i.e. Jesuits, 'though <ordinariely> he be moderate in his speeches as houlding that a point of wisdome'. He had spoken 'roundly of them' to the Flanders nuncio: AAW, A XVI, no. 144, p. 562; see also AAW, A XVI, no. 161, pp. 617–618.

unto D[octor] Bushop. Yo*ur* paynes not only hath deserved much at the handes of the clergy but alsoe hath drawen them to acknowledge a great obligation unto yo*u*. For Gods sake come not away before all be dispatched, especially about b*ishop*s. The confirmation you have gotten of the colledge of Lysbon doth much comfort us. Benedictus Deus. We long to heer of the nomination but, as yo*u* say, we hope it will come in good tyme. I pray God those Jessuetresses[204] have no way given to their cowrses. All indifferent good men wonder they are not clean dissolved. The Jesswetes give owt that either they must dissolve or [*word omitted:* go] to clausure.[205] And M[r] Young[206] the Jesswete <tould me> that the Jesswetes since the beginning of there order had not beene so much wronged in ~~there~~ any thing as in the seeming dependanc[e] the Jessw[e]trices had upon them.[207]

M[r] Georg[e] Gage is <com> six weekes a goe. At first they gave owt he came with the dispensation; now that he had only the coppye of it w*hi*ch, having showed the king, he disliketh two pointes: that his Holl[iness] setteth down for motives inducing hym to dispence viz the Catholicke education of children hoped for; 2[l[y]] tolleration of religion to English Catholicke[s] with some security for the same. And that Georg[e] Gage is to goe to Rome abowt it. This the Jesswetes give owt. If he doe come, I suppose he shall have no letters of creditt from the king or estate, and that hym self is the first mover of the jorney. He must p*ro*cure his comendations from the Spannishe embassadour.[208] In my last[209] I towld you what conferenc[e] I had w*i*th hym [*in margin:* the sayd embassador], having in my company M[r] Broughton (who now is sure for us), M[r] Barker[210] and my nephew.[211] Now I send yo*u*

[204]The members of Mary Ward's institute.

[205]See Littlehales, *Mary Ward*, p. 114; Dirmeier, *MW*, I, pp. 713–714, 716, II, pp. 77–8.

[206]Francis (or John) Young SJ. See CRS, 75, p. 342.

[207]The Jesuit general, Muzio Vitelleschi, tried very hard to prevent John Gerard SJ assisting Mary Ward: ARSJ, Anglia MS 1, *passim*; Dirmeier, *MW*, I, II, *passim*. In June 1621, Vitelleschi had ordered that a book written by John Price SJ in favour of Mary Ward's institute should be neither printed nor circulated in manuscript: ARSJ, Anglia MS 1, fo. 141r; Dirmeier, *MW*, pp. 544–547; H. Peters, *Mary Ward* (Leominster, 1994), p. 289. For the general's directive in early 1620 to Richard Blount SJ to ensure that no member of the Society should be 'mixed with their direction or government', see Chambers, *Life*, II, pp. 13–14; for Blount's orders to this effect which were issued on 19 July 1623, see Dirmeier, *MW*, II, pp. 3–4. For English Jesuits, such as Roger Lee and Andrew White, who were noted supporters of the institute, see Chambers, *Life*, II, pp. 50–51, 53–57; Dirmeier, *MW*, *passim*; *Letter 29*.

[208]Carlos Coloma.

[209]*Letter 8*.

[210]Oliver Almond.

[211]Joseph Haynes.

a coppye of the good archdeacons <of Cambrayes>[212] letters to me, concerninge the embassadours liking of what had past between us. [*Four words deleted.*] <Withe these I write unto hym> secretly to deale w*it*h embassadors that he give Gage no letters of creditt in any thinge to deale in the affayers of the clergye. But I can not beleeve he will come to Rome <about the dispensation>, that matter belonging only to the Count Gundemar, Pater Maistro and yo*ur* self <in the name of th*e* clergy>. Upon his arivall <heer> my nephew spoke with hyme. He seemeth to comend yo*ur* payns and, talking of b*ishop*s, he sayed the pop[e] was a good man but did not understand res transalpinas.[213] See the arrogancy of this fellow in censuring the cheef pastor. Yo*u* must be carefull to keepe this relation of the archdecon secrett. Heer be letters caried up and down w*hi*ch his Hollines should write to the archduches[214] in the behaulf of the Jessuitre[sse]s wherof they bragg much but many beleeve them not.[215]

I have not seene Mr Whitnal.[216] My nephewe telleth me he speaketh wonderfull much good of yo*u* and is desirous to see me.

That relation. [*sic*] How, after yo*ur* first audience, his Hollines should send for yo*u* and tell you that he had h[e]ard [of] yo*u* as a man sent from the body of the clergy. Now, as a private man, he comaunded yo*u* to tell hym yo*ur* opinion of the king, and that yo*u* should awnswere he was not to be trusted, [and] withall advise his Holl[iness] to warn the Catholick kinge not to goe forward w*it*h o*ur* king w*it*hout such assurance as he could not be deceaved. This Doctor Bosvile[217] towld me, having h[e]ard it from [*p. 550*] a very worthye gentleman [*in margin on p. 549:* Mr Baker], seeming to deliver it as come from the Jesswetes. I can not send it you with any other testimony than this. You know

[212] François de Carondelet, archdeacon of Cambrai, who came to London in late 1622 to assist with Carlos Coloma's embassy: CRS, 68, p. 158.

[213] See also AAW, A XVI, no. 153, p. 595 (William Bishop to John Bennett, 26 September/6 October 1622); AAW, B 47, no. 30 (Edward Bennett to John Bennett, 29 September 1622).

[214] Isabella Clara Eugenia, the infanta-archduchess of Austria, and ruler of the Netherlands.

[215] For Isabella's patronage of Mary Ward's institute, see Littlehales, *Mary Ward*, pp. 106–113; Chambers, *Life*, II, p. 92; Dirmeier, *MW*, *passim*.

[216] On 22 August/1 September 1622, William Bishop noted Mr Whetenhall's arrival in London: AAW, A XVI, no. 136, p. 541. A pass was issued to one Thomas Whetenhall in February 1623, permitting him to travel abroad for three years (he had previously, in April 1622, been issued with a licence to stay abroad); this Whetenhall took the oath of allegiance: *APC, 1621–1623*, pp. 192, 427. Thomas Rant recorded in late 1623 'the storye how the Jesuitts would have putt Mr Whitnal (bycause hee was camerado to Mr [John] Bennet) into the Inquisition; but Card[inal] S[anta] Susanna, who knewe him, hindred yt': AAW, B 25, no. 102.

[217] John Bosvile.

that they vent owt ther infection by thear followers soe that, fale it owt as it list, they will escape shott free. [*In margin:* Noat.]

Within these 4 dayes Jenkyn was heer. He called as he came from London. Yo*ur* cosen is very well with all her family. I have written unto her such newes as I had from you. All thinges goe heere very well, wherof in my last I made particular mention. It should seeme you have latly written some letters to me w*hi*ch I have not receaved. All frendes be well and salute yo*u*. I pray remember my best frend[218] and my self to Pater Maistro. I have written to the counte de Gwndemar and acquainted hym w*i*th my lord keepers[219] beinge withe the Spannish embassadour about b*ishop*s, [and] informed [him] of what hath hapned, intreating his helpe. God keepe yo*u*.

Ever yo*ur*s,

Eaton

Edward Bennett[220]

Sept[ember] 14.

As I was writing these my frend came to me and sayd, comend <me> most kindly to my cosen, tell hym that he <doe> lack nothinge. The p*ar*ty that moved hyme to the jorney will not see hym want. God blesse her. As world <the> [*sic, for* the world] hath gon w*i*th us hetherto, we would not have stood withowt her. She is a Mellania[221] unto us. [*In margin*: My old Lady Dormer.]

It is highe tyme o*ur* sup*er*io*ur* be named. Heer is no order taken to helpe any thing that is owt of order nor any body in deed to sett any thing in order. I wonder with what conscience o*ur* opposites labour to hynder sup*er*iority amongest <us>, being soe necessary that withowt it all will [come] to ruine and perdition. Yo*u* must tell his Hollines (wherof I could write many p*ar*ticulars unto yo*u* if I thought they came saffly unto yo*ur* handes) it is heer the comon opinion amongest the clergye that we have no adversaries but the Jesswetes, who in nothing seeke o*ur* good. Therfor thinck [*sic*] that his Hollines can not in co*n*science suffer them to have goverment in any thing that belongeth to the clergye. And, surely, if the cowrse of ther p*ro*ceedinges be not soone and much altered from what it is, the whoale clergy of England wilbe constrayned to p*ro*test to the sea apostolick against them as overthrowers of the cleargy, and soe seek

[218] Lady Elizabeth Dormer.
[219] John Williams, bishop of Lincoln.
[220] In the hand of Thomas Rant.
[221] St Melania (the younger): see D. Atwater, *The Penguin Dictionary of Saints* (Harmondsworth, 1965), p. 242.

means [*words omitted:* to prevent us (?)] from having any thing to doe w*i*th <them> in matter of goverment belonging unto us. Beleve me, it will come to these extremityes if that ther be no order taken w*i*th them, and ordinary jurisdiction [*words omitted:* be not] planted amongest us.

[*p. 551*] It is much marveled heer how Mr Gage came to the coppy of the dispe*n*sation w*hi*ch he showed the kinge and what autority he had to publishe it. For it is imagined that the counte de Gwndemar and Patre Maistro w*i*th yo*u*r self should have had the p*ro*mulgating of it.

*No address.*

[*on p. 552*]

*Endorsed*: Mr Faringt[on]. Septemb[er] 14th.

## 13. William Farrar [Harewell] to [John Bennett], 20/30 September 1622

[*AAW, A XVI, no. 148, pp. 569–570*]

Very reverend and respected sir,

I writt unto you on Satturday last[222] from Brussels, and againe on Wednesday last[223] from hence being then newly come home. What successe I had in that busines you recom*m*ended to me there, I writt at large before, and therefore it <is> needeles to repeate it heere, the shortenes of the time also affording me no laisure thereunto. Since my last <w*hi*ch was but two dayes agoe>, wherein I sent you ~~a copie of~~ a letter[224] ~~from~~ of Mr Broughtons <writt hither> and a copie or two more of other matters, there is another letter come to Mr D*octo*r Champ[ney] from him, wherein he writes that he heares it reported the king is not well pleased w*i*th the forme of the dispensation, the copie w*hi*ch Mr G[eorge] Gage brought him setting downe as motives the education of the children (hoped for by this marriadge) in the Catholick faith, and toleration of religion for Catholickes w*i*th some

[222] AAW, A XVI, no. 144, pp. 561–562.

[223] AAW, A XVI, no. 147, pp. 567–568.

[224] In the margin, Harewell writes: 'by that letter you shall understand that Mr Broughton doth now professe to joyne in the sute of bishops'. For Richard Broughton's letter (AAW, A XVI, no. 135, pp. 539–540), see *Letter 8*.

securitie thereof.[225] This is secretly talked of, and that his Ma*jes*tie is secrettely <also> thereat discontent[ed][226] but doth not outwardly shew it, w*hi*ch (sayth M$^{r}$ Broughton) is to be well liked, if true. It is sayed that M$^{r}$ Gage shall presently returne to Rome about this matter though others thinke there is some other pretence therein. M$^{r}$ Broughton writes he was tould by one that had ~~him~~ it from M$^{r}$ Gage himselfe that he was to returne.

Cardinal Mellino <in the name of the cardinals of the Inquisition> writt a letter to M$^{r}$ President[227] to know who was the author of a booke entituled *English Protestants Plea* etc., whereunto the saied M$^{r}$ President gave his approbation.[228] ~~Whereunto~~ To this letter M$^{r}$ President returned present answer, the same day he receaved <it> [*three words deleted*], informing him and the congregation that the author thereof was one M$^{r}$ Broughton, an assistant.[229] In regard of the notice he had from you by y*our* last of certaine exceptions, w*hi*ch some there seme to take against the booke, it was wished heere that M$^{r}$ President had enlarged himselfe a litle more in his answer, and added a word or two that there was nothing contained therein w*hi*ch might justely be excepted against. I will deale w*i*th him, if I can, to write a second letter to Mel[lino] to that effect so that (if you thinke it good) you may stay that w*hi*ch comes to you in my <last> packett of the 28$^{th}$ of the present. I suppose there is no such hast therein. I thought good to send you the booke it selfe of M$^{r}$ Broughton heere enclosed, that you may see what it is that is excepted [*p. 570*] against. The places are underlined according to the copie w*hi*ch the Jesuits scored as matters of great note and reprehension. It is no marvell they are displeased

[225] For George Gage's return to England with the terms of the dispensation, see PRO, SP 94/25, fo. 199v; BL, Harleian MS 1581, fo. 122v; *CSPV, 1621–1623*, p. 412; McClure, *LJC*, p. 452; *Letter 12*.

[226] For James's objections to the terms of the dispensation, see *CSPV, 1621–1623*, p. 418.

[227] Matthew Kellison.

[228] Richard Broughton wrote to John Bennett on 23 October 1622 that he had heard that Cardinal Giovanni Garzia Millini 'desireth information of the b[ishop] of Londons death'. Nevertheless 'hee that wrote the Protestants Plea had many reasons, as hee thought, to write as hee did'. In particular, he had heard 'for creditt' that John King 'had testified with his owne hand his reconciliation, as many thinke yt was convenient hee should': AAW, A XVI, no. 167, p. 631; see also *Letter 10*. On 24 September/4 October 1622, John Bennett noted that, in 'the last weekes congregacion before the cardinalls', he had been 'called in and amongst other thinges they inquired much concerning the maner of death of King, bishop of London'. Thomas Preston OSB had alleged that he knew nothing of the matter. But he mentioned Broughton's *English Protestants Plea*, which Matthew Kellison 'should approve for the printe, and <sayth> it were needfull the truth were knowne with the author'. Bennett defended Kellison's approbation of the book on the grounds that it related only 'to faith or good maners'; but his interrogators asked 'might we not by him know what the author were, that the truth of the story may be knowne?': AAW, A XVI, no. 151, pp. 588–589.

[229] i.e. an assistant to the former archpriest, William Harrison.

therew*i*th. They would have no mens creditt rise, none talked of but themselves. The monkes have also carped thereat no lesse than the others because he preferres the labours of the clergie before those of the religious.[230] Heere is a letter of procuration come from Mr Colleton w*i*th the handes and seales of the rest of the assistants thereunto, giving power to Mr Newman to accept in their names the donation of Don Pedro,[231] and to oblige the clergie to the performance of all conditions required by the founder. It is made in the Portugall tongue and writt in partchment. <It goes away for Spaine this day.> The newes at Brussels before I came thence was <current> that Heidleberg was taken by Count Tillie[232] <by assalt> and all putt to the sword.[233] W*i*th what blood it will breed in England is doubtefull. I thinke I forgott to write heereof in my last. My L[ord] Vaux came not this way,[234] being (as we are informed) averted from that purpose by the Jes[uits] at St Omers, whither he came w*i*th a full resolution to have taken this place in his way and to <have> seen Mr President. Heere was some provision made for him. His entertainement at S. Omers by the Jes[uits] is reported to <have> been very great and so did a friend of ours also write thence. Mr President and Mr D*octo*r Champ[ney] salute you. The next weeke you shall have some lines from Mr Pres[ident] himselfe, for so he promises, whereby you shall see that (God be thanked) he is now prettily recovered and almost himselfe againe. In hast w*i*th my service to y*ou*r selfe and my freindes w*i*th you, I rest. Doway 30 Sept[ember] 1622.

Yours ever,
W[illiam] Farrar

When I was making up my letter, I was tould that presently uppon the coming forth of this booke of Mr Broughton, w*hi*ch was printed

[230] For one instance of Broughton's tract's abrasive attitude to the regulars, see Broughton, *English Protestants Plea*, pp. 5–6. Broughton had, however, at the time of the appellant controversy, issued publications which were sympathetic to the Society of Jesus. See, e.g., his *An Apologicall Epistle* (Antwerp [false imprint; printed secretly in England], 1601), p. 46; and his *First Part of the Resolution of Religion* (Antwerp [false imprint; printed secretly in England], 1603), pp. 53–54.

[231] Pedro Coutinho.

[232] Jean 't Serclaes, count of Tilly.

[233] For the taking of the elector palatine's capital of Heidelberg, with conventional plunder but not the massacre indicated here, see Cogswell, *BR*, p. 20; Pursell, *WK*, p. 184; *CSPV, 1621–1623*, pp. 467, 469; *DSSD*, pp. 97–98; *HMCMK*, p. 137.

[234] On 18/28 September 1622, William Harewell reported that Lord Vaux had 'newly come over' and that the secular clergy at Douai expected 'him heere this night'. There were 'saied to be come with him (besides some 2,000 come before) 800 soldiers and some 80 gentlemen of note that accompanie him, all very gallant': AAW, A XVI, no. 147, p. 567.

by Heigha*m*[235] at St Omers, the Jesuits made complaint of the printing thereof unto the bishop there, who thereuppon sent the book underlined in the places you shall see to Mr President w*i*th a letter unto him advertizing him what exceptions were taken thereat, and desiring to be informed thereof. Mr President returnes the whole passage in every place of exception, in Latin, w*hi*ch, when the bishop sawe, his censure of that book was that he sawe nothing in <it> that any should take offence at, but that the author spoke honorably of all persons, giving every one their due respect etc. This was the bishop of S. Omers verdict, wherew*i*th the Jesuits, not being satisfied, they threatened to send the book to the nuncio, and it is like they sent <it> up to the cardinals of the Inquisition. And this is the comedie thay have acted.

*No address.*

*Endorsed*: M. Ferar. Septemb[er] 3[o].

## 14. William Bishop to John Bennett, 23 September/ 3 October 1622

[*AAW, A XVI, no. 150, pp. 585–586; part printed in TD, V, pp. ccxlvi–ccxlvii*]

Very worthy s*ir*,

I held my handes the last weeke, hoping that you would have dispatched, and have been ready to come downe with Monsieur d'Aire[236] who, I fear mee, will not stay long there, now he hath obtained Mons*ieu*r Lusons[237] red capp; for that he is wholly his. I begin to feare now lest Mr Gage will proove a cold p*ro*phet, who told us, as I advertised you, howsoever you were faire p*ro*mised, ye[t] that <the> byshop should not be chosen and dispatched till all the covenants about the match were th[o]rough[ly] agreed upon. Yet it may be otherwise, and that they stay onely to heare what their nuncios will report, w*hi*ch, assure yourself, will be in our favour; this nuncio[238] for us here; he[239] in Flanders for D[octor] Kellison. Ere this, I hope you have <received> the commendations, w*hi*ch diverse here, of the greatest ~~great~~ <credit> (considering the absence of the nuncio, and the death of the card[inal] of Retz, byshop of Paris), did very willingly give us, and that in very ample maner; w*hi*ch being joined to the <two>

[235] John Heigham.
[236] Sébastien Bouthillier, bishop of Aire.
[237] Armand-Jean Du Plessis, bishop of Luçon, and now Cardinal Richelieu.
[238] Ottavio Corsini, archbishop of Tarsus.
[239] Giovanni Francesco Guido del Bagno, archbishop of Patras.

cardinals[240] that have been here nuncio, and Bentivolio,[241] 7 yea[rs] before in Flanders (who, besides, doth exceedingly affect D[octor] Kellison), and the archbyshope of Armach,[242] and [the] byshop of Aire, will serve abondantly. And I think that Mons[ieur] Bartin[243] will, if need be, be very foreward for ~~for~~ mee, more much [*sic*] than I am worthy. Besides, one of the chiefest of o*ur* faculties, <the> theolog[ic]all of O*ur* Ladies, and now allso, during the vacation of the byshope, one of the vicar generalls, tels me that he, hearing of the matter, hath written very affectionately in my behalfe to the cardinal of S$^{t}$ Susanna who esteemeth him much.[244] All this I tell you for yo*ur* satisfaction; protesting that I do not, in any case, desire that most weighty burden to light on my shoulders but that the court may not rest misinformed of our simple qualities. Father Archange[245] resalutes you very hartly, and is of opinion <with whom I agree> that it is best that you <to> [*sic*] come down, assoone as you have gotten yo*ur* dispatch for one bishope, that you, wee and they of Doway may conferr togither about the p*ro*ceeding of o*ur* bishop for his officers and of all his affaires; and afterward you may, if you please, returne, if we cannot find a fitt man to send in yo*ur* place; w*hi*ch I feare verely we shall not do. M$^{r}$ Gage, as some suspect, hath put it into the lord kepers[246] head <at least he seemes so conceited> that, if we have bishops, it will be to put them out of their places. But o*ur* byshop shall p*re*tend no more to their bishopricks than our priests do to their benefices, or religious men to their religious houses. And no question but, when he shalbe

[240] Roberto Ubaldini and his successor as nuncio in Paris, Guido Bentivoglio.

[241] In late 1623, Bentivoglio promised Thomas Rant assistance with the secular clergy's suits in Rome: AAW, B 25, no. 102.

[242] Peter Lombard, archbishop of Armagh, who resided in Rome, was a supporter of the secular clergy leadership's agency at Rome. See A. Macinnes, 'Regal union for Britain, 1603–38', in G. Burgess (ed.), *The New British History: founding a modern state 1603–1715* (London, 1999), p. 34; J.J. Silke, 'Primate Peter Lombard and Hugh O'Neill', *Irish Theological Quarterly*, 22 (1955), pp. 15–30; *NAGB*, p. 79. Though he had formerly supported the rebel earl of Tyrone, Lombard had, by the time of Tyrone's death, come to 'favour a rapprochement with the English crown in the hope of achieving some measure of toleration': H. Kearney, *Strafford in Ireland* (Cambridge, 1989), pp. 110–111. Thomas Rant recorded how, in Rome, Lombard discoursed about how much 'the Jesuitts' had 'wrong[e]d the kings title in writinge Dolman', i.e. the *Conference about the Next Succession to the Crowne of Ingland*: AAW, B 25, no. 102; H. Morgan, *Tyrone's Rebellion* (Woodbridge, 1993), pp. 4–5, 182. In September 1622, Lombard had added his voice to those who were trying to persuade the Roman curia that the regime in England would genuinely try to get a toleration through a packed parliament: Gardiner, *NSMT*, p. 177.

[243] Claude Bertin, superior of the French Oratory in Rome.

[244] For Cardinal Scipione Cobelluzio, see Chambers, *Life*, II, p. 140.

[245] William (Archangel) Barlow, a member of the Paris community of the Capuchins. See Allison, RS, p. 183.

[246] John Williams, bishop of Lincoln.

well informed <of> o*ur* manner of p*ro*ceeding, he and his Ma*jes*tie both will rest better conten[t] to have a bishop among us than to let the priests and Catholikes to be swaied by the Jesuits, whom they take for busy bodies and enemies to their p*er*sons and state. And you may promis, if need bee, when our bishop is here consecrated, he shall not enter into England till the Spanish ambassador hath made his way to the said lord keper, yea, and to his Ma*jes*tie also. Catholikes be daily better and better used in England. And S*ir* Edward Cooke being out of the Tower for threatning, as it were, the king that we [*sic for* he] would repent him of shewing to[o] much favour to Catholikes, was by his Ma*jes*tie send [*sic for* sent] back to the Tower, there to lodg[e] till he had learned more witt. Concerning Mr Father Percies conference,[247] it is writen that the lady[248] afterward went to church,[249] and there being two daies conference in the former he was by many reported to have had the better, though many also say the contrary, but in the Saterday he was reported to have had the worse. I have seen the former daies conference set out by himselfe with many additions, what he thought to have said, and yet, I assure [*p. 586*] you, in <my> poore judgment <and in D[octor] Smiths> is [*sic, for* it] was a slight peece of worke, not worthy [of] such an audience wherefor [*word illegible*] inferred [?] very prudently. Were it for nothing els, we have great need of a learned bishop who is able to stand in confractione, or at least that is able to call forth some of the best learned among us to defend Gods truth.[250] Thus much in answer to

[247] For the series of debates held over three days (24–26 May 1622) between the Jesuit John Percy (who had converted the countess of Buckingham to Rome) and leading Protestant divines, as well as the king, see above, pp. 13, 30. For Richard Blount SJ's account (of 8 October 1622) of the disputation between John Percy and Francis White, see AAW, A XVI, no. 154, pp. 597–598; ARSJ, Anglia MS 1, fo. 163r.

[248] Mary Villiers, countess of Buckingham.

[249] The countess's reward from the king for announcing that she was returning to the Church of England was reported to be £2,000. On 22 June 1622, John Chamberlain noted that, on the previous Sunday, she had received communion in the chapel royal 'with both her daughters (though they had receved the weeke before)'. By September, Chamberlain, like others, understood that she had 'relapsed into poperie and makes open profession, wherupon she is sent from court and (as is said) confined to her house at Dalbie in Lecestershire': McClure, *LJC*, pp. 439, 441, 451; see also *Letter 16*. A long letter of October 1622 from Sir George Paul urged her to renounce the Church of Rome: BL, Harleian MS 1581, fos 244r–246v. Rumours and libels circulated about her, including, as Simonds D'Ewes recorded on 10 January 1623, 'a booke [. . .] called "the Chast Matron", in which was discovered all the villanis, witchcrafts and lasciviousnes' of the countess: *DSSD*, p. 113; see also McClure, *LJC*, p. 457; Ruigh, *1624*, pp. 137–138; *CSPV, 1621–1623*, p. 88.

[250] On 18/28 July 1622, Bishop had observed in a letter to Bennett that, 'among the questions which our king is said to have [asked] the Jesuits to be resolved, the chief is whether the pope [can] depose kings. To which, as the report goes, they meane to answer that F[ather] Generall hath forbidden them to treat of that question, which will not satisfy

your letters. I will add this one observation, hoping that you shall have o*ur* bishope, that his buls must passe sure, because that is already granted to all the Irish, as my l[ord] of Armach can tell you, <yet> some 50 crownes or thereabout[s] will neverthelesse be layd out for officers sees. [*In margin:* This is privilegiu*m* pauperem.] Thus with my very harty salutations, I rest.

Yo*urs* alwaies assured,

W*illia*m Byshope

The third of October 1622.

I, fearing Mons*ieu*r d'Aires absence, will write to you hereafter by Monsieur Bertin of the Oratory.

On Michaelmas day F[ather] Sillesden,[251] accompanied with F[ather] Talbot,[252] passed ~~out of England~~ <by this towne> towards Rome. What newes they cary, we heard not, saving that here they gave out that the lay Catholikes were not deliv*er*ed out of prison according to the kings letters patents, w*hi*ch to speake absolutely was false, for that the most of them be out. If some one man in some remote shire be not, that is nothing to the purpose.[253] Their meeting of 45 in one house in London was knowen afterward to the king and very evill taken, enough to have made him fallen out with us all. They excused it and say it was to chuse the said Sillesdon to goe to Rome to be present at a councell of their elect and to be the agent for the English Jesuits there.

Some Protestants of the best intelligence in this towne do report that they saw of late a comission under the kings <broad> seal and under the princes seal passe thorow this town to the Lord Digbie in Spaine, who now is earle of Bristow, to conclude the points of the mariage.[254] I send you a copy of the kings comandement and the bishop of Canterburies exemtion [*sic*] thereof for the framing of preachers

the king. And againe some thinke that his Holines will not take it well that they should be silent in that important point being by a king questioned about it': AAW, A XVI, no. 124, p. 501.

[251] Henry Bedingfield SJ. See CRS, 75, p. 294.

[252] Thomas Talbot SJ. Talbot served as a chaplain to Lord Vaux: ARSJ, Anglia MS 1, fo. 164v.

[253] See *Letter 15*.

[254] John Bennett had been told in March 1622 that Digby's title (he was created earl of Bristol on 15 September 1622, although his promotion was rumoured as early as January of that year) was not to be announced until he arrived in Spain: AAW, A XVI, no. 105, p. 439; see also McClure, *LJC*, p. 422. The count of Tillières ascribed Digby's promotion to Gondomar: PRO, PRO 31/3/56, fo. 39r.

not to speake against the match nor against Catholikes.[255] I further add that the Catholikes have paid nothing for their recusancy [in] the last halfe yeare. [*In margin:* This with M^r [Ir]elands letters by Mons*ieu*r Bernard, my l[ord] of Rhemes[256] chaplaine.]

*Addressed*: A monsieur, Monsieur Bartin, père de la congrégation de l'Oratoire logé a St Louis.
Pour estre donné (si luy plaist) à Mons*ieu*r Bennet, agent pour le cleargé d'Angleterre à Rome.

*Endorsed*: Suarum de fide disp. 19 19 sect 2^a n. 21 propositiones non [*two words illegible*] mentem censura*m* [?] heresis [*word illegible*]. M^r D[octor] Bishop. Octob[er] 3.

## 15. William Farrar [Harewell] to John Bennett, 25 September/5 October 1622 (with postscript by Matthew Kellison)

[*AAW, A XVI, no. 152, pp. 591–594; printed nearly entire in TD, V, p. 122*]

Right worthy and respected sir,

Since my last,[257] w*hi*ch I writt unto you the last weeke by the way of Paris, having but a few daies before sent by the way of Brussels from Paris, we understand that there passed by there of late a coople of Jesuites, by name F[ather] Talbot and F[ather] Silesdon,[258] that are making to Rome.[259] In that place they gave out that the lay Catholickes are not yet released in England. It is not to be doubted but they who, so neere home, and amongst those who are like to know the trueth of matters, are not ashamed to report so manifest untruethes, will, further of[f], be more bould in their relations and reportes. You may, therefore, know this for certaine trueth that (as I have heeretofore writt unto you) all the lay Catholickes that were, in any place in all the kingdome of England, imprisoned meerely for religion are dismissed, freed and sett at libertie by vertue of the king his speciall letters under his broad seale

[255] For the royal directions concerning preaching, see *Letter 11*; and for George Abbot's letter accompanying them and qualifying them, see Shami, *John Donne*, pp. 75, n. 1, 105–106; K. Fincham (ed.), *Visitation Articles and Injunctions of the Early Stuart Church*, 2 vols (Woodbridge, 1994, 1998), I, pp. 213–214; George Abbot, *The Coppie of a Letter sent from my Lords Grace of Canterburie* (Oxford, 1622).

[256] William Gifford, archbishop of Rheims. See Anstr., I, p. 133.

[257] *Letter 13*.

[258] Henry Bedingfield SJ.

[259] See *Letter 14*.

to that effect. This we have for certaine, not onely of such Catholickes are [*sic for* as] were imprisoned for the Catholicke religion in London but even of those in the North, in Lancashire, Herefordshire and, in a word, in all other places and partes of the realme, from whence we had both speciall letters advertizing us thereof; and also divers scholars lately come from those severall partes, who affirme the same; insomuch that they report there be some released in the castle of Yorke who <for their conscience> had suffered 38 yeeres continual imprisonment <there>, others 26, others more ~~for their conscience~~. And although some heere and elsewhere thinke they be not freely and absolutely released, w*i*th[out] any manner of restriction etc, but onely uppon bale, as the com*m*on course of releasement is, yet you know that that manner of releasing uppon bale is, in a sort, equivalent to a free and absolute releasement. And, seeing they are released by the kinges special grant, they cannot be recalled again but by the kinges special com*m*and, and under his or a number of the privie counsell their handes. True it is that we heare there be yet some detained in Lancaster who were com*m*itted heeretofore for printing <of Catholicke bookes> to whom the judges [*p. 592*] (more strict heerein than perhaps they can well justifie) will not permitt this priviledge and favoure of his Ma*jes*tie to be extended, they being com*m*itted <(as they say)> not for matters of religion but for printing, the w*hi*ch is, by a special lawe of <the> realme, prohibited to all (of what religion soever they be) save such as be publickely licensed, w*i*thin the cittie of London onely and the two universities, out of w*hi*ch places, you know, there is no printing permitted or allowed in all England.[260] W*i*thall, we understand at Durrham the bishop[261] of that place, uppon the releasement of the rest of the Catholickes, on his owne authoritie kept still in prison a Catholicke woeman possessed and another in whose house the saied possessed woman had been, at severall times, exercised; w*hi*ch yet was more than he could doe. But it seemes he ought [*sic for* owed] the divell a spight and so ment to keepe him in prison for it.[262] These

[260] William Bishop wrote to John Bennett (in a letter dated either 30 September/10 October 1622 or 10/20 October 1622, but probably the former) that 'the last newes out of England is that all Catholike prisoners are delivered all England over except four printers in Lancaster gayle who are said to be detained under colour of medling in matter of state, though the printers prisoners in London were delivered as well as others', and that 'all priests about London aswell Jesuites as others are out of prison under one pretence or other, saving some fewe in the Clinck who, as it seemes, will not go out': AAW, A XVI, no. 157, p. 609.

[261] Richard Neile.

[262] It is possible that Bishop Richard Neile (who had been involved in suppressing the puritan exorcist John Darrell) was reacting to the circulating reports of the recent attempted exorcism, by Catholic clergy in the Coventry and Lichfield diocese, of William Perry, the 'boy of Bilson'. See Richard Baddeley, *The Boy of Bilson* (London, 1622); A.W. Foster, 'A biography of Archbishop Richard Neile (1562–1640)' (unpublished DPhil thesis, University of Oxford, 1978), p. 21.

two presidents are all that I can heare ~~can~~ <likely to> be alleadged against the generall releasement of all Catholickes, w*hi*ch I thought good to give you notice of, to the end you might be provided against such shameles untruethes and lies as will, perhaps, be given out there in this matter. M$^{r}$ Gage his emploiements are much talked of in England. They say the king and he spend whole howers, sometimes 3 or 4 togeather, in private conference. He gives out he is presently to return in all post hast to Rome.[263]

The king, uppon the newes of the taking of Heydleberg, sent the marques of Buckingha*m* to the Spanish embassadour[264] to expostulate w*i*th him thereabout, betwixt whome there passed a terrible conflict of huge and mightie wordes insomuch that they say they were so loude, in the heate of their reasoning the matter, that they were heard many roomes of[f]. Yet the skirmish ended in peace, and the marques <before he departed> supped with the embassadour.[265]

We are informed that ~~the~~ Tobie Matthew gives out [that] some have raised sinister reportes of him because he will not be drawne to be a slave to the clergie.[266] It seemes some take notice of his Jesuites weedes and his priesthood, w*hi*ch he would gladly conceale, if he could, thereby to carrie matters more smoothely than otherwise he is like, but, I thinke, in vain. Besides other good proofes heereof there ~~be some~~ <is one> in these partes whose ~~parentes have~~ <mother, a

[263] See Gardiner, *NSMT*, pp. 178, 182; *CSPV, 1621–1623*, pp. 485, 490.

[264] Carlos Coloma.

[265] The official Spanish line was that Heidelberg had been taken 'onely to drive those wicked souldiers out of the countrey who lived on the spoile and would not suffer the countrey <men> to till the ground, with reservation of it to the king of England to dispose of for his daughter': AAW, A XVI, no. 157, p. 609. William Harewell reported on 16/26 October 1622 that (as he was informed by William Law, now serving as chaplain to Carlos Coloma) James 'does [. . .] offer Manheim and Frankendale to have Heidleberg delivered againe, which hitherunto he would never offer', although Mannheim (defended, like the other towns, by English troops under Sir Horace Vere) was on the verge of surrender, and fell on 18/28 October: AAW, A XVI, no. 171, pp. 663–664; *CSPV, 1621–1623*, pp. 470, 505; PRO, SP 14/134/13, 14, 15; *DSSD*, pp. 102, 105, 106; Redworth, *PI*, p. 57; Pursell, *WK*, pp. 171, 185–186. For Bristol's unsuccessful diplomatic attempts to save Mannheim from the count of Tilly's forces, see Patterson, *King James VI and I*, pp. 320–321. In Madrid, in February 1623, Bristol offered to the Spanish court that Frankenthal should be put into the archduchess Isabella's hands in return for the abandonment of the siege, with provision to restore it 'si la paix avec l'empereur n'était pas conclue': *CCE*, pp. 117–118. For the treaty signed by James concerning Frankenthal, surrendering it in mid-April 1623 for a specific period to the archduchess (though the government in Brussels decided in April 1624 that this agreement was abrogated by the breach of the Anglo-Spanish marriage treaty), see *CSPD, 1619–1623*, pp. 502, 504, 511, 516, 519, 526, 529, 531, 532, 550, 567; *APC, 1621–1623*, p. 446; BL, Harleian MS 1581, fo. 159r; PRO, C 115/107/8485; *CCE*, p. 125; *CGB*, I, pp. xxi, 293, 300, 304, 312, 456, 492, 495, 508, 509, 528, 534, 543, 547, 555–556. See also *CSPD, 1623–1625*, p. 296, and *passim*; Redworth, *PI*, p. 73; Pursell, ESP, pp. 707, 708; *CCE*, p. 184; *CSPV, 1623–1625*, pp. 458, 465, 468, 470, 476, 481, 485.

[266] i.e. the secular clergy.

lady of good note,> told him that yong Tobie had saied Masse in her house.[267] And yet these men persuade themselves they can walke invisibly. Enough [*p. 593*] of this. In what case Mr President[268] is I leave to his owne relation, and the testimonie you shall have thereof from the subscription beneath. Mr D[octor] Champney salutes you most kindely. In my last, I writt what passed w*i*th the Spanish embassadour in o*ur* sute for bishops, w*hi*ch I hope will come short.[269] If otherwise, you may know he writt uppon mistaking, and now he is of another judgement. God keepe you in health. You are by all o*ur* friendes heere and elsewhere most earnestely entreated not to stirre thence till all thinges be fully settled and (if it be possible) another come to supply y*our* place. In y*our* absence you know how all matters are like to goe.[270] No more at this present but my service to y*our* selfe, P[adre] Maistro, Mr Seton.[271] Adieu.

Y*our*s ever in all service,

W[illiam] Farrar

Doway 5 Octob[er] 1622.

[267] For Mathew's secret ordination, though he was not a Jesuit, see *Letter 3*.

[268] Matthew Kellison.

[269] Joseph Haynes remarked on 12 October 1622 that, the night before, Coloma had told him that the rumour that a bishop had been appointed for England was untrue, because Cardinal Millini had recently written to him 'for to nominate some on[e] whom he thought most fitt to be our archpreist', although Coloma had replied to the cardinal that the English secular clergy were determined to secure an episcopal appointment: AAW, A XVI, no. 158, p. 611.

[270] On 24 September/4 October 1622, John Bennett reported to William Bishop that 'the delay of nomination yet houldeth me; whereof, being weary, I repayred to his Hol[iness] and complayned bitterly, and soe to the cardinals. Some answer his Hol[iness] made at first, as if the danger were not great for a small tyme; to which I replyed that we spent noe daye or weeke in this delay without losse of soules. Wheruppon I insisted very earnestly; soe as his Hol[iness] promised I should forthwith be dispatched. My memoriall was noe lesse earnest than my wordes; which, by comandment from our f[ather], was the next congregacion before himself, within two dayes, readd, and a resolution made, as they conffesse, that I should have speedy satisfaction; but the particulers I cannot yet lerne'. Bennett insisted, however, that the secular clergy would be satisfied only with 'a superior of our owne choice'. In the mean time the secular clergy's adversaries at Rome 'fayne a hundreth chymeras in there owne braynes nothing at all to the matter, and then publish there own fictiones for truth; as, for example, that they here expecte the event of the dispensation before any thing be in this determined. But they knowe litle of the estate of e[i]ther. For our sute dependeth not <at> all of the maraidge; and, I assure you, we had our graunte when here they were doubteffull whether the maraidge would hould or noe': AAW, A XVI, no. 151, pp. 587–588.

[271] William Seton, of Meldrum in Aberdeenshire, a friend of the English secular clergy in Rome. He was attached to the household of Cardinal Scipione Cobelluzio: D. Shanahan, 'The descendants of St. Thomas More: Reverend Thomas More IV, 1565–1625', *London Recusant*, 3 (1973), p. 89. William Bishop pointed out in late December 1623, after the election

[*In Matthew Kellison's hand*]

Deare Sir,

Seing that my recoverie is so deare unto you, these lynes shal serve to shew unto you that I ame living, and not onlie living but (thankes bee to God, his mother, his saintes, and my freinds prayers) soe recovered as I walk abroad about the howse and garden. I congratulate yo*u*r good successe and better hopes of yo*u*r negotiation which, if it should not succeed, yet our countrie and clergie should be never th*e* lesse <bound> to you, yea having used al[l] zeale, industrie and dexteritie and having made matters more known than ever and brought them to <a> better passe than ever before, so that you have at least opened th*e* way for another tyme, and (as we hope) for this tyme. I com*m*end my selfe to yo*u*r prayers there.

Yours own ever,

Matth[ew] Kellison

*No address.*

[*on p. 594*]

*Endorsed*: M^r^ Ferrar. Octob[er] 5^th^.

## 16. William Farrar [Harewell] to [John Bennett], 4/14 October 1622

[*AAW, A XVI, no. 159, pp. 613–614*]

Very reverend and respected sir,

M^r^ D[octor] Champney hath y*our* last of the 12^th^ of September. Y*our* desire for the satisfying of the nuncio[272] heere, and the labouring of his furtherance of y*our* affaires, is in such sort accomplished as I was able

of Maffeo Barberini as Urban VIII, that the new pontiff had been cardinal protector of the Scottish nation, 'and therefore M^r^ Seton is like to be well knowen to him': AAW, A XVII, no. 63, p. 204. Thomas More understood that Seton was, like George Con, 'knowne to his Majestie'. This was because Seton was 'nere of kinn to the late chanceler of Scottland' (Alexander Seton, 1st earl of Dunfermline) and 'most gratfull unto him'. He had 'lyved some yeares in this court wher he hath gott good experience and great frends and acquantance': AAW, A XVIII, no. 55, p. 337. Seton was no friend to the Jesuits. He told Thomas Rant that 'within theis 6 yeeres, ther have byn 2 Jesuitts dyed in the Inquisition for revealinge of confessions', and although 'one of them indeede was gott out to the Jesu, a day before hee dyed [...] bycause his sicknes was in the Inquisition, and his neernes to death ther, wee may say hee dyed ther': AAW, B 25, no. 102.

[272] Giovanni Francesco Guido del Bagno, archbishop of Patras.

to doe it, whereof I presume yo*u* have ere this understood by two of mine. I feare the Jesuites have possessed the eares of that nuncio, or els the Spanish embassadour[273] his letters against y*our* sute (whereof I have already writt unto you once or twice) have made him could [*i.e.* cold] in that affaire. Yet, as I informed you at large, I persuaded my selfe that I left him well satisfied (as also D*oct*or Clement, who is a great man w*i*th him) though I did not finde him desirous to have any dealing w*i*th us in that kinde, save uppon occasion that his sentence and judgement were authentically required by some in ~~there~~ <authoritie in that court> in w*hi*ch case onely he promised his helping hand. But, for that I have writt of this matter and of the manner of my negotiation w*i*th him sufficiently heeretofore, I spare to make a needeles repetition thereof now againe.

It is noe marvell the good fathers make such triumph <there> for the vict[or]ie F[ather] Fisher[274] gott against D*oct*or White. Even in these partes they <gave> out no lesse. But those who are not ashamed of trueth ringe anoth[er] tune. What I writt to you of that matter came from Mr Broug[h]ton and Mr Nelson[275] under their owne handes, and we heard it from divers that came from England as a thing commonly talked of to the litle creditt of the good father. I can not certainely informe you whether the lady[276] was reconciled againe or no.[277] But certaine it is uppon that disputation she went to the church. [*In margin:* my lady of Buckingham.]

D*oct*or Worthington[278] is this day setting forward from hence towardes England. He returned five dayes agoe from Brussels where he lay (and thereabouts) the space of 5 or 6 weekes expecting answer from Rome concerning his congregation, not omitting in the meanewhile to labour the nuntio there in that behalfe. He gives out now to some heere w*i*th whome he is most confident that he hath lately receaved licence from the cardinals to p*ro*ceed w*i*th his congregation untill such time as a superior be appointed <in England> (w*hi*ch he hopes will not be in haste) to whome then it shall belonge to judge of the conveniency of it, and whether it shall be allowed of or no. His designe is to repaire to London w*i*th the best speed he can and from thence to direct his letters to such as have heeretofore given up their names unto him to meet him there, w*i*th whome he hopes to prevaile so farre as also w*i*th others (for to creditt his congregation the more he hath both [*p. 614*] the cardinals letters to shewe and w*i*thall his rules in print) that

[273] Carlos Coloma.
[274] John Percy SJ.
[275] John Jackson.
[276] Mary Villiers, countess of Buckingham.
[277] See *Letter 14*.
[278] Thomas Worthington.

w*i*thin a short time he will so multiplie his companie that the superior who comes heereafter shall not be able to dissolve them though he would.[279] This day I write to M^r^ Sara[280] to give him advertisement heereof and I have promised M^r^ D*octo*r Champney to write to M^r^ Colleton to the same effect. It will not perhaps be amisse for you to shew y*our*selfe <there> in this point according to the directions you have in y*our* instructions. For though there be no great cause to feare that the doctor will be able to bring any great matter to passe in this kinde, yet prevention hurtes nothing.

I send you heereinclosed a peece of Monsieur Carondelett, the archdeacon of Cambray, his letter to M^r^ Provost,[281] word for word in French as it was writt by him, save that for brevities sake I contracted the last paragraffe. The summe of it is this, in English, that he hath, since his coming into England, solicited and brought to ~~passe~~ good issue so many favours w*hi*ch the embassadour[282] hath procured of the king and the honor whereof he may challenge to himselfe, that at this day there is not one prisoner [*in margin:* intellige lay-Catholick] for religion in all England. And that he does now negotiate the same for Scotland; that the king hath recalled the charges and com*m*andes heeretofore given to the judges of the circuit for informing against Catholicks. That the chancelour (bishop of Lincolne),[283] of whome depend all graces and affaires next after the king, hath done him the honour as to favour

[279] On 8/18 October 1622, Caesar Clement wrote to William Harewell that Thomas Worthington had been with him the day before and had told him that 'he wowlde go to Rome for two thinges, the one to informe his Hollines better off this matter of bishops, wherin he <sayed he> was much abused by summe that sowght butt themselves'. His other purpose was 'to sett forwarde the congregation by him begunne, or sodallitie tendinge to reformation'. Clement thought that 'itt were good he wer prevented by givinge warninge' to John Bennett in Rome: AAW, A XVI, no. 161, pp. 617–618. For Worthington's account, written in late August 1624, concerning his quarrel with William Bishop over Worthington's sodality and his refusal to serve as an archdeacon under the authority of Richard Broughton and John Bosvile, see AAW, B 26, no. 111 (modern transcription of AAW, B 26, no. 112); AAW, B 27, no. 42. The hostility of leading secular priests to Worthington dated back to his time as president of the English College at Douai, where he was regarded as a favourer of the Jesuits: *NAGB*, *passim*. It was also thought that he intended to appropriate quasi-episcopal authority to himself in England. In January 1616, Anthony Champney had complained to Thomas More that 'it was given out all over in England' that Thomas Worthington had been created archpriest in place of William Harrison: TD, V, p. clxxxvi. In April 1616, William Rayner remarked from Paris that 'yt hath been here reported that Monsignor Worthington confirmeth people in England', and this rumour was the result 'of soom speaches that D[octor] Worthington himself used to a French bushop that came out of Italie with him to whom he sayd soomthinge about his extraordinarie facultie': AAW, A XV, no. 65, p. 173.

[280] Edward Bennett.

[281] Thomas Harlay, provost of the church of St Gagericus (St Gery) at Cambrai. See CRS, 10, pp. 218, 219.

[282] Carlos Coloma.

[283] John Williams.

and creditt him so much that he saies he (the chancelour) will treate w*it*h no other than himselfe (the archdeacon) in matter appertaining to religion, and in effect grantes him all the favours he demandes of him, etc; that there resort to the embassadours chappell 1,500 or 1,600 Catholicks (at a time, or in a day) to heare Masse.

Mr President[284] writt yesterday both in his owne and the clergies name unto the chapter of Cambray for Monsieur Carondelett his longer stay in England, who w*it*hout licence of the chapter must of necessitie repaire home. He gave them to understand how necessarie Mr Carondelett his presence is in those partes in the behalfe of Cath[olic] religion; and hopes uppon that and other considerations they will condescend to lett him stay longer, for the embassadour himselfe writt to the infanta[285] heere that she would direct her letters to the chapter for the same effect, w*hi*ch she hath done.

F[ather] Rudesind[286] tould me yesterday that the Jesuites write to him from Rome that there is no more done in y*ou*r sute of b*ishop*s than was the first day you came to Rome; and w*it*hall that nothing is like to be done therein, how confident soever you jest of that matter; but we know their trickes.[287] This is all, for the present, but my service and best wishes, whereof I rest.

Y*ou*rs ever,

W[illiam] Far[rar]

Doway 14 Octob[er] 1622.

*No address or endorsement.*

## 17. William Farrar [Harewell] to John Bennett, 11/21 October 1622

[*AAW, A XVI, no. 166, pp. 627–630*]

Very reverend and right worthy sir,

Of the receipt of y*ou*r last, w*hi*ch bare date the 12th of Sept[ember], I writt the last weeke by the way of Paris, according to y*ou*r direction, w*hi*ch as oft as I write I shall heereafter observe. We cannot heere

[284] Matthew Kellison.

[285] Isabella Clara Eugenia, archduchess of Austria.

[286] William (Rudesind) Barlow OSB.

[287] On 14/24 September 1622, William Harewell had informed John Bennett that Rudesind Barlow and the Benedictines were prepared to give their nomination for Matthew Kellison and Richard Smith, but not for William Bishop, for he was, they thought, too 'boisterous': AAW, A XVI, no. 144, p. 562.

understand what this nuncio[288] does in y*our* affaires either one way or another. What was like to be expected of him I have already at severall times sufficiently advertised you since the time I was w*i*th him.

From Paris, M$^{r}$ Ir[eland][289] writes to D*octo*r Champney that F[ather] Ar[changel][290] tould him his brethren from Rome give him notice that, besides the 6 w*hi*ch the clergie hath recom*m*ended and nominated, there be 6 others presented and recommended by those who except against the clergies nomination; and that some have recom*m*ended himselfe (F[ather] Arch[angel]) w*hi*ch he will not heare of. How these thinges goe there, I doubt not but you knowe far better than we heere. Yet I thought it not amisse to let you understand what reportes passe in these partes concerning those affaires. Sig*no*re Chrysogono[291] writt the last week unto M$^{r}$ President[292] to have an information of the state of o*ur* college,[293] <v*iz*> the number of o*ur* schollers, o*ur* institute, the end and fruite of the seminarie, the foundation etc. W*i*thall that he would give him in like sort a particular relation of the other seminaries, colleges and monasteries, both of men and woemen of our <and the Irish and Scotish> nation, resident in the Low Countries, w*hi*ch M$^{r}$ President hath done and is now readie to send him it. We conceave, and not w*i*thout good ground, that the congregation de Propaganda Fide hath writt to the nuncio of these partes to be informed of <all> the seminaries and religious houses of these nations residing w*i*thin his nunciature.[294] And for this cause this information is demanded of M$^{r}$ President not onely of his owne but also of all the rest of these 3 nations. We understand that the like order is come to the superior of the Irish colledge in this towne and that thereuppon they seemed to be inquisitive of the state of o*ur* colledge. Whereby it is gathered that every colledge is to relate not onely of their owne estate and conversation but w*i*thall <of the condition> of all the rest, to the end ~~they~~ superiors be not tyed onely to the relation w*hi*ch each colledge or monasterie shall give of it selfe w*hi*ch might be partiall and too much in it[s] owne favour, but what others also do testifie thereof. That part <of M$^{r}$ Presidents relation>[295] ~~thereof~~ w*hi*ch concernes the Jesuitesses

[288] Giovanni Francesco Guido del Bagno, archbishop of Patras.

[289] Richard Ireland.

[290] William (Archangel) Barlow.

[291] Chrysogono Flacci, secretary to Giovanni Francesco Guido del Bagno. See *CGB*, I, pp. x, 36, and *passim.*

[292] Matthew Kellison.

[293] The English College at Douai.

[294] See AAW, A XVI, no. 169, pp. 635–644, no. 170, pp. 645–662; CRS, 10, pp. 195–206, 390–399.

[295] See Littlehales, *Mary Ward*, p. 112; Chambers, *Life*, II, pp. 50–52; Dirmeier, *MW*, I, pp. 726, 727–729; AAW, A XVI, no. 170, pp. 645–662.

I send you heerinclosed, w*hi*ch I caused to be coppied out in hast whilst I was writing this.

From England we heare there is great trouble about the taking of Heydelberg. The king was at great wordes w*i*th the Spanish embass[ador][296] about it, insomuch that some feared a new storme would have rose against Catholickes. But by such as be newly come out of England (since the generall report there of the taking of Heydelberg) all thinges are quiett, and Catholickes in good peace, w*hi*ch God continue.[297]

[*p. 628*] There is, and that not uncertaine, newes that the palsgrave[298] (who since his flight from the Palatinate till now hath lurked at Sedan w*i*th the duke of Bullion) some ten dayes agoe imbarked himselfe at Calaies.[299] Whither his course was, it is yet [*word omitted:* not (?)] knowne. Some feare he either is [*word omitted:* in], or will (so soone as he can) make for, England. But his entertainement there is like to be but could [*i.e.* cold] by the king and prince.[300]

Out of Spaine there is a fleete coming of 150 saile to keepe the Hollanders in, and to cutt off all their trafficke, the meanes to undoe them quite.[301] Some 60 saile of them were come before Plimmoth (where it is sayd they desired to take in fresh water but could not be permitted). The rest are comming after.[302] Yesterday, we heard that at St Omers there is order taken for provision to furnish the fleete withall. One butcher there hath already killed 500 beeves and poudered them. One baker hath com*m*and to provide 6,000 biskett, another 4,000, besides others etc. But these particulars we had of one

[296] Carlos Coloma.

[297] See *Letter 15*; see also AAW, B 47, no. 30.

[298] Frederick V, elector palatine.

[299] See *CSPV, 1621–1623*, p. 481. In early July 1622, Frederick had dispensed with the services of Mansfelt and Christian of Brunswick, and had withdrawn to Sedan to reside with his uncle, Henri de la Tour d'Auvergne, duke of Bouillon, though Mansfelt and Brunswick had joined him there in August, before leaving for the siege of Bergen-op-Zoom: Pursell, *WK*, pp. 181–185.

[300] See *CSPV, 1621–1623*, pp. 414, 440, 462, 487–488.

[301] See *ibid.*, pp. 476, 478, 479, 480, 483, 485, 495; McClure, *LJC*, p. 455; *CCE*, p. 111.

[302] On 16/26 October, William Harewell had recorded, for John Bennett's benefit, the news sent by Caesar Clement to Matthew Kellison, which he had recently received from William Law, concerning the Spanish fleet. This, combined with the 'newes of the taking of Heydleberg', greatly disconcerted the king, who 'presently called for his councell to know what the meaning heere of should be, and whether they were able to bringe the kingdome in danger'; but the fleet, 'passing on her journey, went forward, with a very prosperous winde, till it arrived uppon our coastes and so 28 ships are arrived at Dunkerk, the rest at Callis'. This was an encouragement to those, such as Harewell, who had been downcast by 'the Marques Spinola his raising of his [si]ege before Bergen op Zome', and it 'opened our eyes to see that surely [a]ll the marques['s] hope laye uppon the coming of this armada', which would 'divert the enemie from Berghen': see AAW, A XVI, no. 171, p. 663; *CGB*, I, p. 261.

who knew the parties and heard it of them, to whome this order was given. I have <not> heard from *ou*r friendes in England now a good space. I expect M^r^ Duckett[303] now every day, uppon whose coming I thinke to provide my self forethw*i*th thitherwards unless Al[mighty] God dispose otherwise of me, w*hi*ch yet I know not. I desire nothing but to fulfill his holy will.

M^r^ President and M^r^ D*octo*r Champney salute you. Let me crave y*ou*r remembrance of me in y*ou*r holy sacrifices, as I forgett you not in mine, remaining yours ever in all service.

W[illiam] Farrar

Doway 21 Octob[er] 1622.

[*on p. 630*]

*Addressed*: Al molto illustre et rev*eren*do sig*no*re, il Sig*no*re Giovanni Benetto, agente del clero di Ingle[t]erra en Roma.

*Endorsed*: M^r^ Ferrar. Octob[er] 21^th^.

## 18. William Bishop to John Bennett, 21/31 October 1622

[*AAW, A XVI, no. 172, pp. 667–668*]

Very wor*shipfu*ll s*i*r,

Yours of October the 10^th^ came speedely to my handes, for the 29 of the same I send [*sic, for* sent] into England the inclosed. I have both earnestly intreated yo*u*r good brother[304] to importune the Spanish ambass[ador],[305] who is both for his letter to Rome and promise to them double bound, to remoove that block out of our way, w*hi*ch he hath cast in it, and, if he find him cold, to seeke unto the l[ord] keeper[306] by some effectual meanes, and to informe him well, and then no doubt but he will rather favour us than our opposites, specially considering that we are for the mariage, and they against it, we all speaking as much honour of his Ma*jes*tie as wee can do, they calumniating his actions, etc.

303 John Ducket, procurator for the English College at Douai. See Anstr., II, pp. 89–90; AAW, A XVI, no. 109, p. 453.

304 Edward Bennett.

305 Carlos Coloma.

306 John Williams, bishop of Lincoln.

I feare lest F[ather] Archangell[307] can do litle with the Frenc[h]e ambassadour[308] in England, who is turned about for the Jesuit[s], I know not by what words, if it be not that they now do leave the Spanish p*ar*ty and fly to the Frenc[h]e, w*hi*ch alone should move the Spanish ambass[ador] to favour them in p*re*judice of them that are their affectionate welwillers. F[ather] Arch[angel] and we may be able to do somwhat with the Cardinall de Surdis[309] if he come hither, as his mother doth looke for him shortly, and some other p*re*lates may then be drawen in to joyne w*i*th him. I meane to sound some of the Sorbon to see if it be fitt to gett our faculties of divinity to write to [his] Holines or the Cardinall Bandini in our cause. I am glad o*ur* testimonies cam[e] safely to yo*ur* hands. God send they may serve to his honour and service in time and place. I do vehemently suspect M$^{r}$ Gage to have suggested to the lord keeper or [the] king himself those calumnies of o*ur* p*re*tensions to the archbishoprickes of Canterbury and Yorke, whereat his Holines was as much touched as we that he would go about to doe such a thing without our kings privity, w*hi*ch questionles he would never have done. That is my first note against M$^{r}$ G[age]. My second [is] that he is credibly reported to <have> sayd to some of o*ur* great ones [?] that the pope was a good man but knew litle of matters on this side of the Alpes.[310] My third I gather out of this w*hi*ch D[octor] Cicill (who holds good intelligence with them) told me that the king and court were indigne, that is, verie offended with some disdaine, with the conditions inserted into the dispensation.[311] This he told me verbatim but did tell me nothing that M$^{r}$ Gage should say for the same, w*hi*ch is to me a good conjecture [*words obliterated*] he is in England. He is for the king rather than for the pope in that matter [*words obliterated*] [of the dispe]nsation and being in deed evill affected to the match lets any thing passe that [*words obliterated:* might serve (?)] to break it of[f]. The like p*ar*t he is like to play in that court. And as I have advised yo[u] [*words obliterated*] tell the Spanish amb[assador], if he beare any good will to the match, let him take heed ho[w] he imploy any such holow harted men in that busines. All this to your self, to make use of as occasion shall serve. I heare that the king and court did mislike that it was put among the motives of the dispensation that their children should be brought up Catholikely till they were seaven yeare old, w*hi*ch is, in my judgment, a very good point, yet rather to be wished than stood

[307] William (Archangel) Barlow.

[308] Tanneguy Leveneur, count of Tillières.

[309] François d'Escoubleau, cardinal de Sourdis.

[310] See *Letter 12*.

[311] See *ibid.*

stifly upon, because when children be past three yeares old they go out of their mothers education and charge, so that she is not bound to see them brought up in her religion, though she be bound to do her best endevour, both by counsell with them and by intreaty with her husband.[312] This, I say, by the way. But if M$^{r}$ Gage returne to Rome to have these points amended <as it is reported he shall> you may lett him alone with it unlesse you shall chance to be requested, for [?] o*ur* king, to assist him, because that wilbe displeasing to that court, and no wise man doth of his own accord thrust himself into other mens busines that is like to p*ro*cure enmity. To worke o*ur* king to say that he likes of a byshop for us may be a hard matter and require more time than it is expedient that o*ur* busines do hang in suspense, for feare God should call his Holines, wherefore do your best to have the man nominated and consecrated, though it be under condition that he not go into England till a faire way be made for him. The Jesuits have their superiour, the Benedictins their[s], so have the recollects. Why should not the cleargy, the noblest portion of the ecclesiasticall state, have theirs? The king cannot justly be offended when the bishope shall neither be intitled to any bishoprick to w*hi*ch he chalengeth right to p*re*sent, nor so much as come into his countrey without his leave; but then, say they, why would we have <one> if he do not go into England. I answer first wee have great hope that we shall gett the king to like it ere it be long. Secondly in the meane season he, with the advise of o*ur* best and wisest men, may continue the best maner of p*ro*ceeding in his goverment and appoint some vicar generals under him, ~~by~~ <among> whom he may devide the goverment of the whole realme, who in his absence may see priests to do their dutie and take heed that no scandall be given neither by priest nor lay Catholikes w*hi*ch, if God grant us liberty, wilbe more necessary to looke unto, quia licentia sumus omnes deteriores. You look for newes but there is litle stirring, albeit o*ur* king was much displeased with the takin[g] of Heidelberge, the chiefe towne in the Palatinate, yet he doth not in any thing lesse [*word obscured*] towards Catholikes. He complained of [*p. 668*] it to the infanta.[313] She exclused [*sic*] herself for that they were enforced, upon the coming downe of Mansfelt into Flanders, to call her forces out of the Palatinate so that she could not [*word omitted:* prevent (?)] the duke of Braviers [*sic*] forces to do what they thought good. O*ur* king hath also send [*sic for* sent] a post into Spaine about

[312] For the negotiation of the clause of the treaty which dealt with this issue, see Gardiner, *NSMT*, p. 338; *CSPV, 1621–1623*, p. 490.

[313] Isabella Clara Eugenia, archduchess of Austria.

the same. God knows whether they will not give the like answer.[314] Yet some Jesuits that came lately from thence thinke that the mariage wilbe shortly concluded, though they be no friends thereunto. Here they say that the king <is in Montpellier and> hath made peace with his rebels. Yet we have no certenty of it, wherefore I referr that to the next.[315] I will in my next com*m*end that to yo*ur* camerado and Mr President[316] w*hi*ch you desire about the booke written for the Jesuitrices. Thus with my very harty com*m*end[ations], I rest ~~yours~~.

Yo*u*rs alwayes assured

W*illia*m Byshope

The last of October 1622.

Mr Gage when he passed by us would not communicate to us anything because the secrecy of the Inquisition was upon them, but it seemes he observed not that secrecy in the court of England for, as I before noted, they did know the p*ar*ticulars of the dispensation.

The reduction of Montpellier and peace made was this day cried upon [*sic*] and downe the streetes.

*Addressed*: Au révérend père, le Père Bartin prestre de la congrégation de l'Oratoire demeurant à St Louis.
Donne le si vous plait à Mons*ieu*r Bennet, agent du cleargy d'Angleterre.
A Rome.

*Endorsed*: Mr D[octor] Bishop.
Octob[er] the last.

[314] In Madrid, the Spaniards offered exactly the same excuse to the earl of Bristol, namely that Mansfelt had caused the withdrawal of Spanish forces from the Palatinate in order to defend Flanders, and that the 'seige of Heidleberge was no way by the consent or knowledge' of Philip IV. On 13/23 October, said Bristol, the Spanish court 'dispatched away letters to the infanta to stopp the emperours and duke of Bavarias proceedings': PRO, SP 94/25, fos 265r, 266r; see also *HMCMK*, pp. 137, 138; *CCE*, pp. 91, 92.

[315] For the peace agreed at Montpellier, see Adams, PC, p. 332; Lockyer, *Buckingham* pp. 229–230; C.J. Burckhardt, *Richelieu and his Age*, 3 vols (London, 1967), I, p. 151. On 10/20 October 1622, William Bishop had observed in a letter to Bennett that Louis XIII was 'said to have made a peace with his rebels which, though most zealous men do dislike, yet it seemes not so bad as some would make it. The townes that held out do yeelde to have their new fortifications beaten downe and do receive Catholike garrison[s] and governour[s]': AAW, A XVI, no. 164, p. 623.

[316] Matthew Kellison.

## 19. William Farrar [Harewell] to John Bennett, 23 October/2 November 1622

[*AAW, A XVI, no. 173, pp. 669–670*]

Very r*everen*d and respected sir,

The last weeke I writt unto you,[317] both by the way of Brussels and Paris, and sent you the coppie of a letter[318] writt unto me from D[octor] Clement. Three days ago Mr President[319] receaved a long letter from y*ou*r brother,[320] relating at large all their proceedinges w*it*h the emb[assador],[321] whereof I have given you advertisement longe agoe. Therew*it*h he also sent the coppie of a letter w*hi*ch Mons*ieu*r Carondelett had writt unto him concerning his <after> dealing with the emb[assador] in the behalfe of the clergie, the w*hi*ch, though I suppose your brother will be carefull to send you, yet for more surenesse sake I thought it not amisse to enclose heerein. D*octo*r Worthington is safely arrived in England, yet passed not w*it*hout suspition. He went in all alone at Dover where the old fox Jones[322] began presently to smell him and tould one Mr Cape,[323] a Catholicke knowne to him, who chanced at that time to be come to Dover to provide shipping for my L[ord] Montague his sonne,[324] that ~~there was~~ some of <his> companie ~~who~~ suspected the old man for what he was and therefore wished him to deale w*it*h him etc. The conclusion was [that] D*octo*r Worthington gave Jones an angell and went his way cleere. My L[ord] Montague his sonne arrived heere on Friday last w*it*h a Benedictin monke[325] his tutor and fower men in his companie. He is going for Spaine, there to spend some time and a great deale of money. He stayed one day heere in towne, not having any com*m*oditie to depart sooner, for his tutor makes as much haste as he can in respect of the season of the yeere.[326] He and his father had been at Wing[327] the latter end of this summer. For now their is great league betwixt both those houses.

[317] AAW, A XVI, no. 171, pp. 663–666 (16/26 October 1622).

[318] AAW, A XVI, no. 161, pp. 617–618.

[319] Matthew Kellison.

[320] Edward Bennett.

[321] Carlos Coloma.

[322] A reference, presumably, to William Jones, clerk of the passage: *CSPD, 1619–1623*, pp. 16, 374, 378, 395, 406, 420, 460, 462.

[323] William Cape. See Questier, *C&C*, p. 392.

[324] Francis Browne, the son of Anthony Maria Browne, 2nd Viscount Montague.

[325] Edward Smith. See Lunn, *The English Benedictines*, p. 229; PRO, SP 16/178/43; Anstr., II, p. 299.

[326] See Questier, *C&C*, p. 392.

[327] The residence of the Dormer family in Buckinghamshire.

The last night Mr George German returned out of England. He left his friendes well and Mr Colleton with them in the countrie. They looke longe for you as also y*our* hostesse Mrs Smith, who is very well, as he sayeth. She hath heard of my returne w*hi*ch was not my fault. Mr Gage is now uppon his way towards Spaine, and from thence to Rome as the report goes. Yet some say his way is straight to Rome.[328] He passed at Dover some 2 or 3 dayes before Mr German. He had 500li for his viaticum.[329] Much speech there is of his employement. Howsoever, whilst he was in England, he was extraordinarely gallant, and still at court, yet had w*it*h him not above one or two men neither in England nor now in his <great> embassie. My conceipt is he is rather for Rome than Spaine because not above 12 dayes agoe there was one Endymion (I know not whether I should putt a Sir before it or no) Porter dispatched from the king for Spaine,[330] a man by the favour of Buckingham raised from small meanes[331] and (if I be not mistaken) Mrs Porter[332] (the Jesuitresse) her sonne. And, now I speake of Jesuitresses, Mr German telles that that broode encreases apace in England, insomuch that in one house in Shoe Lane at London there live 14 of them.[333] They make themselves as sure of the confirmation of their order as if they had it in their pockett.

[*p. 670*] In one of my last[334] I writt we had newes that there <were> 6,000 men levying about London to goe for Holland under the conduct of Colonell Gray[335] but those that came late out of England heare no such matter. All thinges goe in a peaceable course in England. I writt unto you longe since[336] that all the lay Catholicks were for certaine at libertie and that at Yorke some there <were> ~~amongst these~~ that had been prisoners 36 yeeres, some 28 etc. Mr

[328] See *CSPV, 1621–1623*, pp. 485, 490; Gardiner, *NSMT*, pp. 182, 183. For the reasons for Gage's journey via Madrid, see PRO, PRO 31/3/56, fo. 134v.

[329] On 23 September 1622, a warrant was passed to pay George Gage £500 for his employment in the king's service abroad: *CSPD, 1619–1623*, p. 449.

[330] See *CSPV, 1621–1623*, pp. 469, 479; *CSPD, 1619–1623*, p. 451.

[331] Cf. *CSPV, 1621–1623*, p. 439. Porter, a relative of Buckingham, had been appointed a groom of the prince of Wales's bedchamber: Redworth, *PI*, p. 43. For his mission to Spain, see Lockyer, *Buckingham*, pp. 129, 132, 133–134; J.H. Elliott, *The Count-Duke of Olivares* (London, 1986), pp. 205–206.

[332] Angela Porter. See Dirmeier, *MW*, I, p. 731. There is no evidence that she was a member of Mary Ward's institute. I am grateful to Caroline Bowden and to the Bar Convent at York for information on this point.

[333] There is no record of a residence set up by Mary Ward's institute here, and it is unlikely to have existed, certainly not for the numbers of women alleged. Again, I am grateful to Dr Bowden and the Bar Convent for this information.

[334] AAW, A XVI, no. 171, pp. 663–666.

[335] Sir Andrew Gray.

[336] *Letter 15*.

Parrie telles me his father had been prisoner in Flint full 40 yeeres, a longe time of confession of his faith, and therefore worthie the libertie he now enjoyes w*i*th the rest. D*octo*r Bishop solicittes Mr D*octo*r Champney to helpe you w*i*th some advertisements concerning the abuse of the Jesuites goverment of that colledge there that you might fall on bord w*i*th them. But D*octo*r Champney is of opinion that it is not yet time for that matter, and wishes you would not by any meanes medle w*i*th it. Other affaires of importance must be first setled and then that will more easely followe whereas, if you begin now, you will both encomber y*our*selfe in a troublesome businesse and thereby hinder y*ou*r other designes. And w*i*thall, ~~if~~ <though> you should prevaile against them so far as to dispossesse them of that place, <~~yet~~> thinges as yet stand in such sort w*i*th us <as they doe> that there would not be men found to undertake their roomes <and so would [*word illegible*] proove peiora prioribus>. Yet <shall> you [*word deleted*] do well <in [?] the meane[time]> to provide y*our*selfe <full> of [*word deleted*] <all manner of> instructions belonging to that point that, when time shall serve, there want no matter whereon to worke etc. There is not any thing els worth the writing. Mr President comes now to the refectorie. Both he and Mr D*octo*r Champney salute you most kindely. I expect Mr Duckett heere w*i*thin less than ~~these~~ 10 dayes, uppon whose arrivall I shall provide my <selfe> for[th]w*i*th for England, having no occasion to stay heere any longer. In the meane and ever, I rest.

Y*ou*rs to be com*m*anded,

W*illia*m Farrar

2 Novemb[er] 1622.

*No address.*

*Endorsed*: Mr Ferrar the 2 of Novemb[er].

## 20. William Farrar [Harewell] to John Bennett, 30 October/9 November 1622

[*AAW, A XVI, no. 174, pp. 671–674*]

Very reverend and respected sir,

In my last,[337] w*hi*ch was the weeke past, by the way of Brussels, I sent you all the occurrences then worth the writing, togeather w*i*th the

[337] *Letter 19.*

coppie of a letter of Mons*ieu*r Carondelett to y*ou*r brother[338] w*hi*ch y*ou*r brother sent M$^{r}$ President.[339] Since, there occurres no new matter save that M$^{r}$ D*octo*r Bishop writes from Paris that M$^{r}$ Gage, passing that way, tould them the king was highely offended at the clergies sute for bishops and that the Spanish embassadour[340] in Engl[and] had writt to the king of Spaine to hinder the same w*i*th the pope in regard of the k[ing] of Engl[and] his so hainousely taking of that matter. This troubles us heere. But first we know by whose sinistrous and pestiferous suggestion this matter hath been breathed into the kinges eare, to witt the Jesuites darlings. Secondly for that the king is persuaded the clergie seekes to supplant those that at this present possesse the bishoprickes in England; and especially that by this meanes the authoritie w*hi*ch both <he> and his predecessors, even in Catholicke times, have enjoyed in the nomination of bishops and bestowing the bishoprickes independent of the sea apostolicke shall be lost, if not from himselfe, yet from his successors; w*hi*ch is a point whereat the Catholicke princes of England have in former times not a litle stood; and therefore may <now> much more be stood uppon by him. And this ground you may use for the furtherance of y*ou*r sute, giving his Holines to understand that it will be a matter of ~~great~~ <extraordinarie> importance <even> to the sea apostolicke <it selfe> to settle bishops in England now at this present, thereby to regaine that authoritie of bestowing the bishoprickes in England from the kinges who lay claime thereunto. For the popes practice now (w*hi*ch the king certainely will never gainesay for feare of hindering greater matters) will serve for a plea heereafter and the authoritie he hath in this behalfe once taken to himselfe may, without contention or quarrell, be easely continued in aftertimes, for every thing is sooner stopped or hindered at the first, tha[n] <afterwards recalled> when ~~it is~~ by course and practize it is confirmed.

Thirdely it is supposed that the kinges stomacking this matter was but a suddaine passion w*hi*ch afterwardes would passe away w*i*thout leaving any impression in his mind behind it. For what cares the king if the clergie have bishops, so that he receave no prejudice thereby? A wonder lastes but for nine dayes, and surely that fitt of the king (if yet it be true that the k[ing] was really offended at the newes) was of lesse continuance. For even the taking of Heidleberg (uppon the newes whereof the k[ing] fell into an extraordinarie passion of wrath and discontent) stucke uppon his stomacke not above a weeke, as we heare

[338] Edward Bennett.
[339] Matthew Kellison.
[340] Carlos Coloma.

for certaine.[341] And yet <had> the [*p. 672*] kinge great cause to be highely offended and discontented thereat if the circumstance of that businesse be considered. Uppon this rumor of the k[ing's] displeasure w*i*th the clergie, the Jesuites seeme very jolly and cockesure there will be no bishops, insomuch that there was a Jesuite in a certaine place in England who, hearing some talking of bishops which the <clergie> was shortely like to have, used these wordes in plaine termes: they shall have no bishops. We heare also that many other religious in England do so carrie themselfes in this businesse as that they plainely discover they are no friends of b*ishop*s. But this is not to be spoken of. Your brother writt to Mr President that there was a Jesuit[342] knowne to have had three howers privat conference w*i*th Secretarie Calvert, a point worth y*ou*r notice.[343] The Spanish fleete, of w*hi*ch I writt unto you in my last and others before,[344] is vanished away. It never came further, as we heare, than the coast of England about Plimmoth where, having notice they came too late for the service w*hi*ch was intended, they returned, or were (as it is sayed) by speciall order recalled, and com*m*anded backe againe. It is thought they were sent to doe some exploit uppon the Hollanders whilst Spinola should give the onsett uppon Berghen, who being enforced to raise his seege before their comming, all that plott was marr*e*d.[345]

Mr President salutes you, and so doth Mr D*octo*r Champney.

I know not what will become of me, for I am not a litle importuned both by Mr President, D*octo*r Champney and others to stay heere still. But nemo potest duobus dominis servire, and againe in all places I am but servus inutilis, w*hi*ch others will not be persuaded, but I my selfe know it too well. When Mr Duckett comes, whome we expect heere every day, I shall be at some certainetie. Whatsoever become of me, I am y*ou*rs ever in all service.

W[illiam] Farrar

Douay 9 Novem[ber] 1622.

Sir, since the making up of my letter, D*octo*r Champney shewed me a letter of Mr Rouses[346] <216 [*sic*] newly arrived> wherein he writes at large concerning a booke published in Januarie last containinge the

[341] See *Letters 17, 18*.

[342] Francis (or John) Young SJ. See CRS, 75, p. 342.

[343] See *Letter 25*.

[344] The Spanish fleet was mentioned in William Harewell's letter of 16/26 October (AAW, A XVI, no. 171, pp. 663–666), rather than that of 23 October/2 November (*Letter 19*), and also in his letter of 11/21 October (*Letter 17*).

[345] For the raising of the siege of Bergen-op-Zoom, see J. Israel, *The Dutch Republic* (Oxford, 1995), p. 483; *CSPV, 1621–1623*, pp. 472, 480, 486, 488, 548; *CGB*, I, p. 256.

[346] Richard Broughton.

motives of the bishop of London his dying Catholicke.[347] The poste is readie to depart and I have not time to coppie out his letter or the parcells of the saied booke of motives, w*hi*ch M^r^ Rouse gott the sight of and hath sent D*oct*or Champney in his owne hand writing. On Friday next I will send you them both by way of Paris, God willing. In the meane [time], take the title of the foresaid booke, w*hi*ch is this: *The Bishop of London his Legacie, or Certaine motives of D. King late Bishop of London for the change of Religion and dying in the Catholick and Roman Church: penned by himselfe and delivered over to a friend in his life time, with a Conclusion to his Brethren the LL. Bishops of England.*

*No address.*

[*on p. 674*]

*Endorsed*: Ferar. Novemb[er] 9th.

## 21. William Bishop to John Bennett, 5/15 November 1622

[*AAW, A XVI, no. 175, pp. 675–676*]

Very much respected s*i*r,

These are to acknowledg[e] yo*u*rs of October 24th and to give you great thankes for the care you have of the common cause and to praise God for your diligence and patience. God forgive those o*u*r bretherne who, having done litle or nothing in this matter of byshops (w*hi*ch doth most import us), yet cannot but murmur and backbite them who have most furthered it. Well, let us not be weary of well doeing, and they shall have shame enough of their opinions. Yo*u*r camerado did satisfy M. D*oct*or Clement.[348] They that so malitiously informed him and sought to do others <must> sit downe by the losse. Well, to other matters. We are glad of your placing with Monsig*no*r Vives.[349] He will help you, though

[347] See *Letter 10*. In fact, Richard Broughton's letter of 23 October 1622 (AAW, A XVI, no. 167, p. 631) dealt with his own book, *English Protestants Plea*, rather than with George Fisher's *The Bishop of London his Legacy*. For Broughton's defence of the latter book, see AAW, A XVII, no. 3, pp. 9–10 (cited in *Letter 10*).

[348] See *Letter 11*.

[349] Juan Bautista Vives, envoy in Rome for the archduchess Isabella: see Shanahan, 'The descendants of St. Thomas More', p. 91; *CGB*, I, p. 30. Richard Smith wrote to John Bennett on 10/20 October 1622, 'I know him well and, as I think, he wil remember me if you tel him that I was the agent' for the English secular clergy in 1609 and went often, with Thomas More, to visit him, 'and he gave me at my departure a book, De Missione ad Infideles, written by a discalced Carmelite, and hath written to [me] since I came to Paris': AAW, A

not so fervorously as did the bishop of Aire,[350] to whom we will render, at his first arrivall here, all the thanks we can. There is so great reason to p*er*suade his Ma*jes*tie to be favorable to us that I am in very good hope he will be made ours. I have written unto le conde de Gundomar both to yeeld him o*ur* raisons for a byshope and humbly to intreat him that he will write unto our kings Ma*jes*tie in our behalfe, w*hi*ch I pray you to sownd <[*two words obscured*]> and to gett Padre Maestro (to whom I pray you remember my harty comend[ations]) to do the same. Don Balthazar de Zuniga being dep*ar*ted,[351] the conde is like to succeed him in that most honorable place w*hi*ch, if he do, his letters unto the Spanish ambassadour in England[352] (who [?] is over much affected to the Jesuites) will cause him to be more indifferent; howsoever they in Spaine, [*sic*] being now upon the point of conclusion for the match, <the> conde may be requested to put in that for a speciall favour to Catholikes, that his Ma*jes*tie do not resist o*ur* having of bishops, for otherwise how can he be taken to grant us the use of o*ur* religion w*hi*ch cannot be kept in order and peace without our ordinary pastors; w*hi*ch point I have already touched in mine to him. Conde Gundomar is o*ur* patron. He hath been the principall instrument under God to p*ro*cure us that libertie which we already enjoy, wherefore we must fly to him to make it p*er*fect. This point being well recommended to him by you and Padre Maestro cannot but encourage him much to p*ro*ceed in it with ardour. And he principally can effect what we desire both with the Lord Digby (who is now created earle of Bristow) and with our kings Ma*jes*tie. Your brother[353] I know will do in England what he can. And he, accompanied with those his bretherne (unto whom the Sp[anish] ambassador p*ro*mised to repaire what damage soever should come of [*word omitted:* his] letter), pressing the [*word illegible*] to p*er*forme the same, will I hope obtaine it at his handes, he no doubt standing in some awe of Gondomars displeasure, whom he knowes to favour us even in this cause.[354] I am glad that the bishop of Holland[355] comes up to justify his <cause> against the Jesuites for they gave out in Flanders that his evill cariage was made an instance

XVI, no. 163, p. 621. See also *NAGB*, *passim*; AAW, B 26, no. 40A. In December 1623, Vives promised that he would assist Thomas Rant with the secular clergy's current business in Rome: AAW, B 25, no. 102.

[350] Sébastien Bouthillier.

[351] For Zuñiga's recent death, see *CSPV, 1621–1623*, pp. 483, 502.

[352] Carlos Coloma.

[353] Edward Bennett.

[354] For Coloma's second letter to the Spanish ambassador in Rome, withdrawing his objection to the secular clergy's suit for the appointment of a bishop, see AAW, A XVI, no. 177, p. 679; TD, V, p. 91.

[355] Philip Rovenius, vicar apostolic of Holland since 1614, and created archbishop of Philippi in 1620: *CGB*, I, p. 45.

against our havinge bishops as though, for the evill behaviour of one (if it were true), the ordinary institution of Christ and practise of the whole Church should be abrogated and, if you could proove clearly that they had said that they would be gone out of England if we had bishops there, it were alone sufficient to discredit them in all matter of goverment. For, if they cannot endure to live where bishops do governe Gods people, what make they in the Christian world where bishops and none but bishops do governe?[356]

Touching the Jesuitrices, some in Flanders give out that you have ben checked for saying something against them w*hi*ch you could not proove. Whether it be soe or noe, be alwaies wary what you say even against the Jesuite[s] the*m*selves, for that you saw how in the congregation de P*ro*paganda Fide they gott men to speake against a knowen truth; <how> much more would they urge even against a truth that were not well prooved?[357] I have written both to Doway and St Omers to get M[aster] Wilsons booke in their defence and shall send you the principall propositions in it so soone as it comes to my hand[s].[358] A Benedictine of very good credit reported here the last sommer that one of those Jesuitrices (a Benedictine and the

[356]Catholic jurisdictional structures in the Netherlands were problematical in ways rather similar to those in England. The secular clergy who worked in rebel-controlled areas were governed by a vicar apostolic, at this date Rovenius, who was also provisionally bishop of Utrecht, whereas (after 1612) the Jesuits were responsible to the nuncio. As Paul Arblaster explains, 'further confusion was added by the existence of areas under Dutch control which were part of dioceses still largely in loyal territory', in which priests were, of course, governed by diocesan bishops: P. Arblaster, *Antwerp & the World: Richard Verstegan and the international culture of Catholic reformation* (Louvain, 2004), p. 119. On 24 September/4 October 1622, John Bennett had reported that 'here is also in the congregacion de Propaganda Fide informaciones given by the Jesuites against the bishop of Holland', Rovenius, who had recently set out from Flanders for Rome, 'and they would <have> him taken away and noe bishop there. But he hath answered them home. I have seene the objectiones and answeres. The nexte congregacion determineth that matter and I thinke litle for the Jesuites there advantage. They are subjectes to that bishop in many important pointes and he curbeth there insolency.' Also 'there are 200 prestes' whereas the Jesuits numbered only 'some xx[ti], yet would have all in theere owne handes': AAW, A XVI, no. 151, p. 589; *CGB*, I, pp. xxxii, 268–269. For Rovenius, see also *NCC*, pp. 89, 94, 243; Israel, *The Dutch Republic*, pp. 377f. and esp. pp. 381–384; *CGB*, I, pp. xxxi–xxxii, 94 (Rovenius's defence of his actions, offered to Giovanni Francesco Guido del Bagno); AAW, A XVI, no. 180, p. 688.

[357]In a letter of 30 September/10 October 1622, John Bennett had reported to his brother Edward that 'you wrote unto me of a letter published in England as written by his Hol[iness] in approbation of the Jesuitrices', and had asked for a copy of the letter if it could be proved that the Jesuits were publicizing it. John Bennett argued that the pope 'noe way favoureth them but much misliketh them and there institute and <soe> doe all the best of this courte. Yet they will not putt them out of Rome albeit, of late, they were in some danger.' The institute's members 'begge upp and downe here, and that very impudently, to there owne shame and disgrace of there countrey': AAW, A XVI, no. 156, p. 606.

[358]John Wilson, at Saint-Omer, had (said Joseph Haynes) 'written a booke wherin he defendeth them and censureth the spirites that favour them not'. This is a reference, in fact,

priest of the house <in England> being present) did, after Masse, sett her selfe downe in a chaire before the alter and there made them an exhortation; whereas a woman by S[aint] Paules rule should not speake in the congregation. Item M^r^ Harlay, provost of St Gery in Cambrai writt to mee this last weeke that 13 of those women are gathered [*word illegible*] in London into one house[359] and do p*ro*fesse to teach yo[u]ng children. Is not this to irritate the magistrate against all Catholikes? I have written to M^r^ Colleton to take true information of it and to send it to you or me with what speed he can.

M^r^ Biron shalbe for your and his friends sake very welcome to us.[360] The newes of this co[u]ntry is that Montauban [*p. 676*] hath rendred it self to the kings order, is content that all her new fortifications be beaten downe and that all Catholikes be restored to their livings and they must also have the free use of their religion. Rochell will not yeeld to the kings order. The duke of Guise about 12 daies since did give the Rochelers a great overthrow by sea.[361] Out of England no great matter. There is a rumour that M^r^ Mathewe shalbe sworne secretarie unto the prince,[362] who is said also to labour for a parlement to take away the laws against Catholiks because the infanta hath sent him word that she will not come in to have her head stroke of[f], w*hi*ch may be by those wicked lawes enacted against recusantes. Thus with my very harty comend[ations], I rest.

Yo*ur*s alwaies assured,

W*illia*m Bishope

The 15th of November 1622.
Concerning the Benedictins, I once said that it were the better way if they would joyne with us in having of bishops, and that they should

to Richard Gibbons SJ's translation entitled *An Abridgement of Meditations of the Life, Passion, Death & Resurrection of our Lord and Saviour Iesus Christ* (Saint-Omer, 1614); the abridgement in question, by François Solier SJ, is a version of a work by Vicenzo Bruno SJ: see ARCR, II, no. 344; Dirmeier, *MW*, I, pp. 216–218. The book was dedicated by Wilson 'to the vertuous and religious gentlewomen Mistresse Mary Warde and the rest of her devout company in S. Omers'. John Bennett asked for a copy in order to demonstrate Wilson's 'foolery and knavery': Dirmeier, *MW*, I, pp. 216–218; AAW, A XVI, no. 156, p. 606. (Of John Wilson's *The Treasury of Devotion*, which was published at Saint-Omer in 1622, Richard Smith complained to Rome in 1626 that part of this collection had been printed without the proper authorization: ARCR, II, no. 811.) I am very grateful to Caroline Bowden for assistance with this point.

359 See *Letter 19*.

360 On 30 September/10 October 1622, John Bennett had sent word of Biron's impending return from Italy: AAW, A XVI, no. 156, p. 607.

361 See *CSPV, 1621–1623*, p. 519; cf. *HMCMK*, p. 148.

362 See also AAW, A XVI, no. 165, p. 625 (a letter to John Bennett from E. Hewes, of 20 October 1622, mentioning the same rumour, which Hewes did not believe).

be as well chosen and have voices [?] to cho[o]se as wee, if they [?] would be under them. If that did not like them, that we would leave them to the full [*word obscured*] of their puritaynes and only request them to further us in the suite. This hath been repeated over and over to them since, now ten times, and do they yet grudg[e] at it? God amend them.

*Addressed*: Au révérend père, le Père Bartin prestre de la congrégation de l'Oratoire à St Louis.
Donne le (si vous plait) à Mons*ieu*r Bennet agent du cleargy d'Angleterre.
A Rome.

*Endorsed*: Mr D[octor] Bishop. Novemb[er] 15th.

## 22. William Bishop to John Bennett, 5/15 November 1622

[*AAW, A XVI, no. 176, pp. 677–678; postscript to AAW, A XVI, no. 175*]

Since I sealed up my packett, Mr Gage came to visite us who [w]as at his first coming to the king (as he saieth) not much respected because he brought, <as> condition of the dispensation, something that liked them not, yet afterward he was in credit, they meaning to use him for that purpose of mollifying those conditions. And, whereas he was to have been sent straight to Rome, now he is to passe by Spaine[363] and there to see the conclusion of the match and to bring their helpes for o*ur* king with him. He saies that he findes o*ur* king wholy bent to go thorow with the match, and therein to do the Catholikes all the favour that can be reasonably demanded of him. Whereas, if it should not succeed, he must needes deale by way of parlement, that wilbe by the puritans, and so he shalbe driven to condescent [*sic for* condescend] to worse and worse lawes against recusants, otherwise the puritans will do nothing for him. Wherefore, as we love our owne good, we must labour that the match be not hindered. All this is well, and I would his father Jesuits were all of the same mind. He seemes to be much engaged to the king, and very foreward to speake for him, and that the king is not to be pressed to too hard conditions; and, to say the truth, so thinke I too, yet under that faire p*re*tence in generall we must looke to the Catholikes p*ar*ticular present benefitt, as to have some of the Catholike nobility sworne on the privy councell; and that <some> hostages be given for the assurance of p*er*forming,

[363] See *CSPV, 1621–1623*, pp. 485, 490; PRO, SP 94/25, fo. 301v.

w*hi*ch Mr Gage thinkes are not to be stood upon. The former point the king must eas[i]ly do with [*sic for* without (?)] any lett; the second seemes to require their pac[i]ens [*sic for* pacient] consent and therefore more difficult. Well, lett wiser heads than mee thinke well on those and such like points. There was much adoe at the court at the taking of Heidelberge, and for ten daies Mr Gage durst scarce speake to any body. Great talke there was of making a great army and of warr with Spaine as false dissemblers. The king let them alone but, when the heat was blowne over, he staid in his former resolution to linck himself with Spaine and to suppresse the puritans if that commotion were setled. God hold him in that mind. Yea Mr Gage stikes not to say that, if the match go not foreward, he will lay all the fault on the Spaniard (o*ur* king is so reasonable); yea that he never meant it from the beginning. But Mr Cottington, who hath [*word omitted:* been] agent in Spaine this seaven yeares, returning of late into England, assured the king that the Spaniard is as willing to goe foreward as he, so that it is, God willing, moste like to be very shortly concluded.[364] Thus much of Mr Gage.

I heare that the fals[e] byshop of Meath[365] in Ireland, having in his sermon inveighed against the popes Holines, he was told from the d[ep]uty [?] that his Ma*jes*tie [*p. 678*] of Great Britayne had forbidden all preachers to inveigh against the pope. Well then, said he, I will do so no more, and went, as they say, to excuse him[self] to some principall of his auditors therefore.[366] So easy is it <for the kinge> to incline most of [*word deleted*] <his [?]> cleargy not [to] be enemies to o*ur* religion. Yea Mr Gage saith that many of the puritans, seing him to be much made [*sic*] of by the king, seemed to respect him much. One of o*ur* doctors, whom Mr Seton knoweth, told me that the card[inal] of Susanna doth favour o*ur* suite for bishops but would not have it spoken of.[367]

[364]For Francis Cottington's arrival from Spain and his being sworn secretary to Prince Charles, see Redworth, *PI*, p. 44; Lockyer, *Buckingham*, p. 113; *CSPV, 1621–1623*, pp. 336, 485, 490. Digby assured Calvert that Cottington's report of the negotiations in Spain would give 'great satisfaction, notwithstanding any jealousies or doubts which may be raised by the comming of Mr Gage into England with the popes unreasonable demandes': PRO, SP 94/25, fo. 223r. In disgust, Simonds D'Ewes remarked that Cottington 'was newlye come over and had satisfied the king' concerning the Spaniards' intentions, and so 'all the good hopes at court weere dasht': *DSSD*, pp. 102, 101.

[365]James Ussher.

[366]This is, apparently, a reference to Ussher's controversial words in his sermon preached at the swearing in of the new lord deputy, Henry Cary, 1st Viscount Falkland, on 8 September 1622: see Kearney, *Strafford in Ireland*, p. 112; *ODNB*, *sub* 'Ussher, James' (article by Alan Ford).

[367]Cf. *Letter 52*.

The palsgrave[368] that was, is now by the Hollanders p*ro*moted to the bishoprick of Utrick, ~~the~~ to live upon that. And the lady princesse[369] doth by herselfe and [her] folowers seeke to draw wh[at] English or Scottish gentelmen they can to folow her, w*hi*ch [?] breadeth in o*ur* king and prince a great distruste that she p*re*tends to o*ur* crowne before her time, w*hi*ch is no smale motive to them to unite themselves to the Spaniard that by his [*words obliterated*] need be they may withstand both puritans at home and Hollanders abroad.

F[ather] Archang[el][370] will do his best to gett the Frenc[h] ambassadour[371] in England to write to the Fr[ench] ambassadour in Rome[372] to speake for us in that matter of byshops w*hi*ch, if he do, wee will get him to speake much to the purpose for us. It now cometh to my mind, and it may be supposed with some p*ro*bability, that the Jesuits fautors [?] should put into the kings head that great wrong was offered to his regall authoritie to have any man named to be a bishop in his realme without his leave and consent <for> [*three words deleted*] F[ather] Forcer[373] [?] <did> tell M^r^ Missindin[374] that the king had written to my L[ord] Digbie, who is now earle of Bristow, against o*ur* having of bishops without his licence.

O*ur* prince hath sent some token to the y[o]ung [?] infanta, requesting her to come speedely or els he shall <forsooth> languish away with love, as the poets faine.

M^r^ Newman did by the help of law make good his place till F[ather] Kensington,[375] who follows the suit against him, is vanished quite out of sight.[376] Yo*ur* help hath stood him in great stead. We hear [?] even now that all the Rochelers ships to the number of threescore are either sunke or taken or spoiled by the duke of Guyse.[377] This is some recompense for the bad peace [?] w*hi*ch they say is made much to the Hugonots advantage.

[368] Frederick V, elector palatine.

[369] Princess Elizabeth, wife of the elector palatine.

[370] William (Archangel) Barlow.

[371] Tanneguy Leveneur, count of Tillières.

[372] Denis Simon de Marquemont, archbishop of Lyons. See J. Bergin, *The Making of the French Episcopate 1589–1661* (London, 1996), p. 665; D.L.M. Avenel (ed.), *Lettres, Instructions Diplomatiques et Papiers d'état du Cardinal de Richelieu*, 8 vols (Paris, 1853–1877), II, pp. 16–17.

[373] Francis Forcer SJ.

[374] Edward Maddison.

[375] John Laithwait SJ.

[376] For William Newman's report, on 31 July/10 August 1624, of Laithwait's death, see AAW, B 26, no. 99.

[377] See *CSPV, 1621–1623*, p. 519; *Letter 21*.

[*At top of p. 678*] The third of November, when it began to sheet in snow [?].

There is a great fleet of ships come out of Spaine for Flanders w*hi*ch, if they had come a moneth so[o]ner, Spinola had not lost the siege to [*word illegible*] the Spaniards fault.[378]

## 23. William Bishop to John Bennett, 8/18 November 1622

[*AAW, A XVI, no. 178, pp. 681–682; printed in part in TD, V, p. 91*]

Very wor*shipfu*ll s*i*r,

Albeit I did write unto you[379] within these three daies, yet this copy[380] of the legacy of the late <false> bishope of London being sent me from Doway to send unto you, that you may <have> the first presentation of it to the cardinalls that desire it, I do send it away in hast. I like the thing well, yet, because Mr Broughton seemes over fearfull of the publication of it, you may use what moderation you think best in the presentation of it. I have sent yours into England and joyned my owne with them, giving them the best advice I can, specially that they make friends to the prince (who seemes hartely affected to the match) and to give him to understand that whosoever brought that newes unto the kings Ma*jes*tie that his Holines would send him in an archbishop of Canterbury and another of Yorke is no friend to that match but desires the breach of it, but, casting such a bone as that between the popes Holines and his Ma*jes*tie, he must needes be p*re*sumed to make them fall out the one with thother: his Holines with the king, if he should not be willing to p*er*mitt <in his kingdome> the ordinary pastors and pillars of o*u*r religion; and, againe, <to make> the king offended with his Holines for that he should intitle men to the archbishoprikes of England without his privity. If Mr Gage did this prety peece of service (as it seemes he did, for that it was done about his first arrivall to the court and not before) he deserves to be greatly blamed both of the one and of thother: of his Holines, for giving his Ma*jes*tie falsely to understand his <most> modest manner of p*ro*ceeding; and of the king, for that his resisting of bishops may be a just cause of witholding the dispensatio*n* without w*hi*ch the Catholike

[378] See *Letter 20*.

[379] See *Letter 22*.

[380] In the secular clergy agent's papers there is a manuscript copy of the preface of *The Bishop of London his Legacy*, with a part thereof translated into Latin. See AAW, A XVI, no. 85, pp. 303–314, no. 86, pp. 315–318.

king will not proceed in the mariage. If they can beat this well into our princes head they will marr Mr Gages negotiation. And I think that, <if> Cardinal Bandini do but suspect Gage to be such an [*sic*] misinformer of their good meanings to the kings Ma*jes*tie, they will not hereafter use him. But what marvell though a Jesuited man (if not a Jesuite) do use such trickes to breake of[f] the match cunningly w*hi*ch they utterly dislike and have opposed underhand what they could. Truly, to imploy a man that affects not the busines he goeth about is the next way to undoe it. For having <the> credit to be trusted in it, he may eas[i]ly spy out how it is to be marred.

Wherefore <lett> wise men see how they imploy any Jesuited p*er*son in that matter of the match. I am the longer in this point because I have nothing els now to write, wherefore com*m*ending you and our important causes unto the p*ro*tection of our blessed Saviour, I rest.

Yo*ur*s alwaies assured,

W*illia*m Byshope

The 18th of November 1622.

[*on p. 682*]

*Addressed*: Au révérend père, le Père Bartin, prestre de la congrégation de l'Oratoire à St Louis.
Donne le si vous plait à Mons*ieu*r Bennet agent du cleargé d'Angleterre. A Rome.

*Endorsed*: Mr D[octor] Bishop. Novem[ber] 18th.

## 24. Joseph Haynes's relation of his conference with John Williams, bishop of Lincoln, 25 November 1622

[*AAW, A XVI, no. 179, p. 683; printed in TD, V, p. ccliv*]

With warrant from superiors and a letter from the Spanish embassador,[381] I went to the l[ord] keeper[382] and, after acknowledgment of former acquaintance, I made knowne unto him my bussinesse, the substance whereof was sett downe in a letter I had from Mr Benett[383] at Rome, w*hi*ch I did reade unto him. Hee seemed well pleased at it and did not, by his discourse, shewe any dislike of our haveinge

381 Carlos Coloma.
382 John Williams, bishop of Lincoln.
383 John Bennett.

a b[ishop]. He told mee that his Ma*jes*tie was offended w*it*h those b*ishop*s in Ireland ~~for that~~ for that they had sett up a consistorie, and wiped the people there of theire mony; the Protestant b*ishop*s having first fleeced them, the other[s] went closer.[384] I answered that it was not mony w*hi*ch the secular clergie aymed at but goverment, good dis*ci*pline and order amongst them, w*hi*ch could not bee w*it*hout a b[ishop]. He sayd he would deale effectually w*it*h his Majesty and desired a copie of the sayd letter. <This was the> 25 November 1622.

Jo[seph] Heynes

*Endorsed*: My nephew his conference w*it*h my l[ord] keeper.

## 25. Richard Sara [Edward Bennett] to John Bennett, 15 January 1623

*[AAW, A XVII, no. 1, pp. 1–4]*

Good syr,

Immediatly befor Chrismas I sent yo*u* the embassadours[385] letters to Cardinall Melino, to whome also the good archdecon[386] writt wherof I sent yo*u*, in [the] Chrismas hollidaies, <a coppy>,[387] soe that now we hope all impedimentes be removed. I pray write to the good archdecon to whom we are infinitlye bownd. Now they have sett <on> the kinge to take exceptions against D[octor] Kellisons booke of the p*re*late and the prince,[388] because they would hinder his p*ro*motion sed frustra.[389]

[384] See also Hacket, *SR*, part I, p. 94; *Letter 8*.

[385] Carlos Coloma.

[386] François de Carondelet.

[387] AAW, A XVI, no. 181, pp. 689–692 (Carondelet to Cardinal Millini, 27 December 1622, printed in TD, V, pp. cclv–cclx).

[388] Matthew Kellison, *The Right and Iurisdiction of the Prelate, and the Prince. Or, a treatise of ecclesiasticall, and regall authoritie* (Douai, 1617). A second edition had appeared in 1621. In 1624, John Colleton wrote a letter of assurance to King James concerning Kellison's tract. Colleton declared that the 'second impression' of the book (i.e. the second edition) was drawn from the author only 'by reason of certaine exceptions taken' by Thomas Preston (in *A New-Yeares Gift for English Catholikes* (London, 1620)) against the first edition: AAW, A XVIII, no. 104, p. 559.

[389] Kellison was the first choice of those secular clergy who were canvassed for their opinion about those suitable to have episcopal authority conferred on them. This anonymous denunciation of Kellison to the Jacobean regime persuaded Rome to appoint William Bishop instead: Allison, RS, pp. 154–155, 176–177.

The king sent to Mr Colleton a gentleman to wish hyme to enquire the autor of the p*re*late and prince wherin the autor showld write that it was lawfull to kill King James by name. His Ma*jes*ty had not seen the book, owt of w*hi*ch 10 articles were drawen owt, wherof this was on[e]. His Ma*jes*ty alsoe sent to the embassadour by my lord of Buckingham <to complain of his porter who had sould this book>, but the booke being examined ther is nothing fownd in it but the ordinary doctrin of Godes Church de dominio indirecto sum*ma* pontificis over kinges.[390] Soe that all thinges be well pacified; and Doctor Kellison wished [*sic*] to writ to his Ma*jes*ty to give hime account of the argument of the booke and occasions of writing of it. The true autors of this stratagem we knowe not. Great suspition there is the Theatins[391] have had a finger in setting of it forward ~~by th~~[~~e~~] because ther frendes have been busy in it, as Cottington by name, who w*i*th <Secret[ary]> Colvert have opposed them selfes to b*ishop*s and would have made the embassadour[392] beleeve the king would hang any b*ishop*s that came in. But, being sent unto and tould that it will be ill taken they should oppose Gundemar his designes, they excuse them selfes and will no more medle in that bussines. No dowbt his Ma*jes*ty hath ben wrought by Jessuit[i]call means to oppose hyme self but, since he hath been informed by yo*ur* letter, a gentleman tould me from his own mouth that he should say it was necessary the priestes should have bushops ells all would [be] owt of order. These Jesswetes have been soe busye w*i*th the embassadour that he hath no conceit of them. Of this matter of Doctor Kellison I desired Mr Smith to writ some p*ar*ticulars w*hi*ch yo*u* shall receave. They ar much trubled because it is a comon report that ther hath been a Jesswete w*i*th Secretary Calvert, Mr Younge by name, to sett forward this opposition.[393]

All thinges goe heer w*i*th great contentment to his Ma*jes*ty. Syr Endimion Porter is retorned.[394] Boath kinges have agreed upon the

[390] See Kellison, *The Right and Iurisdiction of the Prelate, and the Prince*, esp. chs 7, 8, 9, 10. In early January, Alvise Valaresso reported the news of James's complaint, delivered via Buckingham, to Coloma, concerning the sale, by a porter in his household, of Kellison's book: *CSPV, 1621–1623*, p. 538. John Chamberlain believed it had actually been printed there: McClure, *LJC*, p. 471. According to Chamberlain, the porter was an Englishman. He may, in fact, have been Coloma's chaplain, William Law.

[391] i.e. Jesuits.

[392] Carlos Coloma.

[393] See *Letter 20*.

[394] Porter arrived in London on 2 January 1623: Redworth, *PI*, p. 49; *CSPV, 1621–1623*, pp. 545, 548; *DSSD*, p. 119. His advice that the Spanish match might be successfully concluded, and a settlement achieved in the Palatinate, persuaded Buckingham that he and Prince Charles should travel to Madrid: Adams, PC, p. 333.

conditions of the marraidge.[395] Ther is nothing desyred but the dispe*n*sation. The Jesswetes and ther followers give owt that Gage is gon to Rome abowt that and he will effect all.[396] The priestes and ther followers say that it is Pater Maestro that must effect it, and that Gage doth but intrud[e] hyme self by the countenaunce of Jesswetes, being able to doe nothinge. All indifferent wise men wonder that <the Count> Gwndemar and Pater Maestro will give way to this intruder to have any hand in this bussines knowinge he is an instrument of the Jesswetes boath now and hereafter to truble and make faction for them. It were good [*p. 2*] Pater Maestro did looke into this bussines lest that while they, for manner sake, give way to his forwardnes, he will sett that footinge hereafter for his setters on, that they <will> wish they had never opposed hyme at first. Capite vulpeculas etc. All this Christmas his Ma*jes*ty hath been in this town and no dowbt ~~he~~ hath beene delt w*i*th to showe discontent ~~abowt~~ <against b*ishop*s>, espetially in this rwfflinge abowt Doct[or] Kellisons booke. Yeat ~~she~~ he gave not the least sign of ~~discontent~~ any. Every body crye[s] owt that his Hollines would be pleased p*re*sently to end this good work of b*ishop*s before the ~~dispensation~~ marraidge be concluded as a thinge not dependinge upon it. The lord keep*er*[397] hath beene no back frend to o*u*r bussines because the Jesswetes have no hand w*i*th hyme. But M$^{r}$ Secretary Colvert and M$^{r}$ Cottington, who hath a Jesswette to his brother,[398] have beene very forward against us.

In my letters before Chrismas I sent yo*u* newes of M$^{r}$ W*illia*m Floyer['s][399] good end, w*i*th a letter of George to yo*u*. I looke for hyme every day. His Ma*jes*ty hath been sick of the gowt this Chrismas, as is sayed, but nowe, God be thancked, [is] reasonable well. I pray God

[395] For the contents of and agreement on the marriage articles of December 1622 (concerning the infanta's household and chapel, her servants and the arrangements made for the education of her children, and the legal status of and protection for English Catholics), endorsed by James in January 1623, see Redworth, *PI*, pp. 49, 174–183. On 12/22 February 1623, William Harewell reported to John Bennett that 'it is saied the k[ing] of England at his signing and putting his hand unto the conditions of marriadge concerning religion <seemed to make a pause and> bad[e] the noble men that stood by [to] beare witnesse that he signed those conditions against his conscience. Kings have more fetches than ordinarie men.' Harewell understood also that 'the palatine shall be restored to what the Spaniards possesse of his, and perhaps the rest, but with condition that his children be brought up in the emperours court': AAW, A XVII, no. 6, p. 22.

[396] For puritan ire at rumours spread by Catholics about the dispensation, see *DSSD*, p. 132.

[397] John Williams, bishop of Lincoln.

[398] Sir Francis Cottington's brother, Edward, had entered the Jesuit novitiate in late 1602, although he died shortly afterwards: CRS, 74, p. 148. See also CRS, 54, pp. 63–66; M.J. Havran, *Caroline Courtier* (London, 1973), pp. 3, 13.

[399] Or 'Floyde'.

he have longe life. Ther is a comaund sent to all judges not to medle w*i*th recusantes.

My frend[400] w*i*th all myn[e] [?] salute yo*u*. We are all behowldinge unto her. I pray remember my frend and my service to Pater Maistro. She hopeth yo*u* will come boath together. God keepe yo*u*.

Yo*u*rs,

Rich[ard] Sara

January 15 1622.

It is written unto us that the Jesswetes mean to sett up a seminary at Lysbon in those howses that doe belonge to us and soe sett an altar against ~~the~~ an altar. We doe not desyre they should make up such buildinges for it is to serve them selfes and to oppose us. Lett those howses be joyned to Don Pedro[401] his colledge. If you informe not of this they will breed us truble. Good lord, they thincke upon nothinge but tumultes and scandall. If the sea apostolick takes no order w*i*th them, o*u*r cuntrey wilbe undon. Yo*u* must gett this matter of b*ishop*s sett forward before the maiche be concluded.

[*on p. 4*]

*Addressed*: To the wo*rshipfu*ll my loving frend Mr John Bennett.

[*on p. 2*]

*Endorsed*: Mr Clifton.

## 26. John Bennett to Sir George Villiers, marquis of Buckingham, 24 February/6 March 1623

[*AAW, A XVII, no. 8, pp. 27–30; part printed in TD, V, pp. ccxciii–ccxcv*]

Most excellent and my very good lord,

As to this weighty ~~and importante~~ affayre, soe long dependinge in this courte, I could bringe no other furtherance ~~but~~ <than> such as weake endevoures, ~~issuing out of~~ <accompanied with> an earnest desire of thincrease of Godes honor, ~~accompanied with~~ <and> the service of our prince and countrey, ~~could~~ <~~might~~> <could> affoorde, soe truly could I be very well contente to have lapped upp the memory therof, and joyed in the happy issue, as the effecte

[400] Lady Elizabeth Dormer.
[401] Pedro Coutinho.

of the diligence and industry of others. ~~But I could not be suffered soe to lurk, those poore laboures <must> by busy tonges be brought to lighte and branded I knowe not with what aspersiones of not only unprofitable <for> which I~~ [*deleted:* ~~should~~] <[*deleted:* ~~had~~]> <~~should not complayne~~> [~~but~~] ~~easily have passed over, but hurtefull also to the cause I pretended to advance. And albeit my conscience tould me I sewed noe badd seede and founde the blade incombred with cockle of misreporte~~. [*In margin:* But lurke I might not. I must undergo the ce*n*sures of medling wittes; and, howsoever my co*n*science tould me I had sowed noe bad seed, I found cockle of misreporte cast in.] Yet ayminge, for my parte, at noe private interestes, I resolved to suffre both to growe, in Godes name, knowinge well our supreme and all-seeinge judge would, tyme ynoughe, severe them, thon for his barne, thother for the fyer. ~~But perceaving that myndes guyded whether with mistakinge, misaffection or an overflowing humor of overactive medlinge, I will not judge, had spred this noyse even to the eares of his Ma*jes*ty~~ [*In margin:* But p*er*ceaving that, by overactive diligence, this noyse had bene spread even to the eares of his Ma*jes*ty (whose vassall, though unp*ro*fitable, yet loyall, I am)] and your Ex*cellen*cy, the memory of whose honorable travailes our posterity will blesse, I held [it] my duty to give accountes ~~furst to his Ma*jes*ty, then to your Ex*cellency*~~ <to both>, such as if it cannot recomende much deserte, yet I hope will free my actiones and intentions from all suspecte of cryme. Thus then it fell out.

When furst I arrived here, of his Hol[iness] his power to dispence in our case I found noe doubte made: only, it was aggreed amongst devines [*p. 28*] that to warrant the doinge, as voyd of synne, there must be ~~just~~ <good> cause, inferring special advantage for God his honor, justly hoped, ~~and~~ yea, well assured therby: ells could not ~~his Hol~~[~~iness~~] he lawfully enervate an ecclesiastical decree established for publick good, sith that were an abuse of his authority, graunted [*word deleted*] non ad destructionem, sed ad aedificationem. At my furst audience, his Hol[iness] demaunded what in this behalf we could allege. Soe did the card*ina*ls [*word deleted*]. To satisfy, I pressed by word, and exhibited in writing, the reasones w*hi*ch I send herew*i*th. But this busynesse never wanting stiff and secrete opposition, it was insisted that thoughe ~~it could not be denyed~~ the causes alledged were sufficient, yet what assurance could be had that his Ma*jes*ty would mak[e] good such thinges as therin should be promised? To aunswere this, I added the appendix, w*hi*ch goethe also ~~herewith~~ <w*i*th these>. That, in forcinge and urginge these reasones, we should be importunate: our duty to our prince, our present advantage, our former distresses, were causes pregnant, warranted specially w*i*th the right we had to require remedy from the sea apostolick when, in peaceable maner, and <with> content of all partys, it might be yelded. ~~As~~ If our speeches were feelinge, as issuing from the harte, ~~soe in truth~~ <truly they> were ~~they~~ h[e]ard w*i*th feeling by his Hol[iness] and our hon[ourable] judges, <who> ever showed an ernest desire to give his Ma*jes*ty all satisfaction, and us the releef w*hi*ch <we> soe justly required.

All this <we did, or could, doe> induceth no bond, chalengeth no thankes ~~from us~~. It is due. But P*adr*e Maestro his his [*sic*] faithfull diligence, sollicitude and incessant laboures in this ~~behalf~~ affayre, discovered that affectionat regard of his Ma*jes*ty his service and sincere love to our nation, that many strangers (for all in this matter are not of our judgment) ~~thought it an~~ <deemed it an> excesse, yea blamed it in him. His answere ever was that, thoughe by nation he were not English, yet his harte was English; [*in margin:* and [he] soe much p*re*vayled that, w*i*th his prudence and efficacy, he swayed myndes, if not in affection averted, yet assuredly in judgment opposite]. I ~~protest unto~~ assure yo*u*r Ex*cellen*cy I increase nothing, nor can deliver thon half of what I many tymes h[e]ard and saw. [*p. 29*] Gratitude and honesty bynd us to acknowledge that w*hi*ch, if we did deny or could secrete, this whole court ~~ringeth of~~ <would wittnesse>.

When this important busynesse was brought to the issue w*hi*ch here for the tyme would be expected, I was called uppon by o*ur* Catholicke cleargy of England to supplicate for a sup*er*ior, w*hi*ch nowe they they [*sic*] have wanted above xx$^{ty}$ monthes,[402] and is needffull to preserve peace, discipline and order amongst us. Why they desired that the delegate unknowne, insuficient and never heard of authority of an archprest should should [*sic*] be changed to the caracter, kn[o]wne [?] and receaved jurisdiction of a bishop, and this, w*hi*ch they had xx$^{ty}$ yeres sued for, the enclosed writing will give yo*u*r Exc*ellency* a brief accounte only. I add that, if ever severe discipline were useffull amongst us at this tyme, it is most needeffull to restrayne the overpotent sway of some stirring spirits impatient of limits and boundes, but alsoe w*i*th authority to guyde the zeale of other Catholickes whoe in this calme maye runne into excesses and increase his Ma*jes*ty his difficultyes to there owne harme and hurte of there comon cause. If herin should be neglecte, and therby disorders happen, his Ma*jes*ty hath present remedy, calling the sup*er*ior to accounte, w*hi*ch he cannot avoyd by pretence he wanteth power and meanes of redresse w*hi*ch an archpreest may justly doe. [*In margin:* And this I say <to satisfy such as> [*three words deleted*] ~~reported~~ decried and blamed that [*sic*] ~~though~~ this o*ur* suite <as> unseazonable or out of tyme.]

[402] i.e. since the death of the third of the archpriests, William Harrison.

Sithence we receaved the joyffull newes of the late dispatch in Spayne, his Hol[iness] increased *ou*r congregation w*i*th accesse of two card*ina*ls in place of Card*ina*l Sacrati[403] whoe is absent. These are Ubaldini[404] and Barberini,[405] worthy personages, and [they] shewe greate zeale in this affayer. Two dayes agoe, I had audience w*i*th his Hol[iness], to wytt, the 4th of this p*re*sent. I fynde him the same that [he] allwayes [was]. Having sayd what I purposed, I exhibited the memorial inclosed. But here are greater and more powerffull endevoures w*hi*ch will, I hope, bring this whole treaty on to a speedy conclusion; which God, of his goodnesse, graunt. If I have beene ~~tire~~ tediouse, I conceaved a bonde and necessity. What issueth out of dutiffull affection y*ou*r Ex*cellen*cy will easily p*ar*done. Soe, wishing y*ou*r Ex*cellency* all increase of hon[our] and happinesse, here and hearafter, I rest.

[*on p. 30*]

*Endorsed*: Mr Bennett to the d[uke] of Buckingham.

## 27. William Farrar [Harewell] to John Bennett, 5/15 March 1623

[*AAW, A XVII, no. 10, pp. 33–36*]

Very reverend and most worthy sir,

The last weeke I gave you notice of *ou*r friend Mons*ieu*r Carondelet his visiting Mr President[406] heere and the entertainement he had of us w*i*th the content and satisfaction he receaved therein.[407] The w*hi*ch he hath since very well certified; for at his departure from Cambray towards England, w*hi*ch was w*i*thin three dayes after he went from us, he sent the colledge, for a present, a faire <guilt> cuppe w*i*th a cover in like sort guilt w*hi*ch is valued to be worth some 9 or 10l sterl[ing]. It seemes to be of English worke, and given him by some friends there.

403 Francesco Sacrati.

404 Roberto Ubaldini.

405 Francesco Barberini.

406 Matthew Kellison.

407 On 12/22 February 1623, William Harewell had notified John Bennett that he had been sent to Brussels by Matthew Kellison to meet with François de Carondelet. Carondelet had recently arrived from England 'to treate with the infanta uppon speciall affaires in the behalfe as well of the k[ing] of England as the k[ing] of Spaine'. Harewell saw 'the passe' Carondelet 'had from the k[ing] of England' and said that he had 'done extraordinarie great offices for the clergie of Eng[land] with the infanta' and others, and had defended Kellison against the 'aspersion which was cast uppon him for his booke' (*The Right and Iurisdiction of the Prelate, and the Prince*): AAW, A XVII, no. 6, p. 21; see also *Letter 25*.

I enformed you also by my last, and by my other also of the weeke before, of the licence the chapter hath given him to be absent untill midsomer next and of my being at Cambray to deale w*i*th some of the canons therein. Withall I writt that we had newes out of England that the bishop of Canterburie[408] would resigne his place to the bishop of Lincolne, lord keeper.[409] But it was writt onely as a report, not for <a> certainetie, though it be very probable there is some such matter.

On Satturday last we had di[s]astrous newes from Brussels, w*hi*ch went there for currant, and was verily beleeved of most of our nation in that cittie, to witt that the prince of Wales should be murdered by one of his pages, and the king <surprized and> putt in prison. This newes came from Holland to Brussels, and presently ranne through all these countries. But by Munday we heard that the prince was gone privately out of England disguised into Spaine. This report gave us some hope that the former was false, yet could we not beleeve it, having no greate ground for the same, but ~~the~~ a breeve that the infantas agent[410] in England had writt so much to the governor of St Omers, and he to the abbot of Arras.[411] Yesternight, being Tuesday, we had this most certainely confirmed from Paris by D*octo*r Bishop (our monkes heere receaved as much from theirs there), who writt that the <prince> passed that way the first Sunday in Lent, from whome, for that I presume you will have the same newes particularly, I omitt to adde any more of what comes from him. Over and above w*hi*ch, <Don Carlos>[412] the Spanish emb[assador's] wife residing in Cambray had a letter from her husband in England on Munday morning to the same effect, who moreover writes that the prince his going into Spaine was kept so secrett that he was not made privie thereunto till he was gone; and that he sent a post after him to prevent his coming to Madrid, if it were possible. This newes I doubt not will be the comfortablest unto you that came a long time, as it is to all of us heere. The puritans in England, as the same emb[assador] writes, [*p. 34*] doe mightily storme hereat.[413] But many take this to be one of the greatest pointes of pollicie that the king hath yet shewed for the securing of himselfe and his sonne.

[408] George Abbot.

[409] John Williams.

[410] Jean-Baptiste van Male. Another representative of the infanta, Ferdinand Boischot, had recently arrived in order to negotiate the proposed armistice in the Palatinate: *CSPV, 1621–1623*, p. 577; PRO, PRO 31/3/57, fos 189r–v, 208r–209r.

[411] Philippe de Caverel, OSB, abbot of St Vaast at Arras. See *NAGB*, p. 182; Allison, RSGB, II, pp. 255–256.

[412] Carlos Coloma.

[413] See, e.g., *DSSD*, pp. 121–122.

Newes heareof we expect to heare out of England from *our* friends there, from whome we have not now heard any thing these three weekes or thereaboutes. The last we receaved from you were 15 dayes agoe and bore date the 21 and 28 of Januarie. D*octo*r Bishop writes he had one from you of the 14th of Februarie wherein you advertized him you intended to be shortely downe, w*hi*ch we shall be glad to see. I am now, and shall heereafter be, the more sparing in my writing for that I am in doubt my letters will not find you there. Mr President[414] is well and salutes you most kindely. He sung Masse and evensong on St Gregories day.[415] D*octo*r Champ[ney] and the rest do also remember themselves respective unto you. My self kisse y*our* hands, and rest.

Y*our*s ever in all service,

W*illia*m Farrar

Douay 15 Martii 1623.

I writt unto you in my former letteres of a search w*hi*ch was of late (21 Jan[uary]) in the New Prison at London by com*m*ission from the b[ishop] of Canterburie. The cause thereof (as Mr Nelson[416] writt) was given by the Jesuites who were saied to have printed an answer to the articles or propositions (the last summer given them by the king)[417] against the kinges liking and prohibition, and secretly to have divulged divers copies thereof. What was taken from them, v*iz* their ordinarie bookes, churchestuffe etc., the king promised should be restored unto them againe; and, at that time that notice heereof came unto us, it was also writt that one of the Jesuites there in prison had his chalice and some other of his thinges de facto restored, and expected restitution of the rest.[418]

*No address.*

[*on p. 36*]

*Endorsed*: Perused.

[414] Matthew Kellison.

[415] 12 March.

[416] John Jackson.

[417] See *Letter 14*.

[418] On 20 February/2 March 1623, William Bishop had written to John Bennett that, 'upon suspition of some writings, F[ather] Fishers [John Percy's] lodging was searched in the New Prison, but he', with the prison keeper's connivance, was with 'the countes[s] of Buckingham in Leicestershire', as Bishop had been informed by Richard Broughton, who was resident with the Manners family at Belvoir: AAW, A XVII, no. 7, p. 25; *Letter 29*. Alvise Valaresso noted the confiscation of Percy's books and 'sacred implements' by 'the king's special command', but also, a week later, the restoration to him of 'everything taken from him': *CSPV, 1621–1623*, pp. 573, 578; see also Hacket, *SR*, part I, p. 116; PRO, PRO 31/3/57, fo. 177v.

## 28. William Farrar [Harewell] to John Bennett, 12/22 March 1623

[*AAW, A XVII, no. 11, pp. 37–40*]

Very reverend and right worthy sir,

Since my last of the weeke past,[419] wherein I writt of the prince of Wales his journey into Spaine and the report of the bishop of Canterburie his surrendering his place, we have not receaved any fresh newes from England. All these countries ringe w*ith* the applause of our most noble prince his resolution and adventure for Spaine, and it is the onely subject now of every ones discourse. Much speech there is of his carriadge in Paris, w*hi*ch perhaps you have in part heard from thence. Now we heare that he is safely arrived in Spaine, w*hi*ch we hope is certaine, though we doubt whether any certaine newes could be brought hither from Spaine since his arrivall there, for that is not above 18 dayes since he parted from Paris. It is certaine that the marques of Buckingham, <w*ith*> S*ir* Francis Cottington and M^r^ Endymion Porter, went along w*ith* him,[420] and (as we are credibly informed) not above two more or three at the most.

We have receaved letters from Lou[v]aine of great newes reported there come fresh from Rome; in w*hi*ch letter [*sic*] the partie writes that the day of the date of his saied letter, w*hi*ch was 15 Martii, he sawe a letter from Rome in w*hi*ch was written that M^r^ Gage was arrived at Rome w*ith* other gentlemen coming from England to procure the dispensation, and the partie that shewed him this letter added that he thought that that matter would be sett forward apace (although there had been nothing done in it all this while). And, after, he writes that another partie the same day tould him that M^r^ Gage had procured the dispensation, and that it would be at the court in Spaine by Midlent Sunday. God be thanked M^r^ Gage is so great a man in those mens mouthes. Withall the same partie from Lou[v]aine writes that one (who had the newes from the fathers there) tould him lately that we had now a bishop made, and that the man was M^r^ Benett, but w*hi*ch (sayeth he) I knowe not. And, a few dayes <after>, the same partie tould him againe that now he had for certaine that the clergie had no bishop, nor should have any, because the king (of England) himselfe had written unto the pope against it.[421] These men would faine doe, or at least say, something, but that they falter in both. It is writt from

[419] *Letter 27*.

[420] See *DSSD*, p. 119; Redworth, *PI*, pp. 77–79.

[421] William Bishop had been appointed as bishop of Chalcedon (i.e. as a titular bishop *in partibus infidelium*) in February 1623. The breve for his consecration was issued on 13/23

the same place out of letters from England that Dr Dunne hath of late preached [*p. 38*] at Pauls Crosse by the kinges command,[422] and in his sermon declared publickely that the kinges will was that all persecution of Catholickes should from thence forth cease throughout the realme.

The Jesuites begin now to shew themselves the onely men for the match; though some of them in these parts have not doubted, and that very lately, to say that thinges did not goe in England in that sort, nor so well, as men abroad did thinke and that, if Gondomar did not returne into England this spring, Jordanio converteret*ur* retrorsum. But the prince his going into Spaine hath turned the winde and filled their sailes full for the other course. We have had none from you these three postes. Mr President[423] and the rest salute you, and now longe to see you, praying hartely for y*our* safe returne. I have no more worth the writing. And so, kissing y*our* hands and the handes of Padre Maistro and Mr Seton, I rest.

Y*our*s ever to serve you,

W*illia*m Farrar

Douay 22 Martii 1623.

[*on p. 40*]

*Addressed*: Al molto illustre et rev*eren*do sig*no*re, il Sig*no*re Giovanni Benetto, agente del clero di Ingleterra en Roma.

*No endorsement.*

## 29. William Farrar [Harewell] to John Bennett, 26 March/5 April 1623

[*AAW, A XVII, no. 19, pp. 71–72*]

Very reverend and respected good sir,

Since the last poste, when I writt[424] at large of all occurrences, there hath not arrived any newes heere worth advertising. There have some come to us since then out of England but they bring no more w*i*th

March 1623. The consecration took place in Paris on 25 May/4 June 1623: Anstr., I, p. 37; AAW, A XVII, no. 12, p. 41; TD, V, p. cclxxiii.

[422] See M. Maclure, *The Paul's Cross Sermons 1534–1642* (Toronto, 1958), p. 245.

[423] Matthew Kellison.

[424] *Letter 28.*

them than we had before, and w*hi*ch you have also had from mee. This onely particular we heare above what I have hitherto writt unto you concerning the search that was made in the New Prison, in F[ather] Fisher[425] his chamber, w*hi*ch was (as formerly I have ~~formerly~~ advertized you) to finde out certaine printed bookes privately sett forth by him about the disputation he had w*it*h D*octo*r White, contrarie unto the kinges expresse command given <him> in that behalfe, and for certaine other papers and letters whereof he was suspected.[426] Above this I say we have heard that the saied F[ather] Fisher not being <found> in prison when the saied search was made, but abroad in the countrie by the keepers p*er*mission, the keeper in default of him was com*m*itted prisoner untill the others coming in, w*hi*ch happening a fewe dayes after, F[ather] Fisher, so soone as he was returned to prison, was com*m*itted to close guard, w*hi*ch argued that the state had some pretence against him, otherwise they would not have made shew of such severitie as the times goe now.

The Jesuitesses doe [*word deleted*] swarme in London and other places of England.[427] I writt the last weeke how their mother provinciall, by

[425] John Percy SJ.

[426] See *Letters 14, 27*.

[427] For a copy of the allegations made during this month (March 1623) against Mary Ward by Mary Alcock, see AAW, A XVII, no. 17, pp. 59–62; Dirmeier, *MW*, I, pp. 762–765; Littlehales, *Mary Ward*, pp. 88, 91, 111–112. Alcock's accusations were similar to those presented at Rome by both the secular clergy and others, such as the Benedictine Robert Sherwood: Littlehales, *Mary Ward*, pp. 111–112. Alcock claimed that Mary Ward 'came licke a dutches to visite the Ignatian prisoners att Wisbitche in [a] coache attended with two pages ridinge with her in the sayde coache and two or three attendantes of her owne sexe and was so bowntifulll or rather prodigall that she gave to eache keeper (who wished more suche guests) an angell a peece'. She and her company 'lived att Hungerford Howse in the Strand verye riotouse, with excessive charge bothe for coastlye garments and daintie fare, nott omittinge to dress herselfe and the rest in the newest and most phantasticall maner then (and yeat) used by that companie, videlicet as ieolowe ruffes etc.' In this, they took after Anne Turner, who had been executed (with dramatic shows of repentance) for her part in the murder of Sir Thomas Overbury: 'they seeme to imitate Mris Turnors institution (a sainte latlie hanged att Tiburne for notoriouse crimes, and canonised by my late Lord Cooke), rather than the institution of St Ignatius latelye canonized by Pope Gregorie'. At Hungerford House they 'weare esteemed curtisans and suspected for hoores', as Ward's 'owne brother [William] (nowe called Mr Inglebie) with others will testifie'. Furthermore, 'in imitation of the boyes at St Omers they have playes called actions, manye times, through the helpe of Father [John] Willsons procurement, whearat theire creditors repine, wishing they wowld refraine suche chargable toies and paye theire depts'. Some of the Jesuits urged them on: 'the Ignatians (and namlye Father [Richard] Gibbons, Father [William] Flacke, and Father John Lhoyd [i.e. Floyd] with others before and since the death of Father [Roger] Lea) encoraged and exhorted the sayde companie by sermons and otherwise to dilate and extend themselves though they were butt twoo in a howse'. Mary Ward 'woulde <often> affirme and saye shee was sure, when her order was confirmed, whiche shee kneawe would be shortlye, that manye of her companie by reson of theire worthynes and perfection showld

name N. Bapthrope,[428] passed this way to S[t] Omers w*ith* two other of her societie w*ith* her, and a yong man her servant. They give out that their mother generall is in great grace in the court of Rome and that <her> suite goes on very well, w*ith* expectation shortely to have a good dispatch thereof. In England the puritans are at their wittes endes, having all their common wealth putt out of joynt by the prince his suddaine departure for Spaine. They talke greate wordes, and (as we heare), w*ith* bills sett uppon the Sp[anish] emb[assador][429] his gates, threaten somewhat before May. But they are [*word illegible*]. The princes servantes are gone after him to the number of 80 of his household. Other noblemen have overtaken him by this, whose names I writt you in my last. It is thought he will be backe by the end of May. The marques of Buckingham (as he writt to his wife) is to returne before him, to witt, so soone as the marriadge is past in Spaine. On Sunday next, being Palme Sunday, we hould the quarant howers <of praier> in o*ur* colledge for the good successe heereof in the behalfe of Godes Church and o*ur* countrie.

Heerew*ith* I send you some papers from M[r] Broughton. M[r] President[430] and the rest salute you. We have not heard from you now these 3 weekes, and D*octo*r Bishop [*p. 72*] (as yesterday he writt) not this moneth; w*hi*ch makes us thinke we shall see you shortly, supposing you differ y*our* writing untill you write that good newes we expect, w*hi*ch is that you have y*our* long desired dispatch of all businesses, and are setting forward towards us. I write the more sparingly for that I feare my letters will not finde you there. God send you a happie journey downe. We pray daiely for you. So kissing y*our* handes and the hands of Padre Maistro and M[r] Seton, I rest.

Y*ou*rs ever to serve you,

W*illia*m Farrar

Douay 5 April 1623.

*No address or endorsement.*

be imploy[e]d by his Holines['s] comande and placed in diverse monasteries to reforme other religiouse orders. Therfore it behoved them to take corage and shew themselves more than woemen': AAW, A XVII, no. 17, pp. 59–62; Birch, *CTJI*, I, p. 377; cf. Peters, *Mary Ward*, pp. 354–355; T.J. Dandelet, *Spanish Rome 1500–1700* (London, 2001), p. 180.

428 Barbara Babthorpe.

429 Carlos Coloma.

430 Matthew Kellison.

## 30. William Bishop to Thomas Rant,[431] 14 September 1623

[*AAW, A XVII, no. 40, pp. 141–142*]

Very reverend father,

It falles out so that I cannot, I feare mee, dispatch all my letters of recommendation for you, with all other writings necessary for yo*ur* journey this weeke, unles I, being now out of London, do happely meet with a messenger that goes ~~hence~~ <thither> two daies henc[e] wherefore I do send you inclosed, within F[ather] Bartins letter, one of mine to his Holines in congratulation,[432] and another in thankes giving to Card[inal] Bandini[433] w*hi*ch I pray you send away with the first [op]portunity to the said good father, desiring him to present them at his first leisure. Mr Colleton, with ~~the~~ many other of the better sort of o*ur* cleargy, will send you the like in their own names unto both his Holines and the same cardinall, w*hi*ch, if they come with mine, send them also, I pray you, in yo*ur*s inclosed unto Father Bartin, desiring him in o*ur* names to deliver both togither both to the one and thother. Otherwise send mine away alone I pray <you>, for that they will come rather to[o] late than otherwise. Wee all pray you very hartely to make yo*ur* self ready for the next weeke. You must p*ro*cure for your self the nuncios[434] comendations unto the popes nephew,[435] for we have not yet heard what he is called, and therefore could not write to him. Take your generals[436] comendac*i*ons

[431] For the appointment of Thomas Rant as William Bishop's agent in Rome, see AAW, A XVII, no. 35, pp. 129–130. John Bennett had returned from Rome in the summer of 1623, and accompanied Bishop to Douai in July 1623, on Bishop's journey to England. Bennett came back to England via Brussels in early August 1623 but died almost immediately after he arrived: Anstr., I, pp. 32, 37. For Rant's instructions, as Bishop's agent, see AAW, A XVII, no. 36, p. 131. On 7 November 1623, Arthur Pitts informed Rant that Bishop had dealt with the French ambassador in London, so that letters to Rant might 'passe in his packet' to the French ambassador in Rome, and that Rant should send his letters to London by the same means: AAW, A XVII, no. 50, p. 167.

[432] AAW, A XVII, no. 41, pp. 143–144 (15 September 1623). Bishop's officials had written on 10 September 1623 to congratulate the new pope, Urban VIII (Maffeo Barberini), who had been elected on 27 July/6 August 1623: AAW, A XVII, no. 37, pp. 135–136. See also *Letter 34*. For the Francophile Barberini papacy, see Dandelet, *Spanish Rome*, pp. 188–190.

[433] For William Bishop's letter of 16 September 1623 to Cardinal Bandini, see AAW, A XVII, no. 42, pp. 145–146. Bishop's vicars-general and archdeacons also wrote to Bandini, on 18 September: AAW, A XVII, no. 45, pp. 153–154.

[434] Ottavio Corsini, archbishop of Tarsus.

[435] Cardinal Francesco Barberini, nephew of Urban VIII.

[436] Pierre de Bérulle, the founder and general of the French Oratory. On 17 September 1623, William Bishop wrote to Bérulle concerning Rant's agency in Rome on behalf of the English secular clergy: AAW, A XVII, no. 43, pp. 147–148. See also John Gee, *New Shreds of*

unto the Frenc[h]e ambassador[437] at Rome and to whom els he shall thinke fittest to further yo*ur* negotiation in our behalfe.

The cardinall of Richelieu['s] comendac*io*ns also will do us much good, wherefor I send unto D[octor] Smith to write to him first. Touching yo*ur* charges I will write to Mons*ieu*r de Gamaches[438] that he deliver you one hundreth Frenc[h]e crownes out of that bagg w*hi*ch I gave him to keepe for M^r^ D[octor] Champeney. I do now send you my letter to him, and did the last weeke write to M^r^ D[octor] Champeney to write to the said doctor to the same effect. You must have a man to waite upon you. Wherefore you may <stand in> need of such mony at Paris. When you come to Rome you must take up of the college of Dowaies mony for to serve yo*ur* turne. We will see them paid againe and, albeit I did the last weeke write to D[octor] Champeney to that purpose, yet do you call upon him for a warrant to receive the same mony of their factor at Rome.

It is now a common rumour that o*ur* prince is come home unmaried and unbetrothed,[439] as o*ur* king saith, on his commandement, yet without any meaning to breake of[f] the match, w*hi*ch he desires now more than before, as he hath told the Spanish ambassadors[440] in great earnesnes [*sic*] and caused them so to write into Spaine. The fault is laid on the pope's nuncio in Spaine[441] who, having the dispensation in his handes, would not deliver it till he had received order from his Holines that now is so to do.[442] The king fears lest the Spanish ambassadors here should have certified some thing of the delaies of p*er*formaunce of such favours as he pleased to promise to the Catholikes, and that thereupon they in Spaine did make delaies of the mariage. This I pray you tell the nuncio. Notwithstanding <the rumour of> o*ur* princes returne, his Ma*jes*tie hath given order as we heare <from the Sp[anish] ambassadors house> unto the lord keeper[443] to dispatch p*re*sently the pardons for all Catholikes that please to take it, and to sett all prisoners at liberty, with the suspension of all penall lawes <for time to come and to give> ~~and~~ order to judges and

*the Old Snare* (London, 1624), pp. 51–54, for the copy of a letter, dated 14 September 1623, from John Colleton, Richard Smith, Richard Broughton, and Edward Bennett to Bérulle requesting that Rant might serve as William Bishop's agent. For the probable means of Gee's acquisition of this letter, see Harmsen, *John Gee's Foot out of the Snare*, pp. 109, 161–162; BL, Additional MS 72255, fo. 101v.

437 Noël Brûlart.

438 Philippe de Gamaches, a professor of theology at the Sorbonne. See *Letter 31*.

439 Prince Charles arrived back in England on 5 October 1623.

440 Carlos Coloma and Juan Hurtado de Mendoza, marquis of Inojosa.

441 Innocenzio de Massimi, bishop of Bertinoro.

442 See *CSPV, 1623–1625*, pp. 26, 40; Redworth, *PI*, pp. 102–104.

443 John Williams, bishop of Lincoln.

justices not to execute them.[444] In my next you shall heare whether this be so presently p*er*formed as it is comanded. Thus with my very harty comendaci*o*ns <to your self and> [*two words deleted*] unto all my good friends, I rest.

Yo*ur*s assuredly,
W*illia*m Chalcedon

The 14 of o*ur* September 1623.

[*on p. 142*]

*Addressed*: Au révérend père, le Père Thomas Rant, prestre de la congrégatione de l'Oratoire auprès l'église de S$^t$ Honoré a Paris.

[*on p. 141*]

*Endorsed*: Written: Sept[ember] 14 1623.
Received: Octob[er] 24 1623.
Answered: Nov[ember] 1.

[444]See above, p. 63; Hacket, *SR*, part I, pp. 155–159; *Cabala*, pp. 79–80; PRO, SP 14/152/46, 46.i (for Williams's dealing with the Spanish ambassadors over the pardons, and his attempt to mislead them as to the cause of the delay, i.e. to gain time until Prince Charles returned from Spain). Williams informed Conway on 10 October that, on his own initiative, he had delayed sending out orders to suspend the penal laws against Catholic separatists because of the extent of popular opposition. This was a course which, on 11 October, Conway noted that the king had approved: PRO, SP 14/153/38, 39.

Calvert had written to Conway on 18 August that 'further direction' was needed for the grant of toleration to Catholics. This was because, in the present form of the articles, there was no provision for dispensing Catholics from the oaths of supremacy and allegiance and from 'their coming to church'. On the same day, Calvert was forced to admit that the Spanish ambassadors were so annoyed at the delays to the toleration grant that Inojosa threatened to write to the court in Spain to 'unsay all he hath sayd in his last letters'. The Spaniards also insisted that Lord Zouch should be compelled to take his oath to observe the treaty conditions in order to 'prevent many complaints, which otherwise would come from the Cinque ports, of people landing there to whom the oath of allegiance is administered': PRO, SP 14/151/5, fo. 6r; PRO, SP 14/151/6, fo. 8r–v. The following day, Conway replied that, in spite of James's ire at the Spaniards' demands, clauses concerning the dispensation from the oaths and ecclesiastical conformity would be dealt with, as would Lord Zouch's taking of the oath: *CSPD, 1623–1625*, p. 60; BL, Additional MS 35832, fo. 124r; see also PRO, SP 14/151/27, 43, 60, 61, 62, 63, 79. For the dispensation for Catholics, see PRO, SP 14/151/76, 77; PRO, SP 14/152/4; *CSPD, 1623–1625*, pp. 70, 76; McClure, *LJC*, p. 513. On 7 October, Conway ordered Williams 'to prepare and put in immediate execution the order for enlarging priests', and to inform the Spanish ambassadors thereof: *CSPD, 1623–1625*, p. 89.

## 31. William Bishop to Thomas Rant, 25 September 1623

[*AAW, A XVII, no. 47, pp. 157–160; part printed in TD, IV, pp. cclxxxii–cclxxxiv*]

Very reverend father,

I have at length made ready all that I thought requisite to furnish you in that long and painful journey to Rome. First <you> shall receive a hundreth Frenc[h]e crownes of Mons*ieu*r de Gamaches, one of o*ur* doctors of [the] Sorbon (with whom I left that and more) by this letter w*hi*ch I do write unto him to that effect. If that will not serve, you may take more. Salute also I pray you in my name Mons*ieu*r du Val[445] [and] Mons*ieu*r Filsac[446] my great friend. You may tell them that I have been very joyfully received of all o*ur* cleargy and laity aswell nobles as of the meaner sort; [and] that I have been very busy to reduce the Catholike cleargy <and laity> unto the ordinary goverment of the canons, as neare as I can, without offense of the state. Desire Monsieur Filsac['s] letters of commendation unto the cardinall of S*ant*a Susanna who doth very much esteeme them. Concerning yo*u*r negotiation, the point w*hi*ch may be questioned is my creation of deane and chapter.[447] As for vicar generals and archdeacons, every one teacheth that it lieth in the bishops power to make them; for that he cannot, without their helpe, governe one diocese, much lesse a whole kingdome. Yet these archdeaconries be so cast that the ministers cannot be justly offended with them. For they be not distributed by bishoprics, as theirs are, but by shires; and ours have authority over Catholikes onely, who will not be governed by their archdeacons, and not over any P*ro*testants who be of their flocke. Wherefore the state it self cannot blame us who seeke to order them onely who will not be ordered by their new ~~canons~~ <injunctions> and disorderly ministers. Yea, they must confess that we do them a pleasure, to bring them to live orderly, whom they cannot rule.

Now, concerning deane and chapter, they are in all Catholike country[es] holden for the principall men of the cleargy,

[445] André du Val, a professor of theology at the Sorbonne.

[446] For Jean Filesac (Edmond Richer's successor as syndic of the Sorbonne), see Allison, RSGB, I, pp. 333–334; *NCC*, pp. 174, 241.

[447] For William Bishop's appointment of episcopal officials and his creation of a chapter, see Allison, RS, pp. 149–150.

ordained as to serve God howerly, so to assist the byshope with their counsell and to be an example unto the rest of the cleargy. Wherefore to want them is to want ~~the~~ a principall p*ar*t of the cleargy. Whereupon it followeth that his Holines, giving me the ordinary power and authority of a bishope, doth consequently give me power to institute <a> deane and chapter, as a society of grave learned men, without whom neither the bishope himself, nor the rest of the cleargy, can well consist. Neither is it materiall that I have no cathedrall church to give them residents [*sic*] in, nor revenues to maintaine them; of both w*hi*ch, God be thanked, they can provide for themselves. For it is not the place or maintenance that makes the men fitt for that calling, but the qualit[i]es and giftes w*hi*ch be in the men, w*hi*ch will in time, as we hope, draw the rest after them. The <ancient> byshops in the primitive Church, during the time of p*er*secution, had, no doubt, such worthy men about them as might well have been named a deane and chapter, but it sufficed them to have the matter it self, though not under those tearmes, w*hi*ch were very conveniently brought in afterward. So we do request that we may name the like qualified men by the name of deane and chapter, w*hi*ch are now usuall names all Catholike countries over, yea, and in ours also. Besides, a cathedrall church is so called because the bishop doth make his ordinary residence there, and setteth, as it were, his chaire in that place; for cathedrale doth come of cathedra, the bishops chaire. And what cathedrall church is there without deane and chapter? Finally, the deane and chapter have many priviledges by the canons of the church and, among the rest, one that we do chiefly ayme at w*hi*ch is that episcopall jurisdiction doth remaine among them untill a new bishop be chosen and consecrated. We have but one byshop. If God should call him, then were all piscopall jurisdiction lost in our country unles there be deane and chapter to conserve it. Wherefore, labour, I pray you, very carefully, to obtain of his Holines that he wilbe pleased to confirme and establish our deane and chapter, with power in the chapter, if our bishope should be dead (otherwaies to remaine in the bishop), [*two words deleted*] to cho[o]se a new deane if he that is now chosen by me should hap to dye. [*p. 158*] For this get the popes breve <holding it to be one of the chiefest matters that you <have> now to do>. To give you a brief for yo*ur* own instruction of the manner of <our> new established goverment, thus it is: over all England I have appointed five vicars generals [*sic*], one over the East, Mr Colleton; the second over the South, Mr D[octor] Smith; the third over Wales and the West, Mr Edward

Benet;[448] the fourth over the North w*hi*ch is M$^{r}$ Broughton. <To> the fift I leave the middest of the country, who may be either M[aster] D[octo]r Boswell or M$^{r}$ Arthur Pits, if he come as he promised. There be 20 archdeacons who have, ech one, two shires apeece, saving M$^{r}$ Nelson,[449] who hath the charge of six, and so have <the> two archdeacons of Wales, ech of them, six. Under ~~the~~ every archdeacon are two ~~deacon~~ deanes of the country, decani rurales, in ech shire [who] are to hearken after all the disorders of Catholikes in those shires, and to advertise the archdeacon thereof, that they may be amended. Besides, there shalbe in every shire a notary, to record what the archdeacon there concludeth, and to gather together such thinges as have happened, or shall happen, in the same, concerning <the> Catholike cause.

The deane and chapter are to assist the bishop with their counsell, and to p*re*serve episcopall authority if the bishop should happ to dy.

I desire you to obtaine of his Holines that such of our countrymen as have livinges abroad in other countries may be dispensed withall for their residence there for three years; so that they leave in their places sufficient men to discharge that duty w*hi*ch they were to p*er*forme; ~~and allow~~ <allowing> unto them a sufficient p*or*sion to maintaine them honestly. And, by name, I would request that favour for M$^{r}$ Arthur Pittes, chanon of Remeremont in Lorrayne, who is able to do o*ur* country much good, and [is] willing to labour here, so he may draw some reliefe from his chanonry and not be put out of it for his absence.

I do also send you hereinclosed a copy of faculties granted to the Jesuites at their going into Ireland at the request of Cardinall Arigonio,[450] desiring you to get Cardinal Bandino, or some other of o*ur* friends, to procure me the same, with that last line <set downe in it>, and this only addition that, <what> facultie soever any religious man in o*ur* country hath, I may enjoy and practise the same. This is all that now comes to my mind, w*hi*ch I recom*m*end unto yo*ur* care and diligence. I will not, at the first, find fault with any of the religious mens extraordinary facultates, and how they do communicate the same to ev*ery* meane member of their body. This I leave for hereafter. Thus

[448] William Harewell, in July 1624, described Edward Bennett as 'most about my lord [William Bishop] the time he was heere, and [the] cheefest of his counsell': AAW, B 26, no. 82.

[449] John Jackson.

[450] Cardinal Pompeo Arrigoni. See *NAGB*, pp. 119, 148, 157, 160, 214.

with my very harty com*m*endaci*o*ns, praying o*u*r blessed Saviour to send you a happy journey, I rest.

Yo*ur* affectionate friend,

W*illia*m Byshop of Chalcedon

You must go up to Italy by Lyons lest you be suspected to come from Paris and so put [?] to make you[r] quaranteene.[451] But go first to Lorraine and stay there some few daies that you may take a testimoniall of the city that you go from thence, and so to Basill and Lucerne, where you may have yo*ur* passe signed to testify that you passed along that way.

I do send you <a> copy of all my letters constitutive, of vicars generals [*sic*], of archdeacons, of deane and chapter,[452] that you p*er*use them, and be more ready to defend them if any do impugne them, and a copy also of the instructions w*hi*ch I gave to the archdeacons.[453] All the letters in your comendations are so sealed that you may open them.

M^r^ Doctor Seton followeth the Cardinal de S*anta* Susanna at whose pallace you shall heare of him.[454] He did very greatly help M^r^ Bennet, for he is very expert in all the affaires of that court and mervellous well affected to o*ur* cleargy, wherefore make high account of his friendship.

[*p. 159*] This I give you as a secret instruction, when you have a convenient audience after your first, to let his Holines understand that o*ur* cleargy had no knowledge of Card[inal] Millino['s] election to be o*ur* protector and have since, both in o*ur* sute for byshops and about the college of Lisbo[n], found him to deale against us and so in others [*sic*] matters.[455] Wherefore o*ur* most humble sute unto his Holines is that he wilbe pleased to appoint some other cardinall for

[451] For Thomas Rant's journey to Rome, see *Letter 34*.

[452] AAW, A XVII, no. 30, pp. 117–118, no. 31, pp. 119–120, no. 32, pp. 121–124.

[453] AAW, A XVII, no. 67, pp. 211–212 (1623), 'Instructiones pro archdiaconis maxime cum visitant suas provincias', defining the archdeacon's functions when on visitation. Significantly, the thirteenth article to be observed and implemented reads as follows: 'tam sacerdotes quam laicos exitent ad Deum sancte colendum, et ad debitam regi obedientiam praestandam, pro cujus salute et tranquillo ac prospero regno divinam majestatem quotidie orent, nec non pro Carolo principe et infanta Maria'.

[454] See *Letter 34*.

[455] For the secular clergy leadership's long-standing antagonism towards Giovanni Garzia Millini, cardinal viceprotector of the English nation, see *NAGB*, pp. 13, 158. William Bishop, in a letter to Rant of early January 1624, repeated these accusations and stated that Millini had appointed, at the Jesuits' direction, a visitor of the English College in Rome in September 1623 'who, to gratify the cardinall and the fathers, made no bones to dismisse the scholers', i.e. the anti-Jesuit students ejected from the college (for whom see *Letters 33, 34*): AAW, A XVII, no. 78, p. 249; TD, V, p. cclxxi.

us that will indeed favour and protect us.[456] The like we may truly say of *our* colleges, whom the fathers will thrust out, [if] they can p*re*sently get his furtherance. We had therefore as much need to p*ro*cure those poore scholers a true p*ro*tector. If his Holines demand whom we desire, Card[inal] Bandini is the man to whom we be most bound, and in whom we have the greatest confidence, or whosoever els that is not to[o] much caried by the Jesuites.

[*on p. 160*]

*Addressed*: A monsieur, Monsieur Thomas Rant à Paris.

*Endorsed*: [*on p. 157*] Written: Septemb[er] 25 1623.
Received: Octob[er] 24 1623.
Answ[ered]: Nov[ember] 1.
[*on p. 158*] Theis letters bee w*i*thout date. But they came to my hands October 24 or therabouts, anno 1623. They were written Sept[ember] 25. For M^r Collintons letters and th*em* [?] came togeather. And th*ey* were of that date.

## 32. William Parker [Bishop] to Thomas Rant, 25 November 1623

[*AAW, A XVII, no. 53, pp. 173–176*]

Very reverend and deare s*ir*,

These I send to congratulate yo*ur* arrivall at the holy city where I hope you are by this time, or wilbe very shortly. I have been in some shires over to visit and to give the sacr[ament] of confirmation,[457] where I was very welcome even to the hostes where the fathers of the companie[458]

[456] In March 1624, Bishop again insisted that Millini must be removed, and thought 'it most convenient to request to have Cardinall [Francesco] Barbarino the popes nephew, who is already protector of Scotland', since 'England and Scotland' were 'now made all one kingdome', and William Bishop was himself bishop 'aswell of Scotland as of England': AAW, A XVII, no. 101, p. 327. On 12 March 1624, Bishop's officials set their hands to a formal petition for Millini's replacement by Barberini: AAW, A XVII, no. 105, pp. 341–342; see also AAW, A XVII, no. 110, pp. 355–356, no. 114, pp. 363–364.

[457] For William Bishop's account, of 5 December 1623, of his tours during which he dispensed the sacrament of confirmation, see AAW, A XVII, no. 55, p. 181. On 25 December 1623, Joseph Haynes reported to Rant that Bishop was received 'by al sortes of well meaninge good Catholiques', including the 2nd Viscount Montague. Haynes enclosed a copy of Montague's letter of 1 August 1623 to Bishop 'at his first comminge': AAW, A XVII, no. 29, pp. 115–116. Haynes noted that Montague 'sent for him afterwards to his house where 500 were confirmed with wonderfull joyfull harts to have a Chatholique byshop amongest them': AAW, A XVII, no. 59, p. 191; see also Questier, *C&C*, p. 402.

[458] i.e. Jesuits.

reside. In a word, <from> the greatest of the Catholike nobles unto the meanest of the laity, there was common and great joy for that dignity bestowed on us by his Holines. And whereas some did mutter out [?] that it would be cause of contention <among Catholikes> and much trouble from the state, it prooves, God be thanked, much contrary. For it pleaseth his Ma*jes*tie to winke at it, and all orders of relig[ion] have sent me congratulation by their superiours, either coming to me in presence, as the p*ro*vincials of the Benedictins and of the Society did, and some others by letters very submissively written.[459] So that, o*ur* Saviour be praised, all goes very fairely on. And ~~all the~~ <four> Spa[nish] <extraordinarie> ambassadors[460] and the ordinary of France[461] do applaude o*ur* peacible and orderly p*ro*ceeding, and do much like that I have given no occasion of speech of me in the court. To speake the truth, I do much feare that I shall not be able to give satisfaction to all the shires in England nor be able to visit them in three or four yeares, wherefore I do hartely desire that one more b*ishop* at the least might be chosen for the north country. And the fittest man in my slender judgment wilbe M^r^ D[octor] Champeny, who is a most honest vertuous man, of great zeale, learning and discretion, and not to[o] old, as I take some to bee who were otherwise to be p*re*ferred. He is also that country man.[462] Upon him also I desire that the charge of Scotland may be laid, unles his Holines thinke fitter as I and many other do, to give to the Scottes a bishop of their owne nation.[463] For they will not willingly be under any other. And none of ours doth desire to

[459] On 5/15 June 1623, Rudesind Barlow OSB had written to William Bishop from St Gregory's, Douai, promising obedience to him: AAW, A XVII, no. 21, pp. 81–82; TD, V, pp. cclxxv–cclxxvi.

[460] Juan Hurtado de Mendoza, marquis of Inojosa had arrived in England in June 1623: *CSPV, 1623–1625*, p. 51. For the other Spanish ambassadors at this time (Diego de Mendoza (who landed in October 1623) and Diego de Messia (who arrived, as ambassador from the archduchess Isabella in Flanders, in November 1623)), see PRO, SP 14/153/41, 47; *CCE*, p. 110; *CSPV, 1623–1625*, p. 150; *APC, 1623–1625*, p. 116; McClure, *LJC*, pp. 516, 522; PRO, SP 77/16, fo. 333r. The fourth ambassador (though not 'extraordinary') was, of course, Carlos Coloma: PRO, SP 14/154/27.

[461] Tanneguy Leveneur, count of Tillières.

[462] Anthony Champney came from the North Riding of Yorkshire.

[463] See Allison, RS, pp. 152, 189. Both William Bishop and his successor, Richard Smith, received jurisdictional authority over Scotland as well as England. Despite Bishop's reluctance to accept this responsibility, and despite Scottish Catholics' requests for Scottish prelates, 'no action was taken by Rome until 1653 when a local prefect was appointed for the Scottish mission': Allison, QJ, p. 140. See also AAW, A XVIII, no. 29, pp. 247–248; TD, V, pp. cclxiii–cclxv (a memorandum from David Chambers in 1624 requesting that the bishop of Chalcedon should be relieved of his jurisdiction over Scotland), pp. cclxii–cclxiii (a memorandum by Thomas Rant of 20/30 May 1624, similarly urging that Bishop should not have responsibility for the Scottish Catholics); but cf. AAW, B 26, no. 75 (Matthew Kellison to Thomas Rant, 15/25 June 1624, saying that he was 'not sorie that Scotland is excepted from our b[ishop's] jurisdiction'). Subsequently, in 1626, it was thought that a Scot, John

be troubled with that charge, w*hi*ch will not be well taken of the nation. This point I do not desire that you do yet urge, but to insinuate onely, till I send you full comission from the best of o*u*r cleargy to deale in it wherefore, though you plainly declare that <I> do humbly desire <it> for the good of o*u*r country, yet because more voices may be required to it, do not expresse M. Doctor Champeney by name, that there be no collections made against him. If his Holines please to rely on my credit and yo*u*rs with F[ather] Bartins,[464] Card[inal] Ubaldinall [*sic*], Card[inal] Bentivolio and such others as may be there gotten, then it would bee a fitt season to send him as soone as the infanta shalbe come in, for this sending in one a good while after another is most likely to passe w*i*thout offending o*u*r state. Mr Thomas Sac[kville][465] talkes somwhat idly, as I take it, of having six b*ishop*s and a card[inal]. I would we might [*word omitted:* have] three. Among other yo*u*r charges you must have a speciall care that o*u*r cleargy [*words omitted:* do not] have bishops thrust upon [them] by any trickes of the religious, but that, when it shall please his Hol*in*es to grant us one or two more, that [*sic*] then he will vouchsafe to heare the desires and suffrages of o*u*r cleargy, that no unwelcome <man> be sett over them.

For newes, there came with o*u*r prince out of Spaine an extraordinary ambass[ador], Don Diego de Mendosa,[466] who have [*sic*] been very r[o]ially intertained and is returned.[467] Another [came] from the infanta in Flanders, wonderfully well accompanied, who was also very honorably received.[468] They two and Don Carolo[469] were of late blanquetted [*sic*] by the duke of Buckingham where, the king and prince being p*re*sent, the prince with the kings leave did drinke a health to the infanta of Spaine his mistris, and the king, as they say,

Trumbull, had been appointed to exercise episcopal jurisdiction in Scotland: Questier, *C&C*, p. 429. For Trumbull's arrest and interrogation in August 1626, see AAW, A XX, no. 22, p. 83. Trumbull had a licence from the papal nuncio in Paris 'to administer the sacraments of baptism, penance, the eucharist, extreme unction, and matrimony, throughout Ireland and Scotland' and, with the licence of the bishop of Chalcedon, in England as well: *CSPD, 1625–1626*, pp. 320–321. See also PRO, SP 16/21/71; PRO, SP 16/32/116; PRO, SP 16/36/44; PRO, SP 16/38/15; PRO, SP 16/44/84; PRO, SP 16/525/85. By October 1626, however, Archbishop Abbot was convinced that Trumbull was an impostor. The archbishop claimed to know, 'by certaine intelligence, that their purpose at Rome lately was to make one Muskett [i.e. George Fisher] to bee a bishop in Scotland': AAW A XX, no. 28, p. 101; see also PRO, SP 16/80/10; PRO, SP 16/529/93.

[464] Claude Bertin, superior of the French Oratory in Rome.

[465] The fourth son of Thomas Sackville, 1st earl of Dorset.

[466] See *CSPV, 1623–1625*, p. 150.

[467] Mendoza had departed on 21 November 1623: PRO, SP 14/154/67.

[468] Diego de Messia. The 'ordinary agent of Brussels', Jean-Baptiste van Male, came back to England at the same time: *CSPV, 1623–1625*, p. 150.

[469] Carlos Coloma.

wished all them hanged, and the devill to take them, that were against the match.[470] [*p. 174*] So that the common opinion now is that it is throughly agreed upon and will assuredly hold. Our prince obtained that recusantes should not pay in their halfe yeares rent at this season. And all priests were sett out of prison at his returne home.[471] The lord of Canterb[urie][472] would faine be medling with mee, as some report, and to give an occasion to the Spaniards to breake the match, but it seemes that his Ma*jes*tie will not p*er*mitt it.

Let me heare, I pray you, where you remaine there and what you are like to spend, that I may take order with them at Doway for the discharge of it. I do adventure this letter by the Frenc[h]e ambassad[or] but will shortlie find out the best course, I hope, of sending. [In the] meane season, o*ur* blessed Saviour protect and direct you in all the affaires of this poore Church of England. All yo*ur* friends do salute you and desire to be remembered by you in those holy places.

Yo*ur*s alwaies assured,

W*illia*m Parker al*ias* Chalcedon (so do you write to mee)

The 25 of November stilo veteri.

[*on p. 176*]

*Addressed*: Au très révérend père, le Père Bartin, prestre de l'Oratoire et supérieur de St Louis, pour le Père Th[omas] Rant. A Rome.

*Endorsed*: [*on p. 173*] Written: 25 Novemb[er] 1623.
Received: Jan[uary] 16 1624.
Answ[e]r[ed]: [*sic*].
[*on p. 174*] Received by the hands of Père Bertin, but by the pacquett of France, th*e* 16 Januarii <1624> stilo novo.

This was the first letter I received from my lord since I came to Italye but not the first w*hi*ch hee writt unto mee. For yt appeeres by a letter w*hi*ch Mr Arthur Pitts sente unto mee, dated the 7 of November, that my l*or*d had sente mee a letter dated the 31 of October, and that I never received.

[470]This news was translated into Latin by Thomas Rant to be exhibited to the curia in Rome: AAW, A XVII, no. 55, p. 181.

[471]See PRO, SP 14/153/38.

[472]Archbishop George Abbot.

## 33. Anthony Champney to Thomas Rant, 3/13 and 5/15 December 1623

[*AAW, A XVII, no. 57, pp. 185–188*]

R*everen*d good father,

I have <not> writen unto you since those[473] I wrote after your departure from Paris. These I suppose will find you at yo*ur* journeys end. If our frends in Ingland have beene as slowe in writing to you as to us here, you have heard nothing from them since your departure from Parise. If you have not heard it alreadie, you may understand that upon the 5 of 9$^{ber}$, being Su*n*day, a certayn father of the co*m*panie <called Drewerie>[474] preaching at the French embassatours in London and a great co*m*panie being invited thither, mo[r]e by manie than could enter into the roome ~~about~~, about the middest of the sermon the flore of the chamber, being overcharged, brake and caried w*i*th it the flore of the chamber under it, so that the preacher him self, together w*i*th two other Jesuites and above 90 more, were crushed to death, besides divers that were hurt and brused, of w*hi*ch accident we, haveing notice, sung Mass for the dead and all our prestes sayd Mass for them.[475] Besides one Ladie Webbe,[476] daughter to S*i*r Thomas Treshame, w*i*th one sonn and a daughter, we heare not of anie of note <that were kild>. Of this accident M$^{r}$ Ireland[477] (who is ill w*i*th a quartayn ague) writeth that they (<the fathers>) are blamed for two causes: thon for that they were warned before of the weakness of the howse, in so much that the landlord had charged them not to lay so much as anie nu*m*ber of faggotts;[478] thother because they made so great an assembly at this tyme, whereat the king was offended not a litle, blaming the over bowldness of Catholikes in this begining of his con*n*ivence towards them. Another grave preist writeth that it is

[473] AAW, A XVII, no. 48, pp. 161–162 (3/13 October), no. 51, pp. 169–170 (31 October/10 November).

[474] Robert Drury SJ.

[475] For the 'fatal vespers' in the gatehouse of the French embassy in Blackfriars on 26 October 1623, see above, pp. 64–65. Those Catholics who were opposed to the Society of Jesus did not go so far as to agree with Protestant commentators that the structural failure of the building was an act of providence. But several, like Champney, were clearly unsympathetic. In early January 1624, William Harewell remarked that he hoped the short Latin account (recently sent to Rome) of William Bishop's episcopate in England would, with other documents, 'being well pressed [. . .] lie heavie uppon our adversaries, and crack the master-beame of their creditt': AAW, B 47, no. 89.

[476] Catherine Webb, second wife of Sir John Webb of Odstock and Canford.

[477] Richard Ireland.

[478] According to William Sterrell, the warning was delivered to John Percy SJ: CRS, 68, p. 162.

observed that this father was sent for expressly into Ingland to drawe the world unto them by his preaching, whereunto he is sayd to have hadd a good facultie. And this was his verie first sermon after his arrivall; $2^{ly}$ that this happened upon the 5 of $9^{ber}$ according to the French accompt, w*i*thin whose liberties it happened, w*hi*ch was the day of the powder plott, but after another accompt[479] [*sic*]. 3. That there being a preist, a monk and a frier p*re*sent, none of them were hurt but only the Jesuites kild. 4. There was a great ladie, to wit the Ladie Walingford,[480] who was desireous that a monk showld have preached there that day, but shee was p*er*suaded that he would be out of the towne; nevertheless [she was] towld that, if shee desired to heare it, there would be a good sermon. She ~~cann*o*t~~ <came not> but the monk [*in margin:* M$^{r}$ Hilton[481] ] whome she was made belive would be out of towne came and escaped. Thes[e] be <the> comentaries and glosses made of that dolefull accident, w*hi*ch I write not that I ame of the same opinion but that you may knowe what the world sayth, and use the knowledge thereof as you shall have occasion. M$^{r}$ President[482] is upon urgent occasions of the howse[483] gone into Ingland, not to returne before the spring or somer. These inclosed letters are from two of our p*ro*fessours to the minister of the colledge there, to whom I pray you deliver them and demand answer of them and urg[e] the matter so farr as you [*p. 186*] shall think co*n*venient <and desire to speak your self with Peter Fitton[484] about this matter>. They p*re*tend to have good right <to> the things they demand and do not tak[e] it well they should be put of[f] w*i*th tergiversations. Here is a certayn bruite for the p*re*sent that the match w*i*th Spayn is broken, w*hi*ch we canot belive, for we had letters of the 23 of $9^{ber}$ that the prince hadd sett embrotterers one [*sic for* on] worke to make apparell for the infanta, and that the money w*hi*ch Catholikes were accustomed to pay into the excheker was refused and differed till our ladie day, the infanta being thought will [*sic*] come shortly after. I pray you deliver this inclosed to our agent[485] and com*m*end me most kindly to Father Bertin and, w*i*th my love to yo*u*r self, desiring some ~~memorie~~ remembrance <in your

[479] i.e. 5 November, according to New Style dating.

[480] Elizabeth Knollys (daughter of Thomas Howard, 1st earl of Suffolk), wife of William Knollys, 1st Viscount Wallingford, who was created 1st earl of Banbury in August 1626. He died in May 1632, allowing her to marry Edward Vaux, 4th Baron Vaux: *NCC*, pp. 80–81. In 1628, she was listed as a patron of William Harewell, who was, by then, serving as secretary to Bishop Richard Smith: PRO, SP 16/529/94, fo. 146v.

[481] Thomas (Placid) Hilton OSB.

[482] Matthew Kellison.

[483] The English College at Douai.

[484] Peter Biddulph.

[485] Giovanni Battista Scanarolio.

prayers> when you visit the holy places, I comitt you to Gods holy grace, this 13 of ~~9ber~~ 10ber 1623.

Yo*u*rs ever,

Champney

After I had writen these, I received from Mr Ceton[486] letters signifying a great deale of trouble amongst the scholers in that colledge and the dismission of divers,[487] whereof it seemeth foure or five are yet in Rome, expecting some better issue of theyre business, whoe, because they are gentleme*n* and farr from their freinds, and may be in great want of money or meanes as they have modestly signifyed to my lord[488] and as I suppose to their owne freinds, also I hope I may p*re*sume so much of their freinds will and disposition herein as to wish you to take of S*ign*ore Scanaroglio, our agent there, as for your owne use, so much as may keepe them out of extremitie till we may heare from my lord or theyre owne friends, or that some other order be taken for them there. I knowe not what com*m*ission my lord hath given you co*n*cerning the colledge but, such as you have, use it to the co*m*forth of th*e* dismissed w*i*th the advise of Mr Ceton and other freinds. You must not be afrayd to shew your self agent or p*ro*curator for the clergie where the interest thereof is in question. For so shall you p*re*judice the same and give your adversaries courage to oppose them selves more bitterly agaynst you. Mr Bennett[489] did ever fynd Mr Ceton a true freind and so he sheweth him self still to be your man. Therefore be bowld w*i*th him in that w*hi*ch may appertayn to our clergies affayres. I have here writen to him w*hi*ch you will please to deliver him and so once more I com*m*end you to Gods holy grace. [*Four words deleted in margin.*] You <may> signify to Mr Fitton and his felowes that their letters to my lord, to Mr President and their owne freinds are in my hands and shall, God willing, be w*i*th <the> first comoditie sent [*p. 187*] unto them. [*In margin:* They are alreadie sent.]

Comend me to them and advise them to carie them selves modestly and so as they may be thought to desire nothing but that w*hi*ch is

[486] William Seton.

[487] For the students of the English College in Rome who had been expelled for sedition in the 'Fitton rebellion', see above, pp. 55–57. Peter Biddulph, Thomas Harper, John Faulkner, Anthony Shelley, and Francis Haynes were ejected from the college on 15/25 October 1623. Richard Perkins and Thomas Longueville were thrown out in November: CRS, 37, pp. 185–186, 190–192, 194. For the (undated) letter of appeal, signed by the first five, to William Bishop, see AAW, A XVII, no. 60, pp. 195–198; and for Bishop's answer (of 29 December 1623), see AAW, A XVII, no. 61, pp. 199–200; TD, V, pp. cclxx–cclxxi. See also AAW, A XVII, no. 24, pp. 87–90; TD, V, pp. cclxv–cclxviii.

[488] William Bishop.

[489] John Bennett.

laudable for them to desire. They are not the first that have suffered wrong by such as should have beene their best freinds, and that even in that place. I my self ame wittness of a great deale of such like dealing w*it*h others there, and ame hartely sorie that they are not yet wearie of such woful p*ro*ceeding agaynst their owne children and bretheren. It may be Gods will to pe*r*mitt these things to reduce that howse to their government to whom it belongeth. It is writen to us from Paris that they heare out of Ingland that the mariage is co*n*tracted in Spayn de p*rae*senti by such order as our prince left there for that purpose. And this is co*n*firmed by letters out of Spayn to our Benedictaynes here. This I pray impart w*it*h M$^{r}$ Ceton who in his letter to M$^{r}$ President seemed to be somewhat doubtfull of the issue of that matter be [*sic*] reason of the princes sodayn departure out of Spayn. This 15 of 10$^{ber}$ 1623.

Yo*u*rs as before,

Champney

[*on p. 188*]

*Addressed*: To the r*everen*d Father Thomas Rant.

*Endorsed*: [*on p. 185*] Written: Decemb[er] 15.
Received: January 23.
Answered: [*sic*].
[*on p. 187*] Received this the 23 of Januarye 1624 by Père Bertin or by Scannarolio, I knowe not well w*hi*ch.
[*on p. 188*] Seal the letter that is open. This other that is sealed for the same partie is of like business.

## 34. Thomas Rant to William Bishop, 13/23 December 1623

[*AAW, B 25, no. 103*]

Right hon*ora*ble,

Wearyed with the leangth and fowlnes of the way, uppon St Lucyes daye,[490] I came to Rome, safe and in good healthe, blessed be God. In the whole cours of my journye I rested but one daye, and that was at Thurin, wher the coache for Millan parted not till the second day after my arrivall at Novalese. The passage was open a weeke before I

[490] 13 December.

came, so no quarantene was requisite. When I writt from Paris how I accounted to bee heere by the 21 of November, I was then in the mynde to have gone a good parte of the way by post but, consultinge better with my purse, I founde it necessarye to change advice and to goe common journyes, which are verrye litle ones, in the depth of durte, height of rivers and shortnes of the dayes. And th*e* expence for horshier, coach-hyer, halfe as much more as in sommer tyme, in regarde they imploye halfe as much more tyme and charges than in sommer; for example, from Florence to Rome is but 4 dayes journye in sommer tyme, now they aske six dayes; and that chargeth the passinger with expence for his dyett and lodginge for that surplusage. And this proportion fell out in divers other places.

The first mann I wente to see, after Father Bertin (who exceedinglye healpeth mee) was M$^{r}$ Doctor Seaton, who I fownde so ill that hee kept his bedd but now, thanke God, is upp and able to goe abroade. This indisposition hee is thought to have fallen into by overtravellinge for thos[e] schollars w*hi*ch the Inglishe Colledge put a trick uppon to expell them as seditious.[491] But wee hope [for] their restauration, and wee are now in deliberation w*ha*t cource to take to that purpose. My onlye comminge to towne this wynter gave new life to th*e*m, for they were borne in hande [that] no bodye would bee heere for the clargye till after Esther. All our freinds, w*hi*ch, thanke God, are not fewe nor of th*e* leaste power, sayde <to mee> opportune ad modum venisti.

The next I went to was Card[inal] Bandino who received mee noblye and affectionatlye w*i*th embrasments, and asked particularlye of th*e* comminge into England, freinds, ennemyes, place of aboad, episcopall function and [epis]copall habbit, and was joyed that one was sente hither to looke to th*e* clargy[es] affaires.

Cardinal St Susanna was much plesed w*i*th the letters hee received, assuringe his best healpe in any of o*ur* busines in this courte.[492] Hee reflected uppon my beeinge one of th*e* Oratorye; and asked mee whether I lodged ther. I answered no, for I was an Inglishman, and the number of o*ur* fathers is limmited to six, w*hi*ch they are alreadye. Yow say true, q*uo*th hee; I remember such an agreem*en*t. I am glad y*o*w are of that companye. When I told this to Father Bertin, hee

[491] John Bennett had secured a papal visitation of the college, but the death of Gregory XV in July 1623 intervened and the commission for visiting the seminary was terminated. With the accession of Maffeo Barberini (Urban VIII), a new commission was drawn up, and the new visitor was more favourable to the Jesuit administrators of the seminary. This resulted in the expulsion of the rebel students: TD, V, pp. 100–104; M.E. Williams, *The Venerable English College, Rome* (London, 1979), pp. 29–30.

[492] Rant had visited Cardinal Scipione Cobelluzio on 8/18 December 1623, and the cardinal asked whether 'the Jesuitts and regulars agree well with the bishop': AAW, B 25, no. 102. For Bishop's letter of 13 September 1623 to the cardinal, see AAW, A XVII, no. 39, pp. 139–140.

was much satisfied, alledginge how contrarye an effect my agency will woorke in Rome to that they immagined in France it would. For it cleeres a pointe wherin divers heere did secretlye dowbt that wee are not religious, since one of o*ur* order deales for the secular clargye.

Card[inal] Barbarino, his Holynes['s] nephew, received mee w*i*th much curtesye, and bad[e] mee repaire to him in my occations, and I should well see hee was not onlye a wellwiller but tender of o*ur* cause and exceedinge desirous to healpe it to a good issue.[493] Then I beseecht his l*ordshi*p to gett mee audience of his Holynes. Forthwith hee called to Sig*no*r Georgio Clony,[494] a Scotch gentlemann that follow[s] him, and is in greate favore, to accompanye mee to his Holynes lodgings to see if the tyme weare fitt to kiss his feete. But greater personns and officers, waightinge for audience, made mee come a second tyme. Uppon St Thomas th*e* Apostells day,[495] about two a clock after noon, I was admitted to heeringe, and fownde so favorable and gratious usage that, whil[e] I live, I must remember yt w*i*th all thankfull acknowledgm*ent*. Hee spake w*i*th mee, aboave a full halfe hower, of divers subjects; but principallye of his desire to see that country, w*hi*ch have [*sic*] brought forth so manye glorious martirs, to retorne to the faithe of their forefathers. His verry woords weare: pro salute spirituali gentis vestrae, non pigebit sanguinem propriu*m* effu*n*dere, immo cum apostolo, cupio anathema esse. Next, hee wittnessed a soverain esteeme of o*ur* soveraign, sayinge: cum cardinalitia dignitate constitutus <essem>, et in congregatione de Propaganda Fide, sententiam meam dicturus eram, ubi agebatur de futuris nuptiis, inter filiu*m* regis vestri et sorore*m* regis Catholici, quantum possibilie fuit, steti a parte nuptiaru*m*, nec jam per me stabit, quod optatum finem <non> assequantur; quod potero pro rege Angliae faciam. I proteste before God, I make the matter no better, nor no worse, than his Holynes made yt. In substance thus yt was, though perhaps the woords may have some like difference.[496]

[493] Thomas Rant recorded that Cardinal Barberini had asked him, on 10/20 December 1623, whether the duke of Buckingham and the earls of Rutland and Arundel were Catholics: AAW, B 25, no. 102.

[494] George Con. See Albion, *CI*, *passim*. For correspondence between Rant and Con in the summer of 1625, and Con's promise of assistance for the Collège d'Arras, see AAW, B 47, no. 123.

[495] 11/21 December.

[496] Elsewhere Thomas Rant recorded that on 'St Thomas['s] daye after dinner I had audience of his Holines', to whom he presented letters from William Bishop. The pope asked him what liberties Catholics enjoyed in England, and Rant replied that they could hear Mass in private houses. If the Spanish match were to proceed, however, Mass would be heard in public. The pope asked about Bishop's arrival in England, and whether the king knew of it. Rant said that without doubt he did, since he knew of his consecration (the place, persons, and time) and the joy which Catholics had shown in seeing a bishop whom they

Touchinge y*our* l*ordsh*ips letters, hee sayd, gratissimae sunt nobis episcopi Chalcedonensis litterae, et ipsi respondebo per litteras; w*hi*ch is no smale favore. In the farewell hee bad[e] mee, in all my occations [to] come to him freelye. I should finde him such as I desired for our business. Monsig*no*r Vives is still him selfe, that is, a noble sinceare prelate, affectionate as much as is possible to o*u*r clargie. Wee owe him honore and prayers for the good offices paste and presente. Hee lamented the deathe of Mr Bennet, and so doe 3 or 4 of the cheefe cardinalls, sayinge hee was a worthy personage.

Sig*no*r Ingoli[497] shewd mee y*our* l*ordsh*ips letters, w*hi*ch hee sayes are to bee redd publiq*ue*ly in th*e* congregation de Propaganda Fide. Hee is vostrissimo, and of a sweete disposition, courtious, openn, affectionate.[498]

No letters are yet come to my handes, ether from y*our* l*ordsh*ip or from any other, since I left Paris, yet yow promised I should finde some ready heere to wellcome mee. I have neede of weeklye letters to give accounte of such particularityes as they will aske mee of, concerninge th*e* kinges favoringe or disfavoringe Catholiq*ue*s, concerning the graces or disgraces done to y*our* l*ordsh*ips persone [and] concerninge y*our* actions, imployments, functions, healthe, stay or residence, unitye or dissension with others and particularlye of th*e* Jesuitts. In a woorde, all varietye of information, and thos[e] as particular as cann bee and as frequente as cann bee, not omittinge thos[e] w*hi*ch are com*m*on ther, for they bee not common heere.

Yf supplye of monyes come not quicklye, I shall sone bee at a non plus. Of the 100 crownes I receiv*e*d at Paris, when I came to Rome, I had left but 15; and 50 more I receiv*e*d heere at Rome, w*hi*ch I tooke upp of a gentlemann of my acquaintance at Paris, payinge 6 crownes for th*e* transporte. I am to repay that heere at Candlemas. A long cloake and sotane coste mee 24 crownes of my 50. A rydinge shorte cloake and rydinge suite cost mee 30 crownes of my hundred. The rest in charges. And now my mann healpes to spende the monye faster.

Commendinge my selfe and my busines to y*our* holye prayers, without farder ceremonye, I humblye take leave, <cravinge your

had not seen for many years. Rant argued that James must have allowed Bishop's arrival in the realm, since there was no sign of any official displeasure towards him: AAW, B 25, no. 102.

497 Francesco Ingoli, secretary to the congregation de Propaganda Fide. See *NCC*, pp. 39, 153, 156.

498 Rant wrote that Ingoli advised him to be 'moderate in speakinge of the Jesuitts', unlike John Bennett who had a tendency to be 'transported': AAW, B 25, no. 102.

blessinge and> remayninge y*our* l*ordshi*ps humble servante to his best power.

Thomas Rant

Rome 23 Dec[ember].

I beseeche y*our* l*ordshi*p consider quicklye on[e] that I write to Mr Irlande and, yf hee bee not in towne, ther is no danger to breake upp his letter. I would bee glad to knowe wher y*our* l*ordshi*p stay[s] for the most parte.

*Addressed*: To the right hon*ora*ble [m]y lord bishop of Chalcedon theis.

*Endorsed*: 23 Decemb[er] 1623.
Of Mr Rants first arrivall at Rome.

## 35. William Bishop to Thomas Rant, 18 December 1623

[*AAW, A XVII, no. 58, pp. 189–190*]

Very reverend and much respected father,

About 3 weekes past I did certify you of the occurrents of that time w*hi*ch were very good. But now I must acquaint you with a great alteration, for it pleased his Ma*jes*tie, upon what grownd I know not, to send a post or two into Spaine and there to recall or make stay of the proxy w*hi*ch was left in the Lord Digbies hands to have been deliv*er*ed the day folowing to the king of Spaine to have maried his sister in the name of o*ur* Prince Charles, w*hi*ch recall or stay could not but greatly perplex and trouble the Catholike king and his peeres who had published the same before and p*re*pared extraordinarie solemnit[i]es for the accomplishing of it. We say for o*ur* excuse here that [it] is worthely done because they differred the prince and put him of[f] often when he was there present. Also for that the Cath[olic] king will not promise to restore the Palatinate.[499] They answer that this matter of the Palatinate was never comprehended within the articles of agreement, and to have it thrust in now on the sudden was a signe that we meant not to stand to o*ur* former agreement; besides, all the Palatinate was not in there handes, wherefore they could not restore it if they would; yet ever promised to do their endevour to gett it restored, w*hi*ch they still would do, but could not make it an ingredience of their articles, but would labour that it might be a consequence of it. To thother point of the delay of the marriage whiles o*ur* prince was

[499] See *CSPV, 1623–1625*, pp. 185, 188, 194.

in Spaine, they answer that, assoone as the dispensation was come, they were ready to have finished but staid to heare that o*ur* king had p*er*formed those favours to recusants w*hi*ch in the same dispensation were required. In the meane season his Holines[500] died, and then would not the nuncio deliv*er* the dispensation before he knew the next popes pleasure therein. Nor [*word omitted:* did] the Spaniards accomplish the mariage before they had the dispensation in their handes, w*hi*ch o*ur* prince tooke evill, saying that it was sufficient that they knew the dispensation to be come. Hitherto their reasons, as farr as I can learne. But it is thought by diverse that the duke of Buckingham, o*ur* k[ing's] favorite, falling out with Cou[n]t Olivares, the Spanish kinges favorite, did sollicite o*ur* king to hasten his sonne thence, p*er*suading him that, before they would suffer him to go unmaried, they would not stay for any other confirmatio*n* of the dispensation, w*hi*ch fell out otherwise, and sence their arrivall here the favorite is said to have done both with the king and prince what he can to breake of[f] that mariage and to have prevailed therein. This is the more common opinion, though there be some that thinke it wilbe peeced up againe, one way or other, because it is holden in reason of estate so convenient both for the one king and thother. Buckingham and the Lord Hayes[501] have been with the F[rench] ambassadour, and had long conference with him about matching o*ur* prince in France as many do p*re*sume, thought [*sic for* though] there be no constat of it. Thus much of that unhappy matter.

Touching o*ur* own busines, I am entered into covenant with the Benedictins of the English congregation to hold good correspondence one with another. The Calmelites and Cappucins do promise the like, and the Jesuites a farr of[f] have made some meanes for the same w*hi*ch, if [*word omitted:* it] will come of[f] honestly, we shall p*er*forme.[502] There is not yet any new p*er*secution, but continuance of

[500] Gregory XV.

[501] James Hay, 1st Viscount Doncaster, who had been created earl of Carlisle in September 1622.

[502] For the 'Canones ecclesiastici ad pacem et disciplinam inter clerum saecularem et monachos Benedictinos conservandam a reverendissimo in Christo patre ac domino, D[omino] Gulielmo Episcopo Calcedonensi propositi', see AAW, A XVII, no. 54, pp. 177–180 (an authenticated copy sent to Claude Bertin, superior of the French Oratory in Rome). On 25 December 1623, Joseph Haynes had remarked that 'now we beginne to be much better united than formerly, both preists amongest our selves and religious with us'; via 'spetiall articles [...] in this holy league are we al conjoyned; except only the Jesuits, who have not yet refused, nor yet as we heare doe seeke it, but stand aloofe harkninge what others doe': AAW, A XVII, no. 59, p. 191. On 6 February 1624, William Bishop described how, in the previous year, he had 'made good correspondence with the Benedictins'. He had also received 'letters from the superior of the Franciscans', while the 'Dominicans, Calmelites and Cappucins have congratulated my election and tendred me their obedience and concurrence'. Richard Blount, the Jesuit provincial, had visited him, 'desiring that we

*our* p*ro*vident liberty, God continue it.[503] I certified you that you returne me answer by means of the Frenc[h]e [amba]ssadour in R[ome][504] in the Frenc[h]e ambass[ador] Mons[ieur] de Tillieres['s] packet, [*p. 190*] addressing them to Mons*ieur* Chamberlaine,[505] his English chaplaine, to be delivered to mee.[506] The Jesuites here bragg that four or five of the English scholers be thrust out of the college for having spoken with M^r^ Benett *our* agent there w*hi*ch, if it be true, cannot but be very grievously taken of all *our* body.[507] What, may not they who are bred to serve *our* clergy speake with the agent of the same cleargy?[508] But, say they, he gave them counsell to breake the rules of the college. What rules, I pray you lerne? I answere you shall find none. If the rulers may

might live like good friends together'. Bishop suggested that past antagonisms might be forgotten, but remarked that the secular clergy were 'much offended for the misgovernment of our colleges'. Blount answered 'that he had nothing to do with those goverments but they were under the fathers of the Society who lived in the same country'; he would, however, 'write to them to govern well'. But this 'tooke so small effect that, shortly after, the scholers were thrust out of the college in Rome': AAW, A XVII, no. 96, p. 314; TD, V, p. cclxxv. During the summer and autumn of 1623, the Jesuit general, Muzio Vitelleschi, had voiced extreme suspicion of William Bishop. In August, Vitelleschi warned of the factionalization of the English Catholic community in favour of either Spain or France. In September, he noted how the danger represented by Bishop was increased by Bishop's opportunity to communicate with the king: ARSJ, Anglia MS 1, fos 179r, 181r, 181v, 190v. In January 1624, Vitelleschi congratulated Blount for extricating himself from a meeting with William Bishop and his officials. He advised him that, if English Catholics thought the bishop of Chalcedon's proceedings were unacceptable, they should petition Rome against him. In particular, Vitelleschi rejected what he termed the 'calumnies' spread by Bishop's secretary, William Harewell, about the English College in Rome: *ibid.*, fos 190v, 191r; and in February 1624 he positively instructed Blount to refuse obedience to Bishop: *ibid.*, fo. 191v.

503 On 25 December 1623, Joseph Haynes remarked that 'it is [...] reported that the bitesheepes', i.e. Protestant bishops, 'here, upon the newes of the matches breaking of[f], came to the king for his leave to send abrode the pursevants, but his answer was that he now grew olde and would not persecute any more for religion. If they did otherwaies offend, lett them be punished, so that it is verily thought, whether the match goe forward or no, we shal not be troubled for religion so longe as the kinge liveth, which I wish may be many yeers': AAW, A XVII, no. 59, p. 192.

504 Noël Brûlart.

505 John Varder. See Anstr., II, p. 327. In mid-November 1620, Tillières had secured Varder's release from the New Prison (though on condition that Varder would immediately take himself abroad): *APC, 1619–1621*, p. 314.

506 In March 1624, Bishop remarked that this mode of sending letters was 'the safest and most speedy [...] albeit the Frenc[h]e do not affect the match with Spaine as we do, yet we have in the matter of our hierarchie found more help of Frenc[h]e than of Spanish, and so do remaine indebted unto both': AAW, A XVII, no. 101, p. 327.

507 See *Letters 33, 34*.

508 Anthony Shelley asked how the expelled students, returning to England, were supposed to behave towards the bishop and his officers when they were taught in Rome to question his authority: TD, V, p. 103.

upon such generall accusations expell when they list, yea them that desire to observe most the true end of that college, what murmur will <not> raise in all true <members> of our body, and that deservedly? Wherefore I pray you to speake boldly to his Holines, in all *ou*r names, that he wilbe pleased to have an eye to that stone [?] of offence and to provide that none may be expelled thence on envy or such generall slanders, but that he will give you leave to looke into that disorder that you may informe his Holines of the truth of such matters, for that we send you thither to p*ro*cure remedy thereof as much as for any other matter.[509] Thus, with my very harty com*m*endac*io*ns [*word deleted*] to the reverend Father Bartin and yo*u*r self, with M^r^ Seton and the rest <of> *ou*r friends, I desire you to remember me in those holy places. The 18^th^ of *ou*r December 1623.

Yo*u*r very loving friend,

W*illia*m Byshope of Chalcedon

*Addressed*: Au très révérend père, le Père Bartin supérieur de S^t^ Louis.

Pour estre donné au Père Thomas Rant.

A Rome.

*Endorsed*: [*on p. 189*] Written: Decemb[er] 18 1623.
Received: Febru[ary] 1 1624.

[509]For Bishop's letter to Rant of 29 December 1623, advising the students to stay in Rome until the spring, and telling Rant to petition that their case should be heard by Propaganda Fide, see AAW, A XVII, no. 63, pp. 203–204; TD, V, pp. cclxviii–cclxx; see also *Letter 36*. In a letter of 6 February 1624, Bishop described to Rant how he had recently written, on 15 January, to the pope (AAW, A XVII, no. 81, pp. 267–268; part printed in TD, V, pp. cclxxii–cclxxiii) to request that 'the visit of the college may proceed which his predecessor of happy memory did, motu proprio, begin, and that it may passe by the same <worthy> persons of the congregation de Propaganda Fide whom he appointed'. Other leading secular clergy had done the like (AAW, A XVII, no. 95, pp. 309–312); and Bishop offered his advice as to how Rant should secure their aims and objectives so that the 'notable abuses' in the college might be corrected: AAW, A XVII, no. 96, p. 313; TD, V, pp. 101, cclxxiv. In March 1624, the issue was referred by the pope to Propaganda Fide. The congregation decreed that the expelled students should be sent to Douai and that their expenses should be defrayed by the college in Rome: Anstr., II, p. 291; AAW, B 47, no. 51; AAW, A XVII, no. 122, pp. 389–390; see also *CGB*, I, p. 461. A new college oath was drawn up in August 1624. It was ordered to be published on 11/21 February 1625: AAW, A XVIII, no. 37, pp. 273–274; TD, V, p. cclxxx. For a further petition, of 27 May/6 June 1625, by Thomas Rant that scholars of the English College should not enter the Society, see AAW, B 48, no. 54, fo. 126r–v. A decree was promulgated that a papal licence would henceforth be required by any seminarist who intended to enter a religious order: TD, V, pp. 109, 112–113, cclxxix; AAW, B 26, nos 74, 75; AAW, A XVII, no. 123, pp. 391–392; AAW, A XIX, no. 68, pp. 205–208.

[*on p. 190*] Received by Père Bertin uppon the first daye of Februarye 1624.

## 36. William Bishop to Thomas Rant, 17/27 January 1624

[*AAW, A XVII, no. 86, pp. 281–282*]

Reverend father,

Though I have not as yet received any from you, I cess not to write as occasion requireth. I do now write unto his Holines humbly requesting him to deale with the king Catholike for the rendring of the Palatinate, at leste so much as is in his royall hands, unto *our* king for one of the palatins sonnes that may be brought up Catholikely in the emperours court.[510] We heare now that the Catholike king will condescend thereunto, and I have heard that his Ma*jes*tie of Great Britaine would be content that the said sonne should be brought up in the emperours court and to mar[r]y one of his daughters.[511] This later point is of very great consequence, not onely for continuing the Catholike faith in the Palatinate where it now begins but for us also in England, he being as it were the second and next [to] the prince and his mother. Wherefore his Holines is to be put in mind of it, p*ar*ticularly that he may take order to have it treated of, if it be not already mentioned. The favourite[512] here is mightely against the match, and was like to drave his Ma*jes*tie and the prince from it. The beginning of the p*ar*lement is put of[f] till the twentieth of February.[513]

[510] For William Bishop's letter of 31 January 1624 to Urban VIII urging his assistance in procuring the restitution of the Rhineland Palatinate in order to secure the Anglo-Spanish dynastic treaty, see AAW, A XVII, no. 88, pp. 285–286. A similar letter had been dispatched by Bishop to the king of Spain on 30 January: AAW, A XVII, no. 87, pp. 283–284.

[511] See *CSPV, 1623–1625*, pp. 144, 158–159; see also above, p. 68.

[512] George Villiers, 1st duke of Buckingham.

[513] On 6 February 1624, William Bishop commented that 'at this parlement' it was likely that 'we shall all of us be by proclamation commanded to depart the realm'. He continued that 'all priests and Jesuits' were already 'by proclamation banished out of Ireland and the Catholike bishops also, but the prince is said to excuse it, that it is done by the deputie onely without any warrant from our king': AAW, A XVII, no. 96, pp. 314, 315; TD, V, p. cclxxvi; *CSPV, 1623–1625*, pp. 218–219. This proclamation was dated 21 January 1624 and was brought by Irish Catholics to London to show, in translation, to the marquis of Inojosa, who took it to Prince Charles in order to complain. In Spain, an official protest was made in March to Sir Walter Aston concerning it; and William Trumbull recorded on 19/29 February how a complaint had come from the Spanish ambassadors in London to the authorities in Brussels against the 'newe persecution [. . .] so they are pleased to style it': PRO, SP 94/30, fo. 127r; PRO, SP 77/17, fo. 39r; see also AAW, B 26, no. 10; *CGB*, I, p. 431. A month after it was issued, the Irish proclamation was withdrawn: A. Ford,

The archbishop of Canter[bury],[514] with some others, are in hand already to give comission to pursuivants, but diverse of <the> better sort of the privy counsell do oppose against it and have yet staid it. The good successe against Gabor[515] and Mansfield doth much trouble them that would have the match broken. We begin to feare againe. God Almighty p*ro*tect us.

Mr Harpur[516] is at last arrived here, who hat[h] informed us how all things passed there against the five scholers. We cannot write more p*er*tinently than we [have] done to reduce the visitation unto [the] congregat[ion] de Propaganda Fide who were first charged with it by Pope Greg[ory] the fifteenth of hap[p]y memory.[517] I desire you very hartely to folowe that matter most diligently with all the help of Fa[ther] Bertin and Mr Seton, who hath already dealt in it most kindly, for w*hi*ch I pray you to thank him hartely from me and all our cleargy. Thus, desiring you to remember [*word omitted:* me] in those holy places, I rest.

Yo*u*rs most assuredly,

W*illia*m Bishop of Chalcedon

27 of January <1624> stilo novo.

[*on p. 282*]

*Addressed*: Au très révérend père, le Père Thomas Rant. Soit donnée au très révérend père, le Père Bartin, supérieur de St Louis a Rome.

[*on p. 281*]

*Endorsed*: Written: January 27.
Received: March 25.
Received: 25 March [*sic*].
Delivered his Hol*ine*s letter 27 March.

*The Protestant Reformation in Ireland 1590–1641* (Dublin, 1997), p. 206; C.W. Russell and J.P. Prendergast (eds), *Calendar of the State Papers Relating to Ireland, 1615–1625* (London, 1880), pp. 458f, 464; *HMCMK*, p. 192; AAW, B 26, no. 58.

[514] George Abbot.

[515] See *CSPV, 1623–1625*, pp. 209, 223. For Bethlen Gábor, who had allied himself with the Bohemian rebels against Ferdinand, see G. Parker, *Europe in Crisis* (Brighton, 1980), p. 162; Pursell, *WK*, *passim*.

[516] Thomas Harper, one of the rebel students at the English College in Rome.

[517] See *Letter 34*.

## 37. Anthony Champney to Thomas Rant, 5/15 February 1624

[*AAW, B 26, no. 12*]

Verie r*everen*d and loving s*i*r,

Yo*ur*s of the 10 of Jan[uary] to Mr President,[518] in his absence, came to my hands by the way of Paris. I ame gladd you have received assurance for your money whereof I pray you keepe just accompt. I send you here letters from my lord[519] w*hi*ch yesterday I received. I suppose he hath given you both comission and direction for that matter of the colledge[520] w*hi*ch, as I sayd before <in other letters>, I would have so dealt in as that the dore may not be shut to the clergie frome demanding the colledge to be restored to the clergie when they shall find oportunitie to p*ro*pose that sute. The reasons thereof <I mean of clearing the colledge> you may expect from them for I knowe they are in drawing.

Co*n*cerning the match w*i*th Spayn, whereof no doubt there is as great expectation there as els where, you may knowe that though, since Christmas, it hath beene howlden <as> broken, yet nowe it is generally esteemed to be in more forwardness than before. The difficultie did arise about the Palatinat w*hi*ch the king of Spayne p*ro*miseth to doe what he can for the restitution thereof, w*hi*ch giveth our king good co*n*tentment.[521] The infanta of late hath writen to our prince. The Lord Digbie is stayed in Spayn who <before> was called [*word deleted*] <thence>. Not only the Catholikes do hope well but the heretikes doe feare more than before.[522] Of 12 of the councell, onely three are averted from it, and one of them cometh in.[523] The

[518] Matthew Kellison.

[519] William Bishop.

[520] The English College in Rome.

[521] See *CSPV, 1623–1625*, pp. 201, 207, 208.

[522] Simonds D'Ewes commented, in his diary for 13 February, 'wee had ill newes spread abroad by the papists that the Spanish match should yett proceede': *DSSD*, p. 180.

[523] Anthony Champney likewise recorded, on 20 February/1 March 1624, that (on the basis of a report enclosed in a letter from Kellison) only three of the privy council opposed the Spanish match, and that even Londoners were now in favour of it: AAW, B 26, no. 15. On 31 January, John Chamberlain had observed that 'the junta for forrain affaires sat hard all that weeke' and that it was rumoured that 'they were devided into three parts, five for the Spanish match, viz: lords keper [Williams], treasurer [Middlesex], marshall [Arundel], Weston and Calvert, fowre newters that wold not declare themselves, the duke of Richmond, Hamilton, chamberlain [Pembroke] and Belfast; three directly against yt [. . .] Buckingham [. . .] Carlile and Conway', though the prince was now averse to the match as well, and this was what had broken the deadlock. Pembroke was arguing for the match in order to spite

parlement that was apoynted for the 12 of Febru[ary] is adjorned till the 20 of the same. Cooke and S*ir* Edwin Sandes are sent into Ireland to be occupied there in tyme of parlement.[524] There is a marchant that cometh from London to Parise who sayth that the embassatour[525] hath 80 embrotterers in his howse (but p*er*adventure he exceedeth the nu*m*ber) w*hi*ch argueth p*re*paration for some extraordinarie solemnitie. This is all I can say for the present, but w*i*th my best wishes to yo*ur* self and my love to Father Bertin, I rest this 14 of Feb[ruary] 1624.

I long to heare of the receipt of my letters sent by their <meanes> [*word deleted*] of the Oratorie at Paris w*hi*ch course I will use no more. I pray you deliver this inclosed to the direction [*word omitted:* of], and com*m*end <me> ever most kindly to, Mr Doct[or] Seton and the youthes out of the colledge.

Y*ou*rs ever, Champney

Tell, I pray you, Mr Browne that I have now writen agayn to our agent, S*ign*ore Scanarolio, to pay him 25li everie half yeare.[526]

I have taken notice to our agent of his courtesie towardes you and in Mr President his name have given him thankes.

*Addressed*: R*everen*do admodu*m* pr*estr*e [?] ac d*omi*no, D[omino] Thomae Ranto cleri Anglicani in curia Romana procuratori. Romam.

*Endorsed*: Written: Feb[ruary] 14.
Received: March 25.
Answer[e]d: [*sic*].

Buckingham: McClure, *LJC*, pp. 541–542; Schreiber, *FC*, pp. 56–57; Ruigh, *1624*, p. 41; cf., for Pembroke's position, Adams, FP, p. 156.

[524] See AAW, A XVII, no. 78, p. 249; TD, V, p. cclxxii.

[525] Carlos Coloma.

[526] On 21/31 January 1624, Anthony Champney had written to inform Thomas Rant that 'there is in Rome a young gentleman called Mr John Browne to whome I pray you comend me and tell him that nowe I have writen to our agent to pay him everie six monethes 100 crownes haveing receaved order from his mother for it': AAW, B 26, no. 8. Browne was a cousin of Thomas Roper: *Letter 77*. He appears to have been the individual listed by Thomas Rant as a mourner at Thomas More's funeral in April 1625 (clearly distinguished from Francis Browne, son of the 2nd Viscount Montague, who was also present): D. Shanahan, 'The death of Thomas More, secular priest, great-grandson of St. Thomas More', *RH*, 7 (1963–1964), p. 26; *Letter 85*.

## 38. William Bishop to Thomas Rant, 22 February 1624

[*AAW, A XVII, no. 100, pp. 325–326*]

Deare father,

I have your third [letter] of January the 10th, and do not a litle muse that my first was not come to your hands then. I have written my self to you about six. God send you good dispatch for the deane and chapter because that wilbe as a continuation of episcopall jurisdiction if we cannot gett any more bish[ops], which I trust in God we shall do, ere it be long, by your good aid; and if that chapter were setled and our college visited and reformed by expulsion of them who have robbed us of many fine wits, and the college (as is supposed) of many thousand pounds,[527] then loe we should all joyntly [*two words illegible*] b[ishops].

We daily pray for you and all those good cardinals our patrons. Do not you [forge]tt us in those holy places. I have already written to Card[inal] Farnesio and Barberini[528] and to Monsig[nor] Vives. I will gett [*two words obscured*] to make some faire insinuation to him in [your] [b]ehalfe. I think that [*word obscured*] Mr Setons would place <you> there. He is so hospita[ble]. Now I do write to Card[inal] Ludovisio.[529] If F[ather] Rector[530] should not be some what cholerike he had lost himself; but you <are> wise enough to kepe outward peace with [h]im and yet fol[low] your busines <close> and assist the injured scholers[531] in the best manner you can. Those wandring sisters[532] want not some to magnify their endevoures and to report that they are enlarged to Naples. The scholers letter came in good time and was delivered to his father here in London. I am right glad that P[ère] Bertin is in good health. I pray you thanke him hartely for his kind letter and all the courtesies he hath shewed to our cleargy and mee. Do the like unto Card[inal] Bentivolio both for all former benefits and for his courteous letter to me at this time. Thus much in answer

[527] See AAW, A XVII, no. 96, pp. 313–316; TD, V, pp. cclxxiv–cclxxvi (Bishop's account of the maladministration of the English College at Rome).

[528] For William Bishop's letters of 12 February 1624 to Cardinal Francesco Barberini and 22 February 1624 to Cardinal Edouardo Farnese, see AAW, A XVII, no. 93, pp. 303–304, no. 99, pp. 323–324.

[529] For William Bishop's letter of 19 February 1624 to Cardinal Luigi Ludovisi, see AAW, A XVII, no. 97, pp. 317–318. Ludovisi wrote in reply to Bishop on 6/16 March: AAW, A XVII, no. 108, pp. 351–352.

[530] Thomas Fitzherbert SJ.

[531] i.e. the rebel students at the English College in Rome.

[532] i.e. the members of Mary Ward's institute.

to yo*ur*s. Now to o*ur* newes. Yesterday being the 19th of o*ur* Feb[ruary] the parlement was begun by o*ur* kings Ma*jes*tie. It was <first> put to the 16th, but the duke of Lenoux,[533] dying suddenly that morning in his bed <at Whithall>, thrust it of[f] to the 19th.[534] The duke is lamented of most men as a quiet orderly nobleman who did not wrong any body, and was held for a friend to the Spanish match.[535] His Ma*jes*tie['s] speech was in generall tearmes faire to the par[l]ementary men.[536] He and they be as man and wife. They must not be jaylors of him. He ~~had~~ <did> treated [*sic*] to match his sonne in Spaine, but his beloved Buckingham and his secretarie should acquaint them with their p*ro*ceding therein. He had given the papists more liberty than [here]tofore; yet like a wary horsman, who doth not alwaies use the spurs, but lettes the bridle some times in the horses neck, yet kepes the reins in his own handes. He desired them to see what were best to be done in both those cases and in any other [*word obscured:* matter (?)], yet so as they do remember <alwaies> his prerogatives. This <is> the summe of all I heare as yet. Shortly wee shall have all in print. A constant report is of both Protestants and Catholikes that Co[u]nt Henry de Berge, taking the opportunity of the great frost, is gotten over and encamped nere unto Utrick in Holland, and hath above 20,000 me*n* with him and is like to endanger all that co[a]st.[537] Some speech there is also that another, assisted with the prince of Frizeland,[538] is doeing there and hath already gotten one towne, that

[533]Ludovic Stuart, 1st duke of Richmond and 2nd duke of Lennox.

[534]McClure, *LJC*, p. 545; *DSSD*, p. 181; Thompson, *RD*, p. 1; Hacket, *SR*, part I, p. 173; PRO, SP 14/159/63.

[535]The duke of Lennox was, in fact, generally regarded as a stalwart of the Bohemian faction: Adams, PC, p. 306; Cogswell, *BR*, p. 103. However, Ludovic, the youngest son (born 14 October 1619) of Esmé Stuart, who succeeded to the title as 3rd duke of Lennox, was ordained as a Catholic priest by Richard Smith in 1652 and became almoner to Catherine of Braganza in 1661: Anstr., II, pp. 312–313.

[536]PRO, SP 14/159/55, 56, 57, 58; Hacket, *SR*, part I, p. 91; *LJ*, III, pp. 209–210; *Letter 39*; ED, fos 1r–4r; Lambeth Palace Library, MS 930, no. 81. For the copy of James's speech dispatched to Thomas Rant, see AAW, A XVII, no. 98, pp. 319–322.

[537]Berg's manoeuvre was part of a defensive strategy designed to counter the assembly of Dutch cavalry near Breda under Henry of Nassau: *CGB*, I, pp. xix, 43, 428, 432. On 12/22 February 1624, William Trumbull noted that Berg, 'lieutenant generall of our cavalry (joyned with Don Goncales de Cordova, and 12,000 men, certaine peeces of cannon, and a good quantity of munitions)', had 'already passed the Rheyne and other ryvers', in order to 'make a strong impression into the country of Freezland': PRO, SP 77/17, fos 33r, 39r; see also Israel, *The Dutch Republic*, pp. 386–387; *CCE*, pp. 76, 141, 148.

[538]Enno III, count of East Friesland.

of Harberstade,[539] now duke of Brunswike, by the death of his brother,[540] to witt that he was taken and caried to the [e]mperour, is now recalled. They say onely that <he> doth sue to the emperour for his p*ar*don and wilbecome his servant if he please to accept of his submission.[541]

Tobie Mathew, now knighted for his good service in Spaine,[542] declares himself openly to be for the duke of Buckingh[am] and saith that he hath reason to do as he doth, that is, to be against the Spanish match, and that o*ur* prince was not well used there, and that Cou[n]t d'Olivares is a darke and dull felow. I hope he [*MS torn*] not be for his dealing against Catholikes too. Time will reveale more [*MS torn*]. [Wi]th my very harty comend[ations] I rest.

Your loving friend,

W*illia*m Chalcedon

22 February.

*Addressed*: Au très révérent père, le Père Bertin supérieur de S^t^ Louis, pour le r*évéren*d Père Thomas.
A Rome.

[*on p. 325*]

*Endorsed*: Written: 22 Feb[ruary].
Received: 10 June.

[539] Christian of Brunswick, administrator of the bishopric of Halberstadt. For his employment by the Dutch, see Israel, *Dutch Republic*, p. 483. He had been one of Princess Elizabeth's daughter's godfathers, and was also a cousin of the Stuarts via the marriage of Anne of Denmark's sister Elizabeth: BL, Harleian MS 1581, fos 236r, 436r; Cogswell, *BR*, pp. 239–240; Patterson, *King James VI and I*, p. 29; Pursell, *WK*, p. 148. After getting the better of a skirmish against the count of Tilly in July 1623, Brunswick's army had been destroyed at Stadtlohn by Tilly in August: BL, Harleian MS 1581, fo. 292v; *CSPV, 1623–1625*, p. 80; M. Lee (ed.), *Dudley Carleton to John Chamberlain, 1603–1624* (New Brunswick, NJ, 1972), p. 301; J.V. Polisensky, *The Thirty Years War* (London, 1974), p. 169; Israel, *Dutch Republic*, p. 483.

[540] Friedrich-Ulrich, duke of Brunswick-Wolfenbüttel (d. 1634). See *CGB*, I, pp. 371, 379.

[541] See also AAW, A XVII, no. 94, p. 307.

[542] Back in mid-April 1623, Calvert had written to Buckingham that, in view of the rumoured 'aversenesse' of some of the Roman curia towards the marriage, James had decided that Mathew, 'of whose loyalty and faithfulnesse to his service his Majestie rests very well assured, should instantly make his repayre' to Spain. James believed that, 'by the creditt and reputation which he hath with that party in respect of his profession in religion', Mathew might, in Spain, 'endevor to remove all rubbs arising that way and to satisfy needelesse doubts and jealousies if there bee any'. Mathew would 'bee many other wayes usefull' to the prince there. He had been ordered 'to depend' solely on Buckingham and to take his direction from him 'in all things': BL, Harleian MS 1580, fo. 184r. For the count of Tillières's report of Mathew's purpose in going to Spain ('essayer d'ouvrir les yeux' of Prince Charles 'affin qu'il puisse cognoistre la vérité de nostre religion', and, failing that, to break the match altogether), see PRO, PRO 31/3/57, fo. 204v.

This was the last letter I received.[543]

[*on p. 326*]

*Endorsed*: Written 22 Feb[ruary], received the 10 of Jun[e] by the phisitian of M*on*si[eu]r l'ambassadeur de France, M*on*si[eu]r de Betun.[544] Father Archangel delivered yt to him to bring to Rome.

W[illiam] Chalcedon Feb[ruary] 1624.

## 39. Thomas More to Thomas Rant, 28 February 1624[545]

[*AAW, B 26, no. 14*]

Right wor*shipfu*ll,

It hath pleased our r[ight] hon[ourable] and r*everen*d [lord] to ease me of the care of ordinarie correspondence with you because of my remove from London, and [he] chardgeth me onlie with our affairs in Spayne, which I shall seeke to dischardg[e] as I may.[546] With you alsoe I will not omitt to com*m*unicate as occasion is offered, if I perceave my lines [are] anie thing acceptable to you or avayleable for the com*m*on cause. I know others will have a care to satisfye you in all occurrantes. For my part, though, I am ~~not~~ obliged by your letters to me, yet I wold insinuate unto you that the fearfull parlam*ent*, called principallie to advise with the nobilitie and com*m*ons about the match with Spayne, began upon Thursday the xix[th] of this present. It was putt of[f] twice, once from Thursday the xii[th] of this present to Monday next following, because of the hard frost and deep snowe which contynued three weekes. The second adjourne was from Monday to Thursday when it began. And this was in reguard of the unfortunate and sodaine death of the duke of Richmond, who was a noble man of such worthie disposition that he carryed with him generallie the hartes <of all>, and particulerly the Catholickes, because of his good affection and furtherance of the match with Spayne.[547] The king tooke these unexpected tydinges of the dukes death wonderfullie to hart, it being brought him when he was readie to have sett forward towards the

[543]In fact, as Rant noted in his endorsement of *Letter 42*, Bishop's missive to him of 2 April 1624 was the last letter which came to him from Bishop.

[544]Philippe de Béthune, count of Sully.

[545]The letter concludes with a separate note, in Latin, from More, concerning his cousin Thomas Roper.

[546]See Anstr., I, p. 234.

[547]See *Letter 38*.

parlam*en*t. For the duke, lodging in the court at Whithall, went very well to bed on Sonday night. On Monday morning he complayned of his head and backe, and seeking to take some small repose was sone after fownd dead, to the dismayall of the whole realme. His Ma*jes*tie made a pithie speech to the parlam*en*t of half an howre long,[548] signifying unto his audience the cause of this present assemblie, which was according to the tenour of the writtes dyrected into every shire to advise with his loyall subjects upon certein necessarie pointes and principallie touching the match of his dearest sonne the prince, and the good of his grandchildren, praying the present parlament as they were the representative bodie of the realme, and consequentlie his dear spowse, to sett aside all jealousies and to love him as their spowse, omitting now, because the time of their deliberation was but short, all necessarie questions and brabbles, and seriouslie to attend what may be for the generall peace of Christendome and the peace and tranquillitie of this realme. As for their priviledges, they might be assured he wold never infringe them that be lawfull. Onlie he wold not now have them stand upon anie such unnecessarie delaies and trifleing away of time, but advise him in this important businesse and then he wold doe as he saw cause. He putt them in minde how two or three parlaments had miscarried, and wished them to have more care in [?] this. As for the imputation laid upon him that he meant to suppresse the religion professed, he made his protestation that he never intended alteration of religion, or to digg or root it upp, though he had connyved for a tyme with papist[s] and not proceeded with such rigour as formerlie; yet itt was with that prudence that as a skilfull ryder he had still his hand upon the raines to drawe backe or give head as he thought it best. This was in effect his Ma*jes*ties speech, which the l*or*d keaper, l*or*d of Lincolne,[549] applauded without anie addition,[550] saying onlie that who soe[ver] had heard his Ma*jes*tie needed not to hear a croaking chancelor, as the Lacedemonian who was invited to heare one that co[u]ld represent the tune of a nightingall answered αυτοσ ηκουσα: I ~~have~~ have heard nightingalls them selves; and said his speeches wold be aureo annulo ferreas stallas,[551] to enamell a gold ring with rustie yron. Seeing his Ma*jes*tie had leaft in them τον κεντρον, a pricke and stinge, and soe he concluded that, as Nerva dyed havinge adopted Trajan, least this his mortall deed shold be depraved by anie mortall fact insuing, soe he wold not, by his addinge, seeme to diminish the

[548] See *ibid.*
[549] John Williams.
[550] For Williams's speech, see PRO, SP 14/159/59; ED, fo. 5r–v.
[551] 'Annulum aureum ferreis stellis ferruminare': Hacket, *SR*, part I, p. 175.

im*m*ortall glorie of so dyvine a speech. The speaker of the parlam*en*t is a hott professor, one S*ir* Thomas Crew, a serjeant at law.[552] In his oration after his acceptance by his Ma*jes*tie he made a most bitter and sharpe invective against Catholickes, wishing an exact execution of the penal lawes against them, with the banishment of all preistes and religiouse, of which speech it is sayd that the lo*r*d keaper gave his opinion that it was nether charitable nor according to lawe, nor befitting the present times, nor good for our cowntrie. For charitie wold have us to seeke the conversion, not subversion of our erring neighbours, and that papist[s] shold be wonn by reason and good persuasion and by good examples, and not with terrors and threates made to counterfeit and dissemble. And that the lawes did not require such courses but as were for the peace and tranquillitie of the realme. And that the tymes were now such that we had neede to be at unitie amongst our selves, and the good of our cowntrie wold have frendship manteyned withall seeing that, though we breake with Spayne, yet with whom soever we joyne it is especially with such as professe the same religion with papistes.[553] And one moderate man of the parlam*en*t answered another that wished all Catholickes banished this realme,[554] answered [*sic*] that he saw noe reason in such a project because, suppose all were banished, they might repair to the Palatinate and ther procure the landes and lyvinges of the Protestantes ther [*sic*], and send them hither, w*hi*ch wold not be soe convenient for the realme. Sure it is that the lower howse is marvelouslie bent against religion, and two b*ishop*s made two speeches against my lo*r*d of Ch[alcedon][555] in *p*a*rticu*ler,

[552] See McClure, *LJC*, p. 546; PRO, SP 14/159/60, 64.

[553] See ED, fos 5v–6r, 6r–9v, 9v–13r; *CSPV, 1623–1625*, pp. 234–236, 236–238; cf. Hacket, *SR*, part I, pp. 176, 177–179; PRO, SP 14/159/65, 66, 67; *LJ*, III, pp. 211–213. According to Sir Walter Earle, Williams declared that James had 'never spared the execution of any law but for a greater law, salus reipublicae', and that 'all the laws are yet in force', and there was 'no connivence but for propagation of true religion': ED, fos 11v–12r. Simonds D'Ewes thought that Williams, following Crew, spoke equally boldly against 'the papists', and that previously he had been 'of the popish faction, but now, after the princes returne out of Spaine and the breach of that match, this upstart turned the note of his tune another way': *DSSD*, p. 181.

[554] On 25 February, Sir Thomas Jermyn had 'mooved to intimate to the Lords' what the Commons 'had resolved concerning recusants', *inter alia* 'bannishing the priests out of the kingdom'. Jermyn and other MPs had also suggested barring Catholic recusants from London: Thompson, *HA*, pp. 5, 6.

[555] William Bishop. Thomas More may have meant two MPs in the lower House rather than two bishops. For Richard Dyott's speech in the Commons on 25 February concerning William Bishop's tour through Staffordshire 'with his crosiers, myters and 6 chaplayns' and his confirming 'at one tym 400 in the Roman faith', see Thompson, *HA*, p. 5; *idem*, *RD*, p. 13; ED, fo. 29r; *Letter 42*; for Dyott, see also N. Tyacke, *Anti-Calvinists* (Oxford, 1987), pp. 67, 140–143. Another MP, Christopher Brooke, argued that 'it is treason by the law for

and the president of Doway[556] who is yett hear, procuring some healp towardes the dischardg[e] of the debtes of his house, procured by the backward paym*en*t of the k[ing] of Sp[ain's] pension. And generallie all Catholickes live in daylie fears and dare skantlie keap their owne howses, expecting searches and all extreamities.[557] One M^r^ Harry More, a gentleman of [the] Bishopricke,[558] who had bene somtime prisoner in Yorke upon the statute of persuasion,[559] was sent up prisoner to the Fleet for certeine words disgracefull to the religion professed, *viz*, that Qu[een] Marie of Scotland was a martyre and the trew hiere [*sic*] to this crowne; that Queene Eliz[abeth] was a bastard, and wrongfullie witheld the right from Qu[een] Mary and her issue; and, lastlie, that the religion now professed here came out of K[ing] Henry the eighth his codpeece. This last point was urged most against him as disgracefull to one that was soe worthie a prince and the fowndation of this religion now professed. In conclusion, his judgment in the starr chamber before the parlam*en*t was to loose both ears, to stand two daies upon the pillorie, one in Cheapside, the other at Westminster; to have his nose slitt, to ride through London with his face to the horstaile, to pay, I thinke, ten thowsand powndes fine, and to be prisoner perpetuall. This was executed upon the poor gentleman accordinglie, notwithstanding he alleadged for him self that he had said noe more but what was exstant

seminaries made beyond seas to cum into Engl[and] [. . .] or for any to harbour suche, to avoyd which law this bishopp instituted suche heer': Thompson, *HA*, p. 5; *idem*, *RD*, p. 13.

[556] Matthew Kellison.

[557] William Bishop reported on 5 March that 'they made of late a search all London over upon the second of our March in the night after three persons principally' (Bishop himself, Richard Blount SJ, and Matthew Kellison) but 'found neither them nor any other priest': AAW, A XVII, no. 101, pp. 327–328; see also *CSPV, 1623–1625*, p. 249; PRO, PRO 31/3/58, fo. 49r. In his diary for 2 March, D'Ewes said that 'search was made heere in this cittie, in manye popish howses, for armor': *DSSD*, p. 184. The king, said Bishop, had been told that 'some Catholikes in London had made great provision of muskets and powder, a most gross ly' and all part of the parliament's attempt to break the match with Spain: AAW, A XVII, no. 101, p. 328. (Simonds D'Ewes's diary for 25 February had previously narrated that, following the proposals by MPs in the Commons for 'new lawes', the 'bishopp of London [George Montaigne] alsoe, upon ther instigation, sent about to manye severall howses to have enquirie madde what papists were residing in and about London': *DSSD*, p. 182.) Anthony Champney recorded on 31 March/10 April 1624 that Kellison returned from England in haste, 'upon Good Fryday [. . .] because the lower Howse tooke notice of his being there and there was a search for two nights together thorowe all London by the order of the parliament'. Although 'neither anie one [was] taken nor trobled, nor yet was the search anie way exact but verie sleight [. . .] yet his freinds were of opinione that he showld depart': AAW, B 26, no. 27; Questier, *C&C*, p. 409.

[558] County Durham.

[559] 13 Elizabeth c. 2 ('An Acte agaynste the bringing in and putting in execution of Bulls and other Instruments from the Sea of Rome').

in print in their statute lawes and such other books as were sett forth by publicke authoritie and approbation.[560] Ther was a preist taken two daies since by a bookbinder in London upon occasion that the preist, enterteyning him self upon occasion with the reading of a pamphlett that lay upon the stall intituled A Gag for the Pope,[561] and, being to depart, the bookbinder asked him how he liked the booke. He answered it was a foolish booke and full of lies. Wherupon the bookbinder fetcht the constable and, following him to a Catholicke scriveners shopp, ther apprehended him, carrying [him] first before the l*or*d cheef justice.[562] But, seeing he wold not intermeddle in the businesse, they sayd they must now make somthing of the businesse and soe, carrying him to D*octo*r Montaigne, b[ishop] of London, he is committed, as the report goeth, but it is not knowne to what prison. It is alsoe said that ther is a Jesuit taken at Warwicke whom my l*or*d of Shrewsbury[563] challengeth for his servant. The pr[iest's] name is Mr Hurlston, who hath a brother a Bened[ictine].[564] My l*ord*[565] keapeth marvelouse close. Few knowe wher he is.[566] But I am sure he will not forgett you. I have writt certen reasons whie the government of the colledges shold be given to the clergie and whie the Jesuites are noe fitt [*word obliterated*], which I have sent to my l*or*d to have his approbation and wold have them sent to you to see wh[ether th]er may be made anie use of them, and to be advised from you and our frendes ther wherin they [are] defectuouse and how they may be perfected. I can not yett gett a procuration drawne though [I ha]ve sent, and spoken alsoe with Mr Farrar[567] theraboutes. Onlie I would desire you to informe yourself of the state of thinges and how every thing standeth in the colledge, I mean whether they acknowledg[e] such thinges as I pretend they have. And, if you co[u]ld send me the forme of a procura[tion] drawne by anie notarie, I wold sett my hand ~~therto~~ with Mr Farrars testimonie and others therto. Which I thinke

[560] John Chamberlain commented that Henry More 'laughed all the while' that sentence was being executed in Cheapside: McClure, *LJC*, p. 545. More had also said that Anne Boleyn 'was a whore': *DSSD*, p. 180; see also Whiteway, *Diary*, p. 59; BL, Additional MS 72255, fo. 117v. For the proceedings in the star chamber against More, see PRO, STAC 8/32/20. I am grateful to David Cressy for this reference.

[561] *A Gagge for the Pope, and the Iesuits: or the arraignement, and execution of Antichrist* (London, 1624).

[562] Sir James Ley.

[563] George Talbot, 9th earl of Shrewsbury.

[564] The Benedictine may have been Richard Huddlestone: Anstr., II, p. 164; the identity of the priest is uncertain.

[565] William Bishop.

[566] Alvise Valaresso said on 12/22 March that Bishop had gone to the Spanish embassy: *CSPV, 1623–1625*, p. 249.

[567] William Harewell.

wold be noe bad course, though it will require much time. We all long for an end of this terrible parlam*en*t, and in the mean time keap close, com*m*ending our cause to God and all good men, hoping well that, as the Catholicke cause prospereth in other cowntries, soe it will doe in this. The Hollanders have sent their embass[adors][568] hither, who arryved at London three dayes since, to treat with the king and estate for ayde against the Spanierd.[569] Ther was a report, that is not yett quite laid downe, that Henry van Berge was retyred backe to Brussells from Utreich, wher he had made a passage ~~of~~ over the ryver Isel, with the losse of three thowsand, but the last newes is that he hath fortifyed and secured his passage with two strong bulwarkes that he will not easelie be beaten away, but that at least he will block up Utrech that it shall not be able to range far that way.[570] And it is thought that the Spanierd will hardlie besett Hollend this summer, the emp*er*ors forces comming alsoe to annoy them in Freezland. This newes is said to troble the parlam*en*t very much and, if anie thing make them calme, this will, though ther want not manie that give projectes how to impoverish Spayne and to weaken the force of that kingdome. Howsoever it be trew or false, what is reported of the king of France, it is a wonderfull encoradgment to poor Catholickes to hear that he hath putt all Hugonotts from his cowncell, and in p*articu*ler the chanceler M[r] Seller,[571] with his sonn,[572] and that he hath answered the Vycownt Kensington[573] how if Ingland deal ther for a match they must not expect to finde them more backward in religion than the Spanyerds but that they must exact, if not the same, yet as good conditions for Catholickes. Manie ~~deed~~ deeme, as they faine wold have it, that his Ma*jes*tie, the prince, yea and the duke[574] alsoe, are absolutlie resolved for to match with Spaine, and that, whatsoever the duke or prince doth, it is onlie to drawe the parlam*en*t to yeild consent therto, without which the conditions agreed upon by both kingdomes can not be valide and of force; and the king of Spayne seemeth to condescend to whatsoever is demanded of him, as was declared by a letter he sent which was read in the parlament. For the prince, duke and secretaries of estate, by the kinges order, were

568 François Aerssens and Albertus Joachimi. See Adams, PC, pp. 337–338.

569 See *CSPV, 1623–1625*, p. 233; Adams, PC, p. 337. James received the Dutch ambassadors on 29 February: see *DSSD*, p. 183. For the treaty with the Dutch, see *Letter 47*.

570 See Lee, *Dudley Carleton to John Chamberlain*, pp. 314–315; BL, Additional MS 72255, fos 120r, 122r; *HMCMK*, p. 194; PRO, SP 17/77, fos 41r, 53r.

571 Nicolas Brûlart de Sillery, chancellor of France.

572 Pierre Brûlart, vicomte de Puisieux, secretary of state. See *CSPV, 1623–1625*, pp. 212, 218; Burckhardt, *Richelieu and his Age*, I, p. 155.

573 Henry Rich, 1st Baron Kensington, later 1st earl of Holland.

574 George Villiers, 1st duke of Buckingham.

to impart to the parlament what hath passed hetherto in the matter of the match. Onlie the duke, to curry favour, sayd that whatsoever the k[ing] of Sp[ain] promised, it was never intended sincerlie, but was a fetch to gaine time and to worke his owne ends.[575] We shall, err [*sic for* ere] longe, see what matters will come unto because the king expecteth the parlamentes resolution within this fortnight, it is said before the twelfe of our March. The duke alsoe said that P*a*dre Maestro his comming was alsoe for noe other purpose but to win time. P*a*dre Maestro is not yett come, though he be upon the way, as a post that sett out a day after him from Madrid affirmethe, but it is not known wher he is for the present. Some suppose him to be in Paris.[576] The marquesse of Enojosa expecteth his dispatch by the waye of Flanders, and to be gone hence soe sone as newes com*m*eth that my l*or*d of Bristow is departed from Madrid, who intended to begin his journey upon the first of your March.[577] Noe more but hartie wishes

[575]For Buckingham's speech to members of parliament at Whitehall in the afternoon of 24 February 1624, see PRO, SP 14/159/72–79; Thompson, *HA*, pp. 3–4; *idem*, *RD*, pp. 5–11; ED, fos 16r–26r; *DSSD*, p. 182; Lockyer, *Buckingham*, pp. 180–181; T. Cogswell, 'The people's love: the duke of Buckingham and popularity', in T. Cogswell, R. Cust, and P. Lake (eds), *Politics, Religion and Popularity in Early Stuart Britain* (Cambridge, 2002), pp. 216–219.

[576]See *CSPV, 1623–1625*, p. 242; *CSPD, 1623–1625*, p. 169. For the dispatch in March of a royal safe conduct to Diego de Lafuente via a messenger of the chamber, see PRO, SP 78/72, fo. 60r. At Dover, Matthew Kellison, on his way out of the country, met Lafuente, who, while 'passing thorowe France nere unto Abbeville', had been 'overtaken by 6 horsmen who tooke from him all his letters and instructions. But he sayd the instructions were so favorable for Ingland that he cared not though they were printed, and the miss of them for the present he hopeth will quickly be supplyed by a dooble out of Spayn': AAW, B 26, no. 27; McClure, *LJC*, p. 552; Cogswell, *BR*, p. 198. The Flanders nuncio, Giovanni-Francesco Guido del Bagno, said the incident had taken place at Calais, and that Lafuente was stopped by four men posing as customs officials: *CGB*, I, p. 451. Sir Francis Nethersole heard that some people believed the story of the loss of his papers was a charade in order to 'avoyd the skorne of entering into any negocyation at this time of the day which the ambassadors see is too late': PRO, SP 14/161/36, fo. 56r. See also PRO, SP 14/152/13 (for Lafuente's belief that those who had taken his papers were Englishmen); PRO, PRO, 31/3/58, fo. 67v; PRO, SP 78/72, fo. 113v (for Sir Edward Herbert's note, on 1/11 April 1624, that 'it is told mee from divers that Padre Maestro was robb[e]d of his papers by such as had order afterwards to show them to this king', i.e. Louis XIII); BL, Additional MS 72255, fo. 132r. According to the earl of Kellie on 5 April, the word was that the seizure of the letters was 'bye one of his Majesties embassadours lyeing their', either Kensington or Herbert himself, and that James was incensed: *HMCMK*, p. 197. Sir Edward Conway reported on 30 March that, at a recent audience with James, 'Padre Maestro [. . .] pleaded not the losse of his papers' and 'said he had many good thinges to open, but found the estate of affaires so changed as had rendered those propositions frutelesse': PRO, SP 78/72, fo. 83r. For Lafuente's arrival, see PRO, SP 14/160/58. Del Bagno said that Lafuente's principal objective was to assure 'la securité du comte de Bristol': *CGB*, I, p. 444, 452, 456.

[577]See *CSPV, 1623–1625*, pp. 209, 211; *CSPD, 1623–1625*, p. 169.

of your health and happinesse, commendations, and dutie to all good frendes, and $M^{r}$ Nelsons[578] remembrance to you and soe farewell.

London, February 28, 1624.

Y*ou*rs ever,

Thomas More

*Addressed*: Al m*o*lto r*everend*o sig*no*re et patron mio osservan*issimo* il Sig*no*re Tomasso Rant, Inglese, agente del clero Cath[olico] Inglat*erra*.
Roma.

*Endorsed*: Written: Feb[ruary] 28.
Received: May 16.
Answered: June 4.
Received th*e* 16 of May by the French poste. Card[inal] de La Valette sente it.

## 40. William Bishop to Thomas Rant, 12 March 1624

[*AAW, A XVII, no. 104, pp. 339–340*]

Very reverend and deare sir,

I did write unto <you> the last weeke[579] how the parlement with full consent of both Houses did request the kings Ma*jes*tie to breake of[f] the match with Spaine and treaty for the Palatinate, <to> help the Hollenders and to p*re*pare his navy for the seas, to see his owne havens and other sea coasts well fenced and to looke unto Ireland.[580] His Ma*jes*tie[s] answer was very grave and like a king of greate wisdome and long experience.[581] Albeit he desireth to folow their counsell [*two words deleted*] in all important matters, yet he must see <first> how he should be able to undergo and hold warr against so great a power as was the kings [*sic*] of Spaine, lest, seeing himself to[o] weake, he might onely shewe them his tooth and not be able to bite them. It was now to be considered that the united princes of Germany were brought very lowe, that the Hollenders [were] scarse able to hold out longer without his helpe, w*hi*ch they did even now crave by their ambassadours,[582] [so] that, if warr were once begun, all his imposts

[578] John Jackson.

[579] AAW, A XVII, no. 101, pp. 327–328 (5 March 1624).

[580] See PRO, SP 14/160/33; Thompson, *HA*, pp. 21–23.

[581] For James's speech, delivered at Theobalds on 5 March and reported in parliament on 8 March, see PRO, SP 14/160/30; *CSPV, 1623–1625*, pp. 250–251; Thompson, *HA*, p. 25; *DSSD*, p. 185; *LJ*, III, pp. 246–247, 250–251.

[582] See *Letter 39*.

(w*hi*ch was the best part of his revenues) would p*re*sently decay. That he was already farr in debt to his brother of Denmark and unto others (some say to the summe of sixteen hundreth <thousand> pound[s] sterling) w*hi*ch mony he had imploi[e]d to p*re*serve the Palatinate, to furnish his daughter and her children, and about the princes journey into Spaine, all w*hi*ch they were to repay, as being imploied for the honor of England. Besides, to furnish his navy [and] to set an army a foote would cost a huge summe of money; to repaire his ports and other dangerous sea coasts and to send a garrison into Ireland would not be done [*word deleted*] with smale expences. Let them shew him how these matters might be p*ro*vided for and he would hearken to their counsell for the beginning of warr and, being once entred into it, would not make peace without their advise. They should also have the managing of the money, w*hi*ch they should collect, to se[e] it so imploied as they desired. He gave them this weeke to consider of it. But in fine, as I heare, they will not tell his Ma*jes*tie what mony they will gather, or how, before he hath broke off the mariage. But let him do that <first> and then trust to them for the rest. I do not thinke that his Ma*jes*tie will like of that answer, but will have them, as it is meet, shew him first how the warr shalbe mantained and then yeeld them his answer. Thus stands the matter at this instant. The next weeke will shew more. The lower House is highly offended against on[e] Mr Gerrard that he, being a recusant, crept into the lower House. But he hides <his> head and hath sent to the borow to cho[o]se another burghesse, saying himself to be sick. He was no converted recusant, and so the borow [was] blameles in their choise.[583] It is told me that an English ship carying fifty cast peeces out of Sussex for Flussing was mett by the Dunkerkers and led thither. They wanted

[583] Sir Thomas Gerard, MP for Liverpool, had declined to take the required oaths and had also refused to take communion: Ruigh, *1624*, pp. 89, 259–260; ED, fo. 47v. Holles's diary records that 'complaint was made against Sir Tho[mas] Gerard, chosen burgess for Lerpoole [*sic*] in Lancashire, that he had been long in town', and 'came not to the hows for he would neither swear, nor receave, beeing an obstinate recusant': Thompson, *HA*, p. 18. On 8 March, Gerard 'petitioned to be discharg[e]d, fayning sickness', a manoeuvre which got short shrift from Sir Robert Phelips and Sir Peter Hayman: *ibid.*, p. 25; ED, fos 56v–57r. On 9 March, a sergeant-at-arms was dispatched to find Gerard. Three MPs were appointed to determine whether he was a convicted recusant, and whose names were on his 'writt of election': Thompson, *HA*, pp. 27–28; ED, fos 62v–63r. On 13 March, Sir Arthur Ingram 'mooved that a bill of praemunire' should 'be drawn against' Gerard, though Sir Thomas Hoby was compelled to report 'of the search whether Sir Thomas Gerard were a convict recusant' that 'it could not be found to be so': Thompson, *HA*, p. 34; ED, fo. 81v. Six days later, it was known that he had taken refuge with the Spanish ambassador. On 3 April, MPs were still trying to proceed against Gerard: Thompson, *HA*, p. 60. Subsequently, in October 1625, Gerard was alleged to have used 'traiterous speeches', and was imprisoned in the Tower: *APC, 1625–1626*, pp. 205, 206, 239; PRO, SP 16/7/37, 69, 10, 42, 42.i–iv; PRO, SP 16/11/42.

six peeces and <would> pay honestly for them.[584] Some report that there be above twenty Jesuites fled for savegard unto the Spanish ambassadors house. The Frenc[h]e ambassad*o*r doth <shelter and> borow some of ours, wherefore you must not thinke much that wee do keepe within <with him>, albeit we must alwaies joyne with them whom o*ur* king most respecteth; w*hi*ch some now imagine to be rather the Frenc[h]e than the Spanish, at least the duke of Buckingham so doth, who can do most with the prince and his Ma*jes*tie. Wherefore feare not to send yo*ur* letters to him by the Fr[ench] amb[assador] of Rome;[585] yea, you <may> very truly and lawfully say and tell even the popes Holines that Mons*ieu*r le Count du Tilliers is a very honest and zealous <Catholike>, and favoreth recusants <and priest[s] so> [*word deleted*] <farr forth> as he may, and is very ready to assist us all.[586] I do now write to second you in that pointe of the remove, if it may be, of o*ur* comprotector Car[dinal] Melino,[587] and for o*ur* deane and chapter. I hope the vicar generall will write the next weeke to the same effect. Thus, with my very harty com*m*end[ations], I rest.

Yo*ur*s,

W*illia*m Chalcedon

12 of o*ur* March 1624.

[*on p. 340*]

*Addressed*: Au très révérend père, le Père Bertin, supérieur de S[t] Louys, pour le P[ère] Thomas. A Rome.

*Endorsed*: [*on p. 339*] Written: March 12.
Received: April 25.
[*on p. 340*] Received th*e* 25 Aprill by the bishop of Lyons[588] his servante. Yt came in the pacquett from England. M*onsieu*r de Lion does the affaires of France at Rome and is as [*sic*] ambassador.

[584]See *CSPV, 1623–1625*, p. 250; PRO, SP 14/160/70.

[585]On 16 February 1624, Sir Edward Herbert had reported that the embassy in Rome of Noël Brûlart was 'revoked' and that Philippe de Béthune, count of Sully was appointed in his stead. On 24 April, Herbert noted that Béthune had 'charge to disavow all that' Brûlart 'hath done for the accommodating of the busines of Valtelina and to hold the Spaniard to the Treaty of Madrid': PRO, SP 78/72, fos 36v, 164r; Avenel, *Lettres*, I, p. 725; for the Valtelline, see *Letter 76*.

[586]In early March 1624, Tillières described how he had recently lobbied James at Hampton Court on behalf of English Catholics: PRO, PRO 31/3/58, fo. 44v.

[587]See *Letter 31*.

[588]Denis Simon de Marquemont, archbishop of Lyons.

## 41. Arthur Pitts to Thomas Rant, 19 March 1624

[*AAW, B 26, no. 19*]

R[everend] f[ather],

I wrote unto you a note howe to co*n*vey safely your l*ettr*es to Mr Parker.[589] He since hath satisfyed your doubt. We have a parleme*n*t, violent and of the hotest, for warre, and against us. By the wisdome of our kinge all wilbe for the best. He makes them see their weeke strength in warfare so that, retourni*n*ge home to their residences [and] beinge pressed to geve reason to the hoote spurres of their humeurs [and] why they co*n*cluded not to their expectation of warre and p*er*secutions, they gevinge just reasons, all is lyke to tourne to a greater calme, and the matter of the mariage w*i*th Spayne shall appeare necessary. The kinge his M*ajes*ty gave at the begin*n*inge[590] divers reasons of peace, first that he hath and doeth desire to dye as he hath lived, w*i*th the title of the peacable kinge. Agayne that he would be loth to dye in debt to his brother of Denmarke and others, and, sith warres will bring him further in debt, those must be first payed; that his grand children have not bred but fro*m* him; that his frendes in Germany be downe the wynd and can*n*ot helpe him; that the Hollanders can*n*ot stande unlesse he p*re*sently ayde them (at w*hi*ch his speach in parleme*n*t they storme, though when the m*aste*r of the ceremonies wold have treated them as ambassadors, they sayd we come not nowe in that quality, but as humble petitioners); that subsidies and fiveteenes wilbe longe a leveinge, and for warre that he must have p*re*sent mony; that his enemies we[re] never so potent as nowe; that the cheefe revenu[e] of his estate is the impostes w*hi*ch by warre must cease. All w*hi*ch reasons notw*i*thstandinge, they p*er*sistinge to breake w*i*th Spayne, three dayes since, he sent to them in writinge that his warre can*n*ot be just but against the emperour; for his son*n*e in lawe the others medled not but as collaterals to gayne the estate of Bo[h]emia taken fro*m* him; that before he enter in warre he must trie and solicite others his confederats and fre[n]des. The parleme*n*t this daye are to advise of the meanes for mony.[591] He gave them a caveat not to charge [the]

[589] William Bishop.

[590] See *Letter 40*.

[591] For the tax debates on 19 and 20 March 1624, following James's demand on 14 March for revenue for the waging of war, see Cogswell, *BR*, pp. 203–215; Alexander, *CLT*, pp. 56–58; Thompson, *HA*, pp. 39–49; ED, fos 92v–100r; *LJ*, III, pp. 265–266; *DSSD*, p. 186. Anthony Champney commented on 31 March/10 April 1624 that MPs had, at their meeting with the king at Whitehall on 14 March, urged him to 'brake with Spayn, and offered him to that purpose their goods, lands and lives', but James replied that 'to pay his debts <first>

com*mo*ns, and my L[ord] Scroope, p*re*sident of the North, telleth them that they are so needy there that they must be relieved, and not able to paye. When they urge the goodes of the Catholickes, he scorned yt sayinge, when I am engaged in warre they will goe to church and so fayle me; and that yt will geve occasion to ruyne those of there religion abrode. Yea, the embassador of Venize[592] is sayd to have adv*er*tised o*ur* kinge to co*n*sider that the hard usage of Catholickes here wilbe distastful to their republique. Here hath byne a privat man fro*m* Bavaria[593] to offer the Palatinate to [the] palsgraves eldest son*ne* w*i*th a most advantageouse mariage, who had private co*n*ference as well and dep*ar*ted unknowen.[594] Don Francesco[595] hath byne privatly w*i*th the kinge very often,[596] wherat the duke of Buckingam stormed against the L[ord] Clinton,[597] who answered as resolutely, as one redy w*i*thout his leve to bringe in any that the kinge should cal for. Marvaile not that we write litle newes for ev*ery* day the waves be up and downe. God hath given us a kinge to keepe us as God will have us to stande, inter spem et metu*m*. Expedit eni*m*. Thus in hast, the 19 of March, by o*ur* accompt here. There were some searches in London, but no violence, nor losse, or i*m*prisoneme*nt*, I heard this day fro*m* M^r^ Parker.

*Addressed*: A mons*ieu*r, Monsieur Bertin, supérieur de S^t^ Luys. A Rome.

*Endorsed*: Written: March 19.
Received: Aprill 30.
Answered: June.
This not subscribed letter is written by M^r^ Arthur Pitts. I received yt Aprill 30 or therabouts.
Answered: June 14 or 15.

they must give him 5 subsidies and 10 feefteens, and everie yeare, whilst the warrs lasted, 2 subsidies [*sic*] and 5 feefteenes, at which demand they went their wayes, astonished and wondering': AAW, B 26, no. 27. For the subsidies demanded, see PRO, SP 14/160/89; PRO, SP 14/161/19, 30; Thompson, *HA*, p. 36; Cogswell, *BR*, p. 198; Ruigh, *1624*, pp. 210–211.

592 Alvise Valaresso.

593 Francesco della Rota. See Cogswell, *BR*, p. 133; Pursell, *WK*, pp. 208, 218; PRO, SP 77/17, fo. 1v; *CGB*, I, p. 504; BL, Additional MS 72255, fos 94v, 96v.

594 For Bavaria's diplomatic proposals, see *CSPV, 1623–1625*, pp. 154, 176, 179, 193, 198–200, 203, 204, 208, 209, 212, 215, 216, 218; PRO, PRO 31/3/57, fo. 284r; BL, Additional MS 72255, fo. 101r–v.

595 François de Carondelet.

596 See PRO, SP 14/160/15, 16; *HMCMK*, pp. 199–200; *CGB*, I, pp. 449, 452–453, 462.

597 Pitts intended to refer to Thomas Erskine, 1st earl of Kellie, rather than to Theophilus Clinton, 4th earl of Lincoln. See A. Courtney, 'Court politics and the kingship of James VI & I, c. 1615–c. 1621' (unpublished PhD thesis, University of Cambridge, 2008), pp. 240–241. I am grateful to Alexander Courtney for advice on this point.

## 42. William Bishop to Thomas Rant, 2 April 1624

[*AAW, A XVII, no. 115, pp. 365–366*]

Very rev*erend* father,

Albeit I have not <received> any of yo*u*rs of late yet, the state of *ou*r affaires beginning to alter, I would not omitt to certify you of it. Though our king do yet give faire words to the Spanish ambassadors, nevertheless the common voice goeth that he will breake with Spaine and trait with France about the mariage of the prince. Yea, they say that the Lord Hayes[598] hath already a commission granted him for that purpose[599] and that the Lord Kenchington,[600] captaine of the kings guard, is joyned in commiss[ion] with him, who hath been in France this moneth or more to sound the affection of the Fr[ench] king and his councell concerning the acceptance of that mariage. It then being so p*ro*bable that the match will fall out there, we must seeke to benefite the poore Catholikes by the help of the Frenc[h]e, as we did before by the Spaniards. Wee will write and send to sollicite the principall p*er*sons, dealers in it, that they will not do lesse for the Catholikes their neighbours than Spaine would have done if the match had holden with them.[601] You, *ou*r agent, must also supply[602] to his Holines in all *ou*r names that he will deale with the king of France, the queene mother,[603] Cardinall Richlieu, Mons*ieur*

[598]James Hay, 1st earl of Carlisle.

[599]See *HMCMK*, p. 197; PRO, PRO 31/3/58, fos 63r, 70v (Carlisle had received 'deux commissions, l'une pour une ligue, et l'autre pour le mariage').

[600]Henry Rich, 1st Baron Kensington, later 1st earl of Holland.

[601]A week before, Bishop had already reported that 'the most probable opinion is that' James would 'deale with France for his sonne', and there was 'no doubt but that he and his will do their best endevour to draw in France to assist him in warr for the Palatinate'. Bishop instructed Rant to lobby 'the cardinals our friends' to intervene with the French court to obtain as favourable conditions for Catholics in the treaty as the Spaniards had demanded. In Bishop's opinion, 'they may in deed request more favour for us than did the Spaniard in regard that they do graunt greater favours to their Hugonots than we dare demand': AAW, A XVII, no. 110, p. 355. (This was the line which the French secretary of state, Henri-Auguste de Loménie, seigneur de Villeauxclercs, eventually took over the extent of the toleration to be allowed to English Catholics as part of the Anglo-French marriage treaty: Hacket, *SR*, part I, p. 214.) Bishop believed that, before any dispensation was issued for the marriage, the papacy would demand proof that Catholics had been granted toleration. The count of Tillières, 'a most sound Catholike and a very noble and wise ambassadour, hath very well informed himself of the former conditions' offered to the Spanish court, 'and is able in particular to relate them'. If necessary, the secular clergy would 'provide most honest and sufficient gentlemen to cary them into France and <to> procure his Christian Majestie to effect them'. Bishop was concerned, however, that 'some Frenc[h]e wilbe to[o] precipitate in the busines and suffer them selves to be gulled by some of the Scottish faire promises': AAW, A XVII, no. 110, p. 355.

[602]i.e. supplicate.

[603]Marie de Médicis.

de Guise[604] and Monsieur d'Epernon[605] that they stand stoutly for our Catholikes and suffer not them selves to be deceived by faire words, but send sound Catholikes, witty and trusty men, unto our king to see all thinges promised to the Spaniards in favour of Catholikes to be performed by o*ur* king and councell before the fiances be made. We will assist them with true informations and the best directions we can devise. If p*er*formance go not before of such things that may be done, p*er*haps we shall not obtaine them afterward. For more clearnes: if o*ur* king and the lords of his counsell, if all the bishops and judges, do not bind themselves by oath to see that there shalbe no execution of any penall lawes enacted against Catholike Romans after the match made, and that there shall not <be> any other lawe made afterward against them, matters are not like to go well for us. We shall have faire p*ro*mises and litle p*er*formance. Wherefore it is not amisse to informe his Holines so much, and to request that the dispensation, w*hi*ch must be had for them as well as <it was> for the Spaniard, may stay in the nuncios[606] handes till he heare assuredly from us that that oath especially be taken and cessation of inflicting penalties be published. This much of that matter. Now to the occurrents. The duke of Buckingham caries all before him. His Ma*jes*tie favours him excedinglie and so doth the prince. At an ordinary in Milford Lane, where the greatest lords do often meet, on Saturday the 20th of o*ur* March, there were many of them. The Lord Dorsett[607] began a health to the ruine of Spaine and their folowers, w*hi*ch passed without exception. But ere that day senight his health was impaired and on Easter day, being the 28 of the same, he died.[608] At the same table the earle of Oxford[609] dranke a health to the confusion of papists; or conversion, said some. Divers others said they could not pledg[e] him, for I have many friends papists, said the Lord Scrope. <Nor I, said the e[a]rle of> Essex;[610] my mother and sister are papistes.[611] Nor I, said the earle of Northampton,[612] for my sister[613] is one. And so some others. The said earle of Oxford, on Wenesday

[604] Charles de Lorraine, duke of Guise.

[605] Jean-Louis de Nogaret de La Valette, duke of Epernon.

[606] Bernardino Spada, archbishop of Damietta.

[607] Richard Sackville, 3rd earl of Dorset.

[608] On 22 April 1624, John Jackson recounted Dorset's death to Rant and stressed that he 'was noe frend of ours': AAW, B 26, no. 40A.

[609] Henry de Vere, 18th earl of Oxford.

[610] Robert Devereux, 3rd earl of Essex.

[611] See P. Little, '"Blood and friendship": the earl of Essex's protection of the earl of Clanricarde's interests, 1641–6', *English Historical Review*, 112 (1997), pp. 927–941. Essex's mother was Frances Walsingham, countess of Essex and countess of Clanricarde, and his sister was Dorothy Sherley: *NCC*, p. 209.

[612] William Compton, 1st earl of Northampton.

[613] Margaret Compton, wife of Henry Mordaunt, 4th Baron Mordaunt.

folowing, did runne at the tilt and was cast by his horse, w*hi*ch also fell on him and broke his arme so short atwoo that ~~done~~ <some> yet say he is in danger of death. The admirall Buckingham hath been at the kings ship[s] by Rochester and is about the furnishing of them. He hath made a motion to the parlement to gather up a great summe of mony to victuall them p*re*sently, p*ro*mising to see them paid when the first subsidy shalbe paid in; w*hi*ch they take in evill p*ar*t.[614] The parlement hath p*ro*mised three subsid[i]es and three fifteenes, all to be paid within on[e] yeare, w*hi*ch wilbe a very hard matter for the poorer sort who already are not able to pay their rents.[615] Thus, with my very harty comendac*io*ns, I rest.

Yo*ur*s,

William Chalcedon

2$^{o}$ Aprilis 1624.

[*on p. 366*]

*Addressed*: Au très révérend père, le Père Bartin, supérieur de S$^{t}$ Louis. Pour le r[évérend] Père Th[omas] Rant. A Rome.

*Endorsed*: [*on p. 365*] Written: Aprill 2.
Received: May 28.
This was the last letter hee writt mee.[616]
[*on p. 366*] Received by the French poste who sent yt to S$^{t}$ Leuys th*e* 28 of May, directed in a cover to Père Bertin by the name of Père Bertram. It came nether from M$^{r}$ Lockwood[617] nor from th*e* Oratorye nor by M*onsieu*r Marchand;[618] yet it came from Paris; but I knowe not how. So, beeinge too long uppon the way, I cannot tell who to blame.

[614] See PRO, SP 14/162/4, 12.

[615] See McClure, *LJC*, p. 550; Cogswell, *BR*, p. 215.

[616] William Bishop died on 13 April 1624. For the accounts of his ministry, compiled for dispatch to Rome, see AAW, A XVII, no. 113, pp. 361–362, no. 116, pp. 367–374. John Jackson, on 22 April, observed of Bishop that 'the k[ing] and state never spake against him' and that when the lawyer and vehement anti-puritan Richard Dyott 'did in the parlement lower Howse speak of his going from place to place the last summer in Staffordshire, and confirming hundreds [...] the same man within a while after was put owt of the parlament by the rest of the same howse as one falsly elected': AAW, B 26, no. 40A; Ruigh, *1624*, p. 169; Allison, QJ, p. 141; Russell, *PEP*, pp. 153–154; History of Parliament Trust, forthcoming biography of Richard Dyott (article by Andrew Thrush).

[617] John Lockwood.

[618] See AAW, B 26, no. 11.

## 43. Nelson [John Jackson] to Thomas Rant, 16 April 1624

[*AAW, B 26, no. 34*]

Very r*everen*d and noe less revere*n*ced and beloved sir,

I was not unkinde (as yow write of M^r^ Ire[land] and mee) in being soe long silent, but I omitted or rather differred t*ha*t office upon such grounds as I held for good. For I understood t*ha*t one was by appointment to keep weekly correspondence, w*hi*ch made me the less forward, hoping he wold enforme of all p*ar*ticulers; 2^ly^, M^r^ M[ore] [?] told me himselfe did write and in one of him yow have seen my hande.[619] 3. I was owt of the towne when I shold have written if I had been here, in regard of some perticulers w*hi*ch, after my returne, I thought would be stale before they co[u]ld come unto yow. I co[u]ld alleage diverse others but it is needles to yow to whom I have ever borne soe much faithfull love and respect. This great loss[620] and cross wee have receyved will be noe less bemoaned there than with us, as I think, in regard he was soe worthy a prelate of Gods Church, at th*e* sterne wherof they sit.

Owr parliame*n*t co*n*tinueth as yet. The lawes have passed both th*e* howses.[621] Thc k[ing] promiseth there shall be noe execution of them or th*e* rest. Whether he will passe them or noe is uncertaine, thowgh it

[619] i.e. AAW, B 26, no. 10 (Thomas More to Thomas Rant, 30 January/9 February 1624, with postscript by John Jackson).

[620] i.e. the death of William Bishop.

[621] This is a reference to the 1624 parliament's draft legislation against recusants ('An Act for the Explanation of a Branch of the Statute made in the third Year of the King's Majesty's Reign, intituled, An Act for the better discovering and repressing of popish Recusants'). For its introduction, and the debates over its format, see Thompson, *HA*, pp. 24, 57, 59, 62; *LJ*, III, pp. 248, 249, 252, 278; Thompson, *RD*, pp. 5, 12–13; ED, fo. 170r. On 18/28 June, Thomas More described its contents: 'they provided to disannull all trusts that had bene formerlie used in behalf of Catholickes, laying extreame penalties upon such as did not, w[i]thin a certein time, bring in and discover the said trust, and then procured all grawntes even under the broad seale to be of noe effect, being for benefitt of recusantes, for that everyone shold be, in the tearms of former times, in their monthlie paymentes ether of xx^l^ or two partes of their lyvings. Againe they provided that the king shold take into his handes all the lands and goods of such recusantes as payd two partes and allow the sayd parties a third part out of the exchequer. Further, Catholickes wifes shold alsoe be paid for, and their children above eight years shold be taken from ther parentes and be brought up in some Protestant howses at their parentes chardges. These were some part of their lawes, and I thinke they had dyverse others because, after the former were passed, and the whole companie had supplicated against the recusantes to his Majestie and had procured him to make a bitter speache against Catholickes and to protest his hatred against them, they had xii more pointes to urge against them, but what they were I never heard.' James would not give his assent, of course, but had 'given order, as some say, for the execution of former penall lawes': AAW, B 26, no. 77.

is generally feared he will. I am told th*at* there [is] comaundme*n*t given th*at* all the prince his servants doe receyve on Sunday next. Th*e* penaltie I knowe not, unles it be the losse of his service. Yet I was also told th*at* he said to Padre Maestro, comme*n*d me to the infanta and tell her I will keep my first and last promise to her th*at* there shall be noe p*er*secutio*n*.[622] I wish there were not. But, dura*n*te parl[i]ame*n*to, there is noe hope of helpe. I was also told in secret th*at*, when the imbass*ador*s of Sp[ain][623] alleaged to owr k[ing] th*at* he had declared th*at* he wold break th*e* treaties, his Ma*jes*tie answer[e]d th*at* the howse understood not his [*word illegible*]. For I mean (said he) to break them because they are not in a right forme, and I will againe renue them in a p*er*fecter maner.[624] Yet the lo[rd] of Kensingto*n* is in France, dealing for a match there. And it is dayly expected th*at* the e[arl] of Carlile shall goe w*i*th com*m*ission.[625] I was enformed fro*m* a good hand th*at* Kensington did motion the matter to th*e* q[ueen] mother[626] who sent him to one th*at* is greatest w*i*th th*e* king. He asked th*e* baron if he had com*m*ission. He said noe other than himselfe, for being captaine of the guard he was a com*m*ission. That is noething to us (said the other) but bring a com*m*ission and wee will deall w*i*th yow. Yet I will tell yow beforehand th*at* yow must make account of 2 things. 1. th*at* o*u*r k[ing] will doe noething w*i*thout th*e* popes co*n*sent. 2^ly^, wee expect as good co*n*ditions for religio*n* as Spaine shold have had. Why, said Baro*n* Kensingto*n*, we brake w*i*th Spaine upon th*at* point. And w*i*thout th*at*, said the other, expect noe treatie w*i*th us. The lower House is very violent against Cath[olics] and wold, besides th*e* lawes, have all preists presently banished, and Catholicks also banished 10

[622]See Gardiner, *NSMT*, p. 253.

[623]Carlos Coloma and Juan Hurtado de Mendoza, marquis of Inojosa.

[624]For the anxiety caused by James's response, on 15 March 1624, to a delegation on the previous day from the Lords and the Commons, headed by Archbishop Abbot, concerning the breach of the treaties with Spain (despite Charles's and Buckingham's reinterpretation of James's words), see PRO, SP 14/160/77, 89; *DSSD*, p. 186. However, on 23 March, Abbot delivered the petition of both Houses to break the treaties with Spain, to which James assented: PRO, SP 14/161/19–30, 36; Thompson, *HA*, p. 52; ED, fos 100r–107v; *DSSD*, p. 187. On 16/26 April, Anthony Champney wrote to Thomas Rant that the king had assured the parliament that he would not now treat with Spain any further for any match, and, as for the Palatinate, he would recover it by military means, for which they must provide financially. As for the manner of waging war, however, 'when, and agaynst whome, to wit whether <agaynst> the emperour or duke of Bavier, belonged only to him and his sonn, and therefore he would have no further conference with them thereof'. The wild celebrations in London 'as if the Palatinat had bene alreadie gotten [...] did not please the king, and his dislike did as little please the parliament': AAW, B 26, no. 44.

[625]For the formal instructions issued to Carlisle and Kensington on 17 May 1624, see PRO, SP 78/72, fos 214r–220r.

[626]Marie de Médicis.

myles from London and the court.[627] Yet we hope well, and that the k[ing] will not persecute generally. The French imb[assador][628] is a zealous and worthy nobleman. His brother the count I suppose is with yow, and Monsignor de Lescale with him, to whom I praye present my respect[s] in the best maner, and also to your worthy freind Monsignor Bertine. I mean the next week to send yow the kings 2[d] speech which I did intend a fortnight since to send yow.[629] Your nephew is placed with an other by M[r] Yelverton, whom I co[u]ld never see since yow went, thowgh M[r] Ireland promised to intreat him.[630] God graunt that the deane and chapter be confirmed by his Hol[iness], which will be most needfull in persecution, if any happen, as many fear. It was instituted upon good warrant, yet, to shew our duties, his lordship[631] referred it to his Hol[iness] with humble request he wold confirme the same. I hope one shall be sent to yow shortly, eyther the b[ishop] his secretary[632] or M[r] More.[633] And soe I rest, whose hart and hand you know. 16 Apr[il]. I pray present my respect to that worthy Monsignor Vives. If yow wold have us write to any, send their names, place, stile etc. What is Signor Defendente,[634] a marchant or a cleargy man? In hast, with a 1,000 best wishes and as many intreaties of your prayers.

Nelson

*Addressed*: All molto reverendo pre[te], il Signore Thomaso Rant, agente dell clero Inglese. A Roma. S[t] Luis.

*Endorsed*: Written: Aprill 15 [*sic*] 1624.
Receaved: June 5.
Answered: June 15.

[627] See ED, fo. 113v.

[628] Tanneguy Leveneur, count of Tillières.

[629] See PRO, SP 14/161/24; Cogswell, *BR*, pp. 215–216.

[630] By a letter of 20/30 April 1624, Francis Smith informed Rant that a letter was coming to him from Richard Ireland, 'wherein he certified you of placing your nephewe by order from your sister who requested one M[r] Yelverton to end that business with the consent of M[r] Ireland. The youth likes his master well whoes [*sic*] name is Peter Windor, a taylor in Holburne and a Cath[olic]': AAW, B 26, no. 48; see also Anstr., II, p. 167; *NCC*, pp. 174, 212.

[631] William Bishop.

[632] William Harewell.

[633] Thomas More was, on 28 May 1624, appointed by the episcopal chapter to serve, jointly with Thomas Rant, as the secular clergy's agent in Rome: AAW, A XVII, no. 140, pp. 439–442.

[634] This individual was mentioned to Rant by John Jackson in a letter of 22 April 1624: AAW, B 26, no. 40A.

## 44. John Smith [Colleton] to Thomas Rant, 29 April 1624

[*AAW, B 26, no. 47*]

My very deere sir,

I wrot the last weeke unto yo*u*. The occurrantes since: upon o*ur* Saint Markes daie,[635] o*ur* king, intending to give satisfaction to the parlement men, caused them to appeare before him at Whitehall, where he gave them heartie thankes for the petition they exhibited, both for execution of the lawes against Catholike recusants as also for setting fourth a proclamation for the banishing of all priestes, religious and seculars.[636] And his Highnes granted the one and the other unto them in ample maner w*ith* invective wordes against recusants to the great content and applause of the <saide> auditorie.[637] And, according to the kinges speaches and graunt, we every daie since expected the com*m*inge foarth of the p*ro*clamation.[638] But this daye it is bruted that his Ma*jes*tie, for reasons of state, hath deferred the setting forth of the p*ro*clamatio*n* for thirtie daies or, as others will have it, for fortie. What wilbe the end, O*ur* Lord knowes. But the Catholicke partie is much dismaied, and feareth least his Ma*jes*tie also will let passe and ratifie the newe lawes made against papists w*hi*ch are above measure severe, as intitling the king to all recusants lands and goods of what cauling soever, allowing onlie the third part for there maintenance,

[635] 25 April. In fact, James's reply to the petition against recusants, to which Colleton refers, was delivered at Whitehall on 23 April: PRO, SP 14/163/34; ED, fos 159v–161v (it was reported in the Commons on 24 April). For the petition, itself dated 23 April, see PRO, SP 14/163/32, 33; Ruigh, *1624*, p. 250; McClure, *LJC*, p. 553.

[636] See *Letter 45*. For Sir Robert Phelips's motion on 1 April for a proclamation against recusants, see Thompson, *HA*, p. 57; see also *LJ*, III, pp. 287, 289–290, 291–292, 297–298, 304. For the arguments in the Commons on 6, 7, and 10 April over the formulation of the petition (the Lords and the Commons both produced a draft) concerning the enforcement of the laws against Catholics, and whether it should be done via a proclamation, see Thompson, *HA*, pp. 62, 63–65, 74; PRO, SP 14/162/9–11; see also PRO, SP 14/163/1, 2.

[637] 'Some of the wisest', wrote John Jackson to Thomas More on 22 April, 'think that this satisfaction must eyther bee to graunt but not to execute it (for wee hope there wyll be noe execution therof), or els to tell them that he is to treat with Fra[nce] for his sonne and with Venice and others for <getting> the Palatinate which he cannot doe if he persecute Catholicks; and soe, on Saterday, get the subsidie bill twice read, if it can bee, and shortly after make an end of the parl[iament]. In secret, it is said he enterteyneth yet the matter with Spa[in], and also with Bavaria, and some <wise men> think that, if ever the prince mar[r]y, it will be with Spa[in], thowgh some of France are of an other expectation': AAW, B 26, no. 40A.

[638] See *Letter 45*.

and this to be paid out of the exchecker unto them.[639] Two dayes since, a post came from Spaine and brought warrant for the ambassadours departure,[640] the marquesse, so soone as he could p*ro*vide him selfe and Don Coloma upon the arrivall of the next intended ambassadour, to witt Mendosa, the noble man that attended o*ur* prince in his returne from Spaine, who is apointed leige.[641] Pater Maestro is heere, and hath grace w*ith* o*ur* king and staieth till the com*m*ing of Mendosa, but howe long after is not spoken of. Heer is great adoe and fearefull reports. The lower House have censured foure noblem*en* as unworthie to beare office,[642] namelie the earle of Rutland, lieutenant of the sh[ir]e,[643] the earle of Worchester, lord privie seale, the earle of Northampton, p*re*sident of Wales, the Lord Croope [*sic*], p*re*sident of the Northe.[644]

[639] One week before, on 22 April 1624, Colleton had written that James was resisting the parliament's calls for the newly drawn-up legislation to receive royal assent. The Catholic 'ambassadours protest unto us that his Majestie hath promised them most constantlie that dureing his life there shalbe no more persecution'. James had said that, if the subsidies were to be granted only on condition of oppression of Catholics, he would rather refuse the money: AAW, B 26, no. 42; see also *Letter 43*. On 5 April 1624, Thomas Locke had written to Carleton that 'the recusants (and not the meanest amongst them) give out that the Spanish ambassadors were humble suitors to the king for some mitigation towards recusants, and that the king should promise it in tyme convenient': PRO, SP 14/162/16, fo. 34v.

[640] For Inojosa's departure, see *CSPV, 1623–1625*, p. 373; *CGB*, I, p. 500; and for Coloma's eventual parting, see *CSPV, 1623–1625*, p. 463; PRO, C 115/107/8487; *Letter 57*. According to Sir Balthazar Gerbier (writing much later), the customary royal gifts to the Spanish ambassadors, when they left, allowed some 'malitious tongues' to say that James still credited their accusations against Buckingham: BL, Lansdowne MS 4181, fos 40v–41r.

[641] See *CSPV, 1623–1625*, pp. 366, 377, 413. Diego de Mendoza, Gondomar's nephew, had come from Spain with Prince Charles and had arrived in October 1623, though he had left again in November: *Letter 32*; PRO, SP 14/154/38, 67; *CSPV, 1623–1625*, p. 165; McClure, *LJC*, p. 529.

[642] On 1 April 1624, Sir Edward Coke had moved that the seventh branch of the statute of 1605 (3 James I, c. 5) should be 'revyved [. . .] that no recusant, or [one] that hath a recusant to his wyfe shall beare office': Thompson, *HA*, p. 57. Two days later, Thomas Lovell, elected for Bletchingley, was proceeded against for corruption in the electoral process, and also because he was noncommunicant and his 'mother, his daughter and sunn' were recusants. On the same day it was ordered that 'all knights and burgesses should deliver in wryting the names of all thei knew that boare office in their counties and were recusants, or had wyves so, and children': *ibid.*, pp. 60, 61, see also *ibid.*, p. 83. For proceedings concerning popish and suspected office holders, see ED, fos 163r–164v, 180v–181r; PRO, SP 14/164/46, fos 76v–77r; PRO, SP 14/164/86; PRO, SP 14/165/34, fo. 66v; PRO, SP 14/165/48; TD, V, pp. 152–153; *LJ*, III, pp. 394–396.

[643] Francis Manners, 6th earl of Rutland, was lord lieutenant of Lincolnshire: *LJ*, III, 394.

[644] An undated letter from Sir Henry Constable, 1st Viscount Dunbar to John Kirton, his servant at Burton Constable, noted that the Commons committee 'fell foule upon my lord of Rutland as an absolute papiste' but 'had a query agaynst our presidente [Scrope] for favoringe papistes and not communicatinge, and labors with all violence to have him put from his place': BL, Additional MS 38856, fo. 4r. Rutland had been the only dissenter in the upper House when, at a conference between Lords and Commons on 22 March, a declaration was drawn up to be presented to James on policy towards Spain. Charles had

Count Mansfild was heare of late, had conference with his Majestie and [was] chieflie intertained by our prince. His staie was som ten or twelve daies.[645] Some think the parlement will breake up shortlie, other[s] that his Majestie will dissolve it, as he did the last. Happie for Catholickes if it so prove. M^r^ Doctor Boswell and M^r^ Thomas More <both of the chapter> were not present at the last meeting[646] and, comming since to towne, have given there voices, as you see by the scroles inclosed,[647] which you maie add to the former. We looke earnestlie for letters from you, nor have we received any this moneth or more. Fare you well.

29 of Aprill.

Yours in all,

J[ohn] Smith

*Addressed*: Admodum reverendo d[omino], D[omino] Thomae Ranto, cleri Anglicani agenti. Romam.

*Endorsed*: Written: Aprill 29.
Received: June 26 by Card[inal] de La Valette his pacquett.
Answered: Julye 1.

## 45. Richard Smith to Thomas Rant, 23 May/2 June 1624

[*AAW, B 26, no. 64*]

My very good father,

I am comen to my Cardinal Richeleu for to request him for to help us to get an other bishop in steed of our late deceased,[648] and to obtaine as

laboured to make Rutland change his mind, although Buckingham (Rutland's son-in-law) had defended him: PRO, SP 14/161/30, 36; Ruigh, *1624*, p. 228. For Scrope's occasional conformity, see J.T. Cliffe, *The Yorkshire Gentry* (London, 1969), pp. 174, 200, 202; James Howell, *Epistolae* (London, 1678), part I, section 5, p. 200. Richard Broughton wrote to Rant on 28 April 1624 about the '4 great peeres' and commented that 'all of them' were 'in good grace with our king, our best frend': AAW, B 26, no. 45.

[645] John Jackson reported on 22 April 1624 that Mansfelt, four days previously, had been to 'Tibballs to the k[ing], and came back this evening with the prince' and lodged at 'St James in the <princes quarters>, [in the] next chamber to the prince <in the same chamber which was provided for the infanta>'. Diego de Lafuente had used the opportunity of his interview with James, also at Theobalds, to tell the king 'how daungerous [Mansfelt] may prove to the kingdom': AAW, B 26, no. 40A; see also McClure, *LJC*, p. 556; *DSSD*, p. 192; PRO, SP 14/163/1, 16, 48; PRO, SP 78/72, fos 144r, 146r.

[646] See *Letter 43*.

[647] AAW, B 26, no. 46.

[648] William Bishop. John Colleton had written to Thomas Rant on 22 April 1624 that eleven of the members of the chapter had met and 'we all held it necessarie to petition to

good conditions for Catholiks in case *our* prince marie here in France as the Spaniards had obtained.[649] And he telleth me that he had, befor my coming, *pro*cured that his king had written to his embassadour[650] in Rome for to deale earnestly with his Holines for to give us an other bishop; and that he wold doe what he co[u]ld for the other. Wherfor I pray you visit the French embassador there and set him forward al you can, and if you need any more help from here whiles I am here I wil doe whatsoever lieth in me. And this I can assure you, that *our* back freinds are resolved ether to hinder or to differ [*i.e.* defer] as long as they can that we have no more bishops, and therfor we need follow this matter as hotely as we can, for if it be differred [*i.e.* deferred] it is half denied.[651] Our embassadour, my lord of Carlil, cometh hither to this courte within thes[e] twoe dayes,[652] and both the king and queene mother[653] saye they wil never agree to the mach unles they obtayne

his Hol[iness] for three bishopes at least': AAW, B 26, no. 42; see also AAW, B 26, no. 46; *Letter 44*. However, by 3 June, Colleton had changed his mind. He recommended to Rant that he should solicit the making of two bishops, one of whom should be Matthew Kellison (with the intention that he would eventually reside in the English College in Rome, and become the rector there): AAW, B 26, no. 65. On 7 September 1624, referring to his letter of 3 June and one of the same date addressed to the pope (making the same request), Colleton wrote again to Rant and noted that he had urged that the newly appointed bishops should 'staie, the one in the colledge of Rome, the other in Paris or in the colledge of Douaie, and to governe heere by there under officers till it should please God to calme the storme then violentlie blastering, or mitigate the aversion of his Majestie from the Catholick highe function'. Colleton 'did not name Rome, Paris or Douaie for the places where the bishopes' should live, and used only 'the wordes in partibus transmarinis, but the suite had been easie after his Hol[iness] had yelded to the request' and agreed that those chosen 'might make there staie the one in Rome at the colledge, the other in Paris at the Englishe residence', i.e. the Collège d'Arras, 'or in Douaie', until the time was right for them to go to England. Rant, however, had strongly disagreed, and had not presented Colleton's suit. Colleton had also suggested that the pope should appoint a vicar-general with the powers which the archpriest had enjoyed, but again Rant had vetoed the suggestion: AAW, B 26, no. 118.

[649] Smith, who had been in London, returned to France in May 1624, traversing the Channel at the same time as James Hay, 1st earl of Carlisle, and hurried to the court at Compiègne in advance of Carlisle's arrival there: Allison, RS, p. 170.

[650] Philippe de Béthune, count of Sully.

[651] William Harewell had explained to Thomas Rant in early May 1624 that 'a Catholique of speciall note and qualitie in this land' had written to the pope, immediately after William Bishop's death, to ask for 'religious men to [be] our bishops'. Harewell thought that 'if way should be given to such motions and conceipts of particular persons, and those lay people too', the effect would be to 'have the Church governed not by ecclesiasticall prelates or clergie men but by the laytie [. . .]. Withall, as one moves for one religious order, so will another move and sue for another order and a third person for a third order etc.', and the secular clergy, 'the maine pillar and the very bodie of Gods Church', would be 'cast aside'. Elections of bishops should be governed by canon law, not by 'lay mens privat plottes and projects, not aiming at bonum totius but partis, and their owne privat ends': AAW, B 26, no. 50.

[652] See *CSPV, 1623–1625*, pp. 332, 335, 339; Allison, RS, p. 170.

[653] Marie de Médicis.

as good conditions for Catholikes as Spaine hath obtayned, and I pray you request his Holines to continew the*m* in this good mynd. For otherwise Catholikes in England were undone.[654] I doubt not but befor this you have heard of the p*ro*clamation against priest[s] w*hi*ch was published in England the 8 [*sic*] of their May, and is extreme severe against the*m* and their harbourers.[655] God graunt them patience, and yet, to tell you mine [*sic*] opinion, I rather hope than feare, for the king did clearly shew that he wold never have made this p*ro*clamation if he co[u]ld otherwise have gotten the parlament to graunt him subsidies, w*hi*ch yet their clergie did without any condition at all.[656] And yet the lower House wold not even [*word omitted*] with this but endevoureth to draw the k[ing] to harder lawes against Catholikes. This much I thought to certifie you of, and if herafter there fall out any thing worth yo*ur* notice I shal not omit to let you know it.

2 of June from Compeigne.

Yo*ur*s assured,

R[ichard] Smith

The Jesuites have dealt with the marquis of S. Germain,[657] embass[ador] in England, for to oppose against bishops w*hi*ch, if he doe, you may certifie his Holines that he is no freind to the clergie,

[654]Cf. *CSPV, 1623–1625*, p. 363 (concerning Carlisle's instructions about toleration for Catholics in England).

[655]James had acceded to the demand, in the parliamentary petition of 23 April, for a royal proclamation dealing with Catholic clergy. Though John Colleton had expected, on 29 April, that it would be deferred for a month or more (*Letter 44*) and John Chamberlain claimed on 30 April that the process of securing the measure had stuck, nevertheless Secretary Conway announced in the Commons on 1 May that James had instructed the attorney-general to draw up the proclamation, which was issued on 6 May: ED, fo. 166r. The proclamation stated that, since the Catholic clergy, 'now harboured within this realme', 'by their boldnesse and insolencie', had seduced and withdrawn 'his Majesties subjects, not onely from the religion here established, but also from their obedience and allegiance to his Majestie', James had seen fit to 'charge and command' all of them to take themselves out of his dominions by 14 June 'with the first opportunitie of winde and weather [...] and never after to returne into this realme'. All other such clergy were forbidden to enter the country. The utmost severity of the law would be inflicted on any priests who disobeyed, or any who harboured them: *SRP*, I, no. 252. Alvise Valaresso observed that the proclamation 'was posted up to the sound of trumpets and drums, and a great crowd collected at the Spanish embassy as a sign of contempt for the ambassadors': *CSPV, 1623–1625*, p. 318. Thomas Locke had believed, in early April, that if the law were to be properly enforced there would soon be an exodus abroad of many papists: PRO, SP 14/162/16. But Sir Francis Nethersole thought, on 15 May, that 'the papistes [...] laugh at the proclamation agaynst their priestes, now they are sure the parliament will be ended before their day come[s]': PRO, SP 14/164/86, fo. 142v.

[656]See also Ruigh, *1624*, pp. 248–256; AAW, B 26, no. 71; *Letter 46*.

[657]Juan Hurtado de Mendoza, marquis of Inojosa.

and that he most shamfully reviled our good bishop when he first came to visit him,[658] but that he shold rather give eare to the other embassadors. The Benedictins offer to doe whatsoever they can to p*ro*cure an other bishop, and so doth Fa[ther] Archangel.[659] Agayne, my good father, farewel, in great haste. And I praye you com*m*end me to F[ather] Bertin.

*Addressed*: Au révérend père, D. Thomas Rant, prestre del Oratoir en S. Luis. A Rome.

*Endorsed*: Written: June 2.
Received: June 24.

## 46. John Smith [Colleton] to Thomas Rant, 30 May 1624

[*AAW, B 26, no. 63*]

Right worthie sir,

Yesterdaie, being the 29 of o*u*r Maie, the parlement broke up and is adjourned [?] till the second of Nove*m*ber. His Ma*jes*tie refused to co*n*firme any of the bills or <newe lawes> that were made against recusants, w*hi*ch were many and, beyond belief, severe.[660] What will become of the p*ro*clamation is yet uncertaine. Som hope that before the expiration of the dayes apointed there wilbe published a kind of mitigation or revocation; others thinke that nothing wilbe don, but it shall stand stand [*sic*] still in full force.[661] Our king, talking of late w*ith* the Franche ambassadour,[662] told him that the p*re*sent pope was a marvailous good prelate, wise, myld and judicious, w*ith* other large wordes in his Hol[iness's] com*m*endation. I writ thes[e] by Douaie [*word illegible*] desier to adv*er*tise yo*u* w*ith* the [*word illegible*] of the good newse. On Fridaie I writ by the usuall waie, the Franche ambassadour. I have yo*u*rs of the 12 of yo*u*r Maie, and shall send answere to the pointes thereof, God willing, on Fridaie as I have said. We shall nowe expect weeklie to heare of the former letters addressed upon o*u*r bishopes death. The chapter not co*n*firmed here is no jurisdiction or

[658] In late 1623, Alvise Valaresso had reported that William Bishop's appointment of his officials had provoked the anger of the privy council, but Inojosa intervened and 'himself reproved the bishop': *CSPV, 1623–1625*, p. 165.

[659] William (Archangel) Barlow.

[660] See PRO, SP 14/165/61, fos 141v–143v; ED, fos 204r–207r; PRO, SP 14/167/10; *LJ*, III, p. 424.

[661] See *Letter 45*.

[662] Tanneguy Leveneur, count of Tillières.

superioritie at all: a want that must be supplied *with* speede unlesse havock of discipline be unregarded.

May the 30.

Jo[hn] Smith

*Addressed*: To Mr Thomas Rant, at Rome.

*Endorsed*: Written: May 30.
Received: August 4.
Answered: August 10.

## 47. John Smith [Colleton] to Thomas Rant, 18 June 1624 (with postscript of 25 June 1624)

[*AAW, B 26, no. 68*]

Very deere sir,

It is [a] for[t]night since I wrot,[663] and the cause of my silence was the uncertentie howe things would end. In my last, I advertised that his Ma*jes*tie refused to co*n*firme any of the lawes w*hi*ch the parlement had agreed on against Catholikes. And, where as it was hoped that his Highnes would have reversed or suspended the proclemation for the banishing of priests, the event proved quite co*n*trarie. For, the daie befor the expiration of the time assigned for priests to depart the land, his Ma*jes*tie cauled all the judges before him and straitlie com*m*aunded them to execute *with* rigour all the <old> lawes made against recusantes.[664] This he did on Sundaie last, the 13 of this moneth, and the 14 was the last of the daies w*hi*ch were allowed to priests to prepare themselves. I thinke some eight or neene [*i.e.* nine] seculer and religious accepted of the banishment. On Thursdaie following, the 17 of this p*re*sent, old Father Davis[665] was seased on by the co*n*stable[s] and caried by two porters before the recorder of London.[666] I saie caried by two porters because he could not goe, being above fourescore and almost blind. The recorder com*m*itted him to Newegate, where he lies. On the same daie the Franche ambassadors chaplaine,[667] going in the streetes upon busines, a cu*m*panie of the vulgar cried out and said here is a

[663] AAW, B 26, no. 65 (3 June 1624).

[664] As the count of Tillières noted, this excluded 'celle qui regarde la vie': PRO, PRO 31/3/59, fo. 139v.

[665] William Davies. See *Letter 49*; CRS, 68, p. 171; Anstr., II, pp. 82–83.

[666] Sir Heneage Finch.

[667] It is not clear which individual is referred to here. John Varder was serving as the count of Tillières's English chaplain (*Letter 35*) and, on 22 June 1624, at the insistence of

priest, a Jesuit, and staied him till he told them that he was a Franche man, and no subject of the kings. You see by thes[e] two particulers howe furious the multitude stand, and what extremitie is like to followe.

The king sendeth sixe thowsand men to support the Hollanders.[668] The aerle [*sic*] of Oxford, Southampton, *with* fower more, are coronels, and a Scottishe noble man[669] generall, *which* discont[ent]eth the mightie.[670]

The duke of Buckingham is well recove[re]d and is nowe at courte in no lesse favour both *with* the prince and his father than heretofore.[671]

It is nowe more than <9 neene [*sic*]> weekes since I advertised the death of our bishoppe,[672] and howe destitute we were left of jurisdiction and authoritie. We expect your letters dailie in that point, and shall not a litle marvell if we receive none shortlie from you, our distresses considered. I was tolde this very after noone that the bishoppe of Canterburie,[673] being sued unto by pursivants for making them warrants, answered that they could have none. Good newes, if true, for Catholickes, nowe marvelouslie afraid, would quicklie take heart of grace [?] if pursivantes were suppressed and not againe admitted to ~~authoritie~~ search and ransacke. [*In margin:* The informant[s] are above beliefe busie. There are mo[re] than 250 writ[t]es gone out [?] alreadie.] My next will informe you the certentie. Doctour Richard Smith hath left us and is in Paris *with* his old lord the cardinall.[674] He said before his going he would staie but sixe weekes at most, but I thinke he will not make good that word.

Our Lord be your guid[e] in the businesses. Fare you well.

Yours,

Jo[hn] Smith

18 of June 1624.

Tillières, he received a warrant guaranteeing him freedom from molestation, despite the recent proclamation: PRO, SP 14/168/22.

668 See Alexander, *CLT*, p. 58; Ruigh, *1624*, p. 249; Adams, FP, p. 170; *idem*, PC, p. 349; PRO, SP 78/72, fo. 83v; PRO, SP 94/30, fo. 274r; PRO, SP 94/31, fo. 71v.

669 William Douglas, 7th earl of Morton. See McClure, *LJC*, p. 562; *CSPV, 1623–1625*, p. 333; *HMCMK*, p. 202.

670 For the appointment of regimental officers, see McClure, *LJC*, pp. 562, 565; PRO, SP 14/164/92; PRO, SP 14/165/12; Adams, PC, p. 349; and, for the disputes over precedence among those appointed to lead the new force, see Cogswell, *BR*, pp. 276–277.

671 See PRO, SP 14/168/17, 48.

672 William Bishop.

673 George Abbot.

674 Cardinal Richelieu. For Richard Smith's recent journey to Paris, see *Letter 45*; and for his patronage relationship with Richelieu, see Allison, RS, esp. pp. 168–169; Questier, *C&C*, pp. 212, 378–379, 418, 420, 421, 423, 425.

This letter should have gone the last weeke, but my ill chanch[e] hindered it. The pursevantes have yet no warrants and it is thought they shall have none in respect of the p*re*sent treaty w*ith* France for a matche w*hi*ch wilbe, as most thinke, co*n*cluded eare long, yea very shortlie. The <leiger> ambassadour[675] of France is cauled home by his king very sodenlie and beginneth his journey in post for France tomorowe next.[676] Thes[e] five weekes we have had no letter from yo*u*, w*hi*ch astonisheth and driveth us to feare false dealing some where. Fare yo*u* well, and God blesse yo*ur* doings. June 25. Freindes do all well.

*Addressed*: Admodum r*everen*do patri, D[omino] Thomae Ranto cleri Anglicani agenti.
Romam.

*Endorsed*: Written: June 25.
Received: August 7.
Ans[wered]: Aug[ust] 10.

## 48. John Lockwood to Thomas Rant, 24 June/4 July 1624

[*AAW, B 26, no. 79*]

Rev*eren*d [sir],

I receved yours dated the 4 of June, w*ith* th*e* others inclosed <by Mo*ns*[ieur] Granett>,[677] all w*hi*ch I delivered unto Mr Do*cto*r Champenie who is yett heere w*it*h us in Arras College. They are sent to Doway, and soe for England. The trouble co*n*cerning our college is now before the nu*n*tio[678] heere, who hath imbraced this businesse and is in hoope too mak[e] a good therof [*sic*]. Bothe

[675] Tanneguy Leveneur, count of Tillières. Colleton, recorded Anthony Champney, had 'taken his lodgeinge' in Tillières's residence. Tillières's 'family' temporarily remained there following his departure: AAW, B 26, no. 89.

[676] See *CSPV, 1623–1625*, p. 373; McClure, *LJC*, p. 568. Champney in Paris remarked to Thomas Rant, in a letter of 8/18 July 1624, that 'the count de Tillers is come hither discontented', and the marquis of Effiat went 'in his place, by whose meanes I knowe not, but for our hurt doubtless'. Tillières had informed Champney of the arrest of the priest William Davies on the day before he (Tillières) left the country: AAW, B 26, no. 89; *Letter 49*. For Amerigo Salvetti's surprise at Tillières's recall, see PRO, C 115/107/8486. Dudley Carleton believed that Tillières was 'suddainly revoked for haveing' used 'certaine punctillious language here' about the marriage, 'for which he had no order nor instruction': PRO, SP 14/168/48, fos 67v–68r.

[677] John Lockwood described Granett as 'the banquier of St Benets cloister': AAW, B 26, no. 11.

[678] Bernardino Spada, archbishop of Damietta.

Mr Doctor Champenie and Mr Doctor Reinard ar sworne too stand too his definitive sentence.[679] They have 2 howers appoynted them every day to have ther cause harde before him, which is 7 a clock in the morning and one in the afternoone. Soe sowne as it shall bee ended yow shall understand therof. Ther came to us some 15 days agoe <thos> 4 schollars which were expulsed the English College with yow. They sta[y]ed 2 or 3 days to refresh them selves, and soe were sent for Doway.[680] Doctor Smith hath bene some moneth['s] space att Compien with his cardinal[681] to help all he can to procure by his cardinals meanes, who is one and the cheife (as I heare) of the commissioners appoynted for the intreatie of the macth [*sic*] of England, some good conditions for the Catholiques of England. It is geven fourth that France will stand very resolutly for the good of the Catholiques of England, and that itt is alredie granted that the daughter of France shall have her chappell as large and amplie furnished with clergie men as the infanta of Spayne should have had.[682] My Lor[d] Kinsinton is gone for England to have (as they say) a more ample commission to intreat of the macth [*sic*] heere.[683] This mach is fered will prove a combynation agaynst Spayne (although itt is thought ther will bee no service this yeare), yett notwithstanding the k[ing] of France hath sent for 6 or 7 thowsand Switzers to fortifie his frounter [*sic*] townes in the meane tyme, both towardes Savoy, Lauraine and Picardie. The newes is here that ther shall bee sent 2,500 men into Irland to strenthen that island,[684] and that for the space of 2 days the drumme strok[e] upp to levvye 6,000 men for Holland, but, att the end of thes[e] 2 days, word came to London that the Hollanders in the Indies had hunge upp a dozen of our men, wherupon the drumme was laide downe,

679On 20/30 August 1624, John Lockwood wrote to Thomas Rant, from Paris, that the nuncio had been dealing with the Collège d'Arras for over a month. However, he had left them in the state in which he found them, so that William Rayner 'stayeth still emongst us, wherfore the two younge men that came hether frome Doway this last winter to perfecte ther studies here were redie to be gonne agayne rather than to live in companie with him [...] seing that his impatient course (if itt did continew still as itt did before) would bee noe small hinderance to ther intended course': AAW, B 26, no. 115. For the problems which had been caused in the college by Rayner (Richard Smith's cousin), see *NAGB*, pp. 178, 180–181, 231, 232; *Letters 59, 68*; Questier, *C&C*, p. 401.

680For the arrival at Douai of John Faulkner, Anthony Shelley, and Richard Perkins (on 15/25 June 1624), and Francis Harris (on 6/16 July), see CRS, 10, pp. 229, 230. See also AAW, B 26, no. 91 (Anthony Shelley to Thomas Rant, 13/23 July 1624).

681Cardinal Richelieu.

682For the arrangements which had been made for the infanta's chapel, see above, pp. 46–47.

683See *CSPV, 1623–1625*, p. 373; *Letter 43*.

684Cf. AAW, B 26, no. 85, where Colleton repeated, in his letter to Rant of 16 July 1624, a rumour that 6,000 troops would be sent to Ireland; see also *CSPV, 1623–1625*, pp. 291, 302, 333.

and what this soddayne newes will breede we can not yett tell.[685] We heere that the proclamation for the banishing of all Jesu[i]stes out of England was to tak[e] effect the 14 of June.[686] It is reported that the prince of England ~~hath~~ is much averted from Spayne and that he will be revenged of them. Oould [*sic*] Dr Roger Smith[687] is deed of late. I herd frome Mr Irland of late. He is well and I think that wee shall have him here agayne, if so be wee could gett this Do*cto*r Reynard gone. Thus recom*men*ding too your good prayers in that holy place, I remayne.

Yours always,

Jo[hn] Lo[ckwood]

Paris 4 of July.

*Addressed*: Au rév*éren*d p[ère], Père Thomas Rante. A Rome.

*Endorsed*: Written: Julye 4.
Received: Julye 21.
Answered: [*sic*].

## 49. Richard Smith to Thomas Rant, 22 July/1 August 1624

[*AAW, A XVIII, no. 35, pp. 269–270*]

Very reveren[d] father,

I have *you*rs of the 2 of Julie, w*hi*ch though I answered [it] briefly by Mr More who dep*ar*ted hence towards you ten dayes agoe,[688] yet, becaus[e] this wil come to y*ou*r hands more spedily, I wil answere it agayne. As for b[ishops], if the asking of manie wold be any delay of the matter,

[685] For the Amboyna massacre, which briefly delayed the signing of the treaty with the Dutch, see Cogswell, *BR*, pp. 274, 275; *Letter 75*.

[686] See *Letter 47*. On 15/25 June 1624, Kellison had written to Rant that James had finally taken 'courage and refused to give way to the exequution of lawes against Catholikes and now Catholikes are again as free as ever and in as great troupes flocke publiquelie to the ambassadors howses': AAW, B 26, no. 75. Thomas Locke had sulked to Carleton on 16 June 1624 that 'the Jesuits make no great hast to be gone, though their tyme be out', and that they intended to rely on royal favour: PRO, SP 14/167/70, fo. 109r. Thomas More thought that very few priests had seen fit to obey the proclamation which ordered them into exile: AAW, B 26, no. 77. On 15/25 June, in Paris, Anthony Champney commented that, although the proclamation had been 'fixed upon the Spanishe embassatoures dore', nevertheless Richard Smith had reported that the new French ambassador, the marquis of Effiat, had written to Louis XIII to prevent the execution of the proclamation: AAW, B 26, no. 74.

[687] See *NAGB*, p. 180.

[688] See *CGB*, I, p. 498.

I co[u]ld wish you insisted but upon one, for in time he wil obtayne more. And of the same opinion was Conde Tillier in England that now we were to ask but one. This good conde is called out of England and albeit M^r Colleton and others have written to the k[ing and] q[ueen] m[other] and to others, and I have done al I can, yet I feare he wil not be sent back.[689] The new French embass[ador][690] there hath written hither that *ou*r king hath granted to [*sic*] all that the French demanded, excepting the English Catholiks going to the princesse['s] chapel, w*hi*ch yet he wil not forbid. And in substance the same points are granted to the French for Cath[olics] w*hi*ch were granted to the Spaniards, but not in that forme and maner.[691] My L[ord] Kensinton is not yet returned w[i]th thos[e] articles, w*hi*ch maketh manie here to muse. This day or to morowe [*MS torn*] is looked from England. If the ladie[692] goe to England I think she sha[ll] have divers of y*ou*r congregation.[693] My card[inal][694] promised me to write [*MS torn:* to Cardinal de La] Valette[695] in favour of b*isho*ps, but he is now out of the towne so that I a[m] [*MS torn:* not (?)] sure that he wil remember it this poste, but as soone as I see him I [*MS torn:* shall] get a letter of him. I dare not ask a letter from the k[ing] lest it might be [*MS torn:* thought (?)] offensive to the k[ing] of England.

In any case, demand of his Holines a copie of such informations as wil be given against such as are named for b*isho*ps, w*hi*ch M^r Benet[696] did and obtained, and therby th[e] informers tooke out their informations, confessing that they had bene falsly informed.

[689] For Tillières's recall and departure, see *Letter 47*.

[690] Antoine Coiffier de Ruzé, marquis of Effiat. For his arrival, see PRO, SP 14/169/2, 14; McClure, *LJC*, p. 568; PRO, PRO 31/3/59, fos 157r–158r. Amerigo Salvetti commented that Effiat was 'unexperienced both of countrie and affaire[s]', though, by the second week of July 1624, Salvetti was calling him a 'brave Frenchman': PRO, C 115/107/8486, 8487.

[691] On 13/23 July 1624, Richard Smith had announced that 'the summe for Catholiks is that they shal not be persecuted for practise of their religion in privat'. Buckingham would not agree to more 'lest he shold offend the puritans, of whome he hath made him self head. But if Catholiks carie them selv[e]s moderatly, more in time wilbe graunted': AAW, B 26, no. 90. On 10/20 August, Smith observed that Richelieu 'laboureth al he can to get good conditions for us and hopeth to obtaine' them. The minister La Vieuville had been 'put downe [...] cheefly for having so litle care of the Catholiks of England when he delt for the mach': AAW, B 26, no. 106; see also AAW, B 26, nos 102, 104; Avenel, *Lettres*, II, pp. 20–26; *CSPV, 1623–1625*, p. 443. Carlisle noted how, as a result, 'those who have now the sole managing of the busines will labour all they can' to improve 'the conditions of the treaty to the advantage of this state and Rome': PRO, SP 78/73, fo. 1r–v. See also above, p. 90.

[692] Henrietta Maria.

[693] i.e. the Oratory.

[694] Cardinal Richelieu.

[695] Cardinal Louis Nogaret de La Valette.

[696] John Bennett.

Otherwise by their secret informations they wil stayne any mans credit. A good old priest called Mr N Davis, almost 80 yeares old and almost blind and deafe through age and labors in Gods vinyard, was co*n*demned lately at Newgate, but not executed.[697] Much terror there is, but hope that it is but for a time to content puritans. Six thousand men [a]re to goe to Holland under my L[ords] Southampton, Oxford, Essex and Willougbie.[698] And the prince wil not let my L[ord] Vaux returne to his charge.[699]

Here some give out that o*ur* b[ishop][700] in England was like to have bene [the] cause of a great schisme. But I know that he was [the] cause of greate unitie. For, first, al the laitie were united in him, glad of him, and divers wept for his death, and [*word obliterated*] remitted their temporal debates to his judgment. 2. Al the preists were glad of him, and had now no grudge at the Jes[uits] for hindering the*m* from their natural sup*er*ior. 3. Al the Benedictins joyned hands with him and drew articles [*word obliterated:* for (?)] to avoid al dissentions, and the like was expected of the other religious.[701] 4. The sup*er*ior of the Jes[uits] came to o*ur* b[ishop] w*hich* before they wold not doe,[702] and some of the*m* honorably used him in their houses, and others preached of the

[697] William Davies was reprieved on the way to Tyburn where, according to John Colleton, 'about a 1,000 people went [. . .] to expect his execution': AAW, B 26, no. 95. Alvise Valaresso claimed that the count of Tillières's intervention (as well as 'the king's good disposition') secured Davies's reprieve, although Tillières was on the verge of leaving the country: *CSPV, 1623–1625*, p. 384; see also PRO, SP 14/168/59, 60, 64. Anthony Shelley narrated, on 13/23 July 1624, that 'the holy man was exceeding sorry, and weppe [*sic*] bitterly' at his reprieve, 'sayinge that this was the second time thay had served him soe; for hee had been condemn[e]d once for the same reason, longe before, and delivered. Hee sayd it was his onworthynes whoe did not deserve soe glorius a crowne, and with his constancy and good example did aedify the people exceedingly. When hee was condemned ther was on[e] only man in the roome that cryed God save the kinge, which shoed but litle content that the people tooke at his condemnation': AAW, B 26, no. 91. Sir Francis Nethersole commented, however, that the reprieve of a 'Jesuiste' would 'encourage his fellowes to stay here still and to bring backe those that run away for feare of the proclamation': PRO, SP 14/169/14, fo. 19r. For Davies's own account of the proceedings against him in 1624 (written for Propaganda Fide and attested by two Catholics imprisoned in Newgate), see PRO, 31/9/90, pp. 145–147; for John Colleton's account, see *ibid.*, pp. 157–158.

[698] See *CSPV, 1623–1625*, pp. 333, 353; McClure, *LJC*, p. 567; *Letters 47, 48*.

[699] See *CSPV, 1623–1625*, p. 363; PRO, SP 14/168/40. On 2/12 July 1624, William Trumbull recorded that news had arrived in Brussels of 'Lord Vaux his resolution to staye in England, and not to returne any more to the commande of his English regiment'; and the infanta, on the advice of Inojosa, Coloma, and van Male, had 'given the command of that regiment to Sir Edward Parham': PRO, SP 77/17, fos 231r, 238r. Subsequent missives from Trumbull noted that the English and Scottish forces commanded by Parham and the earl of Argyll were in decline: *ibid.*, fos 353r, 411v–412r, 438r.

[700] William Bishop.

[701] See *Letter 35*.

[702] See *ibid.*

necessitie and com*mo*ditie of a b[ishop] and appointed their people to pray for him. And more was hoped for. Nether can any name any word or deed of o*ur* bishop w*hi*ch was like to cause schisme in England. Thes[e] effects I know did rise of having a b[ishop]. Here is also said that preists in England goe from house to house desiring [*word obliterated:* them] to put away Jes[uits] as enemies to the state, but I doubt not but that is a slan[der]. F[ather] Archangel[703] is not in towne, but as soone as he cometh I wil get him to write to the popes brother.[704]

After I had written thus far, I receaved a letter from M$^{r}$ Ed[ward] Benet of the 7 of their Julie, wherin he saieth that they have no news, w*hi*ch signifieth that p*er*secution is ceased.[705] And that Don Carlos Colombe[706] hath written a marvelous good letter for the clergie to Card[inal] Melino.[707] Trie if he wil shew it to you. I pray you do my

[703] William (Archangel) Barlow.

[704] Cardinal Antonio Barberini, a Capuchin, and brother of Pope Urban VIII. See Allison, RS, pp. 182, 183; *NCC*, p. 107; *Letter 54*.

[705] On 20 June 1624, John Colleton had written to Rant that 'two thousand writ[t]es are alreadie gone out, procured by the promoters, which swarme'; and writs 'ad melius inquirendum' were dispatched 'to sease on the two partes of the landes of Catholikes, to the kings use, and spoile them of all there goods. And thes[e] writs goe within thes[e] two daies into all the shires of the realme, unlesse staie happen to be made by the mediation of the Frenche ambassadour, where of there appeares litle hope': AAW, B 26, no. 72; see also McClure, *LJC*, p. 568; AAW, B 26, no. 83 (Colleton to Rant, 13 July 1624, reporting that the exchequer writs were still 'in readinesse' and emphasizing how severe the judges had been, on their circuits, towards recusants). From Paris, however, on 22 July/1 August, the earl of Carlisle expressed surprise that 'the state of the recusants in England hath been (by some bodie's letters from thence) represented heer under a bitter persecution'. He thought it 'strange' that such claims should even be credible 'while we are in parlie with France': PRO, SP 78/72, fo. 361v. On the same day, he had secured an audience with Louis XIII. Louis had, despite Carlisle's denials, and evidently somewhat tongue in cheek, showed concern at the news of the 'great persecution against the Catholiques in England', and claimed that it was an affront to his honour, especially since the Spanish match negotiations had seen far greater, even if temporary, lenience extended to James's Catholic subjects: PRO, SP 78/72, fos 365v–366r. Carlisle alleged that, even if such rumours were true, James was trying to ensure that any dispensation from statute law against Catholics did not appear to be the result of French pressure, though Louis lamented the internal political disruption caused in France by the rumours of persecution in England: *ibid.*, fo. 366r–v. On 10/20 August, Richard Smith noted that, although by 'the 2 of August, the persecution was not ceased in England', in spite of the king's instructions, 'by this time it is hoped that it is ceased, for bothe the k[ing] and my card[inal] have written effectually to the French embass[ador] there, and he useth diligence therin': AAW, B 26, no. 106.

[706] Carlos Coloma.

[707] On 16 July 1624, John Jackson had reported that Coloma 'liveth solitary; he goeth to none, nor none goe to him'. Also, 'his chappel was robbed 4 or 5 dayes since, but not above x$^{li}$ worth taken. The custodia [*i.e.* tabernacle] was turned upside downe but not opened, which I think was a speciall providence of Our Lord, who was within the same. A silver lamp and other things [were] taken': AAW, B 26, no. 84.

dutie to my good l[ord] of Armach[708] and my kind com*m*endations to F[ather] Berti[n]. Thus with my hartiest to y*ou*r self, I alwaies rest.

Y*ou*rs most assured,

R[ichard] Smith

1 Augusti.

*Addressed*: For M^r^ Rant.

*Endorsed*: Written: August 1.
Received: August 19.
Answered: August 26.

## 50. John Nelson [Jackson] to Thomas Rant, 4 August 1624

[*AAW, B 26, no. 98*]

My reverend good sir,

I have receyved 2 l*ett*res fro*m* yo*w*, as I hope yo*w* have done from me, thowgh [you] me*n*tion but one. I did also write a 3^d^, wherin I had taken exact paynes to enforme yo*w* of many private and speciall points, but finding the same a fortnight after at th*e* Fr[ench] imb[assador's] I did, after a second addition therunto, upo*n* fear of miscariage, tear all. Neyther was my mynde at rest till it was torne, thowgh to this howre I co[u]ld have wished it in yo*u*r hands, and wold have been at th*e* charge of sending w*i*th probable safety. The last newes is th*a*t a speciall post is come fro*m* owr imb[assador][709] in France who, they say, writes th*a*t his Hol[iness] hath willed th*e* k[ing] of Fr[ance] th*a*t he be not hastie in th*a*t match because he cannot as yet receyve any full satisfaction of the breach w*i*th Spayne. Since the k[ing] began his progress he was ill and purged both wayes and, in the fit, I hear, said he died a Romane Cath[olic]. I co[u]ld make [*sic*] lawgh hartely if I durst, thowgh verely the tymes shold rather make me sory. At th*e* last sessio*ns* 2 were comitted to Newg[ate], who refused the oath. At th*e* sessio*ns* before, old Fa[ther] Davise, a sec[ular] pr[iest], [was] co*n*demned, as yow have heard.[710] At th*e* assizes at York 2 gentlewoeme*n* [were] co*n*demned to die for helping a pr[iest] to escape[711] and, upon

[708] Peter Lombard, archbishop of Armagh.

[709] James Hay, 1st earl of Carlisle.

[710] See *Letters 47, 49*.

[711] Ursula and Jane Tankard, of Brampton, Kirkby Ravensworth, co. York, were granted a pardon for harbouring the priest Basil Norton (who was supposed to have gone into exile

it, one of the judges (Denham)[712] fell sick. The other went th*e* rest of th*e* circuite aloan. Judge Cha*m*berlane[713] in Berkshire, at Redding as I take it, chalenged one th*at* he was a papist. He denyed it, saing I goe to church. Th*at* shall not serve, q*uo*th th*e* judge, and made him in his sight receyve the comunio*n*, [and] after th*at* tendred him both th*e* oaths, w*hi*ch fear made him take. All this serv*e*d not. He caus*e*d him to swear th*at* fro*m* his hart he held th*e* rel[igion] of Ing[land] right etc*etera*. This partie, going homeward, fell fro*m* his horse and brake his arme in 3 parts, and now is eyther dead or at th*e* mercy of God. Inditeme*n*ts and presentme*n*ts were never soe many. Comissio*n*s are gone owt and, thowgh it was bruited th*at* there was a stay comaunded, yet I hear it prooves otherwise. Informers are very buisie in vexing Cath[olics]. The spite of the people [was] never soe great, noe not in Q[ueen] Eliz[abeth's] tyme. As Catholicks goe along th*e* streets they crye owt, a papist, a papist, and use other reproaches and molestatio*ns* against the*m*. Gee th*e* minister (I suppose yow know by report who he is, as well as he hath set yow in print),[714] this Gee espied one M$^{r}$ Coale[715] 2 dayes since th*e* 2$^{d}$ of Aug[ust] in Holburne, and presently cryed out a Masspreist, w*hi*ch was enough to rayse th*e* street, and they hayled him before my lo[rd] ma*yor*[716] who te*n*dred him th*e* oath of sup*r*[emacy] and, upo*n* refusall, comitted him to Newg[ate].[717] He had but 12$^{d}$ in his purse whe*n* they tooke him. Many of those who*m* th*e* Jes[uits] gave up as co*n*verted by them are fallen back. There arived, 4 or 5 dayes

in July 1618): Anstr., II, p. 233; CRS, 68, p. 172; PRO, C 231/4, fo. 174r; *APC, 1618–1619*, pp. 202–203; J.C.H. Aveling, *Northern Catholics* (London, 1966), p. 246; see also AAW, B 26, nos 96, 121, 132. The pardon was drawn up for them in late December 1624 as part of the package of toleration measures agreed with the French: PRO, SP 14/177/22.

712 Sir John Denham, a baron of the exchequer.

713 Sir Thomas Chamberlain, a justice of the king's bench.

714 For John Gee, see Harmsen, *John Gee's Foot out of the Snare*. On 20 June 1624, John Colleton instructed Thomas Rant that he should personally write out petitions and memoranda directed to curial officials in Rome, and sign them on behalf of the leading secular clergy in England, because, 'if we sholde pen them here, they maie miscarie, as others that our bishope wrot have done, as now is apparant to the world in Gee his newe booke [i.e. *New Shreds of the Old Snare*], where in the copies of diverse letters are set downe'. Colleton was referring primarily to a letter from William Bishop's vicars-general to Pierre de Bérulle concerning Rant's appointment as the agent of the secular clergy in Rome: AAW, B 26, no. 72; Gee, *New Shreds of the Old Snare*, pp. 51–52; *Letter 30*.

715 Thomas Cole. See Anstr., II, p. 68.

716 Sir Martin Lumley.

717 On Gee's own account, in his Paul's Cross sermon of 31 October 1624, 'not above three moneths since, when I passed along the open street in this citie [. . .] I was set upon by one of that Jesuitical brood, well knowne to mee', with 'a stilletto'. But Gee 'evaded' Cole's (alleged) attack, 'and for his commitment, I had the ayd of the justice of this honourable citie, by the authoritie of [. . .] the lord maior': John Gee, *Hold Fast* (London, 1624), p. 51.

since, one M^r Mors[e][718] from R[ome] who desired to speak with me, and at our first meeting I asked whether he were in the sturrs.[719] He presently told me he was for the Jes[uits] and began to defend them and accuse the schollers. I grew a litle warme therat, having by good chance seen some of your relations. A freind of the Jes[uits] gave owt that I had animated them by lettres. Informe us of the Jesuitrisses and take heed they prevaile not to the overthrow of the cleargy. They got of late from a gentlewoman 2 of her daughters by mear importunitie. What a disgrace (said they) will it be to us if it be knowne that wee can not prevaile with yow, etcetera. She, because she wold not discontent them, against her mynde suffers them to have 2 litle daughters. They report strange things of their being sent for to Naples and entertayned with procession etcetera. The Jesuits freinds give owt that we shall not obtayne b[ishops]. There is a block layed in the way, thowgh all others say that, the sooner it is graunted, the less will be the exception, being the continuing of the succession and of what was formerly done. Sir Tobie Mathew gives owt that the ladie of France[720] is to come to R. agaynst Christmas next and that the k[ing] and q[ueen] accompeny her to Massils.[721] I did write to Doctor Smith and desired him to enforme yow of all. The Fr[ench] imb[assador][722] here said to Mayerne[723] the phisition, as they were sitting downe to the table, that he browght noe Jes[uit] because they medle in state, nor sec[ular] pr[iest] for they wold eyther be drunk in tavernes or lye at the brothel howses, but [only] that good Capucin[724] who then said grace. These be calumnious against all the clergy of Christendome, but that of France especially, who only were in election. They were soe much the more injuriouse because he was a Hugonote to whom they were spoken, and, at that

[718] Henry Morse, who had left the English College in Rome on 9/19 June 1624. He entered the Society of Jesus in 1625: CRS, 37, p. 190; CRS, 75, p. 139.

[719] i.e. the recent disputes in the English College in Rome.

[720] Henrietta Maria.

[721] A reference, perhaps, to Marseille-en-Beauvaisis, east of Rouen.

[722] Antoine Coiffier de Ruzé, marquis of Effiat.

[723] Sir Theodore Turquet de Mayerne.

[724] Ange de Raconis (Angelo Rafaele da Raconiggi) was president and superior of the Capuchin mission in England: AAW, B 26, no. 130. In July 1622, Raconis had informed John Bennett that, while in London, he had dealt with John Jackson, whom he regarded as one of the most learned and judicious among the secular priests: AAW, A XVI, no. 122, p. 496. On 31 August/10 September 1622, Matthew Kellison remarked that Raconis, 'being returned from London, sayd that our k[ing] told him he liked secular priests but not Jesuites': AAW, B 26, no. 120. For Raconis's report from London, dated 29 September 1622, to Propaganda Fide, see PRO, 31/9/90, pp. 124–129.

tyme, Moulins[725] did lye at his howse, to whom in all likelihood he wold relate them when he came home, in infamia*m* religionis.

I suppose yo*w* dare not write us th*e* newes of Spalat.[726] The ballets sing and picture him as burnt.[727] Yea some statesme*n* reported as much. The l[ord] of Kensingto*n*, who*m* some call earle of Holla*nd*,[728] went on Friday last for France.[729] O*u*r soldiers th*a*t goe for the Lowe Countries finde warrs, or at least wounds, in Ingl[and]. At Gravesend they fowght one w*i*th an other, and one having his hand cut and, seeing one of his finger[s] hang by th*e* skin, pull*ed* it of[f] and threw it a way, etc*etera*. An other here slew a captaine to shew his valo*u*r. I hear there is a prophecie th*a*t, in th*e* jubilee year, Ing[land] shall be co*nv*er*t*ed. Thus yow see how I roam up and downe, as matters come to mynde. But I suppose, living soe farr of[f], and having others th*a*t write serious matters, these will serve to recreate yo*u*r spirits. Mr More, if he be come, will excuse me, having in this writte*n* soe much as at this tyme I can. And here, w*i*th my best love and respect, I rest.

Yo*u*rs most assured,

J[ohn] N[elson]

4 Aug[ust].

Some give owt in France th*a*t, if the b[ishop] of Chal[cedon] had lived, there wold have been a schisme in Ingl[and].[730] P*er*haps they say as much there, and add th*a*t fowle slander th*a*t pr[iests] goe fro*m* howse to howse to forbid me*n* to entertaine Jes[uits], breing [*sic*] traito*u*rs, and th*e* fact treason. Card[inal] Mel*in*o hath written a poore, sleight Italia*n* l*ett*re to Mr Coll[eton], stiling him dean of the Ingl[ish] cleargy,[731] and tells him th*a*t the p[ope] caus*ed* 2 of his l*ett*res to be read, of th*e* 15

[725] Pierre du Moulin, for whom see A. Milton, *Catholic and Reformed* (Cambridge, 1995), *passim*; Adams, PC, pp. 289–290; Cogswell, *BR*, p. 40.

[726] For Marc'Antonio de Dominis, archbishop of Spalato, see N. Malcolm, *De Dominis (1560–1624)* (London, 1984); see also above, pp. 28–30.

[727] De Dominis did not die until 30 August/9 September 1624. For the posthumous sentence formally passed on him by the Inquisition, on 11/21 December 1624, see *A Relation Sent from Rome, of the Processe, Sentence, and Execution Done upon the Body, Picture, and Bookes of Marcus Antonius de Dominis, Archbishop of Spalata, after his death* (London, 1624); Malcolm, *De Dominis*, pp. 79, 137.

[728] Henry Rich, 1st Baron Kensington, was created earl of Holland on 24 September 1624.

[729] See *CSPV, 1623–1625*, p. 412.

[730] See *Letter 49*.

[731] See AAW, A XVIII, no. 31, pp. 253–254 (Cardinal Millini to John Colleton, 26 June/6 July 1624). Colleton wrote to Rant on 2 August 1624 that he had received this letter, which arrived in England on 22 July, via the nuncio in Flanders. The cardinal, said Colleton, 'stiled me decanus cleri Anglicani, and wrot that it was his Hol[iness's] pleasure to bestowe that nomination and office upon me till an other were apointed, but gave no one facultie or jurisdiction at all, save onlie authoritie to comfort my brethren and encourage them by my good example': AAW, B 26, no. 96.

and 22 of June, and give[s] him facultie to doe as he doth, that is to exhort the clergy a mantenerse nella fede. Yow shall have a copie of it sent yow. My conjecture is that the p[ope] in congreg[ation] de P[ropaganda] F[ide] ordain[e]d that the d[ean] and chap[ter] shold continew donec etc, and gave him order to signifie soe much, which owt of the abundance of his love he hath thus qualified. I am angry at my selfe that I doe not write both to him and to the congre[gation] that he may reflect on himselfe, and they understand the indignitie.

Yours,

J[ohn] N[elson]

*Addressed*: All molto reverendo signore, il Signore Tomaso Rant, agenti dell clero Inglese.
A Roma.

*Endorsed*: Written: August 4.
Received: Septemb[er] 21.
Answered: Sept[ember] 28.

## 51. John Nelson [Jackson] to Thomas Rant and Thomas More, 27 August 1624

[*AAW, B 26, no. 109*][732]

V[ery] r[everend sirs],

On Saterday the 21 of Aug[ust] I went to the marquess imb[assador] of France[733] and told him I was come in the behalfe of the dean[734] and cleargy: 1. to present our respects. 2. to signifie the causes why he heard not of us sooner, which were 2: owr absence upon owr imployments, and that some came purposely to London to wait on him, and found him gone [on] the progress. He replyed freindly to these. I went on and told him that we tooke notice of his care of religion, and were thankfull for it, and desired that he wold take the cleargy also into his favour and protection, and, if we co[u]ld serve him in any thing, he shold finde us ready. To this he curteously replyed, but knew not what the dean was or any thing of the cleargy till I told him. Then I told him that I had heard that one was sent from the k[ing] of France (Monsieur Berule) to

[732]This letter is discussed in Questier, *C&C*, pp. 415–416.

[733]Antoine Coiffier de Ruzé, marquis of Effiat. Effiat, in his letter of 21 August to the secretary of state, Henri-Auguste de Loménie, seigneur de Villeauxclercs, related that 'le chancellier Brouck m'a amené un prestre seculier qui faict l'office de grand achidiacre' (i.e. Jackson): PRO, PRO 31/3/59, fo. 210v. Fulke Greville, 1st Baron Brooke, had lost the chancellorship of the exchequer to Sir Richard Weston in late 1621.

[734]John Colleton.

R[ome] to procure a dispensation[735] and, if he pleased, wee wold send to our age*nt*[736] to co*n*curr w*i*th him therin. He asked me if I spake this of my owne private motio*n* or fro*m* the dean etc*etera*. To th*a*t I answered th*a*t I came lately fro*m* the dean and was intreated by him to doe these duties. He seemed to take the offer in extraordinarie kinde maner and promised me severall tymes he wold write to his maister of it and of us, and th*a*t now he did see we were not Spaniards etc*etera*. I added also th*a*t we had understood th*a*t the marq[uis] imb[assador][737] of Spaine had done us ill offices at R[ome] by his *lett*res against the having of b*ishop*s,[738] and th*a*t the k[ing] of Fra[nce] his *lett*res came about the same tyme com*m*aunding his imb[assador][739] at R[ome] to deall w*i*th his Hol[iness] effectually about b*ishop*s, w*hi*ch did us a great pleasure, and we desired his Ma*jes*tie shold know o*ur* thankfulnes. He did not understand any thing, eyther th*a*t we had had [*word deleted*] <a bishop or> any other circu[m]sta*n*ces of those points, but gave willing ear to all and promised much kindness and caused a writing to be shewed unto me concerning th*e* good of Cath[olics], w*hi*ch he purposed to procure th*e* k[ing] to subscribe to, being th*e* next day to goe towards Woodstock to meet him; and, after I had read it and liked it, <he> gave me anew many good words and soe dismissed me. I will labo*ur* th*a*t, at his

[735]Richard Smith had written to Thomas More, on 10/20 August, informing him of the departure for Rome of Pierre de Bérulle ('who is my freind and with whome you may deale confidently') in order to secure the dispensation, 'which office the Jes[uits] looked to have had': AAW, B 26, no. 106. For the dispatch of Bérulle to Rome to assist Philippe de Béthune, count of Sully in obtaining the dispensation for the Anglo-French marriage, see Allison, RS, pp. 180–181; Avenel, *Lettres*, II, pp. 18–19; also above, p. 102. On 1 September 1624, John Colleton wrote to Bérulle offering Rant's assistance: AAW, A XVIII, no. 53, pp. 333–334. A letter of the same date to Urban VIII expressed the English Catholics' hope that a dispensation would be granted, and that the pope would remember their Church 'ubi nullus [. . .] pastor episcopus praesidet, sed omnis jurisdictio et regimen jacet hoc tempore': AAW, A XVIII, no. 54, p. 335. This letter, Gordon Albion comments, was dispatched on the advice of Effiat himself: Albion, *CI*, p. 59. Matthew Kellison had written to the same effect on 16/26 August: AAW, A XVIII, no. 49, pp. 325–326; see also AAW, A XVIII, no. 62, pp. 357–358 (Colleton to Urban VIII, 22 September 1624); and above, pp. 102–103. Significantly, George Fisher opined in late October 1624 that, 'if I may creditt report, the French ar very desirous of the match and will, if they can, conclude it uppon any termes, even without a dispensation, if it may <not> be obtained spero tamen meliora': AAW, B 47, no. 156; see also Fisher's letter of 26 November 1624 (*Letter 63*). John Lockwood retailed, on 30 September/10 October 1624, a rumour that Bérulle, on his way to Rome, had all his letters taken from him, allegedly by the 'Spanyereds [. . .] in his hye way towardes Rome, as Padre Maistro was here in Fraunce when he went last for England': AAW, B 27, no. 13; see also *Letter 39*.

[736]i.e. in Rome.

[737]Juan Hurtado de Mendoza, marquis of Inojosa.

[738]See *Letter 45*.

[739]Philippe de Béthune, count of Sully.

returne, others may also goe unto him. I understand th*at*, when it was p*er*ceaved that France stood upo*n* condicions for Cath[olics], th*e* k[ing] shold say to th*e* prince, yow see to what pass yow have brought this business. There are disco*n*te*n*tme*n*ts between the d[uke][740] and p[rince] w*hi*ch I doe gather by some words th*at* the d[uke] spake of the p[rince]. The d[uke] said to a freind of myne th*at* wee papists were strange people th*at* co[u]ld not be co*n*tent to suffer a while that, after, we might be quiet. It seems they desire an other sessio*ns* [*sic*] of parlame*nt*, therby to get money for th*e* payme*nt* of th*e* kings debts, and they fear th*e* purit[ans] will not graunt any new subsidies unles th*e* goods and liberties of Cath[olics] be offred as a sacrifice to appease their malice, and therfore, if the sessions hold, I expect litle cessatio*n* till th*at* be past, if then; w*hi*ch I ad[d] because the purit[ans] doe smell as much and will doe their worst to lay a ground for co*n*tinuing of p*er*sec[ution]. When some of them were told what was done against Cath[olics], they answer[e]d: this is not to hurt yow, but to co*n*tent us. It is thowght th*at* th*e* match w*i*th France will hardly [*word deleted*] <goe on>. I am told th*at* the imb[assador] hath found th*at* by following the Jesuits advise in some point he hath comitted a great errour, and therupo*n* is owt w*i*th them, and desires to co*n*ferr (now) w*i*th th*e* principall of the cleargie.[741] Some have named unto him Mr Coll[eton] and Mr Ben[nett]. Mr Pitts will be one of the fittest, in regard of his language, whe*n* he cometh to towne. Mr Blu*n*t, the provi*n*ciall, was often w*i*th th*e* imb[assador], and others of them also. And Mr Anderson[742] th*e* Scotish Jes[uit] was in th*e* progress, as his chaplein, after the Capucin[743] went for France,[744] whose returne was expected w*i*thin 15 dayes. Fa[ther] Blu*n*t, th*e* provinciall, went to th*e* Spa[nish] imb[assador][745] and told

[740] George Villiers, 1st duke of Buckingham.

[741] See also AAW, B 26, no. 120; Albion, *CI*, pp. 56, 59.

[742] For Patrick Anderson SJ (who died on 24 September 1624), see W. Forbes-Leith (ed.), *Narratives of Scottish Catholics under Mary Stuart and James VI* (London, 1889), pp. 291, 317–347; ARSJ, Anglia MS 1, fos 191r, 201v; AAW, B 26, nos 129, 137 (Thomas Roper's report, of 24 September 1624, that Anderson 'lyethe very dangerously sicke' at the French embassy).

[743] Ange de Raconis. Later, on 14 February 1625, John Jackson wrote to Rant that Patrick Anderson had taken Raconis's place by a 'pretty wile': *Letter 72*.

[744] Alvise Valaresso said he had been assured that Raconis's recall by Richelieu was 'because of some error committed by him, in certain letters, through excess of zeal or lack of judgment': *CSPV, 1623–1625*, p. 424; CRS, 68, p. 169. On 13/23 July 1624, the earl of Carlisle had reported that Raconis had gone to England with the intention of converting the king 'and the whole state [...] to the Romish faith'. Carlisle had learned this 'from a great minister of state, who feares it may occasion scandall there, and yet is not approved heer' in France. Carlisle hoped that Raconis would be recalled as soon as possible 'because publique notice is taken of the man heer', and also because it was believed that he had 'composed a booke of controversies for his Majesties satisfaction': PRO, SP 78/72, fo. 347r. For the damning report on Raconis, written by Effiat to Louis XIII, see PRO, PRO 31/3/59, fos 186v–192r.

[745] Carlos Coloma.

him th*at* such a one, describing ~~Mr Nelson~~ <me>, had been w*i*th th*e* imb[assador] of France and spoken against Spaine.[746] I, understa*n*ding of it, sent Fa[ther] Blu*n*t a message th*at* ~~he~~ <I> found myselfe agreiv*e*d at th*e* wrong he had done me and, if he gave me not the better satisfactio*n*, I wold right myselfe soe as the other shold learne to be better advised and more charitable hereafter.[747] What his answer will be, I knowe not. Perhaps the French imb[assador] shall be aquainted herw*i*th that he may see how they curry favo*ur* w*i*th all sides.

A gentleman of note <and one th*at* was present whe*n* I was w*i*th th*e* Fr[ench] imb[assador]> and a frend to th*e* Jes[uits], hearing of Father Blu*n*ts dealing, was sory and said th*at*, if the Span[ish] imb[assador] had knowne th*e* necessitie by my going and what I sayd, he wold have advised the same. Other matters I must leave till an other time and, w*i*th my best respect to yo*w* both, rest.

Yo*u*rs,

Jo[hn] N[elson]

The 27 of Aug[ust].

*Addressed*: For M$^{r}$ More and M$^{r}$ Rant.

*Endorsed*: Written: August 27.
Received: October 5.
Answered: Octob[er] 21.

## 52. Thomas More to John Nelson [Jackson], 28 August/7 September 1624

[*AAW, B 26, no. 117*]

Right wor*shipfu*ll,

Yours of Julie 16$^{o}$ were most welcome unto me, and I must crave pardon for being soe boysterouse with you, for the want of such

[746] Richard Blount SJ had recently sent a letter of gratitude to Louis XIII: *ibid.*, fo. 181v. On 23 August 1624, however, Effiat complained that 'les lettres du Père Blond me sont non plus de mon goust et particullièrement celle du nonce qui me semble n'est pas asses ample pour venir à la fin desirée'. Effiat had told him bluntly that 'ses affections n'avoient pas rapport à ses promesses': PRO, PRO 31/3/60, fo. 213v. On 1/11 September, Effiat recorded that he and Blount had dined together and 'nous sommes séparés grands amis': *ibid.*, fo. 228v. But, for John Macbreck SJ's report of 31 December 1624 that Effiat was on bad terms with Blount, see ABSJ, Stonyhurst Anglia MS A II, 3, no. 15; ABSJ, Stonyhurst Anglia MS A IV, no. 26, p. 19.

[747] On 15 November 1624, John Jackson complained to Thomas More of Richard Blount SJ's 'wrongful abusing' of him to the 'Spa[nish] imb[assador]': AAW, B 27, no. 47.

necessarie healpes as I wished stay[e]d me long err I co[u]ld take my journey, and I thought all blameworthie in this kinde that did not enquire what was done, and urged not forward the execution of what was resolved upon. You perhaps know not that my commission is limited to one sole matter, and therfore, though I wold, I co[u]ld not follow your affairs in this place for want of your authoritie. And now I am in good hope, his Ho[liness] giving us soe favourable audience as he did, and testifying with tears his tender affection to our cowntrie. I see not but that we shall sone dispatch that principall matter, and soe may returne with expedition. His H[oliness] wished I had had order from you to deal in the matter of dispensation [*in margin:* procure us the like commission] and not onlie from you but alsoe from his Ma*jes*tie and the prince and the lay Catholickes. It wold have bene a dischardg[e] of his conscience if it had bene generallie sued for from thence as it is by France. We expect howrelie F[ather] Berul who writt hither from Turyne upon the 29 of August. He will favour us all he maye and attendeth onlie to the procuring of the dispensation. We are exceedinglie bownd to the French embass[ador] Mons*ieu*r Betune who was our cleargies patrone in their first brunt in time of Clement VIII.[748] I went to visit him with Mr Rant, and ther he discoursed with us above an howre and an half. He it is that in his kinges name furdereth our suite more than we ever co[u]ld, although we finde his Ho[liness] verie readie to give us all satisfaction. To him must we shew our selves gratfull, as alsoe to others in France that favour us. Card[inal] Bandino and the Card[inal] Barbarino be our especiall patrones, and by their means I hope we shall finde singuler comfort in all just demands.[749] Card[inal] S[anta] Susanna is our good frend but he seemeth to be much altered since Mr Jhon Benettes being gone, and inclineth to the favoring of the Jesuites. And soe doth Sig*no*r Ingoli in whom we reposed so great confidence. I have not bene at the colledg[e][750] and the rector[751] telleth Mr Weynman that their is noe place for me. They faine fearfulnesse of our agentes conversation in their colledges because therbie the schollers are moved

[748] i.e. during the 1602 appeal to Rome against the archpriest George Blackwell, when the French diplomatic service, in the person of Philippe de Béthune, assisted the secular clergy who led the appeal. See J. Bossy, 'Henri IV, the appellants and the Jesuits', *RH*, 8 (1965), pp. 80–112; Allison, RS, pp. 170, 180–181.

[749] Anthony Champney requested subsequently, in a letter to Rant of 8/18 December 1624, 'I pray you lett me [know] whether either Card[inal] Barbarino or anie other sayd to you at anie tyme that capitulum cleri Anglicani est chimera. It is tould us Card[inal] Barbarino towld you so, which we would gladly knowe': AAW, B 27, no. 81. Rant tried to set Champney's mind at rest in a letter of 18/28 January 1625: AAW, B 47, no. 49.

[750] The English College in Rome.

[751] Thomas Fitzherbert SJ.

to sedition and tumultes, which is a divelish calumnie to lay their faultes in their government upon our cleargie. Upon Twesday next, one of our schollers, a convictor, defendeth philosophie in the Jesuites schooles and dedicateth his conclusions to Card[inal] Barbarino, the popes nephew. Their will be great solempnitie, and the cost bestowed upon his conclusions is thought will amount to one hundred poundes. He is a convictor and is reputed to have his resolution to be a Jesuite. For such schollers are not comprehended within the prohibition that noe schollers shall enter into religion without his Ho[liness's] especiall licence. For the Jesuitresses they live obscurelie, and in great necessitie in this place, and wold for mear want be driven away, but that the Jesuites underhand mantaine them, I fear me, of our colledge rentes, which is extreamelie in debt. But externallie they wold be accompted their enemies. It is not yett published what they are to doe. C[ardinal] Millino, ther onlie frend, told us when we were with him that he had alwaies bene against that institute. And his Ho[liness] hath said resolutlie aut includantur, aut dissolvantur.[752] And we expect daylie when this shallbe intimated unto them. It is trew what they say, that they have three howses, one here, the other not 4 miles but 40 miles hence, to wit at Perugia, wher the last weeke their cheef patron the bishop[753] dyed, and in what ease he hath leaft them I hear not; the third is at Naples, whereof I hear nothing.[754] Shortlie you will hear more. One prelate in this cittie told me that we shold see some of them err long great bellyed; and when I sayd it co[u]ld not be in these beginnings, because they wold have an especiall care now of their creditt, he said noe more but putt his finger upon his mouth as though he wished us to say nothing but expect the end. But, for their vowes and processional receaving, I take it for a fable as Card[inal] Bandino did alsoe, to whom he signifyed what was reported ther.[755] And everyone wondreth that they can make anie believe what is soe fond and ridiculouse. They have altered ther habit, as it is said, for I have not seen them, and insteed of great hattes they have got the Spanish woemens habit.[756] I thanke you for your newes, and request you to

[752] See Dirmeier, *MW*, II, pp. 77–78.

[753] Napoleone Comitoli, who died on 20/30 August 1624. See Littlehales, *Mary Ward*, pp. 127–128; Dirmeier, *MW*, II, p. 74; Chambers, *Life*, II, pp. 102–103.

[754] See Littlehales, *Mary Ward*, pp. 125–130; Dirmeier, *MW*, II, p. 47.

[755] On 16 July 1624, John Jackson, in London, alerted Thomas More that Mary Ward's institute's members in the capital 'give owt [...] that they have 3 howses there, one in R[ome] and [an] other 4 myle[s] on this side [of] Rome, and one at Naples, and they were sent for and intreated thither and enterteyned with a procession and ringing of bells etcetera, or els that the like was done at Rome and that before the popes face they tooke their [vo]wes in great solemnitie': AAW, B 26, no. 84.

[756] Cf. Chambers, *Life*, II, pp. 6–7; Dirmeier, *MW*, I, p. 606.

write often and in perticuler what occurreth. I presume M^r^ Muskett[757] can send weeklie, to whom committ your letters for me. And soe with my dutie to your right hon[ourable],[758] gyving her and you most humble thankes for the favour shewed to my neece Grace,[759] I take my leave, not forgetting M^r^ Rantes most kinde remembrance, who fealt no smale greife at the miscarriadge of the letter you intended him. He complayneth extraordinarilie of the slacknesse of correspondence, and indeed ther can not be a greater impediment in our negociationes. Farewell. R[ome].

Sept[ember] 7° 1624.

Yours ever most assuredlie,

Th[omas] M*o*re

*Addressed*: To the right wor*shipfu*ll M^r^ Jhon Nelson give these. London.

*Endorsed*: 1624.

## 53. Richard Smith to Thomas More, 2/12 September 1624

[*AAW, B 26, no. 122*]

Right worship*fu*l and deere syr,

Some three weekes agoe I wrote unto you, hoping that that letter shold welcome you to Rome, and now I long to heare of yo*ur* safe arrival and good health w*hi*ch I pray God long continew. On the vigil of O*ur* Ladies nativitie,[760] the mariage betweene o*ur* prince and madame of France was concluded, and signed by both p*ar*ties and with good conditions for Catholiks and in some points better than thos[e] of Spayne. Wherfore I pray you joyne earnestly with Mons*ieu*r Berul (as M^r^ Benet[761] did with P[adre] Maestro) to p*ro*cure the dispensation in the

[757] George Fisher.

[758] A reference, presumably, to Anne Philipson, second wife of Thomas Arundell, 1st Baron Arundell.

[759] For Thomas More's niece, Grace, see D. Shanahan, 'The family of St. Thomas More in Essex, 1581–1640', *Essex Recusant*, 1 (1959), p. 64. Grace More was professed OSB at Cambrai (she took Agnes as her name in religion) on 22 December 1624/1 January 1625: *Letter 61*; AAW, B 47, no. 75; see also B. Weldon, *Chronological Notes containing the Rise, Growth, and Present State of the English Congregation of the Order of St. Benedict* (Stanbrook, 1881), appendix, p. 28.

[760] 29 August/8 September.

[761] John Bennett.

name of the clergie.[762] Mr Benet[763] desireth it and I have written to Mr Colleton and Mr President[764] to authorize you al they can, ~~but I think~~ though I think that not needful, but, becaus[e] it is better and my card[inal][765] desired it, I have written to the*m*. We are much beholden to the said card[inal], not only for thes[e] conditions of the mach but also for his forwardnes to get us a b[ishop]. For he hath earnestly com*m*ended the matter to M*onsieu*r Berul and to the nuntio[766] here, and, seing the mach is concluded, I hope that o*u*r suite of b[ishops] wil not be denied, albeit some of the Jes[uits'] freinds in England give out that such order is taken as we shal have no more in haste, but others of this traine here say we shal have 2 or 3 of whome they hope to get one for the*m*. I wrote to you in my last that I suspected they ment to p*re*fer Mr Jhonson if they could. And what exceptions there are to be made against him both for incontinencie and frailtie in matter of the oathe [*sic*].[767] Deale co*n*fidently with M*onsieu*r Berul, for he is o*u*r freind, and maligned by o*u*r adversaries as wel as we. Co[u]nte Tillier is to be cheefe of [*MS torn:* the] princesse her house and, as I heare, his wife[768] is to be her cheef woman.[769] Wh[o is] to be her confessor, I yet know not. Her b[ishop][770] is a freind of oures and a kinsman of my card*in*al.[771] I need not say how expedient it were that o*u*r b[ishop] were

[762] See AAW, A XVIII, no. 99, pp. 549–550 (draft of a petition to the pope, in More's hand, for the grant of the dispensation).

[763] Edward Bennett.

[764] Matthew Kellison.

[765] Cardinal Richelieu.

[766] Bernardino Spada, archbishop of Damietta.

[767] On 10/20 August, Smith had recorded that 'the Jes[uits] wold have Mr [Cuthbert] Jhonson to be b[ishop], for here is made inquiries of him. Twoe Catholiks told me of his incontinencie with a married woman as a thing certaine and knowne. And he tooke some oathe, for which he escaped death. For which causes my l[ord] of Calcedon [*i.e.* William Bishop] wold not give any office unto him': AAW, B 26, no. 106. For the version of the oath of allegiance which Cuthbert Johnson (serving as chaplain to Margaret Dormer, wife of Sir Henry Constable, the future Viscount Dunbar) had offered to King James in 1610, see *NAGB*, pp. 77, 79, 82. For the rumoured nomination, see Allison, RS, pp. 158–159; and above, p. 86.

[768] Catherine Leveneur (née Bassompierre), countess of Tillières.

[769] See *CSPV, 1623–1625*, p. 507.

[770] Daniel Du Plessis de la Mothe-Houdancourt, bishop of Mende and nephew of Cardinal Richelieu. See C. Hibbard, 'Henrietta Maria and the transition from princess to queen', *The Court Historian*, 5 (2000), p. 23.

[771] On 19/29 September 1624, Carlisle and Kensington alerted Conway that there had been a 'vehement contestation' between Richelieu and Cardinal de La Rochefoucauld, 'as they sate in council, about the nomination of the bishop that should attend Madame into England', with Richelieu 'commending a young, learned and moderate man, the bishop of Mente', and La Rochefoucauld 'as strongly opposing him under pretence that he is an heretique'. The English ambassadors interpreted this as a factional manoeuvre by La Rochefoucauld to secure the appointment of Claude Caylar de Saint-Bonnet de Toiras, bishop of Nîmes and brother of one of the royal favourites, Marshal Toiras, who had

in England before the princesse come, both for respect of Cath[olics] and Protestants, and therfore I pray you urge al you can the naming of him as soone as may be. Because o*ur* former b[ishop] is diversley calum[n]iated I send with this a note of divers good things done by him in his short time. The man who calumniated me to the nuntio, as I wrote in my last,[772] is, as I heare now, Tobie Mathew, who <in Englande> threatened to kil me if I were not a preist, becaus[e] I once said that one reported that he was a priest,[773] so haughtie that ministers sonne and neophite is becomen. And it is very likely that such letters are sent to R[o]me wherfore get, if you [*word omitted:* can] (as M^r^ Benet[774] did), a copie of the accusations that are made against thos[e] that are named. From England they wrote of much p*er*secution, but the k[ing] p*ro*mised the Fre[n]ch embas[sador][775] that there shal be no more after the 5 of their August,[776] and here is comen M^r^ White of Essex,[777] who intendeth to goe to Rome, who knew not of much stirre

petitioned the English to secure the appointment for his brother: PRO, SP 78/73, fo. 144r. For the rivalry between the two cardinals over ecclesiastical appointments, see also Bergin, *The Making of the French Episcopate*, pp. 454–455.

[772] Smith's letter of 10/20 August to More had stated that 'lately hither was a letter written out of England to the nuntio' by 'a nameles fellow [Sir Tobias Mathew] wherin he chargeth me that I am pr[a]eceps, ira fervidus and acerrimus, promotor factionis, contra Jesuitas', and that Smith would, if promoted to episcopal dignity, 'raise a tempest of sedition': AAW, B 26, no. 106. Mathew allegedly also claimed that Smith 'cooperated to the calling out of Co[u]nte Tillieres out of England', which Smith denied: AAW, B 26, no. 105 (Smith to Rant, 8/18 August 1624). Mathew also denounced Richelieu (for insufficient zeal in the cause of English Catholics during the Anglo-French marriage negotiations) in a letter sent to Cardinal Barberini in October 1624: Albion, *CI*, p. 56.

[773] For Mathew's secret ordination, see *Letter 3*; and for the exploitation of this fact by Smith, see Anstr., II, p. 120; Questier, *C&C*, p. 470.

[774] John Bennett. See AAW, B 27, no. 31 (cited in *Letter 58*).

[775] Antoine Coiffier de Ruzé, marquis of Effiat.

[776] On 2/12 September 1624, John Lockwood reported that Louis XIII, 'understanding that the k[ing] of England ment to macth [*sic*] with him, tould him that unlesse hee did discontinew his persecution hee would in no ways entre into conditions of mariag[e] with him, to whom the k[ing] of England replied, requesting him to have patience but untill the 5 of August, which was the day he much solemnized for his delivery <out> of the handes of Go[w]ry, att which tyme he purposed of cessation of persecution': AAW, B 26, no. 121; see also *Letter 54* and above, pp. 98–102. In Sir Richard Weston's account of 23 August, Effiat had insisted on the 'revocacion of the commissions issued out of the exchequer' against Catholics. Weston had replied that this 'could not be don without perticular lettres to every county, which would rayse more bruit and noyse and give more scandall to his Majesties subjects and the parlament than any thing that was don in the treaty with Spayne'. Nevertheless, when the commissions were returned to the exchequer, the king could 'use what grace he pleased', and would intervene in cases where undue rigour had been applied. With this statement Effiat 'seemed to rest satisfied': PRO, SP 14/171/68, fo. 107r. On 1 September, Sir Edward Conway passed to the attorney-general a list of Catholic clergy and laity (among whom were the priests William Davies and Thomas Cole) 'for whom the French ambassador mediates': *CSPD, 1623–1625*, p. 333; PRO, SP 14/172/1.i, fo. 2r.

[777] Richard White. See *Letter 4*.

that daye. If M[r] White come to you, use him kindly, for I hope he is sure to the clergie, and therby <hee> may help you. M[r] Rant hath written downe that the Benedictins request a b[ishop] of their order, but F[ather] Bernard[778] here denieth it.[779] You may know the truth by F[ather] Sebert[780] when he cometh. When occasion serveth, urge how Clement 8 testifieth in his bul[781] that the occasion of dissension betwene the p[riests] and Jes[uits] riseth of their medling in *our* matters and that the*m* selves think it expedient that *our* sup*er*ior shold have nothing to doe with the*m* in governing us. If his Holines wold do the like, al the quarels wold be ended, and otherwise I feare they wilbe endles. After I had written this, talking with M[r] White, he seemed unwilling to be knowne to any Englishman in Rome, but to deal by a Frenchman called Mons*ieu*r de Scala who had bene some times in England with Co[u]nte Tillier. I pray you do my dutie to the good primate of Ireland.[782] And thus, with my hartiest to y*ou*r self, I leave you to the p*ro*tection of *our* sweet Saviour.

12 of 7[ber].

Y*our*s ever and ever,

R[ichard] Smith

*Addressed*: A monsieur, Monsieur Thomas More, prestre Anglois. Rome.

*Endorsed*: Written: Sept[ember] 12.
Received: Sept[ember] ult[imo].
Answered: October.

[778]John (Bernard) Berington OSB. See Lunn, *The English Benedictines* p. 233; Weldon, *Chronological Notes*, pp. 135–136.

[779]Smith's letter of 16/26 September 1624 to Thomas Rant recorded that the English Benedictines in Rome were ready to support the secular clergy's petition for a bishop, and that Robert (Sigebert) Bagshaw OSB would 'further our suite what he co[u]ld': AAW, B 26, no. 141. Subsequently, in a letter of 2/12 December 1624, William (Rudesind) Barlow, president of the English congregation of the Benedictines, who had been lobbied by Anthony Champney for his support, wrote to the cardinals of Propaganda Fide, declaring his order's assent to the appointment of another bishop. He commended, in particular, Smith himself and Matthew Kellison: AAW, A XVIII, no. 83, pp. 413–414; AAW, B 26, no. 141.

[780]Robert (Sigebert) Bagshaw OSB. See *Letter 54*. On 17/27 August 1624, Champney had noted Bagshaw's departure for Rome: AAW, B 26, no. 110; and, on 6/16 September, John (Bernard) Berington OSB wrote to Thomas Rant recommending Bagshaw to him: AAW, B 26, no. 126. Bagshaw was one of those who signed a request, dated 17/27 September 1624, to the pope for the issue of the dispensation for the Anglo-French dynastic treaty, though this petition was never delivered: AAW, B 26, no. 146.

[781]The breve of Clement VIII dated 25 September/5 October 1602. See *NAGB*, p. 5.

[782]Peter Lombard, archbishop of Armagh.

1624 Septem*b*er 12.
D^r Smith. Recea[ved] Septem*b*er 30. Answ[ered] Octo*b*er 7.
By Fr[ance].
Minae Tobiae Mathei.

## 54. Richard Smith to Thomas More, 16/26 September 1624

*[AAW, B 26, no. 142]*[783]

Right worship*ful* and deere syr,

I have y*ou*rs of the 26 of August, written from Rome. Y*ou*r other written from [*word illegible*] I never yet saw. I am most glad th*a*t you are safely comen to Rome and in health, w*hi*ch I pray God to continew, and y*ou*r self to have great care of. I have written unto you twoe or 3 letters, and in my last[784] certified you that the mach betwene England and France was co*n*cluded and signed by the com*m*itties of both p*ar*ties but, the articles being sent to o*u*r king, he hath not yet app*ro*ved them. When notice cometh of his app*ro*bation, Mons*ieu*r Villoclare,[785] one of the French secretaries, is to goe into England to take his oathe.[786] M^r Cape writeth to me from London of the 24 of their August that the p*er*secution for enditing, p*re*senting, convicting and informing was never worse and yet our k[ing] had p*ro*mised the French embass[ador][787] there that there shold be no more p*er*secution after the 5 of their August.[788] Yet Catholiks goe to the embassadours chappells as befor and I heare not of anie searches of houses. But a while agoe M^r Cole, a p[riest], was taken by Gee,[789] and Crosse[790]

[783] This letter is discussed in Allison, RS, pp. 182–183.

[784] *Letter 53*.

[785] Henri-Auguste de Loménie, seigneur de Villeauxclercs. For his appointment, following the dismissal of Puisieux and Sillery, see PRO, SP 78/72, fo. 19r.

[786] On 12/22 September, Carlisle had observed how confident the French were that the match would go forward. He noted that Richelieu 'sent immediately' to the secular clergy's Collège d'Arras 'to invite them to rejoyceing [*sic*] and to blesse that day and to pray for him, for the favour which was then, and by his meanes, procured unto them': PRO, SP 78/73, fo. 163r.

[787] Antoine Coiffier de Ruzé, marquis of Effiat.

[788] See *Letter 53*.

[789] See *Letter 50*. In October 1624, Thomas Cole wrote to Sir Edward Conway that, although Conway had ordered his release from Newgate, the recorder of London refused to accept 'such bayle' as Cole was 'able to procure', since the 'sufficient housholders' who provided it were 'unknowen' to the recorder, and they were also 'Roman Catholiques': PRO, SP 14/173/119, fo. 148r.

[790] Humphrey Cross. See *NAGB*, pp. 43, 77, 89, 218–219; *NCC*, pp. 3, 256, 257.

tooke divers woemen and youthes in their jorney to Dover for to goe over. I heare there hath bene a publik disputation in the French embass[ador's] house, and yet I heare nothing of the successe, w*hi*ch maketh me doubt that it was no better than the former[791] w*hi*ch [the] Jes[uits] had and p*er*haps wold with this recover their honor. More of England I know not, for seldom I have anie letters from thence.

As for the doubtfulnes of his Hol[iness] about making b*ishop*s, I hope that wilbe removed by means of my card[inal],[792] who telleth me that he hath lately written therabout to his Hol[iness] and also to Mons*ieu*r Bethun, and biddeth me not doubt but that he wil obtaine our suite. I have sent you here a letter from F[ather] Archangel[793] to their procurer g*ene*ral,[794] and an other from F[ather] Raconis to the popes brother,[795] and Co[u]nte Tillier hath p*ro*mised me an other to his Holines in oure behalf in this matter and I hope that Mons*ieu*r Bethun and Berul wil overcome al d*iffic*ulties, with whome I pray you be co*n*fident in this matter, and help them al you can in p*ro*cureing the dispensation, about w*hi*ch, if much d*iffic*ultie be made, p*er*haps I shal be sent to Rome, for my card[inal] told me that p*er*haps I might be sent thither, but this to y*ou*r self. As for subscribing my name, I give you ful power, except it be in things w*hi*ch may be to my owne com*m*endation or p*re*ferment. I <have> written to Mr Colleton to send you the seale w*hi*ch you desire. God in heaven speed y*ou*r labours. I have spoken with D[octor] Mailer about that place of Mons*ieu*r Vives, and at the first motion he liked wel of it, but desired some time to consider of it, and saieth that he wil write to you his ful mynd, but as yet he hath not brought me his letter.[796] Mr White[797] and his co*m*panie p*ar*ted from here 8 dayes agoe. He told me th*a*t he wold p*ro*mote our suite for b[ishops] al he co[u]ld.

[791] A reference, perhaps, to John Percy SJ's disputation in May 1622 with the king and leading Church of England divines; see *Letters 14, 16*. Alternatively, Smith may be alluding to Percy's and John Sweet's more recent disputations, in 1623, with Daniel Featley and Francis White, for which see McClure, *LJC*, p. 507.

[792] Cardinal Richelieu.

[793] William (Archangel) Barlow.

[794] For Barlow's letter, see AAW, A XVIII, no. 59, pp. 349–352 (7/17 September 1624).

[795] Cardinal Antonio Barberini.

[796] On 17 May 1624, Sir Walter Aston had reported to Secretary Conway that, 'at the princes being in this court, it pleased [...] Buckingham to have many conferences with one Doctor [Henry] Maylard'. Prince Charles also would 'admitte him sometymes into his presence' because they found 'him [...] a person of very good abilityes, and one that gave extraordinary satisfaction of his affection' in the service of his king and prince, and in particular 'to give light' to the prince concerning the Spaniards' 'unworthy proceedings'. Mayler stayed in Madrid so that 'whylst the business of the match was in any suspence hee might bee ready to assist in any thing that might have required his service'. He had left Madrid (without receiving from the Spanish court 'any kynde of gratuity') on 24 March 1624: PRO, SP 94/30, fo. 264v.

[797] Richard White. See *Letter 53*.

He hath a letter in his com*m*endation to Card[inal] Barberino from o*ur* nonce.[798] Here they looke for news of M*onsieu*r Beruls negotiation for the dispense, and it is said that, as soone as that cometh, my L[ord] Carleil wil goe to England. Mansfeild is dep*ar*ted hence towards Calis, some say for England, others for Holland.[799] The French verily looke th*at* our prince wil come hither if the mach take effect, and p*er*haps our k[ing] expects news from R[ome] of the dispense befor he wil subscribe to the articles. I pray you do my humble dutie to my l[ord] primate,[800] Mons*ieu*r Vives, Mons*ieu*r Berul, and my hartie com*m*endations to M^r Seaton, though unknowne, and to my old acquaintance F[ather] [*word illegible*] if he be alive, and to F[ather] Sebert[801] and al acquaintance. M^r Rant writeth to me of a visit[802] w*hi*ch he thinketh is to be befor C*hri*stmas, but I know [*word omitted:* not (?)] what visit that shal be. I pray you let me know by y*ou*r next. M^r Ireland, who is now with us, told me th*at* Enejosa,[803] being in England, said openly th*at* if the clergie named me for a b[ishop] he wold oppose becaus of my card[inal]. I pray God he oppose not against the matter. Some suspect th*at* my L[ord] Maxwel there helpeth to make a stay for b*isho*ps as M^r Gage was sent for th*at* purpose whiles M^r Benet was there.[804] This letter to the p[ope] is from Co[u]nte Tillier. Now I heare th*at* there is comen a courier from England. P*er*haps he bringeth the kings allowance of the articles. The Jesuite th*at* disputed in the F[rench] embass[ador's] house is Patrick Anderson, a Scot.[805] M^r Rant misunderstood me as if simply I wold have him to sue for one b[ishop], wheras I wish that onely if the striving for many wold delay the suite. This letter to the p[ope] is from Co[u]nte Tillier for b*isho*ps. He sent it sealed and so I know no p*ar*ticulers of it. This letter of M^r Nelson[806] wil give you light of matters in England. I have long time cried upon o*ur* brethren to goe to the F[rench] embass[ador] and I am glad that now at last they have gone to him.[807] It is now 8 dayes th*at* I heare nothing of D[octor] Mailer, and p*er*haps he wil doe nothing. M^r Blacklow[808] wilbe

[798] Bernardino Spada, archbishop of Damietta.

[799] See *CSPV, 1623–1625*, p. 438; PRO, SP 78/73, fo. 162r.

[800] Peter Lombard, archbishop of Armagh.

[801] Robert (Sigebert) Bagshaw OSB.

[802] i.e. an official visitation of the English College in Rome.

[803] Juan Hurtado de Mendoza, marquis of Inojosa.

[804] For Robert Maxwell, 1st earl of Nithsdale's mission to Rome (to assist in the procurement of the dispensation for the Anglo-French marriage), see *CSPV, 1623–1625*, pp. 433, 439, 447, 476; Birch, *CTCI*, I, p. 78; Lockyer, *Buckingham*, p. 232.

[805] See *Letter 51*.

[806] *Ibid.*

[807] See *ibid.*

[808] Richard White. See *Letter 53*.

at Rome before C*hris*tmas, so that you may deale with him y*ou*r self. Mansfeild is gone from here to Calis, some say for England, others for Holland. Co[u]nte Morris hath taken Clevis.[809] One comen lately out of England to the monks in Doway saieth he never knew things so il, and that the archb[ishop] of York[810] his pursivant seaseth both upon Catholiks and so affected. Thus having no more to write, with my hartiest love, I leave you to the p*ro*tection of o*u*r sweet Saviour.

26 of $7^{ber}$.

Y*ou*rs ever as his owne,

R[ichard] Smi[th]

*Addressed*: To M$^{r}$ More.

*Endorsed*: 1624. D[octor] Smith.
September 26.
Recea[ved]: October 15. Answ[ered]: October 21. By Fr[ance].

## 55. George Musket [Fisher] to Thomas More, 23 September 1624

[*AAW, A XVIII, no. 65, pp. 363–366*]

Right r*everen*d s*ir*,

I perceive by your letters dated the 24 and the last of August that our cheife <busines> is yet in the budd and not come to that ripenes and perfection we desire, but we hope shortly to see the fruit of your laborius jorney and to obtaine that wich we all most earnestly desire. Some rumors ar spread abroad that D*oct*or Smith is already designed to that dignity but your letters baring so late date and not intimating any such thing maketh me thinke that thes[e] ar but false reports.[811] If the[y] prove <true> we shall all rejoice and esteeme <it> as a great blessing of Almighty God. The course of the time here is so uneven and uncertaine that we know not our selves in what state we stand. Our feares and hopes ar in equall ballance. In the remote parts of the land, Catholiques suffer great persecution. Ther lands and goods ar

[809] Cf. Israel, *The Dutch Republic*, p. 484.

[810] Tobias Mathew.

[811] For the appointment of Richard Smith to succeed William Bishop as bishop of Chalcedon, see Allison, RS.

seised, 12$^{d}$ for every Sunday[812] rigorously exacted, besides many other aggreevances by promoters in every place.[813] Only we ar free from pursivants wich is some comfort amidst thes[e] troubles. The French ambassador[814] hath labored much with the king for some mitigation of thes[e] extremities and hath received many faire promises but as yet there is no effectuall course taken for the redresse of thes[e] miseries.[815] Yet generally it is reported that the match with France is in great forwardnes, some say concluded, but I cannot beleive this. Certaine it is that the duke is preparing to goe to France. His trunckes ar already at the custome house. The 11$^{th}$ of this moneth ther arrived here a secretary from Spaine.[816] I heard some whispering as though he brought good tidings from thence but I cannot learne what his particular errand is. He is to have audience shortly,[817] wich if it be favorable some say we may expect shortly a great ambassador from thence. Don Carlos[818] will be gone within this fortnight at the farthest. Mansfield arrived here some few daies before the secretary came and

[812]The statutory penalty, under the Elizabethan act of uniformity (1 Elizabeth, c. 2), for absence from church on Sundays and holy days.

[813]See AAW, A XVIII, no. 58, pp. 347–348 (an order for the reporting of recusants at the general sessions at Spittle in Lincolnshire); AAW, A XIX, no. 4, pp. 9–12 ('Complaintes of extremities and wronges done unto the Catholickes in the parishe of Botsworthe in the county of Lincolne by the churche wardens of the sayed parishe by vertue of Sir Nicholas Sanderson his warrantes by worde and writinge'); AAW, A XVIII, no. 64, pp. 361–362 (Robert Turbott [?] to Richard Forster, 23 September 1624, concerning the course taken by Sir Thomas Hoby and Sir David Foulis at Stokesley against Catholics); AAW, A XVIII, no. 75, pp. 395–398. For other letters addresed to Forster, describing sanctions against Catholics in the autumn of 1624, see AAW, A XVIII, no. 66, pp. 367–368, no. 69, pp. 375–376, no. 70, pp. 377–378; see also Questier, *C&C*, p. 422.

[814]Antoine Coiffier de Ruzé, marquis of Effiat.

[815]On 15/25 September 1624, Matthew Kellison recorded that William Lane had written to him (on 3/13 September) that Effiat 'of late, by the mediation of the d[uke] of Buck[ingham], hath gotten some lettres to the lord keeper, the attorney generall and to the chancelor of the exchequer for the suppression of al writtes and commissions sent into the countrie against recusantes. He told the k[ing] plainlie that, if he did <continew> persequution against Catholikes in Ingl[and], then the Fr[ench] k[ing] his master wold persequute in like manner the Hugonotts in France': AAW, B 26, no. 139. The agent for the English College at Douai reported, at the same time, that Effiat had also secured restraints on 'the promotors, informers and pursuivants, soe it is thought the matche will goe forward': AAW, B 26, no. 139. Cf. *Letter 56*.

[816]On 8/18 September 1624, William Trumbull sent news that 'on Tewsday last', Jacques Bruneau, 'secretary of the counsell of Flanders at Madrid [...] passed this way towards England, with the quality of agent for the king of Spaine', in order 'to releive Don Carlos Coloma', and that he would stay there 'untill the comming of another Spanish ambassador': PRO, SP 77/17, fo. 330v; see also *CSPV, 1623–1625*, p. 451; *CGB*, II, p. 657; McClure, *LJC*, pp. 581, 584; PRO, SP 94/31, fo. 168r.

[817]See *CSPV, 1623–1625*, pp. 454, 474.

[818]Carlos Coloma.

hath bin with the king.[819] What his busines is I cannot understand. Some say that he desireth imploiment at sea. The prince lately, as he was hunting, fell from his horse and brused himselfe sorely but, thankes be to God, he is in no danger.[820] Mr Missenden[821] wrighteth from Spaine that the king hath give[n] order that the pension wich was paid yearely by him to the colledge of Doway shall be now paied <by the infanta[822]> by 2,000 escudos per an*num*, and that the arrerages shall be paied by a thousand duckets per an*num* or more as she pleaseth. Before I end, I must <intreat> a favor at your <hands> wich is that you will be pleased to goe to the fathers at Minerva, I meane those of St Dominickes order, by whom I was received into the cheife sodality of Our Lady and to intreat them to give [*p. 364*] me autority to receive into that sodality such as shall desire it at my hands. I might have had <this> favor at my coming from thence but I forgot to aske it. I pray you solicite earnestly in my behalfe. I was admitted into that sodality 17, 18 or 19 yeares agoe by the name of George Fisher or George Ashton, I know not well. If you please to take the paines I doubt not but you will find my name and obtaine this favor for me.[823] Those of the Society have autority to admit into the society or sodality of the conception, and this the[y] chaleng[e] as peculiar to that society, by wich the[y] draw many to them selves, that they must depend only of them. For I have heard they will not admit them unles the[y] promise to depend of them and ther direction.[824] Take this to your consideration and think how this inco*n*venience may be prevented and whether the like priviledge may not be obtained for the clergy. I have solicited Mr Smith[825] many times for such letters as you desire, and he telleth me he hath fully satisfied your expectation. Since the writing of this I understand by me*n* of the best intelligence that the king is pleased at the instance of the French ambassador to compassionate the poore afflicted state of Catholikes and that the order is now drawing up for the staiing of this present persecution, and that such as have had ther goods seased and sold shall have the price of them [re]stored backe. We expect the publication of this order within thes[e] 7 or 8 daies. This mitigation will be some present comfort. Yet I see not any solide foundatio*n* of future hope, but feare that the ensuing

[819] See *Letter 54*.

[820] See *CSPV, 1623–1625*, p. 445.

[821] Edward Maddison.

[822] Isabella Clara Eugenia, archduchess of Austria.

[823] See also AAW, B 26, no. 56 (Fisher to Thomas Rant, 12 May 1625).

[824] For Richard Smith's complaints to Rome in 1626 concerning the Society of Jesus's sodality of the Immaculate Conception, see AAW, B 27, no. 100; AAW, A XXVI, no. 81, pp. 225–226; *NCC*, pp. 47, 72.

[825] Identity uncertain.

parlament will raise the tempest againe to the increase of our miseries. Writts ar allready out for the sum*m*oning of the parliament. I have no more to impart but my best love wich is allwaies yours. Com*m*end me I pray you in most harty manner to M[r] Rant and incourage <him> all you can to <goe> forward and to perfect the good worke he hath begun. He shall have our best petitions to Almighty God for this good successe. I rest.

Yours ever assuredly,

G[eorge] M[usket]

Septemb[er] 23.

*Addressed*: To his wor*shipfu*ll and very worthy freind M[r] Thomas More. Rome.

[*on p. 366*]

*Endorsed*: 1624. Septemb*er* 23. Musket. Recea[ved]: Nov*ember* 8. Answ[ered]: Nov*ember* 9. By Fr[ance].

## 56. George Musket [Fisher] to Thomas More, 1 October 1624

[*AAW, A XVIII, no. 68, pp. 371–374*]

Right r*everen*d s*ir*,

I wrote unto you the last weeke[826] and gave you some hope that the king would take order for the redresse of such <miseries> as Catholiques <suffer> by the extremity of this present persecution, and it was certainly reported that the order was drawing <up> and should be published within [a] few daies, but I see now we ar feed with an empty spoone and that the French ambassador either can doe nothing or will doe nothing, for the persecution daily increaseth and beginneth now to draw neere London and is greater than I have knowne it thes[e] many yeares. Catholiques goods ar seased uppo*n* in most places and sold before their faces. Ther barne dores ar shutt upp and ther corne seased to the king. Petifull complaints come from all parts, and at least <60> petitions have bin preferred by distressed Catholikes to the French ambassador, but he effecteth nothing for them.[827] Besides

[826] *Letter 55*.

[827] On 2 October 1624, Edward Bennett insisted that 'in all places, the justices are busye in making enquiries upon the goodes and landes of recusants': AAW, B 27, no. 2. Eight days

I am crediblely [*sic*] informed that, notwithstanding this extremity of persecution, letters have bin forged by our adversaries (for I know not how it can be otherwise) and generally, in the name of all Catholiques, sent to the French cardinall,[828] president of the councell, to testifie that the[y] suffer no persecution but that Catholiques injoy ther liberty without any molestation[.][829] This proceeding maketh me thinke that ther is juggling in the world and that the French ar deluded with faire words and false reports. For beleive it, *sir*, if you did but heare the complaints and lamentations of Catholikes, and see the miseries they suffer, it would pitty your hart. Neither doe I see any care had of them nor any course taken for ther releife. Only the king giveth faire words. Meane time we ar scourged and vexed intollerably and the promoters ar our cheife persecutors, but, to cover this persecution and give some color of clemency, the pursivants have no warrants; neither ar priests much persecuted nor any imprisoned since M^r^ Coole who was apprehended by Gee and comitted to Newgate. Under this

before, in Antwerp, Henry Clifford believed that the Anglo-French match was doubtful because of the continuing measures against Catholics 'in the remoter parts'. The French ambassador was 'perplexed', but 'Cardinal Richlieu from France wrote a very courteous and frindly lettre assuering our Catholicks in the behalfe of his most Christian Majestie and the queene mother all assistance for their peace and benefite', a reference to Richelieu's formal letter of 15/25 August 1624 to James's Catholic subjects: AAW, B 27, no. 8; Avenel, *Lettres*, II, pp. 29–30. On 10/20 October 1624, Matthew Kellison noted that he had received reports of 300 Catholics proceeded against in Yorkshire, and 700 in Hampshire. On 17 October, Thomas Roper sent word (backed up by Colleton four days later) that, despite rumours of a 'stay of proceedinges' against Catholics, none had yet been released from Newgate. London's lord mayor was seizing Catholics' property. The French ambassador had again been petitioned to intervene (AAW, B 27, nos 20, 25, 23), while, ten days later, John Jackson sent in similar reports from Lincolnshire: AAW, B 27, nos 25, 23, 47; see also *Letter 55*. The French ambassador, wrote Anthony Champney on 18/28 October, had received sixty petitions, and '2,000 are sayd to be falne in the North, partly by the extremitie <of persecution>'. 'Promoters swarm' and 'take <men> in the street by arrest for debt' to the crown: AAW, B 27, no. 31. On 29 October 1624, Thomas Roper, in London, reported that the lord mayor 'seased here uppon many mens goodes, and solde them under' the French ambassador's 'nose, who hathe hetherto prevayled in nothinge for our good' and scarcely had 'patience to heare our complayntes, to which he freely tellethe us that he dothe not geave us any creditte, thoughe our troubles be so appairent', choosing, rather, to rely on the word of the king that there 'shall be no persequution'. Roper added that, 'in the meane tyme, many a hundred have bein utterly undonne, and many [. . .] more are in apparent danger of legall proceedings in the courte of Westminst[er]. There is some stay till Feb[ruary] but 12^d^ a Sunday, indightements and seasures are putt in exequution': AAW, B 27, no. 32; see also *Letter 58*.

[828] Cardinal Richelieu.

[829] John Jackson commented on 15 November 1624 that 'I hear that the Fr[ench] imb[assador] craveth of the Catholicks to informe into France that they think it not convenient to press the k[ing] here to[o] stricktly to points of religion': AAW, B 27, no. 47.

specious pretence of clemency ~~the color~~ towards priests they color ther proceedings and make the world beleive that ther is no persecution at all, wheras those that should entertain and maintaine priests ar spoiled of ther goods and brought to penury.[830] I thought good to intimate thus much least my former informations and such other false reports grounded uppon false hope should make [*p. 372*] you conceive amisse of the present state of things. I wish I could send you better newes, but withall it is fitt you understand <the truth>. The Spanish ambassador Don Carolo[831] is to depart uppon the feast of S[t] Francis,[832] if he hold his apointment wich I thinke he will, for all his carriage is allready gone.[833] The secretary[834] wich came lately out of Spaine hath take*n* a house in the Spitle. To morrow we departe fro*m* Ely House,[835] for it hath pleased him to graunt me also a cha*m*ber at the Spitle. He hath had audience of the king 6 or 7 daies since, and was curteously <intertayned> [*interlineated word obscured*] but Don Carolo departeth without audience bycause he tooke part with the marquez.[836] The duke[837] is not yet gone into France, neither can I heare certainly when he will goe. In hast, [I] comend my selfe to your love and to good M[r] Rant, and desire to heare how matters goe with you. I rest.

Yours assuredly,

G[eorge] Muscott

Octob[er] 1°.

[830] See *Letter 50*. The cynical Francophobe Henry Clifford remarked on 22 October/1 November that 'in England, for the present, there is caulme and, on the sodaine, informers are suppressed, and it is thought such priests and Catholicks as be prisoners shall be released out of hand, and the l[ord] keeper hath order to stay all execution against recusantes'. But, Clifford thought, 'this is to entertaine more plausibly the secretarie of France [*i.e.* Villeauxclercs] who is dayly expected, and it is probable this caulme will endure to February next', when Clifford expected that parliament would assemble, and 'then againe a storme is expected'. The English Catholics' only 'hope is that his Holinesse will not lett things passe without solide meanes setled for our good and peace', for 'the French are sodaine and credulous when the important busines toucheth not themselves directly': AAW, B 27, no. 33.

[831] Carlos Coloma.

[832] 4 October.

[833] See *CSPV, 1623–1625*, pp. 436, 455, 463.

[834] Jacques Bruneau.

[835] The Spanish embassy in London.

[836] Juan Hurtado de Mendoza, marquis of Inojosa. See *CSPV, 1623–1625*, p. 455.

[837] George Villiers, 1st duke of Buckingham.

[*on p. 374*]

*Addressed*: All' ill*ustr*e sig*no*re, il Sig*nor*[e] Thomasso Moro Inglese. Roma.

*Endorsed*: 1624. Octob*er* 1. Musk*et*. Recea[ved]: Novemb*er* 15. Answ[ered]: Novemb*er* 16. By Fr[ance].

## 57. Thomas Roper to Thomas More, 8 October 1624

[*AAW, B 27, no. 10*]

Good cosen,

Yours of the 7th and 14th of Sept[ember] came to my handes at one tyme, our post being gon hence the day before. Otherwise you would have had an answeare a weeke sooner. They came to my handes as I was sitting downe to dinner. I opened them, and that for Sir Francis Cotting[ton][838] I sent presently by my man unto him, for if I had carried it after dinner, as I did intende it, I had missed him, he beinge ready <to sette foote in stiroppe and> to goe to Tibolls[839] where the courte was, as my man delivered him your letter w*hi*ch he readde w*it*h great attention, and thoughe my man told him that I would attende on him my selfe when he retorned, he would notwithstandinge know my lodginge. I was this morninge at his house but yet he is not retorned.[840]

Mr Warde desirethe a ~~forme~~ <coppy> of <a> letter of procura [*sic*] from you, otherwise he feareth if it be made here he shall erre in the manner <and forme>. Yet my [*sic for* me] thinkes, w*it*h a testimony of his life, the old procura should serve w*hi*ch was made to you and me. I thinke it be yet extant.

I doe not heare any suche thinge here as you write concerninge ~~the~~ my cosen George Gag[e][841] who hathe lived this quarter of [a] yeare in Wayles w*it*h his sister Stradlinge,[842] and here amonge us is very litle spoken of, and that w*hi*ch is w*it*h you reported is not beleeved here by any. The lady is in the Low Countreys, and I thinke you will see hir

[838] Thomas More's letter of 28 August/7 September 1624 to Sir Francis Cottington thanked him for his 'singular cowrtesies', and asked him, in effect, whether King James desired English Catholic assistance in obtaining the dispensation: AAW, A XVIII, no. 55, p. 337.

[839] Theobalds.

[840] On 14 October 1624, Thomas Roper further noted that he had gone 'once or twice unto Sir Francis Cotting[ton], but it was not my good fortune to meete with him' because he had gone to the court at Royston, but Cottington knew how to contact Roper if need be: AAW, B 27, no. 15.

[841] See Anstr., II, pp. 120–124; Revill and Steer, 'George Gage I and George Gage II', pp. 141–158.

[842] Elizabeth Gage, wife of Sir John Stradling. For the link between the Gage and the Stradling families, see Questier, *C&C*, p. 80.

shortely where you are, so you see they are very farre distant one from the other. There was in deede a great speeche of a likinge betweene him and my cosen Thatchers[843] widdowe, w*hi*ch was Treshamme,[844] but that would be no great fortune to him.

I am hartely sorry to heare that you can have no tidinges of your ringe and two peeces of golde, and the more it troubleth me that I should be the occasion of your losse. My memory never fayled me in any thinge so muche as it did in this, and there never happened suche a like chanche unto me thoughe I have had often chardge of thinges of great valew, and if Fath[er] Seberte[845] can not helpe my memory I know not what to say or [*sic for* of] my cairelensensesse [*sic*]. If these thinges remayned w*i*th me I feare I might have putte them in a ~~drawer~~ cabinette I had w*i*th severall drawers and some secrette devices, w*hi*ch cabinette I sold at my comminge from Rome to the Jewes, and these thinges taking little place might remayne in some of the sayed drawers, and be forgotten by me, and yet all this is but a surmise and a bare conjecture of myne.

I desire to heare whether you have had satisfaction for your luoghi de monti,[846] and likewise to heare how it passethe w*i*th Mrs Warde.

My Lord Windesor[847] takethe his journey this day for Italy. There goeth w*i*th him Mr Clayton.[848]

My Lord Montague hathe receaved a warrante from the councell for to recaule his sonne from Spayne.[849]

Commende me to my uncle Philippe[850] and lette him know that my Lady Tressam dyed this day seavenight, being some two dayes after M*ichael*mas. I am beholdinge to my uncle for he hathe sette me out here amonge his acquaintance to be a great opposite to the padri,[851] and in that kinde <he> is the most passionat man that ever I knew.

Atkinson betaketh himselfe unto his olde trade, and some few dayes a goe touke one of the padri cauled Bonner (alias Juens)[852] that lived in my neigheboured [*sic*] and released him for ten or eleven pounde.

[843] William Thatcher, son of James Thatcher and Mary Gage.

[844] Anne Tresham, daughter of Sir Thomas Tresham.

[845] Robert (Sigebert) Bagshaw OSB.

[846] See *Letter 75*.

[847] Thomas Windsor, 6th Baron Windsor.

[848] This is a reference, apparently, to James Clayton. See AAW, A XIV, no. 112, pp. 353. He told Thomas Rant in late 1623 that Cardinal 'Bandino sayde to my Lord Windsor' that 'hee could lay downe reasons of state why the kinge of England should bee Catholike', and 'a great kinge', and that it would be possible for the court of Rome to 'recompence his spirituall jurisdiction': AAW, B 25, no. 102.

[849] See Questier, *C&C*, pp. 331, 392–393.

[850] Philip Roper.

[851] i.e. the Jesuits.

[852] John Alexander Evison SJ, whose usual alias was Bonham. See CRS, 74, pp. 163–164; *NCC*, pp. 148, 171, 252.

I heare he had money of one or two before, yet he hathe no warrante to apprehend any.[853]

Some reporte that Sir Alberte Morton shall goe leadger into France at the intercession of my Lady Elizab[eth's] grace, whose servante formerly he was.[854]

There came over a Frenche monsieur[855] some weeke ago, who lodgeth w*i*th the amb[assador],[856] but is no man of note. Only he is a courtier and favoured by that kinge, and goethe gallante. There is preparations made for to receave one other, who is comminge, and sayed to be one of the cheife secretarys of Fra*n*ce.[857] In our cause they doe us very little [*word deleted*] or no good at all, for we are more oppressed now than we have bein this great while, and none escape. Twelve pence the Sunday is commonly exacted. Presentementes and indightementes goe forwarde. Mens goodes are seased on and sold and the monyes returned into the exchequer, and all the [*word deleted*] <favor> the ambassador hathe obtayned is that there is a commission granted <lately> unto the chancelour of the exchequer[858] to this effecte, that suche moneys as are allready leav[i]ed shall be returned into the exchequer. Suche goodes as shall be hereafter seased ar to be redelivered uppon the partyes complainte, geaving his owne bonde for so muche debte unto the kinge as the goodes are prised at.[859] There is noe ease at all but in the pursevantes, who yet have no warrantes.[860] What shall we expecte when the matche is effected if, now it is in treaty, we faire so ill? They say it is done only to content the parlement w*hi*ch now is proroged againe untill the 16 of February.[861] The pretence

[853] Stories about the notorious renegade William Atkinson's ties to the Society of Jesus had circulated ever since the appellant controversy. See Anthony Copley, *Another Letter of Mr. A. C. to his Dis-Iesuited Kinseman, concerning the Appeale, State, Iesuites* (London, 1602), p. 26; Anstr., I, p. 13; see also AAW, B 26, no. 40A.

[854] Morton had served as secretary to Princess Elizabeth, electress palatine.

[855] Guillaume de Bautru. See *CSPV, 1623–1625*, p. 456.

[856] Antoine Coiffier de Ruzé, marquis of Effiat. See Tillières, *ME*, pp. 84–85.

[857] Henri-Auguste de Loménie, seigneur de Villeauxclercs.

[858] Sir Richard Weston.

[859] See PRO, SP 14/172/54 (formal letter of the king to Weston, 24 September 1624, concerning the property of recusant Catholics); see also AAW, A XVIII, no. 73, pp. 385–388.

[860] On 28 October/7 November 1624, Richard Ireland commented that, whereas he had written to Thomas Rant about a month earlier concerning the cessation of the persecution 'upon the relation of letters' received from England, 'it seemeth nowe the relation was grounded upon good words that the French emb[assador] had for the revocation of all writs out of the exchequer against Catholiques. But, since, we doe heare such lamentable complaints both by [. . .] letters, and <by> some gentlemen [. . .] that there is extreme persecution in all parts': AAW, B 27, no. 38.

[861] See *CSPV, 1623–1625*, pp. 456, 462.

is by reason of the rifenesse of the sicknesse,[862] w*hi*ch now the colde weather hath diminished, for wheras there dyed 400 and odd a weeke, this last weeke there dyed but 300 and odd.[863]

It is sayed Sir Roberte Nanton shall be master of the wardes,[864] and Sir Roberte Lee cheife justice treasurer of Engl[and].[865]

Mansefeilde departed hence some two dayes agoe, it is sayed. He is gone for Hollande in one of the kinges shippes. On Satterday last in the night there arrose a very great winde, and so great a storme there was that many shippes were cast a way in the Downes, and one of the kinges was very shridly shaken.[866] Some say that one of the Dunkerkers that lay ther did putte to sea, and was followed by five Hollanders. We heare not yet any thinge of them.[867]

Don Carlos[868] departe[d] hence on Monday last w*i*thout audience.[869] Mansefeildes negotiation was thought to be about a leag[u]e against the House of Austria. It is sayed he shall have from us 9,000 men and 3,000 out of Scottland, and twenty thousande pounde a monthe, as muche from France, and from Venice, Savoy, Holland, Swedland twenty thousand pound more, so in all threescore thousand pounde a monthe.[870]

862 The plague.

863 Cf. McClure, *LJC*, p. 588.

864 See *ibid.*, pp. 580, 582. Naunton had been appointed to the mastership of the court of wards on 30 September 1624: E.B. Fryde, D.E. Greenway, S. Porter, and I. Roy (eds), *Handbook of British Chronology* (London, 1986), p. 112; Schreiber, *The Political Career of Sir Robert Naunton*, pp. 95–96; PRO, SP 78/73, fo. 226r.

865 See McClure, *LJC*, pp. 583, 585, 587. James, Baron Ley was appointed lord treasurer on 11 December 1624: Fryde *et al.*, *Handbook of British Chronology*, p. 108.

866 See PRO, SP 78/73, fo. 226r.

867 See McClure, *LJC*, p. 582.

868 Carlos Coloma.

869 See *Letter 56*.

870 George Fisher recorded on 14 October that 'the councell hath taken order, as I heare for certaine, for the pressing of 1,200 men for Mansfield, who is now at the Hage, but everye day expected in England': AAW, A XVIII, no. 73, p. 386. On the same day, Thomas Roper observed that 'there is a secrette order gon downe <in to the countrey> to the deputy lieutenantes for to use their best endevor and industry towardes the raysinge of souldiers for Mansefeilde' and there were 'some sixteene shippes in readinesse' which some believed would be used as transports: AAW, B 27, no. 15. Also, on 14/24 October, John Lockwood in Paris recorded that Mansfelt, in England, would 'have some say 10, others say 12 or 15, thousand men to helpe to remove, as many conjecture, the seige that is before Breda', which 'doth yett hould out, but by the opinion of most men itt will bee taken [. . .] before itt bee longe': AAW, B 27, no. 28. Five days earlier, Chamberlain believed that Mansfelt would have '8,000 English and 4,000 Scotts under sixe regiments': McClure, *LJC*, p. 582. For James's orders, reported by Conway on 5 October 1624, that Mansfelt should receive £15,000 'in assistance of his charge and arminge of his troope', and £20,000 every month 'soe longe as the accion shall last', and a levy of 12,000 men to be transported at royal expense to France, see PRO, SP 78/73, fo. 225r.

Some say my lord of Somersette shall be permitted to bringe a writte of error against his attaynder whereby the title that my Lord Digby hathe to Sherborne shall be overthrowne.[871]

There is some sixteene shippes preparinge for to sette out. Some conceave they shall goe w*i*th the Hollanders to the Ind[i]es. The prince remaynethe at Ritchemonde and is not very well disposed. He complaynethe somewhat of his faule.[872]

Thus w*i*th my kinde remembrance unto your selfe, M^r^ Rant, M^r^ Seton, Sig*no*r Giov[anni] Battista Portinari,[873] in haste I end.

The 8^th^ of October 1624.

Your assured lovinge cosen,

Th[omas] R[oper]

*Addressed*: All' ill*ust*re sig*no*re, il Sig*no*re Tomasso Moro, Inglese. Roma.

*Endorsed*: Ingl[and]. 1624 Fland*e*rs.
Octob[er] 8.
R[eceived]: Nov*em*b[er] 22.
Ans[wered]: Nov*em*b[er] 23.

## 58. Richard Smith to Thomas More, 14/24 October 1624

[*AAW, B 27, no. 29*]

Right worshi*pfu*l and most deer syr,

I have y*our*s of the 23 of 7^ber^ and am hartely glad of the recoverie of y*ou*r health w*hi*ch I pray you looke unto above al other busines. As for the suite of b*ishop*s, I hope in God by y*our* industrie and good praiers you wil overcome at last, for it is Gods cause and Christs legacie to his Church, and therfor I doubt not but you wil have a good end. Here D[octor] Cecil confesseth that he wrote against me, and yet told me

[871] On 14 October 1624, George Fisher informed Thomas More that 'ther is some whispering [...] that' Robert Ker, earl of Somerset 'is creeping againe into favor wich maketh some suspect that the other [*i.e.* the duke of Buckingham] is declining': AAW, A XVIII, no. 73, p. 385. On 21 October, John Colleton observed that Somerset was pardoned and restored to his honours: AAW, B 27, no. 25; McClure, *LJC*, p. 582 (for Somerset's 'promise not to looke toward the court').

[872] See *Letter 55*.

[873] Giovanni Battista Portenari. Thomas More described him as 'somtime secretarie' to Cardinal Francesco Maria Monti and 'afterward' to Cardinal Luigi Capponi: AAW, A XVII, no. 44, p. 149.

th*a*t he thought me and M^r^ Benet[874] fit men for such a place.[875] Now he forbeareth to come to o*u*r house. Persons accused him for an espie to the Inquis[ition].[876] P*er*haps some thing there might be found against him. M^r^ Benet spake to the pope him self for to have a copie of the accusations, and obtained it, and otherwise it were impo*ssi*ble to see them, and me thinkes it were <reason> that that shold be graunted, els honest me*n* may be slaundered irremediably. I am told for certaine that the French nonce[877] hath written for me, and that he earnestly moved the suite of b*ishop*s.

As for England, very lately came over M^r^ Warner,[878] governor to my L[ord] Peters sonnes[879] who now live at Florence, who assureth me that the F[rench] embass[ador],[880] befor his comming, had obtained a letter of the k[ing] to the chancelour of the exchequer[881] to cease al writts against Catholiks, and that the chancelor had sent writtes into al shires for to stay the p*er*secution of goodes, and that the embas[sador] had p*ro*cured the goodes of 60 or 80 Catholiks to be restored to them. And since his comming we have certaine newes that the parlament

[874] A reference, presumably, to Edward Bennett.

[875] Thomas More had informed Edward Bennett that the calumnies against Matthew Kellison and Richard Smith (and also against William Bishop) were sent to Rome by John Cecil as well as by Sir Tobias Mathew: AAW, B 27, no. 19. (Thomas More reported to John Jackson, from Rome on 30 October/9 November 1624, that Thomas Worthington, in a letter to Thomas Rant, had been the source of the claim that William Bishop, had he lived, would have caused factional division within the English Catholic community: AAW, B 27, no. 42.) These briefings against the leading secular clergy candidates to succeed William Bishop elicited a storm of protest. Anthony Champney, for example, argued in October 1624 that the secular clergy's agents in Rome should demand to be informed of the details of the accusations, 'for it cannot stand with anie right that the accuser be heard and the accused be not permitted to answer for him self. And, though the stile of the Holy Office be not peradventure to produce the reasons, yet the accusation must be knowne <to the accused>, unless they will condemn a man without heareing him, which is agaynst the lawe both <of> God and nature, unless it be in notoriis'. Champney remembered that John Bennett, 'when he was there, demanded the same and obtayned the graunt which, beinge knowne, the accusations were recalled as grownded upon false information': AAW, B 27, no. 31. For an account of the accusations against Smith, see also AAW, B 27, no. 63 (Champney to More and Rant, 17/27 November 1624). For Smith's eliciting of the accusations against himself, see *Letter 59*; Allison, RS, pp. 184–185. For judicial procedure in the inquisition at Rome, see G. Crosignani, 'Richard Smith *versus* Robert Persons SJ: a double denunciation at the Holy Office of *The Judgment of a Catholicke English Man*' (forthcoming in *Archivum Historicum Societatis Iesu*).

[876] For Robert Persons SJ's relationship with John Cecil, see Anstr., I, pp. 64–68.

[877] Bernardino Spada, archbishop of Damietta.

[878] Christopher Walpole SJ. I am very grateful to James Kelly for identifying Walpole, who had been sent to England on 9/19 June 1624: CRS, 37, p. 187; CRS, 75, p. 326.

[879] Edward Petre and Thomas Petre, respectively the fourth and sixth sons of William Petre, 2nd Baron Petre. Again, I am grateful to James Kelly for this reference.

[880] Antoine Coiffier de Ruzé, marquis of Effiat.

[881] Sir Richard Weston. See *Letter 57*.

is p*ro*roged til the 2 of Febr[uary]. A litle befor, Catholiks had bene much trobled, as we understood by letters, and p*er*haps yet are in the north p*ar*tes more remote from London.[882] Don Carlos[883] is comen over and, as some say, without audience of the k[ing].[884] M^r^ Messinden[885] writeth from Spayne that certainly Gondemar is to come to England,[886] where now as agent is the secretarie of Flanders,[887] who, as they say, offereth restitution of the Palatinate for to have the mariage,[888] w*hi*ch p*er*haps maketh the stay in the French mariage, for now o*ur* king demandeth of them assistance for recoverie of the Palatinate. And yet, as F[ather] Archangel[889] saieth, both [the] queene mother[890] and some other great councelors say the French mariage wil take place.[891] I have written long since into England for to get you com*m*ission to sue for the dispensation, but they are sloe in writing, becaus[e] their means of sending hither is not good. If there be a visit of the English colledg[e],[892] I pray you move that al Engl[ish] Jes[uits] may be removed becaus[e] they be nourished in faction and breed the like in the

[882]George Fisher's report of 27 October 1624 to Thomas Rant confirmed that the lord keeper had caused a stay in proceedings against Catholics, though 'how long this mitigation will last I know not, but a stopp is made untill the beginning of the parliament wich is in February'. Fisher feared, however, that 'this is but a preparation to the coming of the secretary of France, whom we expect shortly, who finding a calme here will report to the world the good effects of this treaty and the clemency of our king', and that, since 'policy so raigneth', and 'religion hath allmost no place', in the end, 'howsoever the French bragg of the good conditions, I feare the kings word will be all the security they shall have': AAW, B 47, no. 156; cf. *Letter 57*.

[883]Carlos Coloma.

[884]See *Letter 56*.

[885]Edward Maddison.

[886]On 24 September/4 October 1624, Sir Walter Aston (who had, a month previously, mentioned the rumour of Gondomar's return) reported that, two days before, Gondomar had been instructed to lead another embassy to James. But, by mid-December, Aston was saying that Gondomar would not, in any event, leave until after Christmas. On 24 December/4 January, Aston knew that Gondomar had no desire to go and that his unwillingness had resulted in a serious quarrel with Olivares: PRO, SP 94/31, fos 199r, 233v; BL, Harleian MS 1581, fos 58v, 60r, 65r–v.

[887]Jacques Bruneau.

[888]See *Letter 55*. Bruneau offered that the elector palatine would be restored at a meeting of the imperial electors: *CSPV, 1623–1625*, pp. 465–466.

[889]William (Archangel) Barlow.

[890]Marie de Médicis.

[891]John Lockwood, in Paris, recorded on 14/24 October 1624 that 'now of late ther are new articles proposed on both sydes' by the English and French negotiators, and the match was 'yett no more advanced att this present than itt was when itt was first mentioned'. The reason was, it was reported in Paris, that James had commanded the earl of Carlisle to delay. He had also 'proroged the parlament untill the 2 of Februarie next to come'. All of this was done '(as itt is thoughte) too gaine tyme untill hee heare frome Spayne', in other words anticipating Gondomar's return and a peaceful solution to the problem of the Palatinate: AAW, B 27, no. 28.

[892]The English College in Rome.

scholers.[893] But, if there were speedie hope of a b[ishop], it were good it were differred [*i.e.* deferred] til he were heard, who might speak with more authoritie. The Jes[uits] desired to have P. Arnou[894] sent in F[ather] Beruls place but could not obtayne it. I never saw D[octor] Mailer since I made the p*ro*position to him. Perhaps the offer of a good turne hath turned him from us.[895] I pray you do my dutie to my l[ord] of Armach[896] and Monsig*no*r Vives, and thus with my hartiest to y*our* self I com*m*it you to the p*ro*tection of o*ur* sweet savior.

24 of 8ber.

Y*our*s ever as you know,

R[ichard] Smith

*Addressed*: To the right worship*ful* Mr Thomas More.

*Endorsed*: Oct[ober] 24.
1624 Octob*er* 24.
Smith. Rece[ived]: Nov*em*b[er] 12.
Answ[ered]: Nov*em*b[er] 18.
Fr*an*ce.

## 59. Richard Smith to Thomas More, 28 October/7 November 1624

[*AAW, B 27, no. 40*][897]

Right worship*ful* and deere syr,

I have yo*ur*s of the 7 of 8ber, wherby I p*er*ceave both what paines you take in y*our* sute and how fertil our adversaries are in slanders. The

[893] On 11/21 November 1624, Richard Smith rejoiced at the news of the impending visitation of the college. He had heard from his cousin William Rayner that the pope would visit the college 'in flagello, as it wel deserveth, for, as Mr Fitton saieth, the Hospital [*i.e.* the original foundation] is quite suppressed'. Furthermore, the college was in debt to the tune of 9,000 crowns, and 'yet not half the number' of students 'appointed by Greg[ory] 13['s] bul (which is fiftie)' were accommodated there. Smith argued that 'the alumni shold be repetitors, as it was in our time'. In addition, the 'colledge alone shold not herafter choose our protectors or viceprotectors'. They should not seek to put all Jesuits out of the college, for that would be 'against Greg[ory] 13 his bull'; they should try only to exclude English Jesuits: AAW, B 27, no. 53.

[894] Jean Arnoux SJ, confessor to Louis XIII. See Bergin, *The Making of the French Episcopate*, pp. 437, 438, 440.

[895] Smith noted, on 11/21 November 1624, that Henry Mayler was now 'setled with the bishop of Metz', Henri de Bourbon-Verneuil, 'the king his bastard brother': AAW, B 27, no. 53; Bergin, *The Making of the French Episcopate*, p. 190.

[896] Peter Lombard, archbishop of Armagh.

[897] This letter is discussed in Allison, RS, pp. 184–185.

nonce[898] hath told me (but name him to none) that that w*hi*ch is newly objected against me is that I shold say that the p[ope] can not dare facult*at*es regularibus invitis ordinariis, w*hi*ch, as I p*ro*tested to him, I never thought nor (that I know) ever spoke of anie such matter, w*hi*ch also D[octor] Rainer and M^r^ Ireland testified under their hands in a writing w*hi*ch I gave to him, with w*hi*ch he seemed satisfied, and in truth I think he favoureth me, and withal he told me that he merveiled at this objection becaus[e] some Jes[uits] had certified [h]im that they liked me the best of al thos[e] that are p*ro*posed. My cardinal[899] [*MS torn:* told (?)] me (but this also to y*our* self) that they made me an heretik, and yet [*MS torn*] that the F[rench] embass[ador][900] had written to him that the matter wold be effected a[nd] that Card[inal] de Valette was appointed com*m*issarie for it.[901] God, I hope, who hath raised him to favour this his cause, will bring this matter about in due time. For I feare that this wil not be the last slander. But my comfort is mendacia no*n* diu fall*er*unt. I pray you repaire as often as conveniently you can to the F[rench] embass[ador] and to Card[inal] Valette, and let them know how much the clergie hertofore was beholden to the F[rench] nation for p*ro*curing o*ur* first b[ishop],[902] and p*ar*t[icul]erly to Mons*ieu*r Bethune for his help to the appellants.[903] It were not amisse to suggest how F[ather] Fit[zh]erbert was one of the accusers of my booke against Bel to the Inquis[ition], and how falsly they accused that and yet continew that course.[904] I pray you hartely thank my l[ord] primate[905] and al thos[e] who have given their testimonie of me to the Holie Office, and p*ro*cure, if you can, that Card[inal] Valette make Mons*ieu*r Berul be examined about me becaus[e], as I heare, he is not willing other waies to medle in this matter. My card[inal] is at this p*re*sent very ill at ease and therfor I can not troble him in this matter. I am forced

898 Bernardino Spada, archbishop of Damietta.

899 Cardinal Richelieu.

900 Philippe de Béthune, count of Sully.

901 For the pope's appointment, at Béthune's insistence, of Cardinal Louis Nogaret de La Valette to oversee Smith's case in the Holy Office, rather than of the Holy Office's permanent commissary, Desiderio Scaglia, see Allison, RS, pp. 185–186.

902 William Bishop.

903 See *Letter 52*.

904 For the accusations made against Smith concerning his book *An Answer to Thomas Bels late Challeng* (Douai, 1605), see Crosignani, 'Richard Smith *versus* Robert Persons SJ'; *NAGB*, pp. 8, 140. Edward Bennett had recorded on 31 July 1624 that 'it is heer reported that [...] Fa[ther Thomas] Fitzharbert', who had been associated with Robert Persons in the denunciation of Smith's *Answer*, 'opposeth hym self to bushops, and that he giveth owt my lord of Chalcedon favored the oath. For the first they breake promise with me, for F[ather] Blunt promised me that there society would no way oppose our sute for a successor; and for the second they deserve the Inquisition': AAW, B 26, no. 94.

905 Peter Lombard, archbishop of Armagh.

thus to seek to cleare my self becaus[e] the Jes[uits], as it seemeth, espetially seek to deprive [me of] my good name. Otherwise they shold do me a good turne. That w*hi*ch I feare most is the continuance of their p*er*secution, w*hi*ch is very sore for goods, as three who lately come from England do testifie, and M$^{r}$ Cape, of the 27 of their 7$^{ber}$, saieth never was [it] <so> sore for informers since he hath bene Catholik. Nevertheles, the marriage is here thought to be sure, and my card[inal] told me th*a*t his Hol[iness] findeth the conditions for Catholiks as good as they were with Spaine.[906] Both he and the nonce wold have had me to have come up to you as in the name of the clergie for to sue for the dispense if the time of the year had not beene too far spent. M$^{r}$ Fouler[907] and his companions are now arrived at Lions, and in their way hither, but M$^{r}$ Foscue[908] cam hither the last weeke. My cousin D[octor] Rainer was glad of y*our* salutation and that you hoped that he was not the man that joyned with D[octor] Cecil to oppose. If you please, you may let the cardinals know how F[ather] Persons accused D[octor] Cecil for a spie to the Inquis[ition],[909] and there they may find how he escaped, w*hi*ch I think was but fowly and therfor followeth the Jes[uits] least they shold publish his good tricks. F[ather] Sebert[910] may do you some help and I hope he wil doe it willingly.

After I had writt this, came letters out of England of the 2 of 8$^{ber}$ w*hi*ch reporte extreme p*er*secution for goods. God comfort the*m* for my cardinal can not help the*m*. I sent, to M$^{r}$ Rant, D[octor] Rainer['s] and M$^{r}$ Irelands testimonie that I never taught that w*hi*ch is imputed upon me. Paper faileth me, and therfor no more at this present but O*ur* Lord Jesus be alwaies with you.

7 of 9$^{ber}$.

Y*our*s ever,

R[ichard] Smith

[906] Cf. McClure, *LJC*, p. 589.

[907] A reference, apparently, to Ralph Fowler, a cousin of Peter Biddulph, who had left the English College in Rome on 15/25 February 1624: CRS, 37, p. 202. He took minor orders at Douai on 12/22 February 1625: CRS, 10, p. 234. Nine days earlier, Richard Ireland had recorded receipt of a letter from Anthony Champney 'wherby I understand that M$^{r}$ Fowler is entered among the Benedictins, and soe begineth his novitiatship there': AAW, B 47, no. 120; see also AAW, B 47, no. 49. Fowler also considered entering the Oratory: AAW, B 47, no. 115. But, as Champney pointed out to Thomas More in a letter of 9/19 March 1625, Fowler 'had <made> us belive here he would be a [secular] preist': AAW, B 47, no. 54.

[908] This may be a reference to George Fortescue. See *NCC*, pp. 292, 314.

[909] See *Letter 58*.

[910] Robert (Sigebert) Bagshaw OSB.

*Addressed*: To the right worship*ful* his assured freind Thomas More.

*Endorsed*: Nov[ember] 7.
France. 1624.
Novemb*er* 7. D[r] Smith. Recea[ved]: Novemb*er* 25.
Answ[ered]: Dec*ember* 2.

## 60. John Nelson [Jackson] to Thomas More and Thomas Rant, 5 November 1624

[*AAW, B 27, no. 35*]

My very r*everen*d and revere*n*ced sirs,

I presume yo*ur* loves both to one another and mee also will take in good part th*at* I write but one *lett*re to yow both. I am farr fro*m* London and knowe not how this one will be conveighed. I have written fro*m* tyme to tyme to o*ur* freinds beyond, th*at* yow might fro*m* them be enformed of all occurre*n*ces. I have also written to M[r] Coll[eton] earnestly th*at* he wold eyther himself, or by his secretarye, write every weeke (as I wold doe, were I in his case) and I hear th*at* others about Londo*n* hold correspo*n*dence w*hi*ch makes mee, being absent, forbear to troble yow so oft as I am willing to doe. In my last informatio*n* of Fa[ther] Blu*n*t his trecherous dealing, I omitted to let yow know that he came in at my back when I suspected nothing, having agreed before that I would eyther have private audience or none. I did not then know it was he.[911] But I came after to knowe it. Wee doe wonder here how matters are caried th*at* in France and, as it seems, in R[ome], the p*er*secutio*n* is not beleived. I did write to D[octor] Smith and receyved a *lett*re fro*m* him th*at* we shold hear noe more of th*at* point. Yet, at the same tyme, I receyved one fro*m* M[r] Coll[eton] th*at* Cath[olics] had not been soe p*er*secuted these 60 years.[912] There came forth a proclamatio*n* com*ma*unding persons of qualitie to reside in their countryes, dated th*e* 19[th] of O*cto*ber 1624.[913] One writes to me from Londo*n* th*at*, except the yeare of the battell at Prage,[914] he never knew so p*er*ilous a tyme as this is like to be. And, thowgh there be some small stay of proceedings, yet it is uncertaine and, in th*e* country, litle or noe notice is taken therof. He writes also th*at* some think th*e* Fr[ench] match is dowbtfull,

[911] See *Letter 51*.

[912] John Colleton's letter of 8 October to More and Rant had claimed that the 'persecution holdes still in some degree, thoughe the extremitie be abaited of that it was, worse than at any time for thes[e] threescore yeares, bloud excepted': AAW, B 27, no. 9bb.

[913] *SRP*, I, no. 259.

[914] 1620.

thowgh it is said th*at* o*ur* k[ing] is now co*n*tented that th*e* mariage shall precede the league rather than fayle of both and th*at*, upon Mansfeilds com*m*ing over, who was this last week expected, there shold be 12,000 men pressed and transported w*i*th speed, some say by th*e* end of 9ber. But because there shold be 8,000 maintained by the French, <for the pay> wherof there is yet noe certenty, p*er*haps they will not be sent soe soone.[915] Others will write unto yow of the French archb[ishop],[916] who came hither fro*m* the k[ing] by co*n*sent of his Hol[iness] as it is said, who was at Oxford and w*i*th th*e* k[ing].[917] Yow know I love France but I can not but greive to think th*at* they soe joyne w*i*th enemies to religio*n*,

[915]See *Letter 63*.

[916]Guillaume d'Hugues, Franciscan archbishop of Embrun.

[917]On 29 October, Thomas Roper had reported that 'the archebishoppe of Ambrune is lately comme from our universities. He dothe not seeme to meddle in affaires but rather to observe the courses of thinges': AAW, B 27, no. 32. On 27 October 1624, however, George Fisher had given it as his opinion that 'the archbishoppe of Ambrone (who was sometimes generall of the Fratte Minore) [. . .] hath bin with the king', and James complained to him that 'his Catholique subjects ar too much addicted to the Spaniard, wich discourse pleaseth the French': AAW, B 47, no. 156; Bergin, *The Making of the French Episcopate*, p. 641. For Embrun's fact-finding mission to England, see also *CSPV, 1623–1625*, pp. 479, 480, 486, 493; McClure, *LJC*, p. 586; *CGB*, II, p. 579; PRO, PRO 31/3/61, fos 79r–90r (Embrun's own account, dated March 1635, of the origins and progress of his visit, undertaken in the first instance at the instigation of a Scottish Franciscan but with the backing of Louis XIII). He took part in ceremonies of sacramental confirmation, which disquieted some English Catholics, though John Colleton, it appears, approved. Embrun dispatched an apologia to Rome for his proceedings in England. It replied to the complaints which had been made about him, and which were amplified by the Spaniards in Rome, especially the claim that he had dispensed the sacrament of confirmation without licence. He described his confirming of English Catholics both in their houses in and around London and in the French embassy (where he stayed, for part of his time in the country, with Effiat, even though he initially came as a private individual). He claimed that Colleton had furnished 'les ornaments et aultres choses nécessaires qui luy estoient restés entre les mains par la mort de leur [. . .] évêque'; and 'la chose feult portée aux oreilles du roy par certains puritains principaux': PRO, PRO 31/9/90, p. 201; *Letters 61*, *63*, *68*; PRO, PRO 31/3/61, fos 79v, 89r; Tillières, *ME*, p. 85. Embrun was alleged to have visited both Mansfelt and George Abbot, though Fisher subsequently denied it, as did Embrun in his apology sent to Rome: Tillières, *ME*, p. 85; *Letter 63*; AAW, A XVIII, no. 93, p. 449; PRO, PRO 31/3/61, fo. 89r. On his own account, Embrun made contact with leading Catholics, including the countess of Buckingham and the earl of Rutland. While he was in England, it was rumoured in France that he was labouring to convert King James: PRO, PRO 31/3/61, fos 80v, 81r. On 7 December 1624, Edward Bennett noted that, although Embrun, who had now departed, had 'confirmed heer at least 2,000' ('with what autority we know not'), nevertheless 'by this his Holl[iness] may see what neede heer is of a b[ishop] or rather bushops', and 'the arch[bishop] promised to informe his Holl[iness] of it': AAW, B 27, no. 73. Smith put a different gloss on the archbishop's visit. On 11/21 November, he wrote to More that 'there was in England a French bishop, greatly Jesuited', and that 'perhaps the Jes[uits] wil get that F[rench] bishop to confirme thos[e] noble men or woemen of theirs whome they wold not have to receave that sacrament of our b[ishop]': AAW, B 27, no. 53. Embrun claimed, though, that some Hispanophile English Catholics disliked what he did: PRO, PRO 31/9/90, p. 201. Smith had, in fact, received a letter from Colleton, dated

and in prejudice to religion, for all the victories which those get with whom they joyne hurt the cause of Gods Church. There be 2 tollerated by our state to enforme the French imb[assador]: one M^r^ Foster[918] of Yorkshire (who hath a brother a Jesuite[919]) and one M^r^ Minshaw a lawyer,[920] both Jesuited, and I think the Jes[uits] joyne with the duke upon the hopes they have by his mother,[921] and soe will enforme as shall stand with theire ends. God amend all. There hath been a scandalous report of one Fa[ther] Bartlet a Jesuite in Somersetshire.[922] One Kate Bussy went to the b[ishop] of Bathe[923] etc*etera* and told him what his cariage was towards her. It seems he grew acquainted with her, and eyther made her Cath[olic] or pretended it and, if she were, she is taken and told all. Yet his superiours doe not take him owt of the country.[924] D*octo*r Champ[ney] did write the 9th of Aug[ust] from Par[is] to M^r^ Coll[eton] that I or M^r^ Pitts shold procure an answer of these 2 points from the founder of our residence at Parise:[925] 1. Whether he hath testified to any that he wold not have M^r^ Reyner remooved above all the rest. 2dly whether he hath made a revocation of his gift because his will is not observed; which 2 points Fa[ther] Blunt <vice> provinciall of the Jes[uits] had written thither, and therby hindred the proceeding of the howse. I got that honorable gentleman, the founder, to my lodging, when M^r^ Coll[eton] was present, and read that part

18 November, stating that 'the archb[ishop] of Embrun, who is in England, assureth them that our king wil have no cessation of penal laws til the mariage be consumate'. But Colleton 'addeth withal that the forsaid archb[ishop] saieth that after the mariage we shal have more than we can expect': AAW, B 27, no. 82. For Embrun's advice in November 1624 to Buckingham concerning the link between toleration for James's Catholic subjects and the issue of the dispensation, see BL, Harleian MS 1583, fo. 238v; and for his applause, in a letter of 15/25 January 1625 to Prince Charles, for James's concessions to Catholics, see *ibid.*, fo. 246v.

[918] Richard Forster (knighted in 1649). See *NCC*, p. 121; M. Foster, 'Sir Richard Forster (?1585–1661)', *RH*, 14 (1978), pp. 163–174. Foster speculates that Forster was introduced into royal service by Sir George Calvert: Foster, 'Sir Richard Forster', p. 165.

[919] Thomas (or Seth) Forster SJ. See CRS, 74, p. 176.

[920] For a warrant of November 1624 delivered to 'Richard Minshull and Richard Forster' to carry out unspecified services for the marquis of Effiat, PRO, SP 78/73, fo. 331r. The reference to Minshull may, in fact, indicate the Catholic John Middlemore: see PRO, SP 14/177/37. Thomas Roper explained that Middlemore and Forster would 'be authorised by my lord keeper and the ambass[ador] [. . .] to see the stay of proceedinges, and to repayre uppon occasion to the judges with messadges from them': AAW, B 27, no. 32.

[921] Mary Villiers, countess of Buckingham.

[922] Richard Bartlett SJ. See Anstr., II, p. 18.

[923] Arthur Lake, bishop of Bath and Wells.

[924] In mid-November 1624, Jackson reiterated that he hoped the 'accusation of the Jes[uit] to the b[ishop] of Bath and Wells' was 'undeserved', but 'usually there is noe smoak without some fire': AAW, B 27, no. 47; see also *Letter 72*. Thomas More, in his letter of 15/25 January 1625 to Jackson, asked for further news about this incident: AAW, A XIX, no. 2, p. 3.

[925] i.e. Thomas Sackville, the patron of the Collège d'Arras.

of the letter. To the first point he answer[e]d he never testified or spake any such matter, nor any thing belonging to it. To th*e* 2$^{d}$ he answered, absolutely noe. He had not revoked it. This I testified under M$^{r}$ Colletons hand and my owne, wherby Fa[ther] Blunt is co*n*vinced to be a false informer, an unworthy office for a religious sup*er*ior.[926] Yow may speak this as a testified truth, as also his informing the Sp[anish] imb[assador][927] of my audience.[928] A gentlema*n*, hearing these 3, said th*a*t I had got <such> an advantage against th*e* Jes[uits] as he had not formerly heard of, because they did <soe cuningly> cary their buisinesses as thowgh we had ground to suspect their bad dealing, yet he co[u]ld never see any proofe before against the*m*, w*hi*ch now he did. I receyved yo*ur* l*ett*re (M$^{r}$ Rant) of th*e* 28 of 7$^{ber}$ on the 1 of 9$^{ber}$ and I receyved one fro*m* yow (M$^{r}$ More) since I came into the country. I make the best use of yo*ur* l*ett*res I can. I shew them where they may doe good, and acquaint as many as I can w*i*th th*e* co*n*tents. But I am not acquainted w*i*th what yow write to others, unles [I] sometyme get a sight of M$^{r}$ Colleto*ns* [*sic*] his l*ett*res. Yet I hear yow inform M$^{r}$ Musket.[929] There was a rumo*ur* of Gondomar his returne, but w*i*thout ground as I hear,[930] and some rather think th*a*t the agent[931] who is here will ~~rather~~ depart, at the least if th*e* press of 12,000 [*in margin:* whereof Mansfeild is to be generall] goe on, and I had it fro*m* a good hand th*a*t before the end of 8$^{ber}$ it had passed th*e* hands of the l[ords] of th*e* councell and wanted but th*e* kings hand. Yow have made me long (M$^{r}$ Rant) for th*a*t justificatio*n* of the archb[ishop] of Philippi[932] his bookes, as they in Doway have made me of the booke.[933] [*In margin:* Send it him.] And yow are in th*e* right th*a*t such wares are

[926]Matthew Kellison had alerted Thomas Rant, on 15/25 September 1624, that Colleton and Jackson had confirmed Sackville's answers about the Collège d'Arras; and yet Richard Blount SJ had declared the exact opposite to John Cecil and George Latham SJ: AAW, B 26, no. 139.

[927]Juan Hurtado de Mendoza, marquis of Inojosa.

[928]Presumably John Jackson refers to his audience with the French ambassador, the marquis of Effiat, on 21 August 1624 (see *Letter 51*).

[929]George Fisher.

[930]See *Letter 58*.

[931]Jacques Bruneau.

[932]Philip Rovenius.

[933]Jackson seems to be referring to Rovenius's controversial *Tractatus de Missionibus ad Propagandam Fidem, et Conversionem Infidelium et Haereticorum Instituendis* (Louvain, 1624). On 27 October/6 November 1624, Matthew Kellison had recorded that the religious orders were combining together in an attack on Rovenius's recently published book (which Kellison had in his possession). Kellison expressed the hope that he might 'visit this bishop of Holland, who is in a monasterie not above an Inglish mile from Bruxelles': AAW, B 27, nos 23, 37. For Rovenius's book, see *CGB*, I, pp. xxxii, 525. For the agreement between Rovenius and his critics, worked out initially by Propaganda Fide in May 1623 (dated 5/15 October 1624, and finally confirmed by

very gratefull. But I co[u]ld never get th*a*t booke, w*hi*ch the Jes[uits] set forth in Parise, w*hi*ch as I have heard was not much in favo*u*r of the sea apostolick. Well, I think th*e* Church of God had need to looke to these good fathers fingers ere it be too late. I hope (M^r Mo[re]) yow have yo*u*r treatise against their governme*n*t of seminaries,[934] and I intend by th*e* next to send yow a very good informatio*n* w*hi*ch aloan were sufficient in my opinio*n* to remoove the*m* fro*m* o*u*r colleges. I hope yow will be carefull th*a*t the publishing of the jubilee here may be sent to th*e* cleargy.[935] But we hope yow will send us an other Chalced[onensis] ep[iscopus], ere that tyme, w*hi*ch we have soe much want of, as I can not but mervayle th*a*t any opposition shold hinder it. Owr Lord Jesus prosp*er* yo*u*r labo*u*rs and send us a joyfull meeting.

My freinds take yo*u*r reme*m*brances as they well deserve, in very kind maner, and here, w*i*th my best respects to yow both, I rest, this fifth of 9^ber 1624.

Yo*u*rs in th*e* maner yow knowe,

J[ohn] N[elson]

When Don Carlos Coloma arrived at Calis, caryed in th*e* kings ship, Don Fra*n*cesco[936] met him w*i*th intentio*n* to accompany him to Bruxells, but at th*e* same tyme there came a pacquet fro*m* th*e* infanta,[937] telling [him] th*a*t the order was come fro*m* Spaine th*a*t he must neyther goe to Bruxells nor Cambray but remaine at Gant as the marques del Enojosa is detayned a journey short also of Madrid, upo*n* a motio*n* of o*u*r imb[assador] or agent in Spayne th*a*t they had spoken to th*e* k[ing] against the prince and duke, but I think th*a*t of the prince will not proove soe.[938] However it shewes th*e* k[ing] of Sp[ain] his desire

Propaganda in August 1625), see *CGB*, I, pp. xxxii, 326, 338, 510–511, 575, II, p. 625; AAW, A XVIII, no. 74, pp. 389–394; AAW, A XIX, no. 67, pp. 201–204.

934 It is not clear which document is indicated here. John Jackson may be referring to one of the manuscript accounts of the governance of the English College in Rome, retained in the secular clergy's agent's papers in Rome, e.g. AAW, A XVIII, nos 25, 94, 95, 97.

935 For the jubilee, see AAW, B 26, no. 98; AAW, B 27, nos 47, 107; cf. *CGB*, I, p. 566, II, p. 608.

936 François de Carondelet.

937 Isabella Clara Eugenia, archduchess of Austria.

938 For claims that Inojosa was in disgrace at the Spanish court for his attempt to bring down Buckingham, see AAW, B 27, nos 10b, 14; PRO, SP 14/173/23; see also above, pp. 78–79. For a contrary report, see PRO, SP 14/175/33. On 17/27 July 1624, Sir Walter Aston observed that Inojosa could rely upon Olivares, since Inojosa was 'allied both to the conde and his lady'. Aston, on Conway's orders to secure 'some exemplary justice against the marquis' and, he implied, Coloma as well, did his best to 'negotiate' at Madrid against both ambassadors. Aston assured James that he would 'find that the markes of' his 'distasts are seconded with publike demonstrations' of Philip IV's 'displeasure towards them': PRO, SP 94/31, fos 115r, 197r, 205r. For Aston's accusations, see *CSPV, 1623–1625*,

to give o*u*r k[ing] all possible satisfactio*n* w*hi*ch gives him th*e* greater adva*n*tage if there shold be any breach, w*hi*ch God forbid. Da pace*m*, d*omi*ne, in diebus n*ost*ris.

*Addressed*: To the right worship*fu*ll my very worthy freinds Mr Tho[mas] More and Mr Rant, or eyther of them. At Rome.

*Endorsed*: Written: Novemb[er] 5.
Received: Decemb[er] 17.
Answered: January 1 1625.

## 61. Thomas Roper to Thomas More, 12 November 1624

[*AAW, B 27, no. 43*]

Good cosen,

Mr Muskette[939] did receave one this weeke from you but had no time to answeare it. My company is well. Only your neece is troubled w*i*th a colde. Mansfeilde is here w*i*th us, but lodgethe now at the seigne of the palsgrave in Lombarde Streite. Since his comminge, there hathe bein 3 or 4 severall presses of men in London, and they have raysed some 1,500 or 2,000 men and they have sent into other countreys to levye the rest, w*hi*ch in all must be twelve thousande. It is muche wondered uppon what service they shall goe this winter tyme under such a commander. We have 4 or 5 Catholicke shrifes chosen, whereof some are convicted: Mr Perkins in Barkesheire,[940] Mr Stanforde[941] in Staffordsheire, <and> Sir Henry Sherley in Lestersheire.[942]

There is a rumor that there is order geaven for the restrainte of proceedinges against recusantes but nothinge is don therein, for the persequution is heavy, and never ~~allmost~~ greater if you consider the generality. God comforte us all. And yet some labour to possesse forreners that it is not so, who conceave it is not so great as we make

pp. 412, 413; *CCE*, pp. 177–178. Initially, Aston seemed to get results, for on 24 September/4 October he could report that both ambassadors were forbidden to return to the court in Madrid: PRO, SP 94/31, fos 232r, 255r. For the temporary disgrace (if at all) of Inojosa and Coloma because of their attempted coup against Buckingham earlier in the year, see also *CSPV, 1623–1625*, pp. 300, 301, 303, 309, 395, 449, 463, 472, 484; AAW, B 27, no. 18; PRO, SP 14/173/23; PRO, SP 14/175/33; *CCE*, p. 186; *CGB*, I, p. 539. On 22 October/1 November, Philip officially informed the Flanders administration that Inojosa and Coloma were completely cleared, and that Coloma could resume his duties at Cambrai: *CCE*, p. 187.

[939] George Fisher.

[940] The sheriff of Berkshire, appointed in late 1624, was, in fact, Sir John Blagrave.

[941] Edward Stanford.

[942] For Sir Henry Shirley, see R. Cust, 'Catholicism, antiquarianism and gentry honour: the writings of Sir Thomas Shirley', *Midland History*, 23 (1998), pp. 45, 65; *NCC*, p. 209.

it because there is so great concurse unto the ambass[ador][943] for to receave the sacrament of confirmation w*hi*ch the archeb[ishop][944] there dothe administer,[945] and I thinke is more tollerate[d] to blinde strangers. It is sayed the duke of Buckingh[am] shall ~~have~~ be prince palatine of Munster and lieutennant generall of Ireland.[946] In hast I end.

12 of 9ber 1624.

Yours,

Th[omas] R[oper]

*No address.*

*Endorsed*: Ingl[and]. 1624 Nov*emb*er 2.
Rece[ived] [and] answ[ered]: December 21.

## 62. Richard Smith to Thomas More, 25 November/5 December 1624

[*AAW, B 27, no. 70*]

Right worship*full* and deere syr,

Albeit I wrote unto you by the last ordinarie[947] and also by an extraordinarie since,[948] nor have at this time anie great matter to write, yet wold I not omit to send by this ordinarie to let you know what here wee have. Since, therfor, my last, the mach betwene England and France hath bene published by fires of joy and shooting of artillerie, and the secretarie Villoclare is gone into England to take our kings oathe to keepe the articles.[949] The English Jesuits

[943] Antoine Coiffier de Ruzé, marquis of Effiat.

[944] Guillaume d'Hugues, Franciscan archbishop of Embrun.

[945] See *Letters 60, 63, 68*.

[946] See *CSPV, 1623–1625*, p. 499.

[947] AAW, B 27, no. 53 (11/21 November 1624).

[948] AAW, B 27, no. 60 (16/26 November 1624).

[949] On 7 December 1624, Edward Bennett reported that 'a day agoe the French secretary', Henri-Auguste de Loménie, seigneur de Villeauxclercs, 'arived and was mett by the erle of Dorsett': AAW, B 27, no. 73; see also PRO, PRO 31/3/60, fo. 304r. Henry Clifford understood that, when Villeauxclercs reached Dover, he learned of '3 Catholicks' who had been arrested 'passing [. . .] for England, and there [were] imprisoned and their bookes, beades and other things [had been] taken from them'. Villeauxclercs 'woulde not part thence till these 3 persons were delivered and all their goods restored': AAW, B 27, no. 84. Bennett recorded that 'this day we goe to hime to present our service. Within two dayes he goeth to meete the king at Cambridge where the embassadour is to take his oath abowt the conditions agreed upon. What they be we know not': AAW, B 27, no. 73; see also *CSPV, 1623–1625*, pp. 510, 515; McClure, *LJC*, pp. 589, 591; PRO, SP 14/176/16, 53. For the audience of

agent[950] is gone with him as his chaplen and, as some say, also D[octor] Cecil, for he vanished out of the towne at the same time. The last news of al from M^r Cape were of the begining of the last moneth w*hi*ch told of a fresh renewing of the p*er*secution. But now I hope that is ceased. I can heare nothing fro*m* o*u*r brethren in London. We shal have a good b[ishop][951] ~~from~~ <for> grand almoner to o*ur* princess, and divers English preists for her chaplens, amongst ~~w*hi*ch~~ <whome> I have named you, if you please to accept of it when you returne. The Jesuits give out that they shal have the place of the confes[sor],[952] but that is not certaine, and some report that o*u*r English embass[adors] say they shall passe over their bellies befor that be. It is said that Co[u]nte Carlil is shortly to goe to England, and one Syr [Albert] Morton is to come as leiger here.[953] Out of England is written that the k[ing] had com*m*anded to raise 12 thousand out of hand for to rescue Breda, and yet that Gondamar was dayly expected in England.[954] Thus much for other matters. As for o*u*r owne cause, there is a bul of Greg[ory] 14, made [in] 1591, extant in propi ep*iscop*ali procesii, w*hi*ch forbiddeth anie to make information of thos[e] that are p*ro*posed to be b*ishop*s, besides such [as] are deputed therto by his Holines, and p*ar*ticulerly forbiddeth [*word illegible*] inimicos and aemulos. And yet o*ur* Jes[uits] being both inimici and aemuli, nor being deputed by his Holines, take upon them this office. P*er*haps if you read the bul you may pick thence some thing to y*our* purpose. The other day passed herby a young scholler of that colledg[e] called Hastings,[955] who saieth he came downe for his health, and goeth to Liege to studie. P*er*haps he is sent downe to devide the new order setled in that colledg[e], and therfor it were wel to know whether he was an alumne of the colledg[e] or no, and after to doe as you see convenient.[956] If you heare any thing

Bennett and other leading secular clergymen (including John Colleton, Joseph Haynes, and William Shelley) with Villeauxclercs, in order to acknowledge their obligation to Louis XIII, see AAW, B 27, no. 74. Villeauxclercs promised them that the French court would ensure that the Stuart court delivered on its promises of toleration made in the course of the treaty negotiations. For the confirmation of concessions over religion, secured by Villeauxclercs during his audience with the king at Cambridge, see PRO, PRO 31/3/60, fo. 305v *et seq*; also above, p. 108.

950 A reference, apparently, to George Latham SJ. See *Letter 69*.

951 Daniel Du Plessis de la Mothe-Houdancourt, bishop of Mende.

952 See AAW, A XVIII, no. 86, pp. 419–420 (John Colleton's letter to a cardinal in Rome, 13 December 1624: 'Quare non expedit ut confessarius reginae sit Jesuita').

953 See *CSPD, 1623–1625*, pp. 207, 212, 314, 327, 330.

954 For the progress of Spinola's siege of Breda, see AAW, B 27, nos 72, 88; *CSPV, 1623–1625*, *passim*; see also above, pp. 108–109.

955 Edmund Hastings, alias Manners, son of Sir Henry Hastings, had left the English College in Rome on 1/11 October 1624: CRS, 37, p. 202; CRS, 55, p. 372.

956 On the same day that Smith wrote this letter, Richard Ireland noted that Edmund Hastings had recently arrived in Paris and had 'gone hence to Liege'. He was 'much

of a letter sent thither by Jes[uits] w*hi*ch, they say, was written by a preist,[957] and sent fro*m* house to house to p*er*swade to put out Jes[uits], I pray you make it to be brought out and the place named and p*er*son of whome they had it, for I fear it is forged by them. But F[ather] Leander[958] telleth that, whiles he was in England, he knew 12 preists put out of their places in one moneth by one Jesuit, who asked their patrons whether the preist co[u]ld catechize or preach or give the sp*irit*ual exercises, and, if they co[u]ld [*word omitted:* not], he p*ro*vided them a Jes[uit]. M^r^ Bennet[959] writeth to me that we shold p*ro*cure that o*ur* b[ishop], when God shal give us one, be made vicar to the pope. I think he is made made [*sic*] delegate to him in [*word obscured:* main *or* manie] cases by the co[un]cel of Trent. I pray you confer therof with y*our* freinds. And thus with my hartiest com*m*endations I com*m*it you to the p*ro*tection of o*ur* sweet savior.

5 of 10^ber^.

Y*our*s owne [*sic*],

R[ichard] Smith

*Addressed*: To the right worship*ful*l M^r^ Thomas More.

*Endorsed*: 5 Decemb[er].
Paris. 1624. D*octo*r Smith.
Decemb*er* 5. Recea[ved]: Decemb*er* 27. Answ[ered]: Decemb*er* 30.
De Vicario Apostolico.

## 63. George Musket [Fisher] to Thomas More, 26 November 1624

[*AAW, A XVIII, no. 80, pp. 407–408*]

R*everen*d and very worthy s*ir*,

I cannot persuade my selfe that you have <so> much cause to complaine of our slackenes in writing as you intimate in your last

disappoynted for some meanes, having missed to find Fa[ther] George [Latham] heere': AAW, B 27, no. 69.

957 See *Letter 71*.

958 John (Leander) Jones OSB.

959 Edward Bennett.

of the 2 of Octob[er], for although your extraordinary diligence may be some condemnation of our negligence, yet we should be to[o] much to blame and forgetful of our selves if we should not hold correspondency at this time, especially when it so much concerneth us. I have urged Mr Coll[eton] very earnestly and he telleth me that he hath written unto you every weeke since this intercourse began and given full informatio*n* of the state of all matters here and, for my part, I have writte*n* so many times. True it is I have omitted to wrighte thes[e] last tow weekes, being otherwise imploied abroad. The letters you [have] written [?] to me I have comunicated to Mr Colleton and others, as occasions served, and I hope before this you have received our informations concerning the persecution here wich hath bin very great. And, although now they proceed more moderately, yet we cannot presume of peace but rather feare persecution bycause as yet we cannot perceive that any thing is done effectually by the French in our behalfe, no course taken for the staiing <the execution> of the penall statutes or abolishing the 2 oaths of supremacy and allegiance. What is intended I know not. The tow priests in Newgate who have long expected ther inlargement by mediation of the French ar still in prison. All the ease we find is that we are not molested by pursivants and promotors as formerly we have bin. The French complaine that we fill yours [*sic*] eares with rumors of persecution, but I pray God we have not greater cause to complaine of them for concealing the truth and persuading the world that all persecution is ceased, wheras the matter is farr otherwise. I perceive they earnestly desire this match and, if I be not deceived, they will conclude it uppon any conditions rather than faile, wich whether it will be to the good of our country I leave to your prudent consideration. They condemne us [*word deleted*] also for not sending an agent as we did in the time of the treaty with Spaine to sollicite a dispensation. But you know how to answere this complaint, having fuller comission to deale in this busines.[960] The 21

[960]Thomas Roper added his voice to Fisher's, in a letter written on the previous day (25 November). Roper thought that 'the pressinge of us by the Frenche ambass[ador] (and some say allso the archebish[op] of Ambrune joynethe with him that we are all Sp[a]niardes) turnethe muche to our prejudice, and it is a kinde of justifiinge of the persequution against us. If we might from France receave the like ease we did from Spayne we should as soone be Frenche as Spaniardes; but truly, since the Frenche treaty hathe bein, we have had nothing but a heavy persequution, and yet they labour us <as I am credebly told> to write letters and to certify bothe to Paris and Rome that there is no persequution and to assure his Holinesse that our kinge intendethe well to Catholickes and Catholike religion, wich <in diverse respectes and> in pointe of state <allso> we cannot doe, seinge his Majesty in all his <publicque> speeches and discourses which he maketh <dothe endevor> to make the contrary appeare unto his subjectes; and to sette downe in writinge under our handes the contrary is very dangerous and not fittinge for us to doe. Likewise we are laboured by the ambass[ador] to sollicite and hasten the dispensation': AAW, B 27, no. 58.

of this moneth, bonefiers were at every dore in London in token of joy for the agreement made betwine the tow kings concerning this treaty, and now every houre we expect an extraordinary ambassador from France. The archb[ishop] of Ambrune departed hence this last weeke furnished with the best informations we could give him and accordingly I suppose he will informe the king of France and those ther that ar to deale in this busines.[961] He confirmed many here at severall times, wich was not so well liked by some.[962] But I suppose he did no more than he might well doe. Many here could wish he had come in another fashion and kept the port of a bishoppe, for his being here as a private man in secular habit did somewhat derogate from the dignity of an archb[ishop] and made him lesse esteemed by Catholiques. Also his going to visit Mansfield and Canterbury caused some to mutter. Mansfield hath bin here this fortnight and more, expecting souldiers. At his coming over he was in great danger by sea. The kings shippe wich was to waift him over was cast away by violence of the tempest, in wich were divers English gentlemen and some of Mansfields souldiers to the number of 16[o] all cast away, with some treasure of Mansfields.[963] How much we cannot certainly learne. Since his coming hither, ther arrived uppon the coast of Kent 16 saile, as is reported. In thes[e] shipps ther ar 6,000 Almans or more, as some say.[964] Our souldiers to the number of 1,200 ar, if reportes be true, to joine <with them>. Marry, what enterprize they have in hand no man can imagine. Only the king hath promised the Spanish secretary here that he intendeth no hurt to the king of Spaine nor his dominions. Much muttering [*p. 408*] ther is about thes[e] forraine souldiers, and the more for that wee heare that Brunswike[965] is to be here shortly.

[961] Roper commented that, 'thoughe otherwayes a good man', Embrun 'dothe discover muche passion against Spayne, which makethe him and the discreter sorte of Frenche men to forgette God Allmighties cause, and to say what our state here sayethe and urgethe against us'. Furthermore, at his departure, he was taking with him 'Mr [William] Atkinson the apostata': AAW, B 27, no. 58.

[962] See Tillières, *ME*, p. 85; *Letters 60, 61*. Zuane Pesaro had commented on 19 November 1624 that Embrun had finished his business in England, 'glorying in having publicly performed sacramental functions, a thing that no one has accomplished since the change of religion in these realms', despite complaints from both 'Jesuits and certain Catholics' that he had 'ventured to officiate in another's jurisdiction'. He 'particularly prayed the Catholics' and the religious orders, 'as Béthune requested, to send petitions to Rome to hasten on the dispensation', but the Jesuits had been unwilling to comply: *CSPV, 1623–1625*, p. 501.

[963] On 19/29 November, Henry Clifford reported to Thomas More that Mansfelt escaped with his page and lieutenant, although 100 of his company were drowned: AAW, B 27, no. 64; cf. McClure, *LJC*, p. 586; Whiteway, *Diary*, p. 66.

[964] For the recruiting of these German soldiers, see Whiteway, *Diary*, p. 67; *HMCMK*, p. 219.

[965] Christian of Brunswick, administrator of the bishopric of Halberstadt. He had, two months before, approached the English ambassadors in Paris in order to 'sollicit' their

Mansfield was desirous to land thes[e] souldiers in Kent but the king would not heare of that. Onely he hath given his leave to land 200 at a time, unarmed, to aire themselves. Southampton and his sonne ar both lately dead in the Low Countries.[966] Some rumors ar spread also of Grave Maurice his death, but the[y] ar yet uncertaine. I have no more to impart at this present but my best love to your selfe and good M^r^ Rant.

Yours ever assuredly,

G[eorge] Mus[ket]

Novemb[er] 26.

*Addressed*: To the w*orshipfu*ll his very worthy freind M^r^ Thomas More.

*Endorsed*: Ingl*an*d. 1624. Musk[e]t.
Novemb[er] 26. Recea[ved] [and] answ[ered]: January 11 1625.

## 64. Richard Smith to Thomas More, 23 December 1624/2 January 1625

[*AAW, B 47, no. 21*]

Right worshipful and deere syr,

I have y*ou*rs of the 2 of 10^ber^. And now at the last are the bulls come for to make me b[ishop] of Calcedon, but no jurisdiction at al for England.[967] And therfor I have intreated my cardinal[968] and the nonce[969] to write that I may have the same auth*ority* w*hi*ch my p*re*dec*ess*or had, w*hi*ch was to be ordinarius of England,[970] with the same extrordinarie faculties that the archepriests had, and that in case of necessitie I may confirme sine ornamentis pontificalibus cu*m* solis sacerdotalibus,

'mediation for some employment for him, who otherwise must be forced to accept of the emperours offer of pardon and to serve under him in the contrary quarrel': PRO, SP 78/73, fo. 193r.

[966] Henry Wriothesley, 3rd earl of Southampton, died at Bergen-op-Zoom on 10/20 November 1624, and his son James four days before him, at Rosendal. See Lee, *Dudley Carleton to John Chamberlain*, p. 317.

[967] See AAW, A XIX, no. 5, pp. 13–16 (attested copy of the breve of Urban VIII to Richard Smith, bishop elect of Chalcedon, 25 January/4 February 1625; printed in Dodd, *CH*, III, pp. 7–8).

[968] Cardinal Richelieu.

[969] Bernardino Spada, archbishop of Damietta.

[970] i.e. to have ordinary jurisdiction as a bishop in England.

becaus[e] I can not have the other in some places and occasions.[971] I hope to be consecrated the 6 of this moneth by the nonce and to be gone to England as soone after as I can, and as soone by the next poste I wil send you a com*m*ission in blank, sealed and subscribed by me, for you to put in what you think fit. But in anie case, take no notice as from me that I am the [*MS torn*], his Holines wil have the matter to be as secret as may be, that I may be in England befor o*u*r king know[s] therof. But harken, I pray you, if faculties be already sent to me or no. For p*er*haps they were sent with the bulls, but miscarried by some chance, or it may be thay be sent by this next poste w*hi*ch cometh hither within thes[e] three dayes, and p*er*haps there is some stay for the modification of them. And, if they be modified, doe, I pray you, al you can that I be made ordinarius Angliae, without w*hi*ch my auth*orit*y wilbe nothing.[972]

For England the news is here that, at the coming of Secretarie Villoclare, the Catholik prisoners were set at libertie and al p*er*secution ceased; that our k[ing] hath signed the articles, and given to Villocleere a diamant of 20 thousand crownes, and the prince an other of 10 thousand. Twoe Catholik English say that the p*er*secution is ceased, and one of the*m* addeth that the inquirie was great and general, but not the taking away of goods, and that there are at this p*re*sent foure highe sherives that are recusants.[973] The other, who was one of M^r^ Gage his men, and goe[th] to Rome now, saieth that Mansfeld hath betwene 12 and 15 thousand English souldiors readie to embark and that he is in Dover.[974] The Low Countries are much afraid of him and p*ro*vide wel for him. The duke of Buckingham is made prince of Tiperary in Ireland.[975] From Flanders they write that they hope to have Breda shortly, and that the towne beginneth already to parole [?]. Here is great number of souldiors and much sending of armes and munition towards Calis and some speak that the Hugenots begin to sturre. The good b[ishop] of Ayre[976] hath bene like to die but, God be thanked, now there is hope that he is out of danger. I pray you remember him in y*ou*r devotions.

[971] For Smith's appointment, and the limits imposed by Rome on his jurisdiction, see Allison, RS; Allison, QJ.

[972] In a letter to Thomas Rant of 3/13 February 1625, Smith played down the extent of the authority which he sought, and insisted that he would want to exercise his episcopal judicial authority only in first instance, with a right of appeal allowed to the nuncio in Paris: AAW, B 47, no. 13.

[973] Cf. *Letter 61*.

[974] On 17/27 December 1624, Henry Clifford observed that 'many souldiers of Mansfielde runne away as soone as they have libertie, and one runne [*sic*] into the river and was drowned because he would not be pressed to serve him': AAW, B 27, no. 88. For a similar account by John Chamberlain, see McClure, *LJC*, p. 593.

[975] See *Letter 61*.

[976] Sébastien Bouthillier.

We have a good clergie man[977] apointed to be b[ishop] to Madam[978] in England, and with him shal goe divers good clergie men. The F[rench] k[ing] hath apointed a F[rench] Jesuit for her confessarius, but p*er*haps he wil not hold the place, for the earle of Carlil saieth it wil never be permitted, and is earnest against it.[979] I pray you let this letter be com*m*on to good F[ather] Rant whome I pray to excuse me being so busie for my consecration within thes[e] 3 dayes, and desire him to deale with F[ather] Berul about my faculties aforesaid, but as not knowing any thing of me more than is necessarie. For I know not how his Holines wold take it if it were discovered, and therfor this secresie I com*m*end to you and him above al matters. And by the next I hope I may write to you more plainly. The bulls were here delivered with so litle secresie as I feare they are more knowne than his Holines wold [*sic*], but that was no fault of mine. Thus, with a thousand com*m*endations to you both, I commit you to God. This 2 of Jan[uary] 1625.

Y*ou*rs ever and ever,

R[ichard] Smith

*Addressed*: Au r*évéren*d père, P[ère] Claude Bertin Supérieur du S[t] Louis. Pour Mons*ieu*r Thomas More Anglois. Rome.

*Endorsed*: Paris. 1625. Chalc[e]don. January. 2. Receav[ed]: January 26. Answ[ered]: January 28.

## 65. Thomas Roper to Thomas More, 29 December 1624

[*AAW, B 47, no. 183*]

Good cosen,

This inclosed of M[r] Farring[ton][980] can not take notice of your two letters unto him of the 29[th] of 9[ber] and of 7 Decemb[er] for that they

[977] Daniel Du Plessis de la Mothe-Houdancourt, bishop of Mende.

[978] Henrietta Maria.

[979] On 29 November/9 December 1624, Marc'Antonio Moresini, Venetian ambassador in France, had reported that 'they have agreed upon twenty-eight priests, whom Madame will take with her to celebrate the offices in her church, and a bishop'. There were disagreements about her confessor. The nuncio 'overcame opposition, the queen mother so wishing', and a Jesuit, Barthélemy Jacquinot, was appointed, though his appointment was soon revoked, in part at the insistence of King James: *CSPV, 1623–1625*, p. 507; PRO, PRO 31/3/61, fos 89v–90r; Fraser, *Reports on the Manuscripts of the Earl of Eglinton*, p. 110; see also *Letter 68*.

[980] Edward Bennett.

were yet in my handes when this letter came from him, but, since, I have sent them unto him.

Halberstate,[981] since his coming, is made knight of the Garter and hathe a pension of 2,000[l] graunted him out of the excheq[uer]. It is sayed there shall be raysed another army for him of 15,000, and talke there is of a new presse, but it is not as yet beleeved.[982]

It is thought that Mansef[elt] will remayne yet in Kent these 2 monthes. His shouldiers in passinge throughe the countrey unto him committe many disorders. People shutte uppe their houses and stirre not abroade, no markettes are kepte, nor is there any commerce, and everyone for the present live[s] uppon suche provision ~~and~~ <as> they have in their houses.[983]

Villocleere hathe stayed here a weeke longer than he intended, only to see those thinges perfected w*hi*ch it pleased our kinge to graunte him in favor of his Catholicke subjectes. There was brought him by M[r] Secretary Conway a writinge seigned w*i*th the kinges privat signate w*hi*ch contayned the particulars of his Ma*jes*ties graunte. Uppon perusall thereof the ambass[ador] expressed muche discontentednesse for that he sayed his Ma*jes*ties officers had <not> penned it accordinge unto the kinges graunte. First he excepted maynely against the preamble w*hi*ch seemed to have bein coppied out of some of Queene El[i]zab[eth's] proclamations. The tenor of it was this, vid[elicet], whereas diverse preistes, Jesuites and suche like personnes ~~have~~ for their disloyalty to their ~~prince and~~ soveragne and for many treacherous actiones have bein imprisoned e[t]*cetera*, it is notwithestandinge his Ma*jes*tie[s] pleasure at the entreaty of the ambass[ador] and in contemplation of the matche that they shall be fourtheworthe [*sic for* forthwith] sette at liberty and banished the realme.[984] He disliked that all preistes e[t]*cetera* should be taxed for <suche> heigneous offences and for disloyalty, beinge [*sic for* seeing], as he sayed, no religion thought more obedience to their soveraigne than the Cathol[ic]. And, for banisshement, that was no favor but a great penalty, and his Ma*jes*ties graunte was for their liberty.

[981] Christian of Brunswick, administrator of the bishopric of Halberstadt.

[982] See *CSPV, 1623–1625*, pp. 514, 526, 530; McClure, *LJC*, p. 595; PRO, PRO 31/3/59, fo. 196r.

[983] Thomas Roper had recorded with dismay on Christmas Eve 1624 that Mansfelt's recruits, travelling to their assembly points, caused 'many disorders as they passed'; for example, 'in Hartefortesheere they came to one Sir John Lukes house who, beinge a deputy lieutenant of that sheere, did reprehend them for their insolency. Thereuppon they brake his pate and shrodly beate his men that came to rescue him': AAW, B 27, no. 85. See also *Letter 67*; AAW, B 47, no. 75.

[984] See *Letter 62*; PRO, SP 14/177/11.

Hereuppon Villocleere made his complainte unto the duke. Since, there have bein severall [*word deleted*] <wayes thought on> for to geave him content, and now he hathe a letter under the kinges privat seignat directed to Secretary Conway who hathe order to signifie the kinges pleasure unto my lord keeper,[985] my lord treasurer,[986] M^r^ Attorney[987] and the judges concerninge the present cessation of all proceedinges against recusantes and, <by vertue of> this letter, Secretary Conway gave him severall letters to the sayed officers. It is expected that all prisoners shall be fourthe with delivered.[988]

This day, beinge New Yeares Eve, he tooke his journey for France, havinge leafte behinde a good opinion amonge the Cathol[ics] for his zeale in their cause. And (as some say), if Monsieur Fiats[989] persuasions had taken place, he had not so muche insisted for the performance now of those thinges as he did, ~~but~~ the parlament beinge so nighe at hand. He hathe bein told by some of ~~the~~ our state that they [*sic for* the] papistes have sette him on purposely to breake the matche, w*hi*ch they have great reason to furder, beinge w*i*th a Catholi[c] princesse. The Catholickes desire no more fiats to comme amonge them, but would be gladd to heare of factum est, and be acquainted w*i*th him.

The Dutche agent[990] and the Spanishe agent[991] had joyntly togeather their audience these hollydayes and seemed to have good satisfaction geaven them, none being present at their audience.

Commende me to M^r^ Clayton, who I thinke is arrived ere this at ~~his~~ his journeys ende. Entreate him when he retornethe that he will brinke [*sic for* bring] w*i*th him for me an silver forke for to use at the table, w*hi*ch I desire may be tridens. Here they know not well how to

985 John Williams, bishop of Lincoln.

986 Sir James Ley.

987 Sir Thomas Coventry.

988 According to George Fisher, 'it was long before the ambassador obtained this order in such forme as he desired, insomuch as he rejected tow severall orders sent him under the broad seale, but the third, suting to his expectation, he accepted': AAW, B 47, no. 151. For Zuane Pesaro's account of this confrontation, see *CSPV, 1623–1625*, p. 539. See also PRO, SP 14/177/22 (a memorandum for King James, *inter alia*, to issue letters to both archbishops (for which see PRO, SP 14/177/25–28) to halt high commission proceedings against Catholic recusants and to order a warrant to prevent all process against Catholics); PRO, SP 14/177/23 (a request from the marquis of Effiat that recusants should be released from all pecuniary penalties, be reimbursed for fines levied since the previous Trinity term, and be immune from action against them by secular and ecclesiastical courts); PRO, SP 14/177/36–40 (the warrants to grant Effiat's request); PRO, SP 14/177/29 (James's order, of 26 December, to Lord Keeper Williams to issue writs for the release of imprisoned Catholic clergy); *CSPV, 1623–1625*, p. 551; see also PRO, SP 78/73, fo. 368r; PRO, SP 78/74, fo. 49v.

989 Antoine Coiffier de Ruzé, marquis of Effiat.

990 Presumably Roper intends to refer to Jean-Baptiste van Male, the agent of the archduchess Isabella.

991 Jacques Bruneau.

make them. Likewise una scatula di balle bolognese. I will, when he commethe, retorne him <his> monys w*i*th many thankes.

Commende me to M[r] Rant, Don Anselmo,[992] Don Seberto[993] and the rest of my good freindes.

Yours,

T[homas] R[oper]

Lette my name be hereafter Tho[mas] Browne when you write unto me.

The 29[th] of Dec[ember] 1624.

*Addressed*: All' ill*ust*re sig*no*re, il Sig*no*r Tomasso Moro, Inglese. Roma.

*Endorsed*: Ingl[an]d. 1624. T[homas] R[oper]. Decemb[er] 29. Recea[ved] [and] answ[ered]: Febr[uary] 21 [and] 22.

## 66. Richard Sara [Edward Bennett] to Thomas More, 1 January 1625

[*AAW, B 47, no. 194*]

Right wo*rshipfu*ll and worthy syr,

Having last week written unto you, this day I receaved two from you, thon of the 23 of November, thother of the 30 of the same. I am glad the commission is come to yo*ur* handes, but you tell me not whether it be the com*m*ission for the dispensation, or thother for yo*ur* self. Yo*u* alsoe acknowledge the receit of the breviculus[994] and the canons,[995] whereof, me thinkes, you might make some benefitt at least w*i*th the congregation de P*ro*paganda Fide. The secretary[996] that came last out of Fraunce maketh us beleeve that the articles be very good and that we shall have a generall cessation from all p*er*secution. I suppose upon

[992] Robert (Anselm) Beech OSB.

[993] Robert (Sigebert) Bagshaw OSB.

[994] This is a reference to a Latin account of William Bishop's episcopate in England, sent to Rome by William Harewell in early July 1624. Another copy was dispatched subsequently: AAW, B 27, nos 9, 87; AAW, B 47, no. 89.

[995] i.e. 'Canones ecclesiastici ad pacem et disciplinam inter clerum saecularem et monachos Benedictinos conservandam a reverendissimo in Christo patre ac domino, D[omino] Gulielmo Episcopo Calcedonensi propositi', for which see AAW, A XVII, no. 54, pp. 177–180; *Letter 35*.

[996] Henri-Auguste de Loménie, seigneur de Villeauxclercs.

his return (w*hi*ch I am written unto wilbe within two dayes) they wilbe sent to his Ho[liness] and you shall better know ther the p*ar*ticulars than we heer, soe secrett they be kept. Yo*u* must beare w*i*th me that yo*u* heare not soe soone all occurrantes from me for, beinge in the cuntrey, it is a fortnight sometymes before I doe hear what hapneth [?] in the cowrte, and abowte London, whereof o*ur* frendes, abiding ther, might easily and soone informe yo*u*. I cry unto them to give M^r^ Rant and yo*ur* self correspondence but they still sleepe. This negligence hath undon o*ur* cause. As for assuraunce, I doe think his Ho[liness] doth well not to stand to[o] much upon it but to take the kinge of Fraunce his roiall word. If that we showld break w*i*th Fraunce, and the prince marry som P*ro*testant, we will wish we had some Catholick lady withowt either condition or p*ro*mise. I dowbt not but that many ill suggestions be made ther against our kinge, but surely I can <not> allow of ther information. We take comfort in the insinuation you make that o*ur* b[ishop] is chosen. But we are exceedingly trubled that boath o*ur* agentes (whom we have sent of purpose to deale in that affayer) showld be made such straingers to what is don, and howld you boath, as alsoe the whoale clergye, much dishonored by it. Not that we desyre to knowe it before it is befittinge, but because we all [*word omitted:* are] soe litle regarded that, in o*ur* own affayers, we have not the respect in that cowrte to have o*ur* agent ~~(in our own affayers)~~ trusted. I p*ro*test unto yo*u* boath, if I were where yo*u* are, I showld informe his Ho[liness] and alsoe the congregation de P*ro*paganda Fide how much greved the clergye be at the litle regard [that] is had of them. Againe it breedeth a great inconvenience unto us, this dependance of princes, w*hi*ch his Ho[liness], makinge o*ur* b[ishop] at o*ur* own sute, might redresse. For if the French make hym, as now they doe, the Spaniard will howld hym for there enimye, and soe consequently favour no request he shall make in the behaulf of those colledges we have in ther cuntry. If the Spaniard had made hyme, then the French <lady> (if she become o*ur* princes[s]) would have frowned, and then we had suffered of that syde. All w*hi*ch I say might and may allwayes heereafter be prevented if his Holl[iness] would be pleased to make o*ur* sup*er*iors upon o*ur* own sutes, and not of any princes whatsoever. For then boath sup*er*ior and his clergy showld be held for indifferent to all, and soe w*i*th confidence might intreate the helpe and assistance of all.[997] An exception (p*re*sently upon the

[997] On 1 January 1625, William Harewell also regretted that neither Thomas More nor Thomas Rant had been informed directly of Smith's appointment (even though they were the secular clergy's accredited agents in Rome). Harewell expressed concern at the political implications of the way in which Smith had been appointed: AAW, B 47, no. 89. Edward

b[ishop's][998] death) was made to me by <the> Spanish embassadours against Doct[or] Smith that he was of the French faction. Therefor they sayd they would oppose hyme. [*In margin:* The marquez[999] sayd, if we p*ro*pose him, he would withstand bishops.] And I had much a doe to cleer it. I beseeche you to thinck of this bussines w*hi*ch, beinge <well> vexed in that cowrte, may (it may be) heareafter <move them> to deale better w*i*th us. If I were w*i*th you, I showld say more. I beleeve if Doct[or] Smith be o*u*r b[ishop], and writ in the behalf either of the colledge of Doway or Portingall to Spayn or the Low Cuntres, he wilbe litle regarded, and this because he is made by the French. And soe much of this.

You speake of a restraint feared in his jurisd[ict]ion. I can not imagyn they will restrayn what the canons giveth hyme. As for my L[ord] Mount[ague] his practise, we doe not admire it, although it may seeme strainge, a monk being his sonnes tutor,[1000] he showld seeke to the Jesswetes.[1001] I doe not dowbt but that, er[e] this, yo*u* have fownd my L[ord] Winsor but litle to like them. He p*ro*mised me he would deale confidently w*i*th you boath.[1002] I cowld wishe that such letters as come from us, either to his Ho[liness] or to any of the cardinals, were delivered by yo*u*r self or M^r Rant and not by second p*er*sons, because then you showld have good occasion to urge what in the letters is treated. We hope his Ho[liness] will take order w*i*th these defamers and ~~the~~ not suffer the dead and livinge to be wronged. Me thinges [*sic for* thinkes] they showld either give yo*u* such articles as be given up to awnswer or show there dislik[e] of the defamers by disgracinge of them. I like well of yo*u*r dictamen that the religious who live heer ~~amongst us~~ showld heareafter be examined of the carraidges of bussines amongest us; as also that all o*u*r affayers showld be drawen owt of the Inquisition and handeled in the congregation de P*ro*paganda Fide, being p*ar*ticularly ordayned for these hereticall cuntreis.

Heer is as great sturringe for warrs as ther talk amongest you of it. Brunswick,[1003] Count Mansfeld, as alsoe Towers[1004] be heere.[1005] Great

Bennett lodged another protest about the same matter in a letter of 7 March 1625 to Rant: AAW, B 47, no. 121.

[998] i.e. William Bishop.

[999] Juan Hurtado de Mendoza, marquis of Inojosa.

[1000] See *Letter 19*.

[1001] For the 2nd Viscount Montague's patronage of the Society of Jesus, see Questier, *C&C*, pp. 333, 444–446.

[1002] For Lord Windsor's extant letters to Thomas Rant (one in February 1625, two in June 1625, and one in August 1625), see AAW, B 47, nos 200–203.

[1003] Christian of Brunswick, administrator of the bishopric of Halberstadt.

[1004] Frédéric Maurice de la Tour d'Auvergne, duke of Bouillon, who had succeeded his father, the prominent Huguenot leader, in March 1623: *HMCMK*, p. 162.

[1005] See AAW, B 47, no. 157.

mustering, but whither they goe is unknowen. My frend[1006] giveth you many thankes for y*our* remembraunce of her, and most hartely saluteth yo*u* agayn. I pray reme*m*ber my most kynd respect to good M^r^ Rant, intreating these may serve you boathe, this being all I have to saye owt of this sollitary cuntry. It may be o*ur* frendes at London will tell yo*u* more. O*ur* brethren heer with me salute you boathe. O*ur* Lord keepe yo*u*.

Ever yo*ur*s most assured,

Richard Sarra

1° Januarii 1624.

*Addressed*: For M^r^ More.

*Endorsed*: Ingl*and*. 1625. Sarrha.
January 1°. Recea[ved] [and] answ[ered]: February 21 [and] 22.

## 67. George Musket [Fisher] to Thomas More, 6 January 1625

[*AAW, B 27, no. 91*]

Right w*orshipfu*ll,

I expected to heare from you by the last post, but it is now a fortnight and more, and yet I heare nothing. The last week matters were so doubtfull that I knew not what to wright. Now we have the period of our expectation, for our prisoners ar released and the king hath given order that ther shall be no proceedings in any court against Catholikes for meere matter of religion. This favour we have by the mediatio*n* of the French ambas[sador][1007] who would not depart untill he obtained it under the broad seale. Presently, uppo*n* the dispatch of this order, he departed for France uppo*n* our New Yeares Eve. Brunswicke[1008] hath had very gratious entertainme*n*t here of late. The last weeke he was created knight of the Garter and had a pension of 2,000 per an*num* graunted him by his Ma*jes*tie.[1009] He departed hence uppo*n* New Yeares Day. Mansfield is still uppo*n* the plaines of Dover, training his souldiers, and it is not certaine when he will depart thence. Some report they shall not goe untill the States give security for him that he shall <not> hurt the king of Spaine or any of his

[1006] Lady Elizabeth Dormer.
[1007] Henri-Auguste de Loménie, seigneur de Villeauxclercs.
[1008] Christian of Brunswick, administrator of the bishopric of Halberstadt.
[1009] See *Letter 65*.

territories. In the meane <time> they comitt many outrages, and it is confidently reported that amongst other of ther villanies they have ravished a ladye and her tow daughters. Comission is gone from the king to execute martiall law uppon the*m*, and, as I heare, some of them ar hanged. How many I cannot certainly learne.[1010] Now it is confidently reported here that the earle of Gondomar is coming for England. I cann hardly beleive this, although I heare it reported by those that have reaso*n* to know it.[1011] The next weeke, if any post come fro*m* Spaine, you shall know the certainty. I pray you, send up some comfortable news concerning our manie suites. For we heare nothing at all as yet but what we heare from you. As touching the hospitall,[1012] I suppose M^r^ Collet[on] will send you his opinion. For my part I thinke it fitt his Hol[iness] should be acquainted with it now in the beginning least hereafter they plead prescriptio*n*. Thus, with offer of my love to your selfe and M^r^ Rant, I rest.

Yours assuredly,

G[eorge] M[usket]

Janu[ary] 6.

*Addressed*: To the right wor*shipfu*ll M^r^ Thomas More.

*Endorsed*: Ingla[nd]. 1625.
Musk*e*t. January 6. Recea[ved]: February 21 [and] answ[ered]: [February] 22.

[1010]See *ibid.* On 14 January 1625, George Fisher wrote that Mansfelt's recruits had 'committed in the country many insolencies but that of the ravishing of the lady and her daughters, wich was here for many daies confidently reported, is now as confidently contradicted': AAW, B 47, no. 151. On 5 January 1625, Thomas Roper had complained that 'our cuntrey of Kent sufferethe muche by Mansefeildes shouldiers who have committed many disorders. Some 12 of them brake into my fathers house at Cant[erbury] and some 20 more were brought into the house by the constable and there they remayne and are lodged. Marshall law is now proclamed and, since that, it is sayed some halfe a score have bein hanged. There hathe bein a fleete expected from the East for to transporte them, which now is sayed to be comme to the Downes, being of 80 sayle': AAW, B 47, no. 179. See also McClure, *LJC*, p. 593; PRO, SP 14/176/66. On December 26, Sir John Hippisley, lieutenant of Dover Castle, had told the council that the soldiers committed every kind of outrage, plundering and pillaging their way through the local population: PRO, SP 14/177/18. With the Kentish authorities, Hippisley also reported on 31 December that the officers were failing to enforce discipline: PRO, SP 14/177/48. For similar reports by John Chamberlain, Francis Wilford, and William Jones, see McClure, *LJC*, p. 596; PRO, SP 14/177/33, 34. For the commission for exercising martial law, dispatched subsequently to Hippisley, see PRO, SP 14/181/10, 11; see also PRO, SP 14/181/26, 37. On 13 January 1625, Sir John Ogle and Sir William St Leger assured Conway that the soldiers at Canterbury were now well ordered: PRO, SP 14/181/51.

[1011]See *Letters 58, 73*.

[1012]See *Letter 58*.

## 68. Richard Smith to Thomas More, 7/17 January 1625

[*AAW, B 47, no. 12*]

Right worship*ful* and deer syr,

I have y*our*s of the 16 of 10ber and, by this, I hope you have my last in w*hi*ch I certified you how that I then had receaved my bulls for to be made b[ishop] of Calcedon but yet had no auth*orit*y or jurisdiction for England. Since, I have bene consecrated the 12 of this p*re*sent by the nonce[1013] who did it with much affection and honor to me and invited both me and his twoe assistants[1014] to a very great dinner. He is willing that I shold stay here til my faculties come, and other my freinds counsel me the same, and so I purpose now to doe that I may the better replie if the faculties be not suff*ici*ent, w*hi*ch I onely desire shold be ordinarius Ang[liae] with the same faculties w*hi*ch the archpreists had, and that I may confirme sine pontificalibus cum sacerdotalibus ornamentis in case of necessitie.[1015] My cardinal[1016] hath written by the last for thes[e] faculties and also, as I think, the nonce who p*ar*ticulerly favoureth me. I had hoped that my consecration shold have bene secret and for that end it was done in the chapel of the nonces [*sic*] his house, but one of his men told it to Griffin Floyd and he spreadeth it al about.[1017] My Lord Carlil hath defeated the Jesuit of being confessarius[1018] to our princesse,[1019] and there shalbe ether a doctor of Sorbon or some such other. [*MS obscured:* It] is said our king wil have no religious about her becaus[e] they make vows to strangers. Secretarie Villoclare is dayly looked for here, and it is said the day before his departure from London he went to the prisons and set al Catholiks at libertie.[1020] The d[uke] of Buckingham, now prince of Tiperary, counte palatin of Munster and leiutenant of Ireland,[1021] is making great p*ro*vision for to come hither to espouse the princesse. Don Tomas, sonne to the d[uke] of Savoy, hath married Co[u]nte Soissons sister.[1022] The Hugenots in Poitou are rebelled and have taken twoe

[1013] Bernardino Spada, archbishop of Damietta. See Allison, RS, p. 189.

[1014] Cardinal Richelieu and Claude de Rueil, bishop of Bayonne. See *ibid.*

[1015] See *Letter 64*.

[1016] Cardinal Richelieu.

[1017] For Griffin Floyd, see *NAGB*, pp. 151, 275–276.

[1018] See *Letter 64*.

[1019] Henrietta Maria.

[1020] Thomas Roper informed Thomas More, in his letter of 5 January 1625, that, on 'that day that Villocleere (to whome the recusantes are beholding for his caire <of them>) went a way, the prisoners of Newgate in the morninge came to him to render him thankes': AAW, B 47, no. 179.

[1021] See Lockyer, *Buckingham*, pp. 215–216.

[1022] See *CSPV, 1623–1625*, p. 519; PRO, SP 78/73, fo. 192v.

ilands[1023] before Ro[chelle], twoe litle citties, but the k[ing] sweareth that he wil be revenged of them. As soone as I have faculties I wil send you commission to deale in my name and as soone as I come to England I wil consult with my brethren how to help that colledg[e].[1024] You wold not think what want we are like to have of men, for I feare much [*word omitted:* for (?)] even this litle house[1025] after my leaving it, men are so unwilling to live with my coosin,[1026] and he so hard to be removed, and yet I hope that this house wold be much increased in means if we had suff*ici*ent men that wold live in it. You write that the b[ishop] of Embrun hath confirmed 200 [*sic*] and here is reported [*MS damaged*] that he co*n*firmed 10 thousande.[1027] The French much com*m*end his cariage there. My brethren have written nothing to me of his doings. Now I heare that the reporte of the Hugenots rebellion is doubtful if not true. I pray you inclose this letter to his Holines in a cover and deliver it as soone as you can, I make no mention of you in it becaus[e], as I said, I have my self as yet no com*m*ission for England, and, if he be offended that my consecration be knowne, I pray you tel him that it came not out by my fault. Breda stands as it did. Coloma is to be about Namours with 20 thousand.[1028] Mansfeld is not yet comen out of England and as is said the ports are stopt til he be departed. I pray you let this letter be com*m*on to M[r] Rant, for I gladly use the libertie which he giveth me to write to you both in one. I pray you com*m*end me most respectively to F[ather] Berul and to al freinds, and thus, with my hartiest to you both, I com*m*it you to the protection of o*ur* sweet Savior. I pray you, by yo*ur* next, let me know how much wold be necessarie to mantaine one honestly at Rome. And, when you

[1023]Rhé and Oléron: see *CSPV, 1623–1625*, p. 562.

[1024]The English College in Rome.

[1025]The Collège d'Arras.

[1026]William Rayner. On 11/21 February 1625, Anthony Champney suggested to Smith that, as a last resort, Smith 'co[u]ld procure' Rayner 'the place of chapleine' with Henrietta Maria 'that at least he might live securely without molestation': AAW, B 27, no. 93. On 3/13 March, Smith informed More that he had 'now good hope to remove my coosin' from the college 'with his owne liking, and at a reas[onable] rate, for so he agreed yesterday with me, if his freinds in the towne doe not disswade him from it:, AAW, B 47, no. 15. However, on 19/29 June, Henry Holden reported to Smith that Rayner was 'threatening perpetuall aboad': AAW, A XIX, no. 61, p. 181.

[1027]Cf. *Letters 60, 61, 63*. Embrun himself claimed that he had been permitted to administer the sacrament of confirmation in London, 'où durant le séjour que j'y fis, plus de dix mille Anglois reçeuvent ce sacrament de ma main': PRO, PRO 31/3/61, fo. 81v.

[1028]See *CSPV, 1623–1625*, p. 580. On 3/13 February 1625, Richard Ireland noted that Coloma 'wayteth on' Mansfelt with the troops 'lately levyed in the Lowe Countryes': AAW, B 47, no. 118. For the raising of these troops and for the appointment of Coloma to lead both these soldiers and other imperial troops against Mansfelt, see *CCE*, pp. 197, 204–205; *CGB*, I, p. 576, II, p. 593; PRO, SP 77/17, fo. 18r–v.

may, write to Mr Newman to see what hope there is of a colledge at Lisbon. Farewel a thousand thousand times.

17 of Jan[uary] 1625.

Yo*ur* servant in Christ Jesus,

R[ichard] Chalcedon

*Addressed*: A monsieur, Mons*ieu*r Thomas More chez le r*évéren*d père, P[ère] Claude Bertin, supérieur de St Louis à Rome.

*Endorsed*: Paris. 1625. Chal[cedon].
January 17. Recea[ved]: Febru[ary] 6.
Answ[ered]: Febru[ary] 10.

## 69. Richard Smith to Thomas More, 20/30 January 1625

[*AAW, B 47, no. 11*]

Right worship*fu*l and deere syr,

I have y*ou*rs of the 30 of 10ber and befor this I hope you know that I am appointed succ*ess*or to my l[ord] of Calcedon,[1029] for now they write it from thence to D[octor] Cecil who after such authentical notice, as he said, did take the paines to come to visit me,[1030] as also did F[ather] George[1031] who is now returned out of England with Mons*ieu*r Villoclare, the F[rench] kings secretarie, who hath obtained of o*u*r king that al payments or bonds and such like made by Cath[olics] into the exchequer since the treatie of this mariage should be repaied, that al prisoners be set at liberties, 12d on Sunday remitted, informers put downe and al penal lawes against Cath[olics] ceased, and this our k[ing] hath printed, signed and sealed; and besid[es] he hath sworne that he wil nether directly nor indirectly draw the princesse[1032] from her religion nor hinder her or her trayne in the execution therof, or in the bringing up of her children in her religion. The d[uke]

[1029] William Bishop.

[1030] Smith observed, about three weeks later (on 16/26 February), that John Cecil 'professeth him self a great clergie man, defieth al that say he ever was against the having of b[ishops], and offereth to goe to Rome upon his owne charges for the good of the clergie': AAW, B 47, no. 18.

[1031] George Latham SJ. On 20/30 January, Richard Ireland commented that 'Fa[ther] George Latham hath bene in England' with Villeauxclercs 'and is nowe returned. He hath bene heere to congratulat my l[ord] of Ch[alcedon] [...] and sayth that the king hath promised toleration to Catholiques': AAW, B 47, no. 117; see also *Letter 70*. According to Edward Bennett, Latham, while in England, 'walketh in his habitt': AAW, B 27, no. 74.

[1032] Henrietta Maria.

of Buckingham is looked for here within this moneth or six weeks for to espouse the ladie. And, finally, Mons*ieu*r Villoclare is much com*m*ended for his dealing in England, but not so Fiat.[1033] I am glad that you have so good correspondence fro*m* England, for I had never worse. I feare that both their and my letters are intercepted. Touching the confessor, I have done what I can, and once it was surely held that it should not be a companion[1034] by procurement of my l[ord] of Carlil,[1035] but now they are in hope agayne and, as it seemeth, they hope to worke it by Bucking[ham] his mother,[1036] that from England they shal not be hindered and, if they be not fro*m* thence, it wil not be fro*m* hence. I moved P[ère] Berul himself for that place but he seemed not willing, and I spake to the nonce[1037] and others for him, who liked the notion very wel. What the event wil be God knoweth. Here I see that many feare the Jes[uits] and wil not incurre their hatred for to doe others good. I have heard nothing of that sermon made in England, but F[ather] Persons long since made the like in our colledg[e] at Rome.[1038] If I could learne of it I wold endeavour [*sic*], but as I tel you I can heare nothing from England. M^r^ Rant writeth to me that P[ère] Berul sent him to Card[inal] Valette with a copie of my pre[de]cessor[1039] his faculties w*hi*ch putteth me in hope that I shal soone have mine. I was desirous to have gone to England and expected them there but both the nonce and my cardinal[1040] are of an other opinion w*hi*ch I wil follow. I pray you doe what diligence you can to hasten them and to p*ro*cure that I be ordinarius Ang[liae]. Some Scots wold have me also to have jurisd*ict*ion over their countrie, but that I desire not.[1041] The nonce is ordinarius of both, yet being desired of a Scot to give leave to take orders, he refused becaus[e], as he said, his Holines had forbidden him to practise that auth*orit*y til he had ended some matters w*hi*ch then were consulted in Rome. I pray you also to send me word what i[t] wold cost yearly for to mantayne

[1033]Antoine Coiffier de Ruzé, marquis of Effiat.

[1034]i.e. a Jesuit.

[1035]See *Letter 68*.

[1036]Mary Villiers, countess of Buckingham.

[1037]Bernardino Spada, archbishop of Damietta.

[1038]The identity of Robert Persons's sermon is unclear, but he had (in April 1597) delivered a long speech at Rome to the students of the English college there, condemning those whom he regarded as responsible for the dissensions among English Catholics, and rehearsing many of the arguments which he subsequently deployed during the appellant controversy: P.J. Holmes, '*An Epistle of Pious Grief*: an anti-appellant tract by Robert Persons', *RH*, 15 (1981), pp. 328–335; ABSJ, Collectanea N II, pp. 125–159.

[1039]William Bishop.

[1040]Cardinal Richelieu.

[1041]Cf. *Letter 32*.

one in Rome, for as soone as I come to England I purpose to seek out one who may be instructed by you and assist you in y*our* paynes and save you fro*m* visits that are not necessarie, and succeed you when you shal think fit and not otherwise. You wold not think what d*iffic*ultie I am like to find to get men to keepe up this house,[1042] p*ar*tely upon av*er*sion from my coosin[1043] and p*ar*tely of other humors and want of wil to distaste the*m* selves for the com*m*on good. Ghesse you what we shold doe if that colledg[e][1044] were put into o*ur* hands, how we shold be able to furnish it continually. Now I heare that F[ather] Berul is p*ar*ted fro*m* Rome and wilbe here within this fortnight. God give him a good jorney. I hope he bringeth my faculties. I heare also that the good b[ishop] of Ayre[1045] who so much assisted Mr Benet and our clergies cause is dead. I pray you earnestly com*m*end his good soule to God. I pray you imparte the contents herof to Mr Rant, for I am willing to use the priviledge which you both graunt me to write to you both in one letter, especially sith Mr Ireland writeth to him, so that if ether of us forget any thing the other may supplie it. Com*m*end me I pray you very kindly to [the] l[ord] primate,[1046] Mr Browne, F[ather] Anselme,[1047] Mr White[1048] (whose letter to his brother[1049] is sent) and to al freinds. Thus, with my hartiest to you both, I com*m*it you to the p*ro*tection of o*ur* sweet Saviour.

Paris. 30 of Jan[uary].

Y*our* servant in Christ Jesus,

R[ichard] Chalcedon

*Addressed*: Au r*évéren*d père, P[ère] Claude Bertin, supérieur de St Louis.
Pour Mons*ieu*r Thomas More agent des Anglois à Rome.

*Endorsed*: Paris. 1625. Chal[ce]don.
January 30 Recea[ved]: February 21. Answ[ered]: [February] 24.

[1042] The Collège d'Arras.
[1043] William Rayner.
[1044] The English College in Rome.
[1045] Sébastien Bouthillier.
[1046] Peter Lombard, archbishop of Armagh.
[1047] Robert (Anselm) Beech OSB.
[1048] Richard White.
[1049] Thomas White.

## 70. Thomas Browne [Roper] to Thomas More, 28 January 1625

[*AAW, B 47, no. 184*]

Good cosen,

I have receaved yours of the 28 of Dec[ember] w*i*th some others w*hi*ch have bein disposed of accordinge unto their severall directions.

I have written unto you formerly of Villocleere who hath stoode our good freind. Whilest he was here, there came hether w*i*th him Fath[er] George[1050] but not Doct[or] Cicell. Where he is I know not, but some rather thinke he is gon towardes your partes.

The dukes journey is stayed for a tyme, w*hi*ch makethe us thinke all is not ripe and that the dispens[ation] is not yet comme to France. Yet they say the duke will sett forwarde to be in France against their Easter. Yet all ~~be~~ <is> but conjectures. His brother the lord of Purbeckes wife[1051] is lately brought to bedd of a sonne w*hi*ch the lord dothe not acknowledge to be his, and the generall opinion is that it is Mr Rob[ert] Howardes, a younger sonne to the lord of Suffolke.[1052] The lady is restrained to hir lodginges and hath bein examined by the lord keeper about it and about hir communication w*i*th Lambe,[1053] a famous sorserer, whome formerly my Lord Windesor did prosequute, and had hanged him had he not had extraordinary good freindes who saved his life.[1054] This yonge sonne is to inherite the dukes honnors, I

[1050] George Latham SJ. On 2/12 April 1625, Anthony Champney sent news to Thomas Rant of Christian of Brunswick's sojourn in England, and that 'Father George Lathame, who went with Villoclere as his chaplayn, sayd Mass wittingly before' Brunswick 'in the embassatours presence which, had one of us done [it], would be no less than exco[mmu]nication'. That he 'who gloried to call him self flagellum sacerdotum' should be 'admitted to Mass is either to[o] much indulgence or to[o] much neglect of Gods divin[e] mysteries. That he did this <is> no fable, for we have <it> from one to whom he him self towld <it> and another who served him to Mass, and upon his comman[d] brought a chaire in for' him 'who, askeing Father George whether he was Catholike, answered yea, a sorie one': AAW, B 47, no. 47.

[1051] Frances Villiers, wife of John Villiers, 1st Viscount Purbeck, and daughter of Sir Edward Coke.

[1052] See McClure, *LJC*, pp. 599, 601.

[1053] John Lambe.

[1054] John Chamberlain commented (on 26 February 1625) that Lambe, 'a notorious old rascall' was 'condemned the last sommer at the kings bench for a rape' (of Joan Seger) and was arraigned previously 'at Worcester for bewitching my Lord Windsors ymplement': McClure, *LJC*, p. 601. An account published after Lambe's murder in 1628 recited an indictment against him in 1608 which alleged that he used 'devilish and execrable arts to disable, make infirme and consume the body and strength' of Lord Windsor: *A Briefe Description of the Notorious Life of Iohn Lambe* (Amsterdam, 1628), p. 4.

meane his earledome and baronny and his estate, if he have no isshew mayle himselfe, and therefore the duke stirreth in it as a businesse w*hi*ch concernethe him neere.

On your purification day, in the afternoone, there was some insolency offered to van Male whilest he was at evensonge.[1055] Some unruly people made great noyse at his gate, ringinge often the bell and would not, beinge warned, desiste. Hereuppon some of <his> people issh[e]wed out and some scuffeling there was, w*hi*ch noyse van Male hearinge, came downe himselfe and, as some say, bestirred himselfe and gotte into his house the constable who was one of the most forwardest and did beate <him>. In the meane tyme some of the officers of the parisshe came and so appeased the strife.

Mansfeildes shouldiers are yet on our co[a]st, and lye at ancer in the Downes. He himselfe hathe lately bein at Calais, treatinge to lande his shouldiers thereaboutes, but whither he intendes is not yet knowen.[1056] His shouldiers suffer muche a shippeboarde, especially those Germaines that came to him, who have layen longe at sea, and many of them dye. There is a new presse for 2,000 more to supply the nu*m*ber of the sicke and of those that are runne away.

We say here that his Holinesse is tutto Francese, and that he is entered into league w*i*th other princes who are to assiste him for the recovery of Naples, and that there is a general conspiracy of all the potentates of Europe for to pull downe the House of Austria, w*hi*ch consequently will weaken Catho[lic] rel[igion]. They reporte here likewise that there is a garrison of 2,000 shouldiers in Rome, lodged about Strada Julia[1057] for the better defence of the city against the Spaniards, who are commanded out of Rome, and that his Holinesse is fortifiinge of the Burgo. None of all this I heare from you, w*hi*ch maketh me hope it is otherwise, neither is this answearable to the devotion of this yeare.

[1055] It had been remarked by Alvise Valaresso, back in November 1623, that the residence which van Male had taken was unsuitable because it was 'in a very frequented place', and 'the people coming from his Mass incurred some danger': *CSPV, 1623–1625*, p. 150. However, in the Commons in early April 1624, John Holles complained that there was still 'great resort' of papists to the ambassadors' houses and that 'oure last Lady Day ther was three or 4,000 at Vanmales hows': Thompson, *HA*, p. 55.

[1056] On 19 January 1625, Sir John Ogle and Sir William St Leger had sent word that Mansfelt had received a 'direct prohibition', signed by Louis XIII, against landing his troops in France (primarily to avoid antagonizing Spain) but advising him to 'stand towards the Estates dominions': PRO, SP 14/182/15, fo. 23r; see also *CSPD, 1623–1625*, pp. 454, 457–462; PRO, SP 78/74, fo. 51r; *CGB*, II, pp. 586, 591; Lockyer, *Buckingham*, pp. 224, 227; *Letter 71*.

[1057] The Via Julia, near to the English College.

About London we enjoye a kinde of calme, and yet promoters have some in chaise who rather compounde w*it*h them than stande out w*it*h them, knowinge not what the tymes hereafter will be. In remote partes they are busye in all kinde, and it is feared if the Frenche will be satisfied w*it*h what Sir George Goringe is to deliver them[1058] that then there will ensue a present persequution against the parlam[ent] w*hi*ch is proroged untill the 15 of Marche.

Our cosen the doctor[1059] goethe w*it*h the duke, and is makinge ritch clothes of pluche and velvette w*it*h many gardes of satten lace. M^r^ Sackvell[1060] is muche reformed and goethe moderatly. I saw him yesterday in a suite garded with goulded twiste.

John [*name illegible*] was but to[o] well dealt w*it*hall by me, for after he had spent a yeare in Engl[and] he seemed desirous to retorne, and so I gave [him] 15$^{l}$ or 16$^{l}$ in his purse, w*hi*ch he tooke and spent and went not, but putte himselfe in to other services where he continued not longe, havinge gotten to[o] good an opinion of himselfe and, after he was from me, he borrowed money w*hi*ch yet he owethe me.

In hast I take leave, the 28$^{th}$ of Jan[uary] 1625.

Yours,

Th[omas] Browne

*Addressed*: All' ill*ust*re et molto rev*erend*o sig*no*re, il Sig*no*re Tomasso Moro.
Roma.

*Endorsed*: 28 Jan[uary] 1625.

[1058] See *CSPV, 1623–1625*, p. 568; *Letter 71*.

[1059] Dr John More, the duke of Buckingham's physician. On 20 May 1625, he stood as godparent to Thomas Roper's second son, Thomas. See Harmsen, *John Gee's Foot out of the Snare*, p. 294; McClure, *LJC*, p. 326; A. Hamilton (ed.), *The Chronicle of the English Augustinian Canonesses Regular of the Lateran, at St Monica's in Louvain*, 2 vols (London, 1904–1906), II, pedigree of Roper. He had, allegedly, been involved in the raising of money for the imperial cause against the elector palatine: *CSPV, 1619–1621*, p. 479. Sir Robert Harley had complained, in the Commons on 2 April 1624, that 'ther is a certayn thing in the town call[e]d a popishe physitian, lett him be restrayn[e]d to his hows, and go to no patient; but lett them that can take phisick of no boddy else go to him if they will (meaning [. . .] D$^{r}$ Moore)': Thompson, *HA*, p. 59. On 24 September 1624, Roper had instructed Thomas More that, if he should write to Sir Francis Cottington, John More would deliver the letter: see AAW, B 26, no. 137.

[1060] Identity uncertain.

## 71. Richard Smith to Thomas More, 3/13 February 1625

[*AAW, B 47, no. 10*]

Right worshipful and deere syr,

I have y*ou*rs of the 13 of Jan[uary], and I assure my self that ere this you know that I was consecrated above a moneth agoe b[ishop] of Chalcedon and have al this while expected my faculties w*hi*ch are not yet comen. M^r Berul is arrived and I was at his house to see him, but he was gone forth. If I could have spoken with him, I shold have written some thing to you touching my faculties more than I can doe now. But, for my self, I shal be contented if I have such as my predec*ess*or[1061] had,[1062] and that his Hol[iness] be content that I observe the Councel of Trent, w*hi*ch my cousin Rainer wil not have to bind in England,[1063] nor me to observe, and p*er*haps he speaketh not of himself but of others who wold have no lawes to bind them. Wherfor I pray you know what his Hol[iness's] pleasure is therin, but not as fro*m* y*ou*r self if you can by other means. I pray you get if you can thos[e] articles betwene the b[ishop] of Holland[1064] and the Jes[uits]. M^r Ed[ward] Benet hath certaine articles betwixt them. I know not whether they be thos[e] wherof you write; as also I pray you let me know what that letter of M^r Prat[1065] conteineth and to what purpose it is used. My good cosin[1066] here made great blusterings about it, but

[1061] William Bishop.

[1062] On 3/13 March, Smith wrote to More that his recently arrived faculties were 'sparing ynough, for they are ad beneplacitum sedis Ap[osto]licae, and subordinate to the nonce in France, but I hope they wil serve for the time': AAW, B 47, no. 15.

[1063] Subsequently, this was a position concerning the decrees of the Council of Trent which tended to be associated with the Jesuits: *NCC*, p. 56.

[1064] Philip Rovenius.

[1065] James Pratt. See *Letters 62, 74*. Back in the third week of November 1624, this manuscript letter was known to be in circulation. It alleged that the Jesuits were being evicted from their gentry residences by the seculars: see AAW, B 27, no. 53. More notified John Jackson on 15/25 January 1625 that 'it was my chance to see the coppie of a letter, subscribed by James Pratt, writt to a nobleman whose father keapt in his house a Jesuit who is said to have made an oration to the k[ing] of Spayne in Vallad[olid] Colledg[e], afferming in the name of all the Cath[olics] in Ingland obedience to the said k[ing]'. However, 'this letter seemeth to caste the Jes[uits] as dangerouse men and suspected of the estate and therefore wisheth the nobleman to take order in that matter and not to endanger him self with such parsons. I wold request you to inquire wher you can of such a man as James Pratt', for, More thought, 'the letter is counterfeit and onlie shewed to draw some imputation upon our companie as seeking the displacing of Jesuites and the undoing of such parsons'. More believed that 'it can not be gathered by the letter that the writer was a preist, noe nor soe much as a Cath[olic], which maketh mee suspect false dealing': AAW, A XIX, no. 2, pp. 3–4; see also AAW, A XIX, no. 7, pp. 19–20.

[1066] William Rayner.

the nonce[1067] wold not be knowne to have seene any such. D[octor] Cecil much urged a meeting of some pr[iests] and Jes[uits] before the nonce, and he was inclined therto but, finding that Jes[uits] must be co[mman]ded therto, he is now not so forward. As I think I have written to you already, that [*sic*] I suppose M^r^ Townly[1068] hath repaid the 8^l^ which I lent him becaus[e] so much is given to the man in London to whome I appointed him to pay it. M^r^ Dorington[1069] and M^r^ Hall[1070] are not yet arrived here.[1071] When they come we shal do them what pleasure we can. Thus much touching the contents of y*ou*r letter. Hither are sent from o*ur* prince to Madam[1072] great p*re*sents w*hi*ch some French men value at a million of crownes, others at 800 thousands. The k[ing] is not thought to come so soone as was expected. Mansfeild is p*ar*ted withe his men from England, but as yet we heare not where he is landed. The speech is that he is to land about Bergen up Zome.[1073] F[ather] Barnes hath put forth his booke [*illegible note in margin*] De Equivoc*atio*n*e*, w*hi*ch was condemned in the Indice P*ro*hibitorum befor it came forth, w*hi*ch p*er*haps hath made him take out that p*ar*te of the title (Contra Lessiu*m*).[1074] Here the Jesuit wil goe for confessarius whatsoever become of it, though he be sent back agayne,

[1067] Bernardino Spada, archbishop of Damietta.

[1068] This may be Richard Townley of Norton in Lincolnshire. See AAW, A XIX, no. 109, pp. 387–388, no. 110, pp. 389–390.

[1069] A reference, perhaps, to either Francis or Robert Dorrington. See *NCC*, p. 118.

[1070] On 24 September 1624, Thomas Roper had written to inform More that 'there is gone uppe towardes you one M^r^ George Hall that was your sister Burdes neighbour': AAW, B 26, no. 137. For the return of Dorrington and Hall via Paris (reported by Richard Ireland on 15/25 February 1625), Rheims, and Flanders, see AAW, B 47, no. 124.

[1071] On 30 October/9 November 1624, More had informed John Jackson that 'manie of our cowntrie are come up' to Rome, including Richard White, who 'came with a young Cotton', i.e. a member of the Cotton family of Warblington in Hampshire. The 'Henslowes alsoe come some month after from Florence', while 'from Doway came' not only George Hall but also 'M^r^ North, M^r^ [Richard] Charnock, M^r^ Griffin, M^r^ Shirburne, Damport and others': AAW, B 27, no. 42; see CRS, 10, p. 230.

[1072] Henrietta Maria.

[1073] For Mansfelt's attempt to disembark his infantry, while his cavalry was being marshalled by Christian of Brunswick at Calais, see Lockyer, *Buckingham*, p. 228; *CCE*, p. 204; *CGB*, II, pp. 604, 608, 609.

[1074] John Barnes's *Dissertatio contra Aequivocationes* (Paris, 1625) received approbation from the Sorbonne, though publication was delayed because (as the earl of Carlisle related), after half of the book was printed, the Jesuits informed the papal nuncio, Spada, who complained to the king. A temporary halt was secured to the printing of it, while Spada demanded that the book should be sent to Rome for perusal there. Nevertheless it was available by early 1625, even though it had been censured by the Inquisition on 14/24 December 1624: Allison, RSGB, I, pp. 365–366; ARCR, I, nos 65–67; PRO, SP 78/72, fos 348r, 362r; PRO, SP 78/73, fo. 163v. Smith recorded on 16/26 February that the book was condemned in Rome. But it was 'approved here' both by the Sorbonne and the parlement of Paris, and was 'much esteemed, and surely it decifreth the equivocators and sheweth them to be impostors': Allison, RSGB, I, p. 366. Barnes's book attacked Jesuit attitudes to mental

so they are resolved to put our k[ing] to it, and to hazard the whole matter rather than they shold misse of that office, and yet p*er*haps they may misse of their purpose, but here none wil directly oppose again[s]t them, though it be for the com*m*on good. Besid[es], the ladie, as I heare, liketh not the man who is appointed her confessor.[1075] There is one executed in Roan, for matters touching the k[ing] his person, who hath accused twoe Jes[uits], for w*hi*ch they are in prison and what the event wilbe I know not. A pri*ncip*al Jes[uit] went hence thither for to help them, and an other here in his sermon touched [*sic*] that an order ought not to be worse thought of for the fault of one or twoe.[1076] We heare no more of the rebellion of Soubize, so that it is like that al that matter is [*word illegible*].[1077] I pray you, by y*our* next, confer with M^r^ Rant and send me such a copie of com*m*ission as you think fit, for by that time I hope I shal have my faculties and have com*m*unicated with my brethren in England. Of late, M^r^ Colleton, M^r^ Blunt and the provincial of [the] Bened[ictines] have met and agreed that no newse of the estate of Catho[lics] in England shal be beleved here unles they al write. For hitherto it was a shame how contrarie relations were sent hither. F[ather] George[1078] saieth that F[ather] Rudesind[1079] told him that they were drawne to the articles betwixt my predec*ess*or and them ad redimenda*m* vexatione*m*,[1080] w*hi*ch I beleve not, yet I write that you may know what is said therof. I pray you acquaint M^r^ Rant with this and read his for I have written d*iff*erent things to you. I pray com*m*end me most respectively to my l[ord] primat,[1081] and also to M^r^ Browne and M^r^ White. And thus with my hartiest to y*our* [*word omitted:* self], I com*m*it you to the p*ro*tection of o*u*r sweet Savior.

reservation. Carlisle praised the book's vindication of the 'lives of kings from the fraude of equivocations': PRO, SP 78/72, fo. 362r. For Barnes's dispute with other members of his order over their recently united English congregation, see Lunn, *The English Benedictines*, pp. 108–109.

[1075] See *Letters 64*, *68*.

[1076] A report in the foreign state papers describes how 'a priest at Rouen' was 'broken upon the wheele for having a purpose to kill the king because he ayded heretiques in the Valtelin and Germany'. The two Jesuits accused by him had been brought to Paris, 'but it is thought the thing wilbe smothered, and they brought to no farther question'. The writer believed that the alleged plot 'was partly cause that Mansfield was not suffred to land in France': PRO, SP 78/74, fo. 83r.

[1077] For Benjamin de Rohan, baron of Soubise's rebellion in January 1625, see *CSPV, 1623–1625*, pp. 562, 563, 567, 582, 588; M.P. Holt, *The French Wars of Religion, 1562–1629* (Cambridge, 1995), pp. 185–186; Lockyer, *Buckingham*, p. 230; Elliott, *The Count-Duke of Olivares*, pp. 223, 227; PRO, SP 78/74, fo. 96r; *Letter 72*.

[1078] George Latham SJ.

[1079] William (Rudesind) Barlow OSB.

[1080] See *Letter 35*.

[1081] Peter Lombard, archbishop of Armagh.

13 of Febr[uary].

Y*our* servant in Christ Jesus,

R[ichard] Chalcedon

*Addressed*: To the right worship*ful* M^r Thomas More.

*Endorsed*: Paris. 1625. February 13. L*or*d Chalch[edon].
Recea[ved]: March 6. Answ[ered]: [March] 10.

## 72. [John Jackson] to Thomas Rant, 14 February 1625

[*AAW, B 47, no. 162*]

V[ery] r[everend] s*ir*,

I will not be long in yo*ur* debt. This day I receyved yo*u*rs of w*hi*ch my h[onourable] f[riend],[1082] by who*m* yow are kindly remembred, said that it was short and sweet. Neyther M^r M[ore] nor yo*ur* selfe take notice of two former of myne nor of the relatio*n* co*n*cerning Fa[ther] Blunt and me.[1083] I suspect it is intercepted. Yow must expect no great newes. I have not been in Londo*n* since 7^ber. Concerning matters of religion, they are handled after th*e* wonted maner. Fayre promises, now and then some ease, and by th*a*t tyme the fame therof cometh to th*a*t place, and some desired proceedings therupo*n*, the stream runneth as it did before. The pursuivants range and rage in Yorkshire,[1084] thowgh his Ma*jes*tie did write a l*ett*re to th*e* b[ishop][1085] (at the Fr[ench] imb*assado*rs motio*n*) to the co*n*trary.[1086] M^r Metcalfe, a

[1082] A reference, perhaps, to Thomas Arundell, 1st Baron Arundell.

[1083] See *Letter 51*.

[1084] See AAW, A XIX, no. 4, p. 12 (concerning the enforcement of 'a new commission [. . .] for searching' which had been issued on 23 January 1625 by the 'highe commission to the Blanshardes', for whom see Richard Cholmeley, 'The memorandum book of Richard Cholmeley of Brandsby 1602–1623', *North Yorkshire County Record Office Publications*, 44 (1988), pp. 143, 175, 193, 202, 218, 228).

[1085] Archbishop Tobias Mathew.

[1086] For the king's letter to the archbishop of York, dated 26 December 1624, ordering the suspension of proceedings in the high commission court, see PRO, SP 14/177/27; *Letter 65*. An undated memorandum noted that this letter – and an identical missive to the archbishop of Canterbury – did not extend to the episcopal courts, and so the archbishops should intervene to prevent all process against Catholics there: PRO, SP 14/177/28. Thomas Roper had observed, on 21 January 1625, that the English Catholics were indebted to Villeauxclercs but, 'since his departure, thinges have not bein accordingely performed and, whereas there was a letter written unto the bissh[op] of Yorke by the kinge for a cessation, it was recauled before it was sent, with a promise of more ample satisfaction in another kinde': AAW, B 47, no. 186. (John Hacket implied, in his biography of Lord Keeper Williams, that Williams had

preist, is there co*n*demned since Christmas at a gaole delivery.[1087] The oath [is] tendred at th*e* ports. The informers at Londo*n* served process, as they did of late on th*e* La[dy] Carill and the La[dy] Mulleneux her daughter.[1088] M$^{r}$ Penny w*i*th his nephew M$^{r}$ Mathewes were here of late, and then yow can not doubt of ~~yowr~~ o*u*r often speech of yo*u*r selfe. I excus*e*d yow what I co[u]ld, for both himselfe and his sister mervailed as much they heard not fro*m* yow as yow of his silence. We hear th*a*t his Hol[iness] hath writte*n* to th*e* k[ing] of France to know whether he will avow the proceeding of his generall w*i*th th*e* Grisons; and, if he doe, he must declare himselfe against him. Or, if he had noe com*m*ission, th*a*t he will punish him. The k[ing] hath returned a delatory answer th*a*t, if he have done soe much, he hath exceeded his com*m*ission, but he will not co*n*demne him untill he hear him speak; and soe desires forbearance. O*u*r soldiers th*a*t went w*i*th Mansf[elt] are on th*e* coast of Holla*n*d or [Zeal]a*n*d, but in th*eir* shipps. It is thought to be doone by appointme*n*t that the [*sic*] 2,000 of the French may joyne w*i*th them, [and] that France and Ingl[and] both may equally countenance and avow the action. It is said th*a*t Subize hath taken an other fort call[e]d Bl[a]vet in Britany.[1089] I suppose yow have long since heard of his

managed to persuade Villeauxclercs to moderate his determination to procure concessions for English Catholics: Hacket, *SR*, part I, pp. 213–222, part II, p. 6.)

On 13 February, Williams promised Conway that he would use Conway's warrant to summon 'any of the archbyshopp of Yorke his officers or any one imployed in that highe comission [. . .] upon whom complaint shalbe made for eagernes of proseqution against the Roman Catholiques in this time', and to 'signifie unto them, privatelye and yeat as pressingelye as the occasion shall require, his Majestyes just pleasure for theyr discreet behaviour in the execution of that part of theyre offices in this considerable time of his Majestyes most weightye negociation'. Nevertheless, Williams advised that, if the king wanted to command the judges and JPs 'to be moderate [. . .] in the enquiringe out of Roman Catholiques either by the statute of 12$^{d}$ a Sundaye or by enditements in the quarter sessions', this would require a specific letter from the king telling Williams to issue the necessary order: PRO, SP 14/183/54, fo. 85r. The marquis of Effiat expressed misgivings, and diplomatic protests followed: PRO, SP 78/74, fos 68r–69r, 74r. For the attempt to give assurances to Villeauxclercs concerning the orders directed to Archbishop Mathew, see PRO, SP 14/184/8; PRO, SP 78/74, fo. 80r–v. For Williams's justification, in mid-March, of the regime's proceedings concerning recusants, see *Cabala*, pp. 105–106. On 17 March, Williams remarked to Buckingham that 'you are informed' that copies of the letters to the two archbishops 'are spread abroad in Staffordshire to his Majestyes disadvantage (for soe it is)'. Williams hoped that Effiat might 'thereby [. . .] perceive the bent of the Englishe Catholiques, which is not to procure ease and quietnes to themselves but scandals to their neighbourhinge Protestants and discontentments against the kinge and state': BL, Harleian MS 7000, fo. 174v.

[1087] Brian Metcalf was sentenced on 23 January 1625: Anstr., II, p. 218; AAW, A XIX, no. 4, p. 12; PRO, SP 14/185/54, fo. 84v.

[1088] Mary, the daughter of Sir Thomas Caryll and his wife, Mary (Tufton) of Shipley in Sussex, had married Sir Richard Molyneux of Sefton in Lancashire: Cokayne, *CP*, IX, p. 45. I am grateful to Gabriel Glickman for assistance with this reference.

[1089] See Lockyer, *Buckingham*, p. 230; *CSPV, 1623–1625*, pp. 567, 582; Avenel, *Lettres*, II, pp. 65–66.

taking of the isle by Rochell.[1090] They write th*a*t the e[arl] of Carlile, now kn*igh*t of the Garter, cometh over to hasten the mariage, and th*a*t the d[uke] shall goe to Calis to fetch the la[die]. S*ir* Wa[l]ter Aston is sent for owt of Spaine, some say for writing to o*u*r k[ing] a project about th*e* Palatinate for w*hi*ch the prince is displeased.[1091] Yo*u*r relatio*n* of th*a*t good b[ishop] is gratefull. I praye excuse me w*i*th all respect to M$^{r}$ More at this tyme. I know this shall be com*m*on to both, and the next week, God willing, I will write to him. It seems o*u*r b[ishop][1092] was co*n*secrated before yow knew he had his bulls. M$^{r}$ Penny told me he mervelled th*a*t M$^{r}$ Bartled th*e* Jes[uit] was suffred to stay in th*a*t country, there goe so many speeches of him.[1093] The widowe <M$^{rs}$> Hauker (said he) telleth scurvy and fowl things <of him>; and ther daughters, who are fallen, doe the like. He shold have been at a howse of note this Christmas and a <lay> gentlema*n*, who bare some stroak there, said th*a*t if he came, himselfe wold depart. Thus reformed are the Jes[uits] in Ing[land]. There is a Scotish Jesuite[1094] w*i*th Monsig*nor* Fiat the imb[assador], who in likelyhood got the Capuchines[1095] place by a pretty wile, w*hi*ch I shall write in some other l*ett*re. Now I take my leave of yow both in hartiest maner, and rest.

Yours assured.

Your l*ett*re bears date the 4$^{th}$ of Jan[uary], and I write this the 14$^{th}$ of Feb[ruary]. We had newes 14 dayes since th*a*t the Archd[uke] Charles was dead at Madrid,[1096] and the k[ing] sick. And now it is said in the country th*a*t he is also dead. But we have it by noe letter fro*m* London.

*Addressed*: To the right worship*fu*ll my worthy freind M$^{r}$ Rant, at Rome.

*Endorsed*: Received: 11 Aprill.

[1090] See *CSPV, 1623–1625*, p. 562.

[1091] Cf. *ibid.*, pp. 569, 590, 591.

[1092] Richard Smith.

[1093] See *Letter 60*.

[1094] A letter written on 31 December 1624 by the Scottish Jesuit John Macbreck to Muzio Vitelleschi claimed that the writer had been summoned from Scotland by the marquis of Effiat to take Patrick Anderson SJ's place and to serve as Effiat's confessor: ABSJ, Stonyhurst Anglia A II, 3, no. 15; ABSJ Stonyhurst Anglia A IV, no. 26, pp. 19–20; Forbes-Leith, *Narratives of Scottish Catholics*, p. 314; Foley, VII, p. 483. See also *Letter 75*.

[1095] Ange de Raconis.

[1096] For the death of the archduke (the emperor's brother) at Madrid on 18/28 December 1624, see AAW, B 47, no. 76; *Cabala*, p. 167; BL, Harleian MS 1581, fo. 62r. For the purpose of his recent journey to Spain, see PRO, SP 78/72, fo. 362v; Elliott, *The Count-Duke of Olivares*, p. 218.

## 73. Paul Overton [Peter Snod][1097] to Thomas Rant, 15 February 1625

[*AAW, B 26, no. 13*]

R*igh*t r*everen*d worthy sir,

I have not hetherto tooke uppon <mee> to write unto you, beinge unacquainted, and knowinge the determination of a setled correspondence to bee kept betweene M$^{r}$ More and M$^{r}$ Muskett.[1098] But M$^{r}$ Coleton intimates unto mee that you are desirous more often to bee informed than he can performe, for many imployments. And this is the cause principall that I beginne nowe to intrude my selfe into a correspondence w*i*th you. To beginne with o*ur* generall estate of Catholikes: ~~it~~ you p*er*adventure heare that wee are in security, but it is not soe. Writs are daylie served by informers, excommunications pronounced in publike church by ministers; noe order is given to the judges nowe goinge theire circuits, noe restrainte of exactinge 12$^{d}$ a weeke, and the promise of repayment out of the exchequer is driven of[f] from pe*r*formance w*i*th faire words, ut verbo dicam. Spes alit agricolas. Yet is the French amb[assador][1099] daylie, and earnestly, though frustra, solicited.[1100] The present generall opinion of the duke [of] Buckinghams goeinge for the lady of France is that he sets forward a fortnight or three weekes hence. It is only opinion, yet of good probabilitie. It is conjectured most hast wilbe made least Gondomar, whoe is saide to come hethereward, should trouble the streame. The Viscountes Purbecke hath lately beene in question about

[1097] See Anstr., II, p. 302. Snod had become secretary to the secular clergy's episcopal chapter in 1624.

[1098] George Fisher.

[1099] Antoine Coiffier de Ruzé, marquis of Effiat.

[1100] On 12 March 1625, Secretary Conway sent the attorney-general a list of Catholics presented by Effiat, and asked advice on how 'the king's grace may be most conveniently bestowed, but not in the public way they desire': *CSPD, 1623–1625*, p. 496. On the same day, Archbishop Abbot complained to Conway that Effiat had been told on numerous occasions that a named individual, John Tapper, for whom the French ambassador had evidently interceded, was not in prison for his religion: PRO, SP 14/185/47; see also *CSPD, 1623–1625*, pp. 494, 504; PRO, SP 14/185/95. For the attorney-general's advice concerning the London prisoners whose cases the French ambassador had taken up, see PRO, SP 14/185/54. He argued that each case should be separately investigated, and he advised that presentments and convictions of recusants should not cease but that forfeitures as a result of conviction should be prevented: *ibid.* Williams gave the same advice, in effect, to Buckingham on 13 March: *Cabala*, pp. 105–106.

a man childe of hers nowe come to light, thoughe into the world a yeare since, and ~~that~~ certaine images of waxe, as the dukes and some others, are reported to bee found in her cabinet, uppon w*hi*ch Lambe, the sorcerer formerly condemned in the kings bench for a rape and a murther, is nowe againe close prisoner in the kings bench, and the twoe gentlewomen of the viscountesse in the Gatehouse.[1101] The starre chamber will hereafter discover more of this matter, where it is thought this whole cause shall come to triall. O*ur* parliament is put of[f] till March, and is thought will then be adjourned to Michaelmas. This is the p*re*sent face of ~~our~~ times. Touchinge o*ur*selves, M^r^ Coleton and the rest desire that the motion, alreddy on foote, for fower more b*ishop*s bee followed, and that earnest sute bee made to settle faculties and jurisdiction of goverment uppon some office and the parson bearinge it for the time beeinge, [so] that, if God take away o*ur* b[ishop],[1102] as he did the former,[1103] wee bee not left destitute of order in goverment. Thus, w*it*h my best respect to yo*ur* selfe and M^r^ More, I rest.

Yo*ur*s alwaies to command,

Paule Overton

15 Feb[ruary] 1624.

The inclosed I desire you to deliver if you can, and in most courteous manner commend mee to M^r^ Browne. His mother is in health, redeemed from Jesuitesses.

*Addressed*: To his much respected good freinde M^r^ Thomas Rante, these. Rome.

*Endorsed*: Letters sent to M^r^ Rant and M^r^ More. 1624, 1625. XV. No. XV.

## 74. George Musket [Fisher] to Thomas Rant, 18 February 1625

[*AAW, B 47, no. 155*]

Right w*orshipf*ull,

I have yours of the 18 of Janu[ary] in wich you certifie that the dispensatio*n* is graunted, but no speach <yet> of the coming of the

[1101] See *Letter 70*.
[1102] Richard Smith.
[1103] William Bishop.

lady, although many be of opinion that the match will goe forward, and the duke[1104] still maketh great preparation for that jorney, yet it is uncertaine when he will goe. But that wich most troubleth us is that no effectuall course is taken for the redresse of our miseries. Many still complaine, especially in the North, and Lancaster goale [*sic*] is furnished at this present with 15 prisoners, 2 pr[iests] and 13 lay me*n*,[1105] and no course taken for the[ir] release, nor for the stay of persecutio*n* ther, so that they expect daily more prisoners. And the justices ther ar so forward that they urge the paiment of 12[d] for every Sonday and call poore people before the*m* and tender the oath. And uppo*n* refusall they comitt, insomuch that an honest [?] gentlema*n* of that country told me that he thought he knewe above on[e] hundred wich were fallen away for feare of this danger. Neither must you thinke that they alone ar persecuted, for others in all parts have ther share in thes[e] miseries and know not how to helpe themselves. It is thought the parliame*n*t will be put of[f] untill May, but as yet it is not certainly concluded. Uncertaine rumors ar spread of Mansfield and his forces, some say, and this is more credible that he is not yet landed, and that many of his soldiars ar dead with hunger and cold, and that this expeditio*n* will come to nothing in the end. Ricardus Calcedonensis[1106] is not yet come, but we expect him daily, and hope shortly to injoy him. I know not what to say to that letter of James Pratt.[1107] It is like, as you say, that it was the ground of those scandalous reports you mention, and I [see] no reaso*n* why, <for> the passion of on[e] ma*n*, they should lay an imputatio*n* uppo*n* all priests, as though they terrified Catholikes for keeping of Jesuits if they keepe themselves within ther bounds. I hope we shall live in peace with them. The French ambas[sador][1108] still remaineth <here> and now ther is no speach of his remove, but, to speake truth, he doeth us litle or no good so farr as I can perceive, for wich cause he is not so much respected as others his predecessors have bin.[1109] We ar not yet certaine of the coming of the earle of Gondomar,

[1104]George Villiers, 1st duke of Buckingham.

[1105]On 4 March, Fisher claimed that there were two priests and fifteen lay Catholics imprisoned there: AAW, B 47, no. 159.

[1106]Richard Smith.

[1107]See *Letter 71*.

[1108]Antoine Coiffier de Ruzé, marquis of Effiat.

[1109]Thomas Roper reported to Thomas More, on 12 March 1625, that he had recently 'sent [. . .] some particulars of what had passed in Yorkeshire and Linconsheere about which some <came> uppe hether to seeke remedy, and with much difficulty they obtayned a letter of his Majesties to the justices for their forbearance to proceede furder in suche businesses without expresse leave of his Majestie, to which' the marquis of Effiat 'gave no assistance, beinge much displeased with the recusantes whome he sayed, with their letters, had don him ill offices in France and R[ome] and therefor he would have nothinge to doe with them': AAW, B 47, no. 178.

although some ar of opinion that certainly he will come this spring. If you heare any thing of Ormus[1110] or Brasile, let us be partakers. I have no more to impart but my best love wich is allwaies yours, so I rest.

Yours assuredly,

M[usket] G[eorge]

Febr[uary] 18 1624 co*m*poto Anglicano.

*Addressed*: To the right wor*shipfu*ll M[r] Thomas More.

*Endorsed*: Feb[ruary] 18. Received: 5 Aprill.

## 75. Thomas Roper to Thomas More, 24 February 1625

[*AAW, B 47, no. 181*]

Good cosen,

Your last is of the 25 of Jan[uary]. You will perceave, by this relation I send you, how many suffer for their recusancy, though I presume you are made beleeve otherw[a]ys.

M[r] Bisshoppes name is James, and not Bernaby, that is to be employed into your partes.[1111] We say here that ~~the dis~~ thoughe the dispensation be comme to Paris, yet it is directed to the nuntio[1112] and to remayne in his handes untill the two kinges be agreed, and that it is clogged w*i*th some conditions w*hi*ch are not pleasinge unto us, w*i*thall that the Frenche kinge insistethe to have the same freedome for his Ma*jes*ties subjectes that are Romaine Catholi[cs] that the Frenche Protestants have in France.[1113] The coppy of the dispensation was brought the last weeke by M[r] Carey[1114] and one Seton,[1115] but it geavethe us no content.

[1110] See *CSPV, 1623–1625*, p. 286; PRO, SP 94/25, fo. 348r.

[1111] Six days previously, Roper had written to More that 'it is reported that Barneby Bisshoppe, nephew to our last prelate [*i.e.* William Bishop], shall be employed to your course by his Majestie. He is a humaniste but very unfitte for any negotiation': AAW, A XIX, no. 7, p. 19. See also AAW, B 47, no. 77.

[1112] Bernardino Spada, archbishop of Damietta.

[1113] On 4 March 1625, George Fisher had observed that 'the king of France standeth much <as I heare> uppon conditions for religion and <for> as much toleration as he graunteth his Hugonots in France'. Fisher thought that this would cause James 'to pause at least untill the parliament be ended, wich beginneth the 15 of this moneth, for as yet I cannot heare of any prorogation': AAW, B 47, no. 159; see also Hacket, *SR*, part I, p. 214.

[1114] A reference, presumably, to Thomas Carey.

[1115] Captain John Seton. See *CSPD, 1623–1625*, pp. 249, 486; PRO, SP 78/74, fo. 60v.

There was the last weeke some conference after dinner at the Frenche amb[assador's][1116] betwene Monsieur Molines, the famous minister of France, and one Kelly, a Scottishe man, before the ambass[ador], who allso did argue in defence of our religion. The mannor of the conference was related unto me by one of the padri[1117] who was present w*it*h Father Fissher[1118] (who alwayes is one), yet he ~~hathe~~ <sayed> they were bothe of them there by accident. Yet some are otherwayes persuaded. Monsieur Molines dined w*it*h the ambass[ador] and after dinner the ambass[ador] gave occasion of discourse of matters of religion unto Monsieur Molines who entred into a long discourse, sermon like, runninge throughe many pointes of controversy and was severall tymes interrupted by M^r^ Kelly who required him to pause a while, that he might make some answeare to some one or two pointes of his discourse on w*hi*ch he would insiste, beinge [*sic*] it would be to[o] tedious to answere all he had sayed. And so, after some importunity, they insisted uppon some two heads, whereof marriadge of preistes was one, and so tooke occasion to expounde some generall conseiles. Father Fisher made some one argument or two in forme to w*hi*ch Molines made answeare, and the most of the conference was w*it*h Kelly whome the padri commended to have don well, and to be very readdy in controversies, havinge a good Frenche and Latin tongue. As they were arguinge, Molines sonne was allso arguinge in the same roome w*it*h others, but after some houres or mores discourse they all ended abruptely, for the conference was confused, every one speakinge w*it*hout order, and no judge appointed. At the partinge, the ambass[ador] told Molines that he thought he could have sayed more for his religion, and that he should never persuade him, and so caused him to be accompanyed to his coache.

The Easte India company caused one Greeneberry ~~to~~, a painter, to drawe them a picture wherein they did expresse the great cruelties w*ith*al the Holl[anders] had used against our Ingleshe at Amboina, and this picture they did intende to sette in their haule. The Hollenders complayned to our counsell, who sent for Greeneberry who, understandinge <the cause> thereof, went accompayned [*sic*] w*it*h ten of the committe[e] of the company, who did affirme unto the lords that they had sett him a worke. The counseile have forbidden the picture to be exposed to the vew of the vulgar.[1119]

[1116] Antoine Coiffier de Ruzé, marquis of Effiat.

[1117] i.e. Jesuits.

[1118] John Percy SJ.

[1119] For the Amboyna incident of February 1623 (reported in England in mid-1624), see *Letter 48*; Cogswell, *BR*, pp. 274–275; McClure, *LJC*, pp. 562–563; *CSPV, 1623–1625*, pp. 343,

None of those particulars that were granted to Villocleere are yet performed.

My yonge Lord Dormer[1120] is on Monday next to be married to my lord of Montgomeries daughter[1121] w*it*h little contentment to his freindes.[1122]

One Taylour,[1123] secretary to Conte de Gondemar, arrived here some two dayes agoe, and is gon w*it*h the Spanishe agent[1124] to courte. The reporte is that he hathe written unto the kinge that his Ma*jes*tie will be pleased to send one of his shippes to the Groina for him, he not beinge well able to travell by land.

Sir G[eorge] Colverte, I am tolde, is rectus in C. R.,[1125] and it <is> sayed he intendes to goe <a viaggio> to the New Founde Land where he hathe a share in that plantation.[1126]

I have written two lines ~~to~~ in Italian about your writinge of your luoghi de m*on*ti w*hi*ch <you say> is in the procurer of the colledges

359; PRO, SP 14/168/48; PRO, SP 94/31, fo. 233v. The East India Company wanted the incident made the subject of a stage play, but the Dutch appealed to the privy council to have this prevented: PRO, SP 14/184/22; McClure, *LJC*, p. 602.

[1120] Robert Dormer, 2nd Baron Dormer.

[1121] Anna Sophia, daughter of Philip Herbert, 1st earl of Montgomery.

[1122] See McClure, *LJC*, p. 605. One of Joseph Mead's correspondents observed how John Prideaux, vice-chancellor of Oxford, had 'at the earl of Montgomery's lodging [. . .] bestowed three days in catechizing the young Lord Dormer and the Lady Anne Herbert, and the last Sunday administered the Lord's supper unto them', and then 'married them by special licence of the archbishops; of which young lord much good is conceived, though his mother be an absolute recusant': Birch, *CTJI*, II, p. 503.

[1123] Henry Taylor: see Anstr., II, p. 314; *CSPV, 1623–1625*, pp. 610, 616, 621; AAW, B 47, no. 159. On 10 March, Fisher understood that, following Henry Taylor's return to Spain, Gondomar would travel to England, 'wich I hope will be about Easter or soone after': AAW, B 47, no. 154.

[1124] Jacques Bruneau.

[1125] i.e. the Church of Rome.

[1126] See J.D. Krugler, *English and Catholic: the Lords Baltimore in the seventeenth century* (Baltimore, MD, 2004), ch. 3. On 3/13 February, Richard Ireland believed that Calvert had been imprisoned in the Tower: AAW, B 47, nos 120, 129. For the conferment of Calvert's Irish peerage (Baltimore), noted by John Jackson on 21 February, 'that the world shold not conceyve he was put from his secretariship in disgrace', see AAW, B 47, no. 163; Krugler, *English and Catholic*, p. 74. Calvert had made provision in May 1624 to resign his office to Sir Dudley Carleton, though Secretary Conway suspected him of double dealing and thought that he 'intended to bring the king to take notice that he is excluded from business and therefore desires to be rid of his place', and then James would 'set all again where it was two years since': PRO, SP 14/164/7; Ruigh, *1624*, p. 288, n. 37. In fact, he surrendered his office to Sir Albert Morton: Krugler, *English and Catholic*, p. 68; BL, Additional MS 72255, fo. 165r. On 26 February 1625, Chamberlain noted that Calvert 'is gon into the North with Sir Tobie Mathew which confirmes the opinion that he is a bird of that feather': McClure, *LJC*, p. 603; see also BL, Additional MS 72255, fo. 166v. Calvert was offered the option of remaining a privy councillor if he would take the oath of allegiance, but he refused: McClure, *LJC*, p. 609; *Letter 81*; Krugler, *English and Catholic*, p. 73.

handes. I am confident it was never delivered unto him by me, but if I had it I did deliver it to fath[er] rector who then was Fath[er] Owen,[1127] he beinge dead.[1128] This rector[1129] turnethe you to this Carlo.[1130]

I doe make a question whether these few lines of myne will doe you any good for, if they be disposed to caville, they will stande to have it more authenticall. If Mr Heines had bein in towne, I would have <had> it don by him as protonario apost[olico].

If Mr Clayton be w*i*th you, I pray you tell him that my Lady Appleton[1131] dyed this last night. The 24 Feb[ruary] 1625.

Yours,

T[homas] R[oper]

*No address.*

*Endorsed*: Writt[en]: 24 Febr[uary].
Receaved: 11 Aprill.
Answ[ered]: 19 Aprill.

## 76. Henry Clifford to Thomas More, 25 February/7 March 1625

[*AAW, B 47, no. 70*]

Wor*shipfu*ll and r*everen*d s*i*r,

I have yo*u*rs of the 15 February, and have dispatched the inclosed for England, from whence the last weekes post brought you no *lett*res, and he of this weeke is not yet come. Mr Tho[mas] Roper is very busie in an intricate busines betwene his father and hime, w*hi*ch is com*m*itted to arbitrement, and the last weeke they were all busie abowt it. In England promoters are busie, and the worlde beginns to doubt of the match w*i*th France; upon what grownds I knowe not, for great jewells have bene sent.[1132] Messengers goe up and downe. The earle of Carlile remaines still in France and, by the procuration of the queene mother,[1133] is named knight of Garter. And these assistants of

[1127] Thomas Owen SJ. See *NAGB*, p. 9.

[1128] See PRO, SP 77/13, fo. 145r; see also AAW, B 27, no. 58.

[1129] Thomas Fitzherbert SJ.

[1130] Carlo, as named by Roper, was the procurator in question: AAW, B 27, no. 75.

[1131] Joan Sheldon, wife of Sir Henry Appleton, 2nd baronet, of South Benfleet, Essex. Margaret Roper, sister of William Roper of Eltham (d. 1577), had married Henry Appleton of Dartford.

[1132] See *CSPV, 1623–1625*, pp. 615–619.

[1133] Marie de Médicis.

Mansfielde hath bene jointly from both kings, the one furnishing him w*i*th foot, and the other w*i*th horse, and both w*i*th mony. And it likely th*at* the course [*i.e.* cause] of the delay is to see the effects of this project of Mansfielde. He is by Gertembergh[1134] w*i*th his English expecting his horse from France, who all the last weeke were embarked at Calais.[1135] No <man> suffered to stay on the key while they were shipped. But on Sunday night, 23 February, there was so terrible a north-west winde th*at* it drowned in that haven 3 shipps of the French kings (whereof one was the viceadmirall), a shipp of warre of the Hollanders, and Lambert the com*m*aunder was forced to cutt downe the main mast of his owne shipp, and much spoile did it upon lesser botes. So it was Thursday following before Halberstate[1136] could begin to shipp his horse.[1137] At Flushing also this tempest did much spoile, and cast away a shippe wherein was our English souldiers. At Amsterdame it drowned divers vessells, whereof some were shipps of warre bound for the West Indies. Mansfeeld can not be readie yet these 15 dayes, but our soldiers expect him w*i*th great desire, of whom the countrey is full, sufferinge by them greate spoile and miserie.

I had yesternight a l*ett*re from the leaguer from Captaine Bentley,[1138] who writes that their streangth and new supply would gladly have Mansfielde come nearer. He can doo them no harme, nor in any probable discourse releeve Breda, except God Almightie punish us by this meanes for our sinns, w*hi*ch I hope his mercye will p*re*serve and assist us against the enemies of his truth.[1139]

Both the fleetes of Spaine are now gone for Brasill, and are to meete at Capo Verde. God speede them well.[1140]

Here is a relation of horrible sacrileges, execrable barba[r]ismes and such impiouse insolencies that the French have com*m*itted upon Catholicks and their churches and aultars in the Valteline, as no Turke nor profane beast coulde doo more. O greate miserie th*at* such

[1134] Geertruidenberg. See *CSPV, 1623–1625*, p. 603; *CCE*, p. 206; Lockyer, *Buckingham*, p. 228.

[1135] See *Letter 71*; *CCE*, p. 204.

[1136] Christian of Brunswick, administrator of the bishopric of Halberstadt.

[1137] See *HMCMK*, p. 220.

[1138] A reference, presumably, to Frederick Bentley, who was a cousin of the archpriest William Harrison, and whose father, Edward, had married Catherine, the daughter of Sir William Roper of Eltham and Canterbury. Frederick Bentley fought for the Habsburgs in Flanders: see AAW, B 25, no. 38; Anstr., II, p. 23; Hamilton, *Chronicle of the English Augustinian Canonesses Regular*, II, pedigree of Roper.

[1139] See *CCE*, p. 213.

[1140] See *CSPV, 1623–1625*, pp. 512, 544, 573; *Cabala*, pp. 166–167. On 4/14 March 1625, Clifford expressed the hope that 'the armadas that be gone to Brasill will remoove the Hollander, and ruine him there, being the nation that pester[s] the worlde': AAW, B 47, no. 77.

monsters doo fight and serve under him that hath the name of the most Christian king.[1141]

Breda, no question, is in great affliction, but confideth th*at* Mansfielde will helpe. But the marques[1142] hath sent them word if, at the surrendering of the towne, he finde not a months provision he will leave them to the spoile of the souldiers.

Y*our* brother[1143] is very well and recom*m*ends his love. So are his, as farre as we heare. My wife thanks you for y*our* charitable remembrance, and we both com*m*end us to y*our* good prayers. Wishing you good health and happines.

Andwarp 7° Martii.

Y*our* servant assuered,

Henry Clifford

[1141] On 31 December 1624/10 January 1625, Clifford had commented to More that, in Antwerp, 'they talke that his Ho[liness] is partiall in the Valtelene, and suffers theise forts to be taken by the French without great resistance of his souldiers that keepe them', though on 4 February Thomas Roper informed More that 'here we say that his Hollinesse is offended with the Frenche for their forwardnesse in the Voltolina, and that their generall, the marquise of Cuever, is threatened to be excommunicated'. In Roper's mind, this was connected with a fear that 'the Frenche will bring us into broyles and then leave us, and that they will not be firme to us in the league, which league must needes in effecte turne to the great prejudice of Catho[lic] religion', and so he hoped that 'his Holinesse will nether directly nor indirectly concurre to it': AAW, B 47, nos 83, 182. For the confrontation in the Valtelline, see *CSPV, 1623–1625*, *passim*; J.V. Polisensky, *The Thirty Years War* (London, 1974), p. 163. Since the 'Spanish Road' had, following the duke of Savoy's offensive alliance with the French in 1610, become unavailable as a secure land route for the Habsburg military establishment, the Valtelline was strategically crucial to the Spaniards. It had been taken by the duke of Feria for Spain in November 1620, after the revolt in July of that year by the Catholic inhabitants of the region against the Grisons who ruled over both the Engadine and the Valtelline – the valleys which provided routes between Lombardy and the Tyrol, i.e. northern Italy and Switzerland. In 1593, the Catholics there had made an agreement with the Spaniards to permit the movement of troops across their region. See R. Bonney, *The European Dynastic States, 1494–1660* (Oxford, 1991), pp. 206–208; G. Parker, *The Army of Flanders and the Spanish Road, 1567–1659* (Cambridge, 1972), pp. 70, 73; Cogswell, *BR*, pp. 67, 70; Albion, *CI*, pp. 3–5; PRO, SP 94/24, fo. 37r. The French made clear their determination to see the Valtelline restored to its former state and, following the unsuccessful Treaty of Madrid in April 1621, to ensure the rejection of the articles offered to the Grisons during 1621 and forced on them by Feria in 1622: PRO, SP 78/69, fos 38r, 71v. As Sir Henry Wotton wrote on 8/18 December 1621, the Spaniards, having so successfully taken it, could 'walk (while they keep a foot in the Lower Palatinat) from Milan to Dunkercke upon their own inheritances and purchases, a connexion of terrible moment': L.P. Smith (ed.), *The Life and Letters of Sir Henry Wotton*, 2 vols (Oxford, 1907), II, p. 221. In February 1623, the League of Lyons, between Louis XIII, Savoy, and the Venetians compelled the Spaniards to put the area into the hands of the papacy: Bonney, *The European Dynastic States*, pp. 207–208; Albion, *CI*, pp. 4–5; Pursell, *WK*, p. 196; PRO, SP 78/71, fos 18r, 22v, 50r, 85r; PRO, C 115/107/8495; BL, Harleian MS 1581, fo. 60r–v.

[1142] Ambrogio Spinola, marquis of Los Balbases.

[1143] Cresacre More.

*Addressed*: Al molto illustre signore, sig*no*re mio oss*ervanissi*mo, il r*everen*do sig*no*re, D[omino] Tomaso Moro sacerdote Inglese nella casa de Mons*ieu*r Vives a la Trinita Monte in Roma.

*No endorsement.*

## 77. Thomas Roper to Thomas More, 4 March 1625

[*AAW, B 47, no. 185*]

Good cosen,

I receaved lately two of yours, the one of the first and the other of the 8 of Feb[ruary].

I am gladd you geave me advertisement in your letters of my cosen Browne. His father understandethe the thereof, who is well pleased and sendethe unto me kinde remembrances for lettinge him know from tyme to tyme what you write, I meane as muche as concernethe his sonnes well doinge.

My Lord Maxwell came hither some ten dayes agoe[1144] and hathe often bein w*i*th our duke,[1145] whose journey into France seemethe to be at some staye, and that [*i.e.* because] there is some rubbe in our Frenche treaty. It is sayed that there is a shippe and a pinnace appointed to be sent to the Groina for Gondemar. But I doe not affirme it for certayne. But whosoever [*sic*], I doe not presume that Gondemars journey will be about any matche, but only to continue an amety betwene us and Spayne, to entertayne some reconsiliation or treatys [*sic*] of agreement w*i*th the House of Austria and to hinder this great navy w*hi*ch is preparinge for the West India.

The marquis Hamleton[1146] dyed on Tweuseday last[1147] at his lodginges at Whitehall of a purple fever,[1148] and ended his dayes as befitted a good Christian to doe, for soe am I more than credebly informed, and

[1144] See *CSPV, 1623–1625*, p. 558.

[1145] George Villiers, 1st duke of Buckingham.

[1146] James Hamilton, 2nd marquis of Hamilton.

[1147] Cf. *HMCMK*, p. 222 (Hamilton died early in the morning on Ash Wednesday).

[1148] On 11 March, the Venetian ambassador, Zuane Pesaro, reported that 'it is said that the marquis of Hamilton died a Catholic, but with suspicion of poison, and when alive he rather took sides against the marriage articles, probably not on religious grounds but from opposition to the favourite': *CSPV, 1623–1625*, p. 617; see also McClure, *LJC*, p. 604. The attorney-general dealt on 22 March 1625 with the case of Stephen Plunkett who (though he was not, as had been thought, a 'papist') had been repeating rumours that the marquis had been 'poysoned twelve moneths synce', in 1624: PRO, SP 14/185/95, fo. 171r; A. Fox, 'Rumour, news and popular political opinion in Elizabethan and early Stuart England', *HJ*, 40 (1997), p. 604.

therefore I doe pray for him.[1149] One of the *pa*dri cauled Wood[1150] did the deede.[1151] The drumme is at this present beaten in severall partes of the towne for voluntarie shouldiers for to supply my Lord Willobyes[1152] regiment, but our men are utterly discouraged from goinge, havinge bein very coursely used by the Holl[anders], and now Mansefeilds

[1149]John Chamberlain commented that 'the papists will needs have' Hamilton as 'one of theirs, which neither appeared in his life nor in his death that we can any way learne, but yt is no new thing with them to raise such scandalls and slanders': McClure, *LJC*, p. 605. In late March 1622, the earl of Kellie had remarked that Hamilton's making of 'a matche soe farr as it can be' of his daughter with 'the Lord Digbye his sone' had made many 'think that he is more Spanishe than he was': *HMCMK*, p. 116. The count of Tillières, in mid-May 1622, believed that Hamilton had been 'maltraité de la France, depuis sept ou huit mois' and he was 'presque entièrement retiré et approché de l'Espagne', even though he was accounted 'de la faction puritaine' and a friend of Spain's opponents; and, in mid-June, Tillières hoped that Hamilton could be separated from his 'puritan' friends: PRO, PRO 31/3/56, fos 40r, 58v. Simonds D'Ewes, however, recorded in his diary for early July 1623 that Hamilton had spoken strongly against toleration for Catholics: *DSSD*, p. 146. Tillières recorded the same sentiment from Hamilton in late March 1624, though Hamilton told Tillières that he spoke thus out of deference to Buckingham: PRO, PRO, 31/3/58, fos 65v–66r. On 29 February/10 March 1625, the marquis of Effiat thought that Hamilton 'estoit Catholique en son âme et mort Huguenot': PRO, PRO 31/3/61, fo. 59r. Nine days later, Kellie observed that there were rumours both that Hamilton was 'poysened' and that 'he shuld have dyed a papiste', but 'that is as fals as the uther'. A week later, the rumour was still circulating that Hamilton had 'dyed a papiste and that he had a priste with him and reconcealed himselfe to the pope of Roome'. However, Kellie still did not believe it, for Hamilton was 'more subjecte to his pleasours and the companye of wemen than to preests', and though there was a 'preest with him sume two days before he dyed [. . .] yet I think his besines was more weemens besines than preests affairs'. The rumour was credited because it was spread by Hamilton's Catholic physician, George Eglisham (who subsequently accused Buckingham of poisoning King James): *HMCMK*, pp. 223, 225; R. Cust, *The Forced Loan and English Politics 1626–1628* (Oxford, 1987), p. 183.

[1150]The identity of this Jesuit is uncertain, but John Gee mentions a Jesuit associate of the evangelist John Percy SJ whom he names as 'M[r] Wainman, alias M[r] Wrightman, alias M[r] Wood' (with various other aliases including that of Baker): Gee, *New Shreds of the Old Snare*, pp. 21–22. It is not clear whether this individual should be identified with the Jesuit Alexander Baker (as depicted it seems, under his alias of Wood, in Thomas Scott, *The Second Part of Vox Populi* (np, 1624), p. 54), since Baker was apparently in prison at this point (see Anstr., II, pp. 12–13); but he was obviously not the secular priest Christopher Wainman (*ibid.*, p. 375). Thomas McCoog has suggested that the Jesuit in question might be John Wood (a son, or brother, of James Wood, laird of Boniton), who entered the Society in 1600 but about whom little else is known: ARSJ, Rom. 169, fo. 22v, Rom. 172, fo. 37r. I am very grateful to Dr McCoog for this information.

[1151]In a letter of 18 March, Pesaro said that 'the king spoke wrathfully against the Jesuit who administered extreme unction to the marquis of Hamilton and against the physician who assisted there, but was soon mollified': *CSPV, 1623–1625*, p. 621; see also *CSPV, 1625–1626*, pp. 6–7, for Pesaro's report of 30 March that Archbishop Abbot wanted to take action against 'those concerned in the conversion' but the French ambassador prevented it and so Abbot had 'decided to publish a book praising the marquis as a Protestant'.

[1152]Robert Bertie, 14th Baron Willoughby, later 1st earl of Lindsey.

usadge is farre worse. It is sayed his 12 thousand is comme to 7 thousande. We shall shortely understande what he doethe, for that Brunsewicke[1153] is now gon to him w*i*th his horse from Calais w*hi*ch are sayed to be 1,200 or 1,400.[1154]

The kinge on Satterday last seigned a warrante for the restitution of the bondes which were taken of recusantes since the 5th of Aug[ust] and for the monys w*hi*ch were payed since that tyme into the excheq[uer], but my lord treasurer[1155] sayethe that there is no money in the excheq[uer] so that neither the one nor the other is yet performed.

My awnt Mallory, thankes be to God, is pretty well amended. And so I pray you lette my uncle[1156] know, w*i*th my best remembrance unto him, hopinge he dothe remember me and myne. My wife[1157] ~~will neede~~ <desirethe> to be remembred in his devotions. She drawethe neere hir tyme w*hi*ch will be about the end of Aprill or beginninge of May.

This day came out a proclamation for adjorninge the parla[ment] untill the 20 of Aprill.[1158]

Thus, w*i*th my kinde remembrance unto your selfe, Mr Rant, D[on] Seb[ert],[1159] D[on] Anselmo,[1160] Gio[vanni] Condeno,[1161] Mr Seton and the rest, I end.

Yours,

Th[omas] R[oper]

The 4th Marche 1625.

*Addressed*: All' illustre sig*no*re, il Sig*no*re Thomasso Moro, Inglese. Roma.

*Endorsed*: Tho[mas] More.
Writt[en]: 4 March. Received: 1 May, by Venice post.
Answered: 3 May.

[1153] Christian of Brunswick, administrator of the bishopric of Halberstadt.
[1154] See also AAW, B 47, no. 46; *CCE*, pp. 207–208, 212.
[1155] Sir James Ley.
[1156] Philip Roper.
[1157] Susan, daughter of John Winchcombe of Henwick, Berkshire.
[1158] *SRP*, I, no. 266 (3 March 1625).
[1159] Robert (Sigebert) Bagshaw OSB.
[1160] Robert (Anselm) Beech OSB.
[1161] John Condon. He was one of the mourners at Thomas More's funeral in April 1625: Shanahan, 'The death of Thomas More', p. 26.

## 78. Richard Smith to Thomas More, 15/25 March 1625

[*AAW, B 47, no. 17*]

Right wor*shipfu*ll and deere syr,

I had y*ou*rs of the 24 of Febr[uary] which brought very glad tidings of his Holines['s] desire to uphold the clergie[1162] by declaring that the seminaries are to manteyne that [*i.e.* them], and not instituted for to furnish religious companies, and by his purpose to make al such alumnes for to sweare that they shal not enter into any religion without expresse licence of the sea ap[osto]lik.[1163] If this order be put in practise, our Theatins[1164] wil not be so desirous of o*ur* seminaries where they shal have much paine and no great p*ro*fite, and o*ur* clergie wil soone florish; wherfor God grant that his Hol[iness] put this in execution. My faculties came the last poste but one, and I wold gladly be gone hence, but my cardinal[1165] wisheth me to stay yet a litle, and I doubt not but it is both for my owne, and the com*m*on good, though he tell me not wherin. Of late the mach was like to have broken upon conditions as [*words omitted:* it is] said, w*hi*ch his Hol[iness] had put into the dispensation, w*hi*ch o*ur* king wold not admit,[1166] and I feare that some of o*ur* Theatins seeke under some such good p*re*text to breake al, as is thought they did in the Spanish mach, and may be gathered by thos[e] words of D[octor] Cecil w*hi*ch I have written to you hertofor.[1167] But now, God be thanked, al points are agreed upon and o*ur* duke[1168] expected here within this moneth. I wold M^r^ Benet[1169] had written to me what faculties thos[e] are w*hi*ch he wold have me to have, for by my cardinal his means I hope to obtayne whatsoever is requisite. You wrote to me as archb[ishop] of Chalcedon and so did some to my p*re*dec*ess*or, and indeed Chalcedon was made a metropolitan see

[1162] i.e. the secular clergy.

[1163] See *Letter 35*.

[1164] i.e. Jesuits.

[1165] Cardinal Richelieu.

[1166] See above, p. 110; *Letter 75*; see also AAW, B 47, no. 78.

[1167] On 3/13 March 1625, Smith had informed More that 'D[octor] Cecil tould me that if there be faith in men our Jes[uits] were against the Spanish mach', and 'God grant they be not also against this, and stil dreame of their conquest and booke of reformation', i.e. Robert Persons's notorious discourse about reform of the English Church and state, which had circulated only in manuscript during this period and was eventually published by Edward Gee as *The Jesuit's Memorial for the Intended Reformation of England* (London, 1690), AAW, B 47, no. 15.

[1168] George Villiers, 1st duke of Buckingham.

[1169] Edward Bennett.

by the g*ene*ral counsel held there, and it were for the honor of o*u*r clergie and countrie that I were such, espetially sith Holland hath an archb[ishop] of Philippi.[1170] But in my bul I am named bishop. I pray you see what you can learne of this matter. I rather expect a copie of the comission w*hi*ch you desire than send you a blanc, least as I wrote befor it might fall into enemies hands.[1171] I hope to send you a letter to the F[rench] embass[ador][1172] by this poste, and other letters to the cardinalls I wil send by the next. I am to goe out of this cittie with my card[inal] for thes[e] holie dayes, where I hope p*er*fectly to understand the state of o*u*r matters. M^r^ White his brother[1173] is here with us, and I much wish that he wold come to you, but D[octor] Champney saieth he p*ro*mised them to returne to them after twoe years, and it seem[eth] he expecteth his brother for to make his resolution.[1174] If God send good times in Eng[land] I have great hope to p*ro*cure more b*ishop*s by means of my card[inal] who p*ro*miseth to doe for us al he can, espetially seing, as you write, his Hol[iness] is not averted fro*m* it. I pray you doe my most kind and respective com*m*endations to my L[ord] Winsor, though as yet unknowne to M^r^ Browne, M^r^ Seaton, M^r^ Clinton, D. Anselme,[1175] D. Sebert[1176] and al freinds and acquaintance with you. And thus with my hartiest to y*our* self I leave you to the tuition of o*u*r sweet Savior.

25 of March.

Y*our* servant in Christ Jesus,

R[ichard] Chalcedon

*Addressed*: To the right worship*fu*ll M^r^ Thomas More.

*Endorsed*: Writt[en]: 25 March.
Received: 16 Aprill.
Answered: 21 Aprill.

[1170] Philip Rovenius.

[1171] See AAW, B 47, no. 15 (Smith to More, 3/13 March 1625).

[1172] Philippe de Béthune, count of Sully.

[1173] Thomas White, brother of Richard White.

[1174] Subsequently, on 3/13 August 1625, Richard Ireland wrote that Thomas White 'is readye to come' to Rome 'if my l[ord] [*i.e.* Smith] send him. My l[ord] (as it seemed by his last) expected the consent of his mother and bro[ther] which he had not when he wrote his last': AAW, B 47, no. 113. Thomas White, who had been studying canon law in Paris since April 1624, succeeded More in early 1626 as the secular clergy's agent in Rome: Anstr., II, p. 349.

[1175] Robert (Anselm) Beech OSB.

[1176] Robert (Sigebert) Bagshaw OSB.

## 79. Anthony Champney to Thomas Rant, 4/14 May 1625

[*AAW, B 47, no. 52*]

R*everen*d and beloved s*ir*,

Yours of the 19 of Aprill to Mr President[1177] mentioneth one of the weeke before to my self w*hi*ch is not come, for the miscareing whereof I ame sorie. If <you> would please to send us a copie of Mr Mores will, signed w*i*th your owne hand, that we may see howe we stand w*i*th him and whether he hath left anie thing to this howse, you shall specially oblige us.[1178] If either his brother[1179] or we our selves, or anie other, shall desire a*n* authenticall copie it may be p*ro*cured hereafter as it shall be desired. We like well and com*m*end your indifferencie betwixt this howse and the body of the clergy, and do not wishe you to incurr anie displeasure for your affection to us. I doubt not <but> everie one wilbe well co*n*tent w*i*th that order w*hi*ch our speciall frend hath sett downe, whose sowle God bring to eternall repose. I pray you certefy Mr More at Anwarpe of his brothers will co*n*cerning the payment of the 40 crownes bequeathed to our Franciscanes in like maner as you have sett it downe here, that he may not think that burthen put upon him, nor yet the religiouse me*n* hindered of their legacie.[1180] We thank you hartely ~~for the~~ for the printed decree[1181] you sent us, w*hi*ch

[1177] Matthew Kellison.

[1178] For Thomas More's death and the text of his will, see AAW, A XIX, no. 30, pp. 99–100 (Cresacre More to Thomas Rant, 29 April/9 May 1625); Shanahan, 'The death of Thomas More'.

[1179] Cresacre More.

[1180] Henry Clifford had informed Rant on 22 April/2 May 1625 that Cresacre More would write to him but, in the meantime, 'the watch he requesteth you to accept as a token from him, and what els you like that may by any title descend to him that he had about him. There is alreadye order for the 10li for the church of our English Franciscans in Doway and to other religious frends we have sent to pray for him': AAW, A XIX, no. 28, p. 93.

[1181] AAW, A XIX, no. 9, p. 25 (a decree issued by the Holy Office on the cultus of saints, 3/13 March 1625). George Fisher remarked, on 12 May 1625, that he had received a copy from Rant: AAW, B 26, no. 56. The clergy agent's papers contain a memorandum (never delivered, though shown by Rant to Francesco Ingoli and the secretary of Cardinal Magalotti), dated 10/20 September 1625, against the growing cult of Henry Garnet SJ. The memorandum stated that Garnet died for treason, not for faith, and that his cult would damage the cause of English Catholics. Rant recorded that Ingoli told him not to submit it, and Magalotti's secretary advised that he should present it as a private man, not as agent of the secular clergy: AAW, A XIX, no. 77, p. 235. Rant recorded that, in the previous April, he had made a complaint to the Society in Rome about an inscription under 'Garnets picture in the grand Jesus gallerye' which, referring to Garnet's execution, read 'prop[ter] fidem Catholicam'. It was changed so that it read 'onlye ab haereticis occisus 1606'. Rant remarked that the famous wheatstraw, the relic of Garnet's death and witness to his martyrdom, was still there but was now 'transposed to the right hande, which is the less perspicuous parte of the allye': AAW, B 25, no. 102.

though we must <as we think> thereby be forced to remove some pictures of our martires out of our church, w*hi*ch some hadd bestowed for the ornament thereof, yet are we well co*n*tent therewith. They are the pourtraictes of severall preistes executed in Ingland in this late p*er*secution, set upon the side walles of the church, w*i*thout anie other crownes or glories but only the maner of their execution w*i*th a palme in their hands, w*hi*ch we desire to understand from you whether they are co*m*prised in the decree. We would also knowe what they doe in th*e* colledge there, w*i*th the paynting of their church for so much as p*er*tayneth to the later tymes of persecution. I will send a copie thereof to Mr Messendin[1182] by Mr Ireland that, if he will, he may take [a] copie of it. The copie also of the articles betwixt the bishop of Holland[1183] and the Jesuites was verie welcome and will give my lord[1184] great light howe to p*ro*ceede in his affayres.[1185] But, because this copie is unperfect, <we> intend to send it to the bishop him self to have it p*er*fected and also to entreat him for a copie of the decree of the co*n*gregation,[1186] whereupon these articles are grownded. We <have> hitherto omitted to seeke acquaintance w*i*th him, but, God willinge, we <will> endevour to co*m*pose it, being, as you observe well, verie co*n*venient for us. Mr Blacloe his brother[1187] is come to Parise, so that he may <nowe> resolve w*i*th him self to come to you, if he himself will. For albeit we have great use of him here, and therefore desire much his p*re*sence, according to his p*ro*mise, yet seeing he shall there be imployed for the com*m*on, w*hi*ch we chiefly ayme at, I think we shall resolve to remitt his p*ro*mise, upon co*n*dition he will undertake that charge w*hi*ch truly I doubt not but wilbe for his honour and our countries good. But in the meane while we must entreat your co*n*tinuation, hoping that God will strengthen your corporall forces, according to the desire of your will; that, as by Gods help you have brought our matters to good estate, so you may deliver them to yo*u*r successour who may, by the like help of God, better them dayly. Your judgement of our pension there, and the maner of taking it up, doth jump w*i*th our desires, but the importunitie of freinds will not license us to practice it, w*hi*ch notw*i*thstanding, God willing, we will hereafter observe more strictly. For hitherto, whilst we desire to pleasure freinds, we hurt our selves and troble our agent more than needes. My lord is

[1182] Edward Maddison.

[1183] Philip Rovenius.

[1184] Richard Smith.

[1185] On 12 May 1625, George Fisher wrote to thank Rant for a copy of the articles, and said that he had sent them to Smith: AAW, B 26, no. 56.

[1186] De Propaganda Fide.

[1187] Thomas White, brother of Richard White. See *Letter 78*.

at last gone for Ingland.[1188] God speed him well. Since his departure, came letters to Parise that Mons*ieu*r de Fiat,[1189] ordinarie leger for France in London, is informed, that he hath done him verie ill offices in Parise, and therby is highly displeased w*i*th him. These be the good offices of some back freinds which I doubt not will light upon their owne heades. But they are so co*n*fident in their owne streng[t]h that they think nothing ca*n* hurt them. His back I hope is stronger in Parise than that it ca*n* be swayed with such forgeries. This nu*n*cio[1190] of Bruxelles is gone to Parise to meete there the legate[1191] who, at the writing of our last from Parise, was arrived at Orleance, and the match or marriage was appointed to be solemnised upon Su*n*day last, the 11 of May. Hence I can write you noe newes, nor out of Ingland have we anie; but that our Catholique nobilitie are in difficultie howe to carie them selves at the solemnitie of the coronation, when they are to sweare upon the crowne of S[t] Edward their alleageance to the king; w*hi*ch nowe is done in their service tyme. This case hath beene co*n*sulted at Parise, and the nu*n*cio[1192] will say nothing to it till he heare from Rome w*hi*ch wilbe to[o] long to expect.

M[r] Cooper or Charnock[1193] w*i*th one out of the colledge there, called Ann,[1194] arrived well here upon the 12 of this month. Their other two co*m*panions they left at Parise. The lat[t]er of these went next day towards Ingland. M[r] Charnock acknowledgeth the debt of 20 crownes to M[r] More. M[r] President yesterday tooke phisike, and this day hath beene busied, so that you must accept this as his answer w*i*th his love and myn [*word obscured:* owne] to yo*u*r self, and both our hartie com*m*endacions to M[r] D[octor] Seton w*i*th myn owne to Père Claud Bertin, and so I com*m*itt you to Gods holy p*ro*tection and grace, this 14 of May 1625.

Y*ou*rs ever,

Champney

[1188] See *Letter 80*.

[1189] Antoine Coiffier de Ruzé, marquis of Effiat.

[1190] Giovanni Francesco Guido del Bagno, archbishop of Patras. See PRO, SP 78/75, fo. 85r.

[1191] Cardinal Francesco Barberini. For Barberini's embassy to Paris, see *CSPV, 1625–1626*, p. 44; Hibbard, 'Henrietta Maria', p. 17; PRO, SP 78/74, fo. 96r; PRO, SP 78/75, fos 85v, 300v–301r.

[1192] Bernardino Spada, archbishop of Damietta.

[1193] Richard Charnock. See CRS, 10, p. 236; *Letter 71*. On 7 December 1624, Edward Bennett had asked Thomas More to 'show M[r] Charnock (whose friends I know well) what friendship you can': AAW, B 27, no. 74.

[1194] John Anne. See CRS, 55, pp. 374–375; CRS, 37, p. 203.

*Addressed*: For M[r] Rant.

*Endorsed*: Writt[en]: 14 May.
Received: 7 Juine.
Answered: 7 Juine.

## 80. Richard Smith to Thomas Rant, 12 May 1625

[*AAW, B 47, no. 20*]

Very reverend and deere syr,

God be thanked, and good praiers, I came safely to England the 8 of this moneth after y*our* account and found matters in good termes for Catholiks. For Mon*sieu*r de Fiat,[1195] soone after my coming, obtained of the king letters to the treasurer, chancelor and archb*ishop*s for to surcease al p*er*secution of Catholiks and to set at libertie al prisoners, and restore al moneys taken since Trinitie terme last.[1196] And both he and Conte de Trem received very good words of his Majestie in behalf of Catholiks, and assurance that he wold p*er*forme what he had p*ro*mised.[1197] Nevertheles, becaus[e] as yet the warrants are not published yesterday, some Catholiks were arrested for the 20[l] a moneth and some others cited to appeare befor the comission,[1198] but this I hope wil not continew. The d[uke] of Buckingham is privatly gone to France to meete o*ur* queene who is in her way hither and, as they say, o*ur* king goeth to meete her within thes[e] 2 or 3 dayes. I have written letters to his Holines, to the congreg*ati*on de P*ro*paganda Fide and others, and wil send the*m* as soone as I can by Paris, but this way I take by chance, and am glad to write to you though in haste. If I can I wil send you a com*m*ission now, or els as soone as I can by Paris. I have bene here this forthnight and I heare not that the state taketh any notice of me; yea Mons*ieu*r Fiat offered me divers times to p*re*sent me to his Majestie and the duke, if I wold, but I stay that til the coming of o*ur* queene. F[ather] Blunt hath bene divers times with me, but wil not send any of his for to debate o*ur* matters befor the nonce[1199]

[1195] Antoine Coiffier de Ruzé, marquis of Effiat.

[1196] For Charles I's 'indulgence' of 1 May 1625 in favour of his Roman Catholic subjects, a document of which Lord Keeper Williams was very critical, see Hacket, *SR*, part II, pp. 6–7; PRO, SP 16/2/1–6; PRO, SP 78/75, fo. 117r–v; and for the imprisoned Catholics whose release was promised to Effiat on 28 May 1625 conditionally, i.e. on proof that their imprisonment was solely for religion, see PRO, SP 78/75, fos 39r–v, 116r; see also AAW, A XIX, nos 36, 37.

[1197] For the embassy of Réné Potier, count of Tremes, see PRO, PRO 31/3/61, fos 99r–102r, 103r–v; *CSPV, 1625–1626*, p. 51; Avenel, *Lettres*, II, p. 73.

[1198] i.e. the high commission.

[1199] Bernardino Spada, archbishop of Damietta.

at Paris, but telleth me that al things are wel, and such g*ene*ral good termes. I have given order ~~for al~~ that al the preists in England say 3 Masses for the soule of good Mr More, in whose place I hope to send an other soone after the heats, and then wil expect y*ou*r returne hither wher you shalbe most welcome to me, and enjoye the co*m*panie of y*ou*r good general[1200] and others of y*ou*r brethren for whome his Majestie p*ro*videth a chapel and good lodgings in S. James. In the meane time, com*m*ending my self most hartely to y*ou*r good praiers, I com*m*it you to the p*ro*tection of our sweet Savior.

12 of May.

Y*ou*r servant in Christ Jesus,

R[ichard] Chalcedon

Becaus[e] this com*m*ission is drawne in haste, shew it not unles you have need, for by Paris I wil send you one more formal.

*Addressed*: Admodum reverendo d*omi*no, D[omino] Thoma Rant, congregationis Oratorii presbitero.
Roma.

*Endorsed*: Written: May 12.
Received: June 19.
Answered: June 21.

## 81. Richard Ireland to Thomas Rant, 26 May/5 June 1625

*[AAW, B 47, no. 122]*

R*everen*d and good father,

I have <not> receaved any letter from you by this last post. The banquer[1201] hath not receaved his packett wher[a]s all men that I knowe have receaved theirs. He seemeth to be much troubled, and sayth that it is greatly to his disadvantage.

I have sent your former packets into England where my l[ord] of Ch[alcedon] is well arrived, as you may see by these enclosed packets. He writeth to me th*a*t he hath sent to you directly from England. Mr Black[lo's] brother[1202] maketh great difficultye for th*e* sending of his

[1200] Pierre de Bérulle.
[1201] This appears to be a reference to 'Mons[ieur] Granett' (cited in *Letter 48*).
[1202] Richard White.

bro[ther],[1203] doubting th*at* it may be much to his mothers prejudice and his. My l[ord] hath sent these letters unsealed w*hi*ch I suppose he hath done of purpose that you may understand well the contents of them. I dare not saye th*at* my l[ord] is too credulous for the amendment of our afflicted state. God send all well. But if I had bene of his counsell (thoughe I [*word obscured:* wish (?)] he had farre better counsell than I can give in such a case) under his correction, and likewise of better judgements, he should not have wrote as yet [*word illegible*] hopefully as he doth. If you did heare what the generall opinion is heere to th*e* contrary, and what [*word illegible*] signes there are w*hi*ch bode us noe great good, I doe thinke your [?] feare wold be greater than your hope. Let us commend all, trust God and resigne our selves to His holy will. [*In margin:* Amen.]

Our queene went hence for England on Monday. God speed her well. The duke of Buckingham came sodainly and secretly hether a fewe dayes before her dep*ar*ture.[1204] The duke is heere as yet, and S*ir* Albert Morton, secretary of state, whoe came w*it*h him. They are to goe hence this daye after th*e* queene.

Your old freind S*ir* Geo[rge] Calvert profesed himselfe openly a Catholique before the councell and, as my l[ord] of C[halcedon] writeth to me, had continued in th*e* councell if he wold have taken th*e* oath of allegiance w*hi*ch is tendered to Catho[lics].[1205]

Ther is great doubt of some extraordinary schisme in England for it is thought th*at* preists and Cath[olics] w*hi*ch will take that oath the[re] have great favour; the other must expect nothing but th*e* rigour of th*e* lawe. This is certaine, that Fa[ther] John Barnes hath bene courted heere by the duke, and <hee> was presented to him by th*e* embassadours <of Englande>. Ther ar others, as is sayd, Mr D[octor] Potter,[1206] and Don Michael,[1207] an Italian monke. Some are

[1203] Thomas White.

[1204] See *CSPV, 1625–1626*, pp. 59, 63, 68, 77.

[1205] See McClure, *LJC*, p. 609.

[1206] A reference, presumably, to Jerome Porter OSB. Sir George Goring had recorded on 11/21 March 1625 that 'Docter Potter and Doctor Barnes, both priests [. . .] have bin severall times with me to intreate my mediation for theyre' return to England. They said that, if permission were granted them to return, they would 'doe such service as when his Majesty shall understand the designe thereof and how many of this French Catholique Churche will joyne with them in the publication of such exceptions as they justly have against the popes usurpation', they doubted not but that the king would 'think they doe God and him good service'. They dared not openly voice such sentiments in France, and 'the other night one of them scaped narrowly of being murthered by some of the Jesuits schollers': PRO, SP 78/74, fo. 107v.

[1207] Arthur (Michael) Godfrey OSB. See Lunn, *The English Benedictines*, p. 123; Birch, *CTCI*, I, p. 122.

of opinion that these men shall be putt in place about th*e* queene,[1208] and [the] Oratorians [will be] shortly sent home againe. Sed nolo amplius movere hanc cama[r]inam.[1209]

M^r^ Price came not this waye, but I receaved a letter from him from Dowaye. Heere was an auncient man called M^r^ Browne whoe came to me, in your name, to have my helpe and direction for his journey to Antwerpe and thence to England. He seemeth to be a very kind, honest man and was most thankefull for th*e* litle kindnes I did him.

M^r^ D[octor] Cecilles [*word obscured:* goes (?)] into England as ausmonier to the duchese of Chevreux,[1210] and he purposeth to returne w*it*h her againe w*it*hin 2 moneths. I hope you never forgett my respectfull and kind comendation to M^r^ D*octo*r Seton. And I alwayes include Fa[ther] Sebert[1211] among my freinds notw[i]t[h]standing your differences, w*hi*ch I hope are quickly ended betweene you.

I am heere not tyed as a beare to th*e* stake but sometymes I have cause to thinke that I am tyed w*it*h a beare.[1212] I will doe my best to endure for a tyme thoughe it be very irkesome to me.

M^r^ Lockwood is gone hence to live at Chells, having more profitt and more contentment happily there than he had heere. We are but foure and I wold willingly (unlesse we may be eased of a burden unsupportable) give over my place againe to any honest young man. Heere was one that belonged to my L[ord] Castlehaven in England, whoe desyred me to remember his love and service to you. His name is M^r^ Walgrave,[1213] a gentleman of a good family, and was sometimes

1208 On 25 May/4 June 1625, Anthony Champney had reported that 'Father John Barnes [. . .] being in Parise, saith he is sent for <into> England by our king with promise not only of securitie but also preferment, and saith the king resolveth to make a difference betwixt Catholiques that [. . .] howld opinions favorable to the state, as is that of the oath of alleageance, and others. The first he will favour, thothers contrarie. Doctor Potter is also [. . .] sent for and is to goe in with our queen, who I thinke might better be spared than there imployed. Father Barnes saith he will not goe till he have printed another booke which some thinke wilbe [. . .] in defence or favour of Widdringtons [*i.e.* Thomas Preston's] doctrin, which the parliament of Parise will patronise. It were much to be wished that these men would imploy their wittes and learning for the edification of Gods Church and not for the disquieting thereof': AAW, B 47, no. 48. John Pory claimed, on 1 July 1626, that Porter and Godfrey had 'taken the oath of allegiance, some say of supremacy also': Birch, *CTCI*, I, p. 122.

1209 A reference to Camarina, a town on the south coast of Sicily. For the proverb to which Richard Ireland refers, see W. Smith, *A New Classical Dictionary* (London, 1853), p. 141.

1210 Marie de Rohan, duchess of Chevreuse. For her appointment to accompany Henrietta Maria to England, see Archives des Affaires Etrangères, Paris, Correspondance Politique Angleterre, 32, fos 176r–178r. I am grateful to Michelle Howell for this reference.

1211 Robert (Sigebert) Bagshaw OSB.

1212 Richard Ireland refers here to the conflict among the clergy in the Collège d'Arras.

1213 Charles Waldegrave. George Fisher described him, in October 1624, as 'second sonne to M^r^ Walgrave of Stanningale in Norfolcke and brother to Sir Edw[ard] Walgrave'. Charles had been Fisher's 'schoolefellow in Rome' and was 'on[e] of the prime witts of the colledge'.

scholler of our colledge at Rome. It seemeth he loveth and respecteth you well.

Farewell good father, and remember me as I doe you for, in your love and such remembrances, I doe m[u]ch comfort my self, assuring you that I am as I have found you <the same> [*word illegible*] to me [*two interlineated words illegible*] beyond my meritt in all hartye affection.

Yours to be commanded,

R[ichard] I[reland]

Junii 5$^{to}$ 1625.

Paris.

*Addressed*: Au r*évéren*d p[ère], P[ère] Thomas Rant, d[e]m[euran]t [?] à S$^{t}$ Louis, à Rome.

*Endorsed*: Written: June 5.
Received: Julye 22.
Answered: Julye 28.
And with this, letters to his Holines and card[inals] de Prop[aganda] Fide, dated 26 Maii.[1214]

## 82. Henry Clifford to Thomas Rant, 3/13 June 1625

[*AAW, B 47, no. 82*]

R*everen*d s*ir*,

By the last post I did not write to you, expecting l*ett*res from England, and none came for you then, but now this supply[e]s that defect. I thanke you for yo*u*rs of the 24 of the last, as for the former of the 17 May. Mine have shewed you th*a*t M$^{r}$ More[1215] is gone to Cambray where he is like to reside the moste p*ar*t of this sum*m*er. Yesterday I wrote to him how he was beholding to the love and respect you beare ~~his fam~~ him and his familye, w*hi*ch he will and doth acknowledge,

He was 'a man of extraordinary repute in his county. He came from Rome for his health, and was for some yeares somewhat crasy. For the space of 5 or 6 yeares he followed the court and was in great esteeme with the lord of Northampton [Henry Howard], while he lived. He is lately married and his father hath given him an estate of 300$^{l}$ per annum': AAW, A XVIII, no. 73, pp. 386–387; CRS, 54, pp. 89–90; CRS, 37, p. 121; *NCC*, pp. 266–267.

[1214] AAW, A XIX, no. 33, pp. 107–108 (John Colleton and the vicars-general of Richard Smith to the cardinals of Propaganda Fide, 26 May 1625); AAW, A XIX, no. 34, pp. 109–110 (Colleton and the vicars-general to a recipient (probably a cardinal) in Rome, 26 May 1625); AAW, A XIX, no. 35, pp. 111–112 (Colleton and the vicars-general to Urban VIII, 26 May 1625).

[1215] Cresacre More.

and therefore you have greate reason to keepe th*a*t watch and what els it pleaseth you of his brothers, being likewise a pawne of his love and respect to you.[1216] I thanke you for the p*ro*phesie w*hi*ch I wish you had interpreted all. For what is constered, I shoulde have guessed w*i*thout a com*m*entarie, but com*m*only such matters are fathered on antiquitie, when subtillye they are divulged by moderne witts who, by the concurrence of accidents, conjecture what is likeliest to followe. But this we plainly see th*a*t the maine defender and entire mantainer of the Church and the Catholicke fayth is his Cath[olic] Majestie.[1217] [*In margin:* Nego.] On Thursday $5^{to}$ Junii the Holland forces went out of Breda, [*in margin:* Thank God] and the marques['s][1218] forces entred. They had honorable conditions and marched w*i*th flying colours very gallant and, wholy armed, carried w*i*th them ~~tow~~ <4> peeces of artillerie and two morter peeces. On Tuesday the infanta[1219] came to this towne,[1220] magnificently entertayned. Generally [there] were made bonefires and other feasts of joy for the recoverie of Breda,[1221] whither yesterday morning her hig[h]nes went accomp[anied by] 40 companies of horse and other forces and divers others that went to see the towne and fashion of the leaguer. She carried w*i*th her good store of mony to gratifie the souldiers.[1222] The earle of Oxford is dead at the Hague, sickning upon a fall he had when our English made that rash and unfortunate attempt upon the leaguer of the marques.[1223] Mansfielde is gone w*i*th his forces towards Germanie;[1224] and the Duke Saxe and the Baron Anholt[1225] w*i*th the emperours forces sent by the marques to attend him.

This day our queene is to be in England, for all the gentleman [*sic*] of Kent were com*m*aunded to be at the Downe by Dover to waite upon

[1216] See *Letter 79*.

[1217] In his letter to Thomas More of 31 December 1624/10 January 1625, Clifford had opined that 'it seemes the only protector of the Catholicke Church, under God Almightie and the prayers of the just, is the king of Spaine and howse of Austria': AAW, B 47, no. 83. In another letter to More, six weeks earlier, Clifford had warned that the intentions of the French were good, but 'when they fynde any difficultyes to overcome [. . .] I feare me the execution of their intended good will come short of their wishes, and wee shall fynde but few of them such as worthy Gundemar was, who [. . .] prosecuteth the Catholick cause with his whole heart': AAW, B 27, no. 49.

[1218] Ambrogio Spinola, marquis of Los Balbases.

[1219] Isabella Clara Eugenia, archduchess of Austria.

[1220] Antwerp.

[1221] See *CSPV, 1625–1626*, pp. 69, 71, 72, 78, 80, 83, 101, 111.

[1222] See *CGB*, II, pp. 646, 648.

[1223] See *CSPV, 1625–1626*, pp. 46, 69, 73.

[1224] See Adams, PC, p. 355; Lockyer, *Buckingham*, p. 250; *CSPV, 1625–1626*, p. 46; *CGB*, II, p. 643.

[1225] Johann-Jakob, baron of Bronckhorst and Anholt. See *CSPV, 1625–1626*, p. 122; Lee, *Dudley Carleton to John Chamberlain*, p. 293.

her. Divers ladies went over to Bulleine to attend her, among whom were the Ladye St Johns[1226] and the Lady Savage.[1227] Yet promoters are still busie, and vexe all knowen recusants nor doe, or at least will not, the officers take any notice of the kings promise, w*hi*ch the French assueredly affirme.[1228]

The p*ar*lament is differred [*i.e.* deferred] to our 23 [*sic*] June.[1229] And they still presse w*i*th rigour to supply the great navie w*hi*ch is providing.[1230] In July ambassadours are expected from Spain to condole and congratulate. El Conde Gondamar comes to Paris to treate w*i*th that king abowt the French proceedings.[1231] The Hollanders have had losse at sea by the Spaniards. I bessech you send the enclosed to Fa[ther] Sebert[1232] for it imports [*sic*]. I have ha[d] the 22[li] M[r] Evans[1233] was to make good to M[r] President[1234] at Dou[ai]. [O]ur Lord Jhe*sus* keepe you and so I humbly com*m*end me.

Yo*u*rs,

Henry Clifford

Andw[arp] 13 June 1625.

*No address.*

*Endorsed*: Writt[en]: June 13.
Received: July 3.
Answered: Julye 5.

[1226] Jane Savage.

[1227] Elizabeth Darcy, wife of Sir Thomas Savage, the future 1st Viscount Savage. In December 1622, Jane Savage, their daughter, had married John Paulet, the future 5th marquis of Winchester: Cokayne, *CP*, XII, p. 767; PRO, C 115/107/8485; Redworth, *PI*, p. 43.

[1228] Thomas Roper had noted, on 14 May 1625, that 'promotors are very busye, and this day, in Westminster Hall, did serve Sir Francis Inglefeilde with a writte for his wifes recusancy and some five or six more were so served at the same tyme'. Also 'an attorney was served with a writte for defendinge the causes of six recusantes convicted, the penaltye beinge a 100[l] for eache', which was 'a new strayne in the law not formerly looked into': AAW, B 47, no. 187.

[1229] Following James's death, and because of the determination to secure the Anglo-French marriage treaty, there was a succession of prorogations from 17 May until 18 June: Russell, *PEP*, p. 204.

[1230] See C. Thompson, 'Court politics and parliamentary conflict in 1625', in R. Cust and A. Hughes (eds), *Conflict in Early Stuart England* (London, 1989), p. 177.

[1231] See *CSPV, 1625–1626*, pp. 41, 47, 48, 100, 109, 117; PRO, SP 78/75, fo. 85v.

[1232] Robert (Sigebert) Bagshaw OSB.

[1233] William Evans: see AAW, B 47, no. 87 (Evans to Thomas Rant, 3/13 July 1625).

[1234] Matthew Kellison.

## 83. Anthony Champney to Thomas Rant, 8/18 June 1625 (with postscript by Matthew Kellison)

[*AAW, B 47, no. 55*]

R*everen*d and verie loveing s*ir*,

M^r^ President,[1235] being at this p*re*sent otherwayes occupied, gave me charge to return you answer to yo*u*rs of the 24 of May. D[octor] Cecilles is not like to see you there in hast for he is gone into Ingland w*i*th Madame de Chevereux as her chapleine where, if he fynd footeing to his co*n*tentme*nt*, he is like enough to stay. There hath beene here and at Parise also divers reportes of our younge kings death. What policie there may be in the authores of such fictions, I knowe not. We have not yet seene anie copie of M^r^ Mores will. His brother[1236] is nowe at Cambray and, ere he turn back, we shall desire a sight of that [which] you sent to him. S*ign*ore Scanarolio must not expect his accomptes returned this weeke because we have not p*er*used them further than that [which] I wrote the last weeke. Agnes Fowler is not anie Jesuitess but a good Catholike and descreet woma*n* who com*m*ethe thither upon vowe w*i*th much devotion and resolution, and so you will fynd if I be not deceived. The rate of our scholers, if it be brought under 23^li^, we shall be at overmuch loss by them. Therefore though M^r^ President, to shewe him self not obstinat or peremptorie, did remitt something to the prudence of the judges, yet we hope they <will> consider the matter in some p*ro*portion as it is and not so to favour one part that they may overmuch oppress or wrong thother. M^r^ Fitton[1237] his returne is not yet heard of.[1238]

How matters will goe w*i*th Catholiques <in Inglande> doth not yet appeare, but more feare than hope. P*ro*moters are verie busie and divers troubled, w*hi*ch the embassatoure[1239] sayth shall all be amended by the queenes com*m*ing. The king is between London and Dover, expecting the arrivall of his queene. The countess of Buckinghame w*i*th divers ladies are [*sic*] passed over to Boloigne, where by this day the queene is thought to be arrived. Some say that the ceremonies of mariage must be reiterated agayn at Canterburie. God grant as much constancie in the French Catholikes as our heretikes embassatoures shewed in Parise, who caused the ceremonies to be

[1235] Matthew Kellison.

[1236] Cresacre More.

[1237] Peter Biddulph.

[1238] On 2/12 April 1625, Champney had informed Rant that 'M^r^ Fitton is thinking of going into Ingland to deale with his father and mother and to informe them of the truth, if they will understand it, and so to return': AAW, B 47, no. 49; see also AAW, B 47, nos 46, 90.

[1239] Antoine Coiffier de Ruzé, marquis of Effiat.

celebrated [w]*i*thout the church that they might assist thereat, w*hi*ch done they w*i*thdrewe them selves till Mass was done. We heare that matters goe hard w*i*th the French both in the Valtelin, where they dye for famin, and in Savoy where Prince Thomaso hath had a shrewde shock[1240] and ~~an~~ [*words omitted:* there is (?)] a constant report that the constable[1241] is dead; and that the Hugenotes are insolent in Poitou and Dauphenie; the Spaniards verie strong, so that it is thought that the duke of Savoy may come to blowes in the end.

Gondomare, who was upon his voyage for Ingland, is now come extraordinarie into France[1242] where, if some good end be not made, this is like to proove a troublesome yeare. In Ingland there was never such pressing of men, as well for sea as land, but to what end is not known, whether for offence or defence. The French marchandes from divers places have sent to the king co*m*playning of the loss they sustayn by the arrest of their shippes in all the king of Spayns countries for the money the duke of Guise tooke going to Genova. What wilbe the issu is not yet seene. Yesterday I had one from Mr Messindin[1243] of the 21 of May wherein he writeth as received from Newma*n* at Lisboa that Mr Francis Tregean, a most constant co*n*fessour, in whose howse Mr Cuthbert Mayn, our first martir, was taken, haveing been buried in Lisboa (for in King James his tyme, fynding no remedie of his wronges, he left Ingland and went into Spayn) [in] the yeare 1608, in the church of the casa p*ro*fessa of the Jesuites, upon St Marcs day last, by occasion of having another in the same place, was fownd his bodie <so> entiere and incorrupt that it seemed nothing <was> wanting therein but only life, his fleshe soft and rysing after it was pressed downe and his joyntes limber and plying. And, being buried in St Francis his habit, the habit was wholly co*n*sumed, saveing only so much as covered his secret partes w*hi*ch remayned whole, a spann broad or more.[1244] This it hath pleased God for his owne glorie and the

[1240] For the Spaniards' defeat of Prince Thomas of Savoy, near Asti, see *CSPV, 1625–1626*, p. 42.

[1241] François de Bonne, duke of Lesdiguières, constable of France.

[1242] See *Letter 82*.

[1243] Edward Maddison.

[1244] William Newman had written from Lisbon on 30 April/10 May 1625 that 'a certeyne hermandad or congregation, goeinge to burry one of their brethren in the casa professa of the Jesuittes in this citty of Lisboa, they opened the grave where Mr Francis Trugian (who dyed in this towne) was burryed' in September 1608. The body was said to be incorrupt. On the following day, Newman gained admittance to the church and described what he saw, though he was not certain that the body really was incorrupt. On the Monday following, some of the English Catholics in Lisbon went, at the behest of the Jesuits, to the archbishop to beseech him to set up a commission to see whether all this was natural or 'beyond nature'. The archbishop instructed that a 'junta of physitions and surgeons should be chosen' to deal with this. Newman hoped that this would 'redound to the augmentinge of the glory of

co*m*forth of those that suffer for him to shewe in our days. God grant all may take co*m*forth and example thereby to whose holy grace and p*ro*tection I ever com*m*itt and com*m*end you, and so doth M^r^ President whose lines you may imagin these to be.

Doway this 18 of June 1625.

Y*our*s ever,

Champney

The infanta[1245] is gone to Antwerpe and so to Breda w*i*th good store of money and giftes as well for ordinarie pay as for extraordinarie giftes and presentes.[1246] Howe this whole armye will hereafter be imployed is not yet knowne.

[*Postscript by Matthew Kellison*][1247]

Good Sir, I being otherwise busied, and D[octor] Champney having answered your l*ett*re for mee and imparted al y*ou*r newes, I hope you

the renowned protomartyr of our semynaries, M^r^ Cuthbert Mayne, that was taken in M^r^ Trugian his house and (may piously be beleeved) gave such doctrine in his lyfe, such example by his death and such assistance with his prayers ever after, as brought this great confessor [*i.e.* Tregian] to such perfeccion', when his body lay incorrupt even after seventeen years in a 'common and ordinary grave', in which there were another five bodies which decomposed in the ordinary way: AAW, A XIX, no. 31, pp. 102–103. See also Anstr., I, pp. 224–226. For Ignatius Stafford SJ's account, of 16/26 April 1625, describing Tregian's exhumation and claiming that his body was found 'incorrupt and entire, without corruption in any part', see J. Morris (ed.), *The Troubles of our Catholic Forefathers*, 3 vols (London, 1872–1877), I, pp. 61–63.

[1245] Isabella Clara Eugenia, archduchess of Austria.

[1246] In a letter of 18/28 June to Thomas Rant, Richard Wariner described the infanta's triumphal entry into Breda, for which see also *Letter 82*. Wariner narrated how 'some knavish wittes have sett owt a leafe of paper printed, very conseitedly. The[y] have putt Breda in a coffin and covered it with a moorning clothe. Before goeth Count Morice, who caryeth the crosse (for indeede yt is one of his townes, and therfor he most of all haith lost in this affayre). On eache side of the beere, is of the one, the king of England with a torche in his hand weeping' and on 'the other side is the king of France, then followeth Count Palatin upon an asse, and his wife upon a mule, after whom do follow his 7 children with theyre hattes in their handes like lacquais. After them the estates of Holand on one side, pitifully weeping; on the other the Venetians. All the foresayd personages do complaigne one to another': AAW, B 47, no. 197.

[1247] On 6/16 June 1625, Kellison had written to Thomas Rant a short note to recommend the two bearers of this letter. One of them, he said, was 'sonne to the bishop of Hereford', Francis Godwin. Godwin's son, 'being made a Catholique on this side, hath been oftentymes sent for by his father and mother, and especially his mother who hath written hime persuasive lettres and hath offered him much to return, saying that otherwise he will be [the] cause of her death. And yet, the yong gentleman, fearing least he should be importuned or for[ced] to doe against his conscience, he being now a Catholique, chose rather to live poorelie in this town and to frequent our lessons.' A pension or other subsidy from the English college or from the curia in Rome, said Kellison, would help to sustain his faith: AAW, B 47, no. 133.

will excuse mee. One writeth to mee th*a*t a Theatin[1248] sayd that he that was a principal agent to procure th*e* decree for th*e* new oath did him selfe *pre*sentlie after make sute to be a Theatin. I pray you, good sir, desire Sig*n*or Scanarolio to make th*e* sute of a resignation of a benefice over oure pensions, th*e* which sute I sent to him long since. It is for a frend of myne. M$^{ris}$ Fowler is a verie honest gentlewoman, noe Jesuitesse. Th*e* yong man that confessed to the pope is now heer labouring as he sayth to be [a] Capucin. I bad him to [*word illegible:* dinner (?)]. M$^{r}$ Fitton is not yet returned, w*hi*ch is a sign that he hath much trouble. I pray you comend me to good D[octor] Seaton.

Your own ever,

Mat[thew] Kellison

I wrote to F[ather] Fitzherbert for money, about an 100$^{l}$, w*hi*ch M$^{r}$ Banes gave us, and I desired Sig*n*or Scanarolio to demand it. The next weeke our procurator will send th*e* accountes.

*Addressed*: Admodum rever*en*do domino, D*omi*no Thomae Ranto, cleri Anglicani in curia Romana agenti dig*nissi*mo.

*Endorsed*: Writt[en]: June 18.
Received: Julye 19.
Answered: Julye 19.

## 84. Thomas Roper to Thomas Rant, 17 June 1625

[*AAW, B 47, no. 189*]

Sir,

The letter for David Camerario[1249] is from M$^{r}$ Willson or Tompeson,[1250] one of his countreymen that livethe amonge us here who, hearinge of his unworthy carriadge towardes our nation and clergy, hathe written him a letter of reprehension <and> of advise, and <w*i*thall> geavethe him some freindly admonitions. He was importunat w*i*th me to send it, and assurethe me he namethe no boddy in his letter, thoughe perchance it may doe ~~but little~~ small good and worke little w*i*th him.

[1248] i.e. a Jesuit.

[1249] David Chambers. See *NCC*, p. 58. In June 1625, William Webster described Chambers as 'a Scottes priest, a very honest man who lyved with M$^{r}$ [Thomas] Moore' and others in Juan-Bautista Vives's house in Rome ('a la Trinita de Monte', in the Piazza di Spagna): AAW, A XIX, no. 56, p. 165; AAW, B 27, no. 8; Shanahan, 'The descendants of St. Thomas More', p. 91.

[1250] William Thompson OFM. See *NAGB*, pp. 163, 198; *NCC*, p. 23.

Yet, to satisfye his desire, I wisshe he had it, and by suche meanes as you shall thincke fittinge.

Our queene (after some dayes of expectance) landed on Sonday last, being our 12 of June, at Dover, and that night lay at the castle.[1251] The next day in the afternoone our kinge went from Canterb[ury] unto hir. She, havinge notice of our kinges arrivall, mette him ~~in~~ comminge into the castle uppon a paire of stares and offered to prostrate hir selfe at his feete, but the kinge hindred hir. Then she offered to kisse his hand w*hi*ch he likewise would not suffer hir to doe but, imbracinge hir, kissed hir two or three tymes togeather, and so walked into a roome and passed some howre w*i*th hir in discourse, and then tooke coache and went w*i*th hir that night to Canterb[ury] w*hi*ch was your midsommer eve, and the supper was all flesse. She being advertised by one of hir chapelines of the day, forbore eatinge, and the cause beinge knowen, some whitmeates were presently made readdy for hir, and that night the king and she bedded togeather, and much a doe there was to gett out of the roome an old matrone who attended on the queene, she alleaginge that she had engaged hir promise to [the] queene mother[1252] not to leave hir.[1253] They rested togeather in Canterb[ury] the next day, and the day following went to Cobbam Hall, and yesternight they came to Whitehall by barge, the river beinge full of shippes w*hi*ch discharged their ordinance as hir barge passed by. Of hir trayne there were only 3 persons of note: the duke of Cheverous,[1254] Conte Tilly[1255] and Villocleere.

This day is the first day of the terme and the last, for it is adjourned untill M*ichaelm*as by reason of the ~~sicknesse~~ <plague> of w*hi*ch there dyed this weeke 165, and 31 parishes are infected. Tomorrowe the parlament beginnethe, w*hi*ch it is thought will hold by reason of the kinges occasions of money, especially for his great fleete w*hi*ch is in a manner now in readinesse, and the kinge will be at the parl[iament] himselfe, but goethe privately thether. We have rayne in great abundance and have had [it] bothe before our queenes landinge and since.

Yours,

T[homas] R[oper]

[1251] See *CSPV, 1625–1626*, p. 87; for the allegedly disastrous reception of Henrietta Maria at Dover, see Tillières, *ME*, pp. 89–91.

[1252] Marie de Médicis.

[1253] See *ibid.*, p. 91.

[1254] Claude de Lorraine, duke of Chevreuse.

[1255] Tanneguy Leveneur, count of Tillières.

Indightementes <and> convictions goe forwarde, and penaltyes are imposed uppon recusantes notwithstandinge the matche. At Canterb[ury] some of my kinsefolk and freindes paye yet 12$^{d}$ a Sonday for not going to churche. We cannot but hope that some grace will be shewed them for the queene[s] sake.

[*In margin*]

Some thinke Fiat[1256] will remayne here ledger w*hi*ch pleaseth not your freindes nor others but our state <only>, w*hi*ch will endevor the more to have him here because he is opposed, and for his former service he hathe the order of the Spirito Sancto bestowed on him.[1257]

*Addressed*: All' ill*ust*re sig*no*re, il Sig*no*re Tomasso Rante, Inglese. Roma.

*Endorsed*: Written: June 17.
Received: Julye 24.
Answered: Julye 26.

## 85. George Musket [Fisher] to Thomas Rant, 24 June 1625

[*AAW, B 48, no. 35, fo. 98r*]

Very worthy s*i*r,

Your last of the 7 of June hath given me good satisfactio*n* concerning the secrecy used in our cheife busines. I was too sensible of your disgrace and could not conceive the*n* that it was for our good, but now I am satisfied my selfe <and> I will endeavor to satisfie others. You have deciphered M$^{r}$ Phil[ip] R[oper] sufficiently,[1258] and given M$^{r}$ Browne such a character as we shall easily know him when he cometh.[1259] Notwithstanding M$^{r}$ Philip R[oper's] conceit of those priests[1260] that were sent in with the queene, they have hitherto demeaned themselves so religiously that they have the applause eve*n* of those that stand most affected to the Jesuits and I hope ther exa*m*ple will doe much good.

[1256] Antoine Coiffier de Ruzé, marquis of Effiat.

[1257] See *CSPV, 1625–1626*, pp. 25, 29.

[1258] In a letter of 18 March 1625, Thomas Roper had asked Thomas More to 'commende me to my uncle Philippe who is good company untell he fauleth in to discourse of the padri' (i.e. the Jesuits): AAW, B 47, no. 176.

[1259] Browne had attended the funeral of Thomas More in Rome in April 1625: Shanahan, 'The death of Thomas More', p. 26.

[1260] i.e. Oratorians.

F[ather] Berule especially hath wonn much credit and is esteemed, as he deserveth, a ma*n* of great zeale, but all matters ar yet so unsetled that we know <not> what the issue will be. The parliament, those especially of the lower House, urge eagerly the executio*n* of the penall lawes against the recusants and the confirmatio*n* of such lawes as were made against <the*m*> in the last parlame*n*t, but not confirmed by his M*ajes*tie, also the banishme*n*t of priests.[1261] You know it is but ther wonted proceeding. But ~~the~~ we hope the king will be gratious and rather ease us of our former burden than impose any new inflictions uppon us. Thes[e] parlamentary busines[ses] are but yet in the budd, and it is hard to conjecture what fruit will insue. All of the parliament house have taken the oath of supremacy and the lower House hath ~~to~~ urged to have a generall fast for the cessatio*n* of the plague and good successe of ther busines. But the lords spirituall of the higher <House> opposed this motio*n*, and answered that it apertained to the*m* and not to the parliament to apoint fasts. But they condescended to joine with the*m* in praier for those purposes and to shew that both Houses were in charity notwithstanding some differences betwixt the[m]. They consented all to receive the comunio*n* the next day. I heard also that the lower House moved to have the king open his prerogative that they might know how farr it extended it selfe.[1262] What answere was give*n* I cannot learne. God send good successe to his glory and our countries good. The French will labor what they can to ease our afflictions but how farr they will prevaile is yet uncertaine. During the parliament I suppose they will be able to doe litle. Great part of this weeke hath bin spent in feasting the French and such court compleme*n*ts. Thus abruptly, with offer of my love, I rest.

Yours unfainedly,

G[eorge] M[usket]

June 24.

[1261] Thomas Roper, on 23 June, described the meeting of the parliament on 18 June and narrated that 'in the end of his speeche, his Majestie made a profession of his faithe, assuringe them he would not change nor alter any thinge, but continew in it as his father had don'. But, 'some 2 dayes after', on 20 June, 'Sir Thom[as] Crew, speaker of the lower House, made a speeche and invayed bitterly against recusantes, and thereuppon the lower House did propose unto his Majestie that the penall lawes might be putte in execution against them, to which his Majestie answeared that he would doe what was fittinge, but tolde them withall that was not the businesse for which they were cauled': AAW, A XIX, no. 56, p. 166; see also McClure, *LJC*, pp. 625–626.

[1262] See Thompson, 'Court politics', pp. 172, 174–176. Writing on 25 June 1625, Thomas Roper described the arguments over the proposed fast, the communion, and the royal prerogative, and concluded that 'the common wealthe is sicke and muche distempered': AAW, B 47, no. 190.

*Addressed*: To his very worthy freind M^r^ Thomas Rant.

*Endorsed*: Writt[en]: June 24.
Received: Julye 31.
Answered: Aug[ust] 2.

## 86. Henry Clifford to Thomas Rant, 12/22 August 1625

[*AAW, A XIX, no. 70, pp. 211–212*]

R*everen*d good s*ir*,

I am, thanks be to God, after two months returned home, where I finde many kinde l*ett*res of yo*u*rs but, newly arrived, have not yet time to p*er*use them. I left our countrey exceedingly infected, but cheifly London wherein these last weekes dyed, as the note was brought this day, 4,557 and moste, yea all, this number of the plague. For Westminster and Stepney are not counted in this reckning.[1263] Notw*i*thstanding this greate contagion, the parlament is continued at Oxford, to assist the king w*i*th mony, who wants it by meanes of the greate expences for the late helps of Holland w*i*thout any benefite, and the setting forth of this greate armada, w*hi*ch from England hath 120 shipps and from Holland 30. So in al 150, w*hi*ch makes the king of Spaine to be about him. Yet divers are of opinion th*a*t this navie will not goe forth, although it be in a manner readie at Plimmouth, p*ar*tly as I say for wants of mony, p*ar*tly for the late victories of the Spaniard here upon Breda, at Genoa upon the French, and at Brasile upon the Hollander, whose fleete being victorious is much encoraged against any enemie.[1264] And w*i*thall the greate pestilence in England will be a hinderance to putt the souldiers and marriners togeather w*i*thout infection, some of the shipps being alreadie infected. The queene remaines very Catholicke, and the bishop and Mons*ieu*r Berule, her confessour, doe their duties very well, being still about her, although at my com*m*ing away the rest of the Oratorie remained at S^t^ James, much discontented. There is no other chappell than private chambers.

[1263] On 26 July/5 August 1625, George Fisher had sent Thomas Rant a graphic account of the plague, and said that he was in London 'to attend the sicke and cheifly to releive the necessity of the poore' and that 'we ar called uppon daily, the number of the sicke is so greate'. The count of Tillières interpreted the plague as a providential judgment on the English for continuing to persecute Catholics, contrary to the treaty made with the French: Tillières, *ME*, p. 92.

[1264] See *CSPV, 1625–1626*, pp. 122–123, 138. The Dutch had occupied Bahía, the capital of Brazil, but the Spaniards had recently recovered some of their losses: see G. Parker, *Spain and the Netherlands, 1559–1659* (London, 1979), p. 55; Elliott, *The Count-Duke of Olivares*, pp. 215, 236; *CCE*, pp. 176–177, 222; *CGB*, II, p. 653.

Buckingham doth all, for the king w*i*thout him will doe nothing. The p*ar*lament is very busie to heape more burdens and afflictions uppon Catholicks. The duke of Chevre[use] they say hath doone good offices w*i*th the king to stay these violences, brought to it upon the honour to keepe promises and for reason of state than of any inclination in himselfe. I coulde doe no busines in England because all fri[e]nds were so farre disp*er*sed by meanes of the sicknes. [*In margin:* This towne hath also many howses infected.] I sent yo*ur* l*ett*res for England yesterday w*hi*ch were many, w*hi*ch shoulde be of the 2 of this. God Almightie keepe you.

Andwarpe, 22 April.

Yours,

Henry Clifford

*No address.*

*Endorsed*: Written: Aug[ust] 22.
Received: Sept[ember] 11.
Answered: Sep[tember] 13.

# INDEX

Note: Newsletters and other papers included in this volume are indexed in **bold** type.